Cultural history of Bhāratam Janam

-- Indus Script metalwork catalogs

S. Kalyanaraman

Library of Congress Catalog Number 2016901900

0-9911048-5-4 ISBN-10

978-0-9911048-5-7 ISBN-13

Cultural History of Bhāratam Janam

-- Profiles of culture, civilization, Indus Script metalwork catalogs in a framework of Itihāsa from Vedic times, 8th millennium BCE

Objective

An objective of this monograph is to provide resources, including examples from Indus Script Corpora, for data mining.to identify profiles of culture, civilization with particular reference to technological advances contributed by Indian Meluhha artisans and seafaring merchants -- Bhāratam Janam -- during the Bronze Age.

This is a note on ancient data mining systems of Indus writing techniques by metalworkers, Bharatam Janam: with raised script on copper/bronze tablets, incisions on hard surfaces and free-hand writing on metal surfaces with herbal/metallic paint (perhaps ferric oxide pigment).

Data mining techniques of computer science widely used in Information Technology and Wi-Fi cellular/mobile communication system of the present day can be paralleled by the techniques demonstrated by artisans who created and used the Indus Script writing system on over 7000 inscriptions of ca. 3rd millennium BCE (5000 years ago). The techniques used on Indus Script could be of value to enhance data security through advanced cipher systems in cryptology, the study of codes, or the art of writing and decrypting cipher keys.

"Data mining is an interdisciplinary subfield of computer science. It is the computational process of discovering patterns in large data sets ("bigdata") involving methods at the intersection of artificial intelligence, machine learning, statistics, and database systems."(1.*"Data Mining"ACM SIGKDD. 2006-04-30.* 2. Clifton, Christopher (2010). *Encyclopaedia Britannica; definition of Data Mining.* 3.Hastie, Trevor; Tibshirani, Robert; Friedman, Jerome (*2009*). *"The elements of statistical learning: Data mining, inference, and prediction"*)

Resources of the earth which yield products of utilitarian and exchange value provided new forms of recording life activities of ancient Meluhha artisans of Bharatam. Products made such as s'ankha bangles, s'ankha libation vessels, s'ankha trumpets and cakra or vajra (wheel or Vajra adorning the Soma Yaga Yupa as a ring) are sacred and become divine attributes in temples. Nataraja the cosmic dancer is adorned with a damaru drum and flames of fire, Somaskanda form of S'iva is adorned with antelope [mlekh 'goat' rebus: milakkhu 'copper', meluhha (Bharatam Janam)] and paras'u 'metal axe'.These are abiding cultural markers of a civilization which reinforce the divinity in everyone of the worshippers in a temple which is kole.l 'temple' rebus: kole.l 'smithy, forge' (Kota)..

Sarasvati River Basin is the epicenter of culture and civilization of Bhāratam Janam from Vedic times.

Bhāratam Janam is the story of a civilization, of Sarasvati's children.

This is validation of the presence of Vedic culture in Sarasvati River Basin from recent findings of a yajnakunda at Binjor (near Anupgarh). The Yajnakunda yielded an octagonal yupa which has been mentioned in Rigveda (RV 1.162.6) and described in Satapatha Brahmana, a vedic text as **अष्टाश्रि** 'having eight corners', an emphatic cultural marker to evidence the performance of a Soma Yaga at the site. Details of the Yupa and चषाल are presented from Indus Script corpora and evidences of punch-marked and cast coins from ancient mints.

The Indus Script seal found in Binjor has been deciphered and is seen to be a documentation of mintwork. This decipherment is consistent with thousands of seals of. Indus Script Corpora deciphered as documentation, *catalogus catalogorum*, of सुवर्णक 'a कर्ष of gold MBh., gold, yellow brass, lead' and other metalwork.

The overall total number of inscriptions of Indus Script Corpora may be over 7,000 from all sites (if cognate hieroglyphs are identified in 'Persian Gulf type' circular seals and many pictorial motifs of cylinder seals of Ancient Mesopotamia (Near East), of Dong Son Bronze Drum *cire perdue* hieroglyphs on tympanum (Far East) and artifacts such as Gold disk of Kuwait Museum, Warka vase, Samarra plaques (pace Denise Schmandt-Besserat), Tukulti Ninurta fire-altar and Assur tin-road from Assur to Kultepe, tin ingots of Haifa, Nahal Mishmar *cire perdue* artifacts dated to ca. 5th millennium BCE – all signifying metalwork deploying Indus Script hieroglyphs. Hieroglyphs are also presented as objects in the round as exemplified by trefoils on Sivalinga base, on shawl of 'priest-kjing' (Mohenjo-daro), standard (lathe PLUS brazier), a hieroglyph-multiplex ubiquitously signified on over one thousand seals in front of a one-horned young bull with a pannier. Such hieroglyphs are also shown carried in processions as proclamations of stellar inventions of the Bronze Age. The greatest of these inventions was the invention of the cipher for a writing system (*mlecchita vikalpa*). Data mining of these evidences yields profiles of knowledge systems of ancient times which continue to be the संस्कृति weltanschuaang, the civilized frontier of a period earlier than ca 5th millennium BCE.

Somnakay (Gypsy), *samanom* (Santali) 'gold' metaphor for wealth creation

samanom = an obsolete name for gold (Santali)

This monograph demonstrates that the yupa discovered in Binjor and Kalibangan (ca. 2500 BCE) is a Vedic tradition, which is evidenced as continuum in historical periods, in 19 Yupa inscriptions of Rajasthan (Maukhari), Mathura, Allahabad and East Borneo documenting the performance of *bahusuvarNaka* Soma Yaga; बहुसुवर्णक costing or possessing much gold (Ramayana). suvarṇa सुवर्ण -र्णम् 1 Gold. -2 A golden coin (*-m.* also); नन्वहं दशसुवर्णान् प्रयच्छामि Mk.2 -माक्षिकम् a kind of mineral substance सुवर्णकम् 1 Brass, bell-metal. -2 Lead. -3 Gold. -कर्तृ, -कार, -कृत् *m.* a goldsmith. (Samskritam. Apte) suvárṇa ' of bright colour, golden ' RV., n. ' gold ' AV., *suvarṇaka* -- ' golden ' Hariv. 2. saúvarṇa- ' golden ' ŚrS., n. ' gold ' MBh. -- In many cases it is impossible to distinguish whether a NIA. form is derived from *suvárṇa* -- or *saúvarṇa* -- : they are therefore listed below together. [su -- 2, várṇa -- 1]1. Pa. *suvaṇṇa* -- ' of good colour ', n. ' gold ', *soṇṇa*<-> ' golden ', n. ' gold '; NiDoc. *suv́arna* ' gold '; Pk. *su(v)aṇṇa* -- , *soṇṇa* -- n. ' gold ', *suvaṇṇia* -- ' golden '.2. Pa. *sōvaṇṇa* -- , °*aya* -- ' golden '; Pk. *sō(v)aṇṇa* -- n. ' gold ', Ap. *sōvaṇa* -- n.1 or 2. Gy. gr. *sovnakáy*, wel. *sōnakai*, rum. *somnakáy* m. ' gold ', Ḍ. *son* m.; -- (Kaf. forms ← Ind. NTS ii 276) Ash. *sun*, Wg. *sū̃n*, Kt. *sun* f., Pr. *sü*; <-> Dm. *sōn*, Paš.lauṛ. *sū˘wan*, Gmb. *sō' n*, Gaw. *sōṇ, sūṇ*, (→ Sv. *son* NOPhal 47), Kal. *sū̃ṛa, sū̃ŕä*, Phal. *suāṇ*, Sh.gil. *sọn* m., koh. *sonŭ* m., gur. *son* m., dr. jij. *sōṇ* m., pales. *lēlo swā̃ṛə*' gold ', gil. (Lor.) *sōno* ' golden ', koh. gur. *sōṇų* ' beautiful '; K. *sŏn* m. ' gold ', rām. *sōnu*, kash. pog. *sŏnn*, ḍoḍ. *sŏṇṇā*, S. *sõnu* m. ' gold ' (*sõnõ* ' golden '), L. *sonā* m., P. *sonā, soinā, seonā, siūnā* m., WPah.bhad. *sunnō*, khaś. *sɔnnu* n., jaun. *sūnō*, Ku. *suno*, gng. *sun*, N. *sun*, A. *xon, xonā*, B. *sonā*,

Or. *sunā*, Mth. *son*, *sonā*, Aw.lakh. *sonu*, Bhoj. H. *sonā* m., OMarw. *sauno*, OG. *sovana*, *sonaüṁ* n., G. *sɔnũ* n., M. *sonẽ* n. (*sonā* ' golden '), OSi. (Brāhmī) *sovaṇa*, Si. *suvan* -- *na*. -- Early ← Sk.: Paš.chil. *swāren*' gold ', dar. *surun*, Shum. *suárin*, Kho. *sórum* (with -- *m* from *droxum* ' silver '; → Yid. *suwōrum*).suvarṇakāra -- , *suvarṇataruka -- , *suvarṇadhara -- , suvarṇamaya -- , suvarṇavarṇa -- ; -- sauvarṇika -- .Addenda: suvárṇa -- . 1. WPah.kṭg. *súnnɔ*, kc. *suno* m. ' gold '.2. saúvarṇa -- : Garh. *sonu* ' gold ', OMarw. *sonaü* m.suvarṇakāra m. ' goldsmith ' Mn. [suvárṇa -- , kāra -- 1]Pa. *suvaṇṇakāra* -- m. ' goldsmith ', NiDoc. *suv́arnakara*, Pk. *suvaṇṇaāra* -- , *suṇṇaāra* -- , °*ṇāra* -- m., Sh. (Lor.) *suniār* m., K. *sŏnar*, *sŏnuru* m., S. *sonāro* m., L. *sunārām*., awāṇ. *suniārā*, P. *suneār*, °*rā* m., Ku. N. *sunār*, A. *xonāri*, Or. *sunāra*, °*ri*, Bi. Mth. Bhoj. Aw.lakh. *sonār*, H. *sonār*, *sun*° m., G. M. *sonār* m., Ko. *sonāru*; -- Si. *suvaru*< **suvanaru*?Addenda: suvarṇakāra -- : WPah.kṭg. (kc.) *sənār* m. ' goldsmith ', Garh. *sunār*; -- Md. *sunāru* ← G. M. (CDIAL 13519, 13520)

The roots of the Indian Civilization in 8th millennium BCE (and cultural continuum into historical periods) was suggested by BR Mani and KN Dikshit in an International Conference held in Chandigarh from 27th to 29th October, 2012. The suggestion was based on archaeological reports and chronological dating of sites such as Mehrgarh in Baluchistan, Rehman Dheri in Gomal plains, Jalilpur and Harappa in Punjab, Bhirrana, Baror, Sothi, Nohar, Siswal, Banawali, Kalibangan, Girawad and Rakhigarhi in India.

The cultural remains of Bhirrana (a site on the Sarasvati/Ghaggar-Hakra river valley) date from 7380 BC to 6201 BCE and represent Hakra Ware Culture. Hakra Ware was also attested in the Hakra river basin of Cholistan sites by excavation of sites such as Ganweriwala and Bahawalpur. What is referred to as Ghaggar-Hakra river basins is the Vedic Sarasvati River Basin.

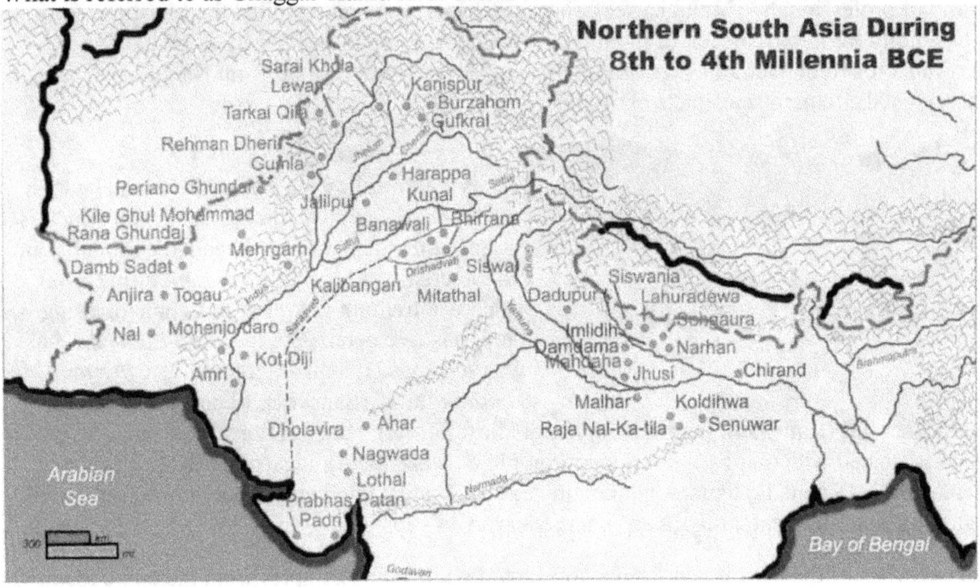

'Bhāratam janam', of the Chandas in Rigveda can be interpreted as 'bhārata folk' as in the ṛṣi's mantra:.*viśvāmitrasya rakṣati brahmedam bhāratam janam* RV 3.53.12. (Trans. This prayer, *brahma*, of *viśvāmitra* protects bhārata folk'.).

य इ॒मे रोद॑सी उ॒भे अ॒हमिन्द्र॑मतुष्टवम् ।
वि॒श्वामि॑त्रस्य रक्षति॒ ब्रह्मे॒दं भार॑तं॒ जन॑म् ॥ 12 ॥

RV 3.53.12 I have made Indra glorified by these two, heaven and earth, and this prayer of *viśvāmitra* protects Bharata folk. [Made Indra glorified: *indram atuṣṭavam*-- the verb is the third preterite of the casual, I have caused to be praised; it may mean: I praise Indra, abiding between heaven and earth, i.e. in the firmament].

The metaphor of heaven and earth is related to the Soma Yaga Yupa which is चषालः caṣālḥ godhūma गोधूम, as Vajra, and *axis mundi* metaphorically climbed by the yajnika to reach upto heaven, i.e. attain amrtatvam 'immortality'. The Yupa is a signifier of metalwork to produce purified soma, ams'u अंशु 'filament' cognate ancu 'iron' (Tocharian). चषालः caṣālḥ godhūma गोधूम is annam in pyrolysis/carburization to harden metal alloys in a smelting process.

Excellence in evolving knowledge systems related to minerals, metals and alloys was matched by a brilliant invention: a writing system.

The following is a potsherd which could perhaps signify the earliest writing system of the world. This statement may be contested but the excavators of HARP (Harappa Archaeological Research Project which began in 1986) have, with exemplary diligence, dated the potsherd to ca. 3300 BCE. As of now, there is no other evidence of a writing system earlier than this date has been reported from anywhere. A writing system was necessary to match the pace of inventions of new alloys and cire perdue (lost wax) techniques being perfected during the Early Bronze Age which created a new guild of professionals – Meluhha seafaring merchants who had travelled the Maritime Tin Road extending from the Tin Belt of th globe from Hanoi, Vietnam (exemplified by Dong Son bronze drums found in over 200 sites of Far East) to Haifa, Israel (not far from Nahal Mishmar which produced cire perdue artifacts of 5th millennium BCE).

This is a glyph showing five petals on a Harappa potsherd dated to ca. 3300 BCE, a glyph which is variant of the depiction on Shahdad cylinder seal. Characteristic of *tabernae montana* tulip flower which is a fragrant flower used as hair-dressing is that it has five petals. So, the word *tagaraka* has two meanings: 1. 'hair fragrance'; 2. *tabernae montana* 'tulip' (Sanskrit). Rebus: A homonym *tagara* means 'tin' (Kannada); tagromi 'tin, metal alloy' (Kuwi); takaram tin, white lead, metal sheet, coated with tin (Ta.); tin, tinned iron plate (Malayalam); tagarm tin (Kota); tagara, tamara, tavara id.(Kannada) tamaru, tamara, tavara id. (Tamil): tagaramu, tamaramu, tavaramu id. (Telugu); ṭagromi tin metal, alloy (Kuwi); tamara id.

A brief overview of the deciphered script is presented with some examples from the embedded Indus Script Corpora. The word 'mleccha' denotes copper in Samskritam. Hence, the appropriateness of interpreting *mlecchita vikalpa* as metalworkers' speechforms, sprachbund in ancient India of *Bhāratam Janam*.(a phrase by Rishi Visvamitra which identifies the ancestors of Sarasvati's children, i.e. the people who nurtured a civilization on the banks of Rivers Sarasvati and Sindhu from ancient times).

इतिहास (इति-ह-आस , " so indeed it was ") , talk , legend , tradition , history , traditional accounts of former events , heroic history S3Br. MBh. Mn. &c

The cultural continuum of pōtṟ पोतृ as a priest of Vedic tradition is evidenced in the veneration of ancestors: போத்தி pōtti 'grandfather, Malabar priest'. In ancient times of Sarasvati-Sindhu civilization, he was priest of *dhǎvaḍ* 'iron-smelters' (root: *dhāu* 'ore') with Indus script hieroglyphs signifiesपोतृ,'purifier' of dhātu, dhāū, dhāv 'red stone minerals'. This is evidenced by the Indus Script hieroglyphs signified on the limestone statue.

போற்றன் pōṟṟaṉ, *n.* prob. id. Grandfather; பாட்டன். (நாமதீப. 189.) போத்தி pōtti, *n.* < போற்றி. 1. Grandfather; பாட்டன். *Tinn.* 2. Brahman temple- priest in Malabar; மலையாளத்திலுள்ள கோயிலருச் சகன்.போற்றி pōṟṟi, < id. *n.* 1. Praise, applause, commendation; புகழ்மொழி. (W.) 2.Brahman temple-priest of Malabar; கோயிற் பூசைசெய்யும் மலையாளநாட்டுப் பிராமணன். (W.) 3. See போத்தி, 1.--*int.* Exclamation of praise; துதிச்சொல்வகை. பொய்தீர் காட்சிப் புரையோய் போற்றி (சிலப். 13, 92).போற்றுநர் pōṟṟunar, *n.* < போற்று-. 1. Relatives, kinsmen; சுற்றத்தார். போற்றா ருயிரினும் போற்றுந ருயிரினும் (பரிபா. 4, 52). 2. Those who understand; நன்குணர்வார். வேற்றுமை யின்றது போற்றுநர்ப் பெறினே (பரிபா. 4, 55).போற்று[1]-தல் pōṟṟu-, *5 v. tr.* 1. To praise, applaud; துதித்தல். (பிங்.) போற்று மடி யாருண்ணின்று நகுவேன் (திருவாச. 5, 60). 2. To worship; வணங்குதல். (பிங்.) 3. To protect, cherish, keep with great care; பாதுகாத் தல். போற்றி னரியவை போற்றல் (குறள், 693).

पोतृ pōtṟ Purifier Mohenjo-daro priest statue hieroglyphs and Harappa Indus Script tablet with 24 dots cartouche deciphered

A unique mold-made faience tablet or standard (H2000-4483/2342-01) was found in the eroded levels west of the tablet workshop in Trench 54 of Harappa by HARP Team. On one side is a short inscription under a rectangular box filled with 24 dots. The reverse has a narrative scene with two bulls fighting under a thorny tree.

खांडा (p. 202) [khāṇḍā]A jag, notch, or indentation (as upon the edge of a tool or weapon). (Marathi). Such dots are seen on many metallic artefacts of Sarasvati-Sindhu civilization.

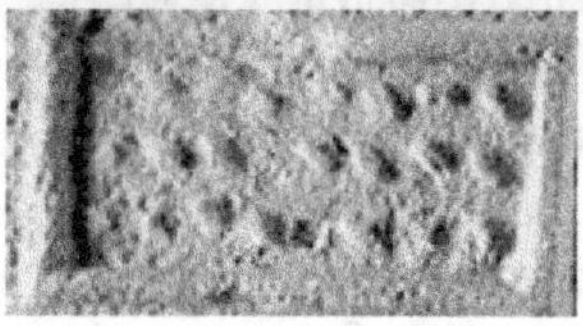

Rectangle with 12 dots on Harappa faience tablet; deciphered: metalcasting artisans

dula 'pair' Rebus: dul 'cast metal' PLUS baroṭi 'twelve' Rebus: bharata 'alloy of copper, pewter, tin'. Thus together, copper-pewter-tin-alloy metal casting. PLUS कारु [kāru 'twelve' Rebus: 'artisans' Thus, metal casting artisans.

Hieroglyph: A pair of twelve dots: dula 'pair' Rebus: dul 'cast metal' PLUS कारु [kāru] *m* (S) A common term for the twelve बलुतेदार q. v. Also कारुनारु *m pl* q. v. in नारुकारु. Rebus: कारु [kāru] *m* (S) An artificer or artisan. बाराकारू (p. 576) [bārākārū] *m pl* The twelve कारू or बलतेदार. See बलुतेदार.बलोतें, बलोतेदार, बलोता or त्या (p. 567) [balōtē, mbalōtēdāra, balōtā or tyā] Commonly बलुतें &c.

Hieroglyph: गोटा [gōṭā] *m* A roundish stone or pebble. 2 A marble (of stone, *lac*, wood &c.) Rebus 1: खोट (p. 212) [khōṭa] *f* A mass of metal (unwrought or of old metal melted down); an ingot or wedge. Rebus 2: goTa 'laterite (ferrous ore)' [khōṭasāḷa] *a* (खोट & साळ from शाला) Alloyed--a metal. (Marathi) Bshk. *khoṭ* ' embers ', Phal. *khūṭo* ' ashes, burning coal '; (CDIAL 3931)

PLUS कारु [kāru] 'twelve' Rebus: 'artisan' dula 'pair' rebus: dul 'cast metal' Thus, the 24 dots signify: ingot, laterite metalcasting artisan. The faience tablet of Harappa on both sides signifies through hieroglyph-multiplexes a catalog of metallurgical competence of the metalsmiths, laterite (ferrous) metalcasters.

Rebus 2: गोठघोळणी [gōṭhaghōḷaṇī] *f* A goldsmith's instrument for forming गोठ (metal bracelet).गोट [gōṭa] *m* (H) A metal wristlet. An ornament of women. 2 Encircling or investing

Pair of bulls deciphered as copper-pewter-tin-alloy metalcasters

Ka. kōḍu horn, tusk, branch of a tree (DEDR 2200). Rebus 2: खोट [khōṭa] alloyed ingot (Marathi). *koḍ* 'artisan's workplace'.

dula 'pair' Rebus: dul 'cast metal' Hieroglyph: *barad, balad* 'ox' Rebus: भरताचें भांडें (p. 603) [bharatācē mbhāṇḍēṃ] *n* A vessel made of the metal भरत. 2 See भरिताचें भांडें.भरती (p. 603) [bharatī] *a* Composed of the metal भरत.भरत (p. 603) [bharata] *n* A factitious metal compounded of copper, pewter, tin &c. Thus, the pair of bulls (ox) signified: copper-pewter-tin-alloy metalcasters

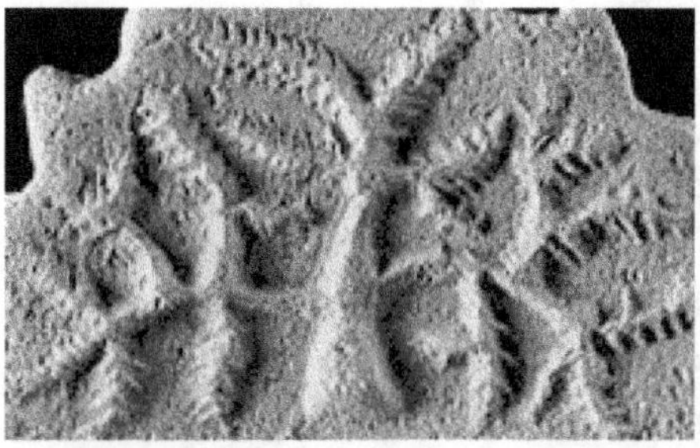

Lealess tree on faience tablet. Deciphered: metal alloy turner

Hieroglyph: *khōṇḍa* 'leafless tree' (Marathi). Rebus 1: *kõdār* 'turner' (Bengali)

Hieroglyph: kut.i, kut.hi, kut.a, kut.ha a tree (Kaus'.); kud.a tree (Pkt.); kur.a_ tree; kar.ek tree, oak (Pas;.)(CDIAL 3228). kut.ha, kut.a (Ka.), kudal (Go.) kudar. (Go.) kut.ha_ra, kut.ha, kut.aka = a tree (Samskritam) kut., kurun: = stump of a tree (Bond.a); khut. = id.(Or.) kut.amu = a tree (Telugu)

Text on Harappa faience tablet deciphered. alloy metal, copper-pewter-tin alloy, supercargo-scribe, portable furnace.

From r. aya 'fish' Rebus: aya 'metal (alloy)' PLUS aDaren 'lid' Rebus: aduru 'unsmelted metal' Thus, together, unsmelted alloy metal. baraDo 'spine' Rebus: bharata 'alloy of copper, pewter, tin'; karNIka 'rim of jar' Rebus: karNI 'supercargo' karNIka 'scribe'; karava narrow-necked jar' Rebus: karba 'iron' kharva 'nidhi of Kubera'. कंकवा (p. 123) [kaṅkavā] *m* A sort of comb. See कंगवा. कोंगें (p. 180) [kōṅgēṃ] *n* A long sort of honeycomb.Rebus: kanga 'portable furnace' Rebus: kangar 'large brazier': ***kāṅgārikā** ' poor or small brazier '. [Cf. kāgni -- m. ' a small fire ' Vop.: ka -- 3 or kā -- , aṅgāri --] K. *kā̃gürü, kā̃gar* f. ' portable brazier ' whence *kangar* m. ' large do. ' (or < **kāṅgāra* -- ?); H. *kā̃grī* f. small **portable** brazier '.(CDIAL 3006)

Who are the 12 बलुतेदार, public servants of a village in ancient India?

बलुतेदार or बलुता (p. 567) [balutēdāra or balutā] or त्या *m* (बलुतें &c.) A public servant of a village entitled to बलुतें. There are twelve distinct from the regular Government officers पाटील, कुळकरणी &c.; viz. सुतार, लोहार, महार, मांग (These four constitute पहिली or थोरली कास or वळ the first division. Of three of them each is entitled to चार पाचुंदे, twenty bundles of Holcus or the thrashed corn, and the महार to आठ पाचुंदे); कुंभार, चाम्हार, परीट, न्हावी constitute दुसरीor मधली कास or वळ, and are entitled, each, to तीन पाचुंदे; भट, मुलाणा, गुरव, कोळी form तिसरी or धाकटी कास or वळ, and have, each, दोन पाचुंदे. Likewise there are twelve अलुते or supernumerary public claimants, viz. तेली, तांबोळी, साळी, माळी, जंगम, कळवांत, डवऱ्या, ठाकर, घडशी, तराळ, सोनार,

चौगुला. Of these the allowance of corn is not settled. The learner must be prepared to meet with other enumerations of the बलुतेदार (e. g. पाटील, कुळ- करणी, चौधरी, पोतदार, देशपांड्या, न्हावी, परीट, गुरव, सुतार, कुंभार, वेसकर, जोशी; also सुतार, लोहार, चाम्हार, कुंभार as constituting the first-class and claiming the largest division ofबलुतें; next न्हावी, परीट, कोळी, गुरव as constituting the middle class and claiming a subdivision of बलुतें; lastly, भट, मुलाणा, सोनार, मांग; and, in the Konkaṇ, yet another list); and with other accounts of the assignments of corn; for this and many similar matters, originally determined diversely, have undergone the usual influence of time, place, and ignorance. Of the बलुतेदार in the Indápúr pergunnah the list and description stands thus:--First class, सुतार, लोहार, चाम्हार, महार; Second, परीट, कुंभार, न्हावी, मांग; Third, सोनार, मुलाणा, गुरव, जोशी, कोळी, रामोशी; in all fourteen, but in no one village are the whole fourteen to be found or traced. In the Paṇḍharpúr districts the order is:--पहिली or थोरली वळ (1st class); महार, सुतार, लोहार, चाम्हार, दुसरी or मधली वळ (2nd class); परीट, कुंभार, न्हावी, मांग, तिसरी or धाकटी वळ (3rd class); कुळकरणी, जोशी, गुरव, पोतदार; twelve बलुते and of अलुते there are eighteen. According to Grant Duff, theबलतेदार are सुतार, लोहार, चाम्हार, मांग, कुंभार, न्हावी, परीट, गुरव, जोशी, भाट, मुलाणा; and the अलुते are सोनार, जंगम, शिंपी, कोळी, तराळ or वेसकर, माळी, डवऱ्यागोसावी, घडशी, रामोशी, तेली, तांबोळी, गोंधळी. In many villages of Northern Dakhaṇ the महार receives the बलुतें of the first, second, and third classes; and, consequently, besides the महार, there are but nine बलुतेदार. The following are the only अलुतेदार or नारू now to be found;--सोनार, मांग, शिंपी, भट गोंधळी, कोर- गू, कोतवाल, तराळ, but of the अलुतेदार & बलुते- दार there is much confused intermixture, the अलुतेदार of one district being the बलुतेदार of another, and vice versâ. (The word कास used above, in पहिली कास, मध्यम कास, तिसरी कास requires explanation. It means Udder; and, as the बलुतेदार are, in the phraseology of endearment or fondling, termed वासरें (calves), their allotments or divisions are figured by successive bodies of calves drawing at the कास or under of the गांव under the figure of a गाय or cow.)(Marathi)

पोतदार (p. 532) [pōtadāra] *m* (P) An officer under the native governments. His business was to assay all money paid into the treasury. He was also the village-silversmith.पोतदारी (p. 532) [pōtadārī] *f* (P) The office or business of पोतदार: also his rights or fees.पोतनिशी [pōtaniśī] *f* (P) The office or business of पोतनीस.पोतनीस [pōtanīsa] *m* (P) The treasurer or cash-keeper.पोतेचाल [pōtēcāla] *f* (Treasury-currency.) The currency in which the public revenue is received. 2 Used as *a* Of that currency; as पोतेचालीचा (रूपया-पैसा- नाणें &c.) Coin or money admitted into or issued from the Government-treasury; sterling money of the realm.पोतेझाडा [pōtējhāḍā] *m* Settlement of the accounts of the treasury.पोथी [pōthī] *f* A book, a pamphlet, a manuscript.

Hieroglyph: पोंथ [pōntha] *m n* (Or पोंत) A seton. 2 Applied to the hole of a ploughshare.पोत [pōta] *m f* A bead of glass and, sometimes, of gold and of stone. 2 *m* A neck-ornament of females made of these beads. पोत [pōta] *m* (or P) A link composed of rolls of coarse cloth. This portion, together with the विडी or iron handle, constitute the मशालor torch. 2 The head, end, point (of a tool, stick &c.): also the end or extreme portion (of a thing gen.) 3 *m* A seton; and fig. the hole of a फाळ or ploughshare. पोतडी [pōtaḍī] *f* पोतडें *n* (पोतें) A bag, esp. the circular bag of goldsmiths, shroffs &c. containing their weights, scales, coins &c.पोतंडी [pōtaṇḍī] *f* A little thing (as a nut, a pebble,) or a small quantity (as of sugar, flour, grain) put up in a corner of a cloth and confined by a knot; thus forming a knob or ball. 2 Medicaments tied up in a corner of a cloth, to be dabbed on the eye or other part: also a cloth rolled up into a ball, heated, and applied to foment. *v* दे,लाव,

also पोतंडीनें or पोतंडीचा शेक.पोतें [pōtēṃ] *n* (or P) A sack or large bag. 2 The treasury or the treasure-bags of Government. 3 The treasure-bag of a village made up for the district-treasury.पोतेखाद [pōtēkhāda] *f* Wastage or loss on goods (as on sugar &c.) from adhesion to the containing sack or bag.

NOTE: A **seton** or **seton stitch** is, in medicine, a procedure used to aid the healing of fistulae (abnormal connections between two epithelium-lined organs or vessels). The trefoil may be an orthographic construction of three setons or three holed circles.

I suggest that the trefoil is read: pot-ti, the suffix -ti signifying three (Pali) tri- (Samskritam)

Thus, the shawl worn on the statuette decorated with trefoils leaving the right-shoulder bare signifying a priest becomes a phonetic determinative of the reading of the trefoil as potR. पोत [pōta] *n m* (H Quality; or formed by redup. out of सूत with which word it is generally conjoined in use.) Weftage or texture (of cloth); quality as respects closeness, firmness, body. Ex. सूत- पोत पाहून धोत्र घ्यावें.

போத்தி pōtti, *n.* < போற்றி. 1. Grandfather; பாட்டன். *Tinn.* 2. Brahman temple- priest in Malabar; மலையாளத்திலுள்ள கோயிலருச் சகன்.போற்றி pōṟṟi, < id. *n.* 1. Praise, applause, commendation; புகழ்மொழி. (W.) 2.Brahman temple-**priest** of Malabar; கோயிற் பூசைசெய்யும் மலையாளநாட்டுப் பிராமணன். (W.) 3. See போத்தி, 1.--*int.* Exclamation of praise; துதிச்சொல்வகை. பொய்தீர் காட்சிப் புரையோய் போற்றி (சிலப். 13, 92).

पोतृ [p= 650,1] प/ओतृ or पोतृ, *m.* " Purifier " , N. of one of the 16 officiating priests at a sacrifice (the assistant of the Brahman ; = यज्ञस्य

शोधयितृ Saly.) RV. Br. S3rS. Hariv.N. of विष्णु L. **पोत्री a***f.* N. of दुर्गा Gal. (cf. पौत्री).(Monier-Williams. Samskritam)

Slide harappa.com 41. Priest king.

Seated male sculpture, or "Priest King" from Mohenjo-daro (41, 42, 43). Fillet or ribbon headband with circular inlay ornament on the forehead and similar but smaller ornament on the right upper arm. The two ends of the fillet fall along the back and though the hair is carefully combed towards the back of the head, no bun is present. The flat back of the head may have held a separately carved bun as is traditional on the other seated figures, or it could have held a more elaborate horn and plumed headdress.

Two holes beneath the highly stylized ears suggest that a necklace or other head ornament was attached to the sculpture. The left shoulder is covered with a cloak decorated with trefoil, double circle and single circle designs that were originally filled with red pigment. Drill holes in the center of each circle indicate they were made with a specialized drill and then touched up with a chisel. Eyes are deeply incised and may have held inlay. The upper lip is shaved and a short combed beard frames the face. The large crack in the face is the result of weathering or it may be due to original firing of this object.

Material: white, low fired steatite

Dimensions: 17.5 cm height, 11 cm width

Mohenjo-daro, DK 1909

National Museum, Karachi, 50.852

Marshall 1931: 356-7, pl. XCVIII

Ta. potti garment of fibres, cloth. *Ka.* potti cloth. *Te.* potti bark, a baby's linen, a sort of linen cloth; pottika a small fine cloth; podugu a baby's linen.*Kol.* (*SSTW*) pot sari. *Pa.* bodgid a short loincloth. / Cf. Skt. potikā-, Pkt. potti-, pottiā-, etc(DEDR 4515) pōta2 m. ' cloth ', *pōtikā* -- f. lex. 2. *pōtta -- 2 (sanskrit- ized as *pōtra* -- 2 n. ' cloth ' lex.). 3. *pōttha -- 2 ~ *pavásta*<-> n. ' covering (?) ' RV., ' rough hempen cloth ' AV. T. Chowdhury JBORS xvii 83. 4. pōntī -- f. ' cloth ' Divyāv. 5. *pōcca -- 2 < **pōtya* -- ? (Cf. *pōtyā* = *pōtānāṁ samūhaḥ*Pāṇ.gaṇa. -- *pṓta* -- 1?). [Relationship with *prōta* -- n. ' woven cloth ' lex., plōta -- ' bandage, cloth ' Suśr. or with *pavásta* -- is obscure: EWA ii 347 with lit. Forms meaning ' cloth to smear with, smearing ' poss. conn. with or infl. by *pusta* -- 2 n. ' working in clay ' (prob. ← Drav., Tam. *pūcu* &c. DED 3569, EWA ii 319)]

1. Pk. *pōa* -- n. ' cloth '; Paš.ar. *pōwok* ' cloth ', *pōg* ' net, web ' (but lauṛ. dar. *pāwāk* ' cotton cloth ', Gaw. *pāk* IIFL iii 3, 150).

2. Pk. *potta* -- , °*taga* -- , °*tia* -- n. ' cotton cloth ', *pottī* -- , °*tiā* -- , °*tullayā* -- , *puttī* -- f. ' piece of cloth, man's dhotī, woman's sāṛī ', *pottia* -- ' wearing clothes '; S. *potī* f. ' shawl ', *potyo* m. ' loincloth '; L. *pot*, pl. °*tã̄* f. ' width of cloth '; P. *potṛā* m. ' child's clout ', *potṇā* ' to smear a wall with a rag '; N. *poto*' rag to lay on lime -- wash ', *potnu* ' to smear '; Or. *potā* ' gunny bag '; OAw. *potaï* ' smears, plasters '; H. *potā* m. ' whitewashing brush ', *potī* f. ' red cotton ', *potiyā* m. ' loincloth ', *potṛā* m. ' baby clothes '; G. *pot* n. ' fine cloth, texture ', *potũ* n. ' rag ', *potī* f., °*tiyũ* n. ' loincloth ', *potṛī* f. ' small do. '; M.*pot* m. ' roll of coarse cloth ', n. ' weftage or texture of cloth ', *potrẽ* n. ' rag for smearing cowdung '.

3. Pa. *potthaka* -- n. ' cheap rough hemp cloth ', *potthakamma* -- n. ' plastering '; Pk. *pottha* -- , °*aya* -- n.m. ' cloth '; S. *potho* m. ' lump of rag for smearing, smearing, cloth soaked in opium '.

4. Pa. *ponti* -- ' rags '.

5. Wg. *pōč* ' cotton cloth, muslin ', Kt. *puč*; Pr. *puč* ' duster, cloth ', *pū´čuk* ' clothes '; S. *poco* m. ' rag for plastering, plastering '; P. *poccā* m. ' cloth or brush for smearing ', *pocṇā* ' to smear with

earth '; Or. *pucā̆ra, pucurā* ' wisp of rag or jute for whitewashing with, smearing with such a rag '.Addenda: pōta -- 2. 2. *pōtta -- 2: S.kcch. *potyo* m. ' small dhoti '.(CDIAL 8400)

Ma. poṭṭi chicken pox. *Ko.* poṭ- (poc-) (hand) blisters from friction or hard work; poṭḷ a blister. *To.* pïṭ- (pïṭy-) (hand) blisters by friction. *Tu.* poṭlapustule, blister; puṭla id., bubble. *Te.* poṭamarincu to rise or swell up, as a boil. *Pa.* poṭka pimple. *Ga.* (P.) poṭ- to blister. *Go.* (SR.) boṭṭā, (G.) boṭṭa, (Mu.)boṭka, (Tr.) bōṭṭā, bottā blister (*Voc.* 2622); (LuS.) botta a boil. *Pe.* poṭka blister, protuberance on tree. *Kui* poḍosi, poṭkori blister; āḍi-puṭi smallpox pustule; bṛōga pimple, small boil. *Kuwi* (P.2) poṭka boil. *Malt.* poṭka sores on the feet. *Br.* pūtuṛō blister. / Cf. Skt. (*lex.*) poṭika- pustule, boil.(DEDR 4496)

Trefoil of Indus Script Corpora and Siva, Dance step of Ganesa, of Cosmic Dancer

Three strands, *tri-dhātu* is an Indus Script hieroglyph on पोतृ *pōtṛ* 'purifier priest' to signify *dhā̆vaḍ, dhamaga* 'smelter, blacksmith' working in alloy of three mineral ores.

Lokokti and Lokottara renderings of Indus Script Corpora messages. Siva and Ganesa as cultural identifiers of Bharatam Janam are evidenced by Indus Script hieroglyph-multiplexes signified on sculptural friezes and writing systems in a stunning continuum of nearly 4 millennia, from ca. 3300 BCE (Harappa potsherd with *tabernae montana* hieroglyphs) to Candi Sukuh Sivalinga and Ganesa iconography of 15th century. There are emphatic indicators of the veneration of the Cosmic Dancer Siva-Nataraja and Ganesa of the GaNa-s shown also on Bhutesvar cultural friezes in the context of smelting processes. The smelting processes date back to Indus Script hieroglyphs of trefoil *tri-dhātu* signifiers of metalwork. Metalwork in *kole.l* 'smithy' evolves into *kole.l* 'temple' venerating that Dancer of cosmic phenomena which find mirror images on smithy-forge work by smiths, Bharatam Janam, 'metalcaster folk'.

पोतृ *pōtṛ* 'purifier priest', adorned with the hieroglyphs of one dotted circle, two dotted circles and three dotted circles is: *dhā̆vaḍ* m. 'iron-smelter' and *dhamaga* 'blacksmith'. He wears two *paṭṭi* tied to a dotted circle, one on his forehead and another on his right shoulder. Rebus rendering is: *paṭṭi* 'hamlet, village'. Thus, पोतृ *pōtṛ* is *bhaṭṭāraka* 'arhat' of the village. The smithy is *kole.l,* the temple is *kole.l* He is the smelter, blacksmith working with three *dhātu, tri-dhātu* in a process which is a metaphor of the cosmic dance of the Cosmic Dancer engaged in dissolution and regeneration. The forge and the anvil are the dance-steps of smiths Bharatam Janam, metalcaster forlk, replicating with mere earth and stone in fire of the smelter, this cosmic dance.

Remarkably precise orthographic evidence is provided by the engraver of Sarasvati-Sindhu civilization who created the limestone statue of priest. This evidence is intended to signify *dhātu* 'strand' rebus: *dhātu* 'element or mineral ore (ochre, 'red pigment containing hydrated iron oxide' subjected to smelting to produce *muhã* 'ingot' or *muhã* 'quantity of metal produced at one time in a native smelting furnace'. A variant of ochre containing a large amount of hematite, or dehydrated iron oxide, has a reddish tint known as "red ochre". The words in Meluhha (Prakritam or Indian *sprachbund*) lexis to denote this red element are: Pk. *dhāu* -- m. ' metal, red chalk '; N. *dhāu* ' ore (esp. of copper) '; Or. *ḍhāu* ' red chalk, red ochre ' (whence *ḍhāuā* ' reddish '; M. *dhāū*, **dhāv** m.f. ' a partic. soft red stone ' (whence *dhā̆vaḍ* m. ' a caste of iron -- smelters ', *dhāvḍī* ' composed of or relating to iron '); -- Si. *dā* ' relic '; -- S. *dhāī* f. ' wisp of fibres added from time to time to a rope that is being twisted ', L. *dhāī̃* f.(CDIAL 6773). **dhā́tu** n. ' substance '

RV., m. ' element ' MBh., ' metal, mineral, ore (esp. of a red colour) ' Mn., ' ashes of the dead ' lex., 'Pa. *dhātu* -- m. ' element, ashes of the dead, relic '; KharI. *dhatu* ' relic '(CDIAL 6773).

The hieroglyph 'dotted circle' or a single strand is: **dhā´tu** strand of rope ' (cf. *tridhā´tu* -- ' threefold ' RV., *ayugdhātu* -- ' having an uneven number of strands ' KātyŚr.). [√dhā]S. *dhāī* f. ' wisp of fibres added from time to time to a rope that is being twisted ', L. *dhāī̃* f. (CDIAL 6773)

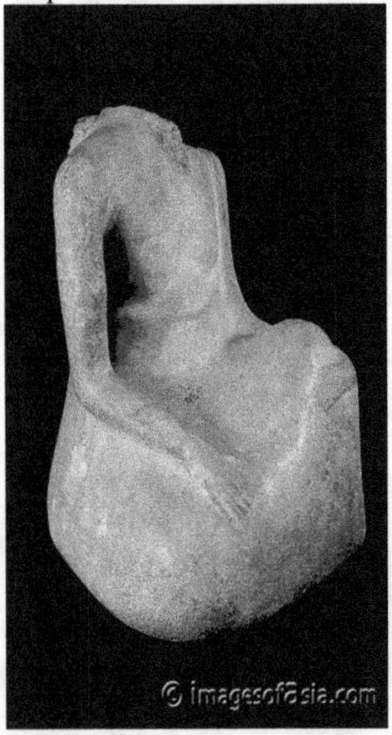

This hieroglyph also signifies rebus *dhamaga* (from root *dhma*) 'blacksmith' (Prakritam): dhma 'blow': dhamá in cmpds. ' blowing ' Pāṇ., *dhamaka* -- m. ' blacksmith ' Uṇ.com. [√dham] Pa. *dhama* -- , °*aka* -- m. ' one who blows ', Pk. *dhamaga*<-> m.; K. *dam* m. ' blast of furnace or oven, steam of stewing '; -- Kho. Sh.(Lor.) *dam* ' breath, magical spell ' ← Pers. *dam.* dhámati ' blows ' RV. [√dham]Pa. *dhamati* ' blows, kindles ', Pk. *dhamaï*, °*mēi*; K. *damun* ' to roar (of wind), blow up a fire '; S. *dhãvaṇu* ' to blow (with bellows), beat (of pulse) '; P. *dhauṇā* ' to blow (with bellows) ', WPah.khaś. rudh. *dhamṇū*, G. *dhamvũ.* -- Kt. *dəmō* -- , Pr. -- *lemo*-- ' to winnow ' rather < dhmāyátē. -- Kho. (Lor.) *damik* ' to work a charm on ' deriv. *dam* ' charm ' ← Pers. rather than < **dhāmayati.* -- Ext. -- *kk* -- or X MIA. *phukk* -- , *phuṁk* -- s.v. *phūtka -- : L. *dhaũkaṇ* ' to blow (with bellows) '; P. *dhauk(h)ṇā,dhaũk(h)ṇā* ' to blow (with bellows), bellow, brawl '; Ku. *dhaũkṇo* ' to blow, breathe ', *dhaũkalo* ' bellows '; H. *dhaũknā* ' to blow (with bellows), breathe on, pant '.dhamana n. ' blowing with bellows ' lex. [√dham] K. *damun* m. ' bellows '. -- Ash. *domótilde;* ' wind ' (→ Pr. *dumũ*'), Kt. *dyīmi*, Wg. *damútildemacr;*, Bashg. *damu*; Paš.lauṛ.*dāmā´n*, kuṛ. *domón*, uzb. *damūn* ' rain ' (< ' *storm ' → Par. *dhamā´n* ' wind ' dhamanī f. ' bellows ' KātySm., ' sort of perfume ' Bhpr. [√dham] Pk. *dhamaṇī* -- f. ' bellows ', S. *dhãvaṇi* f., H. *dhaunī* f., G. *dhamaṇi* f. (whence *dhamaṇvũ* ' to blow with bellows '); -- K. *daman*, dat. °*müñü* f. ' bad smell (esp. of stale curd or other bad food) '.(CDIAL 6730-2, 6734) ध्मातृ [p= 520,3] *m.* a blower , smelter or melter (of metal) RV. v , 9 , 5 *n.* a contrivance for blowing or melting ib. धमक [p= 509,3]*m.* " a blower " , blacksmith (as blowing the forge) Un2. ii , 35 Sch. See above: Pāṇ., *dhamaka* -- m. ' blacksmith ' Uṇ.com. [√dham] Pa. *dhama* -- , °*aka* -- m. ' one who blows ', Pk. *dhamaga*<-> m.

"Mohenjo-daro, a seated male figure with head missing. On the back of the figure, the hair style can be partially reconstructed by a wide swath of hair and a braided lock of hair. A cloak is draped

over the edge of the left shoulder and covers the folded legs and lower body, leaving the right shoulder and chest bare. The left arm is clasping the left knee and the hand is visible peeking out from underneath the cloak. The right hand is resting on the right knee which is folded beneath the body." -- Shahid Hussain Raja https://www.pinterest.com/pin/423620527183266625/

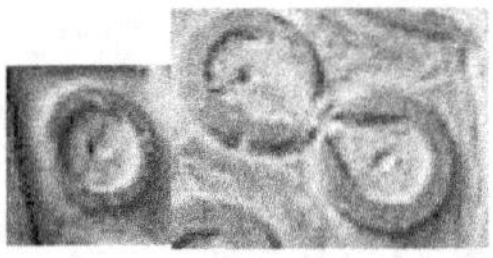

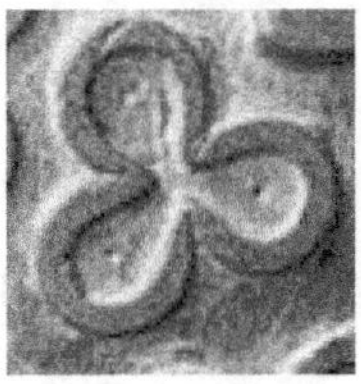

I suggest that a dotted circle is an orthographic signifier of one strand; two dotted circles joined together as orthographic signifiers of two strands; three dotted circles joined together as orthographic signifiers of three strands.

This orthographic rendering of the hieroglyphs can be vividly seen on the dotted circles shown on the uttariyam (shawl) of the priest statue of Mohenjodaro.

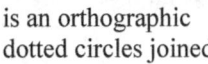

A single dotted circle pierced through with a string or band is shown 1. on the right shoulder; and 2. on the forehead.

The most common form of braid is the 3-strand braid. The technique is diagrammed below.

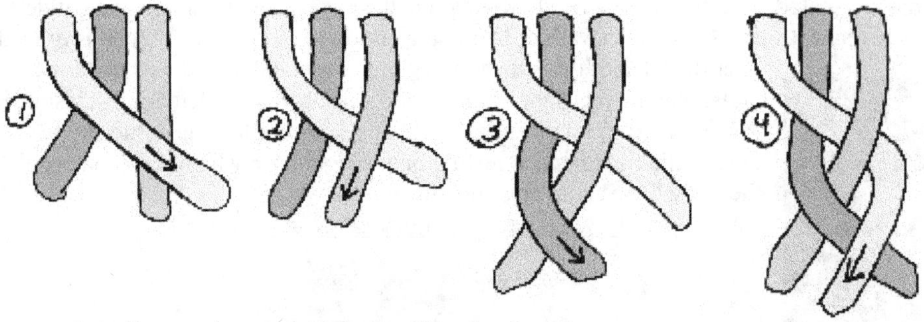

Source: http://www.virtue.to/articles/braiding.html

A three-strand braid, using hair, rope, or cord appears as follows:

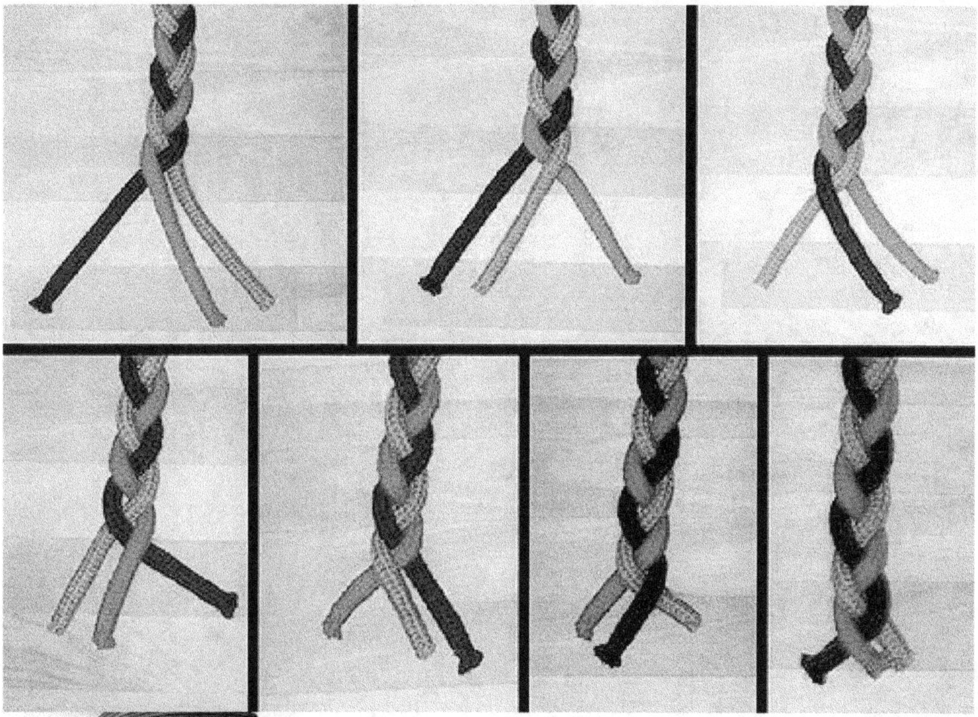

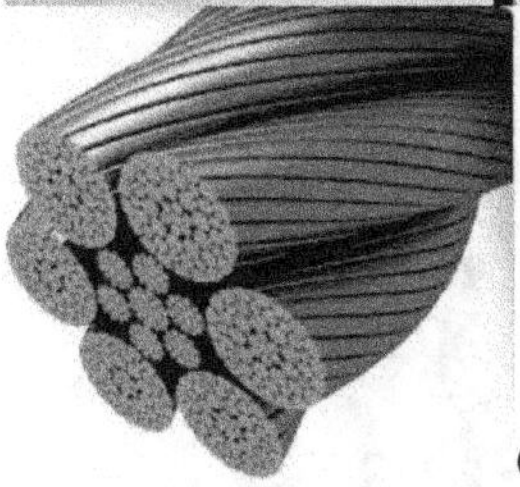

Cross section of a steel rope is explained by the folowing diagram of types of wire rope showing cross sections and construction.:

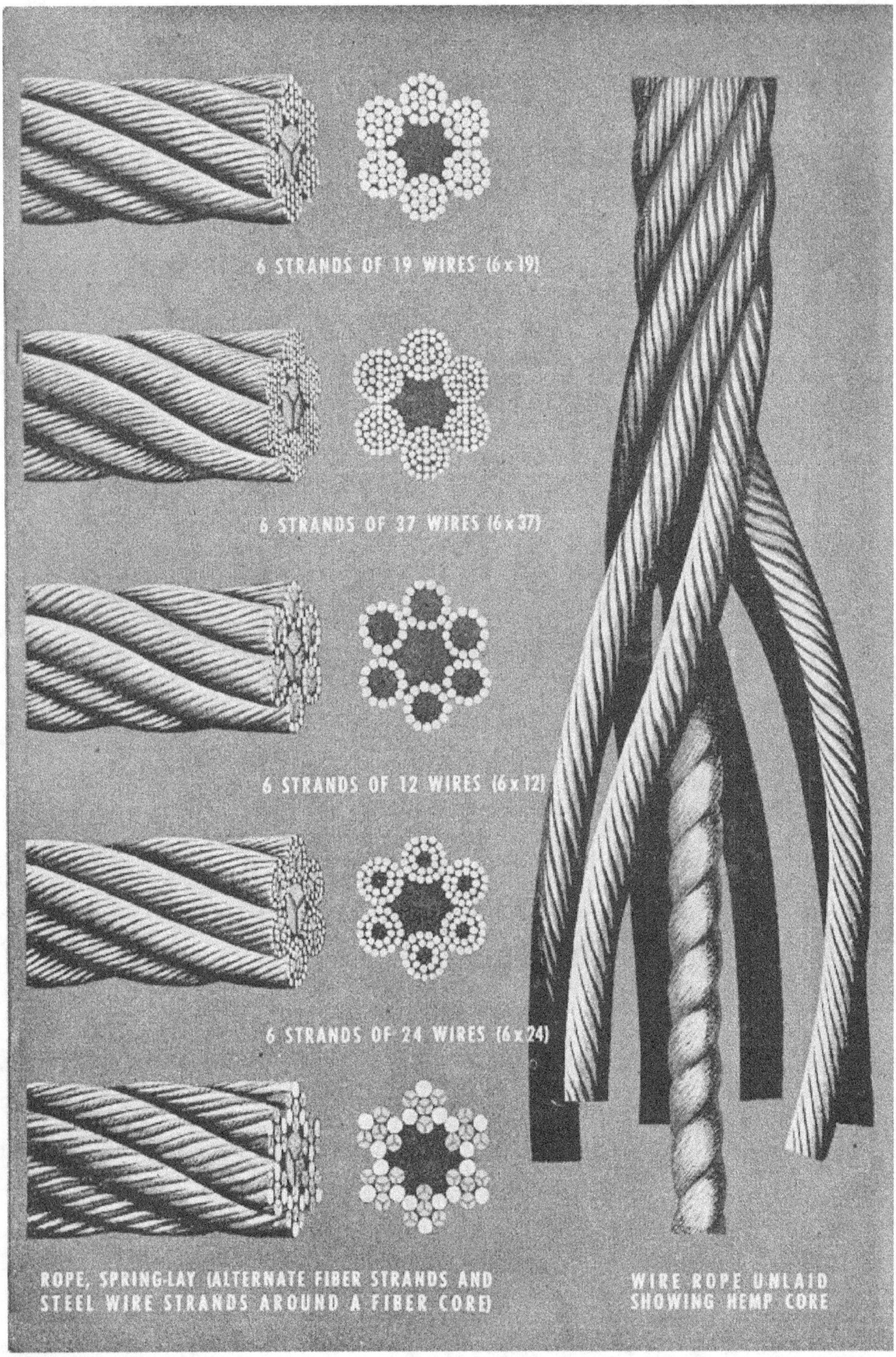
6 STRANDS OF 19 WIRES (6 x 19)
6 STRANDS OF 37 WIRES (6 x 37)
6 STRANDS OF 12 WIRES (6 x 12)
6 STRANDS OF 24 WIRES (6 x 24)
ROPE, SPRING-LAY (ALTERNATE FIBER STRANDS AND STEEL WIRE STRANDS AROUND A FIBER CORE)
WIRE ROPE UNLAID SHOWING HEMP CORE

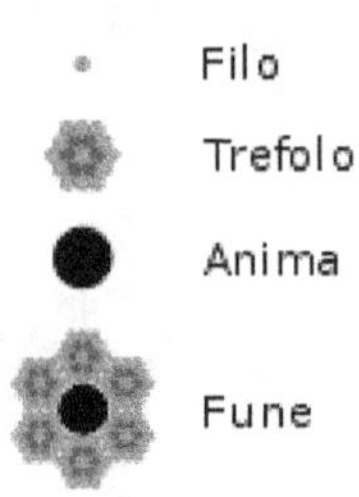

Italiano: Schema interno di una fune 6x19. Wire: filo, Strand: trefolo, Core: anima, Rope: fune
Wire-Strand-Core-Rope
English: Diagram showing construction of 6x19 fibre core flexible wire rope.
Source: https://commons.wikimedia.org/wiki/File:6x19_wire_rope_construction-en.svg

6 denotes number of strands that make up the rope
19 denotes number of wires that make up each strand

Steel wire rope (right hand lay) "**Wire rope** consists of several strands laid (or 'twisted') together like a helix. Each strand is likewise made of metal wires laid together like a helix. Initially wrought iron wires were used...Manufacturing a wire rope is similar to making one from natural fibres. The individual wires are first twisted into a strand, then six or so such strands again twisted around a core. This core may consist of steel, but also of natural fibres such as sisal, manila, henequen,jute, or hemp. This is used to cushion off stress forces when bending the rope." https://simple.wikipedia.org/wiki/Wire_rope

Rope that is used for holding ships in port

Close-up of a rope

Hieroglyph of dotted circle on the fillet on the forehead, right shoulder

பட்டா[3] paṭṭā, *n.* < U. *paṭṭa.* Outer rim of a wheel; வண்டிச் சக்கரத்தின் மேலிட்ட இரும்புப் பட்டம்.

9366 bhaṭṭa2 m. ' mixed caste of bards ' lex. [Cf. *bhaṭa* -- m. ' mixed caste ' lex., *bhaḍa* -- m. Cat., *bhaṇḍa* -- m. BrahmavP.Pk. *bhaṭṭa* -- m. ' bard '; K. *bāṭh*, dat. °*ṭhas* m. ' bard, panegyrist ', S. *bhaṭu* m., P. *bhaṭṭ* m., Ku. N. A. B. *bhāṭ*, Or. *bhāṭa*, Bhoj. Aw.lakh. H. G. M. *bhāṭ* m., Si. *bäṭṭayā*; -- S. *bhaṭiṇī* f. ' woman of this caste ', P. *bhaṭṭaṇ*, °*ṇī* f., N. *bhaṭini*, H. *bhāṭan* f.; -- N.*bhaṭyāunu* ' to lead a chorus '.
bhaṭṭāra -- see bhártr̥ -- .Addenda: bhaṭṭa -- 2: WPah.kṭg. (kc.) *bhā`ṭ* m. ' poet and singer ', kṭg. *bhā`ṭṭəṇ*, kc. *bhāṭiṇ* f. ' his wife '; Garh. *bhāṭ* ' bard '.

bhaṭṭārikāmaṭha 9367 bhaṭṭārikāmaṭha m. ' name of a quarter of Śrīnagar ' Rājat. (PW). [*bhaṭṭāra* -- s.v. bhártr̥ -- , maṭha --]K. *Bràḍimar* m. < **baṭarimar*?பட்டன் paṭṭaṉ, *n.* < *bhaṭṭa.* 1. Learned man, scholar; புலவன். மறைநான்கு முன் னோதிய பட்டனை (திவ். பெரியதி. 7, 3, 6). 2. Brāhmin-priest of a temple; கோயிலருச்சகன். 3. Spiritual master, god; சுவாமி. ஆலநிழலமர் பட்டனை (தேவா. 926, 1). 4. See பட்டர்பிரான். தண்புது வைப்பட்டன் சொன்ன (திவ். பெரியாழ். 3, 8, 10).

பட்டாசாரி paṭṭācāri, *n.* < *bhaṭṭa* *பட்டாசாரியன் paṭṭācāriyaṉ , n. < id. +. 1. See பட்டன், 1, 2. (W.) 2. founder of a sub-sect of Mīmāṁsakas; மீமாஞ்ச மதத்தினுள் ஒரு பகுதிக்கு ஆசிரியன். (சி. போ. பா. பக். 44.)* பட்டாமணியம் paṭṭā-maṇiyam, *n.* < U. *paṭṭā பட்டாரகன் paṭṭārakaṉ, n. < bhaṭṭāraka. 1. Deity; கடவுள். (பிங்.) திருநந்திக்கரை பட் டாரகர் (T. A. S. iii, 206). 2. One who attained the stage of Arhat; அருகபதவி பெற்றோர். நமி பட்டாரகர் (தக்கயாகப். 375, உரை). 3. Spiritual preceptor; ஞானகுரு. (பிங்.) முகுந்தோத்தம பட் டாரகர் (T. A. S. iii, 44). பட்டாவளி[1] paṭṭāvaḷi, n. < paṭṭaāvali. 1. List of successive spiritual heads, as among Jains; பட்டம்பெற்ற குருமாரின் தலைமுறை வரிசை. (I. M. P. Md. 42.)*

பட்டி[3] paṭṭi , n. < bhaṭṭi. The Prime Minister of Vikramāditya of Ujjayinī; விக்கிர மாதித்தன் மந்திரி.

பட்டி[2] paṭṭi, n. < paṭṭikā. 1. [K. paṭṭi.] Cloth; சீலை. (பிங்.)

2. Puttee, cloth wound round the legs in place of high boots; கணைக் காலிலிருந்து முழங்கால்வரை சுற்றிக்கட்டிக்கொள்ளும் கிழிப்பட்டை. *Loc. 3. Bandage, ligature;* புண் கட்டுஞ் சீலை. பட்டிகட்டுதல் *(*தைலவ. தைல*. 128). 4. Hemming;* மடிப்புத்தையல். *Loc.*

பட்டிகை[3] *paṭṭikai, n. < paṭṭikā. 1. Woman's girdle, belt of gold or silver;* மேகலை. *(*சூடா.*)* *(*S. I. I. *ii, 144.) 2. A belt;* அரைக்கச்சை. தொகை விரிபட்டிகைச் சுடருஞ் சுற்றிட *(*கம்பரா. கடிமண. 65). 3. Stays for the breast; முலைக் கச்சு. (சூடா.) 4. See பட்டி[2] 1, 3. (W.) 5. A shoulder-strap, used in yogic postures; தோளிலிடும் யோகபட்டி. தோளிலிடும் பட்டிகையும் (பெரியபு. மானக்கஞ். 23). 6. An ornamental structure around the wall, as in the inner sanctuary of a temple; கருப்பக்கிருகம் முதலியவற்றின் மதிலடியைச்சுற்றி அமைக்கப்படும் அலங் காரவேலையுள்ள பகுதி. தம்மிசை யிலங்கு பட்டிகையு மைஞ்ஞூறு விற்கடை (மேருமந். 1133).

பட்டி[1] paṭṭi, n. prob. படு[1]-. 1. [K. M. paṭṭi.] Cow-stall; பசுக்கொட்டில்.(பிங்.) 2. [K. M. paṭṭi.] Sheep-fold; ஆட்டுக்கிடை. (W.) 3. A measure of land, as sufficient for a sheep-fold; நிலவளவு வகை. (J.) 4. [K. paṭṭi.] Cattle-pound; கொண் டித்தொழ. 5. [T. paṭra, K. paṭṭi.] Hamlet, village; சிற்றூர். (நாமதீப. 486). 6. Place; இடம். (பிங்.)

Metmuseum.

Nataraja with *damaru* ‘drum’ and agni ‘fire’ on his hands. Bronze.

Achyuta, Narasimha, Adhokshaja with s'ankha, cakra, gada on their hands.

Vishnu with सुदर्शन चक्र Sudarshana Cakra in his right rear hand. Standing Figure of Vishnu, 10th century. Gilt bronze (high copper content) Brooklyn Museum

Parvati and Somaskanda carrying an antelope and paras'u on his hands. Bronze

पवि [p= 611,2] *m.* (perh. orig. " brightness , sheen " ; cf. पावक and Un2. iv , 138 Sch.) the tire of a wheel (esp. a golden tire on the chariot of the अश्विन्s and मरुत्s) RV. AitA1r. the metallic point of a spear or arrow ib. the iron band on a सोम-stone ib. a thunderbolt Naigh. ii , 20 an arrow Nir. xii , 30 क्षुर--पवि [p= 331,3] *mfn.* sharp-angled , sharp-edged , very sharp AV. xii , 5 , 20 and 55 TS. S3Br. Suparn2. *m.* (इस्) a sharp-edged wheel-band MaitrS. i , 10 , 14 (= Ka1t2h. xxxvi , 8 ; = Nir. v , 5) *m.* N. of a sacrifice performed in one day (एका*ह) S3a1n3khS3r.

चक्र [p=380,3] *n.* (Ved. rarely *m.* ; g. अर्धर्चा*दि ; fr. √ चर्? ; √1. कृ Pa1n2. 6-1 , 12 Ka1s3.) the wheel (of a carriage , of the Sun's chariot [RV.],of Time [i , 164 , 2-48] ; °क्र/अं- √चर् , to drive in a carriage S3Br. vi) RV. &c a discus or sharp circular missile weapon (esp. that of विष्णु) MBh. R. Sus3r. Pan5cat. BhP. the wheel of a monarch's chariot rolling over his dominions , sovereignty , realm Ya1jn5. i , 265 MBh. i , xiii BhP.ix , 20 , 32 VP.

<karaD>(Z),,<kanaD>(Z) {N} ``^sheaf of ^straw". #16160.(Munda)

kaṇḍa -- m.n. ' joint of stalk, stalk (Pali); *kā̃ḍ* m. ' stalk of a reed, straw '(Kashmiri); *kā̃ḍ* n. ' trunk, stem ' (Marathi); Or.*kāṇḍa, kā̃ṛ* ' stalk (Oriya);*kā̃ṛā* 'stem of muñja grass (used for thatching) (Bihari); *kānā̃* m. ' stalk of the reed Sara ' (Lahnda)(CDIAL 3023).

काड [kāḍa] n f Thrashed or trodden stalks of leguminous plants, pulse-straw. 2 f Straw (of wheat, नाचणी, उडीद, वरी and others). 3 C The chaff and bits that fall from rice-straw on beating or shaking it. 4 C Plants of rice left over from a transplantation. 5 Peeled stalks of अंबाडी or ताग. 6 n Legumes gen. (Marathi)

कांडें [kāṇḍēṃ] n (कांड S) Stalks and heads of corn once trodden or thrashed (as thrown or reserved for a second treading or thrashing).कंडारणें [kaṇḍāraṇēṃ] n An instrument of goldsmiths,--the iron spike which is hammered upon plates in reducing them to shape. 2 The handle of a ploughman's whip. 3 The central and thick part of a दावें. 4 A little indented instrument, used to cut flowers and figures out of paper. 5 A cudgel or club. 6 A large and coarse ornamental ring. Esp. used with सरीचें, गोट्याचें, कड्यांचें&c. as सरीचेंक0 7 A barber's nail-parer. (Marathi)

kā´ṇḍa (*kāṇḍá* -- TS.) m.n. ' single joint of a plant ' AV., ' arrow ' MBh., ' cluster, heap ' (in *tṛṇa* -- *kāṇḍa* -- Pāṇ. Kāś.). [Poss. connexion with gaṇḍa -- 2makes prob. non -- Aryan origin (not with P. Tedesco Language 22, 190 < *kṛntáti*). Prob. ← Drav., cf. Tam. *kaṇ* ' joint of bamboo or sugarcane ' EWA i 197] Pa. *kaṇḍa* -- m.n. ' joint of stalk, stalk, arrow, lump '; Pk. *kaṁḍa* -- , °*aya* -- m.n. ' knot of bough, bough, stick '; Ash. *kaṇ* ' arrow ', Kt. *kåṇ*, Wg. *kāṇ, kŕãdotdot;*, Pr. *kə̃*, Dm. *kǟn;* Paš. lauṛ. *kāṇḍ, kāṇ*, ar. *kōṇ*, kuṛ. *kō̃*, dar. *kā̃ṛ* ' arrow ', *kā̃ṛī* ' torch '; Shum. *kō̃ṛ, kō̃* ' arrow ', Gaw. *kāṇḍ, kāṇ*; Kho. *kan* ' tree, large bush '; Bshk. *kā`'n* ' arrow ', Tor. *kan* m., Sv. *kā̃ṛa*, Phal. *kōṇ*, Sh. gil. *kōn* f. (→ Ḍ. *kōn*, pl. *kāna* f.), pales. *kōṇ*; K. *kā̃ḍ* m. ' stalk of a reed, straw ' (*kān* m. ' arrow ' ← Sh.?); S. *kānu* m. ' arrow ',°*no* m. ' reed ', °*nī* f. ' topmost joint of the reed Sara, reed pen, stalk, straw, porcupine's quill '; L. *kānā̃* m. ' stalk of the reed Sara ', °*nī˜* f. ' pen, small spear '; P. *kānnā* m. ' the reed Saccharum munja, reed in a weaver's warp ', *kānī* f. ' arrow '; WPah. bhal. *kān* n. ' arrow ', jaun. *kā̃ḍ*; N. *kā̃ṛ* ' arrow ', °*ṛo* ' rafter '; A. *kā̃r* ' arrow '; B. *kā̃ṛ* ' arrow ', °*ṛā* ' oil vessel made of bamboo joint, needle of bamboo for netting ', *kẽṛiyā* ' wooden or earthen vessel for oil &c. '; Or. *kāṇḍa, kā̃ṛ* ' stalk, arrow '; Bi. *kā̃ṛā* ' stem of muñja grass (used for thatching) '; Mth. *kā̃ṛ* ' stack of stalks of large millet ', *kā̃ṛī* ' wooden milkpail '; Bhoj. *kaṇḍā* ' reeds '; H. *kā̃ṛī* f. ' rafter, yoke ', *kaṇḍā* m. ' reed, bush ' (← EP.?); G. *kā̃ḍ* m. ' joint, bough, arrow ', °*ḍũ* n. ' wrist ', °*ḍī* f. ' joint, bough, arrow, lucifer match '; M. *kā̃ḍ* n. ' trunk, stem ', °*ḍẽ* n. ' joint, knot, stem, straw ', °*ḍī* f. ' joint of sugarcane, shoot of root (of ginger, &c.) '; Si. *kaḍaya* ' arrow '. -- Deriv. A. *kāriyāiba* ' to shoot with an arrow '.kā´ṇḍīra -- ; *kāṇḍakara -- , *kāṇḍārā -- ; *dēhīkāṇḍa -- [< IE. **kondo* -- , Gk. kondu/lo*s* ' knuckle ', ko/ndo*s* ' ankle ' T. Burrow BSOAS xxxviii 55] S.kcch. *kāṇḍī* f. ' lucifer match '? (CDIAL 3023) *kāṇḍakara ‘ worker with reeds or arrows ’. [kā´ṇḍa -- , kará -- 1] L. *kanērā* m. ‘ mat -- maker ’; H. *kā̃ḍerā* m. ‘ a caste of bow -- and arrow -- makers ’.*kāṇḍārā ‘ bamboo -- goad ’. [kā´ṇḍa -- , ā´rā --]Mth. (ETirhut) *kanār* ‘ bamboo -- goad for young elephants.(CDIAL 3024,3025)

kā´ṇḍīra ‘ armed with arrows ’ Pāṇ., m. ‘ archer ’ lex. [kā´ṇḍa --] H. *kanīrā* m. ‘ a caste (usu. of arrow -- makers) ’.(CDIAL 3026)

*kaṇḍa ‘ pounding ’, *kaṇḍīkarōti* ‘ pounds, brays ’ Car. [√kaṇḍ1]Pk. *kaṁḍa* -- m. ‘piece, fragment ’; Or. *kaṇḍā* ‘ husked grain ’. -- Deriv. Pk. *kaṁḍārēi* ‘ scrapes, engraves ’; M. *kā̃ḍārṇē̃, karā̃ḍṇē̃* ‘ to gnaw ’, *kā̃ḍārṇē̃* n. ‘ jeweller's hammer, barber's nail -- parer ’. (CDIAL 2683)
kaṇḍáyati, *káṇḍati*1 ‘ separates chaff from grain ’ Dhātup. [√kaṇḍ1]
Pk. *kaṁḍaï*, pres. part. °*ḍiṁta* -- ‘ threshes rice &c. ’; P. *kaṇḍnā* ‘ to beat mercilessly ’; A. *kā̃riba* ‘ to clean (grain) ’; B. *kā̃ṛā* ‘ to clean finely (as rice) ’; Or. *kāṇḍibā, kā̃ṛibā*‘ to husk grain, beat ’, H. *kā̃ḍnā, kā̃ṛnā* ‘ to trample, tread on, crush ’; M. *kā̃ḍṇē̃* ‘ to husk rice by pounding in a mortar ’. A. *kā̃riba* also ‘ to husk paddy ’ (CDIAL 2686).

kaṇḍita ‘ dislocated ’ Apte. [√kaṇḍ1] Pk. *kaṁḍia* -- ‘ threshed ’; A. *kā̃rī* ‘ cleaned (of grain) ’.(CDIAL 2687)

Tu. kandůka, kandaka ditch, trench. *Te.* kandakamu id. *Konḍa* kanda trench made as a fireplace during weddings. *Pe.* kanda fire trench. *Kui* kanda small trench for fireplace. *Malt.* kandri a pit. (DEDR 1214)

Pa. kandi (*pl.* -l) necklace, beads. *Ga.* (P.) kandi (pl. -l) bead, (pl.1215 Pa. kandi (pl. -l) necklace, beads. Ga. (P.) kandi (pl. -l) bead, (pl.) necklace; (S.2) kandiṭ bead. (DEDR 1215)

kaṇḍa‘stone (ore)(Gadba)’. . Ga. (Oll.) kanḍ, (S.) kanḍu (pl. kanḍkil) stone (DEDR 1298).

Allographs:
kaṇḍa ‘arrow’ (Skt.) H. kā̃ḍerā m. ‘ a caste of bow -- and arrow -- makers (CDIAL 3024). Or. kāṇḍa, kā̃ṛ ‘stalk, arrow ’(CDIAL 3023).

खांडा [khāṇḍā] *m* A jag, notch, or indentation (as upon the edge of a tool or weapon). (Marathi)

kāṇḍa‘water’.

kaṇḍ ‘backbone’ (Lahnda);

Si. *kaṭa* ‘ throat, mouth ’ (X skandhá -- in SigGr. *kaṇḍa* ‘ neck ’) (CDIAL 2680).

 A hieroglyph on m0304 inscription: A खांडा *khāṇḍā* ‘jag’ infixed inside *kanka* ‘rim of jar’ glyph is read as the phrase: *kaṇḍa kanka*, ‘furnace account, scribe’. The rim-of-jar is the most frequently occurring hieroglyph in the corpora of Meluhha hieroglyphs (aka Indus writing). This hieroglyph is read rebus: Glyph: *kaṇḍa kanka*, 'rim of jar' Rebus: furnace account, scribe. cf. *kul -- karṇī* m. ‘village accountant’ (Marathi); *karṇikan* id. (Tamil)கணக்கு kaṇakku, n. cf. gaṇaka. [M. kaṇakku] 1. Number, account, reckoning, calculation, computation (Tamil) kaṇḍ ‘fire-altar’ (Santali) *kaṇḍa*, furnace (fire-altar, consecrated pit). khondu id. (Kashmiri)

m1656 Mohenjodro Pectoral. kāṇṭamகாண்டம் kāṇṭam, *n.* < *kāṇḍa*. 1. Water; sacred water; நீர். துருத்திவா யதுக்கிய குங்குமக் காண் டமும் (கல்லா. 49, 16). <kanda> {N} ``large earthen water ^pot kept and filled at the house". @1507. #14261.(Munda)
Rebus: *khāṇḍā* 'metal tools, pots and pans' (Marathi)

<lo->(B) {V} ``(pot, etc.) to ^overflow". See <lo-> `to be left over'. @B24310. #20851. Re<lo->(B) {V} ``(pot, etc.) to ^overflow". See <lo-> `to be left over'. (Munda) Rebus: loh 'copper' (Hindi) The hieroglyph clearly refers to the metal tools, pots and pans of copper. Thus, the two words read together Rebus:lōkhaṇḍa लोखंड Iron tools, vessels, or articles in general (Marathi). *khaṇṭi* 'buffalo bull' (Tamil) Rebus: *khā̃ḍ* '(metal) tools, pots and pans' (Gujarati)கண்டி kaṇṭi buffalo bull (Tamil) kaṇḍ 'buffalo'; rebus: kaṇḍ 'stone (ore)'.

lokhā̃ḍ 'overflowing pot' Rebus: 'tools, iron, ironware' (Gujarati)
ayaskāṇḍa is a compound attested in Pāṇini; the word may be semantically explained as 'metal tools, pots and pans' or as alloyed metal.

Kāru 'crocodile' (Telugu). Rebus: artisan (Marathi) Rebus: *khar*'blacksmith' (Kashmiri) *kola*'tiger' Rebus: *kol* 'working in iron' (Tamil).

Mohenjo-daro seal m0304. The

platform is atop two stacks of hay
(straw).
Kur. kaṇḍō a stool. Malt. kanḍo stool, seat. (DEDR 1179) Rebus: kaṇḍ = a furnace, altar (Santali) H. *lokhaṇḍ* m. 'iron tools, pots and pans'; G. *lokhā̃ḍ* n. 'tools, iron, ironware', the word *khaṇḍ* denotes 'tools, pots and pans and metal-ware'.

Ta. takar sheep, ram, goat, male of certain other animals (yāḷi, elephant, shark). பொருநகர் தாக்கற்குப் பேருந் தகைத்து (குறள், 486).Ma. takaran huge, powerful as a man, bear, etc. Ka. tagar, ṭagaru, ṭagara, ṭegaru ram. Tu. tagaru, ṭagarů id. Te. tagaramu, tagaru id. / Cf. Mar. tagar id. (DEDR 3000). Rebus 1: tagromi 'tin, metal alloy' (Kuwi) takaram tin, white lead, metal sheet, coated with tin (Ta.); tin, tinned iron plate (Ma.); tagarm tin (Ko.); tagara, tamara, tavara id. (Ka.) tamaru, tamara, tavara id. (Ta.): tagaramu, tamaramu, tavaramu id. (Te.); ṭagromi tin metal, alloy (Kuwi); tamara id. (Skt.)(DEDR 3001). trapu tin (AV.); tipu (Pali); tau, taua lead (Pkt.); *tū̃* tin (P.); ṭau zinc, pewter (Or.); tarūaum lead (OG.); *tarvũ*(G.); tumba lead (Si.)(CDIAL 5992). Rebus 2: damgar 'merchant'.

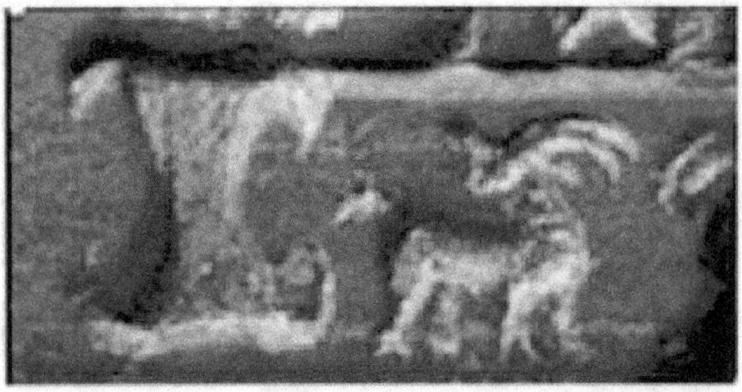

The pair of antelopes have their heads turned backwards. క్రమ్మర *krammara.* adv.

Again. క్రమ్మరిల్లు or క్రమరబడు Same as క్రమ్మరు.krəm back'(Kho.)(CDIAL 3145) Rebus: karmāra 'smith, artisan' (Skt.) kamar 'smith' (Santali) The two antithetical antelopes thus denote:*tagar kamar*'tin artisan, tin smith, tin merchant.'

Thus, the scribe on the Nagarjunakonda sculpture can now be named: *kaṇḍa kanka* -- 1. *kanka, karṇaka*'engraver, scribe' -- a remarkable continuum of the legacy of writing systems which originated in Sarasvati-Sindhu civilization ca. 3500 BCE.

kaṇḍa kanka is lit. a stone scribe account, an engraver of a writing system with representations of messages using Meluhha hieroglyphs.

The cartouches shown atop haystacks (stack of straw), on the Nagarjunakonda sculptural fragment depicting the 'scribe' are relatable to the same rebus readings as Meluhha hieroglyphs.

The engraver, scribe is shown holding a wedge on the Nagarjunakonda sculptural frieze: The phrase, *tanana mleccha* may be related to: (i) tah'nai, 'engraver' mleccha; or (ii) tana, 'of (mleccha) lineage'. 1. See Kuwi. *tah'nai*'to engrave' in DEDR and Bsh. *then, thon*, 'small axe' in CDIAL: DEDR 3146 *Go.* (Tr.) *tarcana*(Mu.) *tarc-* to scrape; (Ma.) *tarsk-* id., plane; (D.) *task-*, (Mu.) *tarsk-/tarisk-* to level, scrape (*Voc.*1670). Alternative: *kõda* 'young bull-calf'. koḍe 'young bull' (Telugu) खोंड [khōṇḍa] m A young bull, a bullcalf. Rebus: kõdā 'to turn in a lathe' (B.) **कोंद** *kōnda*'engraver, lapidary setting or infixing gems' (Marathi)

Asian
Bronze
Stylus

The images are only used as an example to show the nature of the stylus (possibly Roman). These are NOT an archaeologically attested, provenienced artifacts. Scribe uses a metal -- bronze stylus -- pointed needle (Pen, *nib* as in *ib*, 'iron') to engrave writing on palm-leaves.

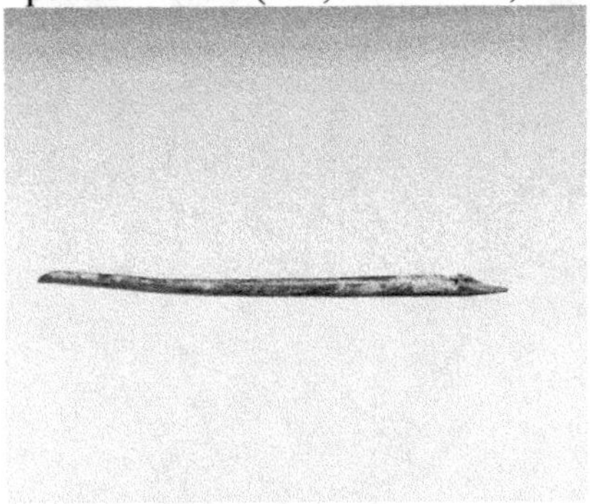

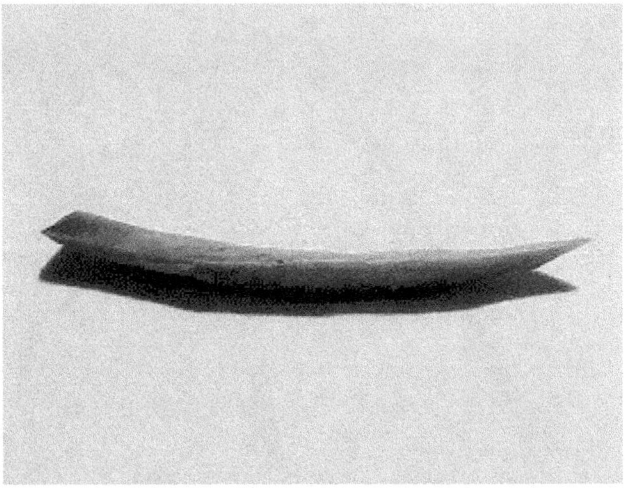

Paleolithic Burin This small flint tool comes from the area of Amiens, France. It dates from the Magdalenian period of the Upper Paleolithic, or late Old Stone Age, about seventeen to eleven thousand years ago. The tool, called a "burin" was used for engraving on bone, antler, and stone. It shows how finely the people of the Upper Paleolithic could shape and retouch their stone tools.

The people of the European Upper Paleolithic, often called Cro-Magnons, were anatomically modern humans, Homo sapiens. Dr. Wilson adopted the accepted classificaitons of their culture at the time, which was a scheme of three stages. Each stage is defined by a characteristic technological complex and named for a French archaeological site in which that complex was found: The Aurignacian first, the Solutrean following, and finally the Magdalenian. This sequence takes in the period of 40,000 to 11,000 years ago, and we now know that it applies only to Europe.
If you would like to know more about the peoples or tools related to this treasure, follow the link to a longer article in the Wilson Museum Bulletin, Vol. 4, No. 28.

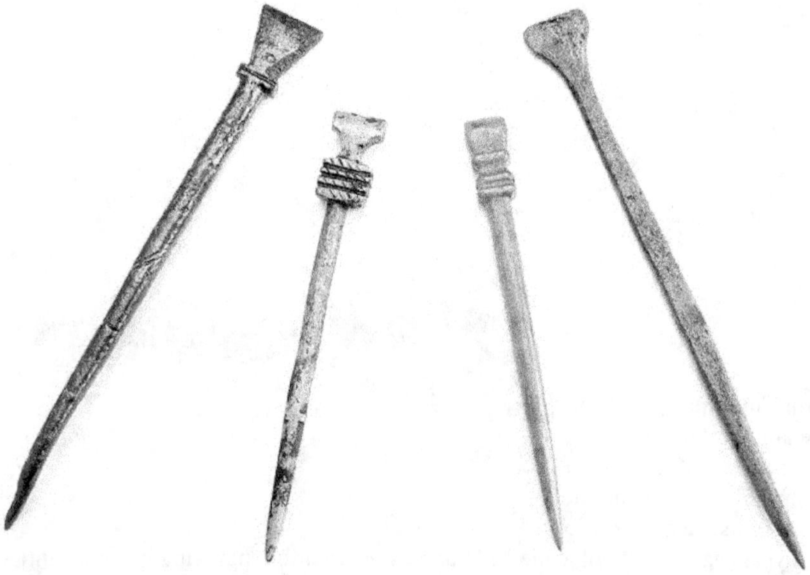

Examples of 4 Medieval styluses for writing on wax tablets. Two are made of iron, one brass and one bone stylus.

Plate 6.20 Metal styluses recovered from the urban mound, unstratified (courtesy of Mr. A.Rathnayake of Kataragama).

Metal styluses, Katargama (Sri Lanka)

Stylus with steel tip & sheath (Sri Lanka).

Borobudur temple frieze. Narrative of the Siddhartha Gautama becoming an

ascetic. At the bottom write is a scribe holding a stylus.

The palmyra leaves were used as paper to write books in ancient India. The letters were written with an iron stylus.

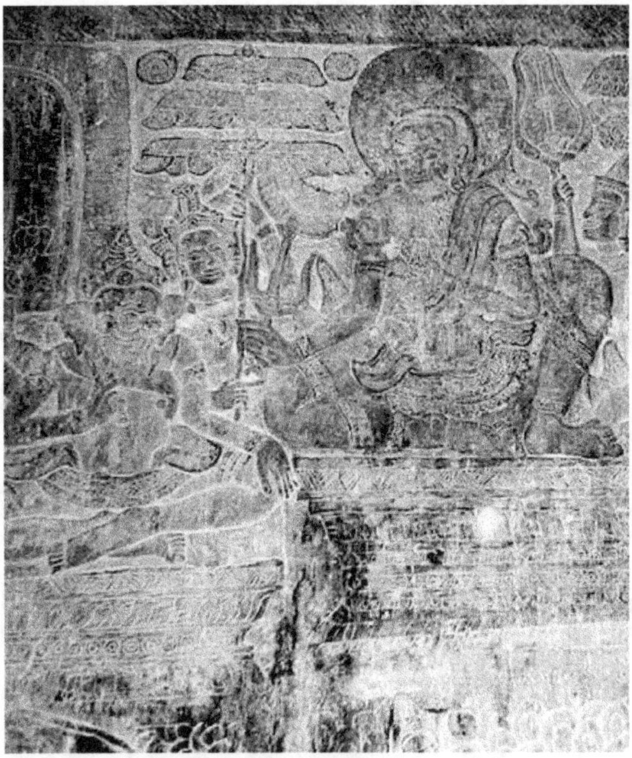

'trunk of elephant' rebus: karba 'iron' (Kannada)

Depiction at Angkor Wat of Vyasa narrating
the Mahabharata to Ganesha, his scribe.

\

Halebidu Sculpture. Ganesa holds one of his broken tusks on his right hand, depicting him as a scribe (engraver). This is an abiding metaphor in Hindu civilization tradition. (*ibha*'elephant'
Rebus: *ib*'iron' (Santali) karibha

Stone sculpture of the divinity of learning Sarasvati, holding the Vedas, a lotus, a waterpot, and prayer beads, 12th century, from Pallu, Rajasthan, Delhi National Museum

Sarasvati 6th cent.

Saraswati , black stone Chalukya dynasty (12 century CE)

Sarasvatī, 10th century, India
From Mathurā, Stone CarvingH = 68.6 cm, The British Museum
Writes Ludvik.: "She holds a zither in her natural hands, and a rosary and palm-leaf manuscript wrapped in cloth in her additional right and left hands." Zither is a stringed musical instrument. At her feet is her vehicle (Skt. = Vāhana), the haṃsa, a fowl resembling a goose or swan. In India, she is often shown playing a vina (zither) and often depicted with four arms.

Vajra Sarada, Pala Period ca. 8th Century, Nalanda Archaeological Museum, Biha

Sarasvati shown on caSAla 'snout' of varAha, a data mining metaphor for knowledge systems..

A revised reading of Sohgaura copper plate inscription which was first read by JF Fleet in 1907

गो-धूम **'wheat**, earth-smoke' of चषालः **caṣāla** of Yupa yields soma as elaborated in Satapatha Brahmana. Sohgaura inscription seems to refer to loads of caSAla received in the two warehouses.

Sohgaura copper plate inscription with top line of Indus Script hieroglyphs.

Text as read by JF Fleet (1907). I suggest that the expression Chathchu-medama-bhAlakAnam should be read: caSAla meDa bhArakANam. I suggest that caSala meDa bArakAna can be translated as 'loads of caSAla' or loads of wheat chaff, and meD 'iron') mentioned in Sohgaura copper plate inscription in Brahmi script. The sixth hieroglyph from the left on the top register signifies a railing with a yupa PLUS caSAla, together with two hieroglyphs signifying warehouses, two koṬThAgAra..

Text.

1 Savva-ti-yānamahāmaggānaṁ sāsane Manavasi-tikē
2 Dasilimatē Usagāmē=va ēte duve koṭṭhāgālāni
3 Tiyavani-Mathulā-Chaṁchu-medama-bhālakānaṁ vā-
4 lā kayyiyaṁti atiyāyikāya nō gahitavvāya

The first hieroglyph is a tree on a railing: kuTi 'tree' rebus: kuThi 'smelter'. ఈటె [īṭe] *īṭe*. [Tel.] n. A dart, a spear may be signified by iSTaka इष्टिका [p= 169,3] *f.* = /इष्तका q.v. L. इष्टका [इष्-तकन् टाप् Uṇ.3.148] 1 A brick; Mk.3. -2 A brick used in preparing the sacrificial altar &c. लोकादिमग्निं तमुवाच तस्मै या इष्टकी यावतार्वा यथा वा Kaṭh.1.15. -Comp. -गृहम् a brick-house. -चयनम् collecting fire by means of a brick. -चित *a.* made of bricks; Dk.84; also इष्टकचित; cf. P.VI.3.35. -न्यासः laying the founda- tion of a house. -पथः a road made of bricks. -मात्रा size of the bricks. -राशिः a pile of bricks.इष्टिका iṣṭikā इष्टिका A brick &c.; see इष्टका. This may be signified by the word 'Eto'. Read on line 2 of the text. Thus, the reading Eto duvo koTThAgAlAni is: ITe duvo koTTAgAra meaing: two warehouses with इष्टिका. The objective of the inscription is thus to signify the facilities for Yaga made available to itinerant artisans.

Sarasvati is a divinity of eloquence, connected with inspired thought -- *dhī* closely linked with *vāc* as speech and knowledge --and exemplifies the Meluhha traditions of vernacular and writing systems unraveled by the Bronze-Age Meluhha hieroglyph cipher evidenced by about 7000 epigraphs found in the Ancient Near East.

*Vāk*is called the language of Bharatas, *Bhāratī*. It is the voice, it is the vernacular and music. *brahma vai vāk,* mantra or chandas is speech. (ABr. 4.21.1) Hence, Sarasvati or *Brāhmī*can be related to both the literary and vernacular versions: Sanskrit and Mleccha (Meluhha). *Vāk* is the power behind all actions (RV 10.125.4-6). This power makes her to claim in a monologue: I am the *Rāṣṭrī*(that is, feminine form of *Rāṣṭram*- - the stable, lighted path bountiful in waters).

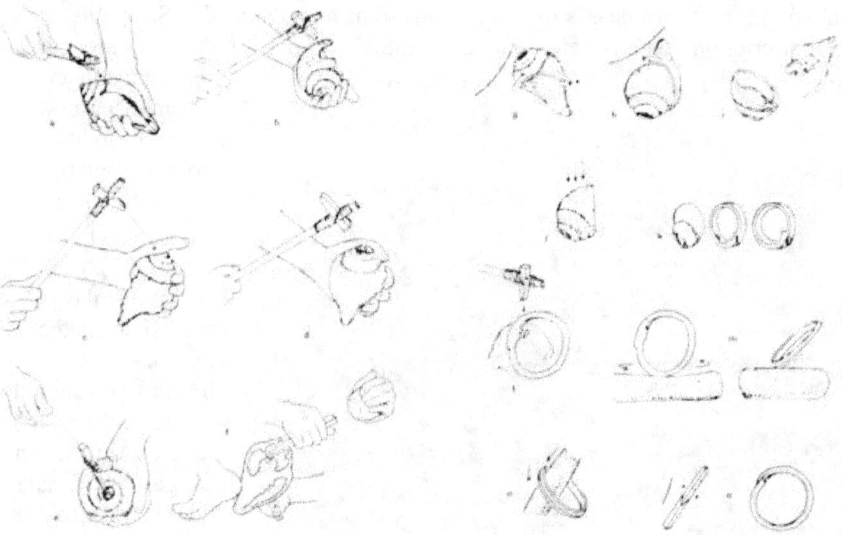

(After Fig.6. Bangle manufacture with Turbinella pyrum, Kenoyer, 1984)

http://www.persee.fr/doc/paleo_0153-9345_1984_num_10_1_4349

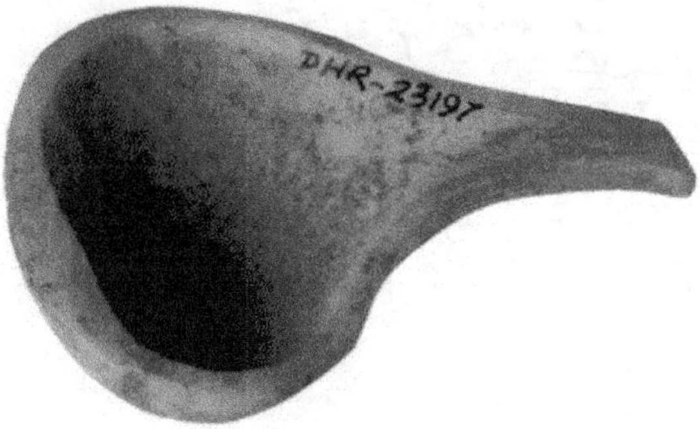

'Ladle' of Conch Shell, Chicoreus ramosus,from Dholavira, Gujarat,during excavations of 1989-2005

Conch shell. Signature tune of culture of Bharatam Janam.

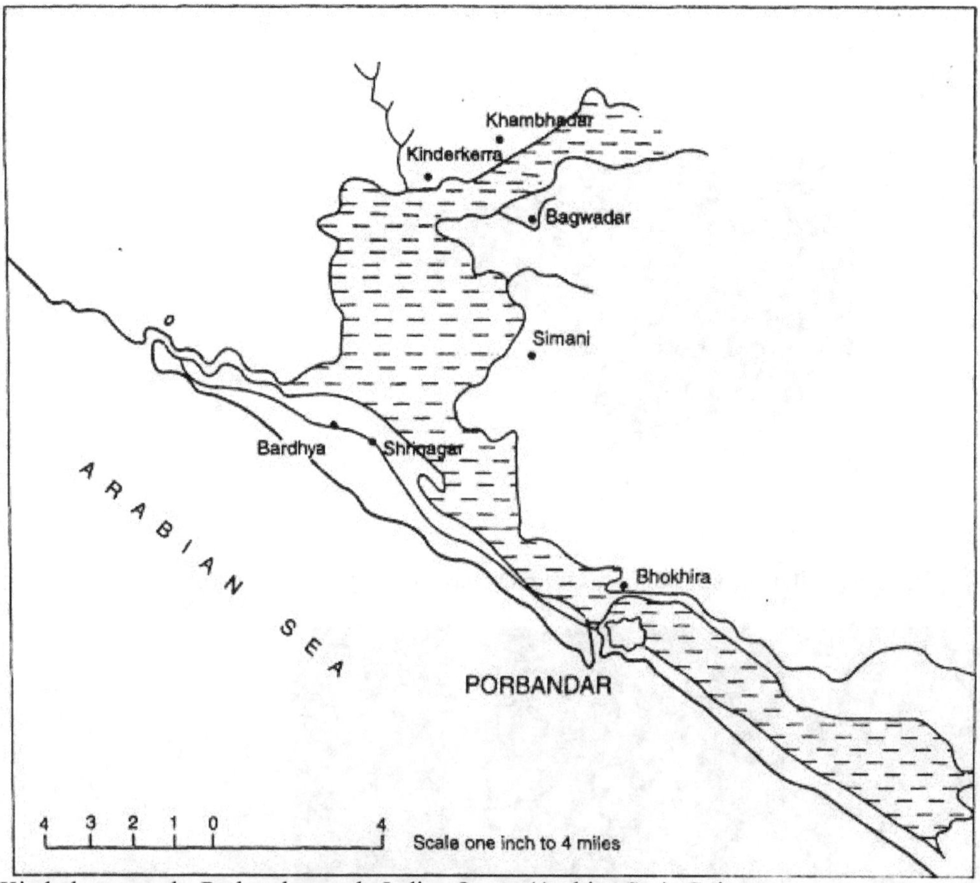

Kinderkerro on the Porbandar creek. Indian Ocean (Arabian Sea), Gujarat.

Kinderkerro shell objects. (AS Gaur and Sundaresh, A late Harappan port at Kindr Kheda on the Saurashtra Coast, in: *Man and Environment* XXX(2)-2005, pp. 44-48)

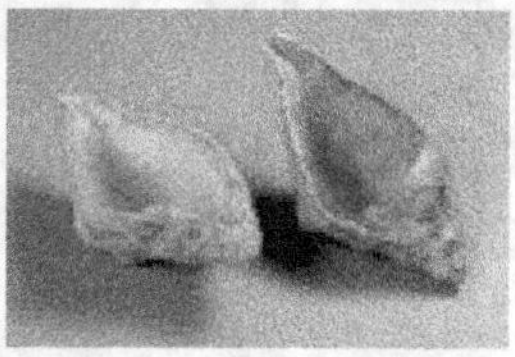

Vessel, pouring, 1, & 2, from royal tombs, ur. Conch shell. Sumerian. Royal tomb (PG 1819) & PG 143, royal cemetery, Ur, Mesopotamia. Philadelhpha U. Mus. 18.5x18cm. Cleveland Museum of Art http://library.clevelandart.org/node/201048

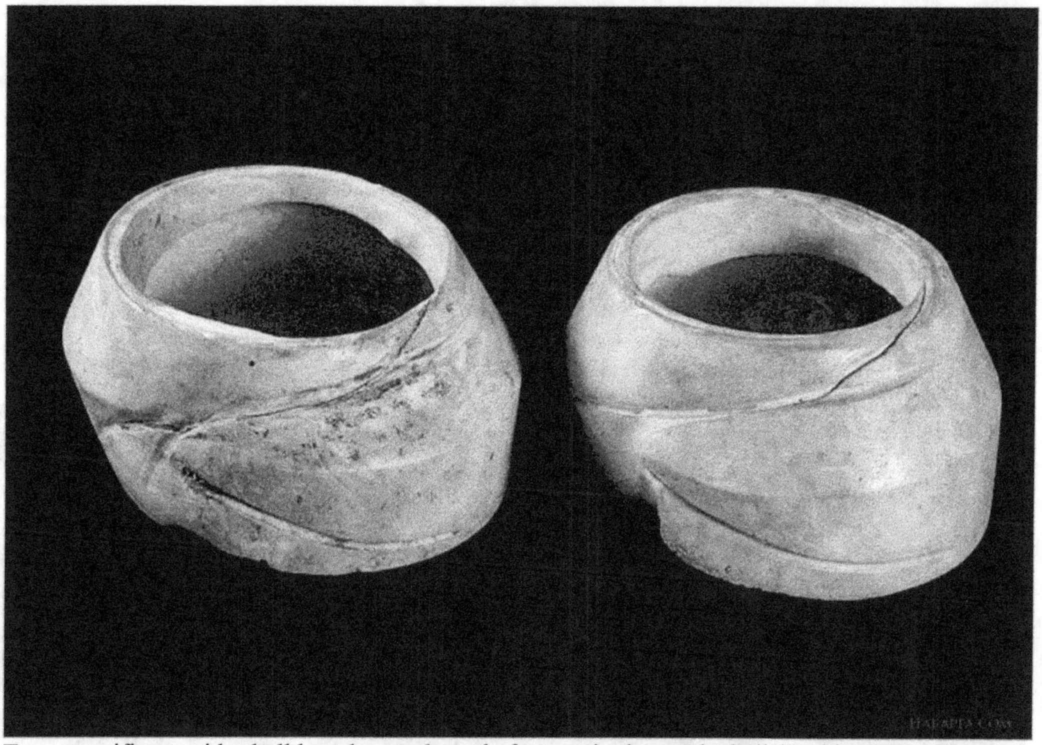

Two magnificent wide shell bangles, each made from a single conch shell (Turbinella pyrum) found at Harappa. "The use of marine shell in the manufacture of ornaments and ritual objects provides one of the most striking examples of the continuity between the Indus cities and later cultures in South Asia. Along the coastal regions of Makran, Kutch and Gujarat, the conch shell or Turbinella pyrum was collected throughout the period following the decline of Indus cities. Later, with the rise of cities in the northern sub-continent this marine shell became common at inland sites in the Gangetic region as far north as Taxila. As Mauryan contacts expanded to the south, some shell may have been collected from South Indian waters and traded to workshops throughout peninsular India." (Mark Kenoyer, Ancient Cities, p. 182). https://www.harappa.com/blog/two-wide-shell-bangles

Seal made of sankha shell. Dwaraka.

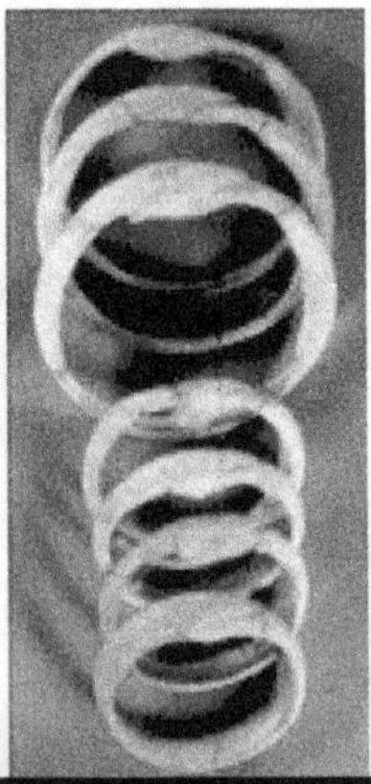

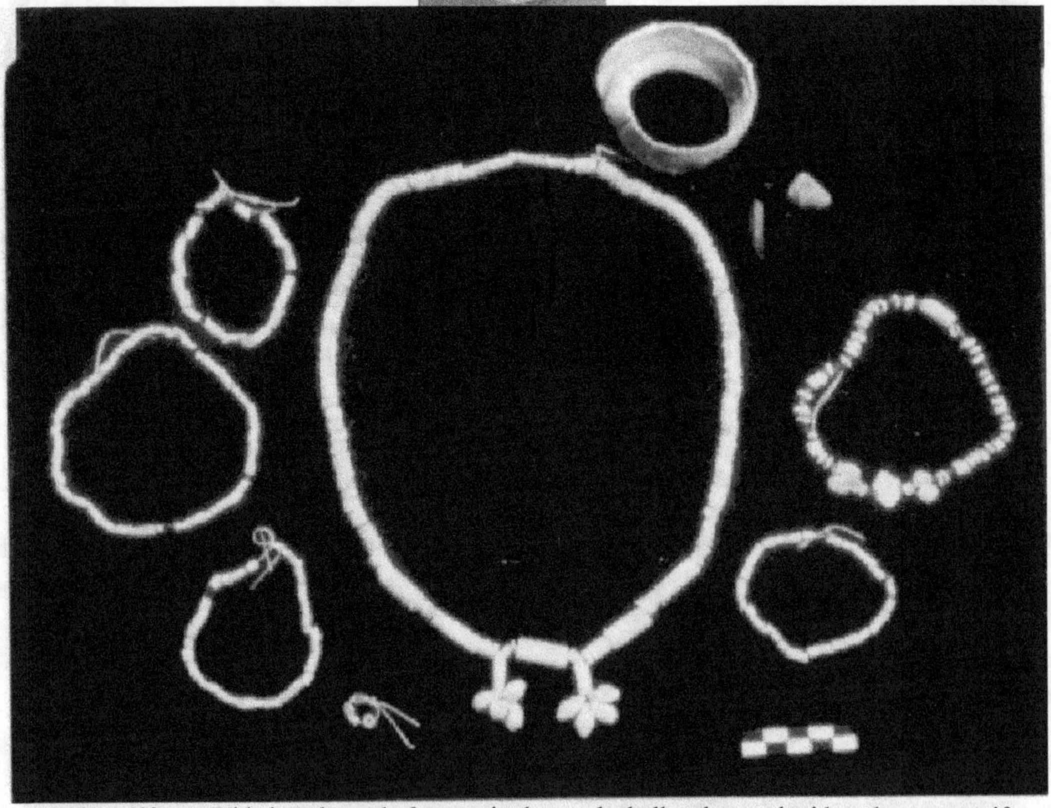

S'ankha artifacts: Wide bangle made from a single conch shell and carved with a chevron motif, Harappa; marine shell, Turbinella pyrum The wide bangleof s'ankha was found in a burial, Nausharo, dated to ca. 6500 BCE.

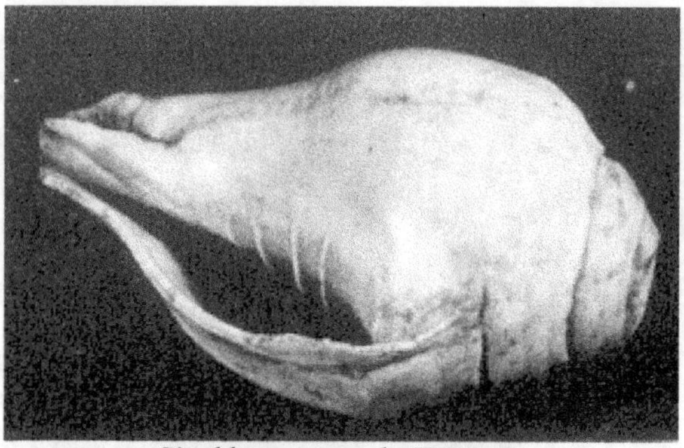

S'ankha as a conch. Harappa.

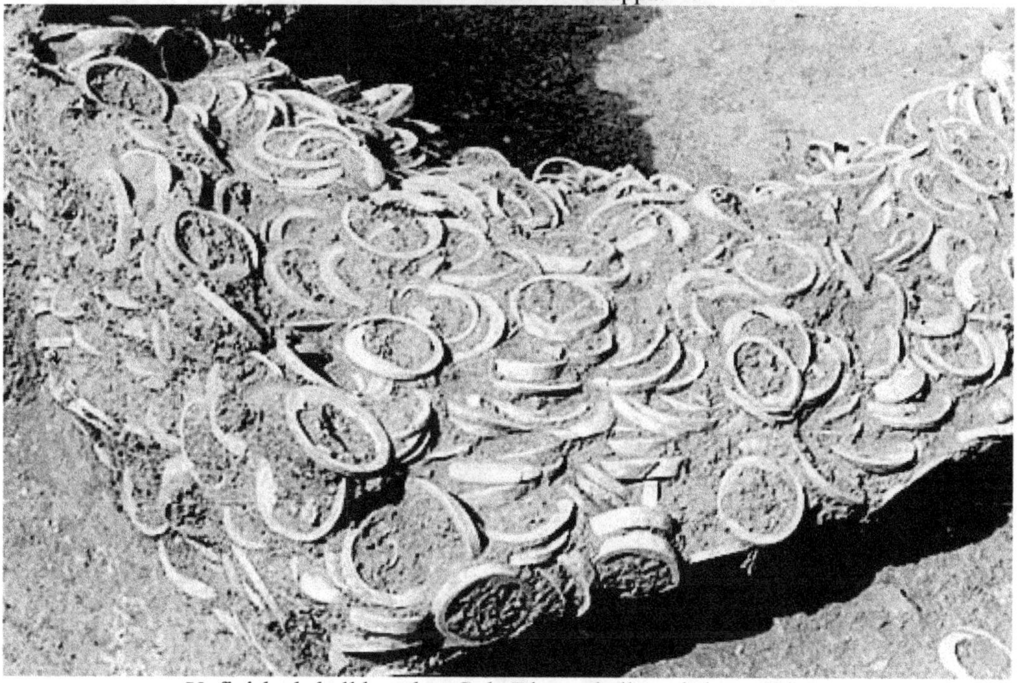

Unfinished shell bangles. Gola Dhoro shell workshop, Gujarat

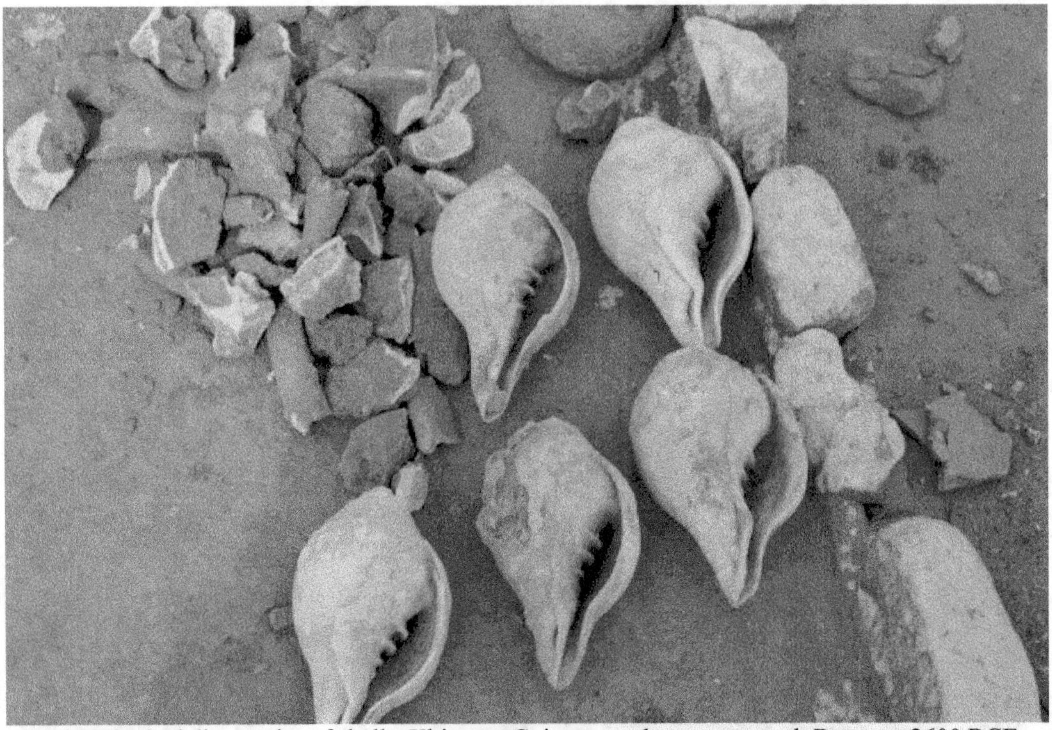

Archaeological discoveries of shells. Khirsara, Gujarat, at the pottery yard. Between 2600 BCE and 2200 BCE..

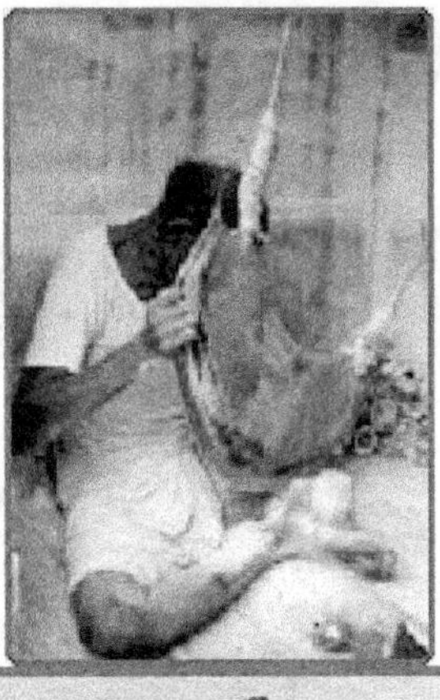

S'ankha artifacts: Wide bangle made from a single conch shell and carved with a chevron motif, Harappa; marine shell, Turbinella pyrum (After Fig. 7.44, Kenoyer, 1998) National Museum, Karachi. 54.3554. HM 13828. Seal, Bet Dwaraka 20 x 18 mm of conch shell. Seven shell bangles from burial ofan elderly woman, Harappa; worn on the left arm; three on the upper arm and four on the forearm; 6.3 X 5.7 cm to 8x9 cm marine shell, Turbinella pyrum (After Fig. 7.43, Kenoyer, 1998) Harappa museum. H87-635 to 637; 676 to 679. Modern lady from Kutch, wearing shell-bangles.

6500 BCE. Date of the woman's burial with ornaments including a wide bangle of shankha. Mehergarh. Burial ornaments made of shell and stone disc beads, and turbinella pyrum (sacred conch, s'an:kha) bangle, Tomb MR3T.21, Mehrgarh, Period 1A, ca. 6500 BCE. The nearest source for this shell is Makran coast near Karachi, 500 km. South. [After Fig. 2.10 in Kenoyer, 1998]. S'ankha wide bangle and other ornaments, c. 6500 BCE (burial of a woman at Nausharo). Glyph: 'shell-cutter's saw'

Turbinella pyrum —śankha-bangle found in a woman's grave in Mehergarh, dated to c. 6500 BCE, yes 7th millennium BCE; the type of shell found nowhere else in the world excepting the coastline of Sindhu sāgara upto to the Gulf of Mannar

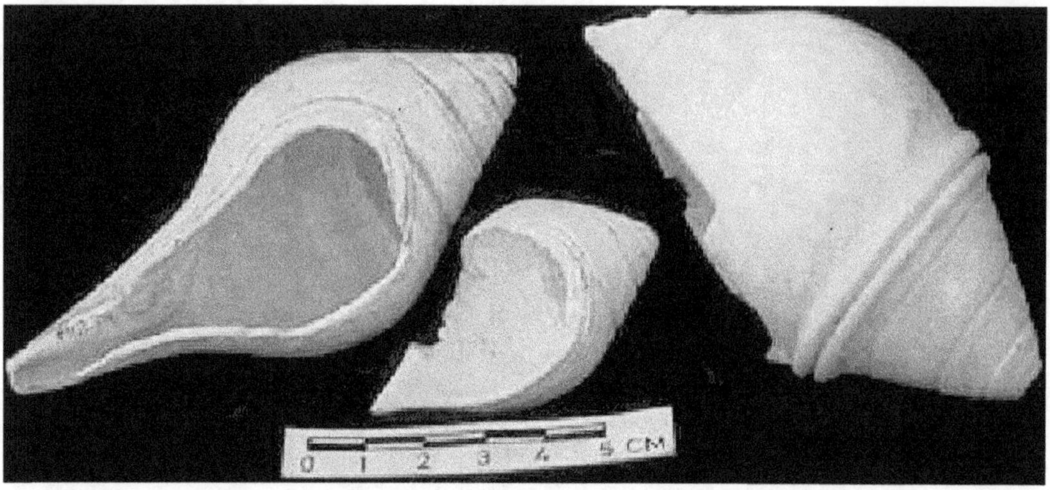

Libation vessels made of the conch shell Turbinella pyrum. One of these is decorated with vermilion filled incised lines. A single spiraling design is carved around the apex and a double incised line frames the edge of the orifice. This type of vessel was used in later times for ritual libations and for administering sacred water or medicine to patients.

Material: marine shell, Turbinella pyrum
Dimensions of the left vessel: 11.4 cm length, 5.4 cm width, 4.7 cm height.
Mohenjo-daro, DK 8538
Mohenjo-daro Museum, 52.2114, MM5073
Kenoyer 1983: 183-4, fig. 3-15, 5.Source: Harappa.com

Candi Sukuh

Pylon with womb-shaped sculptural relief, Candi Sukuh. Bhima, a hero of the Mahabharata, who stands opposite a pedestaled god within a horseshoe-shaped arch.The figures are sculpted in wayang puppet style, resembling theirleather-puppet counterparts in posture, costume, and sideways presentation.

Kneeling Bhima with club. Candi Ceto.

Consecrated Ganggasudhi sivalinga, Candi Sukuh

Pannenborg-Stutterheim's studies based on descriptive and iconographic studies, point to a Mahabharata narrative adapted in Javanese texts.
Candi Sukuh temple was consecrated by Bhre Daha in 1440 CE celebrating Bhima, an embodiment of the philosophy of life alternating between death and rebirth in an eternal cycle, a cosmic dance. King Kertanagara's role in unifying Majapahit Empire, founded on Dharma-Dhamma is recorded in history. Some refer to Candi Sukuh as a temple venerating Tantrik Saivism as 'Bhima cult'. Bhre Daha belonged to the tradition of royal purohita Bhagawan Ganggasudhi, associated with the royal house of Girindrawardhana. Gangga sudhi is rebus for kanga sudhi 'purification by brazier, kanga'.

Stutterheim, WF, 1935, Indian influences in Old-Balinese Art, London, The India Society argues for the iconography of Candi Sukuh and Candi Ceto based on Mahabharata narratives in Javanese texts. The episodes relate to the narration of Bhima's birth from a caul in *Bhima Bungkus* and other Mahabharata episodes from *Bhima Suwarga*.

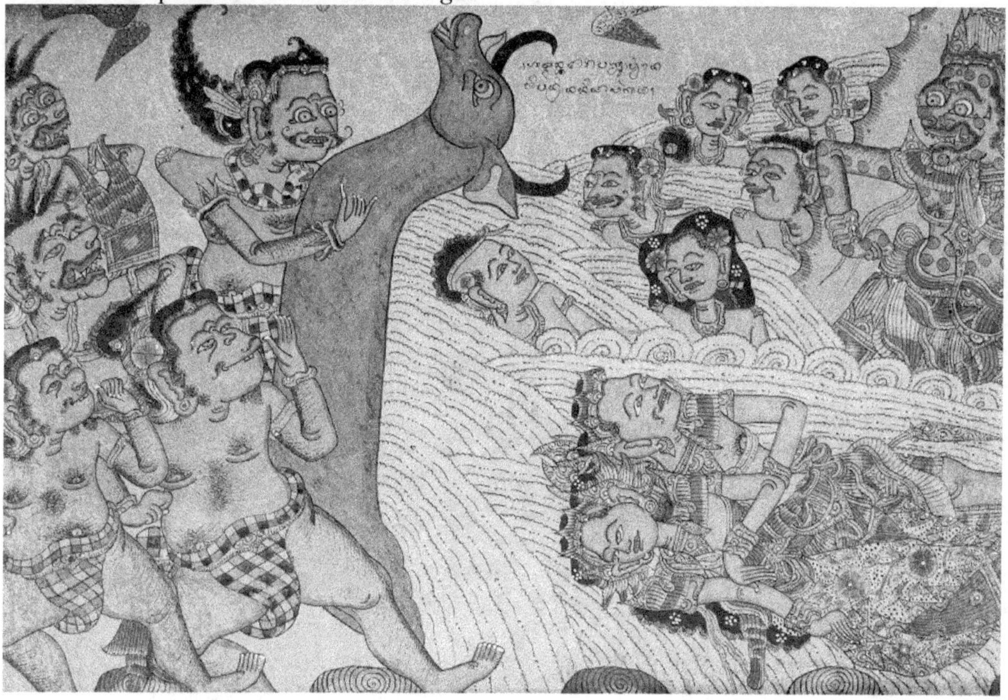

Paintings in Bali based in Bhima Suwarga. Bhima rescues the Atman of Pandu from hell with guidance from Siva.

I suggest that the narrative of dhā̆vaḍ, dhamaga 'smelter, blacksmith' working in alloy of three mineral ores in Indus Script hieroglyphs is a cultural idiom signified on Candi Sukuh sculptural narratives. The connecting link is Siva and Ganesa, as shown by the ekamukha sivalinga and gana on Bhutesvar reliefs shown in the context of a smelter.

A tree associated with smelter and linga from Bhuteshwar, Mathura Museum. Architectural fragment with relief showing winged dwarfs (or gaNa) worshipping with flower garlands, Siva Linga. Bhuteshwar, ca. 2nd cent BCE. Lingam is on a platform with wall under a pipal tree encircled by railing. (Srivastava, AK, 1999, Catalog of Saiva sculptures in Government Museum, Mathura: 47, GMM 52.3625) The tree is a phonetic determinant of the smelter indicated by the railing around the linga: kuṭa, °*ṭi* -- , °*ṭha* -- 3, °*ṭhi* -- m. ' tree ' Rebus: *kuṭhi* 'smelter'. *kuṭa,* °*ṭi* -- , °*ṭha* -- 3, °*ṭhi* -- m. ' tree ' lex., °*ṭaka* -- m. ' a kind of tree ' Kauś.Pk. *kuḍa* -- m. ' tree '; Paš. lauṛ. *kuṛā́* ' tree ', dar. *kaṛék* ' tree, oak ' ~ Par. *kōṛ* ' stick ' IIFL iii 3, 98. (CDIAL 3228)

Worship of Siva Linga by Gandharvas - Shunga Period - Bhuteshwar - ACCN 3625.The Curzon Museum of Archaeology, Museum Road or Murari Lal Rajpal road, Dampier Nagar, Mathura, Uttar Pradesh, India.

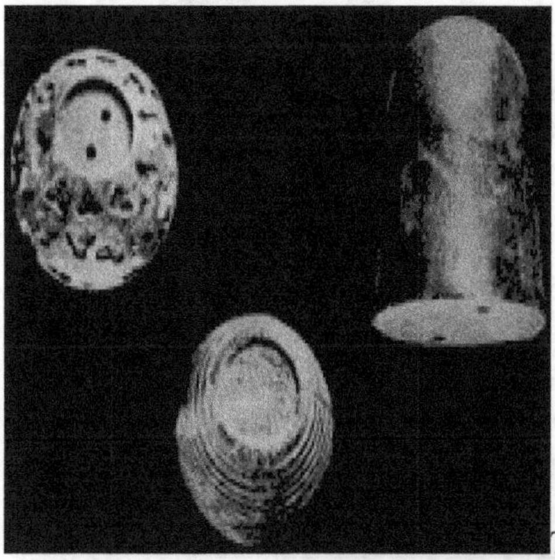

The base is decorated with 'trefoil' indicating three perforations or three strands: *tri-dhātu* signifying three mineral ores, *tri-dhātu*.

Lingam, grey sandstone in situ, Harappa, Trench Ai, Mound F, Pl. X (c) (After Vats). "In an earthenware jar, No. 12414, recovered from Mound F, Trench IV, Square I
Terracotta sivalinga, Kalibangan.

Ekamukha Sivalinga Relief with Ekamukha linga. Mathura. 1st cent. CE (Fig. 6.2). This is the most emphatic

representation of linga as a pillar of fire. The pillar is embedded within a brick-kiln with an angular roof and is ligatured to a tree. Hieroglyph: kuTi 'tree' rebus: kuThi 'smelter'. In this composition, the artists is depicting the smelter used for smelting to create *mũh* 'face' (Hindi) rebus: *mũhe* 'ingot' (Santali) of *mēḍha* 'stake' rebus: *meḍ* 'iron, metal' (Ho. Munda). मेड (p. 662) [mēḍa] *f* (Usually मेढ q. v.) मेडका *m* A stake, esp. as bifurcated. मेढ (p. 662) [mēḍha] *f* A forked stake. Used as a post. Hence a short post generally whether forked or not. मेढा (p. 665) [mēḍhā] *m* A stake, esp. as forked. 2 A dense arrangement of stakes, a palisade, a paling. मेढी (p. 665) [mēḍhī] *f* (Dim. of मेढ) A small bifurcated stake: also a small stake, with or without furcation, used as a post to support a cross piece. मेढ्या (p. 665) [mēḍhyā] *a* (मेढ Stake or post.) A term for a person considered as the pillar, prop, or support (of a household, army, or other body), the *staff* or *stay*. मेढेजोशी (p. 665) [mēḍhējōśī] *m* A stake-जोशी; a जोशी who keeps account of the तिथि &c., by driving stakes into the ground: also a class, or an individual of it, of fortune-tellers, diviners, presagers, seasonannouncers, almanack-makers &c. They are Shúdras and followers of the मेढेमत q. v. 2 Jocosely. The hereditary or settled (quasi fixed as a stake) जोशी of a

village.मेंधला (p. 665) [mēndhalā] *m* In architecture. A common term for the two upper arms of a double चौकठ (door-frame) connecting the two. Called also मेंढरी & घोडा. It answers to छिली the name of the two lower arms or connections. (Marathi)
मेंढा [*mēṇḍhā*] A crook or curved end rebus: *meḍ* 'iron, metal' (Ho. Munda)
The association of dwarfs, gaNa is consistent with the interpretation of Ganesa iconography with elephant trunk: karibha 'elephant trunk' (Pali) rebua: karba 'iron' (Tulu); ib 'iron' (Santali) kara 'trunk' khAr 'blacksmith'. Siva's gaNa are Bharatam Janam, metalcaster folk engaged with पोतृ pōtṟ 'purifier priest' to signify dhā̆vaḍ, dhamaga 'smelter, blacksmith' working in alloy of three mineral ores. The garland depicted on Bhutesvar sculptural friezes signifies: dhAman 'garland, rope' rebus: dhamaga 'blacksmith', dhmAtr 'smelter'.

Candi Sukuh and Candi Ceto narratives are a cultural continuum of the veneration of Skambha, the fiery pillar of light as a metaphor for the cosmic dance of dissolution and regeneration. The message of the narratives of Indus Script hieroglyphs and of Candi Sukuh/Candi Ceto are the same: liberation of the Atman as the Cosmic Dancer renders in rhythm and dance the Cosmic phenomena finding expression in kole.l 'smithy' i.e. kole.l 'temple'.

The narratives documented in Indus Script Corpora from ca. 3300 BCE find their echoes in Candi Sukuh of 15th century, validating the stunning significance of the Atharva Veda Skhamba Sukta (AV X.7).

The aniconic Sivalinga form gets expression in the form of Cosmic Dancer.

Cosmic Dancer, Nataraja sculptural frieze, Ellora caves. Kailasha temple.

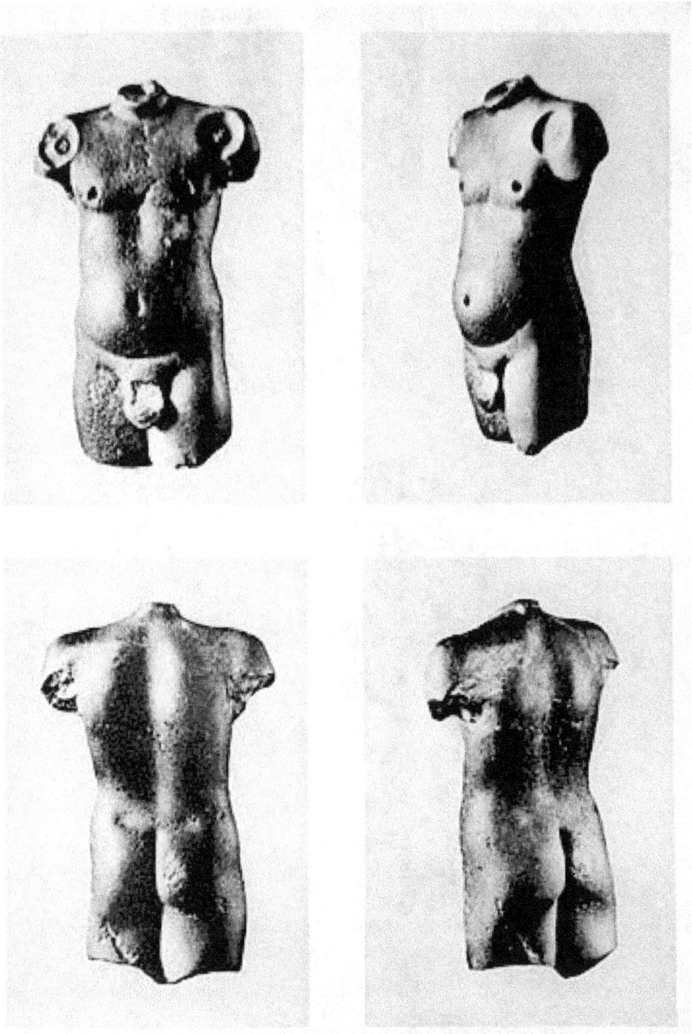

Statue of red stone. Torso of male. Harappa.

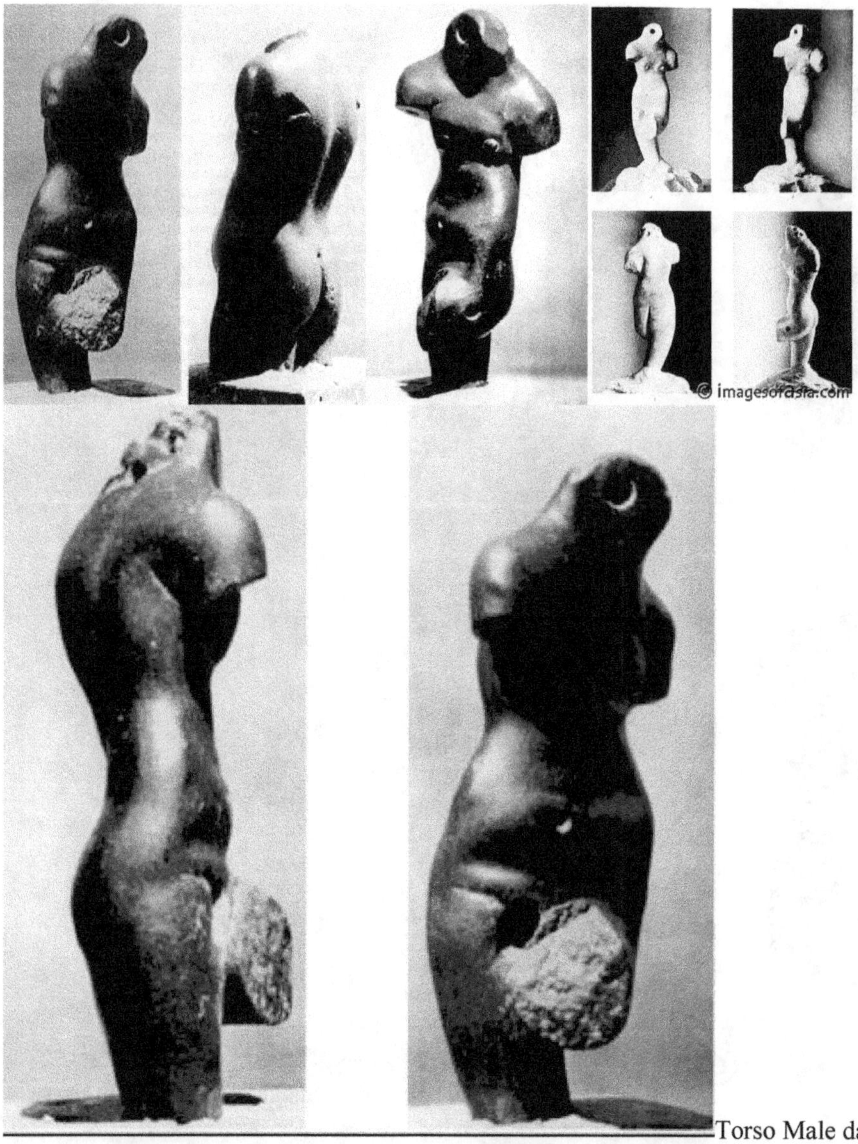

Torso Male dancer. Harappa. Grey limestone, ht 4 inches-National Museum, New Delhi

Candi Sukuh frieze. The scene in bas relief The scene depicted Bhima as the blacksmith in the left forging the metal, Ganesa in the center, and Arjuna in the right operating the tube blower to pump air into the furnace.

The dance step of the male torso of Harappa and the dance step of the elephant-headed Ganesa on Candi Sukuh frieze are explained in a remarkable hieroglyph on a Bhirrana potsherd and a Mohenjodaro tablet:

 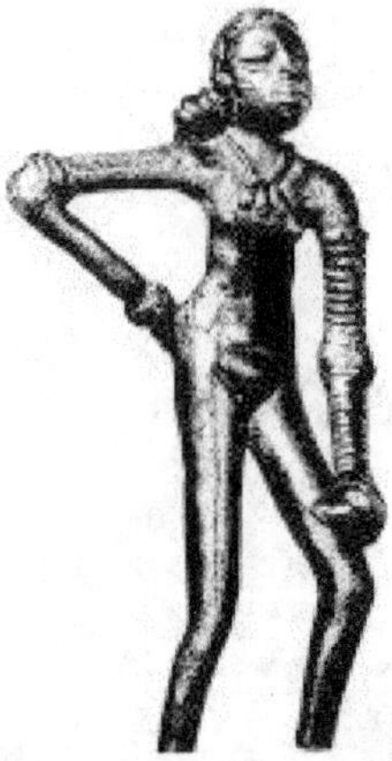 Dance-step in a cire perdue bronze statue, Mohenjodaro replicated on a Bhirrana potsherd. **The red potsherd with the engraving resembling the Dancing Girl bronze figurine of Mohenjodaro, found at Bhirrana.**

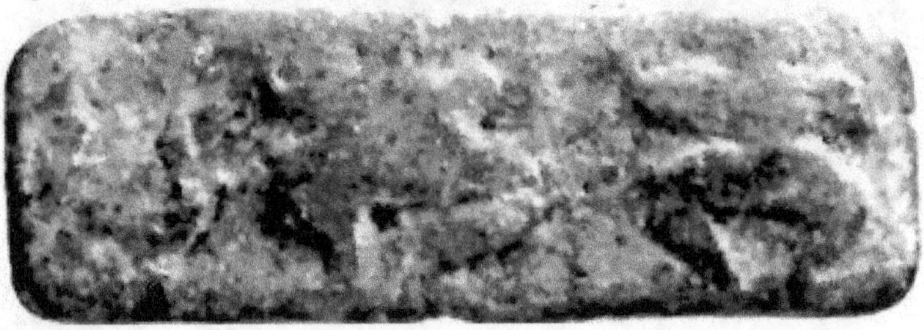 m0493Bt Pict-93: Three dancing figures in a row. Text 2843 Glyph: Three dancers. Kolmo 'three'; meD 'to dance'

Rebus: kolami 'furnace, smithy'; meD 'iron'

Sign 44 (this glyph could be compared with the orthography of three dancers in a row; the glyph is a ligature showing a 'dance step' and a rimless pot). Glyphs: meD 'dance' (Remo); rebus: meD 'iron'; bat.a 'pot'; bat.hi 'furnace'.

So, why a dancing girl? Because, depiction of a dance pose is a hieroglyph to represent what was contained in the pot. The glyph encodes the mleccha word for 'iron': med.

Glyph: meD 'to dance' (F.)[reduplicated from me-]; me id. (M.) in Remo (Munda)(Source: D. Stampe's Munda etyma)Ta. meṭṭu (meṭṭi-) to spurn or push with the foot. Ko. meṭ- (mec-) to trample on, tread on; meṭ sole of foot, footstep, footprint. To. möṭ- (möṭy-) to trample on; möṭ step, tread, wooden-soled sandal. Ka. meṭṭu to put or place down the foot or feet, step, pace, walk, tread or trample on, put the foot on or in, put on (as a slipper or shoe); n. stepping, step of the foot, stop on a stringed instrument; sandal, shoe, step of a stair; meṭṭisu to cause to step; meṭṭige, meṭla step, stair. Koḍ. moṭṭī footprint, foot measure, doorsteps. Tu. muṭṭu shoe, sandal; footstep; steps, stairs. Te meṭṭu step, stair, treading, slipper, stop on a lute; maṭṭu, (K. also) meṭṭu to tread, trample, crush under foot, tread or place the foot upon; n. treading; maṭṭincu to cause to be trodden or trampled. Ga. (S.3) meṭṭu step (< Te.). Konḍa maṭ- (-t-) to crush under foot, tread on, walk, thresh (grain, as by oxen); caus.maṭis-. ***Kuwi*** (S.) **mettunga** steps. ***Malt.*** **maḍye** to trample, tread. (DEDR 5057)

Mĕrhĕt́. Iron.
Mĕṛhĕt́ idena. The iron is rusty.
Ispat mĕṛhĕt́. Steel.
Dul mĕṛhĕt́. Cast iron.
Mĕṛhĕt́ khanḍa. Iron implements.

Rebus: meD 'iron' (Mundari. Remo.) Santali glosses

The dance step of Ganesa (elephant head ligatured to a dancing person) on Candi Sukuh frieze is also explained by the gloss: meD 'dance step' rebus: meD 'iron'.

Ganesa ligature with head of an elephant is a memory recollected from Indus Script hieroglyph-multiplex tradition:

Ganesha, late 7th–8th century. Central Vietnam. Lent by Museum of Cham

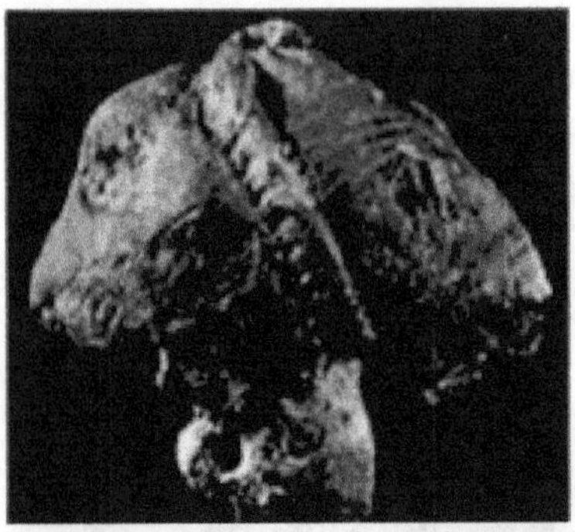

Terracotta. Tiger, bovine, elephant, Nausharo NS 92.02.70.04 h. 6.76 cm; w. 4.42; l. 6.97 cm. Centre for Archaeological Research Indus Balochistan, Musée Guimet, Paris

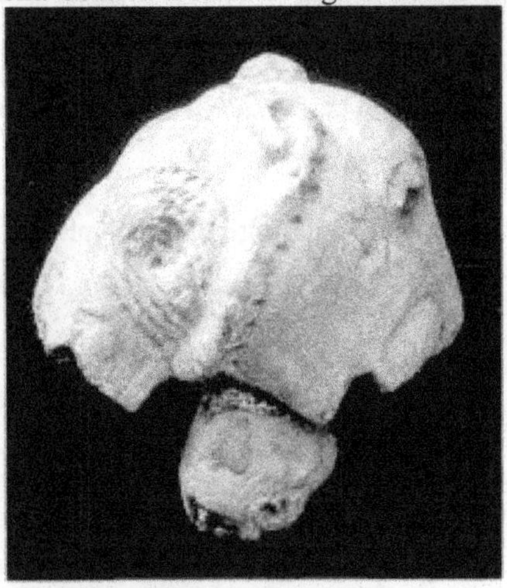

Fig. 6. L'objet composite zoomorphe (Nausharo, période III : NS 92027004) : vue de profil (photo C. Jarrige).

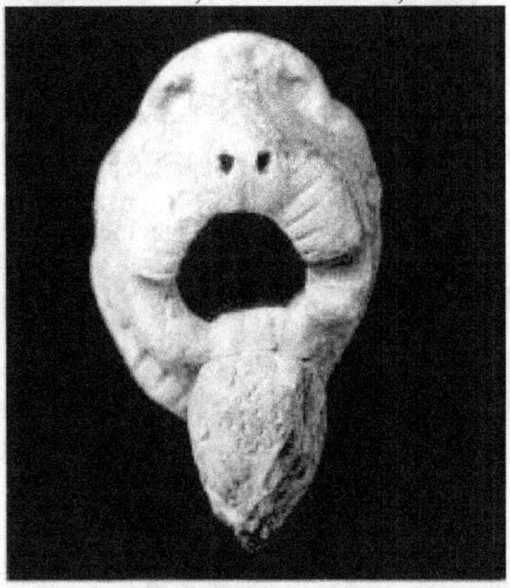

Fig. 7. La tête de félin vue de face (photo C. Jarrige).

Three-headed: elephant, buffalo, bottom jaw of a feline. NS 91.02.32.01.LXXXII. Dept. of Archaeology, Karachi. EBK 7712

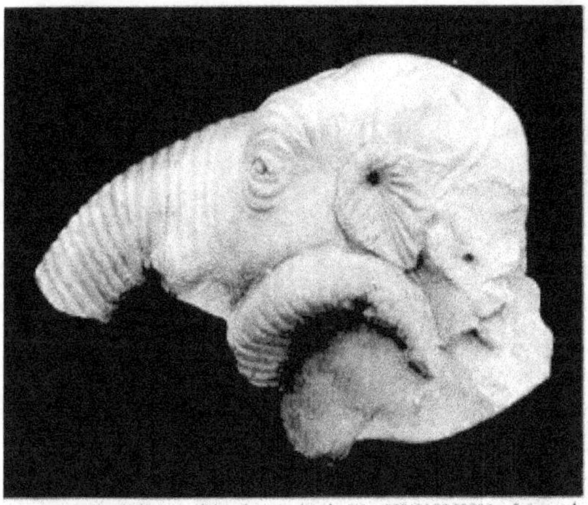

Fig. 1. La tête d'éléphant (Nausharo, période III : NS 91023201), côté gauche (photo C. Jarrige).

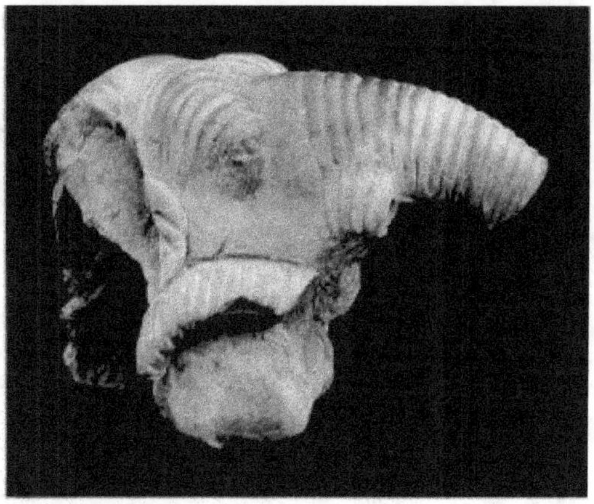

Fig. 2. La tête d'éléphant, côté droit (photo C. Jarrige).

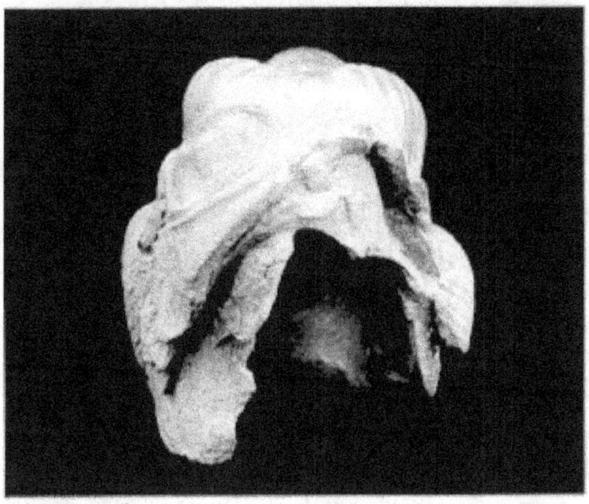

Fig. 3. Vue arrière (photo C. Jarrige).

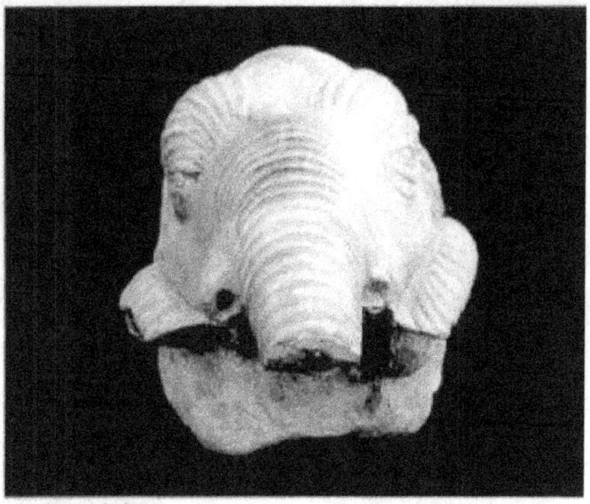

Fig. 4. Vue de face (photo C. Jarrige).

Source:
Une tête d'éléphant en terre cuite de Nausharo (Pakistan)
In: Arts asiatiques. Tome 47, 1992. pp. 132-136. Jarrige Catherine
http://www.persee.fr/web/revues/home/prescript/article/arasi_0004-3958_1992_num_47_1_1330

The elephant head ligatured with a buffalo at Nausharo is a curtain-raiser for the practice of ligaturing in Indian tradition for *utsava bera* 'idols carried on processions'. The phrase *utsava bera* denotes that processions of the type shown on Mesopotamian cylinder seals or Mohenjo-daro tablets are trade processions for *bera* 'bargaining, trade'. Thus, the processions with hieroglyphs may be part of trade-exchange fairs of ancient times. It is significant that the utsava bera of Ganesa is shown together with a rat or mouse -- as *vāhana*: ibha 'elephant' Rebus: ib 'iron'. *mūṣa* 'rat, mouse' Rebus: *mūṣa* 'crucible'. Thus both rat/mouse and elephant face ligatured to a body, are Meluhha hieroglyphs related to metallurgical processes.

sangaDa 'joined animals' rebus: sangara 'proclamation': karibha 'elephant trunk' (Pali) Rebus: karba 'iron' (Tulu) ib 'iron' (Santali) kara 'trunk of elephant' Rebus: khAr 'blacksmith' ranga 'buffalo'

Rebus: ranga 'pewter'. kola 'tiger' Rebus: kolle 'blacksmith' kol 'working in iron' kole.l 'smithy, temple' kolimi 'smithy, forge'.

The dance step of elephant-headed Ganesa shown on Candi Sukuh sculptural hieroglyph-multiplex can thus be deciphered as: karibha 'trunk of elephant' rebus: karba 'iron' ib 'iron' meD 'dance step' rebus: meD 'metal, iron, copper'.

Pali language refers to *milakkha* 'copper workers', cognate Meluhha (in Sumerian/Akkadian cuneiform texts). The phonetic transform *mleccha ~~ meluhha* is evidenced by the Pali text forms: *milakkha rajanam* 'copper colored'; *milakkha bhasha 'mleccha* or *meluhha* language*'* and the well-attested *s-h* transforms from Sindhi to Avestan (Old Indo-Iranian or Old Persian). The early use of the expression in Manusmriti is a reference to *mleccha* language as a form of speech distinguished from *ārya* speech: the expressions used are: *ārya vācas, mleccha vācas*. One form of speech refers to grammatically correct literary expression and the other form of speech refers to mispronounciation, ungrammatical expressions in speech forms. This distinction is elaborated by Patanjali and also in Satapatha Brahmana which refers to an expression by Asura: *he'lo, he'lava* which expression has been found relatable to boatmen songs of ancient times with the refrain *'elo, elelo'*. Such an interpretation is valid in the context of Meluhha seafaring merchants attested in Ancient Near East as a contact area of the Meluhha or Sarasvati-Sindhu (Hindu) civilization.

Meluhha, mleccha was the ancient language of *Bharatam Janam*, 'metalcaster community'. [Derived from the glosses: *bharatiyo* 'metalcaster' (Gujarti); भरती (p. 603) [*bharatī*] *a* Composed of the metal भरत.भरताचें भांडें (p. 603) [*bharatācē mbhāṇḍēṃ*] *n* A vessel made of the metal भरत. 2 See भरिताचें भांडें.भरत (p. 603) [*bharata*] *n* A factitious metal compounded of copper, pewter, tin &c. Note: The page reference is to Molesworth lexicon of Marathi.]

Itihasa of *Bharatam Janam*, 'Ancient history of Bharata people' can be understood and appreciated from Art History recorded on Tin Road artifacts of sculptural reliefs (such as seals with Indus writing or reliefs and sculptures on structures such as stupa or temple walls and entrances).

I suggest that this phrase of self-designation, clear identity of the people as bhāratam janam is a reference to the artisans who had invented the new techniques of alloying metals and metal casting. Archaeological evidence from Nahal Mishmar is stunning. The artifacts found in a cave there were metal castings of exquisite artistry made using cire perdue (lost-wax casting) technique.

Cylinder seal of Shu-ilishu, interpreter for Meluhha. Cuneiform inscription in Old Akkadian. Serpentine. Mesopotamia ca 2220-2159 BCE H. 2.9 cm, Dia 1.8 cm Musee du Louvre, Departement des Antiquites, Orientales, Paris AO 22310

शब्दकल्पद्रुमः śabdakalpadruma -- excerpts for selected etyma embedded --validates the Indus Script cipher as mlecchita vikalpa, Meluhha cipher caṣāla on Yupa, gōdhūma, āyasamutpati, 'production of metal'. This ancient encyclopaedic text also validates mleccha bhāṣā as the spoken language of Bhāratam janam. Mleccha is cognate Meluhha documented in cuneiform texts of Ancient Near East, see for example the Shu-ilishu cylinder seal.

Vātsyāyana notes about himself after writing down Vidyāsamuddeśa:

> 'After reading and considering the works of Babhravya and other ancient authors, and thinking over the meaning of the rules given by them, this treatise was composed, according to the precepts of the Holy Writ, for the benefit of the world, by Vatsyayana, while leading the life of a religious student at Benares, and wholly engaged in the contemplation of the Deity. This work is not to be used merely as an instrument for satisfying our desires. A person acquainted with the true principles of this science, who preserves his Dharma (virtue or religious merit), his Artha (worldly wealth) and his Kama (pleasure or sensual gratification), and who has regard to the customs of the people, is sure to obtain the mastery over his senses. In short, an intelligent and knowing person attending to Dharma and Artha and also to Kama, without becoming the slave of his passions, will obtain success in everything that he may do.'

Vidyāsamuddeśa includes three of the 64 arts related to language communication: dēśá bhāṣā jnānam, akṣára muṣṭíka kathanam, mlecchita vikalpa: expressions which can be translated as: language speech forms, messaging by hand/wrist gestures, mleccha (meluhha) cipher.

Mlecchita vikalpa may be interpreted as a 'contrivance' to alternatively signify speech, i.e. 'cipher'. Such a cipher or mlecchita vikalpa is employed in Indus Script Corpora. Mlecchita has three meanings: 1. indistinct or mispronunciations in speech; 2. made by copper workers: 3. metalwork e.g mlecchāśa = mlecchabhojanam. mlecchāśya = production of āyasam or metal or copper (āyasamutpatirasya); mlecchabhohjanam means 'gōdhūma' which is the caṣāla on Yupa which signifies a Soma Yaga. āyasam means 'loha', 'metal'.Thus, mlecchāsya means 'production of metal or metalwork.

शब्दकल्पद्रुमः notes in reference to the geographical spread of mleccha speakers that they constituted the Bhāratam Janam and were all over Bhāratam. The spoken form of the language is called mleccha bhāṣā. This language or Prakritam is signified by Indus Script hieroglyphs in the Corpora.

Tracing the language roots of Bhāratam Janam on the banks of River Sarasvati system speaking a form of Proto-Prakritam a metalwork lexis emerges. This is traceable in many languages of Indian *sprachbund*. A unique writing system was based on Proto-Prakritam. This was called Meluhha in cuneiform texts and *mlecchita vikalpa* (i.e. alternative representation of mleccha) in Vatsyayana's treatise on Vidyasamuddesa (ca 6th century BCE). The principal life-activity of artisan guilds of Bhāratam Janam was metalwork creating metalcastings, experimenting with creation of various forms of ores, metals, alloys, smelters, furnaces, braziers and other tools and making metal implements. The result was a veritable revolution transiting from chalcolithic phase to metals age in urban settings. This legacy finds expression in the famed, non-rusting Delhi iron pillar which was originally from Vidisha (Besanagara, Sanchi). Archaeologically-attested presence of Bhāratam Janam dates from ca. 8th millennium BCE. The use of a writing system dates from ca. 4th millennium BCE (HARP). Rigveda. In RV 3.53.12, Rishi Visvamitra states that this mantra (brahma) shall protect the people: visvamitrasya rakshati brahmedam Bhāratam Janam. The word Bharata in the expression is derived from the metalwork lexis of Prakritam: bharata '*bhārata* 'a factitious alloy of copper, pewter, tin'; *baran, bharat* 'mixed alloys (5 copper, 4 zinc and 1 tin)'. Thus, the expression Bhāratam Janam can be deciphered as 'metalcaster folk', thus firmly establishing the identity of the people of India, that is Bharat and the spoken form of their language Prakritam ca. 3500 BCE.

आयस, क्ली, (अयस् + अण् ।) लौह । इति

भरतः राजनिर्घण्टश्च ॥ अयोनिर्म्मितादौ, त्रि ॥

(यथा महाभारते, --

"आयसं हृदयं मन्ये तस्य दुष्कृतकर्म्मणः" ।

यथा मनुः, ८ । ३१५ ।

"शक्तिं चोभयतस्तीक्ष्णामायसं दण्डमेव वा" ।

रघुवंशे, १७ । ६३ ।

"स चकर्ष परस्मात् तदयस्कान्त इवायसम्" ।

(अयोजनितार्थे यथा, --

"विपाके कटु शीतञ्च सर्व्वश्रेष्ठं तदायसम्" ॥

इति वैद्यकचक्रपाणिसंग्रहे ॥)

आयसी, स्त्री, (अयसा निर्म्मिता । अयस् + अण् +

ङीप् ।) लौहमयकवचः । तत्पर्य्यायः । अङ्गरक्षिणी

२ जालिका ३ जालप्राया ४ । इति हेमचन्द्रः ॥

म्लेच्छित [p= 838,1] *mfn.* = म्लिष्ट Pa1n2. 7-2 , 18 Sch. म्लिष्ट [p= 837,3] *mfn.* spoken indistinctly or barbarously Pa1n2. 7-2 , 18

वि--कल्प 1 [p= 950,1] *m.* (for 2. » under वि- √क्ळृप्) an intermediate कल्प , the interval between two कल्पs. (q.v.) BhP.*m.* (for 1. » [p= 950,1]) alternation , alternative ,
option S3rS. Mn. VarBr2S. &c (°पेन *ind.* " optionally ")variation , combination , variety , diversity , manifoldness Ka1tyS3r. MBh. &contrivance , art Ragh. वि- √ क्ळृप् [p= 955,2] *A1.* -कल्पते , to change or alternate , change with (instr.) AV. MBh. &c ; to choose one of two alternatives , proceed eclectically VarBr2S.

A set of Prakritam glosses from शब्दकल्पद्रुमः (compiled by Radhakantadeva Bahadur) are embedded. Source: https://sa.wikisource.org/wiki/शब्दकल्पद्रुमः

One excerpt is of significance defining the shape of Yupa and caSala: स यूपः तस्य शिरसि वलयाकृत्यिर्डमरुकाकृतिर्वा यः (trans. 'the Yupa atop which a ring in the shape of Damaru).

The upper right hand of Nataraja, Cosmi Dance shown on a bronze image with a Damaru, an hour-glass shaped small drum. This explains the octagonal shape of the hour-glass shaped Vajra held by Vajrapani on sculptures.

Vajra with octagonal bases. Relief fragment. Dipamkara Jataka with Buddha & Vajrapani. Butkara, Swat, 1st-2nd cent. CE c., Museo Nazionale d'Arte Orientale 'Giuseppe Tucci', Roma, dep. IsIAO, Inv. MNAOR 1127, MAI B 65;79 (after Bussagli, M.,1984, L'Arte del Gandhara, Torino, p.146)

Note: Vajrapani holds a Vajra of eight-angles.

क्लृप्तः, त्रि, कल्पनार्थकृपधातोः कर्म्मणि क्ते क्लृपादेशः ।

नियतः । कृतकल्पनः । कल्पनं सामर्थ्यं तद्विशिष्टः ।
यथा, "अवश्यक्लृप्ताभिः पर्व्वतत्वचत्वरत्वादितत्तद्ध-
र्म्मावच्छिन्नाधिकरणताव्यक्तिभिरेवोपपत्तौ" । इति
जगदीशः ॥ (यथा, मनौ । ११ । २७ ।
"इष्टिं वैश्वानरीं नित्यं निर्व्वपेदब्दपर्य्यये ।
क्लृप्तानां पशुसोमानां निष्कृत्यर्थमसम्भवे" ॥)

चषालः, पुं, (चष्यते वध्यतेऽस्मिन् । चष + "सानसि-
वर्णसीति ।" उणां । ४ । १०७ । इति आल
प्रत्ययेन निपातनात् साधुः ।) यूपकटकः । इत्य-
मरः । २ । ७ । १८ ॥ यज्ञसमाप्तिसूचकं पशु-
बन्धनार्थं यज्ञभूमौ यत् काष्ठमारोप्यते स यूपः
तस्य शिरसि वलयाकृतिर्डमरुकाकृतिर्व्वा यः
काष्ठविकारः सः । यूपमूलेविहितलोहवलयश्च ।
इति केचित् । इति भरतः ॥ मधुस्थानम् । इति
संक्षिप्तसारे उणादिवृत्तिः ॥

कटकः, पुं, क्ली, (कटति वर्षति अस्मिन् मेघ इति ।
अथवा कट्यते निर्गम्यते अस्मात् निर्झरिण्या-
दिभिः "कृञादिभ्यः संज्ञायां वुन्" । ५ । ३५ ।
उणां इति वुन् ।) पर्व्वतमध्यभागः । तत्पर्य्यायः ।
नितम्बः २ । इत्यमरः ॥ २ । ३ । ५ ॥ मेखला ३
इति भरतः ॥ (यथा रघुः । १६ । ३१ । "मार्गै-
षिणी सा कटकान्तरेषु वैन्ध्येषु सेना बहुधा
विभिन्ना" ॥) वलयः । चक्रम् । इत्यमरः ॥ २ ।
६ । १०७ । हस्तिदन्तमण्डनम् । सामुद्रलवणम् ।
राजधानी । इति मेदिनी ॥ नगरी । इति
शब्दरत्नावली ॥ सेना । इति हेमचन्द्रः ॥ (यथा
हितोपदेशे १ । ३३२ । "स च दिग्विजयक्र-
मेणागत्य चन्द्रभागानदीतीरे समावेशितकटको
वर्त्तते" ॥) सानुः । पर्व्वतस्य समभूभागः । इति
विश्वः ॥
("गिरिकूटेषु दुर्गेषु नानाजनपदेषु च ।
जनाकीर्णेषु देशेषु कटकेषु परेषु च" ॥
इति महाभारतम् ४ । २४ । १२ ।)

यूपकटकः, पुं, (यूपस्य कटक इव ।) यज्ञसमाप्ति-
सूचकं पशुबन्धाद्यर्थं यज्ञभूमौ यत् काष्ठमारो-
प्यते स यूपः तस्य शिरसि वलयाकृतिर्डमरुका-
कृतिर्वा यः काष्ठविकारः सः । यूपमूले निहित-
लोहवलय इति केचित् । इति भरतः ॥ तत्-
पर्य्यायः । चषालः २ । इत्यमरः । २ । ७ । १८ ॥

म्लिष्टं, क्ली, (म्लेच्छ + क्तः + "क्षुब्धस्वान्तध्वान्तलग्न-
म्लिष्टविरिब्धेत्यादि ।" ७ । २ । १८ । इति
निपातितम् ।) अस्पष्टवाक्यम् । तत्पर्य्यायः ।
अविस्पष्टम् २ । इत्यमरः । १ । ६ । २१ ॥

म्लेच्छ, कि देश्योक्तौ । इति कविकल्पद्रुमः ॥ (चुरा०-
वा भ्वा०-पर०-अक०-सक० च-सेट् ।) देश्या
ग्राम्या उक्तिर्देश्योक्तिरसंस्कृतकथनमित्यर्थः ।
कि, म्लेच्छयति म्लेच्छति मूढः । अन्तर्विद्यामसौ
विद्वान्न म्लेच्छति धृतव्रत इति हलायुधः ॥
अनेकार्थत्वादव्यक्तशब्देऽपि । तथा चामरः ।
अथ म्लिष्टमविस्पष्टमिति । म्लेच्छ व्यक्तायां वाचि
इति प्राञ्चः । तत्र रमानाथस्तु । म्लेच्छति वटु-
र्व्यक्तं वदतीत्यर्थः । अव्यक्तायामिति पाठे कुत्-
सितायां वाचीत्यर्थः ।
'तत्सादृश्यमभावश्च तदन्यत्वं तदल्पता ।
अप्राशस्त्यं विरोधश्च नञर्थाः षट् प्रकीर्त्तिताः ॥'
इति भाष्यवचनेन नञोऽप्राशस्त्यार्थत्वात् इति
व्याख्यानाय हलायुधोक्तमुदाहृतवान् । इति
दुर्गादासः ॥

म्लेच्छः, पुं, (म्लेच्छयति वा म्लेच्छति असंस्कृतं वदतीति । म्लेच्छ् + अच् ।) किरातशवरपुलिन्दादिजातिः । इत्यमरः ॥ पामरभेदः । पापरक्तः । अपभाषणम् । इति मेदिनी । छे, ६ ॥ म्लेच्छादीनां सर्व्वधर्म्मराहित्यमुक्तं यथा, हरिवंशे । १४ । १५ -- १९ ।

"सगरः स्वां प्रतिज्ञाञ्च गुरोर्व्वाक्यं निशम्य च ।
धर्म्मं जघान तेषां वै वेशान्यत्वं चकार ह ॥
अर्द्धं शकानां शिरसो मुण्डयित्वा व्यसर्जयत् ।
जवनानां शिरः सर्व्वं काम्बोजानान्तथैव च ॥
पारदा मुक्तकेशाश्च पह्लवाः श्मश्रुधारिणः ।
निःस्वाध्यायवषट्काराः कृतास्तेन महात्मना ॥
शका जवनकाम्बोजाः पारदाः पह्लवास्तथा ।
कोलसर्प्याः समहिषा दार्व्वाश्चोलाः सकेरलाः ।
सर्व्वे ते क्षत्त्रियास्तात धर्म्मस्तेषां निराकृतः ॥
वशिष्ठवचनाद्राजन् सगरेण महात्मना ॥"

शकानां शकदेशोद्भवानां क्षत्त्रियाणाम् । एवं जवनादीनामिति । अत्र जवनशब्दस्तद्देशोद्भववाची चवर्गतृतीयादिः । जवनो देशवेगिनोरिति त्रिकाण्डशेषाभिधानदर्शनात् ॥ * ॥ तेषां म्लेच्छत्वमप्युक्तं विष्णुपुराणे । तथाकृतान् जवनादीनुपक्रम्य ते चात्मधर्म्मपरित्यागात् म्लेच्छत्वं ययुरिति । बौधायनः ।

"गोमांसखादको यश्च विरुद्धं बहु भाषते ।
सर्व्वाचारविहीनश्च म्लेच्छ इत्यभिधीयते ॥"
इति प्रायश्चित्ततत्त्वम् ॥ * ॥
अपिच । देवयान्यां ययातेर्द्वौ पुत्त्रौ यदुः तुर्व्वसुश्च ।

शर्म्मिष्ठायां त्रयः पुत्राः द्रुह्युः अनुः पुरुश्च ।
तत्र यदुप्रभृतयश्चत्वारः पितुराज्ञाहेलनं कृत-
वन्तः पित्रा शप्ताः । ज्येष्ठपुत्रं यदुं शशाप तव
वंशे राजा चक्रवर्त्ती मा भूदिति । तुर्व्वसु-
द्रुह्य्वनून् शशाप युष्माकं वंश्या वेदवाह्या म्लेच्छा
भविष्यन्ति । इति श्रीभागवतमतम् ॥ * ॥
("असृजत् पह्नवान् पुच्छात् प्रस्रावाद्द्राविडान्
शकान् ।
योनिदेशाच्च यवनान् शकृतः शवरान् बहून् ॥
मूत्रतश्चासृजत् काञ्चीञ्छरभांश्चैव पार्श्वतः
पौण्ड्रान् किरातान् यवनान् सिंहलान् वर्व्वरान्
खशान् ॥
चियुकांश्च पुलिन्दांश्च चीनान् हूनान् सके-
रलान् ।

ससर्ज्ज फेनतः सा गौर्म्लेच्छान् बहुविधानपि ॥"
सा वशिष्ठस्य धेनुः । इति महाभारते । १ । १७६ ।
३५ -- ३७ ॥) अन्यच्च । "शकजवनकाम्बोज-
पारदपह्नवा हन्यमानास्तत्कुलगुरुं वशिष्ठं
शरणं ययुः । अथैतान् वशिष्ठो जीवन्मृतकान्
कृत्वा सगरमाह । वत्स वत्सालमेभिर्जीवन्मृत-
कैरनुसृतैः । एते च मयैव त्वत्प्रतिज्ञापालनाय
निजधर्म्मद्विजसङ्गपरित्यागं कारिताः । स
तथेति तद्गुरुवचनमभिनन्द्य तेषां वेशान्य-
त्वमकारयत् । जवनान्मुण्डितशिरसोऽर्द्धमुण्डान्
शकान् प्रलम्बकेशान् पारदान् पह्नवांश्च श्मश्रु-
धरान्निःस्वाध्यायवषट्कारानेतानन्यांश्च क्षत्त्रि-
यांश्चकार । ते चात्मधर्म्मपरित्यागाद्ब्राह्मणैश्च
परित्यक्ता म्लेच्छतां ययुः ।" इति विष्णुपुराणे । ४ ।
३ । १८ -- २१ ॥ * ॥ प्रकारान्तरेण तस्योत्-
पत्तिर्यथा, --
सूत उवाच ।
"वंशे स्वायम्भुवस्यासीदङ्गो नाम प्रजापतिः ।
मृत्योस्तु दुहिता तेन परिणीतातिदुर्मुखी ॥
सुतीर्था नाम तस्यास्तु वेनो नाम सुतः
पुरा ।
अधर्म्मनिरतः कामी बलवान् वसुधाधिपः ।
लोकेऽप्यधर्म्मकृज्जातः परभार्य्यापहारकः ॥
धर्म्मचारप्रसिद्ध्यर्थं जगतोऽस्य महर्षिभिः ।
अनुनीतोऽपि न ददावनुज्ञां स यदा ततः ॥
शापेन मारयित्वैनमराजकभयार्द्दिताः ।
ममन्थुर्ब्राह्मणास्तस्य बलाद्देहमकल्मषाः ॥

तत्कायान्मथ्यमानात्तु निपेतुर्म्लेच्छजातयः ।
शरीरे मातुरंशेन कृष्णाञ्जनसमप्रभाः ॥"
इति मत्स्यपुराणे । १० । ३ -- ८ ॥ * ॥
म्लेच्छभाषाभ्यासनिषेधो यथा, --
"न सातयेदिष्टकाभिः फलानि वै फलेन तु ।
न म्लेच्छभाषां शिक्षेत नाकर्षेच्च पदासनम् ॥"
इति कौर्म्म्ये उपविभागे १५ अध्यायः ॥ * ॥

तस्य मध्यमा तामसी गतिर्यथा, मानवे ।
१२ । ४३ ।
"हस्तिनश्च तुरङ्गाश्च शूद्रा म्लेच्छाश्च गर्हिताः ।
सिंहा व्याघ्रा वराहाश्च मध्यमा तामसी
गतिः ॥"
(मन्त्रणाकाले म्लेच्छापसारणमुक्तं यथा, मनु-
संहितायाम् । ७ । १४९ ।
"जडमूकान्धवधिरांस्तैर्य्यग्योनान् वयोऽति-
गान् ।
स्त्रीम्लेच्छव्याधितव्यङ्गान् मन्त्रकालेऽपसार-
येत् ॥"
"अथवा एवंविधा मन्त्रिणो न कर्त्तव्याः । बुद्धि-
विभ्रमसम्भवात् ।" इति तद्भाष्ये मेधातिथिः ॥
म्लेच्छानां पशुधर्म्मित्वम् । यथा, महाभारते । १ ।
८४ । १५ ।
"गुरुदारप्रसक्तेषु तिर्य्यग्योनिगतेषु च ।
पशुधर्म्मिषु पापेषु म्लेच्छेषु त्वं भविष्यसि ॥")

म्लेच्छजातिः, स्त्री, (म्लेच्छस्य जातिरिति षष्ठी-
तत्पुरुषः म्लेच्छरूपा जातिरिति कर्म्मधारयो वा ।) गोमांसखादकबहुविरुद्धभाषकसर्व्वाचारविहीनवर्णः । यथा, --

"गोमांसखादको यस्तु विरुद्धं बहु भाषते ।
सर्व्वाचारविहीनश्च म्लेच्छ इत्यभिधीयते ॥"

इति प्रायश्चित्ततत्त्वधृतबौधायनवचनम् ॥

अपि च ।

"भेदाः किरातशवरपुलिन्दा म्लेच्छजातयः ॥"

इत्यमरः । २ । ४० । २० ॥

अन्यच्च ।

"पौण्ड्रकाश्चौड्रद्रविडाः काम्बोजा शवनाः
शकाः ।
पारदाः पह्लवाश्चीनाः किराताः दरदाः
खशाः ॥
मुखबाहूरुपज्जानां या लोके जातयो बहिः ।
म्लेच्छवाचश्चार्य्यवाचः सर्व्वे ते दस्यवः स्मृताः ॥"

इति मानवे १० अध्यायः ॥

म्लेच्छदेशः, पुं, (म्लेच्छानां देशः म्लेच्छप्रधानो देशो वा ।) चातुर्व्वर्ण्यव्यवस्थादिरहितस्थानम् । तत्पर्य्यायः । प्रत्यन्तः २ । इत्यमरः । २ । १ । ७ ॥ भारतवर्षस्यान्त प्रतिगः प्रत्यन्तः । म्लेच्छति शिष्टाचारहीनो भवत्यत्र म्लेच्छः अल् । स चासौ देशश्चेति म्लेच्छदेशः । किंवा म्लेच्छयन्ति असंस्कृत वदन्ति शिष्टा-

चारहीना भवन्तीति वा पचाद्यचि म्लेच्छा
नीचजातयः तेषां देशो म्लेच्छदेशः । भारतवर्ष-
स्यान्तः शिष्टाचाररहितः कामरूपवङ्गादिः ।
उक्तञ्च ।
चातुर्व्वर्ण्यव्यवस्थानं यस्मिन् देशे न विद्यते ।
म्लेच्छदेशः स विज्ञेय आर्य्यावर्त्तस्ततः पर-
मिति ॥"
इति भरतः ॥
(अपि च, मनुः । २ । २३ ।
"कृष्णसारस्तु चरति मृगो यत्र स्वभावतः ।
स ज्ञेयो यज्ञियो देशो म्लेच्छदेशस्ततःपरम् ॥")

म्लेच्छभोजनः, पुं, (भुज्यतेऽसौ इति । भुज् + ल्युट् । म्लेच्छानां भोजनः । (गोधूमः । इति त्रिकाण्डशेषः ॥

म्लेच्छमण्डलं, क्ली, (म्लेच्छानां मण्डलं समूहोऽत्र ।) म्लेच्छदेशः । इति हेमचन्द्रः ॥

म्लेच्छमुखं, क्ली, (म्लेच्छे म्लेच्छदेशे मुखमुत्पत्ति-रस्य । इत्यमरटीकायां रघुनाथः ।) ताम्रम् ।
इत्यमरः । २ । ९ । ९७ ॥ (तथास्य पर्य्यायः ।
"ताम्रमौदुम्बरं शुल्वमुदुम्बरमपि स्मृतम् ।
रविप्रियं म्लेच्छमुखं सूर्य्यपर्य्यायनामकम् ॥"
इति भावप्रकाशस्य पूर्व्वखण्डे प्रथमे भागे ॥
"ताम्रमौडुम्बरं शूल्वं विद्यात् म्लेच्छमुख-
न्तथा ॥"
इति गारुडे २०८ अध्याये ॥)

म्लेच्छाशः, पुं, (म्लेच्छैरश्यते इति । अश् + कर्म्मणि + घञ् ।) म्लेच्छभोजनः । गोधूमः । इति केचित् ॥

म्लेच्छास्यं, क्ली, (म्लेच्छे म्लेच्छदेशे आस्यमुत्पत्ति-रस्य ।) ताम्रम् । इति हारावली ॥

म्लेच्छितं, क्ली, (म्लेछ् देश्योक्तौ + क्तः ।) म्लेच्छ-भाषा । अपशब्दः । तत्पर्य्यायः । परभाषा २ । इति हारावली ॥

विकल्पः, पुं, (विरुद्धं कल्पनमिति । वि +
कृप + घञ् ।) भ्रान्तिः । (यथा, देवीभाग-
वते । १ । १९ । ३२ ।
"विकल्पोपहतस्त्वं वै दूरदेशमुपागतः ।
न मे विकल्पसन्देहो निर्व्विकल्पोऽस्मि सर्व्वथा ॥")
कल्पनम् । इति मेदिनी । पे, ॥ (यथा, भाग-
वते । ५ । १६ । २ ।
"तत्रापि प्रियव्रतरथचरणपरिखातैः सप्तभिः
सप्त सिन्धवः उपक्लृप्ताः । यत एतस्याः सप्त-
द्वीपविशेषविकल्पस्त्वया भगवन् खलु सूचितः ॥"
संशयः । यथा, रघुः । १७ । ४९ ।
"रात्रिन्दिवविभागेषु यथादिष्टं महीक्षिताम् ।
तत्सिषेवे नियोगेन स विकल्पपराङ्मुखः ॥"
नानाविधः । यथा, मनुः । ९ । २२८ ।
"प्रच्छन्नं वा प्रकाशं वा तन्निषेवेत यो नरः ।
तस्य दण्डविकल्पः स्याद्यथेष्टं नृपतेस्तथा ॥")
विविधकल्पः । स च द्विविधः । व्यवस्थितः ।
ऐच्छिकश्च । सोऽप्याकाङ्क्षाविरहे युक्तः । तथा
च भविष्ये ।
"स्मृतिशास्त्रे विकल्पस्तु आकाङ्क्षापूरणे सति ॥"
इच्छाविकल्पेऽष्टदोषाः । यथा, --

"प्रमाणत्वाप्रमाणत्वपरित्यागप्रकल्पना ।
प्रत्युज्जीवनहानिभ्यां प्रत्येकमष्टदोषता ॥"
व्रीहिभिर्यजेत यवैर्यजेत इति श्रूयते । तत्र
व्रीहिप्रयोगे प्रतीतयवप्रामाण्यपरित्यागः ।
अप्रतीतयवाप्रामाण्यपरिकल्पनम् । इदन्तु पूर्ब्ब-
स्मात् पृथक् वाक्यं अन्यथा समुच्चयेऽपि याग-
सिद्धिः स्यात् । अतएव विकल्पे न उभयः
शास्त्रार्थ इत्युक्तम् । प्रयोगान्तरे यवे उपा-
दीयमाने परित्यक्तयवप्रामाण्योज्जीवनं स्वीकृत-
यवाप्रामाण्यहानिरिति चत्वारो दोषाः । एवं
व्रीहावपि चत्वारः । इत्यष्टौ दोषा इच्छा-
विकल्पे । तथा चोक्तम् ।
"एवमेवाष्टदोषोऽपि यद्व्रीहियववाक्ययोः ।
विकल्प आश्रितस्तत्र गतिरन्या न विद्यते ॥"
इति ॥

एकार्थतया विविधं कल्प्यते इति विकल्पः ।
तस्मादृष्टदोषभिया उपोष्य द्वे तिथी इत्यत्र
न इच्छाविकल्पः किन्तु व्यवस्थितविकल्पः ।
इत्येकादशीतत्त्वम् ॥ (अवान्तरः कल्पः । यथा,
भागवते । २ । ८ । ११ ।
"यावान् कल्पो विकल्पो वा यथा कालोऽनु-
मीयते ॥"
देवता । यथा, भागवते । १० । ८५ । ११ ।
"वैकारिको विकल्पाना प्रधानमनुशायि-
नाम् ॥"
"विविधं आधिदैवाध्यात्माधिभूतभेदेन कल्प्यन्ते
इति विकल्पा देवास्तेषां कारणं वैकारिकः
सात्त्विकोऽहङ्कारश्च त्वम् ॥" इति तट्टीकायां
स्वामी ॥)

Source: https://sa.wikisource.org/wiki/शब्दकल्पद्रुमः

The 'goat' carried by Meluhhan is metonymy denoting the special life-activity of the artisan-seafaring merchant: Hieroglyph: *mṛēka* 'goat' Rebus: Meluhha 'copperworker' (*mleccha* 'copper' (Samskritam); *milakkhu rajanam* 'copper colored' (Pali) ***Ka.*** **mēke** she-**goat; mē** the bleating of sheep or goats. ***Te.*** **mē̃ka, mēka** goat. ***Kol.*** **me·ke** id. ***Nk.*** **mēke** id.
Pa. **mēva**, (S.) **mēya** she-goat. ***Ga.*** (Oll.) **mēge**, (S.) **mēge** goat.***Go.*** (M) **mekā**, (Ko.) **mēka** id. ? ***Kur.*** **mēxnā (mīxyas)** to call, call after loudly, hail. ***Malt.*** **méqe** to bleat. [***Te.*** **mṟēka** (so correct) is of unknown meaning. ***Br.*** **mēḻh** is without etymology; see MBE 1980a.] / Cf. Skt. **(*lex.*)** **meka-** goat. (DEDR 5087). http://a.harappa.com/sites/g/files/g65461/f/201402/Shu-ilishus-Cylinder-Seal.pdf

Hieroglyph: *mṛēka* 'goat' Rebus: Meluhha 'copperworker' (*mleccha* 'copper' (Samskritam); *milakkhu rajanam* 'copper colored' (Pali)

Culture and civilization are explained by two terms in Samskritam: संस्कृतिः and विज्ञानम्. The roots of civilization are to be traced from the banks of Rivers Sarasvati and Sindhu. The cultural manifestations are found in all parts of Eurasia – āsetu himachalam, from Indian Ocean communities to Himalayan communities. Data mining Indus Script Corpora evidences 1. vedic culture continuum in Eurasia -- ancient Bharatam, Near East and Far East; and 2. material advances made during the Bronze Age resulting in a significant changes in social groupings of people, idea of the community and life-activities of the people in the expansive region. These are exemplified by Chanhu-daro which was called the 'Sheffield of Ancient India' by Ernest JH Mackay, the archaeologist who reported discoveries of exquisite pots and pans, implements, tools and weapons of bronze made in that community.

Sarasvati-Sindhu (Hindu) Civilization bronze artifacts from Chanhu-daro

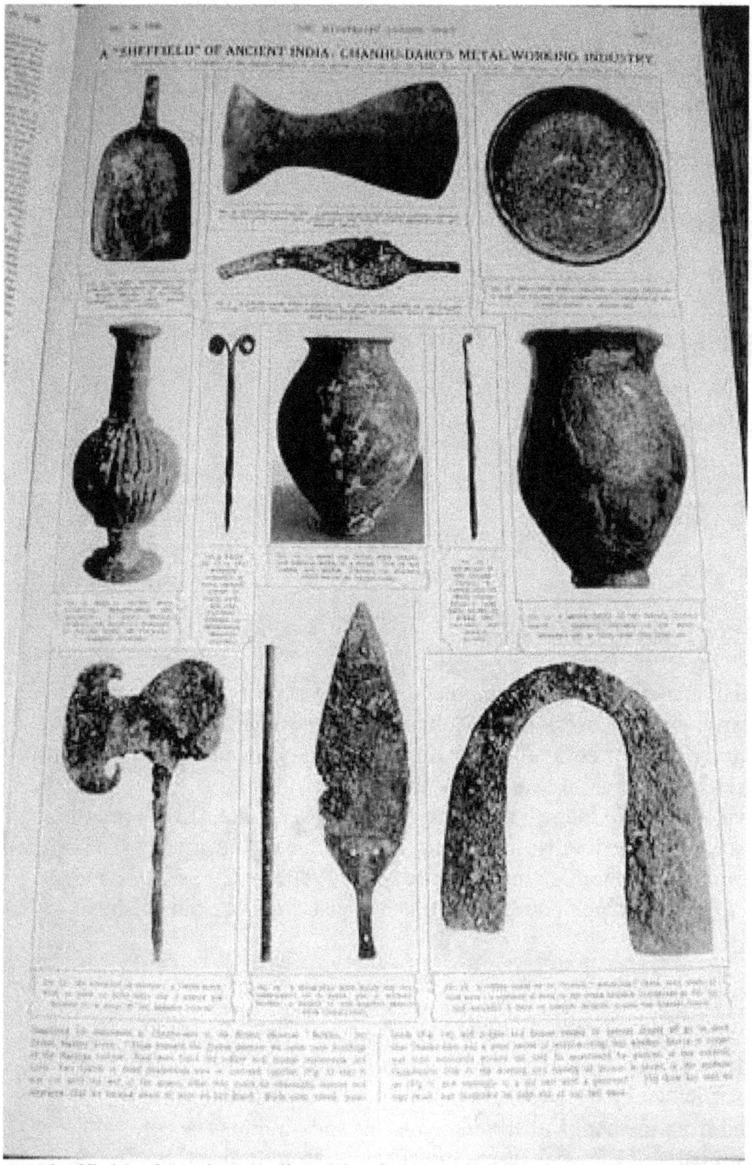
A "SHEFFIELD" OF ANCIENT INDIA: CHANHU-DARO'S METAL-WORKING INDUSTRY

A 'Sheffield of Ancient India': Chanhu-Daro's Metal working Industry. Illustrated London News 1936 – November 21st, p.909. 10 x photos of copper knives, spears , razors, axes and dishes.

Chanhu-daro was a site on the right bank of Vedic River Sarasvati.

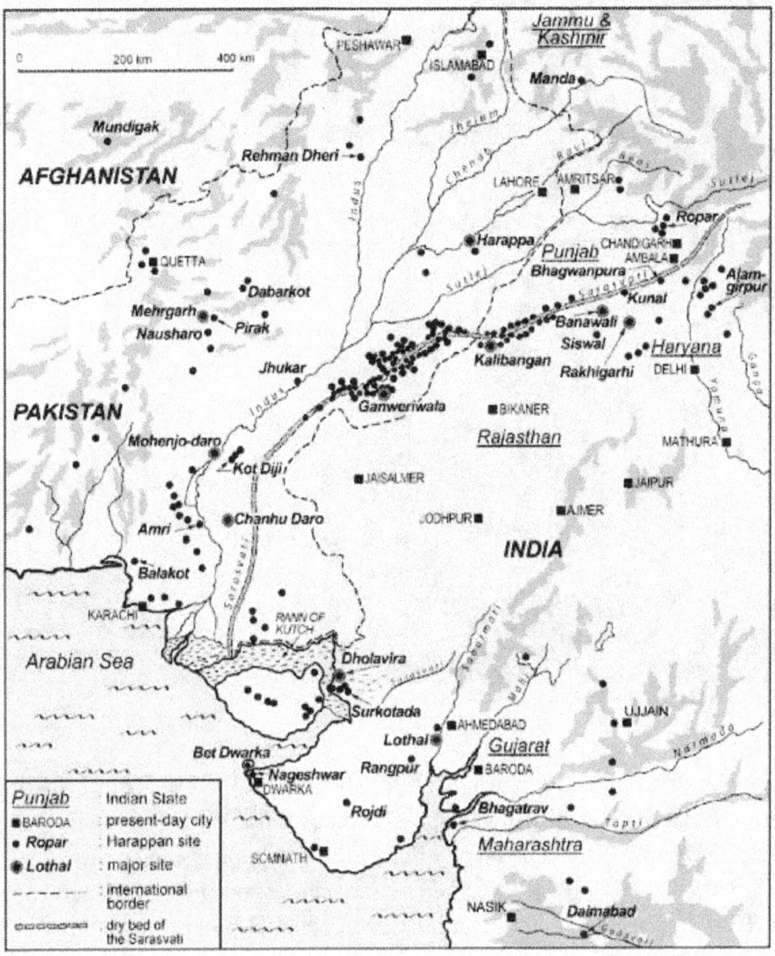
Jammu &
Kashmir
0
200 km
400 km
PESHAWAR
ISLAMABAD
Manda
Mundigak
Rehman Dheri
AFGHANISTAN
Jhelum
Chenab
Ravi
Beas
Sutlej
LAHORE
AMRITSAR
Ropar
Harappa
Punjab
CHANDIGARH
AMBALA
Bhagwanpura
Alam-
girpur
QUETTA
Dabarkot
Mehrgarh
Nausharo
Pirak
Kunal
Banawali
Siswal
Kalibangan
Haryana
Rakhigarhi
DELHI
Jhukar
Indus
Ganweriwala
BIKANER
PAKISTAN
Mohenjo-daro
Rajasthan
MATHURA
Kot Diji
JAISALMER
JAIPUR
AJMER
Chanhu Daro
JODHPUR
Amri
INDIA
Balakot
Sarasvati
KARACHI
RANN OF
KUTCH
Arabian Sea
Dholavira
Sabarmati
Mahi
Surkotada
UJJAIN
AHMEDABAD
Lothal
Gujarat
Narmada
Bet Dwarka
Rangpur
BARODA
Nageshwar
DWARKA
Rojdi
Bhagatrav
Tapti
Punjab : Indian State
BARODA : present-day city
Ropar : Harappan site
Lothal : major site
international border
dry bed of the Sarasvati
SOMNATH
Maharashtra
NASIK
Daimabad
Godavari

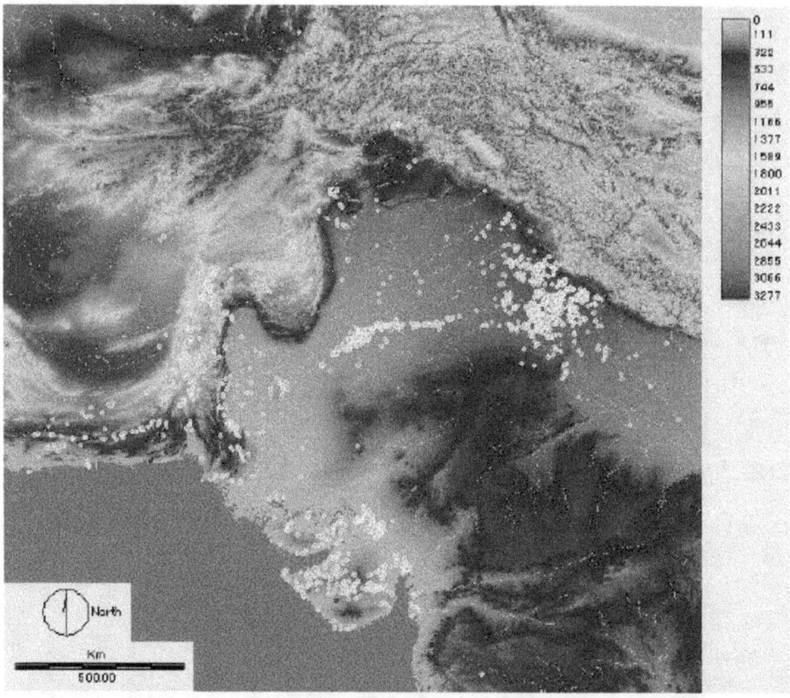

Map of Indus civilization sites (Map by Hirofumi Teramura, Indus Project, RIHN)

संस्कृतिः saṃskṛtiḥ from saṃskṛ संस्कृ To refine, polish; वाण्येका समलंकरोति पुरुषं या संस्कृता धार्यते Bh.2.19; Śi.14.5. saṃskārḥ संस्कारः Any faculty or capacity. Effect of work, merit of action; फलानुमेयाः प्रारम्भाः संस्काराः प्राक्तना इव R.1.2. The faculty of recollection, impression on the memory; संस्कारमात्रजन्यं ज्ञानं स्मृतिः T. S. **-पूत** *a.* **1** purified by sacred rites; purified by refinement or education. संस्कृतिः 1 = संस्कार perfection, determination, culture; संस्कारक *a.* Consecrating, purifying, refining &c.

vijñānam विज्ञानम् 1 Knowledge, wisdom, intelligence, under- standing; यज्जीव्यते क्षणमपि प्रथितं मनुष्यैर्विज्ञानशौर्यविभवार्यगुणैः समेतम् । तन्नाम जीवितमिह ... Pt.1.24;5.3; विज्ञानमयः कोशः 'the sheath of intelligence' (the first of the five sheaths of the soul). **-2** Discrimination, discernment. **-3** Skill, proficiency; प्रयोगविज्ञानम् Ś.1.2.
From: Vijñā विज्ञा 9 U. **1** To know, be aware of; विजानन्तो$प्येते वयमिह विपज्जालजटिलान्न मुञ्चामः कामान् Bh.3.21. Worldly or pro- fane knowledge, knowledge derived from worldly ex- perience (opp. ज्ञान which is 'knowledge of Brahma or Supreme Spirit'); ज्ञानं ते$हं सविज्ञानमिदं वक्ष्याम्यशेषतः Bg.7.2;3.41;6.8; (the whole of the 7th Adhyāya of Bg. explains ज्ञान and विज्ञान; vijñātiḥ

विज्ञातिः *f.* Knowledge; न विज्ञातेर्विज्ञातारं विजानीयाः Bri. Up.3.4.2.

संस्कृतिः saṃskṛtiḥ**, cultural,** vijñānam विज्ञानम् **civilizational frontier**

The frontier extends from Hanoi, Vietnam to Haifa, Israel, paralleling the stretch of the Nagadhiraja Himalaya from Hanoi to Teheran. This was the ancient Maritime Tin Route which predates Silk Road by two millennia. Data mining of the catalogs in the Corpora (as *catalogus catalogorum*) evidences the vedic cultural continuum in civilizational advances of Sarasvati-Sindhu civilization from ca. 3500 BCE recorded in archaeo-metallurgical artifacts of use of metal alloys and *cire perdue* lost-wax metal castings – an invention of unsurpassed brilliance in advances of knowledge systems, transmuting mere earth and stones into utility objects of hardened metal, pots and pans, metal implements, tools and even weapons. This material, technologicalc creative brilliance of human endeavor by artisans and enquirers is matched by the stunning metaphors of वाक् *vāk* (Rigveda 10.125) and *skambha* (Atharvaveda X.7) – vAk as rASTrI, vasUnAm samgamanI, skambhस्कम्भ् 'to create, to support' in a transmutation process signified by *axis mundi*, paralleling the cosmic dance of the supreme divine. राष्ट्री [p= 879,2] *f.* a female ruler or sovereign or proprietress

RV. AitBr. राष्ट्र [p= 875,2] *mn.* (fr. √ राज् ; g.

अर्धर्चा*दि ; *m.* only MBh. xiii , 3050) a kingdom (Mn. vii , 157 one of the 5 प्रकृतिs of the state) , realm , empire , dominion , district , country RV. &c a people , nation , subjects

Mn. MBh. &c (Monier-Williams) No wonder, Prakritam has a gloss which denotes both a temple and a smithy-forge: *kole.l* (Kota language), as a profound tribute to the cosmic dancer.

Two sites alone account for 4723 inscriptions (Mohenjo-daro 2134 and Harappa 2589), all included in the embedded compendium, titled. Vāk and Mlecchita Vikalpa (Select inscriptions from Indus Script Corpora).

Prakritam was वाक् vāk and a cipher, as writing system was mlecchita. Derived from this word वाक् vāk is व्याहृत *p. p.* Said, spoken, uttered. -तम् 1 Speaking, talking. -2 Inarticulate speech or song; रसज्ञाने तु जिव्हेयं व्याहृते वाक् तथोच्यते Mb.12.21.32. -3 Information, instruction. व्याहृतिः भूर्भुवः सुवरिति वा एतास्तिस्रो व्याहृतयः T. Up.1.5.1; वेदत्रयान्निरदुहद्भूर्भुवःस्वरितीति च Ms.2.76 Vyāhṛitis are three: भूर्, भुवस् and स्वस् or स्वर् usually repeated after *om.*

Indus Script Corpora in *mlecchita vikalpa* 'cipher rendered by mleccha 'copper' workers) can be summarized as व्याहृतिः vikalpa, an alternative rendering – in writing --of proclamations of metalwork in hieroglyph-multiplexes, as hypertexts. A synonym for vāk 'speech' is भाषा bhāṣā derived from भाष् 1 Ā. (भाषते, भाषित) 1 To say, speak, utter. Ancient cuneiform texts and ancient Indian texts. categorized a speech form as Meluhha, Mleccha language. Patanjali explains the term mleccha as characterized by mispronunciations and ungrammatical forms which are common in speech forms as compared with prosody of chandas used in Vedic texts, Rigveda and Samaveda, in particular.

Metalwork lexis of Prakritam was recorded on seals, sculptural reliefs by artisans, artists of ancient India, as hieroglyphs read rebus to signify and to document Bronze Age metalwork life-activities.

Mleccha or Meluhha was a speech-form, भाषा [भाष्-अ] speech, talk; as in चारुभाषः. -2 Language, tongue; सत्या न भाषा भवति यद्यपि स्यात् प्रतिष्ठिता Ms.8.164. -3 A common or vernacular dialect; (*a*) the *spoken* Samskṛtam language (opp. छन्दस् or वेद); विभाषा भाषायाम् P.VI.1.181; (*b*) any Prākṛita dialect (opp. संस्कृत) भाषित-ईशा Sarasvatī; N.11.16.

Semantics of प्राकृत [p= 703,1] are related to language or speech of a people of ancient times; the word is derived from प्र-कृति original , natural , artless , normal , ordinary , usual (SBr.); provincial, vernacular, Prakritic (Vcar.); unrefined (Mn. viii , 338 MBh.); (in सांख्य) belonging to or derived from प्रकृति or the original element; any provincial or vernacular dialect cognate with Sanskrit (esp. the language spoken by women and inferior characters in the plays , but also occurring in other kinds of literature and usually divided into 4 dialects viz.शौरसेनी , माहाराष्ट्री , अपभ्रंश and पैशाची) , Ka1v. Katha1s. Ka1vya7d. &c. (Monier-Williams) तद्भवस्तत्समो देशीत्यनेकः प्राकृत- क्रमः Kāv.1.33; also 34, 35; त्वमप्यस्माद्दशजनयोग्ये प्राकृतमार्गे प्रवृत्तो$सि Vbप्रकृतेरयं प्रकृत्या निर्वृत्तो वा अण्] 1 Original, natural, unaltered, unmodified, ordinary प्राकृत इव परिभूयमानमात्मानं न रुणत्सि K.146; Bg.18.28. कार्षापणं भवेद्दण्डयो यत्रान्यः प्राकृतो जनः Ms.8.336 भाष्यम् [भाष्-ण्यत्] N. of the great commentary of Patañjali on Pāṇini's Sūtras. This commentary explains the characteristics of Mleccha as language, which may be called parole 'spoken form' (French) as distinct from langue 'literary, grammatical form' (language) (Samskrtam.Apte)

Indus script cipher, the method of messaging, data substitution paralleling *cire perdue* casting method

A good example of mlecchita vikalpa, cipher-writing is provided by Narmer palette in Egyptian hieroglyphs. N'r 'cuttle-fish' and M'r 'awl' are two hieroglyphs read together as Narmer, signified the name of an Egyptian emperor, Narmer.

Narmer Palette, rebus method

Connections between glyphs and intended meanings are provided by the rebus method. If two similar sounding words have different meanings -- one, pictorial meaning and the other metallurgical meaning -- and if this happens consistently for hundreds of word-pairs, the application of the rebus method for writing is a reasonable deduction. Similar was the method used on Narmer palette in Egypt. N'r meant 'cuttle fish'; M'r meant 'awl'. Together, they gave the Emperor's name and so, N'r + M'r pictorials are shown in front of this person.

The Narmer Palette (Great Hierakonpolis Palette) Cairo J.E. 14716, C.G. 32169 Hierakonpolis (Horus Temple 'Main Deposit') h. 63,5 cm dated from ca. 31st century BCE.[1] The Egyptologist Bob Brier has referred to the Narmer Palette as "the first historical document in the world". (Brier, Bob. *Daily Life of the Ancient Egyptians*, A. Hoyt Hobbs 1999, p.202). At the top of both sides of the Palette are the central serekhs bearing the rebus symbols n'r (catfish) and m'r (chisel) inside, being the phonetic representation of Narmer's name. The Narmer Palette is a 63-centimetre tall (2.07 ft), shield-shaped, ceremonial palette, carved from a single piece of flat, soft dark gray-green siltstone.[2]

It appears that the entwined snakes has a Sumerian connection.

The glyph of entwined snake-hoods together with an eagle appear on a Uruk cylinder seal.

Jasper cylinder seal and clay impression: monstrous lions and lion-headed eagles, Mesopotamia, Uruk Period (4100

BC–3000 BC). Department of Oriental Antiquities, Richelieu wing, ground floor, room 1a, case 2 MNB 1167 Louvre.

The glyphs include two entwined snake-hoods with faces of a feline and a winged feline shown between the entwined tails of the animals.

This is a scene from a ceremonial make-up palette c. 3300 BCE. Two jackals face standing up face each other. Two snakes flanking a circle have tiger-heads in place of the snake-hoods, licking a ram. Some suggest that this may be an import from Sumer to the Nile Valley. Source: The depiction of rams in the context of faces of tigers is a metallurgical determinative that the sharpness, tempered metal sought to be achieved by the process of alloying is related to copper. Hence, the tiger glyphs could connot bronze or arsenic alloys of copper. A pair of tiger glyphs then indicate cast bronze or arsenic alloys – cast perhaps into bun ingots or cast into weapon or tool shapes hardened enough to be made with sharpened edges.[3]

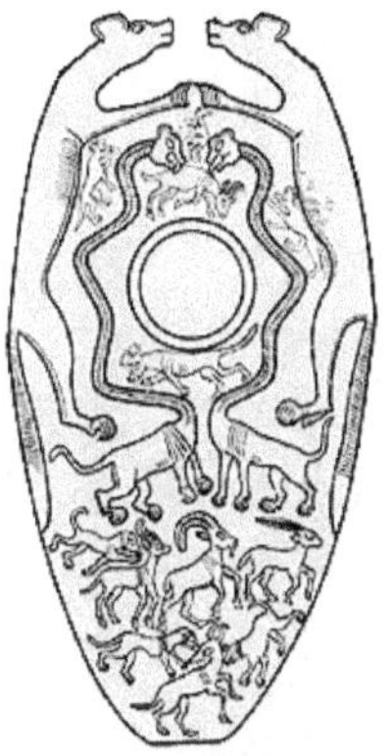

By the Early Dynasty III period, the Mesopotamian craftsmen had mastered the techniques for working copper, lead, silver, gold and tin. The Royal Cemetery at Ur has yielded a corpus of metal work where true tin bronze is found, apart from the common arsenical bronze and precious metals: gold, silver and electrum. Metal blades were produced in many sizes to serve as arrows, spears, daggers. Also found are sickles and hoes. Axes come in many shapes and sizes, some cast and some hammered with the tang beaten round a haft. Muhly (1983) quotes a passage from the late third millennium Laws of Eshnunna that a workman issued with tools for the harvest must return the same weight of metal at the end of the season, even if some of it is scrap. This is an indication that temples had metalsmithies where metal could be melted down and recast. Sumerian Simug was the metalsmith. In the Ur III period, the royal mausoleum of Shulgi at Ur yielded scraps of gold leaf which seem to have been part of architectural decoration, as was the case in the Jemdat Nasr period where the altar of the Eye temple at Tell Brak was decorated with gold leaf. The texts state that large numbers of metal-workers were employed by both the temple and the palace to produce a whole range of goods from tools to jewellery. These workers at Ur worked in groups under a foreman who reported to a general overseer. An assay office issued the metals to the foreman and weighed the finished article before counter-signing the receipts issued by the general overseer. In provincial towns, the governor himself issued metal from the treasury. Private metal merchants handled the supply of raw materials.[4]

The motif snake-hoods ligatured with tiger faces, is similar to the entwined snake hoods shown on Narmer Palette c. 31st century BCE.

Below the procession shown on Narmer Palette, two men are holding ropes tied to the outstretched, intertwining necks of two serpopards confronting each other, mythical felines with bodies of leopards (or more likely lionesses or tigers, given that there are no spots indicated) and snakelike necks. The circle formed by their exaggeratedly curving necks is the central part of the Palette, which is the area where the cosmetics would be ground.

These animals have been considered an additional symbol for the unification of Egypt, but it is a unique image in Egyptian art and there is nothing to suggest that either animal represents an identifiable part of Egypt, although each had lioness war goddesses as protectors and the intertwined necks may represent the unification of the state. Similar images of such mythical animals are known from other contemporaneous cultures, and there are other examples of late-predynastic objects (including other palettes and knife handles) which borrow similar elements from Mesopotamian iconography.[5]

The Narmer Palette (Great Hierakonpolis Palette) Cairo J.E. 14716, C.G. 32169 Hierakonpolis (Horus Temple 'Main Deposit') h. 63,5 cm dated from ca. 31st century BCE.[6] The Egyptologist Bob Brier has referred to the Narmer Palette as "the first historical document in the world".[7] At the top of both sides of the Palette are the central serekhs bearing the rebus symbols n'r (catfish) and m'r (chisel) inside, being the phonetic representation of Narmer's name. The Narmer Palette is a 63-centimetre tall (2.07 ft), shield-shaped, ceremonial palette, carved from a single piece of flat, soft dark gray-green siltstone.[8]

Obverse side

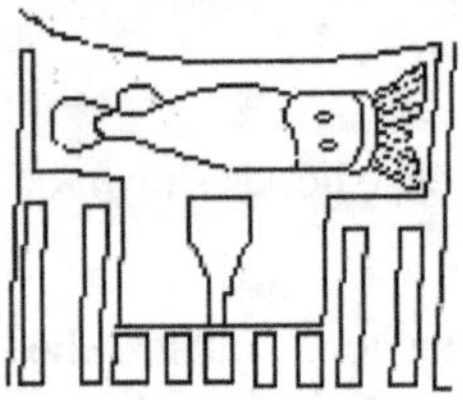

The obverse side of the Narmer Palette shows some images which parallel images used in Uruk. The bottom registers shows a bull and two entwined snake-hoods. At the top of both sides of the Palette are the central serekhs bearing the rebus symbols *n'r* (catfish) and *m'r* (chisel) inside, being the phonetic representation of Narmer's name.[9] The serekh on each side are flanked by a pair of bovine heads with highly curved horns, thought to represent the cow goddess Bat.

Below the bovine heads is what appears to be a procession, with Narmer depicted at almost the full height of the register (a traditional artistic representation emphasizing his importance) shown wearing the Red Crown of Lower Egypt, whose symbol was the papyrus. The first two standard-bearers on the procession carry poles superfixed with

hieroglyphs of 'bird + scarves'. baṭa = quail (Santali) Rebus: baṭa = furnace (Santali) bhrāṣṭra = furnace (Skt.) baṭa = a kind of iron (G.) bhaṭa 'furnace' (G.) baṭa = kiln (Santali). WPah.kṭg. dhàṭṭu m. ' woman's headgear, kerchief ', kc. dhaṭu m. (also dhaṭhu m. ' scarf ', J. dhāṭ(h)u m. Him.I 105). dhaṭu m. (also dhaṭhu) m. 'scarf' (WPah.) (CDIAL 6707) Rebus: dhatu = mineral (Santali) dhātu 'mineral (Pali) dhātu 'mineral' (Vedic); a mineral, metal (Santali); dhāta id. (G.) H. dhāṛnā 'to send out, pour out, cast (metal)' (CDIAL 6771).

He holds a mace and a flail, two traditional symbols of kingship. To his right are the hieroglyphic symbols for his name.

Behind him is his sandal bearer, whose name may be represented by the rosette appearing adjacent

to his head, and a second rectangular symbol that has no clear interpretation but which has been suggested may represent a town or citadel.[10] Immediately in front of the pharaoh is a long-haired man, accompanied by a pair of hieroglyphs that have been interpreted as his name: *Tshet* (this assumes that these symbols had the same phonetic value used in later hieroglyphic writing). Before this man are four standard bearers, holding aloft an animal skin, a dog, and two falcons. At the far right of this scene are ten decapitated corpses, with heads at their feet, possibly symbolizing the victims of Narmer's conquest. Above them are the symbols for a ship, a falcon, and a harpoon, which has been interpreted as representing the names of the towns that were conquered.

At the bottom of the Palette, a bovine image is seen knocking down the walls of a city while trampling on a fallen foe. Because of the lowered head in the image, this is interpreted as a presentation of the king vanquishing his foes, "Bull of his Mother" being a common epithet given

to Egyptian kings as the son of the patron cow goddess.[11] This posture of a bovine has the meaning of "force" in later hieroglyphics.

Reverse side

Repeating the format from the other side, two human-faced bovine heads, thought to represent the patron cow goddess Bat, flank the serekhs. Some authors suggest that the images represent the vigor of the king as a pair of bulls.

A large picture in the center of the Palette depicts Narmer wearing the White Crown of Upper Egypt, whose symbol was the flowering lotus, and wielding a mace. To his left is a man bearing the king's sandals, again flanked by a rosette symbol. To the right of the king is a kneeling prisoner, who is about to be struck by the king. A pair of symbols appear next to his head, perhaps indicating his name or indicating the region where he was from.

Above the prisoner is a falcon, representing Horus, perched above a set of papyrus flowers, the symbol of Lower Egypt. In his talons, he holds a rope-like object which appears to be attached to the nose of a man's head that also emerges from the papyrus flowers, perhaps indicating that he is drawing life from the head. The papyrus has often been interpreted as referring to the marshes of the Nile Delta region in Lower Egypt, or that the battle happened in a marshy area, or even that each papyrus flower represents the number 1,000, indicating that 6,000 enemies were subdued in the battle.

Below the king's feet is a third section, depicting two naked, bearded men. They are either running or are meant to be seen as sprawling dead upon the ground. Appearing to the left of the head of each man is a hieroglyphic sign, the first a walled town, the second a type of knot, likely indicating the name of a defeated town.[12]

Kafajeh vase fragment. The vase was found in level IX of the Sin temple. It carries a contest scene typical of Mesopotamian prototypes.[13] The top register shows two tigers standing on their hindlegs held back by a person, with bovine-hoofs, in the middle. The bottom register shows a pair of 'buildings'.

These tiger motifs and two tigers standing on their hindlegs and facing each other on the Sumerian or Narmer palettes are comparable to *kola*, the jackals or tigers shown on the Harappa tablet h1971.

h1971B Harappa. Three tablets with identical glyphic compositions on both sides: h1970, h1971 and h1972. Seated figure or deity with reed house or shrine at one side. Left: H95-2524; Right: H95-2487.

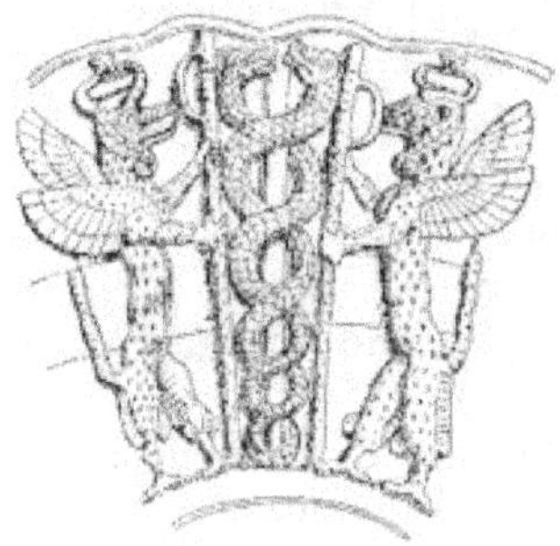

[quote]"Gudea's libation vase", 21st cent BCE[14]

The vase carries an inscription across the figures which establishes it as a gift to the god Ningishzida by Gudea, lord of Lagash. Ningishzida was a minor deity, a special patron of Gudea. Ningishzida is depicted in several works as presenting Gudea to Nin-girsu, the patron deity of Lagash. The scene is a large caduceus, two snakes twining around a central staff, flanked by two genii. The caduceus is interpreted as the god Ningishzida himself. [unquote]

Rebus readings: Glyph: *kola* 'tiger'. Rebus: *kol* 'pañcaloha, alloy of five metals, working in iron'. Glyph: when the head of the tiger is elongaged to appear like a snake's hood: Glyph: 'snake's hood': *paṭam*. Rebus: *padm* 'temper, sharpness (of metal)'. If the ram glyph denotes *melakku* 'copper'. or meḍ 'metal', the tiger glyph denotes an alloy of minerals: kol. When elongated like a snake's hood, the tiger represents a sharpened, tempered alloy – *padm kol* -- which can produce sharp tools, sharp as the edge of a knife and weapons. Pair of snake-hoods is relatable to the glyph: dula 'pair'. Rebus: dul 'cast (metal). Thus a pair of tigers with elongated necks made to look like snake-hoods cnnote 'cast alloy tempered metal.' Such a snake-hood is shown on Indus script inscriptions by the tail of a composite animal to look like a snake's hood.

A tiger tied to a rope as shown on Egyptian hieroglyphs is an abiding metaphor which also signifies on a Kalibangan terracotta cake found in a fire-altar a smelting process. The terracotta cake shows a tiger tied to a rope and dragged by a person.

Pl. XXII B. Terracotta cake with incised figures on obverse and reverse, Harappan. On one side is a human figure wearing a head-dress having two horns and a plant in the centre; on the other side is an animal-headed human figure with another animal figure, the latter being dragged by the former.

Decipherment of hieroglyphs on the Kalibangan terracotta cake:

bhaTa 'warrior' rebus: bhaTa 'furnace'
kolmo 'rice plant' rebus: kolimi 'smithy, forge'
koD 'horn' rebus: koD 'workshop'

kola 'tiger' rebus: kolle 'blacksmith', kolhe 'smelter' kol 'working in iron'

The tiger is being pulled to be tied to a post, pillar. Hieroglyph: *Ka.* kunda a pillar of bricks, etc. *Tu.* kunda pillar, post. *Te.* kunda id. *Malt.* kunda block, log. ? Cf. Ta. kantu pillar, post. (DEDR 1723) Rebus: (agni)kuNDA 'fire-altar, vedi'.

Hieriglyph: *meṛh* **rope tying to post, pillar: mēthí** m. ' pillar in threshing floor to which oxen are fastened, prop for supporting carriage shafts ' AV., *°thī* -- f. KātyŚr.com., *mēdhī* -- f. Divyāv.

2. mēṭhī -- f. PañcavBr.com., *mēḍhī* -- , *mēṭī* -- f. BhP.1. Pa. *mēdhi* -- f. ' post to tie cattle to, pillar, part of a stūpa '; Pk. *mēhi* -- m. ' post on threshing floor ', N. *meh(e)*, *miho*, *miyo*, B. *mei*, Or. *maï* -- *dāṇḍi*, Bi. *mẽh*, *mẽhā* ' the post ', (SMunger) *mehā* ' the bullock next the post ', Mth. *meh*, *mehā* ' the post ', (SBhagalpur)*mīhā̃* ' the bullock next the post ', (SETirhut) *mẽhi bāṭi* ' vessel with a projecting base '.2. Pk. *mēḍhi* -- m. ' post on threshing floor ', *mēḍhaka*<-> ' small stick '; K. *mīr*, *mīrü* f. ' larger hole in ground which serves as a mark in pitching walnuts ' (for semantic relation of ' post -- hole ' see kūpa -- 2); L. *meṛh* f. ' rope tying oxen to each other and to post on threshing floor '; P. *mehṛ* f., *mehaṛ* m. ' oxen on threshing floor, crowd '; OA *meṛha*, *mehra* ' a circular construction, mound '; Or. *meṛhī*,*meri* ' post on threshing floor '; Bi. *mẽṛ* ' raised bank between irrigated beds ', (Camparam) *mẽṛhā* ' bullock next the post ', Mth. (SETirhut) *mẽṛhā* ' id. '; M. *meḍ(h)*, *meḍhī* f., *meḍhā* m. ' post, forked stake '.mēthika -- ; mēthiṣṭhá -- . mēthika m. ' 17th or lowest cubit from top of sacrificial post ' lex. [mēthí --]Bi. *mẽhiyā* ' the bullock next the post on threshing floor '.mēthiṣṭhá ' standing at the post ' TS. [mēthí -- , stha --] Bi. (Patna) *mẽhṭhā* ' post on threshing floor ', (Gaya) *mehṭā*, *mẽhṭā* ' the bullock next the post '.(CDIAL 10317 to, 10319) Rebus: meD 'iron' (Ho.); med 'copper' (Slavic)

Note the Isapur yupa which show ropes in the middle and on the top to tie an animal as shown on the Kaibangan terracotta cake. In the case of the Kalibangan terracotta cake, the hieroglyph shows a kola, 'tiger' tied to the rope. The rebus reading is kol 'working in iron'. The work in iron is signified by the post, yupa: *meḍ(h)*, 'post, stake' rebus: *meḍ* 'iron', med 'copper' (Slavic).

Thus, the terracotta cake inscription signifies a iron workshop smelter/furnace and smithy.

The recording of an inscription on a terracotta cake used in a fire-altar continues as a tradition with inscriptions recorded on Yupa, 'pillars' of Rajasthan, Mathura, Allahabad and East Borneo indicating the type of yajna's.Yupa, often an octagonal-shaped pillar, is a signifier of Soma Yaga, as evidenced by the octagonal yupa found in Binjor fire-altar.

Discovery reported from Binjor (a site near Anupgarh, on the banks of Vedic River Sarasvati) excavations in April 2015 by ASI. The fire altar, with a yasti made of an octagonal brick. Photo:Subhash Chandel, ASI. This is a signifier of a Soma Yaga according to the details elaborated in Satapatha Brahmana, a Vedic text. Binjor (4MSR) site is near Anupgarh, Rajasthan, where River Sarasvati forks off (bheda). One channel flows southwards, another flows westwards to join Sindhu (Bahawalpur province, Ganweriwala). The image provided by LANDSAT is a stunner which pins the bheda mentioned in Mahabharata: one is camasobheda, another is nAgobheda (could be close to Little Rann).

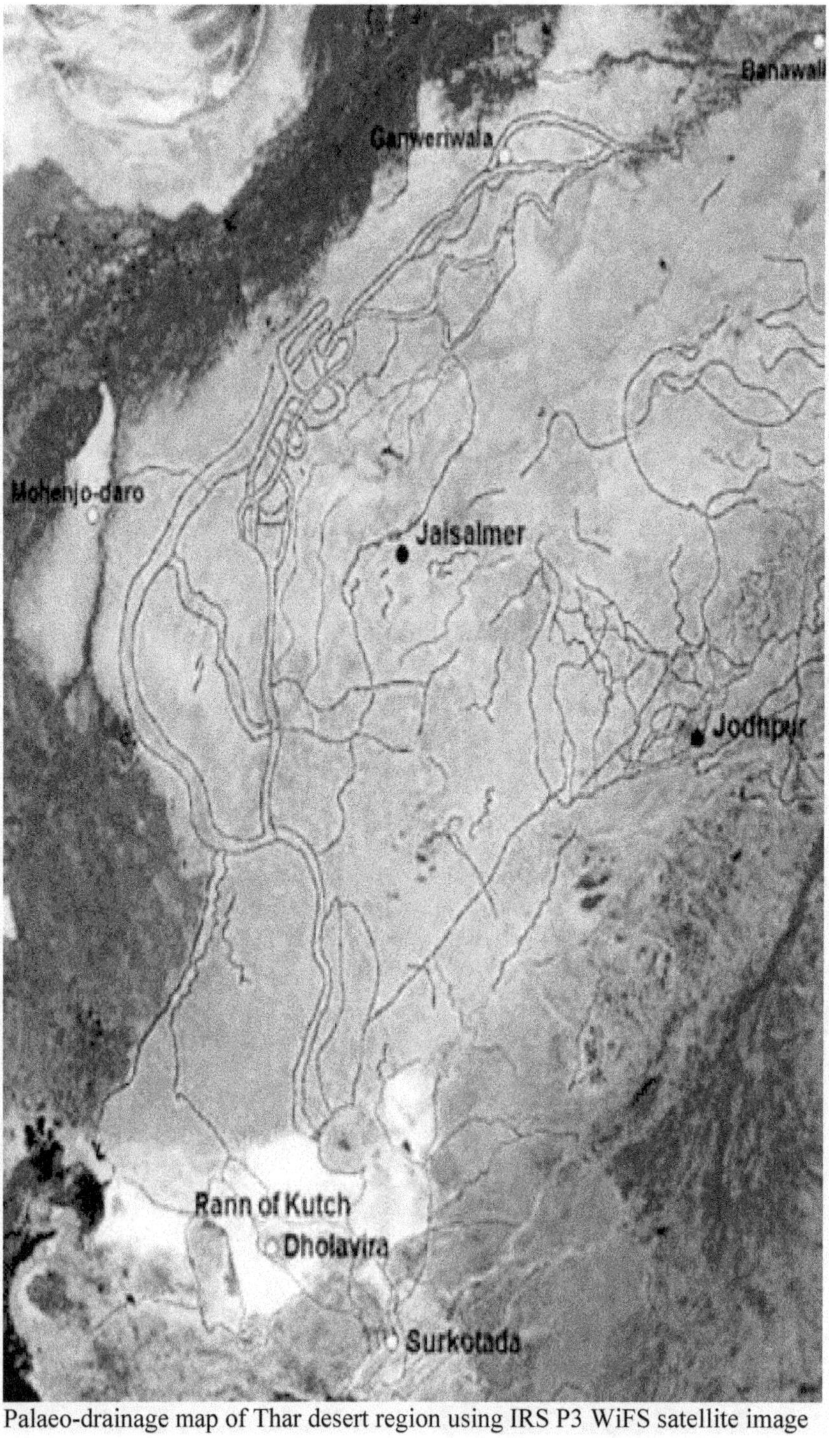

Palaeo-drainage map of Thar desert region using IRS P3 WiFS satellite image

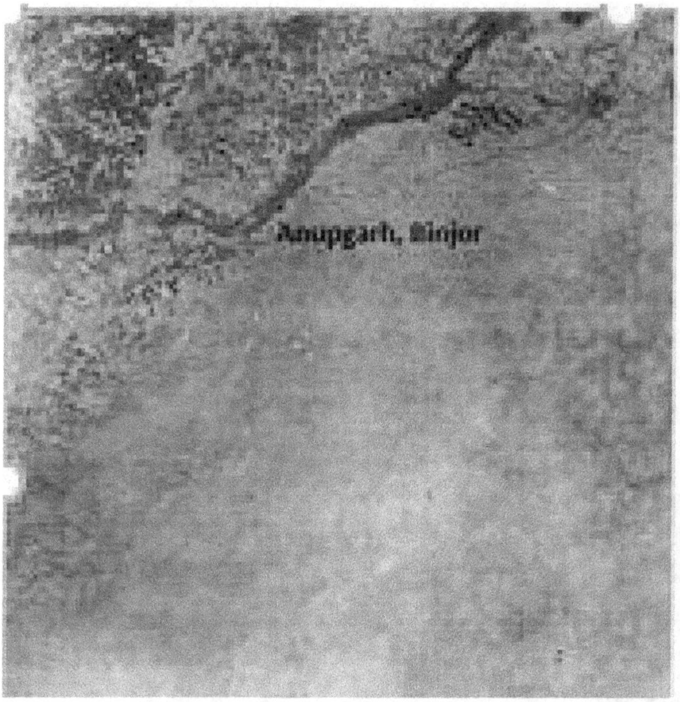

Landsat image showing the bifurcation of River Sarasvati at Anupgarh (Binjor) -- one channel flowing westward into Bahawalpur province and paleochannel flowing southwards towards Jaisalmer. Near Anupgarh Sarasvati bifurcates and both channels come to an abrupt end at Marot and Beriwala (in Bahawalpur Distt of Pakistan) from where Sarasvati is likely to have extended through the Hakra/Nara bed to the present Runn of Kachchh.
The location of the Binjor archaeological site (4MSR) is significant in identifying the desiccation point of Vedic River Sarasvati.

A LANDSAT image shows clearly the bifurcation of the River Sarasvati into two channels, one channel flowing westwards towards Ganweriwala (Bahawalpur Province) and another flowing southwards towards Surkotada/ Dholavira (Gujarat). The River Sutlej had joined River Sarasvati at Shatrana as a tributary. This tributary emanating from Manasarovar glacier in the Himalayas, took a 90-degree turn westwards at Ropar (another archaeological site with a site museum). This 90-degree turn is evidence of the impact of plate tectonics resulting in the River Sutlej changing its course abandoning the supply of glacial waters to River Sarasvati/Drishadvati drainage system.

Thus, Binjor (4MSR) site is a time marker for the River Sarasvati as a navigable channel prior to 1900 BCE, allowing for the trade indicated by the Bijnor seal of metal implements which might have been carried by seafaring merchant caravants across the Persian Gulf.

It is likely that the Binjor site was visited by Balarama during his pariyatra as the text says he visited the camasobheda, nAgodbheda and paid homage to ancestors, Rishis.

The discovery results in a paradigm shift in our understanding of the Vedic cultural continuum. It is revolutionary, announced in April 2015 by the students of Inst. of Archaeology, National Museum, Delhi. The yupa is octagonal as exactly described in Satapatha Brahmana (aSTAs'ri, 'eight angles'). Yupa + cashAla is the signature tune of a Soma Yaga (like VAjapeya). The cashAla is also mentioned in Sohgaura copper plate (JF Fleet struggles to read the Brahmi text in a brilliant exposition in 1907). It is wheat chaff in pyrolisis/carburization, like crucible steel making. 19 yupa inscriptions have been found in Rajasthan, Allahabad, East Borneo (Mulavarman, Pallava grantha script Samskritam).

Buddha attended by Padmapani and Vajrapani, dated to the year 3 of the Kanishka era, ca. 130 CE, Ahicchatra, India What Vajrapani is carrying is a Vajra with octagonal bases (like an hour glass). This is the orthography of cashAla described in Satapatha Brahmana as aSTAs'ri (eight angles).

Vajra with octagonal bases. Detail of the stele with Buddha, Vajrapani and Padmapani, Ahichchatra, Uttar Pradesh, year 3 of Kanishka era, ca. 130 CE. Delhi Museum. Acc. No. L. 5525. The caShAla is what Vajrapani carries on sculptures. Vajra or Indra dhvaja which Nivedita wanted to be made part of the national flag. Now we have to re-read KV Sharma's account of Vedic culture in Sangam literature.

Locus. Binjor is close to Anupgarh where River Sarasvati forks off (bheda). One channel flows southwards, another flows westwards to join Sindhu (Bahawalpur province, Ganweriwala). The image provided by LANDSAT is a stunner which pins the bheda mentioned in Mahabharata: one is camasobheda, another is nAgobheda (could be close to Little Rann). It is likely that the Binjor site

was visited by Balarama during his pariyatra as the text says he visited the camasobheda, nAgodbheda and paid homage to ancestors, Rishis.

Railing crossbar with monks worshiping a fiery pillar, a symbol of the Buddha. Worship at the throne in front of fiery pillar of light (Sivalinga, as yupa), ca. 3rd cent. CE, Amaravati Stupa, Amaravati, Andhra Pradesh.

Naga worshippers of fiery pillar, Amaravati stup Smithy is the temple of Bronze Age: *stambha, thãbharā* fiery pillar of light, Sivalinga. Rebus-metonymy layered Indus script cipher signifies: *tamba, tā̃bṛā, tambira* 'copper'

दिवो यः स्कम्भो धरुणः स्वातत आपूर्णो अंशुः पर्येति विश्वतः ।
सेमे मही रोदसी यक्षदावृता समीचीने दाधार समिषः कविः ॥ 2 ॥ 9.074.02 The supporter of heaven, the prop (of the earth), the Soma-juice who, widely spreading, filling (the vessels), flows in all directions-- may he unite the two great worlds by his own strength; he has upheld them combined; (may he) the sage (bestow) food upon (his worshippers). [The prop of the earth: cf. RV. 9.089.06; may he unite: yaks.at = sam.yojayatu; a_vr.ta = by its own unaided strength.]

Inscriptions are recorded on many 'tablets' with upto six sides. Harappan 'miniature tablets' are incised flat plates of steatite. Mohenjodaro has yielded engraved copper tablets. Moulded terracotta or faience tablets occur with many repeated texts produced in bas-relief. "On one particular moulded tablet (existing in several identical copies), we see an anthropomorphic deity sitting on a low dais, flanked on either side by a kneeling man and a snake; one of these supplicant men has both his hands raised in worship, while the other is giving what looks like a sacrificial vessel to the deity. Another moulded tablet (again available in several copies) has a similar offering scene, except that here the kneeling worshipper holds out the pot towards a tree. On both tablets the sacrificial vessel looks exactly like the U-formed Indus sign." (Parpola, 1996).

Mohejodaro, tablet in bas relief (M-478)

M-488 A

M-488 B

M-488 C

The pictorial of a kneeling 'worshipper' is echoed in the script signs, ligatured with the 'pot' sign:

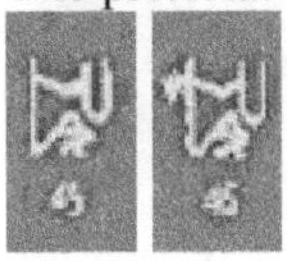

Ornamental 'endless knot', *svastika* & other hieroglyphs on Indus Script corpora, on *āyāgapaṭṭa* अयागपट्ट signify *dhmātṛ, dhamaga* 'smelters of ores'

The monograph demonstrates that ornamental 'endless knot', svastika & other hieroglyphs on Indus Script corpora, on *āyāgapaṭṭa* अयागपट्ट 'homage tablet', signify *dhmātṛ, dhamaga* smelters of zinc and other metallic ores.

In Indus Script Corpora, 'endless knot' hieroglyph can be read with two hieroglyph components: 1. strand of rope or string; 2. twist: *dām* 'rope, string' rebus: *dhāu* 'ore' rebus: मेढा [*mēḍhā*] A twist or tangle arising in thread or cord, a curl or snarl (Marathi). Rebus: *meḍ* 'iron, copper' (Munda. Slavic) *mẽṛhẽt, meḍ* 'iron' (Munda).

Dotted-circle and trefoil hieroglyphs on the shawl of the statue of Mohenjo-daro priest are interpreted as orthographic signifiers, respectively, of: 1. single strand of string or rope; 2. three strands of string or rope. The glosses these hieroglyphs signify are, respectively: 1. Sindhi *dhāī* f. ' wisp of fibres added from time to time to a rope that is being twisted ', Lahnda *dhāī̃* id.; 2. *tridhā́tu* -- ' threefold ' (RigVeda).

Priest of dhā̆vaḍ 'iron-smelters' with Indus script hieroglyphs signifies पोतृ,'purifier' of dhāū, dhāv 'red stone minerals'

The inscription on Mohenjo-daro copper plate m1457 shows two hieroglyphs: 1. svastika; 2. ornamental figure of twisted string. Both hieroglyphs are read rebus in Meluhha:

satthiya 'svastika glyph' rebus: *sattva, jasta* 'zinc' PLUS *dām* 'rope, string' rebus: *dhāu* 'ore'; मेढा [mēḍhā] A twist rebus: mẽṛhẽt, meD 'iron'(Santali.Mu.Ho.). The archaeo-metallurgical interpretation is that this inscription signifies zinc metallic ore, sphalerite.

Orthography of a hieroglyph-multiplex on a Jaina āyāgapaṭṭa अयागपट्ट: The hieroglyph-multiplex has the components of: fish, rope, two molluscs; the mollucs and fish-tail are tied together by the rope.

Hieroglyphs: *dām* 'garland, rope': Rebus 1: *dhamma* 'dharma' (Pali); Rebus 2: *dhamaga* 'blacksmith'; *dhmātṛ* 'smelter'

Hieroglyphs: *hangi*, 'mollusc' tied to a fish: *ayira* 'fish' Rebus; *ariya, ayira* 'person of noble character'.

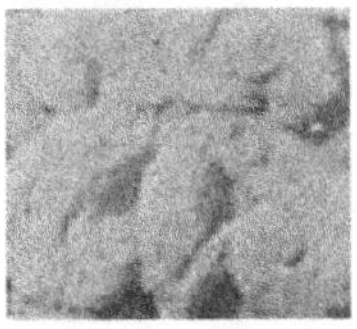

Hieroglyphs: *hangi* 'mollusc' + *dām* 'rope, garland' *dā̃u* m. 'tying'; *puci* 'tail' Rebus: *puja* 'worship'

Rebus: *ariya sanghika dhamma puja* 'veneration of arya sangha dharma'.

Copper plate m1457
h182 tablet in bas-relief
m488A prism tablet

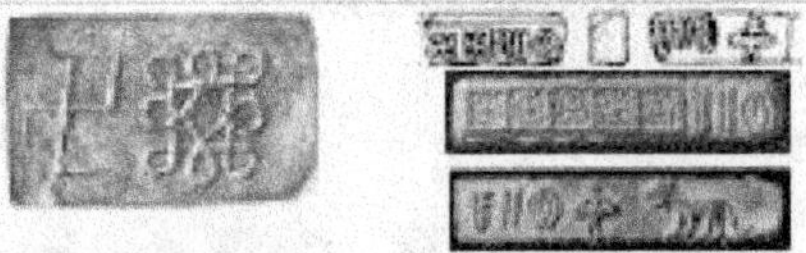

ḍan:gara, ḍan:gura public notice by a crier who beats a tom-tom (Ka.) **iṭan:kā ram** = left-hand side of a double drum (Ta.lex.) [Note a drummer glyph] Rebus: ṭhākur , ḍhangar blacksmith (Mth.)(CDIAL 5488).

- *svostiko* pewter (Kannada); jasta = zinc (Hindi) **yasada** (Jaina Pkt.)
- **merhao** = to entwine itself, wind round, wrap around, roll up (Santali.lex मेढा mēḍhā] menda A twist or tangle arising in thread or cord, a curl or snarl. (Marathi) (CDIAL 10312). Rebus: med 'iron' (Ho.)

m1356, m443 tablet
Hieroglyph: मेढा [mēḍhā] 'a curl or snarl; twist in thread' (Marathi) .L. meṛh f. 'rope tying oxen to each other'.
मेढा [mēḍhā] A twist or tangle arising in thread or cord, a curl or snarl.(Marathi) mer.ha = twisted, crumpled, as a horn (Santali.lex.) meli, melika = a turn, a twist, a loop, entanglement; meliyu, melivad.u, meligonu = to get twisted or entwined (Te.lex.) [Note the endless knot motif]. Rebus: med. 'iron' (Mu.) sattva 'svastika glyph' Rebus: sattva, jasta 'zinc'.

The 'endless knot' hieroglyph on m1457 Copper plate of Mohenjo-daro has also orthographic variants of a twisted string.

The 'endless knot' hieroglyph can be interpreted as composed of two related semantics: 1. strand of rope or string; 2. twist or curl

Twisted rope as hieroglyph:

dhā´tu *strand of rope ' (cf. tridhā´tu -- ' threefold ' RV., ayugdhātu -- ' having an uneven number of strands ' KātyŚr.) S. dhāī f. ' wisp of fibres added from time to time to a rope that is being twisted ', L. dhāī̃ f.(CDIAL 6773) Rebus: dhā´tu n. ' substance ' RV., m. ' element ' MBh., ' metal, mineral, ore (esp. of a red colour) ' Mn.Pk. dhāu -- m. ' metal, red chalk '; N. dhāu ' ore (esp. of copper) '; Or. ḍhāu ' red chalk, red ochre ' (whence ḍhāuā ' reddish '; M. dhāū, dhāv m.f. ' a partic. soft red stone ' (whence dhā̆vaḍ m. ' a caste of iron -- smelters ', dhāvḍī ' composed of or relating to iron ')(CDIAL 6773).

Mohenjo-daro. m1457 Copper plate with 'twist' hieroglyph. Mohejodaro, tablet in bas relief (M-478) The first hieroglyph-multiplex on the left (twisted rope):

m478a tablet

கோலம்[1] kōlam, *n.* [T. *kōlamu*, K. *kōla*, M. *kōlam*.] 1. Beauty, gracefulness, hand- someness; அழகு. கோலத் தனிக்கொம்பர் (திருக் கோ. 45). 2. Colour; நிறம். கார்க்கோல மேனி யானை (கம்பரா. கும்பக. 154). 3. Form, shape, external or general appearance; உருவம். மானுடக் கோலம். 4. Nature; தன்மை. 5. Costume; appropriate dress; attire, as worn by actors; trappings; equipment; habiliment; வேடம். உள்வரிக் கோலத்து (சிலப். 5, 216). 6. Ornament, as jewelry; ஆபரணம். குறங்கிணை திரண்டன கோலம் பொறாஅ (சிலப். 30, 18). 7. Adornment, decoration, embellishment; அலங்காரம். புறஞ்சுவர் கோலஞ்செய்து (திவ். திருமாலை, 6). 8. Ornamental figures drawn on floor, wall or sacrificial pots with rice-flour, white stone-powder, etc.; மா, கற்பொடி முதலியவற்றாலிடுங் கோலம். தரை மெழுகிக் கோலமிட்டு (குமர. மீனாட். குறம். 25).

The hieroglyphs on m478a tablet are read rebus:

kuTi 'tree'Rebus: kuThi 'smelter'

bhaTa 'worshipper' Rebus: bhaTa 'furnace' baTa 'iron' (Gujarati) This hieroglyph is a phonetic deterinant of the 'rimless pot': baṭa = rimless pot (Kannada) Rebus: baṭa = a kind of iron (Gujarati) bhaṭa 'a furnace'. Hence, the hieroglyph-multiplex of an adorant with rimless pot signifies: 'iron furnace' bhaTa.

bAraNe ' an offering of food to a demon' (Tulu) Rebus: baran, bharat (5 copper, 4 zinc and 1 tin) (Punjabi. Bengali) The narrative of a worshipper offering to a tree is thus interpretable as a smelting of three minerals: copper, zinc and tin.

Numeral four: gaNDa 'four' Rebus: kand 'fire-altar'; Four 'ones': *koḍa* 'one' (Santali) Rebus: *koḍ* 'artisan's workshop'. Thus, the pair of 'four linear strokes PLUS rimless pot' signifies: 'fire-altar (in) artisan's wrkshop'.

Circumscript of two linear strokes for 'body' hieroglyph: dula 'pair' Rebus: dul 'cast metal' *koḍa* 'one'(Santali) Rebus: *koḍ* 'artisan's workshop'. Thus, the circumscript signifies 'cast metal workshop'. meD 'body' Rebus: meD 'iron'.

khareḍo = a currycomb (G.) Rebus: kharādī 'turner' (Gujarati)

The hieroglyph may be a variant of a twisted rope.

dhāu 'rope' rebus: dhāu 'metal' PLUS मेढा [mēḍhā] 'a curl or snarl; twist in thread' rebus: mẽṛhẽt, meḍ 'iron'. Thus, metallic ore.

kōlam, *n.* [T. *kōlamu*, K. *kōla*, M. *kōlam*.] 'ornamental figure' Rebus: *kol* 'working in iron'

The inscription on m478 thus signifies, reading hieroglyphs from r.:

Tree: kuThi 'smelter'

Worshipper: bhaTa 'furnace'

Four linear strokes + rimless pot: kanda baTa 'fire-altar for iron'

Circumscript two linear strokes + body: meD koDa 'metal workshop'Currycomb:khareḍo 'currycomb' rebus: kharādī 'turner'; dhāu 'metal' PLUS mẽṛhẽt, meḍ 'iron'; kol 'working in iron'. Together, the two hieroglyphs

signify metalworker, ironsmith turner.

m0478b tablet

erga = act of clearing jungle (Kui) [Note image showing two men carrying

uprooted trees] thwarted by a person in the middle with outstretched hands

Aḍaru twig; aḍiri small and thin branch of a tree; aḍari small branches (Ka.); aḍaru twig (Tu.)(DEDR 67). Aḍar = splinter (Santali); rebus: aduru = native metal (Ka.) Vikalpa: kūtī = bunch of twigs (Skt.) Rebus: kuṭhi = furnace (Santali) *ḍhaṁkhara* — m.n. 'branch without leaves or fruit' (Prakrit) (CDIAL 5524)

Hieroglyph: *era* female, applied to women only, and generally as a mark of respect, wife; hopon era a daughter; era hopon a man's family; manjhi era the village chief's wife; gosae era a female Santal deity; bud.hi era an old woman; era uru wife and children; nabi era a prophetess; diku era a Hindu woman (Santali)

•Rebus: er-r-a = red; eraka = copper (Ka.) erka = ekke (Tbh. of arka) aka (Tbh. of arka) copper (metal); crystal (Ka.lex.) erako molten cast (Tu.lex.) agasa_le, agasa_li, agasa_lava_d.u = a goldsmith (Te.lex.)

kuTi 'tree' Rebus: kuṭhi = (smelter) furnace (Santali)

heraka = spy (Skt.); eraka, hero = a messenger; a spy (Gujarati); er to look at or for (Pkt.); er uk- to play 'peeping tom' (Ko.) Rebus: erka = ekke (Tbh. of arka) aka (Tbh. of arka) copper (metal); crystal (Ka.lex.) cf. eruvai = copper (Ta.lex.) eraka, er-aka = any metal infusion (Ka.Tu.) eraka 'copper' (Kannada)

kōṭu branch of tree, Rebus: खोट [khōṭa] f A mass of metal (unwrought or of old metal melted down); an ingot or wedge.

Hieroglyph: Looking back: *krammara* 'look back' (Telugu) *kamar* 'smith, artisan' (Santali)

kola 'tiger, jackal' (Kon.); rebus: *kol* working in iron, blacksmith, 'alloy of five metals, panchaloha' (Tamil) kol 'furnace, forge' (Kuwi) kolami 'smithy' (Telugu)

^ Inverted V, m478 (lid above rim of narrow-necked jar) The rimmed jar next to the tiger with turned head has a lid. Lid 'ad.aren'; rebus: aduru 'native metal' karnika 'rim of jar' Rebus: karni 'supercargo' (Marathi) Thus, together, the jar with lid composite hieroglyhph denotes 'native metal supercargo'. karn.aka = handle of a vessel; ka_n.a_, kanna_ = rim, edge; kan.t.u = rim of a vessel; kan.t.ud.iyo = a small earthen vessel; kan.d.a kanka = rim of a water-pot; kan:kha, kankha = rim of a vessel

Comparable hieroglyph of kneeling adorant with outstretched hands occurs on a Mohenjo-daro seal m1186, m478A tablet and on Harappa tablet h177B:

Rebus readings: *maṇḍa* ' some sort of framework (?) '. [In *nau - maṇḍḗ* n. du. ' the two sets of poles rising from the thwarts or the two bamboo covers of a boat (?) ' ŚBr. Rebus: M. *mā̃ḍ* m. ' array of instruments &c. '; Si. *maḍa -- ya* ' adornment, ornament '. (CDIAL 9736) *kamaḍha* 'penance' (Pkt.)Rebus: *kampaṭṭam* 'mint' (Tamil) *battuḍu*. n. A worshipper (Telugu) Rebus: *pattar* merchants (Tamil), perh. Vartaka (Skt.)

Mohenjo-daro seal. m0301 baradh 'bull' (Gujarati); baddi (Nahali)
Sign 48: baraḍo = spine, the backbone, back (Gujarati)
Glyph: baraḍo = spine; backbone; the back; baraḍo thābaḍavo = lit. to strike on the backbone or back; hence, to encourage; baraḍo bhāre thato = lit. to have a painful backbone, i.e. to do something which will call for a severe beating (G.lex.) man.uk.o a single vertebra of the back (G.)

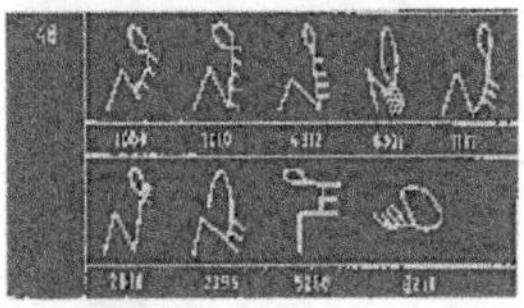

Rebus: baraḍo (vardhaki). Rebus: baraḍo, vardhaka 'carpenter, mason' (Santali. Sanskrit) *baḍhi* 'a caste who work both in iron and wood' (Santali)**barduga = a man of acquirements, a proficient man (Ka.)** Rebus: bharatiyo = a caster of metals, a brazier; bharatar, bharatal, bharatal. = moulded; an article made in a mould (G.) bharata = casting metals in moulds; bharavum = to fill in; to put in; to pour into (G.lex.) bhart = a mixed metal of copper and lead; bhartīyā = a barzier, worker in metal; bhaṭ, bhrāṣṭra = oven, furnace (Skt.)

maruḍiyo = one who makes and sells wristlets, and puts wristlets on the wrists of women (G.lex.) maraḍa = twisting; a twist; a turn; marad.avum = to twist, to turn; maraḍāvum = to bend; maroḍa = a twist, a turn; writhing, a bend; maroḍavum = to writhe, to twist, to contort; to bend (Gujarati)

bhāraṇ = to bring out from a kiln (G.) bāraṇiyo = one whose profession it is to sift ashes or dust in a goldsmith's workshop (G.lex.) baran, bharat (5 copper, 4 zinc and 1 tin)(P.B.) In the Punjab, bharata = a factitious metal compounded of copper, pewter, tin (M.) In Bengal, an alloy called bharan or toul was created by adding some brass or zinc into pure bronze. bharata = casting metals in moulds; bharavum = to fill in; to put in; to pour into (G.lex.) Bengali. ভরন [bharana] n an inferior metal obtained from an alloy of coper, zinc and tin.

bharaḍo a devotee of Śiva; a man of the bharaḍā caste in the brāhman.as (G.) baraṛ = name of a caste of jat- around Bhaṭiṇḍa; baraṛaṇḍā melā = a special fair held in spring (Punjabi) bharāḍ = a religious service or entertainment performed by a bharāḍī; consisting of singing the praises of some idol or god with playing on the ḍaur (drum) and dancing; an order of aṭharā akhāḍe = 18 gosāyī group; bharāḍ and bhāratī are two of the 18 orders of gosāyī (M.lex.) bārṇe, bāraṇe = an offering of food to a demon; a meal after fasting, a breakfast (Tu.lex.) barada, barda, birada = a vow (Gujarati) vrata id. (Sanskrit) Rebus: bhāraṇ = to bring out from a kiln (G.) bāraṇiyo = one whose profession it is to sift ashes or dust in a goldsmith's workshop (G.lex.) baran, bharat (5 copper, 4 zinc and 1 tin)(P.B.) In the Punjab, bharata = a factitious metal compounded of copper, pewter, tin (M.) In Bengal, an alloy called bharan or toul was created by adding some brass or zinc into pure bronze. bharata = casting metals in moulds; bharavum = to fill in; to put in; to pour into (G.lex.) Bengali. ভরন [bharana] n an inferior metal obtained from an alloy of coper, zinc and tin.

m1186 seal. *kaula*— m. 'worshipper of Śakti according to left—hand ritual', *khōla*—3 'lame'; Khot. *kūra*— 'crooked' BSOS ix 72 and poss. Sk. *kōra*— m. 'movable joint' Suśr.]

Ash. *kṓlə* 'curved, crooked'; Dm. *kōla* 'crooked', Tir. *kṓolə*; Paš. *kōlā́* 'curved, crooked', Shum. *kolā́ṇṭa*; Kho. *koli* 'crooked', (Lor.) also 'lefthand, left'; Bshk. *kōl* 'crooked'; Phal. *kūulo*; Sh. *kōlu̯* 'curved, crooked' (CDIAL 3533).

Rebus: **kol** 'pancaloha' (Tamil)

bhaTa 'worshipper' Rebus: bhaTa 'furnace' baTa 'iron' (Gujarati)

saman 'make an offering (Santali) samanon 'gold' (Santali)

minDAl 'markhor' (Torwali) meDho 'ram' (Gujarati)(CDIAL 10120) Rebus: me~Rhet, meD 'iron' (Mu.Ho.Santali)

heraka 'spy' (Samskritam) Rebus:eraka 'molten metal, copper'

maNDa 'branch, twig' (Telugu) Rebus: maNDA 'warehouse, workshop' (Konkani)\karibha, jata kola Rebus: karba, ib, jasta, 'iron, zinc, metal (alloy of five metals)

maNDi 'kneeling position' Rebus: mADa 'shrine; mandil 'temple' (Santali)

dhatu 'scarf' Rebus: dhatu 'mineral ore' (Santali)

The rice plant adorning the curved horn of the person (woman?) with the pig-tail is kolmo; read rebus, kolme 'smithy'. Smithy of what? Kol 'pancaloha'. The curving horn is: kod.u = horn; rebus: kod. artisan's workshop (Kuwi)

The long curving horns may also connote a ram on h177B tablet:

h177B

4316 Pict-115: From R.—a person standing under an ornamental arch; a kneeling adorant; a ram with long curving horns.

The ram read rebus: me~d. 'iron'; glyph: me_n.d.ha ram; min.d.a_l markhor (Tor.); meh ram (H.); mei wild goat (WPah.) me~r.hwa_ a bullock with curved horns like a ram's (Bi.) me~r.a_, me~d.a_ ram with curling horns (H.)

Ganweriwala

tablet. Ganeriwala or Ganweriwala (Urdu: گنےریوالا Punjabi: گنیریوالا) is a Sarasvati-Sindhu civilization site in Cholistan, Punjab, Pakistan.

Glyphs on a broken molded tablet, Ganweriwala. The reverse includes the 'rim-of-jar' glyph in a 3-glyph text. Observe shows a person seated on a stool and a kneeling adorant below.

Hieroglyph: kamadha 'penance' Rebus: kammata 'coiner, mint'.

Reading rebus three glyphs of text on Ganweriwala tablet: brass-worker, scribe, turner:

1. kuṭila 'bent'; rebus: kuṭila, katthīl = bronze (8 parts copper and 2 parts tin) [cf. āra-kūṭa, 'brass' (Skt.) (CDIAL 3230)

2. Glyph of 'rim of jar': kárṇaka m. ' projection on the side of a vessel, handle ' ŚBr. [kárṇa --]Pa. kaṇṇaka -- ' having ears or corners '; (CDIAL 2831) kaṇḍa kanka; Rebus: furnace account (scribe). kaṇḍ = fire-altar (Santali); kan = copper (Tamil) khanaka m. one who digs , digger , excavator Rebus: karanikamu. Clerkship: the office of a Karanam or clerk. (Telugu) káraṇa n. ' act, deed ' RV. [√kr̥1] Pa. karaṇa -- n. 'doing'; NiDoc. karana, kaṁraṁna 'work'; Pk. karaṇa -- n. 'instrument'(CDIAL 2790)

3. khareḍo = a currycomb (G.) Rebus: kharādī ' turner' (G.)

Hieroglyph: मेढा [mēḍhā] A twist or tangle arising in thread or cord, a curl or snarl (Marathi). Rebus: meḍ 'iron, copper' (Munda. Slavic) mẽṛhẽt, meD 'iron' (Mu.Ho.Santali)

med' 'copper' (Slovak)

Santali glosses:

Mẽrhẽt'. Iron.
Mẽṛhẽt' icena. The iron is rusty.
Ispat mẽṛhẽt'. Steel.
Dul mẽṛhẽt'. Cast iron.
Mẽṛhẽt' khanḍa. Iron implements.

Relief with Ekamukha linga. Mathura. 1st cent. CE (Fig. 6.2).This is the most emphatic representation of linga as a pillar of fire. The pillar is embedded within a brick-kiln with an angular roof and is ligatured to a tree. Hieroglyph: kuTi 'tree' rebus: kuThi 'smelter'. In this composition, the artists is depicting the smelter used for smelting to create *mũh* 'face' (Hindi) rebus: *mũhe* 'ingot' (Santali) of

mēḍha 'stake' rebus: *meḍ* 'iron, metal' (Ho. Munda). मेड (p. 662) [mēḍa] *f* (Usually मेढ q. v.) मेडका *m* A stake, esp. as bifurcated. मेढ (p. 662) [mēḍha] *f* A forked stake. Used as a post. Hence a short post generally whether forked or not. मेढा (p. 665) [mēḍhā] *m* A stake, esp. as forked. 2 A dense arrangement of stakes, a palisade, a paling. मेढी (p. 665) [mēḍhī] *f* (Dim. of मेढ) A small bifurcated stake: also a small stake, with or without furcation, used as a post to support a cross piece. मेढ्या (p. 665) [mēḍhyā] *a* (मेढ Stake or post.) A term for a person considered as the pillar, prop, or support (of a household, army, or other body), the *staff* or *stay*. मेढेजोशी (p. 665) [mēḍhējōśī] *m* A stake-जोशी; a जोशी who keeps account of the तिथि &c., by driving stakes into the ground: also a class, or an individual of it, of fortune-tellers, diviners, presagers, seasonannouncers, almanack-makers &c. They are Shúdras and followers of the मेढेमत q. v. 2 Jocosely. The hereditary or settled (quasi fixed as a stake) जोशी of a village.मेंधला (p. 665) [mēndhalā] *m* In architecture. A common term for the two upper arms of a double चौकठ (door-frame) connecting the two. Called also मेंढरी & घोडा. It answers to छिली the name of the two lower arms or connections. (Marathi)

Relief with Ekamukha linga. Mathura. 1st cent. CE shows a gaNa, dwarf with tuft of hair in front, a unique tradition followed by Dikshitar in Chidambaram. The gaNa is next to the smelter kuTi 'tree' Rebus: kuThi 'smelter' which is identified by the ekamukha sivalinga. *mũh* 'face' (Hindi) rebus: *mũhe* 'ingot' (Santali) *mũhā̃* = the quantity of iron produced at one time in a native smelting furnace of the Kolhes; iron produced by the Kolhes and formed like a four-cornered piece a little pointed at each end; mūhā mẽṛhẽt = iron smelted by the Kolhes and formed into an equilateral lump a little pointed at each of four ends;*kolhe tehen mẽṛhẽt ko mūhā akata* = the Kolhes have to-day produced pig iron (Santali). *kharva* is a dwarf; *kharva* is a nidhi of Kubera. *karba*'iron' (Tulu)

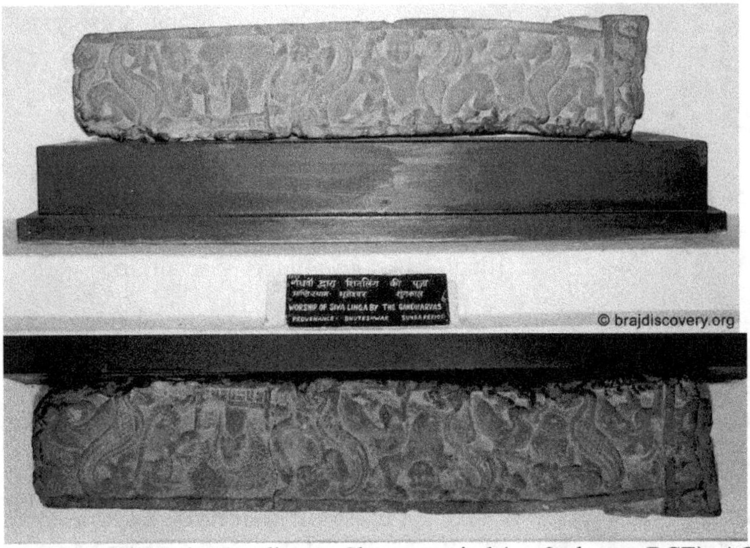

Worship of linga by Gandharva, Shunga period (ca. 2nd cent. BCE), ACCN 3625, Mathura Museum. Worship signified by dwarfs, Gaṇa (hence *Gaṇeśa* = *Gaṇa* + *īśa*).

This relief shows puja to tree: Hieroglyph: kuTi 'tree' Rebus: kuThi 'smelter' (smithy). The complex of hieroglyph readings rebus: kole.l 'smithy' rebus: kole.l 'temple'. The hieroglyph composition of tied fish-tail pair emerges out of the roof of the brick kiln (smelter). This ligaturing is comparable to the ligature of Ekamukha linga emerging out of the sloping roof brick-kiln.

The worship of a smithy (smelter) as a temple is also seen in the artistic representations in Mathura in the context of worship of Sivalinga (Ekamukha siva linga); this is a remarkable affirmation of Bauddham, Jaina and Hindu traditions as composite gestalt of ancient Bharatam Janam venerating natural phenomena as an extension of cosmic-consciousness order called dharma-dhamma..:

Linga worship relief. Bhutesvara, Mathura. 1st cent. BCE (Fig. 5.1) The ling is in the centre of a brick-kiln. In the backgrouns a tree is shown. A pair of dwarfs holding rope venerate the linga. A tree associated with smelter and linga from Bhuteshwar, Mathura Museum.

Architectural fragment with relief showing winged dwarfs (or gaNa) worshipping with flower garlands, Siva Linga. Bhuteshwar, ca. 2nd cent BCE. Lingam is on a platform with wall under a pipal tree encircled by railing. (Srivastava, AK, 1999, Catalog of Saiva sculptures in Government Museum, Mathura: 47, GMM 52.3625) The tree is a phonetic determinant of the smelter indicated by the railing around the linga: **kuṭa**, °*ṭi* -- , °*ṭha* -- 3, °*ṭhi* -- m. ' tree ' Rebus: *kuṭhi* 'smelter'. ***kuṭa,*** °*ṭi* -- , °*ṭha* -- 3, °*ṭhi* -- m. ' tree ' lex., °*ṭaka* -- m. ' a kind of tree ' Kauś.Pk. *kuḍa* -- m. ' tree '; Paš. lauṛ. *kuṛā´* ' tree ', dar. *kaṛék* ' **tree**, oak ' ~ Par. *kōṛ* ' stick ' IIFL iii 3, 98. (CDIAL 3228).

In *Atharva Veda skambha* (AV X.7-8) is a celestial scaffold, supporting the cosmos and material creation. It is *axis mundi.*

The worship of a smithy (smelter) as a temple is also seen in the artistic representations in Mathura in the context of worship of Sivalinga (Ekamukha siva linga); this is a remarkable affirmation of Bauddham, Jaina and Hindu traditions as *weltanschaang* of ancient Bharatam Janam venerating natural phenomena as an extension of cosmic-consciousness order called dharma-dhamma..:

Atharva Veda Skambha Sukta predates archaeology of Sarasvati Sindhu civilization. The civilization dates from ca. 8th millennium BCE (pace BR Mani's article) https://friendsofasi.wordpress.com/writings/the-8th-millennium-bc-in-the-lost-river-valley/ There is no mention of linga in Rigveda. S'is'nadeva is wrongly interpreted as phallus worshipper. Yaska's and Sayana's seems to be the correct interpretation. Gopinatha Rao and RS Bisht ar in error when they deduce phallus-worship. What is worshipped is the temple which is the smithy-forge-- kole.l This is consistent with the decipherment of the entire Indus Script Corpora as*catalogus catalogorum* of metalwork. and the veneration of skambha as sivalinga in Bhuteswar and Mathura and in Amaravati

"The Dhruvaberas in all Siva temples is the Linga surmounted upon the Yoni or the piNDikA (pedestal)...Int he praise of Skambha, we meet with the following passages, namely, 'Where Skambha, generating brought PurANapurusha into existence' and 'Skambha in the beginning shed forth that gold (hiraNya, out of which HiraNyagarbha arose) in the midst of the world' and lastly 'He who knows the golden reed standing in the waters is the mysterious PrajApati.' From the first two of the three passages quoted above, we see that one of the functions of Skambha is to beget HiraNyagarbha, or PurANapurusha, the god of reproduction. He pours forth his golden seed in begetting PrajApati. The original of the third passage runs thus: Yo vetasam hiraNyayam tishThantam salile veda sa vai guhyah PrajApatih."(pp.56-57)

"...a brief account contributed by Mr. RD Banerji to the Annual of the Director General of Archaeology for 1909-1910. About the linga of Bhita Mr. Banerji writes, 'The top of it is shaped as the bust of a male holding a vase in his left hand, while the right is raised in the abhaya mudrA posture. Below this bust, where the waist of the figure should have been, are four human heads, one at each corner. From the mode of dressing the hair and the large rings worn in the lobes of the ears, it appears that these are the busts of females. They are more or less defaced, but still retain sufficient detail to admit of identification. The upper part of the hed of the male is broken, only the portion below the nose being extant. The male figure wears a loth which is thrown over the left shoulder, the folds being shown by a double line running over the breast. The vase held in the left hand resembles to some extent, the ointment vessel found in the figures of Bodhisatvas of the Gandhara school. The left ear of the male figure bears the circular pendants, which may be earrings. In front, immediately below the heads of two females, the phallus is marked by deeply drawn lines. To the upper left of this is the inscription...The lower part of the tsone is shaped as a tenon to be fitted in a mortice. The inscription is in a good state of preservation, and with the exception of the last three letters, can be deciphered very easily.' The translation of the inscription is given by Mr. Banerji as follows: 'The lings of the sons of Khajahuti, was dedicated by Nagasiri, the son of VaseThi. May the deity be pleased.' (The text of this inscription reads as follows: Khajahuti putanam l[im]go patiThApito vAseThi-putena NagasirinA piyayta[m] d[e]vatA.). From the description given by Mr. Banerji it is evident that it is a Mukhalinga having five faces corresponding to the Is'Ana, Tatpurusha, Aghora, Vamadeva and Sadyojata aspects of Siva. In the description of Mukhalingas given...the face representing Is'Ana should be on the top, while the other four should face the east, south, west and north respectively. The four faces of the four cornes which Mr. Banerji believes may be of females are really those of male figures...With the help of the (inscription) characters, Mr. RD Banerji has correctly guessed the age of the Linga to be the first century BCE. The second most ancient Linga is the one discovered by me (T Gopinatha Rao) at Gudimallam."(pp.63-65)

Three views of the Bhita lingam: stone. ca. 1st cent. BCE

Five-headed Mukhalinga embedded in a yoni;Budanilkantha, Nepal

Peninsular Siam lingas ca. 7th century CE

Photograph from Malleret, L., L'archaeologie du delta du Mekong, Paris, 1959;
Ekamukhalinga from JaiyA, National Museum, Bangkok

Ekamukhalinga from Vat Sak Sampou

"The JaiyA ekamukhalinga is divided into three parts in accordance with the prescriptions in the Siva Agamas. The base, BrahmabhAga, is cubic in form and is 47.8 cms. High. The middle section, the ViSNubhAga, is octagonal in shape and is approximately 43 cm. High. The topmost

section, the RudrabhAga, is cylindrical and is approximately 51 cms high, while the superimposed face measures 29.5 cms from the bottom of the chin to the top of the jaTA. The two lower sections of the linga would not normally be visible, since they would be enclosed in the pedestal (pIThikA)...One of the singular features of these pre-Angkorian mukhalingas is the fusing of the jaTA with the filet on the gland of the RudrabhAga (fig.2)...There is, however, an ekamukhalinga from Vat Sak Sampou (fig. 3) which displays a coiffure which is very muh like that worn on the JaiyA linga." (O'Connor, SJ, 1961, *An ekamukhalinga from Peninsular Siam, The Journal of the Siam Society*. The Siam Society. pp. 43-49).
http://www.siameseheritage.org/jsspdf/1961/JSS_054_1e_OConnor_EkamukhalingaFromPeninsularSiam.pdf

Linga with One Face of Shiva (Ekamukhalinga), Mon–Dvaravati period, 7th–early 8th century. Thailand (Phetchabun Province, Si Thep) Stone; H. 55 1/8 in.
Octagonal form of ViSNubhAga and the occurrence of pancamukhalinga is consistent with the tradition of *pancaloha* 'five dhAtu or five mineral alloy' images as utsavaberas.

I suggest that the mukha on the linga is read rebus from the hieroglyph: **mũh** 'a **face**'
Rebus: **mũh,muhã 'ingot'** or **muhã** 'quantity of metal produced at one time in a native smelting furnace.' This reaffirms the association of the octagonal brick of Binjor fire-altar with the Skambha as linga or vajra which participates in the process of smelting dhAtu, 'ores'.

Face on Bhuteswar sivalinga & face with body of a hunter on Gudimallam sivalinga.

Siva stands on the shoulders of a stumpy dwarf or goblin, gaNa. Ananda Coomaraswamy sees similarity of the goblin figure with 'kupiro yakho' (Kubera yaksha) of Bharhut.

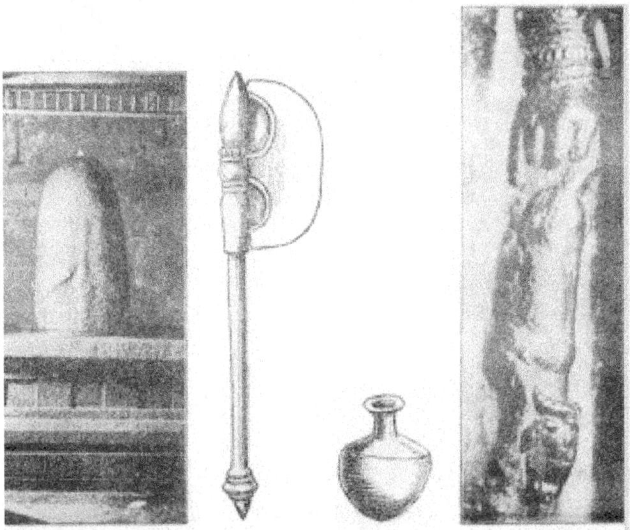

(Fig. 1.) (Fig. 2.) (Fig. 3.) (Fig. 4.)

Plate V. “The figure of Siva has two arms, in the right one of which a ram is held by its hind legs and with its hed hanging downwards (fig.4, Pl. V); in the left one is held a water-pot (fig. 3, Pl. V); and a battle-axe (paqras'u) rests upon the left shoulder (fig. 2, Pl.V)”(Gopinatha Rao, TA, 1997, Elements of Hindu iconography, Vol. 2, Pt 1, Delhi, Motilal Banarsiddass, p.66).

Hieroglyph: Ram on Siva's right hand: Dm. *mraṅ* m. ‘markhor’ Wkh. *merg* f. ‘ibex’ (CDIAL 9885) Tor. *miṇḍ* ‘ram’, *miṇḍā̃l* ‘markhor’ (CDIAL 10310) Rebus: *meḍ* (Ho.); *mẽṛhet* ‘iron’ (Munda.Ho.)

Mẽṛhẽt́. Iron.
Mẽṛhẽt́ idena. The iron is rusty.
Ispat mẽṛhẽt́. Steel.
Dul mẽṛhẽt́. Cast iron.
Mẽṛhẽt́ khanḍa. Iron implements.

Santali glosses.

Origin of the gloss *med* 'copper' in Uralic languages may be explained by the word *meD* (Ho.) of Munda family of Meluhha language stream:

Sa. <i>mE~R~hE~'d</i> `iron'. ! <i>mE~RhE~d</i>(M).
Ma. <i>mErhE'd</i> `iron'.
Mu. <i>mERE'd</i> `iron'.
~ <i>mE~R~E~'d</i> `iron'. ! <i>mENhEd</i>(M).
Ho <i>meD</i> `iron'.
Bj. <i>merhd</i>(Hunter) `iron'.
KW <i>mENhEd</i>@(V168,M080)

http://www.ling.hawaii.edu/austroasiatic/AA/Munda/ETYM/Pinnow&Munda

— Slavic glosses for 'copper'

Мед [Med]*Bulgarian*

Bakar *Bosnian*
Медзь [medz']*Belarusian*
Měď *Czech*
Bakar *Croatian*
Kòper*Kashubian*
Бакар [Bakar]*Macedonian*
Miedź *Polish*
Медь [Med']*Russian*
Meď *Slovak*
Baker*Slovenian*
Бакар [Bakar]*Serbian*
Мідь [mid'] *Ukrainian*[unquote]
http://www.vanderkrogt.net/elements/element.php?sym=Cu
Miedź, med' (Northern Slavic, Altaic) 'copper'.

One suggestion is that corruptions from the German "Schmied", "Geschmeide" = jewelry. Schmied, a smith (of tin, gold, silver, or other metal)(German) result in *med* 'copper'.

Hieroglyph of a worshipper kneeling: *Konḍa* (BB) meḍa,
meṇḍa id. *Pe.* meṇḍa id.*Manḍ.* meṇḍe id. *Kui* meṇḍa id. *Kuwi* (F.) menda, (S. Su. P.) meṇḍa, (Isr.) meṇḍa id.
Ta. maṇṭi kneeling, kneeling on one knee as an archer.
*Ma.*maṇṭuka to be seated on the heels. *Ka.* maṇḍi
what is bent, the knee. *Tu.* maṇḍi knee. *Te.* maṇḍī kneeling on one knee. *Pa.*maḍtel knee; maḍi kuḍtel kneeling position. *Go.* (L.) meṇḍā, (G. Mu. Ma.) Cf. 4645 Ta.maṭaṅku (maṇi-forms). / ? Cf. Skt. maṇḍūkī- (DEDR 4677)

So, why a dancing girl? Because, depiction of a dance pose is a hieroglyph to represent what was contained in the pot. The glyph encodes the mleccha word for 'iron': med.

Glyph: meD 'to dance' (F.)[reduplicated from me-]; me id. (M.) in Remo (Munda)(Source: D. Stampe's Munda etyma) meṭṭu to tread, trample, crush under foot, tread or place the foot upon (Te.); meṭṭu step (Ga.); mettunga steps (Ga.). maḍye to trample, tread (Malt.)(DEDR 5057) మెట్టు (p. 1027) [meṭṭu] *meṭṭu*. [Tel.] v. a. &n. To step, walk, tread. అడుగుపెట్టు, నడుచు, త్రొక్కు. "మెల్ల మెల్లన మెట్టుచుదొలగి అల్లనల్లనతలుపులండకు జేరి." BD iv. 1523. To tread on, to trample on. To kick, to thrust with the foot.**మెట్టిక** *meṭṭika*. n. A step , మెట్టు, సోపానము (Telugu) Rebus: meD 'iron' (Mundari. Remo)

It is possible that there were earlier versions of this iconography on utsava bera in bronze or other copper alloys in the Sarasvati-Sindhu civilization tradition of making *cire perdue* sculptures and taking them on processions.

Siva as Nataraja is associated with two characteristic orthographic components: flowing expanding jaTa (hair-locks) and flames emanating from Sivalinga.

A skambha linking heaven and earth, a fiery pillar of light. The following three ricas of Rigveda also refer to and explain the metaphor of skambha as a prop which upholds heaven and earth; RV 9.89.6 places it in the context of purification of Soma, reinforcing the possibility that the Skambha signified the impeller of the purification process of yajna -- a process which is replicated in the purification of metals in a smelter/funace/fire-altar:

इन्द्रो॑ः दि॒वः प्रति॑मानं पृथि॒व्या विश्वा॑ वेद॒ सव॑ना॒ हन्ति॒ शुष्ण॑म् ।
म॒हीं चि॒द्द्यामात॑नो॒त्सूर्ये॑ण चा॒स्कम्भ॑ चि॒त्कम्भ॑नेन॒ स्कभी॑यान् ॥ 5 ॥

10.111.05 Indra, the counterpart of heaven and earth, is cognizant of all sacrifices, he is the slayer of S'us.n.a; he spread out the spacious heaven with the sun (to light it up); best of proppers, he propped up (the heaven) with a prop. [Propped up the heaven with a prop: Satyata_ta_ = that which is stretched out by the true ones, the gods; or, ta_ti as a suffix, that which is true, i.e., heaven].

दि॒वो यः स्क॒म्भो ध॒रुण॒ः स्वा॑तत॒ आपू॑र्णो अं॒शुः प॒र्येति॒ वि॒श्वत॑ः ।
सेमे म॒ही रोद॑सी यक्षदा॒वृता॑ समीची॒ने दा॑धार॒ समिष॑ः क॒विः ॥ 2 ॥

9.074.02 The supporter of heaven, the prop (of the earth), the Soma-juice who, widely spreading, filling (the vessels), flows in all directions-- may he unite the two great worlds by his own strength; he has upheld them combined; (may he) the sage (bestow) food upon (his worshippers). [The prop of the earth: cf. RV. 9.089.06; may he unite: yaks.at = sam.yojayatu; a_vr.ta = by its own unaided strength]. विष्टम्भो दिवो धरुणः पृथिव्या विश्वा उत क्षितयो हस्ते अस्य । असंत्त उत्सो गृणते नियत्वान्मध्वो अंशुः पवत इन्द्रियाय ॥ 6 ॥ 9.089.06 The prop of heaven, the support of earth-- all beings (are) in his hands; may (Soma) the fountain (of desires) be possessed of horses for you (his) adorer; the filament of the sweet-flavoured (Soma) is purified for (the sake of winning) strength.

A terracotta cake is a *piṇḍa* पिण्ड [p=625,2] m. (rarely n.) any round or roundish mass or heap , a ball , globe , knob , button , clod , lump , piece (cf. अयः-, मांस- &c) RV. (only i , 162 , 19 and here applied to lumps of flesh)
TS. S3Br.&c; n. (L.) iron; steel (Monier-Williams. Samskritam). What archaeometallurgical functions were served by the terracotta cakes offered as *piṇḍa* पिण्ड in fire-altars? One possibility is that the terracotta cakes (of circular and triangular shapes) served the functions of *piṇḍika*a which is a support base for the Sivalinga which is a divine impeller of the cosmic dance of transmutation occurring in a fire-altar.

Lembuswana, Candi-Sukuh linga are Indus Script hieroglyph-multiplexes, Harappa is Hariyupiya, 'with golden yupa' link with Sangam age; Indus Script Corpora signify metalwork.

Yupa octagonal brick of Bijnor fire-altar, Kalibangan evokes the name Hariyupiya cited in Rigveda, or Harappa 'with golden yupa' and over a thousand Indus Script inscritptions of metalwork.

Griffith notes translating Rig Veda (RV 6.27.5-6) ricas that Hariyupia (having golden sacrificial posts), is the name of a town. It is the scene of the defeat of the Vrivavants by Abhyavartin Caayamana. "In aid of Abhyavartin Cayamana, Indra destroyed the seed of Varasikha. At Hariyupia he smote the vanguard of the Vrcivans, and the rear fled
freightened"

Like the UJjain coin which shows hieroglyphs of yupa, Hariyupiya may denote a place with yupas, commemorating celebration of yaga-s in fire-altars. Thus, Griffith's interpretation of Hariyupiya as a reference to golden posts in front of fire-altars is valid.

Yupa tradition together with the performance of yaga-s links Sangam age with Sarasvati-Sindhu civilization.

Nettimaiyar, one of the oldest poets of Sangam period, wonders ,"Oh! Pandya! please tell me whether the number of Yupa posts you installed more? Or the number of enemies you defeated more? Or the praises by the poets more?"

Verse 224 parised the greatest of the Chola kings Karikalan for installing the tall Yupa post. Other Sangam texts also refer to Karikalan, Perunarkilli and Mudukudumi Peruvazuthi who performed many yaga-s and used yupa: Purananuru verses 15 and 224; Maduraikanci line 27; Pathtrupathu 67-10.

See: http://swamiindology.blogspot.in/2012/03/madagascar-india-link-via-indonesia.html

Ujjain coin with yupa post http://www.speakingtree.in/blog/rig-vedic-hariyupia-and-indus-valley-harappa-rig-veda-mystery-7

Pallava trace their ancestry to As'vatthama, son of Drona, Brahmin-warrior of Mahabharata. Varman, like Mulavarman of Java (East Borneo) of Kutei kingdom are Brahmin royalty who belong to Bharadvaja gotra.

«The illustrious lord-of-men, the great Kuṇḍuṅga, had a famous [4] son, Açvavarman [*by name*], who, like unto Aṃçumant, [5] was the founder of a noble race. His were three eminent sons resembling the three sacrificial fires. Foremost [6] amongst these three and distinguished by austerity, strength, and self-restraint [7] was the illustrious Mūlavarman, the lord-of-kings, who had sacrificed a Bahusuvarṇaka [8] sacrifice. For that sacrifice this sacrificial post has been prepared by the chief amongst the twice-born». [9]

Translation of a Mulavarman yupa inscription by Vogel

बहु--सुवर्णक [p= 726,1] *mfn.* costing or possessing much gold R.

"Both the scholarship and the workmanship of our yupa inscriptions ber testimony to a considerable degree of Hindu culture in Eastern Borneo during the period to which they belong."(Vogel, J.Ph., 1918, The **Yupa** inscriptions of King **Mula-Varman**, from Kotei (East Borneo). JSTOR embedded p.218)

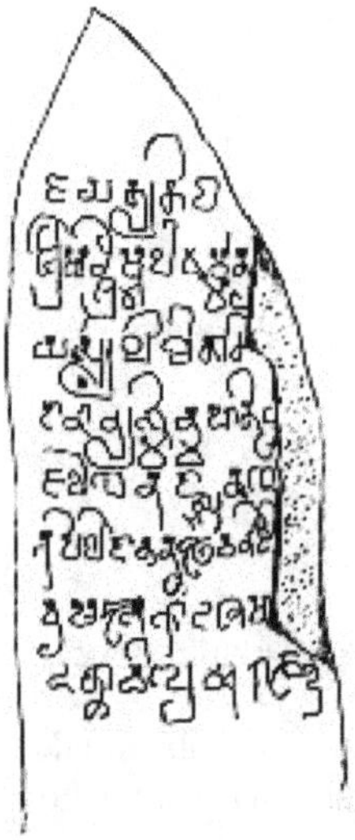

The Kutai Prasasti (Yupa) of Mulavarman

These days the former palace of the Sultan of Kutai (or Kutai Kertanagara as some call it) is a museum.

From left: CDU Vice-Chancellor, Professor Barney Glover, Consulate of the Republic of Indonesia, MrBambang Daranindra, Administrator of the Northern Territory, Tom Pauling, Governor of East Kalimantan, Dr Awang Faroek Ishak and Territory Minister for Business and Employment, Trade, Asian Relations, Rob Knight

Lembuswana, the symbol of Kalimantan, Borneo islands

"The Lembuswana is a legendary creature appearing in Kutai mythology. It is described as being a lion-headed horse with an adorning crown, having an elephant-like trunk, a pair of Garuda wings, and fish-like scales.

In legend of this creature is the guardian of the Mahakam River, and the vehicle of Mulawarman - king of the Kutai kingdom approximately 1500 years ago. It is also the vehicle of princess Karang Melenu.

This creature is a symbol of Kutai Kartanegara city, its head and body symbolizing power of the king, and its trunk symbolizing Ganesha - the god of intelligence." http://cryptidz.wikia.com/wiki/Lembuswana

'Paksi leman gangga yakso" 'Fattened bird Kanga yaksha' Hieroglyph: kaṅká m. ' heron ' VS. [← Drav. T. Burrow TPS 1945, 87; onomat. Mayrhofer EWA i 137. Drav. influence certain in *o* of M. and Si.: Tam. Kan. Mal. *kokku* ' crane ', Tu. *korṅgu*, Tel. *koṅga*, Kuvi *koṅgi*, Kui *kohko*]Pa. *kaṅka* -- m. ' heron ', Pk. *kaṁka* -- m., S. *kaṅgu* m. ' crane, heron ' (→ Bal. *kang*); B. *kā̃k* ' heron ', Or. *kāṅka*; G. *kā̃kṛū̃* n. ' a partic. ravenous bird '; -- with *o* from Drav.: M. *kõkā* m. ' heron '; Si. *kokā*, pl. *kokku* ' various kinds of crane or heron ', *kekī* ' female crane ', *kēki* ' a species of crane, the paddy bird ' (*ē*?).(CDIAL 2595) Rebus: kanga 'brazier'

यक्ष [p=838,2] *n.* a living supernatural being , spiritual apparition , ghost , spirit RV. AV. VS. Br. Gr2S3rS. (accord. to some native Comms. = यज्ञ , पुजा , पूजित &c) *m.* N. of a class of semi-divine beings (attendants of कुबेर , exceptionally also of विष्णु ; described as sons of पुलस्त्य , of पुलह , of कश्यप , of खसा or क्रोधा ; also as produced from the feet of ब्रह्मा ; though generally regarded as beings of a benevolent and inoffensive disposition , like the यक्ष in कालिदास's मेघ-दूत , they are occasionally classed with पिशाचs and other malignant spirits , and sometimes said to cause demoniacal possession ; as to their position in the Buddhist system » MWB. 206 , 218) Up. Gr2S. Mn. MBh. &c

yakṣá m. ' a supernatural being ' MaitrUp. (n. ' mani- festation ' RV.), *yakṣī* -- , *yakṣiṇī* -- f. MBh.Pa. *yakkha* -- m. ' a supernatural being ', *yakkhī* -- , *yakkhiṇī* -- f., Pk. *jakkha* -- m., *jakkhiṇī* -- f.; Ash. *yuš, yüš* ' ogre ', *yuštrī'k* ' ogress ' (+ **strī´**--); Kt. *yuṣ* ' female demon ', Wg. *yūṣ*; Pr. *yuṣ* ' demon '; Kal.rumb. *Jaç* ' female demon '; Sh. (Lor.) *yaç* m. ' demon ', *yaçini* f., *y****lç***(*h*)*olo* ' demon like a bear ', (Grahame Bailey) *yaçhăl&lacutebrev;tu* ' mad ', *yaçhălyār* f. ' madness '; K. *yĕch, yẹ̆ch* m. ' a kind of fairy ', *yĕchiñ* f.,*yochu* m. ' a spirit '; P. *jakkh* m. ' demigod, devout worshipper ', f. ' ogress '; H. *jāk* m. ' demon ', *jakhnī* f. ' female demon in the service of Durgā '; OG. *jākha, jākhala* m. ' demon '; M. *j̈akhīṇ, j̈ākīṇ* (with *ã* after *ḍãkīṇ* s.v. **ḍākinī** --) f. ' ghost of a woman who died in childbirth or drowned herself ', *j̈ākhīṇ, j̈ãkhīṇ* f. ' old and ugly woman ', *j̈akhāī* -- *j̈ukhāī* f. ' two female fiends, minor deities and demons in general ' (f. from m. **jākhā*); Si. *yak* -- *ā* ' demon ', *yakin* -- *ī, yakinna* f. (with *a* for *ä* after m. *yak* -- *ā*); -- Kho. *ẓoç* ' unruly (of children), knotty, complicated ' BelvalkarVol 98 with (?); Ku. *jākhaṛ* ' idiot '; N. *jakkhu* ' huge '; -- Bi. *jāk* ' a cowdung cake called *mahāde* placed on a grain heap to ward off evil eye '?
YAJ ' sacrifice ': iṣṭá -- 2, íṣṭi -- 3, yajuṣyà -- Add., yajñá -- , yajñíya -- , yājñiká -- .Addenda: yakṣá -- : S.kcch. *jakh* m. ' demi -- god '.(CDIAL 10395)

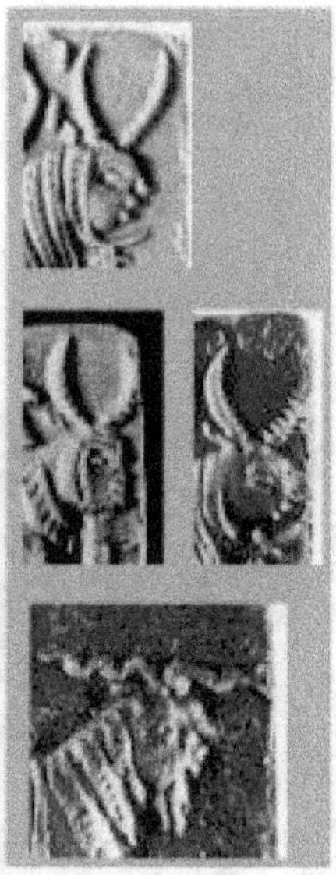

m1186 (DK6847) [Pleiades, scarfed, framework, *ficus religiosa* , scarfed

person, worshipper, twigs (on head), horn, markhor, human face ligatured to markhor, stool, ladle, frame of a building]

Mohenjo-daro seal. Ligaturing components: horns of zebu, human face, tail-hood of serpent, elephant tusk, scarves on neck, bovine forelegs, feline hind legs.

paṭa 'hood of snake'. *Rebus: padm* 'tempered, sharpness (metal)'. nāga 'serpent' Rebus: nāga 'lead (alloy)' Vikalpa: kulA 'hood' rebus: kol 'working in iron'

mũh 'face' Rebus: *mũhe* 'ingot'. *khũṭ* 'zebu'.khũṭ 'community, guild' (Munda)

ibha 'elephant' Rebus: ib 'iron'. Ibbo 'merchant' (Gujarati).

ḍhangar 'bull' Rebus: *dhangar* 'blacksmith' (Maithili) *ḍangar* 'blacksmith' (Hindi)

kol 'tiger' Rebus: kol 'working in iron'.

dhaṭu m. (also *dhaṭhu*) m. 'scarf' (WPah.) Rebus: *dhatu* 'mineral (ore)'

Rebus reading of the 'face' glyph: mũhe 'face' (Santali) mũh opening or hole (in a stove for stoking (Bi.); ingot (Santali) mũh metal ingot (Santali) mũhã̄ = the quantity of iron produced at one time in a native smelting furnace of the Kolhes; iron produced by the Kolhes and formed like a four-cornered piece a little pointed at each end; mūhā mẽṛhẽt = iron smelted by the Kolhes and formed into an equilateral lump a little pointed at each of four ends; kolhe tehen mẽṛhẽt ko mūhā akata = the Kolhes have to-day produced pig iron (Santali.lex.) kaula mengro 'blacksmith' (Gypsy) mleccha-mukha (Skt.) = milakkhu 'copper' (Pali) The Sanskrit loss mleccha-mukha should literally mean: copper-ingot absorbing the Santali gloss, mũh, as a suffix

The composite animal (bovid) is re-configured by Huntington. http://huntington.wmc.ohio-state.edu/public/index.cfm

In a scintillating study of the orthography of Indus Script, Dennys Frenez & Massimo Vidale provide an insight comparing two hieroglyph components on Indus Script corpora: 1. elephant trunk and 2. hand of a person seated in penance

m1177, m1175, m300

Metalwork provides a framework for defined meaning of words used in the vernacular and continued use of such words in writing systems using what Frenez and Vidale call 'symbolic hypertexts' as on Indus Script provide the evidence for Indus Script decipherment of Indus Script Corpora as c*atalogus catalogorum* of metalwork. (Dennys Frenez & Massimo Vidale, 2012,Harappa Chimaeras as 'Symbolic Hypertexts'. Some Thoughts on Plato, Chimaera and the Indus Civilization in: *South Asian Studies* Volume 28, Issue 2, pp. 107-130).

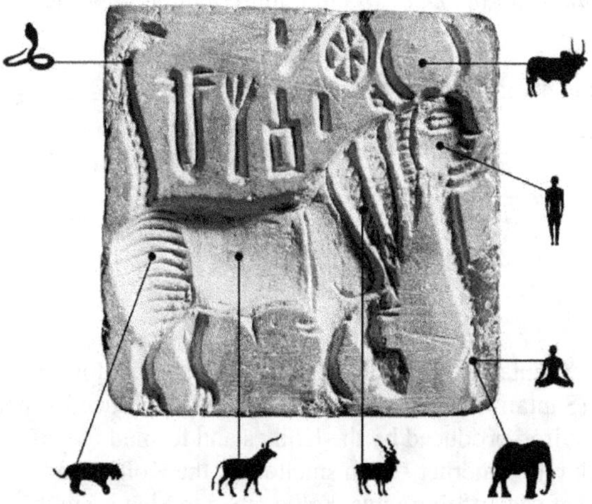

Meluhha (Prakritam) glosses which decipher the hieroglyph components are consistent with this insight of Frenez and Vidale comparing the snout of the elephant's trunk with the hands of the person seated in penance: karabha 'trunk of elephant' (Pali) kara 'hand' (Rigveda). Gujarati gloss expands the semantics of 'hand' to include *karā̃* 'wristlets, bangles'.

It is remarkable that samples of orthography on seated persons in penance on Indus seals, the hands are decorated with wristlets and bangles. Obviously, the artisan is conveying the gloss: *karā̃* 'wristlets, bangles' while signifying the hand: kara (Rigveda. Prakritam. Pali)

Hieroglyph: karabha 'trunk of elephant' (Pali) 2803 karin m. ' elephant '. [See karabhá --]Pa. *karin* -- m., Pk. *kari* -- , °*iṇa* -- m., °*iṇī* -- , °*iṇiyā* -- f.; <-> Si. *kiriyā* ← Pa.(CDIAL 2803)

Hieroglyph: hand: karál ' doing, causing ' AV., m. ' hand ' RV. [√kr̥1]

Pa. Pk. *kara* -- m. ' hand '; S. *karu* m. ' arm '; Mth. *kar* m. ' hand ' (prob. ← Sk.); Si. *kara* ' hand, shoulder ', inscr. *karā* ' to ' < *karāya.* -- Deriv. S. *karāī* f. ' wrist '; G. *karā̃* n. pl. ' wristlets, bangles '.(CDIAL 2779)

Rebus: karba, ajirda karba 'iron' (Tulu) (Note: cognate of *ajirda* is *ayas* 'metal', aduru 'native metal').

The 'ram' glyph shows the animal with curved, long horns and sometimes also gets ligatured with a human face on some Indus script inscriptions. The human face is also read rebus in mleccha (meluhha): *mũhe* 'face' (Santali); rebus:*mũh* ingot (Santali); opening or hole (in a stove for stoking (Bi.)mũhā̃ = the quantity of iron produced at one time in a native smelting furnace of the Kolhes;

iron produced by the Kolhes and formed like a four-cornered piece a little pointed at each end; mūhā mẽṛhẽt = iron smelted by the Kolhes and formed into an equilateral lump a little pointed at each of four ends; kolhe tehen mẽṛhẽt ko mūhā akata = the Kolhes have to-day produced pig iron (Santali.lex.) kaula mengro 'blacksmith' (Gypsy) mleccha-mukha (Skt.) = milakkhu 'copper' (Pali) The Sanskrit loss mleccha-mukha should literally mean: copper-ingot absorbing the Santali gloss, mu~h, as a suffix. See used in cmpds. (Telugu): మ్లేచ్ఛముఖము mlēchha-mukhamu. n. Copper, రాగి. మ్లేచ్ఛము mlēchhamu. n. Cinnabar. ఇంగిలీకము.

Thus, a 'ram' glyph ligatured with 'human face' glyph reads: mũh meḍh 'ram face'; rebus: (metal) ingot merchant. It is notable that *meḍ, meḍho* has two rebus meanings: 1. iron (metal); 2. merchant.

Elephant, trunk of elephant: kar-ibha, ib; rebus: karba 'iron'; ib 'iron'.

Ka. bisu (becc-), besu, bese to unite firmly, solder; join, be united; bisu soldering; bisuge, besage, besavu, besike, besige, besuge id., state of being soldered or firmly united, close connexion, composition; beccu state of being soldered or united. *Tu.* besigè soldering gold or other metal. (DEDR 5468)

Hieroglyph: *rā̃go* 'buffalo': raṅku m. ' a species of deer ' Vās., °*uka* -- m. Śrīkaṇṭh.Ku. N. *rā̃go* ' buffalo bull '? (CDIAL 10559)

raṅga3 n. ' tin ' lex. [Cf. nāga -- 2, vaṅga -- 1]Pk. *raṁga* -- n. ' tin '; P. *rā̃g* f., *rā̃gā* m. ' pewter, tin ' (← H.); Ku. *rāṅ* ' tin, solder ', gng. *rā̃k*; N. *rāṅ*, *rāṅo* ' tin, solder ', A. B. *rāṅ*; Or. *rāṅga* ' tin ', *rāṅgā* ' solder, spelter ', Bi. Mth. *rā̃gā*, OAw. *rāṁga*; H. *rā̃g* f., *rā̃gā* m. ' tin, pewter '; Si. *ran̆ga* ' tin '.(CDIAL 10562)

On mED 'copper' in Eurasian languages:

Wilhelm von Hevesy wrote about the Finno-Ugric-Munda kinship, like "Munda-Magyar-Maori, an Indian link between the antipodes new tracks of Hungarian origins" and "Finnisch-Ugrisches aus Indien". (DRIEM, George van: Languages of the Himalayas: an ethnolinguistic handbook. 1997. p.161-162.) Sumerian-Ural-Altaic language affinities have been noted. Given the presence of Meluhha settlements in Sumer, some Meluhha glosses might have been adapted in these languages. One etyma cluster refers to 'iron' exemplified by meD (Ho.). The alternative suggestion for the origin of the gloss med 'copper' in Uralic languages may be explained by the word meD (Ho.) of Munda family of Meluhha language stream.

It is possible to infer why *Gaṇeśa* is rendered iconographically with an elephant trunk ligatured to a human body. The tradition has evolved in Indian sprachbund which defines kole.l as a smithy/forge and kole.l as 'temple' with the invocation of *Gaṇeśa* before any human undertaking or endeavour, praying for the successful completion of the tasks of the worshipper in perfection, without any hindrances, impediments, obstructions or blemish. The mantra of the Rigveda RV 2.23.1 explains the tradition: *gaṇānāṃ tvā gaṇapatiṃ havāmahe* is a celebration of the *kaví* ' wise ' RV., m. ' wise man, poet ' RV., °*ika* -- m. lex. Pa. Pk. *kavi* -- m., Pk. *kaï* -- m., Si. *kivi* ES 25 but ← Pa.(CDIAL 2964).

It is this mantra of the Rigveda tradition which finds expression in some hieroglyph-multiplexes of Indus Script Corpora of metalwork. The hieroglyph-multiplexes include depictions such as an elephant trunk ligatured to the body of an antelope, the face of a human, scarfs on neck (dhatu 'scarf' rebus: dhatu 'mineral'), forelegs of a hoofed bovine, hindlegs of a feline, horns of a zebu (*bos indicus*), tail as hood of a snake -- all signifying metalwork components.

Example of hieroglyph-multiplex on Indus Script Corpora. (Note: the strands of rope signify Sindhi. *dhāī* f. ' wisp of fibres added from time to time to a rope that is being twisted ', Lahnda. *dhāī̃* f. rebus: धावड dhavaḍa 'iron smelters'; *kaṁḍa*-- m. ' backbone '(Prakritam) rebus: khaNDa 'metal implements'; karNika 'rim of jar' rebus: karNika 'supercargo'.)

The lokottara analytical framework provides a basis for the narration of ancient history of Bhāratam Janam who were remarkable metalworkers who have handed down a tradition of signifying work as worship.

That the creators of the Indus Script Corpora are Bhāratam Janam is evidenced by the finds of two terracotta toys at Nausharo. The toys show sindhur (red vermilion) on the mAng or hair-partings, a tradition to signify married status of a woman which is an abiding tradition of Bhāratam Janam.

Nausharo: female figurines. Wearing sindhur at the parting of the hair. Hair painted black, ornaments golden and sindhur red. Period 1B, 2800 – 2600 BCE. 11.6 x 30.9 cm.[After Fig. 2.19, Kenoyer, 1998].

This is the most emphatic evidence attesting that the writing system evidenced by Indus Script Corpora and the underlying Proto-Prakritam language of the inscriptions are the heritage of Bhāratam Janam. The same Bhāratam Janam continue to use the hieroglyph-multiplexes of Indus Script on punch-marked and cast coins all over Bhāratam, during the historical periods.

I have suggested, based on the fact the the largest tin belt of the globe is in Mekong river delta, that a cultural sprachbund of tin bronzes and related metalcastings as cultural markers can be traced along the Tin Maritime Road from Hanoi to Haifa which predates the Silk Road by about 2 millennia -- from Dong Son bronze drums to Nahal Mishmar cire perdue arsenical bronze artifacts of 5th millennium BCE.

Candi Sukuh as a temple for worship of Siva linga evidences remarkable narrative sculptures from Mahabharata heroes, and narrative of metalwork in smelter/smithy/forge. An example is a frieze showing a dancing Ganesha.

The scene in bas relief The scene depicted Bhima as the blacksmith in the left forging the metal, Ganesha in the center, and Arjuna in the right operating the tube blower to pump air into the furnace.

Pl. 1 Relief of smithy at Candi Sukuh, central Java. On the left, a smith forging a weapon. Person on left (Bhima) is surrounded by tools and weapons and is forging a sword.In the center, a dancing elephant-headed figure. Far right, an assistant operating the traditional double-piston bellows of Southeast Asia.

Pl. 2 Detail of Pl. 1 showing smith grasping tang of weapon with bare hand. Note the blade rests on the smith's knee. There is no hammer in the upraised hand.

Pl. 3 The elephant-headed figure, almost crtainly Ganesha, wears a crown and carries a small animal, probably a dog (jackal looking backwards?)

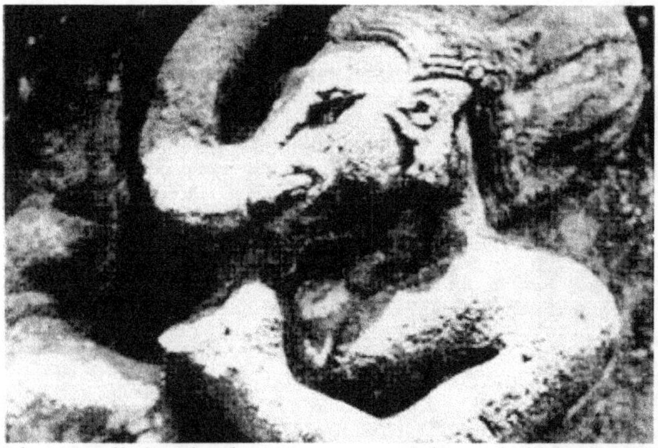

Pl. 4 Detail showing bone rosary or rattle carried by Ganesha.

<kanpati> {NB} ``^temple". *Loan. @N0028. ??not in De. dict. -Ganapati? #10821.

గణపతి [gaṇapati] *gaṇa-pati*. [Skt.] n. A name of the god Gaṇēsa. వినాయకుడు.

ఇభము [ibhamu] *ibhamu*. (Skt of *elephant*. Gr. *elephas*.] An elephant. ఇభయాన *ibhayāna*. n. A graceful woman, *i. e*., a woman with an elephant's easy and luxurious rolling gait. ఇభి *ibhi*. n. A she-elephant ఇభ్యుడు *ibhyuḍu*. A ruler, rich man. (A. ii. 125.)

ibbo 'merchant' (Gujarati. Desi).

gaṇá m. ' troop, flock ' RV. [Poss. (despite doubts in EWA i 316) < **gr̥ṇa* -- ' telling ' (cf. *gr̥̄nti -- and esp. gaṇáyati ' tells one's number (of troop of flock) ' Kāś. -- √g&rcirclemacr;3]Pa. Pk. *gaṇa* -- m. ' troop, flock '; Tor. (Biddulph) *gan* m. ' herd '; K. *gan* m. ' beehive ' = *mã̄cha* -- *gan* m.; WPah. bhal. *gaṇ* m. pl. ' bees '; Si. *gaṇaya* ' company ' EGS 52 but prob. ← Pa.(CDIAL 3988).

గణము [gaṇamu] *gaṇamu*. [Skt.] n. A flock, multitude, or assemblage, a tribe, class or troop. వర్గము, సమూహము. A prosodial foot, such as భగణము a dactyl. గణములుకట్టు to scan. గణములు పోయినవి or తప్పినవి the metre is imperfect. A troop of inferior deities, considered as Siva's attendants, and under the special superintendence of Gaṇēsa: whence his name గణేశుడు, గణపతి or గణాధిపుడు. A body of troops consisting of 27 war-chariots, 27 elephants, 81 horses and 135 infantry men. గణార్చన *gaṇārchana*. n. Worship of the demigods attending on Siva.

గాణాపత్యము (p. 0363) [gāṇāpatyamu] *gāṇā-patyamu*. [Skt.] n. The worship of Ganapati.

గణి [gaṇi] *gaṇi*. [Skt.] n. One who knows the Vedas completely. సాంగముగా వేదాధ్యయనము చేసినవాడు.

Candi Sukuh. Gana.

Candi Cetho. Lingga shows a pair of balls at the top of the penis -- to be read rebus as Meluhha hieroglyph composition: lo-khaNDa, penis + 4 balls; Rebus: iron, metalware.

The four balls of the penis are also clearly shown on a 6 ft. tall linga inscribed with 1. a sword; and 2. inscription in Javanese, referring to 'inauguration of the holy ganggasudhi...'

लोखंड [lōkhaṇḍa] *n* (लोह S) Iron. लोखंडाचे चणे खावविणें or चारणें To oppress grievously.
लोखंडकाम [lōkhaṇḍakāma] *n* Iron work; that portion (of a building, machine &c.) which consists of iron. 2 The business of an ironsmith.

लोखंडी [lōkhaṇḍī] *a* (लोखंड) Composed of iron; relating to iron. 2 fig. Hardy or hard--a constitution or a frame of body, one's हाड or natal bone or parental stock. 3 Close and hard;--used of kinds of wood. 4 Ardent and unyielding--a fever. 5 लोखंडी, in the sense Hard and coarse or in the sense Strong or enduring, is freely applied as a term of distinction or designation. Examples follow.
लोखंडी [lōkhaṇḍī] *f* (लोखंड) An iron boiler or other vessel. 2 A large scandent shrub, Ventilago Maderaspatana. Grah.
लोखंडी काव [lōkhaṇḍī kāva] *f* A red ochre or earth.
लोखंडी चुना [lōkhaṇḍī cunā] *m* A term for strong and enduring chunam-work.
लोखंडी छाप [lōkhaṇḍī chāpa] *m* (Iron type.) A term, according to popular apprehension, for *Leaden types* and for *Printing;* in contrad. from दगडछाप Lithography.
लोखंडी जर [lōkhaṇḍī jara] *m* (लोखंड & जर) False brocade or lace; lace &c. made of iron.लोह [lōha] *n* S Iron, crude or wrought.

खांडा [khāṇḍā] *m* A kind of sword, straight, broad-bladed, two-edged, and round-ended.

खांडेकरी [khāṇḍēkarī] *m* A man armed with the sword called खांडा.

खेंड [khēṇḍa] *f* A sort of sword with a rounded and weighty extremity.
खंडोबा [khaṇḍōbā] *m* A familiar appellation of the god खंडेराव. सोळा गुणांचा खं0 (Marathi)
Psht. *guṇḍ* ' round ', Pers. *gunda* ' ball of leaven ', *gund* ' testicle ' < **gr̥nda* -- NTS xii 263. -- See also gaḍu -- 1, gaṇḍu -- , *giḍa -- , *gilla -- , kanda --]1. Pa. *gaṇḍa* -- m. ' swelling, boil, abscess '; Pk. *gaṁḍa*<-> m.n. ' goitre, boil ', NiDoc. *gaṁḍa*(CDIAL 3997)
गंडा[gaṇḍā] *m* An aggregate of four (cowries or pice). (Marathi) <ganDa>(P) {NUM} ``^four''. Syn. <cari>(LS4), <hunja-mi>(D). \*Sa., Mu.<ganDa> `id.', H.<gA~Da> `a group of four cowries'. %10591. #10511.<ganDa-mi>(KM) {NUM} ``^four''. |<-mi> `one'. %10600. #10520. Ju<ganDa>(P) {NUM} ``^four''. gaṇḍaka m. ' a coin worth four cowries ' lex., ' method of counting by fours ' W. [← Mu. Przyluski RoczOrj iv 234]S. *gaṇḍho* m. ' four in counting '; P. *gaṇḍā* m. ' four cowries '; B. Or. H. *gaṇḍā* m. ' a group of four, four cowries '; M. *gaṇḍā* m. ' aggregate of four cowries or pice '.(CDIAL 4001)

gōla1 m. ' ball ' BhP., °*aka* -- m. ' ball ' BhP., ' glans penis ' Sāy., °*likā* -- f. ' little ball ' SāmavBr. (CDIAL 4321) Rebus: kol 'working in iron'(Tamil)Rebus: *kāṇḍa*. Water; sacred water (Samskritam. Tamil)

Go<kanDa>(A) {N} ``^sword''. Gu<ka~Da> {N} ``^sword''. *Des.<kaNDa>(GM) `sword'. Re<khanDa>(B) {N} ``^sword''. \*Des.<khOnDa:>.<kanDa>(A) {N} ``^sword''. #15910. <ka~Da> {N} ``^sword''. \*De.<kaNDa>(GM) `sword'. @N0670. #10791. <khanda>>:. #16501.<pet = khanda>E145 {N} ``a ^sword worshipped as the symbol of an important local deity''. @B28440. #16512.<khanDa>(B) {N} ``^sword''. *Des.<khOnDa:>. @B07650. #16521. Re<paTkaNDa>(F) {N} ``sacred ^Great_^Sword worshipped in Remo ritual as the symbol of an important local diety''. Cited also as <pet = khanda>E145.

Pl. 6 Linga discovered at Candi Sukuh and now in Museum Pusst, Jakarta (from CJ van der VLie, Report of 1843).Linga is six feet long, five feet in circumference. Old Javanese inscription: 'Consecration of the Holy Gangga sudhi...the sign of masculinity is the essence of the world.' Sword is carved in relief on the shaft of the linga.

mēṇḍhra -- m. ' penis '(Samskritam)(CDIAL 9606).Rebus: *meḍ* 'iron' (Ho.)

ibha m. ' elephant ' Mn. Pa. *ibha*-- m., Pk. *ibha*--, *iha*--, Si. *iba* Geiger EGS 22: rather ← Pa.(CDIAL 1587).Rebus: ib 'iron' (Santali) karibha 'trunk of elephant' Rebus: karba 'iron' (Kannada). *meḍ* 'step', 'dance step' rebus: *meḍ* 'iron' (Ho.)

K. *khāra* -- *basta* f. ' blacksmith's skin bellows '; -- S. *bathī* f. ' quiver ' (< **bhathī*); A. Or. *bhāti* ' bellows ', Bi. *bhāthī*, (S of Ganges) *bhāthī*; OAw. *bhāthā* ' quiver '; H. *bhāthā* m. ' quiver ', *bhāthī* f. ' bellows '; G. *bhāthɔ*, *bhātɔ*, *bhāthṛɔ* m. ' quiver ' (whence *bhāthī* m. ' warrior '); M. *bhātā* m. ' leathern bag, bellows, quiver ', *bhātaḍ* n. ' bellows, quiver '; <-> (X bhráṣṭra -- ?) N. *bhāṭi* ' bellows ', H. *bhāṭhī* f. OA. *bhāthi* ' bellows ' (CDIAL 9424). Rebus: Pk. *bhayaga* -- m. ' servant ', *bhaḍa* -- m. ' soldier ', *bhaḍaa* -- m. ' member of a non -- Aryan tribe '; Paš. *buṛī´* ' servant maid ' IIFL iii 3, 38; S.*bharu* ' clever, proficient ', m. ' an adept '; Ku. *bhaṛ* m. ' hero, brave man ', gng. adj. ' mighty '; B. *bhaṛ* ' soldier, servant, nom. prop. ',.kcch. *bhaṛ* ' brave '; Garh. (Śrīnagrī dial.) *bhɔṛ*, (Salānī dial.) *bheṛ* ' warrior '.G. *bhaṛ* m. ' warrior, hero, opulent person ', adj. ' strong, opulent ' (CDIAL 9588).

The writing system continued among metallurgists who created the mints for early coins; in India, these were punch-marked coins of many janapadas (republics). Kota language documents the smithy as a temple. Kole.l means, 'smithy, temple in Kota village (Kota); kwala.l Kota smithy (Toda)(DEDR 2133). Koles were iron-smelters. The scribe was karṇaka (kanka in mleccha) represented rebus by the rim of a jar. This glyph becomes the glyph used with the highest frequency on Indus script epigraphs. The scribe had arrived as an artisan with capability and skills to write on copper plates and to inscribe/punch-mark on early coins with incised Meluhha speech.

Snarling iron, anvil -- *kolimi kōnda kharādī* smithy, engraver, turner -- as read from Chanhudaro inscribed tool

Indus Meluhha Writing inscription on a Chanhu-daro snarling alloy (ingot) has an inscription writing with five

Snarling iron, 2529H, ASI, Central Antiquities Collection. 74.1/48

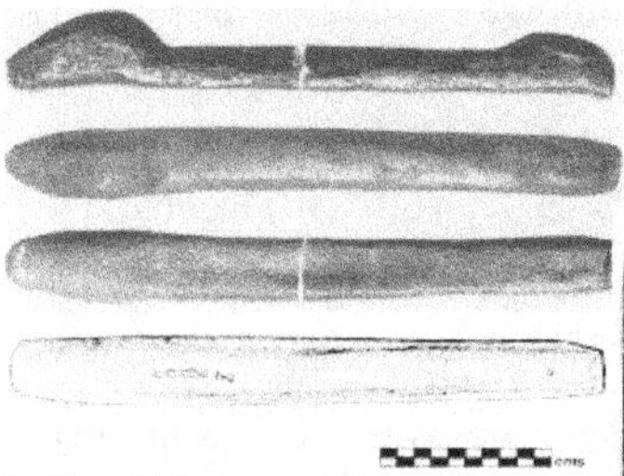

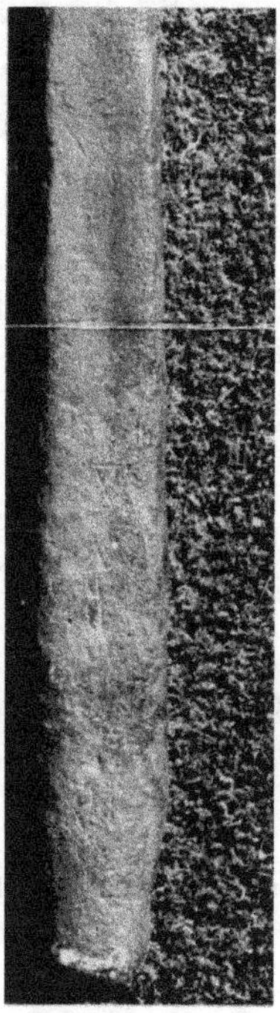

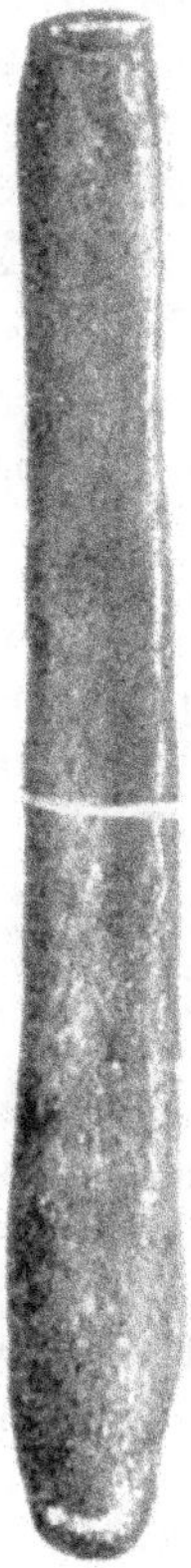

Snarling irons from the first quarter of the 20th century, after Otto 1922: 45 fig. 41-2. Used like special anvils for the raising of metal vessels.

The Chanhu-daro snarling alloy (ingot) has an inscription writing with five

using Indus (Meluhha) glyphs and a dot

glyph. Chanhujodaro39A1 Chanhudaro39A2

Text of inscription 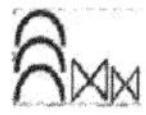

Three piled up U glyphs, two 'drum' glyphs. *koṇḍa* bend (Konkani)

Enclosure signs of the field: ( ) *kuṭila* = bent, crooked (Skt.Rasaratna samuccaya, 5.205) Humpbacked *kuḍilla* (Pkt.) Rebus: *kuṭila, katthīl* = bronze (8 parts copper and 2 parts tin) [cf. āra-kūṭa, 'brass' (Skt.)

koṇḍa bend (Konkani) Rebus: *kõdā* 'to turn in a lathe'(B.) **कोंद** *kōnda* 'engraver, lapidary setting or infixing gems' (Marathi) Allograph: *kọ̃ḍu* m. 'large cooking pot'(Kashmiri) *kolmo* 'three' Rebus: kolimi 'smithy/forge'. Thus, the inscription describes the snarling iron, as a forger's, lapidary's tool.

Dula 'pair' rebus: *dul* 'cast metal'PLUS *Ta. karaṭi, karaṭi-ppaṟai, karaṭikai* a kind of drum (said to sound like a b 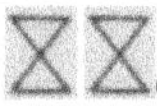 ear, karaṭi). *Ka. karaḍi, karaḍe* an oblong drum beaten on both sides, a sort of double drum. / Cf. Skt. *karaṭa-* a kind of drum. (DEDR 1264). Rebus: करडा [karaḍā] Hard from alloy--iron, silver &c. (Marathi) *kharādī* ' turner, a person who fashions or shapes objects on a lathe' (Gujarati)

கரடி² karaṭi, *n.* [T. *gariḍi*, K. *garuḍi*.] 1. Fencing; சிலம்பம். 1262 *Ta.* karaṭi, karuṭi, keruṭi fencing, school or gymnasium where wrestling and fencing are taught. *Ka.* garaḍi, garuḍi fencing school. *Tu.* garaḍi, garoḍi id. *Te.* gariḍi, gariḍī id., fencing. గరిడి [gariḍi] or గరిడీ *gariḍi*. [Tel.] n. Fencing, sword play. సాము. A dancing school, a fencing school. సాముకూటము. గరడీల సాము, or గరిడీవిద్య sword play, gymnastics. A place చోటు. Nearness. సమీపము, చెంత. గరిడిముచ్చు a rogue who pretends to be a good man. మంచివానివలె దగ్గిరనుండి సమయము చూచి దొంగిలించే దొంగ. (కళా. ii.) Rebus: करडा [karaḍā] Hard from alloy--iron, silver &c. (Marathi)

Kalibangan065E Kalibangan065a Text 8024

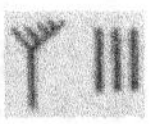

Rebus 1: करडा [karaḍā] Hard from alloy--iron, silver &c. (Marathi) karaḍo, karāḍī 'a goldsmith's tool' (Gujarati) kharādī ' turner, a person who fashions or shapes objects on a lathe' (Gujarati) Rebus 2: karaḍu, kharaḍe, karḍu 'rough, as an account' (Kannada); kharaḍem a rude sketch, foul copy' (Marathi)

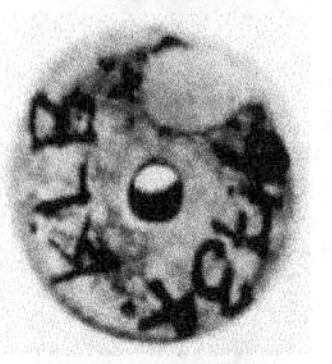

khareḍo = a currycomb (G.) खरारा [kharārā] *m* (H) A currycomb. 2 Currying a horse. (Marathi)

The dot glyph is a notch upon the edge of the bronze snarling tool read rebus as: खांडा [khāṇḍā] *m* A jag, notch, or indentation (as upon the edge of a tool or weapon). Rebus: *kāṇḍa* 'tools, pots and pans and metal-ware'.

There are 3 U glyphs: *kolmo* 'three' (Munda) Rebus: *kolimi* 'forge, smithy' (Telugu). *baṭhu* m. ' large pot in which grain is parched' (Sindhi) Rebus: *bhāṭhā* ' kiln '(Awadhi). The three U glyphs together read: *kolimi bhāṭhā* 'forge, smithy (with) smelter/furnace'.

The pair of glyphs preceding the 3 U glyphs are comparable to the pair of feet shown on some seals (discussed further in this note).

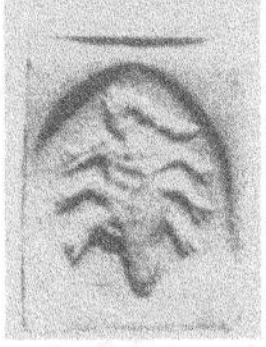

aṭai அடை 'anvil' (Tamil) combined with the U glyph which is *baṭhu* yields the compound lexeme: பட்டடை¹ *paṭṭaṭai*(Tamil); cognate *paṭṭaḍi* smithy, forge (Kannada)

The inscription on the 'snarling iron' of Chanhudaro can thus be read as: *kolami paṭṭaḍi* 'anvil for smithy/forge'. The inscription accurately describes in Meluhha (Mleccha) language the function served by the anvil for raising vessels in a smithy/forge.

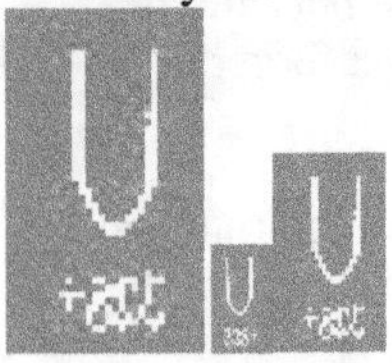

Reference to *aṭai, aḍi* அடை 'anvil' yields the clue to the rebus readings of 'feet, footprint' glyphs which occur on seals, discussed further in this note.

Tepe Yahya. Seal impressions of two sides of a seal. Six-legged lizard and opposing footprints shown on opposing sides of a double-sided steatite stamp seal perforated along the lateral axis.

Lamberg- Karlovsky 1971: fig. 2C Shahr-i-Soktha Stamp seal shaped like a foot.

Glyph: *aṭi* foot, footprint (Tamil) Rebus: *aḍe, aḍa, aḍi* the piece of wood on which the five artisans put the article which they happen to operate upon, a support (Kannada)

Glyph: araṇe 'lizard' (Tulu) Rebus: eraṇi f. ' anvil ' (Gujarati); aheraṇ, ahiraṇ, airaṇ, airṇī, haraṇ f. (Marathi)

Glyphs: six (numeral): आर [āra] A term in the play of इटीदांडू,--the number six. Rebus: āra 'brass'.

Alternative: Glyph: bhaṭa 'six' (G.) rebus: baṭa = kiln (Santali) baṭa = a kind of iron (Gujarati) [Note: six legs shown on the lizard glyph]

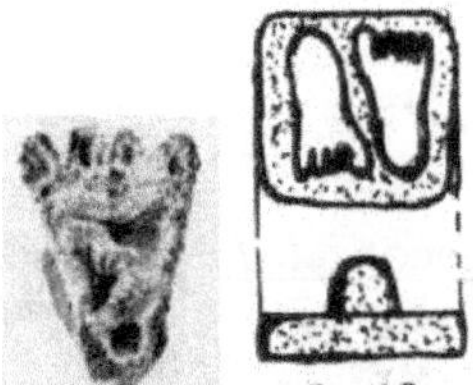

Ia. 18

The rebus readings are: āra 'brass' *aṭai-kal* 'anvil', *airaṇ* 'anvil', that is, brazier's anvil.

Shahdad seal (Grave 78)

Meluhha (Mleccha) glosses from Indian *sprachbund*:

Ta. aṭi foot, footprint, *Ma.* aṭi sole of foot, footstep, measure of foot, *Ko.* aṛy foot (measure); *Ka.* aḍi foot, measure of foot, step, pace,*Tu.* aḍi bottom, base; kār aḍi footsole, footstep; *Te.*aḍugu foot, footstep, footprint, step, pace, measure of a foot, aḍi-gaṟṟa sandal, wooden shoe. *Ga.* (S.2) aḍugu footstep (< Te.). *Go.* (G.) aḍi beneath (Mu.) (DEDR 72)
Rebus: *Ta.* aṭai prop. slight support; aṭai-kal anvil. *Ma.* aṭa-kkallu anvil of goldsmiths. *Ko.* aṛ gal small anvil. *Ka.* aḍe, aḍa, aḍi the piece of wood on which the five artisans put the article which they happen to operate upon, a support; aḍegal, aḍagallu, aḍigallu anvil. *Tu.* aṭṭè a support, stand. *Te.* ḍā-kali, ḍā-kallu, dā-kali, dā-gali, dāyi anvil. (DEDR 76).

அரணை Ta. araṇai typical lizard, Lacertidae; smooth streaked lizard, Lacerta interpunctula. Ma. araṇa green house lizard, L. interpunctula. Ka. araṇe, rāṇe, rāṇi greenish kind of lizard which is said to poison by licking, L. interpunctula. Tu. araṇe id. (DEDR 204). Rebus: eraṇi f. ' anvil ' (Gujarati)

M0592 copper plate.

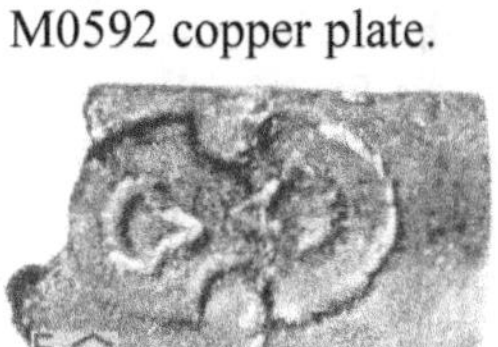

Double-axe hieroglyph. Compare with double-axe (together with axe and dagger) of finds in a Ur grave.[15]

4407 Field Symbol 129

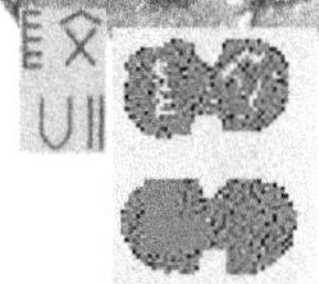

h818At

h818Bt

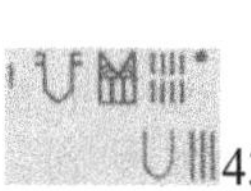

4376

h817At

h817Bt

 h971Ait  h971Bit 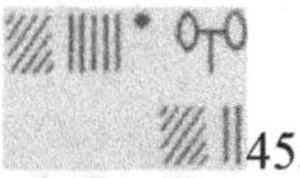4557

h232A 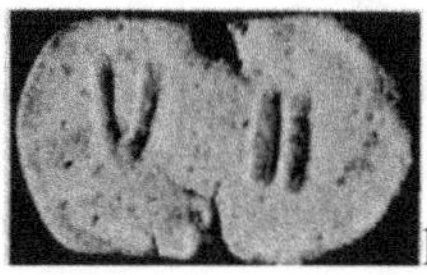h232B tablet in bas relief 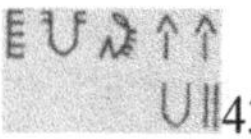4368 Harappa tablets in the shape of double-axe

tabar 'a broad axe' (Punjabi). Rebus: *tam(b)ra* 'copper'

Deux représentations du dieu Soma

http://www.anthropologieenligne.com/pages/sacrificeI_2.html (Note: No literary source has been cited for this identification).

The RV Sukta 10.177 is also called Māyābheda Sukta; devata is Māyābheda in Pravargya yajna. The full text of the Sukta, transliteration, translation (based on Sayana and Wilson) are appended.

After *gharma* is taken out of the furnace hot milk is offered to As'vins. The prayer is offered on three consecutive days preceding the *upasad; gharma* or *mahavira* pot and implements used are carried in procession to *uttaravedi* and buried there. *gharma or ukhA Mahavira vessel is the head of Makha, head of the yajna and* is the sun, the all-seeing eye.

SBr. (14.1.1-5) explains: "The ods, Agni, Indra, Soma, Makha, Vishnu and the Vis've DevAh perform a sacrificial session that whoever amongst them through austerity, fervour, faith, sacrifice and oblations would first encompass the end of the sacrifice would be the most excellent amont them and the glory should then be common to them all. Vishnu obtained it." Our all-encompassing hero (mahAn VIrah) has fallen... Dadhyanc AtharvaNa knew...how the head of the sacrifice is put on again...Dadhyanc AtharvaNa with a horse's head taught them (As'vins) the sweet (secret)(SB. 14.1.1.11-18, 25). The decapitated divinity in Tandya Brahmana is Makha. Taittiriya Aranyaka calls him Makha Vaishnava. Vishnu is the sacrifice; Makha is Vishnu. (SB 14.1.1.6; SB 14.1.1.13). Dadhyanc's horse's head was submerged in S'aryaNAvat. (RV 1.84.14). (See: Kramrisch, Stella, 1975, The Mahavira vessel and the plant Putika, in: *Journal of the American Oriental Society*, Vol. 95, No. 2 (Apr-Jun 1975), pp. 222-235).

Deux représentations du dieu Soma

RV_1,084.14a icchann aśvasya yac chiraḥ parvateṣv apaśritam |

RV_1,084.14c tad vidac charyaṇāvati ||

RV 1.84.14: Wishing for the horse's head hidden in the mountains, he found in S'aryan.a_vat.

Ekamukha linga seen in Bhuteshwar next to a smelter and tree (kuTi 'tree' rebus: kuThi 'smelter') may be comparable to the mukha seen on gharma, Mahavira pot.

प्रवर्ग्य [p= 693,2] *m.* a ceremony introductory to the सोम sacrifice (at which fresh milk is poured into a heated vessel called ,महा-वीर or घर्म , or into boiling ghee) Br. S3rS. MBh. &c *n.* N. of a सामन् A1rshBr (Monier-Williams) घर्म gharma The प्रवर्ग्य ceremony A cauldron, boiler.Sunshine; A cavity in the earth shaped like a boiler. -A hot day. Ved. A sacrifice. pravargyḥ प्रवर्ग्यः A ceremony preliminary to the Soma sacrifice; प्रवर्ग्यं शास्त्रतः कृत्वा Rām.1.14.4; Bhāg.3.13.37. (Apte. Samskritam) ప్రవర్గ్యము (p. 0843) [pravargyamu] *pra-vargyamu.* [Skt.] n. A certain ceremony or sacrifice. అగ్నిష్టోమాద్యంగ భూతమైనయాగవిశేషము.

ప్రవర్గ్యుడు *pra-vargyuḍu.* n. An officiating priest. పురోహితుడు.

(3)	177	(म.10, अनु.12)
ऋषिः पतङ्गः प्राजापत्यः	छन्दः जगती 1, त्रिष्टुप् 2-3	देवता मायाभेदः

पतङ्गमक्तमसुरस्य मायया हृदा पश्यन्ति मनसा विपश्चितः |
समुद्रे अन्तः कवयो वि चक्षते मरीचीनां पदमिच्छन्ति वेधसः || 1 ||
पतङ्गो वाचं मनसा बिभर्ति तां गन्धर्वोऽवदद्गर्भे अन्तः |
तां द्योतमानां स्वर्यं मनीषामृतस्य पदे कवयो नि पान्ति || 2 ||
अपश्यं गोपामनिपद्यमानमा च परा च पथिभिश्चरन्तम् |
स सध्रीचीः स विषूचीर्वसान आ वरीवर्ति भुवनेष्वन्तः || 3 ||

r.s.i: patan:ga pra_ja_patya; devata_: ma_ya_bheda; chanda: tris.t.up, 1 jagati_

RV_10,177.01a pataṅgam aktam asurasya māyayā hṛdā paśyanti manasā vipaścitaḥ |
RV_10,177.01c samudre antaḥ kavayo vi cakṣate marīcīnām padam icchanti vedhasaḥ ||
RV_10,177.02a pataṅgo vācam manasā bibharti tāṃ gandharvo 'vadad garbhe antaḥ |
RV_10,177.02c tāṃ dyotamānāṃ svaryam manīṣām ṛtasya pade kavayo ni pānti ||
RV_10,177.03a apaśyaṃ gopām anipadyamānam ā ca parā ca pathibhiś carantam |
RV_10,177.03c sa sadhrīcīḥ sa viṣūcīr vasāna ā varīvarti bhuvaneṣv antaḥ ||

10.177.01 The wise behold their mind; (seated) in their heart the Sun made manifest by the illusion of the asura; the sages look into the solar orb, the ordainers (of solar worship) desire the region of his rays. [Illusion of the asura: asurasya = the supreme Brahma devoid of all disguise; aktam ma_yaya_ = united, to knowledge, all-knowing].

10.177.02 The Sun bears the (sacred) word in his mind the Gandharva has spoken it, (abiding) within the womb; sages cherish it in the place of sacrifice, brilliant, heavenly ruling the mind. [Sacred word: va_k: the three Vedas;*Taittiri_ya Bra_hman.a* 3.12.9: in the morning the deity moves in the sky with the hymns of the R.k, he abides at noon in the Yajurveda, at his setting he is extolled with the Sa_maveda; the sun moves accompanied by the three Vedas; gandharva: from gah (voices), and dhr. (to hold) = the breath of life].

10.177.03 I beheld the protector (the Sun), never descending, going by his paths to the east and to the west; clothing (with light) the (four) quarters of heaven and the intermediate spaces, he constantly revolves in the midst of the worlds.

Excerpts from a blogpost in Manasatarangini:

[quote]

In the great pravargya ritual the mAhAvIra pot containing the milk of a cow and a goat, i.e. the gharma offering, is intensely heated until it starts glowing. When the pot starts glowing the hotar looks at it starts reciting the sUkta RV 10.177 (In some traditions in south India they only recite RV 10.177.1 & 3). This sUkta is traditionally referred to as the mAyAbheda sUkta. Regarding this the sUkta the shaunakIya R^igvidhAna redacted by the early vaiShNava viShNukumAra states:

pata~Ngam iti nityam tu japed aj~nAna bhedanam |

mAyA bhedanam etaddhi sarva mAyAH prabAdhate ||

He should constantly do japa of the [mantra-s beginning with] pata~Nga that destroys ignorance. It is breaks the [spell of] mAyA and drives away all mAyA.

shAmbarIm indrajAlAm vA mAyAm etena vArayet |

adR^iShTAnAm cha sattvAnAm mAyAm etena bAdhate || RVdh 4.115-116

By this he should block mAyA be it of the shambara or the indrajAla variety; By this he repulses the mAyA of the unseen ones and of the consciousness.

This prayoga is interesting because it uses the term shAmbarI in the sense of a magical prayoga, which is closer to its use in the sense we encounter it in the temporally later tantra texts. But of course the mAyA of shambara has a very old precedence, primarily in a negative sense, in the R^igveda itself:

tvaM divo bR^ihataH sAnu kopayo .ava tmanA dhR^iShatA shambaram bhinat |

yan mAyino vrandino mandinA dhR^iShach ChitAM gabhastim ashanim pR^itanyasi || RV 1.54.4

You shook the pinnacle of the high heavens; with your own valor you rent apart shambara,

when exhilarated with the flowing soma juice you battled with the sharp, radiating thunderbolt those wielding mAyA.

This might be compared to the mAyA of other dAnava-s and dasyu-s like vR^itra:

indro mahAM sindhum AshayAnam mAyAvinaM vR^itram asphuran niH |

arejetAM rodasI bhiyAne kanikradato vR^iShNo asya vajrAt ||

indra threw down vR^itra who sprawled across the great sindhu: both the celestial hemispheres trembled in terror of the manly warrior's vajra when he roared.

On the other hand the mAyA of indra and other deities is clearly praised in the R^igveda:

maho mahAni panayanty asyendrasya karma sukR^itA purUNi |

vR^ijanena vR^ijinAn sam pipeSha mAyAbhir dasyUMr abhibhUty ojAH ||

[The ritualists] express wonder at the great deeds of this great one, the numerous glorious acts of indra; Through his might the surpassed the mighty, of unsurpassed might, with his mAyA powers he pounded the dasyus....

mAyAbheda sUktam (RV 10.177):

pata~Ngam aktam asurasya mAyayA hR^idA pashyanti manasA vipashchitaH |

samudre antaH kavayo vi chakShate marIchInAm padam ichChanti vedhasaH ||

vipaShchitaH = seers, plural subject; manasA= by their mind, instrumental; hR^idA= by heart, instrumental of hR^id; pata~Ngam= bird, singular object; aktam= anointed; asurasya=asura's, genitive singular; mAyayA= by mAyA; singular instrumental; pashyanti= see, 3rd person plural present, parasmai.

samudre= in ocean, locative; antaH= inside; kavayaH= kavi-s, vocative plural; vi chakShate= 3rd person singular present, atmane; marIchInAm= rays, genitive plural; padam= station, accusative singular; vedhasaH= ritualists; plural subject; ichChanti= 3rd person plural present, parasmai.

Here the terms vipashchit, vedhas and kavi all refer to the ritualist-mantra composer-sages who are participating in the rite.

The seers see with their minds and with their heart the bird anointed with the mAyA of the asura; O kavi-s, from within the ocean he shines forth, the ritualists seek the station of [his] rays.

Here the pata~Nga, by vaidika metaphor, is the sun and he is "anointed" with rays by the mAyA of the asura who is none other than the deva savitA (Indeed hiraNyastUpa A~Ngirasa praises savitA thus: vi suparNo antarikShANy akhyad gabhIravepA asuraH sunIthaH | RV 1.35.7a. The golden eagle, lit up the mid-regions, the one from the wavy depths, the good asura). Even when not visible he shines from within the ocean. The meditating on him the ritualists seek the "station" of his rays, which could figuratively mean the illumination of his rays. This effectively is parallel to the image presented by the famed sAvitrI R^ik of vishvAmitra that used in the saMdhyA ritual, where in the rays of the deva savitA are sought to illuminate the mind of the meditator. This connects to the fact that one of the prime deities of the gharma offering is savitA (the deva-s offered the gharma are: ashvin-s, vAyu, indra, savitA, bR^ihaspati and yama).

....

pata~Ngo vAcham manasA bibharti tAM gandharvo .avadad garbhe antaH |

tAM dyotamAnAM svaryam manIShAm R^itasya pade kavayo ni pAnti ||

pata~NgaH= singular, subject; vAcham= holy utterance/incantation, object; manasA= singular instrumental; bibharti= bears, 3rd person singular present, parasmai; tAM= that, accusative feminine; gandharvaH=subject; avadat= uttered, 3rd person singular past, parasmai, garbhe= in the womb, locative singular, antaH= inside;

tAM= that, accusative feminine, dyotamAnAM= radiant; svaryam= celestial; manIShAM= mental creation, i.e., incantation, object; R^itasya= of the R^ita, genitive; pade= in the station, locative;

kavayaH=kavi-s, nominative plural; ni pAnti= take in [literally drink in], 3rd person plural present, parasmai.

The bird holds the incantation (vAk, the holy utterance) in the mind; the gandharva had uttered within the womb. That radiant, celestial incantation the kavi-s take in at the station of the R^ita (i.e. the universal laws).

Here the bird, i.e., the sun is said to hold the incantation, which is uttered by the gandharva within the womb, which represented by the world hemispheres. But for the ritualist the external sun is also homologized with the "light" of mental enlightenment; hence the synesthetic metaphor of the sun holding it in the mind. This enlightenment leads to the utterance of the mantra-s within, which is expressed by the metaphor of the gandharva [For an explicit statement of this internal homology see below]. The gandharva here is the sun as indicated in other R^igveda mantra-s such as:

Urdhvo gandharvo adhi nAke asthAd vishvA rUpA pratichakShANo asya |

bhAnuH shukreNa shochiShA vy adyaut prArUruchad rodasI mAtarA shuchiH || RV 9.85.12

High to the zenith as the gandharva risen, beholding all these varied forms.

His rays have shone widely with brightness: the pure one has lit both the worlds, the parents.

This gandharva also specifically relates to the gandharva-s invoked at the pravargya after the mahAvIra pot is finally disposed. Here the ritualists as a chorus utter a series of yajuSh incantations which include the formulae:

rantir nAmAsi divyo gandharva | tasya te padvad dhavirdhAnaM | agnir adhyakShA | rudro.adhipatiH ||

you are ranti by name, the celestial gandharva, the havirdhAna is your foot messenger, agni your president, rudra is your overlord !

vishvAvasur abhi tan no gR^iNAtu | divyo gandharvo rajaso vimAnaH | yad vA ghA satyam uta yan na vidma | dhiyo hinvAno dhiya inno avyAd | prAsaM gandharvo amR^itAni vochad | (prAnA vA amR^itAH ||)

vishvAvasu, proclaim it to us, the celestial gandharva who measures out the heavens. Whether we know the truth already or not, he who has impelled our inspired intellect also have these thoughts inspired. The gandharva has proclaimed he immortal one. The prAna-s are immortal.

Thus, the mantra-s of the mAyAbheda sUkta are closely related to the inspiration that is received as result of the rite which is supposed to be proclaimed by the celestial gandharva. The gandharva in Vedic tradition has a mysterious nature and can take possession of individuals during which he can make revelations via the possessed medium. This relates to the earlier R^ik where the sun(bird) is said to be covered by mAyA, thus making it fit to be described as a gandharva. Like the possessing gandharva-s, the solar gandharva-s ranti and vishvAvasu confer knowledge to the ritualists. This is what is alluded to when they are described as drinking the gandharva's proclamation at the seat of the universal laws. This seat of the R^ita is in essence the ritual arena – the uttaravedi which is homologized with the universe. Indeed the incantation used in the pravargya when he sets down the mahAvIra pot at the conclusion of the ritualist utter the formula:

chatuHsraktir nAbhir R^itasya | (iyam vA R^itam | tasyA eSha eva nAbhiH |)

Quadrangular is the center of R^ita. This [the uttaravedi] is the R^ita; the pravargya is its root.

……….

apashyaM gopAm anipadyamAnam A cha parA cha pathibhish charantam |

sa sadhrIchIH sa viShUchIr vasAna A varIvarti bhuvaneShv antaH ||

apashyaM= saw; 1st person singular past, parasmai; gopAm= guardian, object; anipadyamAnam=never resting; A cha parA cha= northern and southern (eastern and western); pathibhiH= paths, instrumental; charatam= moving;

sa= he; sadhrIchIH= approaching; viShUchIH= departing; vasAnaH= clothes [or in this context taking on appearances], singular nominative; A varIvarti= revolves, 3rd person singular, parasmai; bhuvaneShu= in worlds, locative plural; antaH= inside.

I saw the never-resting guardian, moving along the northern and southern [eastern and western] paths. He, in his approaching and departing apparitions (or: clothing the sadhrIchI= antarikSha and the viShuchI= dyaus [with his rays]), continually revolves in midst of the worlds.

The taittirIya AraNyaka explains:

apshyaM gopAM ity Aha | prANo vai gopAH | prANam eva prajAsu vi yAtyati | "apashyaM gopAM ity Aha | asau vA adityo gopAH | sa hiimAH prajA gopAyati | tam eva prajAnAM goptAraM kurute ||

"I saw the guardian" so he recites. The guardian is the prANa. [If he meditate thus] he has the prANa flowing into all reproducing life. "I saw the guardian" so he recites. The yonder Aditya is the guardian for he guards all this reproducing life. [If he mediates thus] he makes a protector for all life forms.

This explanation establishes clearly the duality that is implied in these mantra-s i.e. homologizing of the external sun with the internal prANa which is also described as a bird (e.g. the haMsaH). It also holds for the rest of the R^ik: Both the prANa and the sun are seen as never-resting. The paths taken by the sun might be interpreted as the rising and the setting (i.e. eastern and western). But we prefer the explanation of the northern and southern paths because traditionally these are the two paths or ayana-s of the sun. The eastern and western one are part of the same path after all. The prANa is similarly seen as having the inhalation and exhalation as its two paths. The sadhrIchIH and viShUchIH in the case of the sun might be interpreted as the visible apparition during the day with the bright clothing or the invisible one at night with the dark clothing. However, it is has also been connected with water – i.e. the one which draws water away from the earth and the one which supplies waters in the form of the rains. The inward prANa similarly is dry and the outward one is wet. Finally like the sun is seen as revolving within the world, the prANa is seen as constantly revolving within an organism.

…

This shows that the Hindu tradition of meditative practices connecting the observation of the prANa with the celestial solar movement or penetration by solar light (as seen in the daily saMdhyopAsanA) was also related to the mantra-s in the context of the pravargya ritual. Moreover it also became clear to us that the mAyAbheda sUkta is closely linked to the pravargya rite and was most probably composed precisely for that rite. However, the mAyA and asura in this context are meant in a largely positive sense as that of savitA. The mystery of this mAyA may be seen as being discerned by the ritualists who realize the homologies between the prANa and sUrya. It was only later in the vidhAna tradition that the mAyA acquired a negative connotation. Even latter the advaitin-s interpreted it in the sense they understood mAyA.

[unquote]

https://manasataramgini.wordpress.com/2013/07/02/the-mayabheda-sukta/

h1973B h1974B Two tablets. One side shows a person seated on a tree branch, a tiger looking up, a crocodile on the top register and other animals in procession in the bottom register. kāru 'crocodile' (Telugu). Rebus: artisan (Marathi) Rebus: khar 'blacksmith' (Kashmiri) kola 'tiger' Rebus: kol 'working in iron'. Hieroglyph: heraka 'spy' Rebus: eraka 'copper'. *khōṇḍa* 'leafless tree' (Marathi). Rebus: *kõdār* 'turner' (Bengali) kuTi 'tree' rebus: kuThi 'smelter'. Hieroglyph: barad, balad, 'ox' Rebus: baran, bharat (5 copper, 4 zinc and 1 tin)(Punjabi.Bengali). भरत (p. 603) [bharata] *n* A factitious metal compounded of copper, pewter, tin &c.भरतखंड (p. 603) [bharatakhaṇḍa] *n* (S) भरतवर्ष *n* S A division of the globe,--that from the Himálaya range to the ocean, India.भरतशास्त्र (p. 603) [bharataśāstra] *n* S The shástra of the drama, the authoritative treatise upon dramatic composition and representation. 2 Used freely in the sense of The *laws* of the drama and of scenic exhibition.भरताचें भांडें (p. 603) [bharatācē mbhāṇḍēṃ] *n* A vessel made of the metal भरत. 2 See भरिताचें भांडें.भरती (p. 603) [bharatī] *a* Composed of the metal भरत. A hieroglyph to signify भरत (p. 603) [bharata] is: barad, balad 'ox'.

Looking back: krammara 'look back' Rebus: kamar 'smith, artisan'.

Animals in procession are hieroglyphs signifying metalwork

meḍho a ram, a sheep (G.)(CDIAL 10120); mRdu 'iron' Rebus: *muṇḍa* 'iron' (Sanskrit) mRdu, 'soft iron'
adar ḍangra 'zebu'
H. *muḍḍhā* m. ' shoulder ', *mū̃ḍhā* m. ' lump, hump, shoulder ' Or. *muṇḍā* ' lump '.(CDIAL 10189) Rebus: *muṇḍa* 'iron' (Sanskrit) mRdu, 'soft', *kuṇṭha*, 'hard', kad*āra* 'brittle' are three varieties of *muṇḍa loha*(Vagbhata, *Rasaratnasamuccaya*, 69-74). *muṇḍitam*, *muṇḍa loham* 'iron'; *muṇḍajam* 'steel' (Sanskrit) Thus, zebu reads rebus: *kuṇṭha munda (loha),* a type of iron native metal. (Vagbhata, *Rasaratnasamuccaya*, 69-74). पोळी [pōḷī] dewlap. Rebus: Russian gloss, *bulat* is cognate *pola* 'magnetite' iron in Asuri (Meluhha). Magnetite is the most magnetic of all the naturally occurring igneous and metamorphic rocks with black or brownish-black with a metallic luster. These magnetite ore stones could have been identified as *pola* iron by Meluhha speakers. Kannada gloss *pola* meaning 'point of the compass' may link with the characteristic of magnetite iron used to create a compass.*pŏlāduwu* made of steel; *pŏlād* प्वलाद् or *phōlād* फोलाद् मृदुलोहविशेषः] m. steel (Gr.M.; Rām. 431, 635, *phōlād*). *pŏlödi pōlödi phōlödi* लोहविशेषमयः adj. c.g. of steel,

steel (Kashmiri) urukku what is melted, fused metal, steel.(Malayalam); ukk 'steel' (Telugu)(DEDR 661) This is cognate with famed 'wootz'steel. "Polad, Faulad" for steel in late Indian languages is traceable to Pokkhalavat, Polahvad. Pokkhalavat is the name of Pushkalavati, capital of Gandhara famed for iron and steel products. पोळें [pōḷēṃ] 'honeycomb' (shown as a pictorial motif on Lothal Seal 51).

Lothal Seal 51

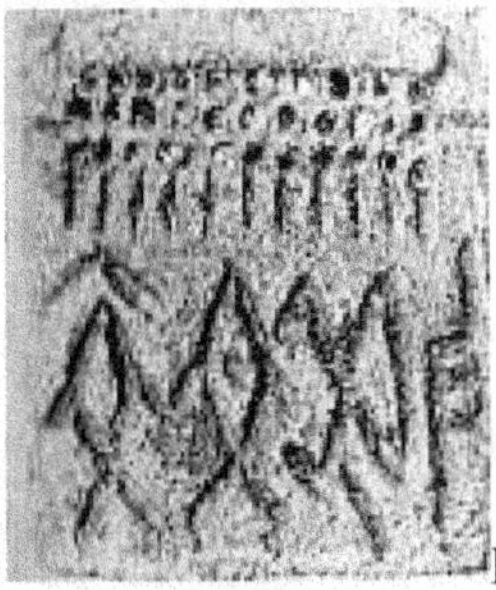Lothal seal 51 Hieroglyph: *pōḷī,* 'dewlap, honeycomb' *pola, 'zebu'* *Rebus: pola,* 'magnetite'

ibha 'elephant' (Skt.); rebus: ib 'iron' (Ko.)
kolo 'jackal' (Kon.)

pola (magnetite), *gota* (laterite), *bichi* (hematite), three types of ferrite ores are signified by hieroglyphs:

pola 'zebu', *gota* 'round object', *bichi* 'scorpion'..

One side of a molded tablet m 492 Mohenjo-daro (DK 8120, NMI 151. National Museum, Delhi. A person places his foot on the horns of a buffalo while spearing it in front of a cobra hood.

kulā ''hooded serpent' Rebus: kol 'working in iron' kolle 'blacksmith' kolhe 'smelter' *kulā* ' winnowing fan, hood of a snake ' (Assamese)(CDIAL 3350)

Hieroglyph: kolsa = to kick the foot forward, the foot to come into contact with anything when walking or running; kolsa pasirkedan = I kicked it over (Santali.lex.)mēṛsa = v.a. toss, kick with the foot, hit with the tail (Santali)
kol 'furnace, forge' (Kuwi) kol 'alloy of five metals, pancaloha' (Ta.) •kolhe (iron-smelter; kolhuyo, jackal) kol, kollan-, kollar = blacksmith (Ta.lex.)•kol'to kill' (Ta.)•sal 'bos gaurus', bison; rebus: sal 'workshop' (Santali)me~ṛhe~t iron; ispat m. = steel; dul m.

= cast iron; kolhe m. iron manufactured by
the Kolhes (Santali); meṛed (Mun.d.ari); meḍ (Ho.)(Santali.Bodding)

nAga 'serpent' Rebus: nAga 'lead'
Hieroglyph: rā̃go ' buffalo bull '

Rebus: Pk. raṅga 'tin' P. rā̃g f., rā̃gā m. ' pewter, tin ' Ku. rāṅ ' tin, solder 'Or. rāṅga ' tin ', rāṅgā ' solder, spelter ', Bi. Mth. rā̃gā, OAw. rāṁga; H. rā̃g f., rā̃gā m. ' tin, pewter 'raṅgaada -- m. ' borax ' lex.Kho. (Lor.) ruṅ ' saline ground with white efflorescence, salt in earth ' *raṅgapattra ' tinfoil '. [raṅga -- 3, páttra --]B. rāṅ(g)tā ' tinsel, copper -- foil '.
paTa 'hood of serpent' Rebus: padanu 'sharpness of weapon' (Telugu)

Hieroglyph: kuntal ' spear '. 2. *kōnta -- . [Perh. ← Gk. konto/*s* ' spear ' EWA i 229]1. Pk. *kuṁta* -- m. ' spear '; S. *kundu* m. ' spike of a top ', °*dī* f. ' spike at the bottom of a stick ', °*diṛī*, °*dirī* f. ' spike of a spear or stick '; Si. *kutu* ' lance '.
2. Pa. *konta* -- m. ' standard '; Pk. *koṁta* -- m. ' spear '; H. *kõt* m. (f.?) ' spear, dart '; -- Si. *kota* ' spear, spire, standard ' perh. ← Pa.(CDIAL 3289)

Rebus: kuṇṭha munda (loha) 'hard iron (native metal)'

Allograph: कुंठणें [kuṇṭhaṇēṃ] *v i* (कुंठ S) To be stopped, detained, obstructed, arrested in progress (Marathi)

Tablet. Crocodile above. Peson kicking and spearing a bison, near a seated,horned (with twig) person.Harappa. Harappa Museum, H95-2486 Meadow and Kenoyer 1997
karA 'crocodile' Rebus: khAr 'blacksmith' (Kashmiri)
kamaDha 'penance' (Prakritam) Rebus: kammaTa 'mint, coiner'
kUtI 'twigs' Rebus: kuThi 'smelter'
muh 'face' Rebus: muhe 'ingot' (Santali)

poliya 'citizen, gatekeeper of town quarter' Hieroglyph: *pola 'zebu'*

Pola festival in Bharatam, buffalo in sacred dairy, temple, zebu, *bos indicus* dedicated to the gods in Indus Script hieroglyphic tradition signifying magnetite

Hieroglyph: पोळ [pōḷa] *m* A bull dedicated to the gods, marked with a trident and discus, and set at large. பொலியெருது poli-y-erutu , *n.* < பொலி- +. 1. Bull kept for covering; பசுக்களைச் சினையாக்குதற் பொருட்டு வளர்க்கப்படும் காளை. (பிங்.) கொடிய பொலியெருதை யிருமூக்கிலும் கயி றொன்று கோத்து (அறப். சத. 42). 2. The leading ox in treading out grain on a threshing-floor; களத்துப் பிணையல்மாடுகளில் முதற்செல்லுங் கடா. (W.) பொலி முறைநாகு poli-muṟai-nāku, *n.* < பொலி + முறை +. Heifer fit for covering; பொலியக்கூடிய பக்குவமுள்ள கிடாரி. (S. I. I. iv, 102.)

Rebus 1: pōḷa 'magnetite, ferrous-ferric oxide Fe3O4'.

Rebus: cattle festival: पोळा [pōḷā] *m* (पोळ) A festive day for cattle,--the day of new moon of श्रावण or of भाद्रपद. Bullocks are exempted from labor; variously daubed and decorated; and paraded about in worship. "Pola is a bull-worshipping festival celebrated by farmers mainly in the Indian state of Maharashtra (especially among the Kunbis). On the day of Pola, the farmers decorate and worship their bulls. Pola falls on the day of the *Pithori Amavasya* (the new moon day) in the month of Shravana (usually in August)." https://en.wikipedia.org/wiki/Pola_(festival) Festival held on the day after Sankranti (= kANum) is called pōlāla paNDaga (Telugu).

The early Prakritam form of the word signifying a village, temple, sacred dairy may be *poḷ* m. ' bull dedicated to the gods ': poḷy sacred dairy (Toda) since the related gloss poLa signifies a bull set at liberty. B. *polā* ' child, son '; M. *poḷ* m. ' bull dedicated to the gods '; Si. *pollā* ' young of an animal '.4. Pk. *pōāla* -- m. ' child, bull '; A. *powāli* ' young of animal or bird '. (CDIAL 8399)

pallī -- 1, °*li* -- f. ' small village ' Kathās., ' hut ' lex. [← Drav. Tam. *paḷḷi* T. Burrow TPS 1946, 10: see padra --]Pk. *palli* -- f. ' small village '; Si. *päla* ' hut '. -- Or. *pa(h)lā* ' tiny hut made of leaves ' rather < pallava -- 1.pallī -- 2 f. ' a measure of grain ' KātyŚr.com (CDIAL 7972)palya n. ' sack for corn ' KātyŚr., *palla* -- 1 m. ' large granary ' Suśr., *pallī* -- 2 f. ' measure of grain ' KātyŚr. com. [EWA ii 235, 236 with lit. separates *palya* -- from *palla* -- 1. -- Cf. *palla --2?] Pk. *palia* -- , *palla* -- , °*aga* -- m. ' round sack for grain '; S. *palu* m. ' place attached to a house for storing grain ', *palī* f. ' a mat bag for grain '; L. *pall*, *pallā* m. ' stack of straw or grain, two concentric walls of grass ropes on masonry cylinder of a well between which earth from the well is placed '; P. *pall* f. ' large bamboo bin (holding 200 -- 300 maunds) ', *pallā* ' cloth spread for holding grain '; WPah.khaś.*pallā* ' udder of cow or buffalo (as opposed to those of sheep and goats) '; Ku. *pālī* ' small wooden dish ', *pallo* ' basket work interwoven with grass and leaves for thatching ', *palaṛo* ' one of the baskets of a balance ', *palyālo* ' a wooden vessel '; A. *pal* ' a bamboo basket for catching fish ', *palā* ' rattan basket for pressing mustard oil '; B. *pālaï* ' granary, rick of corn, stack of straw or hay '; H. *pālā* m. ' stack of corn ', *pallā* m. ' grain sack, cloth spread for grain '; G. *pālī* f. ' any measure of capacity, a measure of 4 seers '.(CDIAL 7963) *Ta.* paḷḷi hamlet, herdsman's village, hermitage, temple (esp. of Buddhists and Jains), palace, workshop, sleeping place, school, room. *Ma.* paḷḷi hut, small settlement of jungle tribes, public building, place of worship for Buddhists or foreigners, mosque, royal couch. *To.* poḷy sacred dairy, matrilineal sib, Badaga house; -oḷy in: wïsoḷy dairy of a particular grade, whose dairyman is wïs̱ o·ḷ. *Ka.* paḷḷi, haḷḷi settlement, abode, hamlet, village; (K.2) paḷḷiru to rest, inhabit. *Koḍ.* paḷḷi hut of a Poleyë or Me·dë (both low castes). *Tu.* paḷḷi mosque; haḷḷi hamlet, small village. *Te.* palli village, hut; palliya, palle small village; (inscr.) paḷḷi = palli. *Pa.* palli village (only in place names). *Kur.* pallī, in: eṛpā-pallī household, family

establishment (eṛpā house). / Cf. Skt. pallī-, pallikā- small village, esp. a settlement of wild tribes, hut, house; Turner, *CDIAL*, no. 7972. (CDIAL 4018)
'zebu' poLa 'magnetite'

Bemrose, Collo., Derby.

FIGURES OF ANIMALS MADE FOR POLA FESTIVAL.

Toy animals made for the Pola festival especially celebrated by the Dhanoje Kunbis. (Bemrose, Colo. Derby - Russell, Robert Vane (1916). The Tribes and Castes of the Central Provinces of India: volume IV. Descriptive articles on the principal castes and tribes of the Central Provinces. London: Macmillan and Co., limited. p. 40).

Some artifacts of Sarasvati-Sindhu Civilization point to the possibility that the celebration of pola cattle festival may be traced to the cultural practices of 3rd millennium BCE.

Picture 27.2

Copper chariot was found by M.S. Vats, the Director of the ASI, at Harappa. Dates back to 3000 BCE "(Vats) found several pieces of a small copper chariot, about two inches in height. Hreconstructed it from those several pieces or parts. The wheels are missing, so are the yoke and the axle. The man sitting inside has braided his long hair into a knot. Mr. Vats claims this to be the first miniature model of a chariot in the worlld." https://aryaninvasionmyth.wordpress.com/2012/10/01/3/

Copper model of a passenger box on a cart, Chanhudaro, ca. 2,000 BCE

Harappan Chariot toy kept at the Brooklyn University Museum

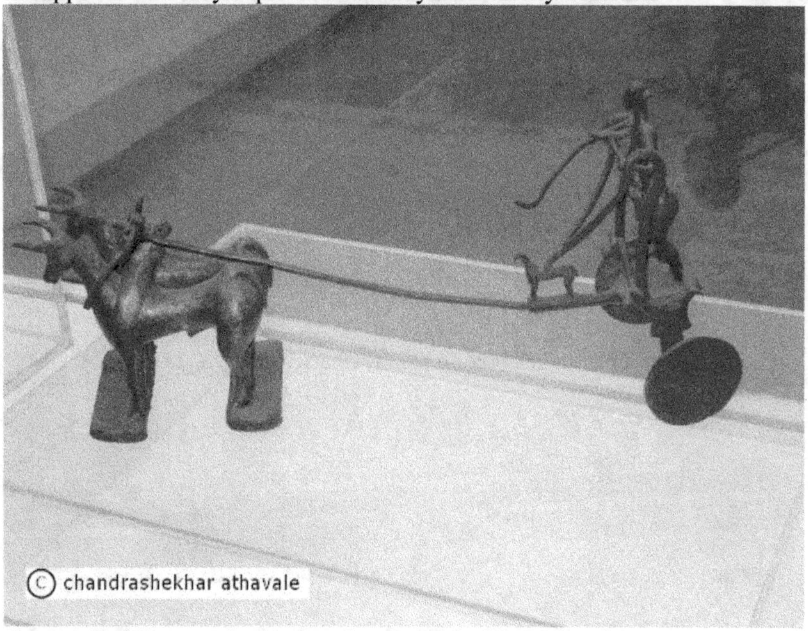

Oxen pulled Bronze chariot found at Daimabad in Maharshtra
chandrashekharasandprints.wordpress.com

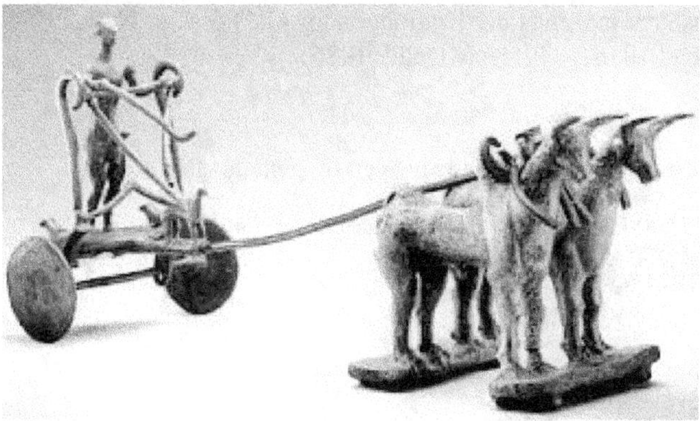

Daimabad bronze chariot. c. 1500 BCE. 22X52X17.5 cm.

Buffalo. Daimabad bronze. Prince of Wales Museum, Mumbai.

Daimabad bronzes. Buffalo on four-legged platform attached to four solid wheels 31X25 cm.; elephanton four-legged platform with axles 25 cm.; rhinoceros on axles of four solid wheels 25X19

cm. (MK Dhavalikar, 'Daimabad bronzes' in: Harappan civilization, ed. by GL Possehl, New Delhi, 1982, pp. 361-6; SA Sali, Daimabad 1976-1979, New Delhi, 1986).

That zebu, *bos indicus*, is an exclusive legacy of South Asia is proven by genetic studies.

Nausharo: céramique de la période I (c. 2500 BCE) cf. Catherine Jarrige

http://www.waa.ox.ac.uk/XDB/tours/indus6.asp

After the domestication of the zebu, *bos indicus*, deployment of the hierolyph of zebu on Indus Script Corpora is a significant advance in archaeometallurgy documentation.

The writing system depicting a hieroglyph multiplex of a zebu tied to a post with a bird perched on top is based on the rebus rendering of the Prakritam glosses: Hieroglyph: पोळ [*pōḷa*], 'zebu' Rebus: magnetite, citizen. baTa 'quail' Rebus: baTha 'furnace'. The messaging on Nausharo pots of a magnetite furnace for metalwork continues on seals and tablets including copper plates as metalwork catalogs.

The Prakritam gloss पोळ [*pōḷa*], 'zebu' as hieroglyph is read rebus: *pōḷa*, 'magnetite, ferrous-ferric oxide';*poliya* 'citizen, gatekeeper of town quarter'.

Data mining techniques & decipherment of over 240 Indus Script inscriptions on copper tablets and metal

Ancient data mining techniques of ca. 3rd millennium BCE are demonstrated by hieroglyphic cipher (picture writing) signified on 250 deciphered metal tablets, tools, gold pendant, gold fillets of Sarasvati Civilization, dated to ca. 3rd millennium BCE. All these inscriptions of the Indus Script Corpora are *catalogus catalogorum* of metalwork -- a veritable data mine for advances in computational and data encryption processes.

A parallel is seen in multi-layered metaphors in Vedic texts, for e.g. on Yupa and caSAla which signify smelting processes using wheat chaff for caburizing/pyrolysis to harden metals. The idea of multi-layering is likely to be a key component in further strengthening encryption systems for data security.

Data security systems devised by ancient artisans of India could help improve present-day data security systems with tight encryptions of data which are crucial for cyber security.

Ras-al-Junayz. Copper seal.

Harappa. Raised script. H94-2198. [After Fig. 4.14 in JM Kenoyer, 1998]. Eight inscribed copper tablets were found at Harappa and all were made with raised script, a technique quite different from the

Rick Willis and Vasant Shinde hypothesise the possibility that copper plate printing (i.e. transfer of pigment) might also have been used with such writing on metal tablets. http://www.ancient-asia-journal.com/articles/10.5334/aa.12317/ "The principles of printing were perhaps known to Indus Valley artisans through the ancient technique of *ajrakh*, printing fabric with woodblock designs. It is possible that the copper plates were created firstly to maintain a permanent record of the standard designs on seals and tablets, and furthermore provide a cheap and portable means to distribute standard designs to craftsmen that carved seals in the Indus Valley region. To test this idea, an experimental trial printing was carried out with the plates by Marco Luccio, an artist and master printer based in Melbourne, Australia. Two printing inks were tested: 1) a water-based ink with ferric oxide as the pigment, and 2) an oil-based ink with carbon black. Prints were first trialled with rag paper, but then were printed on tussah silk cloth and parchment, materials which were likely available in the third millennium BC. Almost no organic materials, such as cloth, leather or wood have survived from Indus civilisation, although impressions of woven fabric have been found on terracotta vessels (Kenoyer, J. M. (1998). *Ancient cities of the Indus Valley Civilization.* Oxford: Oxford University Press. p.159). "

Rick Willis and Vasant Shinde demonstrate the printing on tussah silk from a copper template of the types found in Sarasvati-Sindhu Civilization:

Simple ferric oxide and carbon black inks print on tussah silk taken from an inscribed copper plate. Demonstration in 2012 (After Fig. 13 in Willis & Shinde, opcit.) One possibility is that such prints from inscriptions on metal were taken on birch-bark documents as demonstrated in ancient epigraphical evidence. This lends credence to the manuscript discussed in a thesis. (Zuberbühler, L. (2009). A comparison of a manuscript with the Indus script. Unpublished Bachelor Thesis In: Department of Linguistics and Literary Studies Institute of Linguistics, University of Bern.)
Historical periods also evidence of printing on textiles using such transferance of pigments from templates.

Detail of a classic Gujarati patola of double ikat from the early 19th century. LACMA textile collections.

Example of Gujarat Ajrak printing. Women from the Khatri community whose ancestors migrated from Sindh, Pakistan to Kutch, Gujarat.

Such a khati'spinner' rebus: khati 'wheelwright' is shown on a sculptural frieze in Louvre Museum. Louvre Excerpt *Fragment of the bas-relief called "The spinner"* Susa Neo-Elamite period Bitumen mastic Remarkable condition H 9.3 cm; L 13 cm Sb 2834 Feline legs of stools: kola 'tigr' rebus: kol 'working in iron' kolhe 'smelters'
A. *kulā* ' **winnowing fan**, hood of a snake ';
B. *kul*, °*lā* ' winnowing basket or fan '; Or.*kulā* ' winnowing fan ', °*lāi* ' small do. '; Si. *kulla*, st. *kulu* -- ' winnowing basket or fan '. (CDIAL 3350) Rebus: kol 'working in iron' kolle 'blacksmith' kolimi 'smithy,

forge'. baTa 'six' rebus: bhaTa 'furnace' aya 'fish' rebus: aya, ayas 'iron, metal'. Hieroglyph: गोटा [gōṭā] *m* A roundish stone or pebble. 2 A marble (of stone, *lac*, wood &c.) Rebus 1: खोट (p. 212) [khōṭa] *f* A mass of metal (unwrought or of old metal melted down); an ingot or wedge. Rebus 2: goTa 'laterite (ferrous ore)' [khōṭasāḷa] *a* (खोट & साळ from शाला) Alloyed--a metal. (Marathi) Bshk. *khoṭ* ' embers ', Phal. *khūṭo* ' ashes, burning coal '; (CDIAL 3931)
Indus Script Corpora evidences are presented which document metalwork, mintwork, lapidary/turner/joiner work from over 240 copper/bronze tablets, hieroglyphs painted on a gold pendant, incised gold fillet, raised script on gold dick -- all of which signify writing on metal of Indus Script Corpora.

The catalogs of metalwork, include repeated references to मृदुकृष्णायसम् soft-iron, rendered in Prakritam phonetic forms as: *mẽṛhẽt, meḍ, med* (Indian *sprachbund* and Slavic languages)

A decipherment has been posited based on the functions served by the writing system. The functions are to document metalwork, listing resources, lapidary/turner/joiner techniques and metal casting techniques.

Devices used are to mirror objects/images with joinings or compositions into hieroglyph-multiplexes.

Mirroring of images in the writing system is a device to signify that cire perdue (lost-wax) technique is used for casting metal objects or sculptures.

"The 240 copper tablets from Mohenjo-daro are a rare category of Indus objects, because they show a clear interdependence between the inscription on the obverse and the iconographic animal r human-shaped motif on the reverse. Numerous tablets form sets of identical tablets. In some sets, a single sign appears on the reverse instead of an iconographic motif. By comparing tablets having the same inscription on the obverse side but different reverse sides, it is possible to link these single signs with their corresponding iconographic motifs."(Asko Parpola, 2015, *The roots of Hinduism: the early Aryans and the Indus Civilization*, OUP, pp.282-283) Parpola proceeds to present such a pair of tablets from two sets C6 with 14 examples and B19 with 7 examples:

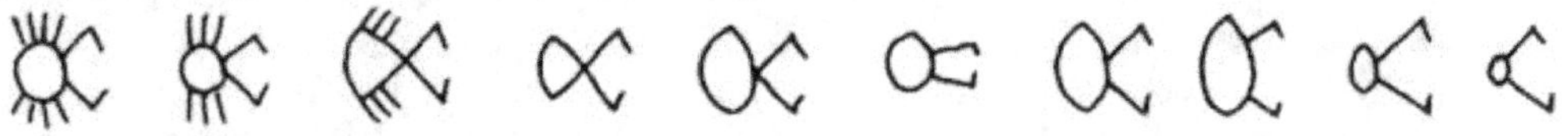

Variants of the 'crab' hieroglyph (sign). After Fig. 21.14 in Asko Paropla, 2015 opcit. After Fig. 13.13 in: **Parpola, Asko, 1994**. Deciphering the Indus script. Cambridge: Cambridge University Press., p. 232

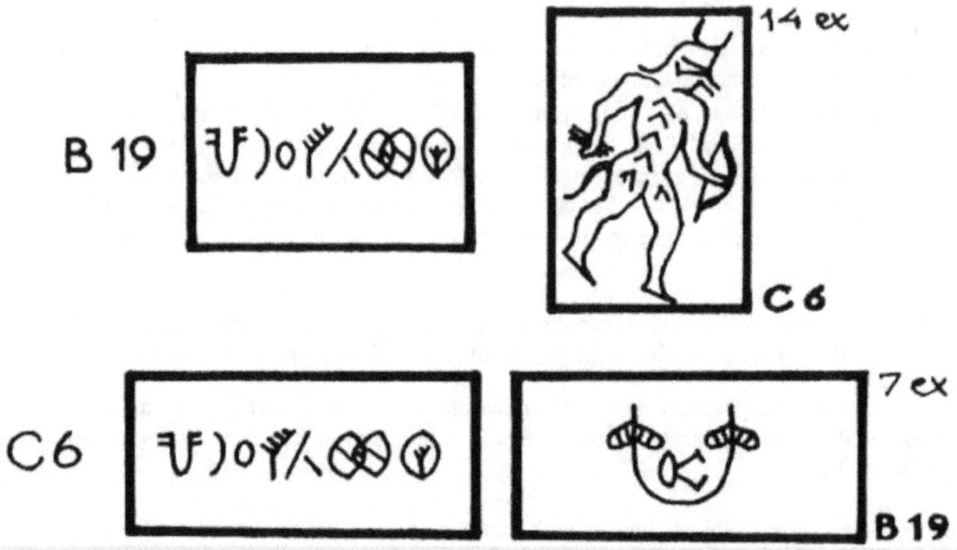

After Fig. 21.15 Parpola, 2015 opcit. A 'pictorial translation' of an Indus sign: the identical inscriptions on the obverse sides correlate the 'horned archer' on the reverse of the type B-19 (there are fourteen identical tablets of this type) and the 'fig+crab' sign on the reverse of the type C-6 (there are seven identical tablets of this type) among the copper tablets from Mohenjo-daro. After **Asko**, **1994**. Deciphering the Indus script. Cambridge: Cambridge University Press.,p. 234, fig. 13.13.

The hieroglyph-multiplex of fig+crab (shown as Sign 124 Parpola concordance) occurs on other Indus Script inscriptions as shown in the following examples, with variant orthographic renderings of the components:

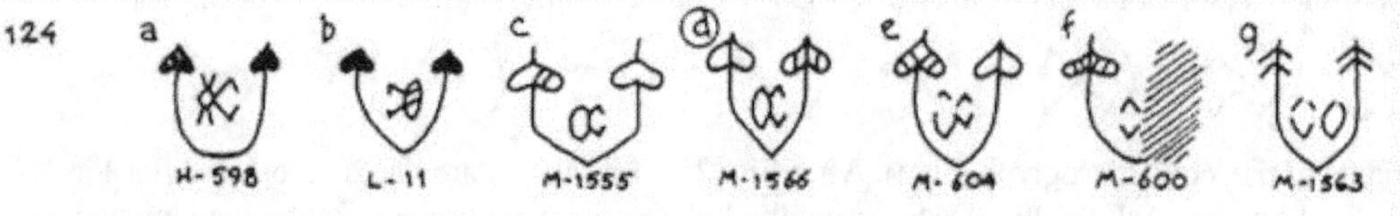

Variants of Sign 124 Parpola concordance. After Fig. 11 in
Parpola http://www.thehindu.com/multimedia/archive/00133/_A_Dravidian_Soluti_133901a.pdf

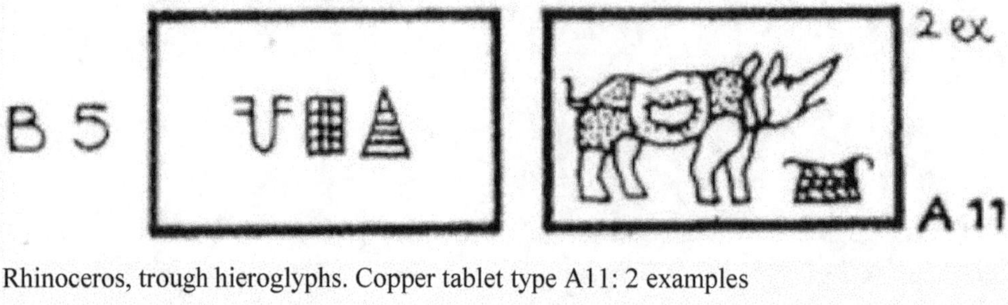

Rhinoceros, trough hieroglyphs. Copper tablet type A11: 2 examples

Asko Parpola, 2008, Copper tablets from Mohenjo-daro and the study of the Indus script, pp. 132-139 in: Eri Olijdam & Richard H Spoor (eds.), *Intercultural relations between south and southwest Asia: Studies in commemoration of ECL During Caspers (1234-1996)*. BAR Interntional Series 1826. Oxford: Archaeopress.

Asko Parpola, 1992, Copper tablets from Mohenjo-daro and the study of the Indus script in: *Proceedings of the second international conference on Moenjodaro,* ed. IM Nadiem, Karachi. Department of Arhaeology

Pande, BM, 'Inscribed copper tablets from Mohenjo-daro: a preliminary analysis' in: D. Agrawal/A. Ghosh eds., Radiocarbon and Indian Arcaheology, Bombay 1973, tablet no. 38.
See: https://www.academia.edu/737300/A_New_Copper_Tablet_from_Mohenjo-daro_DK_11307_ Paul Yule analyses the stratigraphic and archaeological context of this find.

See:

1. Parpola, A. 1992 Copper Tablets from Mohenjo-daro and the study of the Indus Script. In: *Proceedings of the Second International Conference on Moenjodaro*, edited by I. M. Nadiem, pp. Karachi, Department of Archaeology.

2. Pande, B. M. 1979 Inscribed Copper Tablets from Mohenjo daro: A Preliminary Analysis. In Ancient Cities of the Indus, edited by G. L. Possehl, pp. 268-288. New Delhi, Vikas Publishing House PVT LTD.

3. Pande, B. M. 1991 Inscribed Copper Tablets from Mohenjo-daro: Some Observations.Puratattva (21): 25-28.

Brij Mohan Pande had first analysed (1979 and 1991) the importance and significance of copper tablets with unique sets of inscriptions. This contribution is just scintillating and was later (1992) followed up by Asko Parpola identifying 36 groups. The find by HARP recently, of a copper tablet -- and duplicates -- (bas relief with raised script) in Harappa was a stunner, together with 31 and 22 sets of duplicate tablets with identical inscriptions.

Iron pillar at Delhi, India, containing 98% wrought iron

Unique Coiled Copper-alloy Necklace

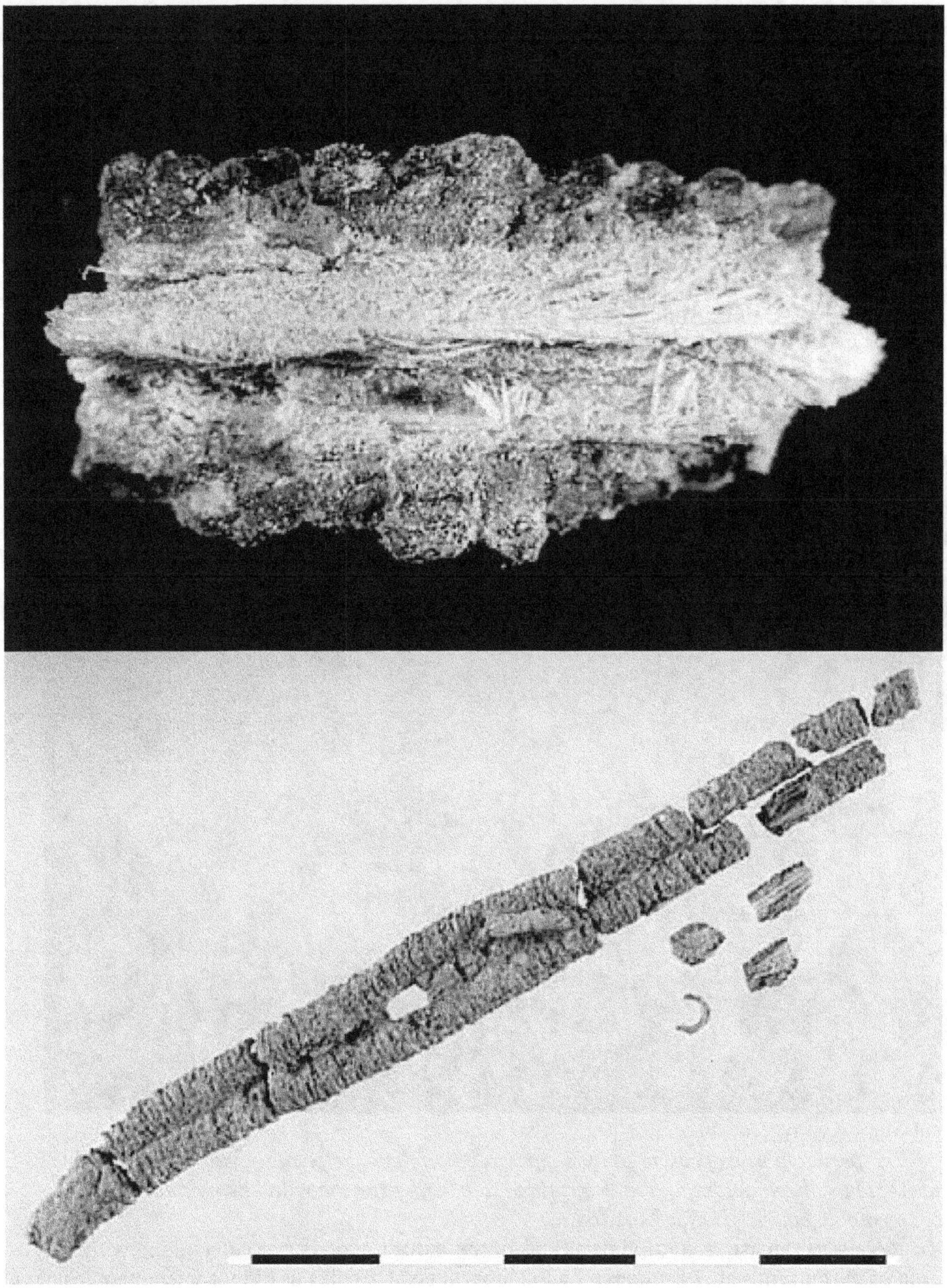

- This unique discovery of a coiled copper-alloy wire necklace (H2000/2242-01) dating to Harappa period 3B (circa 2450-2200 BC) is the earliest evidence for silk in South Asia. It has traces of fibers preserved on the inside. Recent studies indicate that the fibers are from the wild silk moth,

Antheraea mylitta, commonly called "Tussar" silk today (Irene Good, J. M. Kenoyer and R. H. Meadow 2008).
Its discovery demonstrates that silk production may have first been used to make fine threads for necklaces and only later used for weaving fabrics. The copper wire on this necklace is also among the earliest evidence for finely made wire in the Indus Valley. This type of wire is likely to have been made by drawing the wire through a series of graduated perforations.
For two papers on the silk discovery see Ancient Textiles of the Indus Valley Region and New Evidence for Early Silk in the Indus Civilization.
See also Composite Tubular Gold Bead.

https://www.harappa.com/blog/unique-coiled-copper-alloy-necklace

Ancient Textiles of the Indus Valley Region

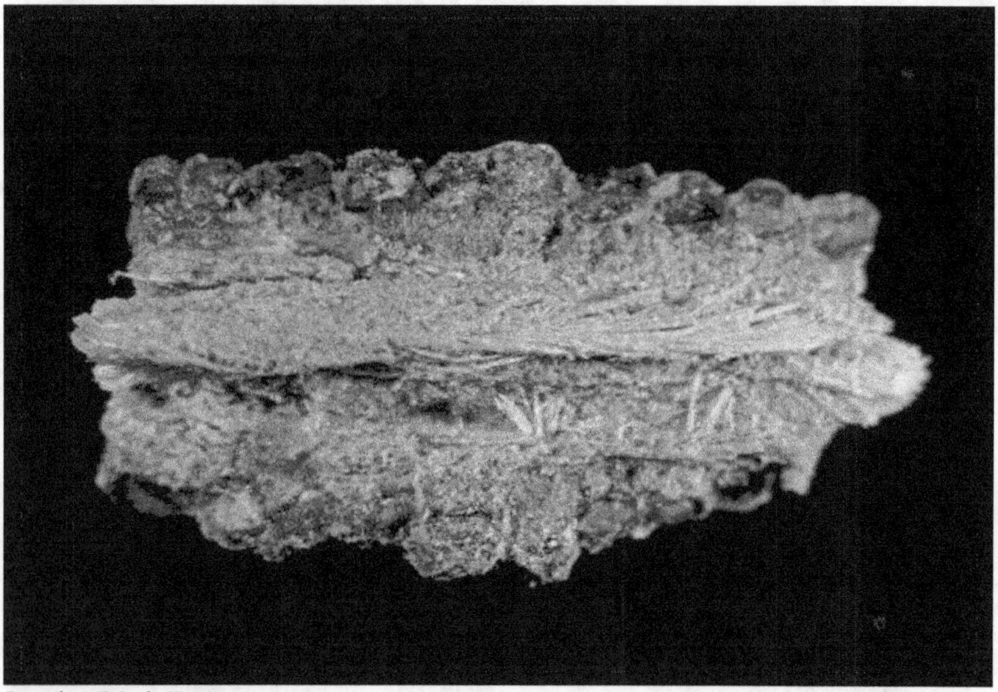

Jonathan Mark Kenoyer
Above: Fiber pseudomorphs preserved by copper salts on the interior of the coiled copper necklace that have been analyzed and determined to be silk from the wild silk moth, Antheraea mylitta, commonly called "Tussar" silk today.
A brief overview of the major cultural traditions of the Indus region is presented along with a discussion of the current state of research on the most ancient textiles used by ancient peoples of this region. The most common fibres used in the Indus Valley appear to have been cotton, but various types of wool and possibly jute or hemp fibres were also used. Most recently, the discovery of silk thread inside copper beads from the site of Harappa indicates that wild silk was also known to the ancient inhabitants of the region, though there is no evidence to suggest that it was woven into fabric. In the following article a brief overview of the major cultural traditions of the Indus

region will be presented along with a discussion of the current state of research on the most ancient textiles used by ancient peoples of this region.

Kenoyer2004 IndusTextilesfinal.pdf

https://www.harappa.com/content/ancient-textiles-indus-valley-region

New Evidence for Early Silk in the Indus Civilization

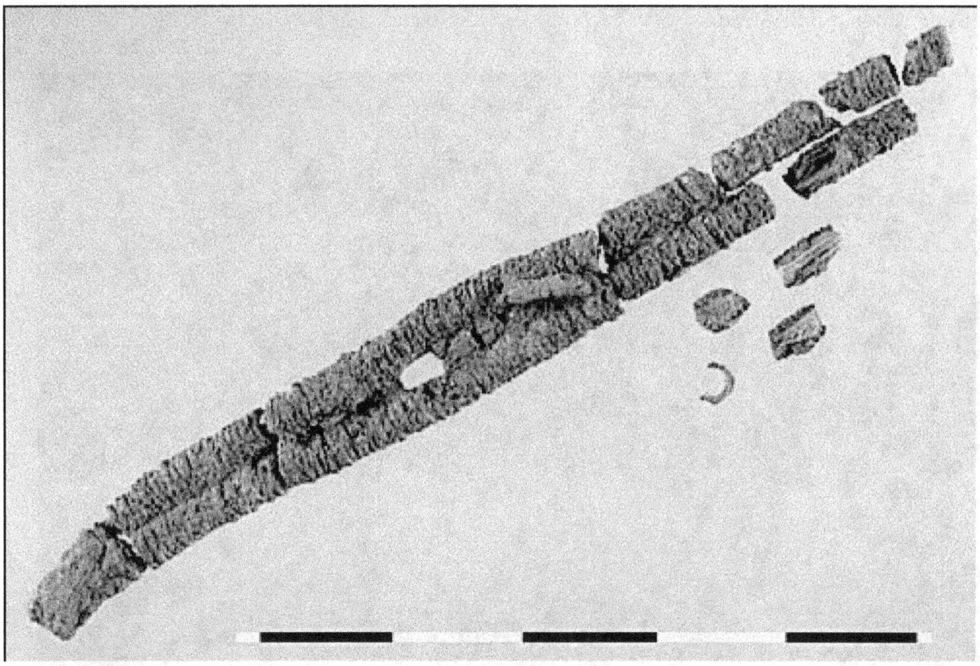

Irene Good

Jonathan Mark Kenoyer

Richard H. Meadow

Above: Coiled copper-alloy wire necklace discovered at Harappa in 2000 with traces of silk fibers preserved on the inside

The Indus Civilization, c. 2800–1900 bc, was one of the great urban riverine civilizations of the ancient world. Current understanding of this cultural phenomenon is that it emerged out of earlier diverse, regional cultures that interacted with each other economically and socially. Settlements of the Indus Civilization spread over a vast area, centred on the Indus and Ghaggar-Hakra river systems of Pakistan and northern India. From the Himalaya and Hindu Kush to the coastal regions of Kutch and Gujarat, westward into Baluchistan and eastward into northwestern India, sites identified with the Indus Civilization are distributed across an area larger than that of Mesopotamia or of Egypt.

Also included is a response to Ji-Huan He:

"We are grateful for the opportunity to hear readers' views concerning our joint paper on archaeological evidence for early silk in the Indus Civilization (Good et al. 2009), and are equally grateful for the opportunity to respond to one particular reader's comments on our findings: Mr Ji-Huan He (2010), who writes 'Silk is of China and China is of Silk'."

Good Kenoyer Meadow 2009 Indus Silk.pdf

Good Kenoyer and Meadow 2011 Silk Response.pdf

https://www.harappa.com/content/new-evidence-early-silk-indus-civilization

Composite Tubular Gold Bead

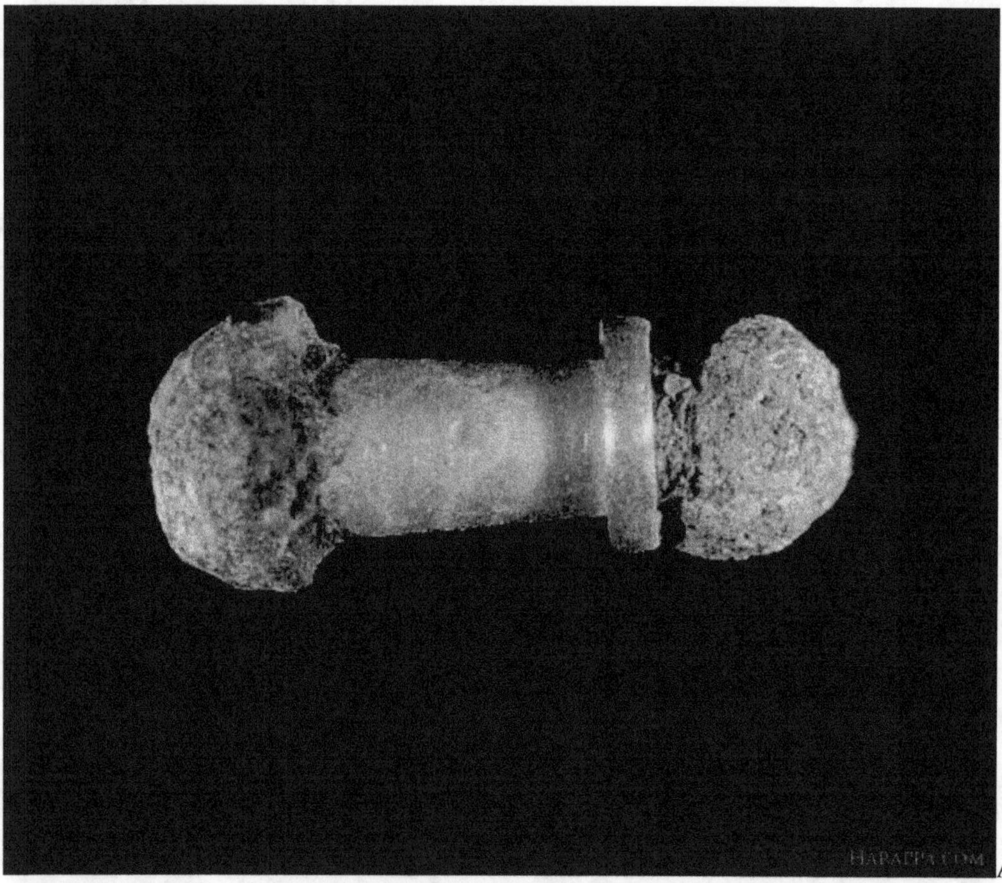

A composite tubular gold bead found on Mound AB at Harappa in 2000. Greenish corroded copper-alloy from an interior wire covers part of the gold bead. "Gold was easily obtained from the sands of the upper Indus river where it is still panned by itinerant miners. Another source of gold was along the Oxus river in northern Afghanistan where a trading colony of the Indus cities has been discovered at Shortughai. Situated far from the Indus Valley itself, this settlement may have been established to obtain gold, copper, tin and lapis lazuli, as well as other exotic goods from Central Asia," (J.M. Kenoyer, Ancient Cities of the Indus Valley Civilization, p. 96).

Art

See: http://www.ancient-asia-journal.com/articles/10.5334/aa.12317/

...
See: http://www.messagetoeagle.com/curious-ancient-copper-plates-and-the-mystery-of-indus-valley/
https://www.academia.edu/8886084/Copper_plates_of_Indus_Script_and_rebus_Meluhha_readings
http://www.ancient-asia-journal.com/articles/10.5334/aa.12317/#aff-1

meḍ(h), *meḍhī* f., *meḍhā* ' post, forked stake '; *meṛh* f. ' rope tying oxen to each other and to post on threshing floor ' (See the rope tied to a tiger on Kalibangan terracotta cake found in a fire-altar; kola 'tiger' rebus: kol 'working in iron'; kohle 'smelters'.)

Binjor octagonal brick as a skambha, pillar **mēthí** m. ' pillar in threshing floor to which oxen are fastened, prop for supporting carriage shafts ' AV., °*thī* -- f. KātyŚr.com., *mēdhī* -- f. Divyāv. 2. **mēṭhī** -- f. PañcavBr.com., *mēḍhī* -- , *mēṭī* -- f. BhP.1. Pa. *mēdhi* -- f. ' post to tie cattle to, pillar, part of a stūpa '; Pk. *mēhi* -- m. ' post on threshing floor ', N. *meh(e)*, *miho*, *miyo*, B. *mei*, Or. *maï* -- *dāṇḍi*, Bi. *mēh*, *mēhā* ' the post ', (SMunger) *mehā* ' the bullock next the post ', Mth. *meh*, *mehā* ' the post ', (SBhagalpur)*mīhā̃* ' the bullock next the post ', (SETirhut) *mēhi bāṭi* ' vessel with a projecting base '.2. Pk. *mēḍhi* -- m. ' post on threshing floor ', *mēḍhaka*<-> ' small stick '; K. *mīr*, *mīrü* f. ' larger hole in ground which serves as a mark in pitching walnuts ' (for semantic relation of ' post -- hole ' see kūpa -- 2); L. *meṛh* f. ' rope tying oxen to each other and to post on threshing floor '; P. *mehṛ* f., *mehaṛ* m. ' oxen on threshing floor, crowd '; OA *meṛha*, *mehra* ' a circular construction, mound '; Or. *meṛhī*,*meri* ' post on threshing floor '; Bi. *mēṛ* ' raised bank between irrigated beds ', (Camparam) *mēṛhā* ' bullock next the post ', Mth. (SETirhut) *mēṛhā* ' id. '; M. *meḍ(h)*, *meḍhī* f., *meḍhā* m. ' post, forked stake '.mēthika -- ; mēthiṣṭhá -- . **mēthika** m. ' 17th or lowest cubit from top of sacrificial post ' lex. [mēthí --]Bi. *mēhiyā* ' the bullock next the post on threshing floor '.**mēthiṣṭhá** ' standing at the post ' TS. [mēthí -- , stha --] Bi. (Patna) *mĕhṭhā* ' post on threshing floor ', (Gaya) *mehṭā*, *mēhṭā* ' the bullock next the post '.(CDIAL 10317 to, 10319)

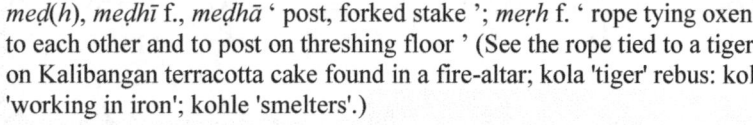

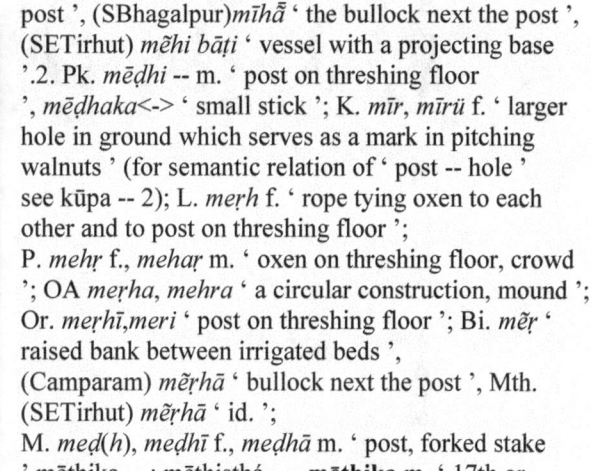

Why are animals shown in pairs?

dula 'pair' (Kashmiri); rebus: dul 'cast metal' (Mu.)

Thus, all the hieroglyphs on the gold disc can be read as Indus writing related to one bronze-age artifact category: metalware catalog entries.

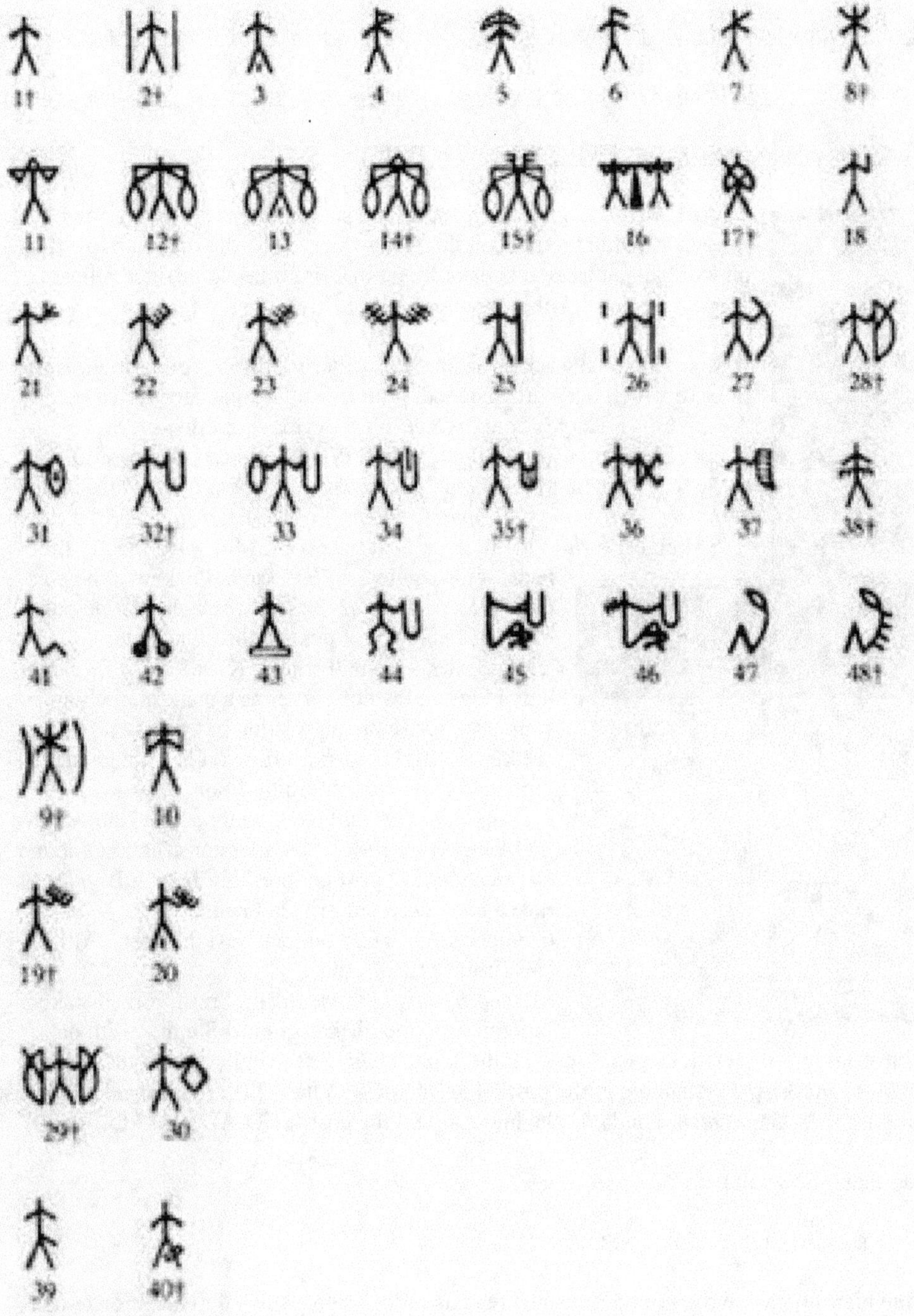
1† 2† 3 4 5 6 7 8†
11 12† 13 14† 15† 16 17† 18
21 22 23 24 25 26 27 28†
31 32† 33 34 35† 36 37 38†
41 42 43 44 45 46 47 48†
9† 10
19† 20
29† 30
39 40†

mēd ‘body’ (Kur.)(DEDR 5099) Rebus: meḍ ‘iron’ (Ho.) खांडा [*khāṇḍā*] *m* A jag, notch, or indentation (as upon the edge of a tool or weapon)(Marathi). Rebus: *kāṇḍa* ‘tools, pots and pans and metal-ware’ (Marathi) Thus, *meḍ kāṇḍa 'iron implements'.*

Ligature: Stool or plank/seat

Sign 43: Kur. *kaṇḍō* a stool. Malt. *kanḍo* stool, seat. (DEDR 1179) Rebus: kaṇḍ 'fire-altar' (Santali) *kāṇḍa* ‘tools, pots and pans and metal-ware’ (Marathi) + *kāṭi* 'body stature; Rebus: fireplace trench. Thus, furnace for metals in mint. Thus, fire-altar metalware furnace.

Alternative: PLUS mēd ‘body’ (Kur.)(DEDR 5099) Rebus: meḍ ‘iron’ (Ho.)
Thus, *meḍ kāṇḍa 'iron implements'.*

Ligature: crab, claws

Sign 36: : mēd ‘body’ (Kur.)(DEDR 5099); meḍ ‘iron’ (Ho.) Thus,

meḍ dhātu 'iron ore'

Alternative Sign 36: *kāṭi* 'body stature; Rebus: fireplace trench. Thus, furnace for metals in mint + *kamaḍha* ‘crab’ Rebus: *kammaṭa* ‘mint, coiner’. *ḍato* = claws of crab (Santali) Rebus: *dhātu* ‘mineral ore’. Thus mineral ore mint, coiner.

kamaḍha ‘archer, bow’ Rebus: *kammaṭa* ‘mint, coiner’. dula 'two' Rebu: dul 'cast metal'. Thus metal castings mint. + kāṭi 'body stature; Rebus: fireplace trench. Thus, furnace for metal castings in mint. Alternative reading could be: *mēd* ‘body’ (Kur.) Rebus: *meḍ* ‘iron’ (Ho.) PLUS *dul* 'cast metal' PLUS *kammaṭa* 'mint' Thus, together, cast iron mint.
Similarly, in all the following hieroglyph-multiplexes, the 'body' hieroglyph can be deciphere and explained:as

mēd ‘body’ (Kur.) Rebus: *meḍ* ‘iron’ (Ho.)

Sign 28: Archer. Ligature one bow-and-arrow hieroglyph

kamaḍha ‘archer, bow’ Rebus: *kammaṭa* ‘mint, coiner’. + *kāṭi* 'body stature; Rebus: fireplace trench. Thus, furnace for metals in mint.  Ligature hieroglyph: 'lid of pot'

aḍaren

'lid of pot' Rebus: aduru 'unsmelted, native metal' + kāṭi 'body stature; Rebus: fireplace trench. Thus furnace for aduru, unsmelted, native metal.Ligatures: water-carrier + lid of pot

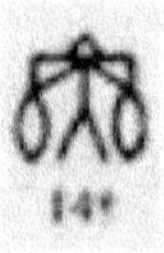
Sign 14: *kuṭi* 'water-carrier' Rebus*: kuṭhi* 'smelter/furnace'+

kāṭi 'body stature; Rebus: fireplace trench +
aḍaren'lid of pot' Rebus: aduru 'unsmelted, native metal' + kāṭi 'body stature; Rebus: fireplace trench. Thus furnace for aduru, unsmelted, native metal. Thus, furnace-smelter for unsmelted, native metal.

Ligature: water-carrier

Sign 12: *kuṭi* 'water-carrier' Rebus*: kuṭhi* 'smelter/furnace'+ kāṭi 'body stature; Rebus: fireplace trench. Thus, smelter furnace.

Ligatures: water-carrier + notch
Sign 13: *kuṭi* 'water-carrier' Rebus*: kuṭhi* 'smelter/furnace'+ kāṭi 'body stature; Rebus: fireplace trench. + खांडा [*khāṇḍā*] *m* A jag, notch, or indentation (as upon the edge of a tool or weapon)(Marathi). Rebus: *kāṇḍa* 'tools, pots and pans and metal-ware' (Marathi) + kāṭi 'body stature; Rebus: fireplace trench. + kāṭi 'body =stature; Rebus: fireplace trench. Thus, smelter-furnace metalware.

Ligatures: water-carrier (as in Sign 12) + rim of jar

Ligature: rim of jar Rebus: *kanda kanka* 'fire-trench account, *karṇi* supercargo' *Tu.* kandůka, kandaka ditch, trench. *Te.* kandakamu id. *Konḍa* kanda trench made as a fireplace during weddings. *Pe.*kanda fire trench. *Kui* kanda small trench for fireplace. *Malt.* kandri a pit. (DEDR 1214).

'rim-of-jar' hieroglyph Rebus: *kanka* (Santali) karṇika 'scribe'(Sanskrit) *kuṭi* 'water-carrier' Rebus*: kuṭhi* 'smelter/furnace'.+*kāṭi*'body stature; Rebus: fireplace trench. Thus, smelter furnace account, supercargo.

Ligature 'two spoked wheels'

Spokes-of-wheel, nave-of-wheel *āra* 'spokes' Rebus: *āra 'brass'*. cf. erka = ekke (Tbh. of arka) aka (Tbh. of arka) copper (metal); crystal (Kannada) Glyph: *eraka*'nave of wheel' Rebus: eraka 'copper'; cf. erka = ekke (Tbh. of arka) aka (Tbh. of arka) copper (metal); crystal (Kannada) *dula* 'two' Rebus: *dul* 'cast metal'. Thus, moltencast copper castings ++ kāṭi 'body stature; Rebus: fireplace trench. Thus, furnace for copper metal castings.

Ligature hieroglyph 'corner'

kanac 'corner' Rebus: *kañcu* 'bronze' + *kāṭi* 'body stature; Rebus: fireplace trench. Thus, furnace for bronze castings.

Ligatures: corner + notch

Sign 31: *kana, kanac* = corner (Santali); Rebus: *kañcu* = bronze (Telugu) PLUS
खांडा [*khāṇḍā*] *m* A jag, notch, or indentation (as upon the edge of a tool or weapon). Rebus: *kāṇḍa* 'tools, pots and pans and metal-ware' Thus, bronze metalware. + *kāṭi*'body stature; Rebus: fireplace trench. Thus, furnace bronze metalware castings.

Ligature hieroglyph: 'stick' or 'one'

Sign1 Hieroglyph: काठी [kāṭhī] *f* (काष्ट S) (or शरीराची काठी) The frame or structure of the body: also (viewed by some as arising from the preceding sense, Measuring rod) stature (Marathi)
B. *kāṭhā* ' measure of length '(CDIAL 3120).
H. *kāṭhī 'wood'* f. G. *kāṭh* n. ' wood ', °*ṭhī* f. ' stick, measure of 5 cubits '(CDIAL 3120). + kāṭi 'body stature; Rebus: fireplace trench.The 'stick' hieroglyph is a phonetic reinforcement of 'body stature' hieroglyph. Alternatively, koḍ 'one' Rebus: koḍ 'workshop'+ kāṭi 'body stature; Rebus: fireplace trench.. Thus, workplace of furnace fire-trench.
Rebus: G. *kāṭɔrɔ* m. ' dross left in the furnace after smelting iron ore '.(CDIAL 2646)
Rebus: kāṭi , *n.* < U. *ghāṭī*. 1. Trench of a fort; அகழி. 2. A fireplace in the form of a long ditch; கோட்டையடுப்பு காடியடுப்பு kāṭi-y-aṭuppu , *n.* < காடி&sup6; +. A fireplace in the form of a long ditch used for cooking on a large scale; கோட்டையடுப்பு.
Rebus: S.kcch. *kāṭhī* f. ' wood 'Pa. Pk. *kaṭṭha* -- n. ' wood '(CDIAL 3120).
Sign 37 Hieroglyph: WPah.kṭg. *ṭōṭ* ' mouth '.WPah.kṭg. *thótti* f., *thótthər* m. ' snout, mouth ', A. *ṭhõt*(phonet. *thõt*) (CDIAL 5853).
Rebus:

tutthá n. (m. lex.), *tutthaka* -- n. ' blue vitriol (used as an eye ointment) ' Suśr., *tūtaka* -- lex. 2. *thōttha -- 4. 3. *tūtta -- . 4. *tōtta -- 2. [Prob. ← Drav. T. Burrow BSOAS xii 381; cf. *dhūrta* -- 2 n. ' iron filings ' lex.]1. N. *tutho* ' blue vitriol or sulphate of copper ', B. *tuth*.2. K. *thŏth*, dat. °*thas* m., P. *thothā* m.3. S.*tūtio* m., A. *tutiyā*, B. *tũte*, Or. *tutiā*, H. *tūtā*, *tūtiyā* m., M. *tutiyā* m. 4. M. *totā* m.(CDIAL 5855) *Ka.* tukku rust of iron; tutta, tuttu, tutte blue vitriol. *Tu.* tukků rust; mair(ů)suttu, (*Eng.-Tu. Dict.*) mairůtuttu blue vitriol. *Te.* t(r)uppu rust; (*SAN*) trukku id., verdigris. / Cf. Skt. tuttha- blue vitriol (DEDR 3343).
Sign 2: dula 'pair' Rebus: dul 'cast metal' + kāṭi 'body stature; Rebus: fireplace trench. Thus furnace for metal casting. koḍ 'one' Rebus: koḍ 'workshop'. Thus, furnace workshop.

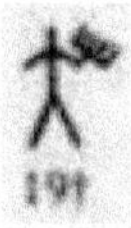
Ligature: harrow

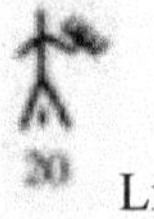
Ligatures: harrow + notch (between legs) Allographs: Signs 18, 39 

Sign 18: खांडा [*khāṇḍā*] *m* A jag, notch, or indentation (as upon the edge of a tool or weapon)(Marathi). Rebus: *kāṇḍa* 'tools, pots and pans and metal-ware' (Marathi) + kāṭi 'body stature; Rebus: fireplace trench. Thus, furnace for metalware castings of unsmelted, native metal.

Ligature component in hieroglyph 'harrow'

Sign 19: *aḍar* 'harrow'; rebus: *aduru* 'native unsmelted metal' (Kannada) + kāṭi 'body stature; Rebus: fireplace trench. Thus, furnace for native metal.

Sign 20: खांडा [*khāṇḍā*] *m* A jag, notch, or indentation (as upon the edge of a tool or weapon)(Marathi). Rebus: *kāṇḍa* 'tools, pots and pans and metal-ware' (Marathi) + kāṭi 'body stature; Rebus: fireplace trench. Thus, furnace for metalware castings of unsmelted, native metal.

 Ligature hieroglyph 'currycomb'

kSign 38: *hareḍo* = a currycomb (Gujarati) खरारा [*kharārā*] *m* (H) A currycomb. 2 Currying a horse. (Marathi) Rebus: करडा [*karaḍā*] Hard from alloy--iron, silver &c. (Marathi) *kharādī* ' turner' (Gujarati) kāṭi 'body stature; Rebus: fireplace trench. Thus, fireplace for hard alloy metal.

Ligature hieroglyph 'foot, anklet'

Sign 40: toṭi bracelet (Tamil)(DEDR 3682). Jaina Skt. (*IL* 20.193) toḍaka- an anklet (Sanskrit) *khuṭo* ' leg, foot ', °ṭī ' goat's leg ' Rebus: *khōṭā* 'alloy' (Marathi) Rebus: tuttha 'copper sulphate' + kāṭi 'body stature; Rebus: fireplace trench. Thus smelted copper sulphate alloy.

Ligature hieroglyph 'rimless pot + ladle'

Sign 34:
muka ‘ladle’ (Tamil)(DEDR 4887) Rebus: *mũh* ‘ingot’ (Santali) *baṭa* = a kind of iron (G.) *baṭa* = rimless pot (Kannada) Thus, iron ingot.+ kāṭi 'body stature; Rebus: fireplace trench. Thus, iron ingot furnace.

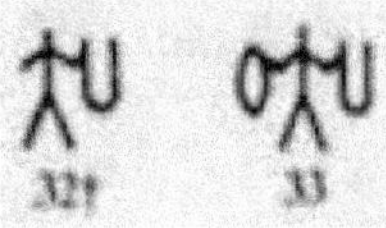
Ligatures: rimless pot + hollow or ingot

Sign 32: *baṭa* = rimless pot (Kannada) Rebus: *baṭa* = a kind of iron (G.)+ *kāṭi* 'body stature; Rebus: fireplace trench. Thus, iron furnace
Sign 33: As for Sign 32 + dulo 'hole' Rebus: dul 'cast metal' Thus, furnace iron castings.

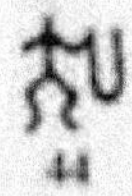
Ligatures: rimless pot + dance step

Sign 44: meṭ sole of foot, footstep, footprint (Ko.); meṭṭu step, stair, treading, slipper (Te.)(DEDR 1557). Rebus: *meḍ* ‘iron’(Munda); मेढ meḍh‘merchant’s helper’(Pkt.) *meḍ* iron (Ho.) *meṛed-bica* = iron stone ore, in contrast to bali-bica, iron sand ore (Munda) + *kāṭi* 'body stature; Rebus: fireplace trench. Thus, iron furnace.

Ligatures: rimless pot + wire mesh

Sign 35: *baṭa* = rimless pot (Kannada) Rebus: *baṭa* = a kind of iron (G.)+ *kāṭi* 'body stature; Rebus: fireplace trench + *akho* m. ‘mesh of a net’ Rebus: L. P. *akkhā* m. ‘ one end of a bag or sack thrown over a beast of burden ’; Or. *akhā* ‘ gunny bag ’; Bi. *ākhā*, *ā̃khā* ‘ grain bag carried by pack animal ’; H. *ākhā* m. ‘ one of a pair of grain bags used as panniers ’; M. *ā̃khā* m. ‘ netting in which coco -- nuts, &c., are carried ’, *ā̆khẽ* n. ‘ half a bullock -- load ’ (CDIAL 17) అంకెము [aṅkemu] *ankemu*. [Telugu] n. One pack or pannier, being half a bullock load. Thus, a consignment or packload of furnace iron castings.

Ligature: warrior + *ficus religiosa*

Sign 17: *loa* ‘*ficus religiosa*’ Rebus: *lo* ‘iron’ (Sanskrit) PLUS unique ligatures: लोखंड [lōkhaṇḍa] *n* (लोह S) Iron. लोखंडाचे चणे खावविणें or चारणें To oppress grievously.लोखंडकाम [lōkhaṇḍakāma] *n* Iron work; that portion (of a building, machine &c.) which consists of iron. 2 The business of an ironsmith.लोखंडी [lōkhaṇḍī] *a* (लोखंड) Composed of iron; relating to iron. (Marathi)*bhaṭa* ‘warrior’ (Sanskrit) Rebus: *baṭa* a kind of iron (Gujarati). Rebus: *bhaṭa* ‘furnace’ (Santali) Thus, together, th ligatured hieroglyph reads rebus: *loa bhaṭa* ‘iron furnace’

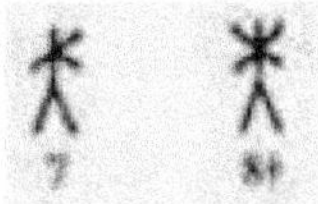
Ligature 'armed body stature' or 'horned body stature'

Sign 8:*bhaṭa* 'warrior' (Sanskrit) Rebus: *baṭa* a kind of iron (Gujarati). Rebus: *bhaṭa* 'furnace' (Santali) + kāṭi 'body stature; Rebus: fireplace trench. Thus, furnace for a kind of iron.

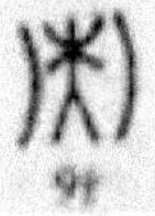

Ligatures: two curved lines

Sign 9: Read rebus as for Sign 8 PLUS Ligature hieroglyphs of two curved lines
dula 'pair' Rebus: dul 'cast metal + ()kuṭila 'bent' CDIAL 3230 kuṭi— in cmpd. 'curve', *kuṭika*— 'bent' MBh. Rebus: *kuṭila, katthīl* = bronze (8 parts copper and 2 parts tin) [cf. *āra-kūṭa*, 'brass' (Sanskrit) +*bhaṭa* 'warrior' (Sanskrit) Rebus: *baṭa* a kind of iron (Gujarati). Rebus: *bhaṭa* 'furnace' (Santali) + kāṭi 'body stature; Rebus: fireplace trench. Thus, furnace bronze castings.

Ligature hieroglyph: 'roof' Allograph: Sign 10

Sign 5: *mūdh* ' ridge of roof ' (Assamese)(CDIAL 10247) Rebus: *mund* 'iron' + *kāṭi* 'body stature;

Rebus:fireplace trench. Thus, furnace for iron Ligature hieroglyph 'flag'

Sign 4: *koḍi* 'flag' (Ta.)(DEDR 2049). Rebus 1: *koḍ* 'workshop' (Kuwi) Rebus 2: *khŏḍ* m. 'pit', *khŏḍü* f. 'small pit' (Kashmiri. CDIAL 3947). + kāṭi 'body stature; Rebus: fireplace trench. Thus, furnace workshop.

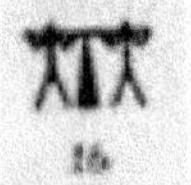

Sign 16:dula 'two' Rebus: dul 'cast metal' + + kāṭi 'body stature; Rebus: fireplace trench +*koḍi* 'summit of mountain' (Tamil). Thus, furnace for metal casting. *mēḍu* height, rising ground, hillock (Kannada) Rebus: *mẽṛhẽt, meḍ* 'iron' (Munda.Ho.) Thus, iron metal casting. The ligaured hieroglyph of Sign 11 is a ligature with two mountain peaks. Hence *dul meḍ* 'iron casting'

Ligature hieroglyph 'paddy plant' or 'sprout'

kolmo 'paddy plant' Rebus: *kolami* 'smithy, forge' Vikalpa: *mogge* 'sprout, bud'
Rebus: *mũh* 'ingot' (Santali) dolu 'plant of shoot height' Rebus: dul 'cast metal' + kāṭi 'body stature; Rebus: fireplace trench. Thus furnace smithy or ingot furnace.

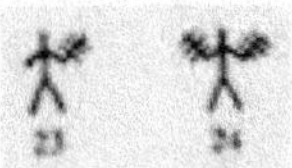

Ligature hieroglyph: 'three short strokes on a slanted stroke'

Signs 23, 24: dula 'two' Rebus: dul 'cast metal' *dhāḷ* 'a slope'; 'inclination of a plane' (G.); *ḍhāḷiyum* = adj. sloping, inclining (G.) Rebus: *ḍhālako* = a large metal ingot (G.) *ḍhālakī* = a metal heated and poured into a mould; a solid piece of metal; an ingot (Gujarati) + kāṭi 'body stature; Rebus: fireplace trench' Thus ingot furnace for castings. Three short strokes: kolom 'three' Rebus: kolami 'smithy, forge'. Thus it is a place where artisans work with furnace for metal castings.

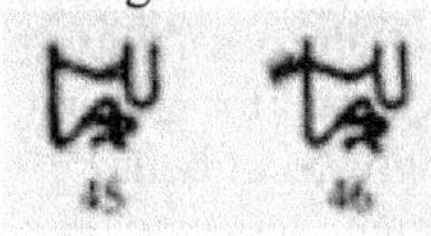
Ligatures: Worshipper + rimless pot + scarf (on pigtail)

Signs 45, 46: A variant of 'adorant' hieroglyph sign is shown with a 'rimless, broad-mouthed pot' which is *baṭa* read rebus:*bhaṭa* 'furnace'. If the 'pot' ligature is a phonetic determinant, the gloss for the 'adorant' is *bhaṭa* 'worshipper'. If the 'kneeling' posture is the key hieroglyphic representation, the gloss is *eragu* 'bow' Rebus: *erako* 'moltencast copper'. Thus moltencast copper furnace. + *dhaṭu* m. (also dhaṭhu) m. 'scarf' (Western Pahari) (CDIAL 6707) Rebus: *dhatu* 'minerals' (Santali). Thus Sign 46 read rebus: moltencast copper minerals furnace.

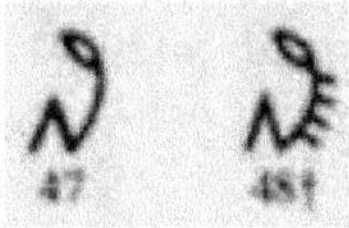
Hieroglyphs: backbone + four short strokes

Signs 47, 48: *baraḍo* = spine; backbone (Tulu) Rebus: *baran, bharat* 'mixed alloys' (5 copper, 4 zinc and 1 tin) (Punjabi) +
gaṇḍa 'four' Rebus: *kaṇḍ* 'fire-altar'. Thus, Sign 48 reads rebus: *bharat kaṇḍ* 'fire-altar', furnace for mixed alloy called *bharat*(copper, zinc, tin alloy),

'Backbone, spine' hieroglyph: *baraḍo* = spine; backbone; the back; baraḍo thābaḍavo = lit. to strike on the backbone or back; hence, to encourage; baraḍo bhāre thato = lit. to have a painful backbone, i.e. to do something which will call for a severe beating (Gujarati)bārṇe, bāraṇe = an offering of food to a demon; a meal after fasting, a breakfast (Tulu) barada, barda, birada = a vow (Gujarati)bharaḍo a devotee of S'iva; a man of the bharaḍā caste in the bra_hman.as (Gujarati) baraṛ = name of a caste of jat- around Bhaṭiṇḍa; bararaṇḍā melā = a special fair held in spring (Punjabi) bharāḍ = a religious service or entertainment performed by a bharāḍi_; consisting of singing the praises of some idol or god with playing on the d.aur (drum) and dancing; an order of aṭharā akhād.e = 18 gosāyi_ group; bharād. and bhāratī are two of the 18 orders of gosāyi_ (Marathi).

Decoding 'ram' glyph of Indus script, meḍh: rebus: 'helper of merchant'

An aspect of metalwork of the Bronze Age which should receive detailed attention of archaeo-metallurgical researchers is the competence demonstrated by artisans of Sarasvati-Sindhu civilization to inscribe on metal.

Such evidences of inscriptions on metal presented in this note, reinforce the validity of decipherment of almost the entire set of 7000 inscriptions on Indus Script Corpora as *catalogus catalogorum* of metalwork.

Such inscriptions on metal are not merely those found on copper plates but also on metal objects themselves such as silver seals, axes, chisels, knives, spearheads, daggers, tin ingots, copper alloy ingots, celts.

'Illiteracy' experts (yet assuming expertise in judging the functions of Indus Script) should recognize the metallurgical competence of artisans who inscribed 'illiterate' hieroglyphs on metal. The experts can also keep their prize money for themselves after going through 1) the possibility demonstrated by Rick willis that copper plates with inscriptions could have been used for printing; 2) short size of Indus Script inscriptions may be due to words signified by hieroglyphs of both pictorial motifs and signs (NOT syllables or alphabets as assumed by the prize compilers who seek 50-sign inscriptions). Such printing may have duplicated segments of the *catalogus catalogorum* as announcements of metalsmiths' competence in alloying metals and metalcastings. (It is a cop-out to pronounce Rick Willis' finds as forgery, without proper investigation). (For a thread on the topic of illiteracy, see: https://groups.yahoo.com/neo/groups/Indo-Eurasian_research/conversations/messages/17026) Since the experts are capable of reading hieroglyphs on the figures presented in this note, the rebus renderings of decipherment are not repeated. They can be read from the trilogy of a serial decipherer S. Kalyanaraman, Sarasvati Research Center, Herndon: 1.*Indus Script Cipher -- Hieroglyhphs of Indian Linguistic Area*(2010) 2. *Indus Script: Meluhha metalwork hieroglyphs* (2014) 3. *Philosophy of Symbolic forms in Meluhha cipher* (2014).

HARP excavations discovered 8 unique cast copper tablets with inscriptions using raised script which is presented juxtaposed to a copper seal of Ral-al-Junayz with Indus Script hieroglyphs:

Ras-al-Junayz. Copper seal.

Harappa. Raised script. H94-2198. [After Fig. 4.14 in JM Kenoyer, 1998]. Eight inscribed copper tablets were found at Harappa and all were made with raised script, a technique quite different from the

The inscription on the cast copper tablet is read as: dul 'cast metal', khoT 'alloy ingot', bharata, 'alloy of coper, pewter, tin'.Hieroglyphs:dula 'pair' Rebus: dul 'cast metal'; goT 'seed' Rebus: khoT 'alloy ingot'. खोट (p. 212) [khōṭa] *f* A mass of metal (unwrought or of old metal melted down); an ingot or wedge. (Marathi) baraDo 'spine' Rebus: भरत (p. 603) [bharata] *n* A factitious metal compounded of copper, pewter, tin &c. (Marathi) karava 'pot' Rebus: kharva 'wealth'; karba 'iron'; karNaka 'rim of jar' Rebus: karNI 'supercargo'; karnIka 'scribe'.

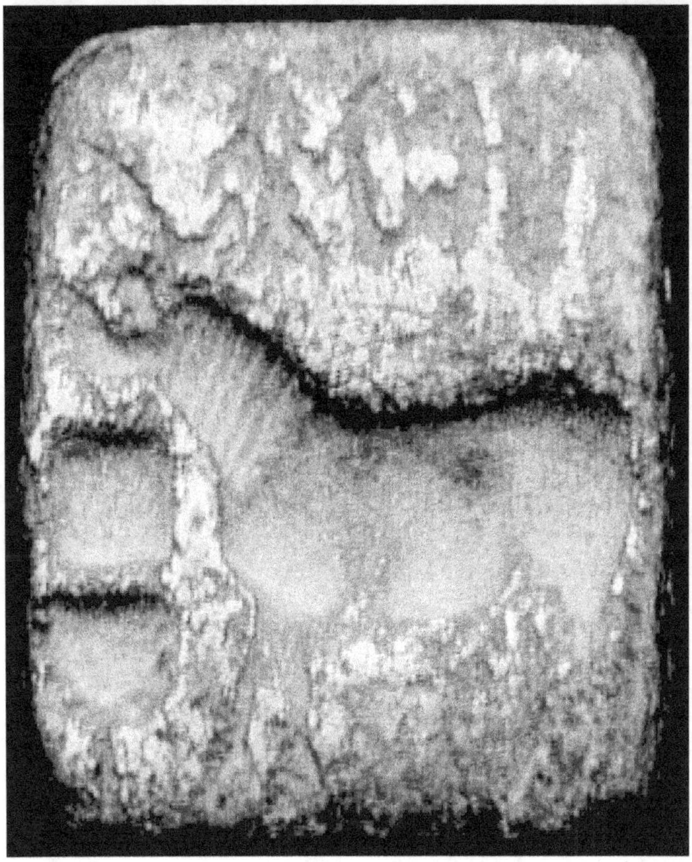

Mohenjo-daro Siver seal. m1199 Mackay 1938, vol. 2, Pl. XC,1; XCVI, 520

Slide 209. harappa.com Inscribed lead celt or ingot fragment from the Trench 54 area (H2000-4481/2174-321). The object was apparently chiseled to reduce its size. Lead may have been used as an alloy with copper, for making pigments, or as medicine.

Altyn-depe. Silver seal. Pictograph of ligatured animal with three heads. Hieroglyph: sangaDa 'joined animals' (Marathi) Rebus: sangāṭh संगाठ् । सामग्री m. (sg. dat. sangāṭas संगाटस्), a collection (of implements, tools, materials, for any object), apparatus. Given examples of similar joined animals, it may be surmised that the three animal hieroglyphs are: ranku 'antelope' Rebus: ranku 'tin'; krammara 'look backwards' Rebus: kamar 'smith'; barad 'ox' Rebus: bharat 'alloy of copper, pewter, tin'; kondh 'one-horned young bull' Rebus: kondh 'turner'.

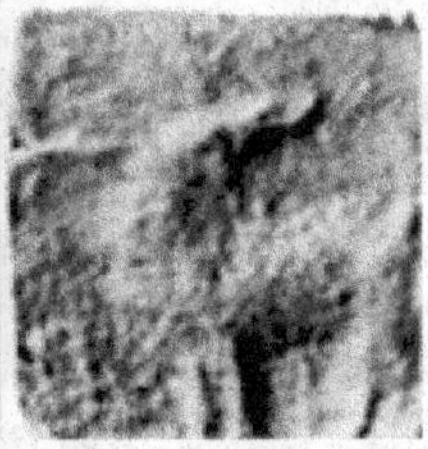

m0438, m1449, m1452, m1486, m1493, m1498, m1501; m0582 (123 copper tablets)

One lead celt with a hazy inscription has also been found in Harappa (HARP project).

Mohenjo-daro. Copper seal. National Museum, Nev Delhi. [Source Page 18, Fig. 8A in: Deo Prakash Sharma, 2000 *Harappan seals, sealings and copper tablets*, Delhi, National

A painted inscription occurs on a Mohenjo-daro gold pendant:

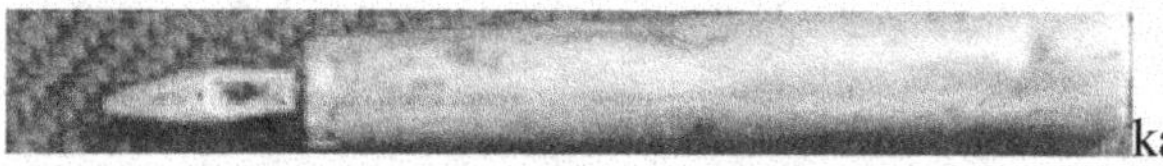

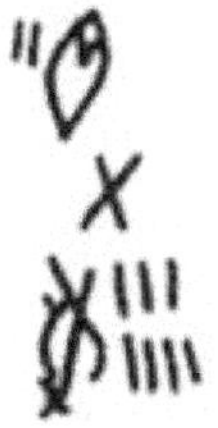

kanac 'corner' Rebus: kancu 'bronze'; sal 'splinter' Rebus: sal 'workshop'; dhatu 'cross road' Rebus: dhatu 'mineral'; gaNDa 'four' Rebus: khanda 'implements'; kolmo 'three' Rebus: kolami 'smithy, forge'; aya 'fish' Rebus: aya 'iron'(Gujarati) ayas 'metal' (Rigveda) Gold pendant with Indus script inscription. The pendant is needle-like with cylindrical body. It is made from a hollow cylinder with soldered ends and perforated joint. Museum No. MM 1374.50.271; Marshall 1931: 521, pl. CLI, B3 (After Fig. 4.17 a,b in: JM Kenoyer, 1998, p. 196).
Copper tablet (H2000-4498/9889-01) with raised script found in Trench 43
Source:http://www.harappa.com/indus4/351.html

"For example, the characteristic square steatite seals with animal motifs and short inscriptions

begins in late Period 2 as noted above, is found in 3A and continues into Period 3C, but the carving style for both the animal motifs, and the inscriptions shows stylistic changes. The greatest variation and widespread use of such seals appears to be during Period 3B. Small rectangular inscribed tablets made from steatite begin to appear at the beginning of Period 3B and by the end of 3B there is a wide variety of tiny tablets in many different shapes and materials. They were made of fired steatite or of molded terracotta or faience. Some of the steatite tablets were decorated with red pigment and the faience tablets were covered with a thick blue-green glaze. These various forms of inscribed tablets continued on into Period 3C where we also find evidence for copper tablets all bearing the same raised inscription."
http://www.harappa.com/indus4/print.html Kenoyer and Meadow date the Period 3 between c.600 BCE – 1900 BCE.(Period 3A c.2600BCE -2450BCE; Period 3B c.2450BCE – c. 2200BCEl Period 3C c. 2200BCE -1900BCE) This particular inscription on the tablet is one of the most frequently occurring texts in Indus Script corpora, in particular the hieroglyphs of 'back-hone + rim-of-jar'.

A list of Inscribed metal tools

Broken axe, Chanhu-daro (C-40) inscribed on both sides.
Ingot. Chanhu-daro (C-39)
Chisel. Kalibangan (K-121). Wt. 210 g.
Parallels broken chisel (tang) Mohenjo-daro (DK-7856). Wt. 165/343 g/
Axe. Kaibangan (K-122). Wt. 476 g.
Parallels axe Mohenjo-daro (DK-7835). Wt. 1910.030 g.
Knife. DK-7800
Spearhead DK-7857
Axe. DK-7855. Wt. 262 g.

(Note: Of the five metal objects from Mohenjo-daro, four were found 'at the low level 24.4 ft.[and one (copper knife) was found 18.4 ft. below datum. (Mackay 1938: 454; Vol. II. Pl. CXXVI #2.3 and 5, Pl. CXXVII #1, Pl. CXXXI; Vol. II. Pl. CXXXIII#1).Mackay 1938: Vol. 1, p. 348, Vol. 2, Pl. XC,1; XCVI, 520.
see: Pettersson, JS, 1999, Indian Journal of Historyh of Science, 34(2): 89-108http://www.new.dli.ernet.in/rawdataupload/upload/insa/INSA_2/20005a61_89.pdf

Chanhu-daro Pl. LXXIV and Mohenjo-daro: copper and bronze tools and utensils (an inscriptions line mirrored on a zebu seal)

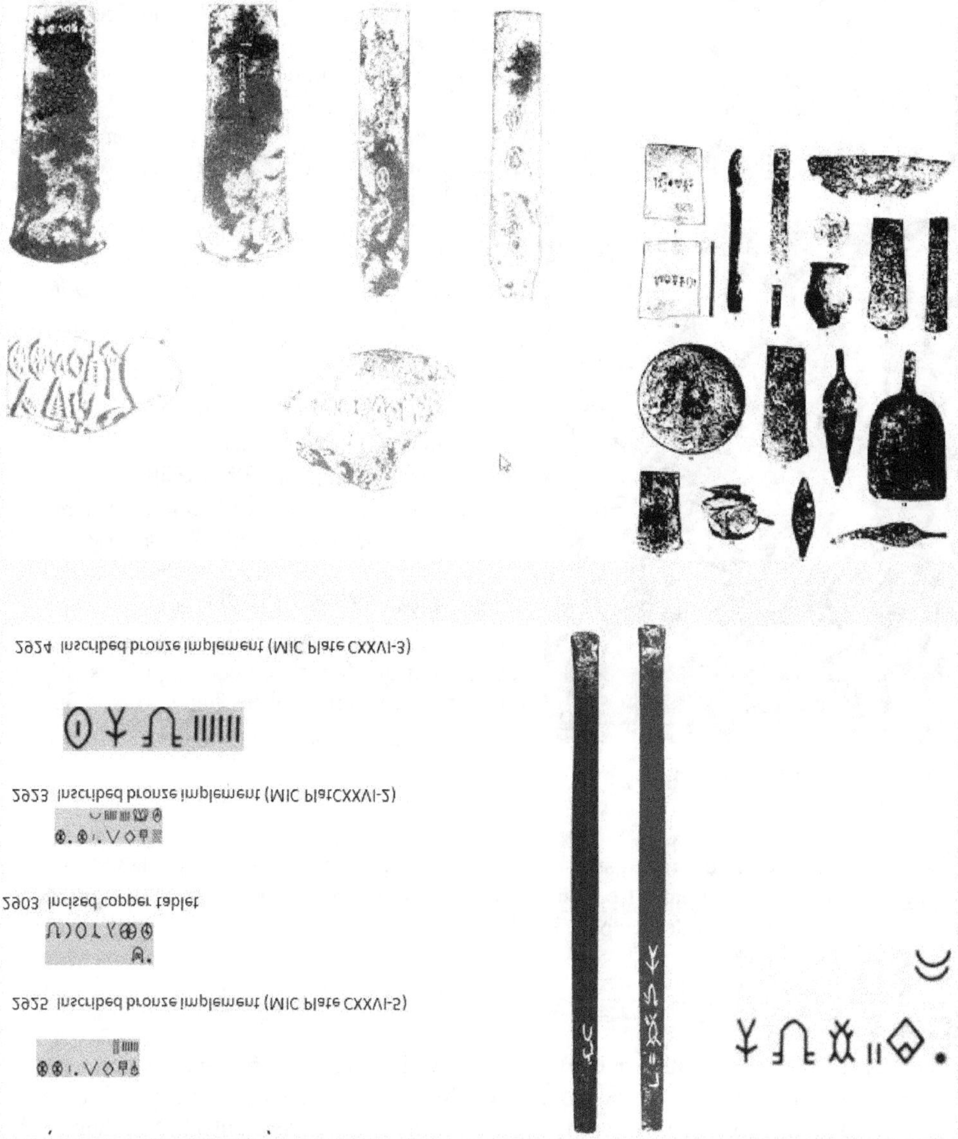

Chanhu-daro, Pl. LXXIV & Mohenjo-daro: copper and bronze tools and utensils (an inscription line mirrored on a zebu seal)

A report from an archaeological excavation at Banawali indicates that a seal with the inscription with hieroglyphs such as: horned tiger, standard device and other hieroglyphs such as body, fish was found in a silversmith's residence:

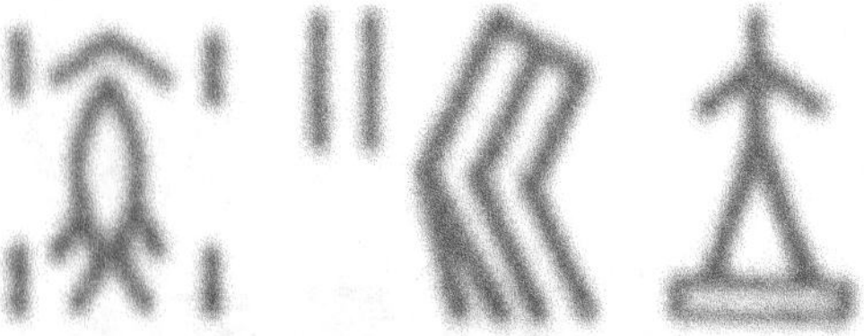

Banawari. Seal 17. Text 9201. Hornd tiger PLUS lathe + portable furnace. Banawali 17, Text 9201 Find spot: "The plan of 'palatial building' rectangular in shape (52 X 46 m) with eleven units of rooms…The discovery of a tiger seal from the sitting room and a few others from the house and its vicinity, weights ofchert, and lapis lazuli beads and deluxe Harappan pottery indicate that the house belonged to a prominent merchant." (loc.cit. VK Agnihotri, 2005, *Indian History*, Delhi, Allied Publishers, p. A-60) Message on metalwork: kol 'tiger' (Santali); kollan 'blacksmith' (Ta.) kod. 'horn'; kod. 'artisan's workshop' PLUS śagaḍī = lathe (Gujarati) san:gaḍa, 'lathe, portable furnace'; rebus: sangath संगथ् । संयोगः f. (sg. dat. sangüṭsü association, living together, partnership (e.g. of beggars, rakes, members of a caravan, and so on); (of a man or woman) copulation, sexual union. sangāṭh संगाठ् । सामग्री m. (sg. dat. sangāṭas संगाटस्), a collection (of implements, tools, materials, for any object), apparatus, furniture, a collection of the things wanted on a journey, luggage, and so on. --karun -- करुन् । सामग्रीसंग्रहः m.inf. to collect the ab. (L.V. 17).(Kashmiri)

The Technique -

Most plates that are classed as engraved start out by having parts of the main design etched first. (See Etching.) Etching gives a greater freedom and ease in laying down bold areas of design, the finishing and detail then being added by pure engraving.

The engraver used a burin (illustration above), or graver, which was a prism shaped bar of hardened steel with a sharp point and wooden handle. This was pushed across the surface of the plate away from the artist, the palm was used to push the burin and it was guided by the thumb and forefinger. The action of engraving produced thin strips of waste metal and left thin furrows in the plate's surface, to take the ink. Any burr left on the edge of the engraved lines was removed with a 'scraper'.[unquote]

Inscriptions on tin ingots

Tin ingots in the Museum of Ancient Art of the Municipality of Haifa, Israel (left #8251, right #8252). The ingots each bear two inscribed Cypro-Minoan markings. (Note: I have argued that the inscriptions were Meluhha hieroglyphs (Indus writing) denoting ranku 'tin' dhatu 'ore'. See: The Bronze Age Writing System of Sarasvati Hieroglyphics as Evidenced by Two "Rosetta Stones" By S. Kalyanaraman in: *Journal of Indo-Judaic Studies* Volume 1: Number 11 (2010), pp. 47-74.) See:

ranku 'liquid measure'; *ranku* 'antelope' Rebus: *ranku* 'tin' (Santali) *dhatu* 'cross' Rebus: *dhatu* 'mineral ore' (Santali).

ran:ku = tin (Santali)

- *ran:ku* = liquid measure (Santali)
- *ran:ku* a species of deer; *ran:kuka* (Skt.)(CDIAL 10559).

- *dāṭu* = cross (Te.); dhatu = mineral (Santali)
- Hindi. *dhāṭnā* 'to send out, pour out, cast (metal)' (CDIAL 6771).

These two hieroglyphs -- ranku, dhatu -- were inscribed on two tin ingots discovered in port of Dor south of Haifa from an ancient shipwreck. They are allographs. Both are read in Meluhha (Mleccha) of Indian *sprachbund*:
ranku 'liquid measure'; *ranku* 'antelope'.Rebus: *ranku* 'tin'. An allograph to denote tin is: tagara 'ram' Rebus: tagara 'tin'. Rebus: damgar 'merchant' (Akkadian)

Another tin ingot with comparable Indus writing was reported by Artzy:

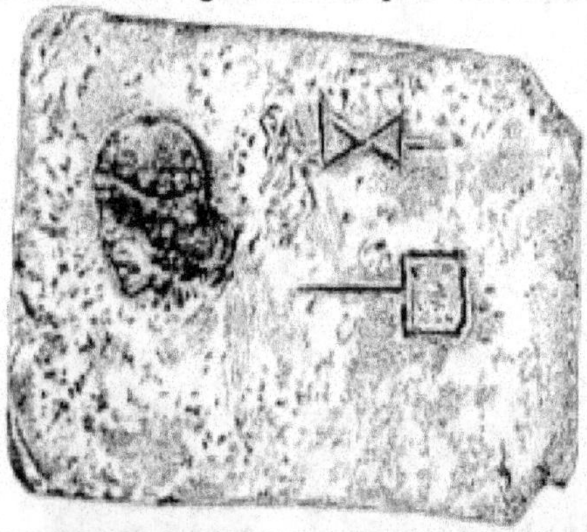

Fig. 4 Inscribed tin ingot with a moulded head, from Haifa (Artzy, 1983: 53). (Michal Artzy, 1983, Arethusa of the Tin Ingot, Bulletin of the American Schools of Oriental Research, BASOR 250, pp. 51-55)
https://www.academia.edu/5476188/Artzy-1983-Tin-Ignot

The two hieroglyphs incised which compare with the two pure tin ingots discovered from a shipwreck in Haifa, the moulded head can be explained also as a Meluhha hieroglyph without assuming it to be the face of goddess Arethusa in Greek tradition: Hieroglyph: mũhe 'face' (Santali) Rebus: mũh 'ingot' (Santali). The three hieroglyphs are: ranku 'antelope' Rebus: ranku 'tin' (Santali) ranku 'liquid measure' Rebus: ranku 'tin' (Santali). *dāṭu* = cross (Te.); dhatu = mineral (Santali) Hindi. *dhāṭnā* 'to send out, pour out, cast (metal)' (CDIAL 6771). [The 'cross' or X hieroglyph is incised on both ingots.]

That the artisans had the competence to create such inscriptions in bas relief (as raised script), on copper is also evidenced by the multiple solid copper tablets found in Harappa and reported by HARP. An example is provided by Kenoyer who was in the HARP project team:

Kalibangan 122A

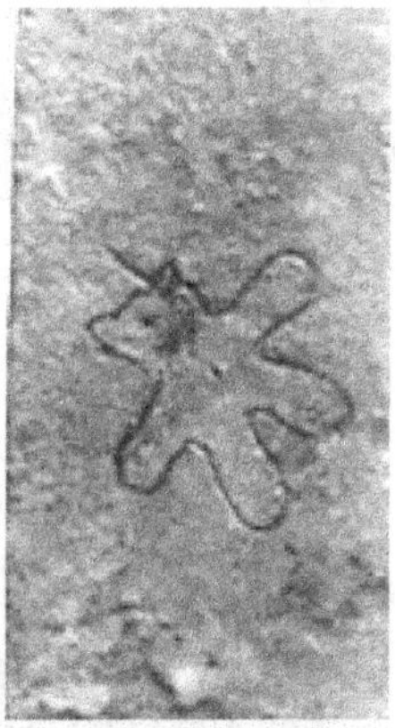

m0475 Inscribed metal place (One-horned young bull PLUS octopus)

"Rendered in strict profile, standing before what might be an altar, the bull is by far the most popular motif in the Indus Valley glyptic art; there is virtually no v ariation in either the style or the iconographic details among the individual examples. The shoulder of the bull is emphasized by an upside-down doubly outlined heart shape that has been interpreted as painted decoration on the body of the bull, but is more likely an artistic convention for representing the muscles of the bull's shoulder."[After Fig. 38 in Holly Pittman, 1984, p. 84].

Mohenjo-daro. Silver seal (After Mackay 1938, vol. 2, Pl. XC,1; XCVI, 520). Two silver seals at Mohenjo-daro, two copper seals at Lothal and at Ras al-Junayz in Oman are rare uses of metal for making seals.

Stamp seal and a modern impression: unicorn or bull and inscription,, Mature Harappan period, ca. 2600–1900 B.C. Indus Valley Burnt steatite; 1 1/2 x 1 1/2 in. (3.8 x 3.8 cm)

http://www.metmuseum.org/toah/ho/02/ssa/ho_49.40.1.htm

m0315 Silver seal

An evidence for the continued use of Indus Script hieroglyphs comes from Ramurva copper bolt.

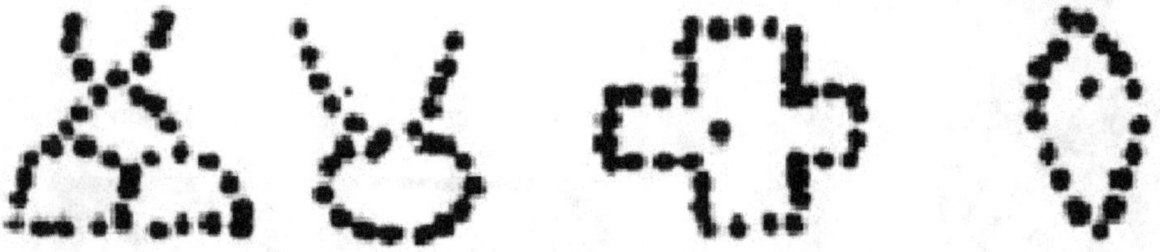

Hieroglyphs:

goT 'seed' Rebus: khoT 'alloy ingot'. खोट (p. 212) [khōṭa] *f* A mass of metal (unwrought or of old metal melted down); an ingot or wedge. (Marathi) kanda 'fire-altar' Rebus: khaNDa 'metal implements'; goT 'round object' Rebus: khoT 'alloy ingot' PLUS bhaTa 'rimless pot' Rebus: bhaTa 'furnace'; dhanga 'mountain-range' Rebus: dhangar 'metalsmith' PLUS bhaTa 'rimless pot' Rebus: bhaTa 'furnace'. Thus, the inscription on the Rampurva copperbolt provides technical specification on the metal object, the copper bolt: that it was made of an alloy ingot (from) furnace, (made by) metal implements metalsmith.

Who knows? The metalsmith might have worked for Asoka or Asoka's predecessors (earlier than 3rd cent. BCE), as Allchin surmises.

Rampurva copper bolt "The starting place for the inquiry is the Rampurva copper bolt at present in the Indian Museum, Calcutta. This was discovered in 1880 by Cunningham and H.B. Garrick. It was buried beside the fallen southerly pillar on which was engraved a set of Asoka's pillar edicts. The pillar and its lion capital were subsequently fully excavated by Daya Ram Sahni. The more northerly Rampurva pillar is that associated with the famous bull capital. The bolt was examined by Cunningham who concluded that there could be n doubt of its being original and that it must have served to hold the lion capital in place upon its pillar. It is probable that other Asokan pillars and capitals bear mortises for similar bolts. This one is described as barrel shaped, of pure copper measuring 2 ft. ½ in. in length, with a diameter of 4 5/16 in. in the centre, and 3 5/8 in. at each end. Cunningham makes no mention of any marks upon the bolt, but Durga Prasad published an impression of four marks. They are made of lines of impressed dots and include the hill-with-crescent, the taurine or Nandipada, and the open cross:

Here then these signs occur upon an object which must have been made by craftsmen working for Asoka or one of his predecessors." (F.R. Allchin, 1959, Upon the contextual significance of certain groups of ancient signs, *Bulletin of the School of Oriental and African Studies*, London.)

Sohgaura copper plate inscription as a survival of Sarasvati hieroglyphs and writing system

The Sohgaura copper plate refers to a pair of kos.t.ha_ga_ra (dva_ra kot.t.haka); the two storehouses described as tri-garbha (i.e. having three rooms) are illustrated on line 1. (Fleet, JRAS, 1907). The illustrations indicate that the three rooms are in three storeys, with supporting pillars clearly seen. The inscription refers to the junction of three highways named Manavati, in two villages called Dasilimita and Usagama. The storehouses were made at this junction for the goods of people using the highways, which are indicated in line 3 by mentioning the three places to and from which they led. One of the names give is reognized by Fleet as Chanchu. (Fleet, JRAS, 63, 1894 proceedings, 86, plate, IA 25. 262; cf. Sohgaura copper plate/B.M. Barua. The Indian Historical Quarterly, ed. Narendra Nath Law. Reprint. 41)
Some glyphs on line 1: kut.hi = tree; rebus: kut.hi = smelting furnace; kos.t.ha_ga_ra = storehouse; s'u_la = spear; cu_l.a = kiln; kan.d.kanka = rim of jar; rebus: copper furnace; bat.a = quail; rebus: kiln.

The top line is a set of hieroglyphs (from left to right).

Tree = kut.i; rebus: kut.hi 'smelter, furnace'
Warehouse = kot. (kos.t.hagara)
Spear = cu_la; rebus: cu_lha 'furnace'
Mountain-summit = ku_t.amu ; rebus : ku_t.a 'workshop'
Wide-mouthed pot on mountain-summit = bat.i; rebus: bat.hi 'furnace')
Rim of jar = kan.d.; rebus: kand. 'fire-altar'
Tree = kut.i; rebus: kut.hi 'smelter, furnace'
Bird on branch: bat.a 'quail'; rebus: bat.a 'furnace'; d.a_l. 'branch of tree'; rebus: d.ha_l.ako 'large metal ingot' [The glyptic composition refers to a kut.hi which can produce metal ingots]
Warehouse = kot. (kos.t.hagara)

The brahmi epigraph on the lines following the top line refers to two kos.t.hagara set up for itinerant merchants (smiths?) at the junction of three roads.
Some devices used on punch-marked coins also occur as the first line of the Sohgaura copper plate inscription. (Fleet, J.F., The inscription on the Sohgaura Plate, JRAS, 1907, pp. 509-532; B.M. Barua, Sohgaura copper plate, Indian Historical Quarterly, Vol. X, 41).

Sohgaura or Soghaura is a village on the right bank of River Rapti, about fourteen miles south-east from Gorakhpur. The plate measures 2 ½ X 1 7/8 inches. The copper plate was cast in a mould. The writing is NOT incised, but in bold, high relief. (JRAS 1907, p. 527). "In the first place, this archaeological find affords the oldest known and clear example of the use of a copper-plate as a material for writing, especially for inscribing a record in Brahmi characters…Secondly, the record has its uniqueness and importance for the standard of Brahmi characters which it presents, the standard which, in the opinion of Dr. Fleet, 'refers it to at any rate an early date in the Maurya period, BC 320 to about 180'…

Non-religious nature of sign graphs on Sohgaura copper plate

"Lastly, with regard to its subject-matter, the inscription is found to be a public notification about the judicious use of certain things in two storehouses by persons carrying on traffic along the high roads leading to S'ra_vasti, or it may be, by persons carrying on traffic by all the three kinds of vehicles along the high roads, in times of urgent need…What we owe to Dr. Fleet's study of the nature of the devices (used on the top line of the copper plate) is the recognition in all of them a significance other than that of religious symbols. To quote him in his words: 'Two of them obviously represent the storehouses themselves, which are shown as shed with double roofs. The lower roof in each case is supported by four rows of posts; and these perhaps stand for four rows of posts, the front posts hiding, those behind them. In the other devices I recognize, not religious emblems, Buddhist or otherwise, -- (I mean, not religious emblems employed here as such), -- nor Mangalas, auspicious symbols, but the arms of the three towns mentioned in L3 of the record.'…" (BM Barua, 1929, The Sohgaura copper-plate inscription, ABORI, vol. 11, 1929, pp. 31-48).

The text of the inscription (which is considered by some to of pre-Mauryan days, i.e. circa 4th century BCE) refers to some famine relief measures and notifies the establishment of two public storehouses at a junction of three great highways of vehicular traffic to meet the needs of persons (apparently merchants and metal-workers) using these roads. The first line which is full of glyphs or devices should relate to the inscription and the facilities provided to the traders. Next to the symbol of the kos.t.haagaara is a s'u_la (spear). This is phonetically cuula 'kiln' for metals to be heated and copper/bronze/brass vessels and tools, worked on by metalsmiths. Similarly, the first glyph of a tree on a platform can be read as kuti 'tree'; another word kuti in Santali means a 'furnace' for melting metals. The other devices are: three peaks mounted by a rimless pot, a rim of a jar, a tree branch with a bird perched on top. These can also be explained in the context of Sarasvati heiroglyphs and the context of metals/minerals-trade.

The second symbol from the left and the second symbol from the right may refer to a kos.t.haagaara. Ko.s.thaagaara is a pair of storehouses are referred to by this name in the Sohgaura plaque inscription, and illustrated on the same plaque (Fleet, The tradition about the corporeal relics of Buddha, JRAS, 1907, pp. 341-363: I find a mention of a place named Chanchu, which I take to be the same one, in the Sohgaura plate (JASB, 63, 1894. proceedings, 86, plate; IA, 25. 262). That record, as I understand it, is a public notification relating to three great highways of vehicular traffic…It notifies that at the junction, named Manavasi, of the three roads, in two villages named Dasilimata and Usagama, storehouses were made for the goods of people using the roads. It indicates the roads by mentioning in line 3, the three places to and from which they led; as regards the junction of them.). They are described as trigarbha, having three rooms; Fleet discusses this at length, but it is evident from the illustrations that these rooms are on three storeys, for the storehouses are represented as small three-storeyed pavilions; it is true that the roof of the top storey is "out of the picture," but its supporting pillars can be clearly eeen. For another use of

garbha as designating chambers of a many-storeyed building, see Ananda K. Coomaraswamy, Indian Architectural Terms, Journal of the American Oriental Society, Vol. 48, no. 3, SEPT 1928, pp.250-275.
The devices on the top line of the Sohgaura copper plate can be read rebus as hieroglyphs, as in the case of Sarasvati hieroglyphs: 1. tree, kut.i (as smelting furnace); 2. tree twigs, kut.i (as smelting furnace); 3. cup, bat.i (as a furnace for melting iron ore); 4. bird, bat.a (as iron or metal); 4. two kos.t.ha_ga_ra (as storehouses), comparable to a sign graph with four posts used on Sarasvati epigraphs (so called Indus inscriptions); three mountains with a U graph on top summit. The presence of furnace facilities for working with metal tools in the two warehouses can be explained in the context of the types of conveyances, parts of which may require mending and to work/tinker on metallic articles and wares of itinerant merchants who need such publicly provided facilities in times of emergency as the s'a_sana in Brahmi writing notes.

kut.hi kut.a, kut.i, kut.ha a tree (Kaus'.); kud.a tree (Pkt.); kur.a_ tree; kar.ek tree, oak (Pas;.)(CDIAL 3228). kut.ha, kut.a (Ka.), kudal (Go.) kudar. (Go.) kut.ha_ra, kut.ha, kut.aka = a tree (Skt.lex.) kut., kurun: = stump of a tree (Bond.a); khut. = id. (Or.) kut.a, kut.ha = a tree (Ka.lex.) gun.d.ra = a stump; khun.t.ut = a stump of a tree left in the ground (Santali.lex.) kut.amu = a tree (Te.lex.)

kut.i, 'smelting furnace' (Mundari.lex.).kut.hi, kut.i (Or.; Sad. kot.hi) (1) the smelting furnace of the blacksmith; kut.ire bica duljad.ko talkena, they were feeding the furnace with ore; (2) the name of e_kut.i has been given to the fire which, in lac factories, warms the water bath for softening the lac so that it can be spread into sheets; to make a smelting furnace; kut.hi-o of a smelting furnace, to be made; the smelting furnace of the blacksmith is made of mud, cone-shaped, 2' 6" dia. At the base and 1' 6" at the top. The hole in the centre, into which the mixture of charcoal and iron ore is poured, is about 6" to 7" in dia. At the base it has two holes, a smaller one into which the nozzle of the bellow is inserted, and a larger one on the opposite side through which the molten iron flows out into a cavity (Mundari.lex.) cf. kan.d.a = furnace, altar (Santali.lex.)

kut.i = a woman water-carrier (Te.lex.) kut.i = to drink; drinking, beverage (Ta.); drinking, water drunk after meals (Ma.); kud.t- to drink (To.); kud.i to drink; drinking (Ka.); kud.i to drink (Kod.); kud.i right, right hand (Te.); kut.i_ intoxicating liquor (Skt.)(DEDR 1654).

The bunch of twigs = ku_di_, ku_t.i_ (Skt.lex.) ku_di_ (also written as ku_t.i_ in manuscripts) occurs in the Atharvaveda (AV 5.19.12) and Kaus'ika Su_tra (Bloomsfield's ed.n, xliv. cf. Bloomsfield, American Journal of Philology, 11, 355; 12,416; Roth, Festgruss an Bohtlingk, 98) denotes it as a twig. This is identified as that of Badari_, the jujube tied to the body of the dead to efface their traces. (See Vedic Index, I, p. 177).

bat.i = a furnace for melting iron-ore (Santali.lex.) bhat.t.hi_ = [Skt. bhr.s.ti frying; fr. bhrasj to fry] a kiln, a furnace; an oven; a smith's forge; a stove; the fireplace of a washer-man;a spirit still; a distillery; a brewery (G.lex.)
bat.i = a metal cup or basin; bhat.i = a still, a boiler, a copper; dhubi bhat.i = a washerman's boiler; jhuli bhat.i = a trench in the ground used as a fireplace when cooking has to be done for a large number of people (Santali.lex.)

bat.a = a quail, or snipe, coturuix coturnix cot; bon.d.e bat.a = a large quail; dak bat.a = the painted stripe, rostraluta benghalensis bengh; gun.d.ri bat.a = a small type, coloured like a gun.d.ri (quail); ku~k bat.a = a medium-sized type; khed.ra bat.a = the smallest of all; lan.d.ha bat.a = a small type

(Santali.lex.) bat.ai, (Nag.); bat.er (Has.); [H. bat.ai or bat.er perdix olivacea; Sad. bat.ai] coturnix coromandelica, the black-breasted or rain-quail; two other kinds of quail are called respectigely: hur.in bat.ai and gerea bat.ai (Mundari.lex.) vartaka = a duck (Skt.) batak = a duck (G.lex.) vartika_ = quail (RV.); wuwrc partridge (Ash.); barti = quail, partridge (Kho.); vat.t.aka_ quail (Pali); vat.t.aya (Pkt.); bat.t.ai (N.)(CDIAL 11361). varta = *circular object; *turning round (Skt.); vat.u = twist (S.)(CDIAL 11346) bat.er = quail (Ku.B.); bat.ara, batara = the grey quail (Or.)(CDIAL 11350).
bat.ai = to divide, share (Santali) [Note the glyphs of nine rectangles divided.]
bat.a; rebus, bat.a 'iron' bat.a = a kind of iron (G.lex.) bhat.a = a furnace, a kiln; it.a bhat.a a brick kiln (Santali)

This note has presented two continuities from Sarasvati civilization: 1. use of punches to mark devices on punch-marked coins and 2. use of copper plate to convey message related to an economic transaction.

This continuity of tradition is linked by the metallurgical tradition of s'reni/artisan guilds working with metals, minerals and furnaces to create copper/bronze artifacts and terracotta or s'ankha bangles and ornaments of silver, copper or semi-precious stones such as agate, carnelian or lapis lazuli. The code of the writing system which was employed on Sarasvati hieroglyphs with 5 or 6 sign graphs constituting an inscription, is the same code which was employed on devices of punch-marked coins (produced in mints belonging to guilds) and on copper plate s'a_s'ana-s or historical periods of pre-mauryan times in India, like the evidence presented by Sohgaura copper plate. Since this plate contains a Brahmi inscription, this constitutes a Rosetta stone to explain the meanings of the sign graphs or glyphs employed on the top line of the plate in the context of the facilities provided in two warehouses to traveling caravan merchants or rive-faring merchants.

Harappa. Molded terracotta tablet. Tree on 'ingot'. kuTi 'tree' Rebus: kuThi 'smelter'.

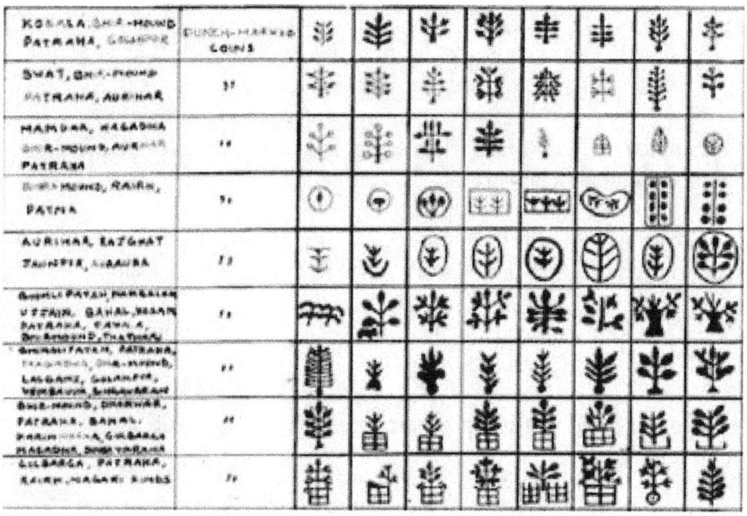

Tree shown on a tablet from Harappa.
[Pl. 39, Tree symbol (often on a platform) on punch-marked coins; a symbol recurring on many tablets showing Sarasvati hieroglyphs].

<u>Prakritam base for Indus Script inscription related to metalwork on a copper plate and contact areas of seafaring Meluhha merchants</u>

Mirror: http://tinyurl.com/q5aqwjr

A copper plate from Mohenjo-daro with inscription demonstrates the connection between a pictorial motif and associated text of Indus Script inscriptions.

The copper plate kept in Lahore Museum has -- on the obverse --a hieroglyph-multiplex of rhinoceros + trough which is deciphered as 'Excellent implements of metalworkers guild'.

On the reverse of this plate is the following inscription (photo from Lahore Museum):
Bronze plate with inscription. Sarasvati-Sindhu civilization Lahore Museum. (This is referred to as Copper plate on Indus Script Corpora).

On the obverse of this copper plate inscrition is a hierolyph-multiplex: rhinoceros PLUS trough:

kANDa 'rhinoceros' Rebus: khaNDa 'metal implements' pattar 'trough' Rebus: pattar 'metalworker (goldsmith) guild'.

The text of the inscription is supercargo, scribe documenting three types of ayas 'iron, metal':
Hieroglyph: fish 'aya' Rebus: aya 'iron' ayas 'metal'

Hieoglyph-multiplex: fish PLUS lid: aya 'fish' Rebus: aya 'iron, metal' adaren 'lid' Rebus: aduru 'native unsmelted metal'

Hieroglyph-multipled: fish PLUS notch: खांडा [khāṇḍā] m A jag, **notch** Rebus: ayaskhāṇḍa 'excellent implements: tools, pots and pans, metalware'

Hieroglyph-multiplex: fish PLUS oval as parenthesis circumscript PLUS horn: aya 'fish' Rebus: aya 'iron, metal' PLUS goTa 'round' Rebus: khoT 'ingot' koD 'horn' Rebus: koD 'workshop'

Hieroglyph: rim of narrow-necked jar: karava 'narrownecked jar' Rebus: kharva 'nidhi, karba 'iron'; karNaka 'rim of jar' Rebus: karNI 'supercargo', karNIka 'scribe'.

Thus, the text message is: Metalworker guild workshop supercargo scribed, ingot (of) native unsmelted metal, excellent metal implemets.

Second line on Texts 3415, 3318:

kanac 'corner' Rebus: kancu 'bronze'
koDi 'flag' Rebus: koD 'workshop'
sal 'splinter' Rebus: sal 'workshop'
meD 'body' Rebus: meD 'iron' PLUS koDa 'one' Rebus: koD 'workshop'
dula 'pair' Rebus: dul 'cast metal' PLUS khaNDa 'rectangle divisions' Rebus: khaNDa 'excellent metal implements' Thus the text message on this line is: excellent metal imlements (from) iron, bronze workshop

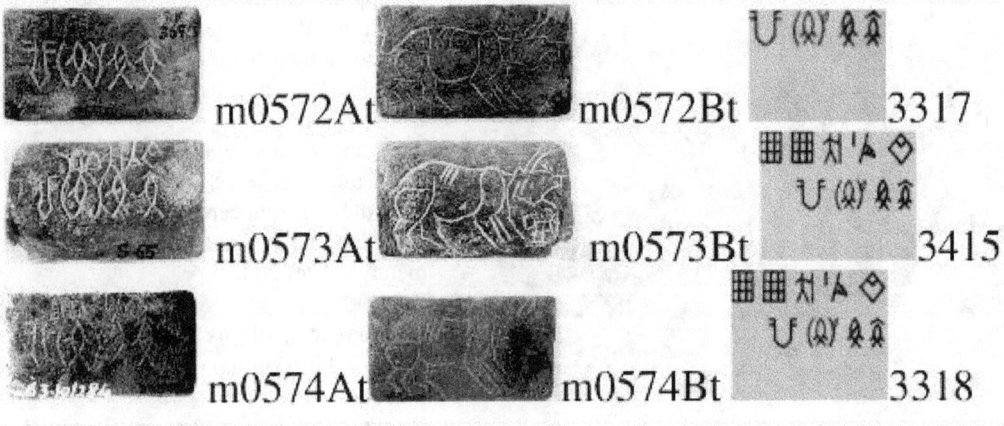

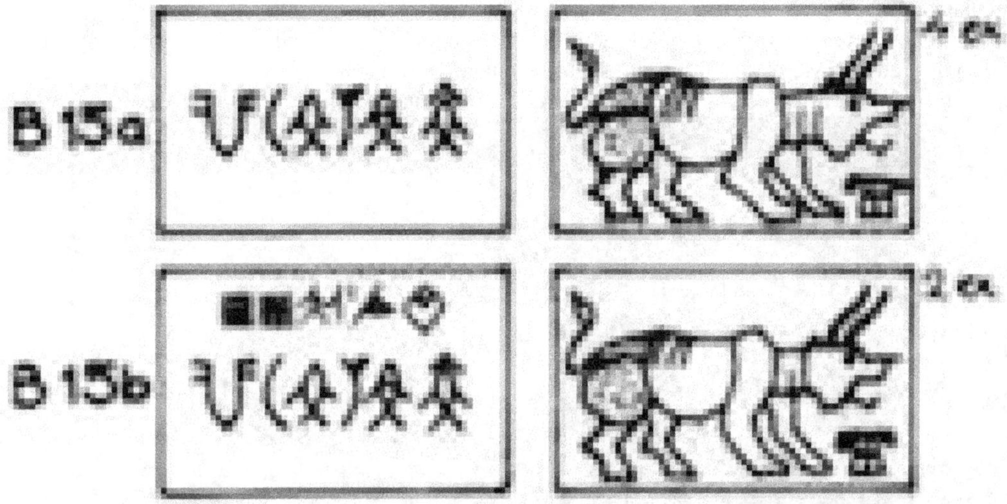

The contact area of the metalworkers extended beyond Persian Gulf into Mesopotamia as demonstrated by Dilmun seal finds with Indus Script from sites along the Persian Gulf and also on the banks of the doab: Tigris-Euphrates in Mesopotamia:

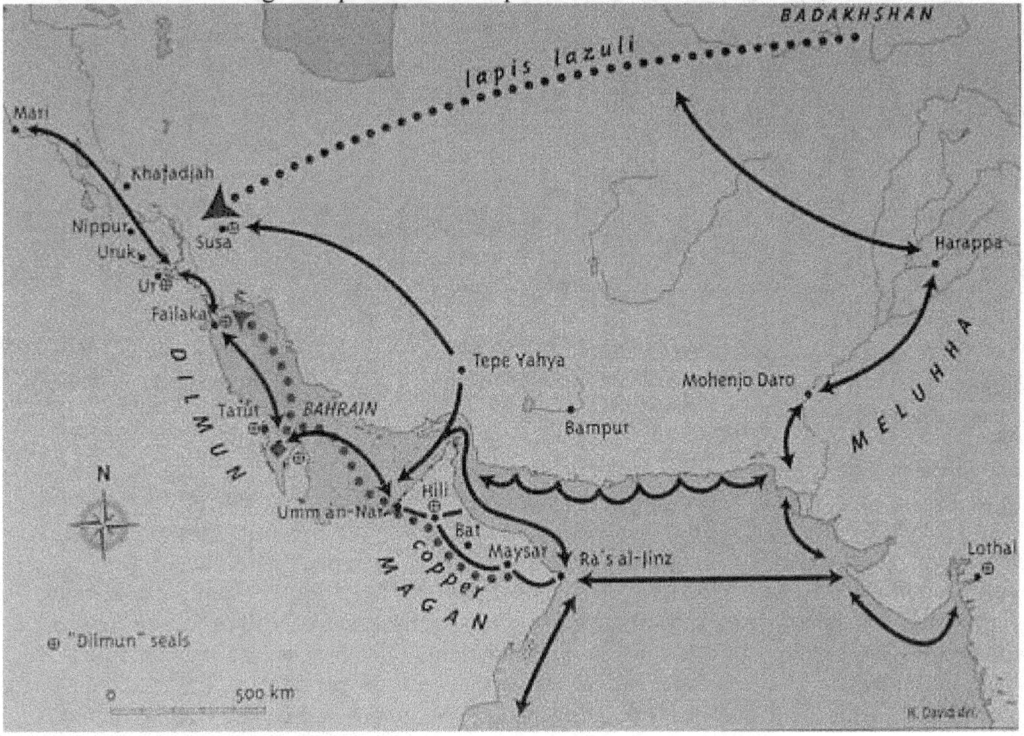

Dilmun Seals: Persian Gulf find sites. "Dilmun is understood to embrace the eastern coastline of Arabia including the island of Failaka opposite Kuwait to the island of Bahrain (cf. p. 15. Harriet Crawford & Michael Rice, editors. *Traces of Paradise, the Archaeology of Bahrain, 2500 B.C -300 A.D.* London. Published by the Dilmun Committe for an exhibit from the Bahrain National Museum. Printed June 2000)."
http://www.bibleorigins.net/DilmunMaganMeluhhaBahrainFailakaCrawford.jpg

The language of the civilization is Prakritam which provides the spoken forms of Samskritam glosses related to metalwork. Many of these glosses are relatable to the Indo-European languages. It is suggested that Meluhha (Prakritam speakers) metalworkers had extensive contact with the region of the Indo-European languages in Eurasia as presented in the following map:

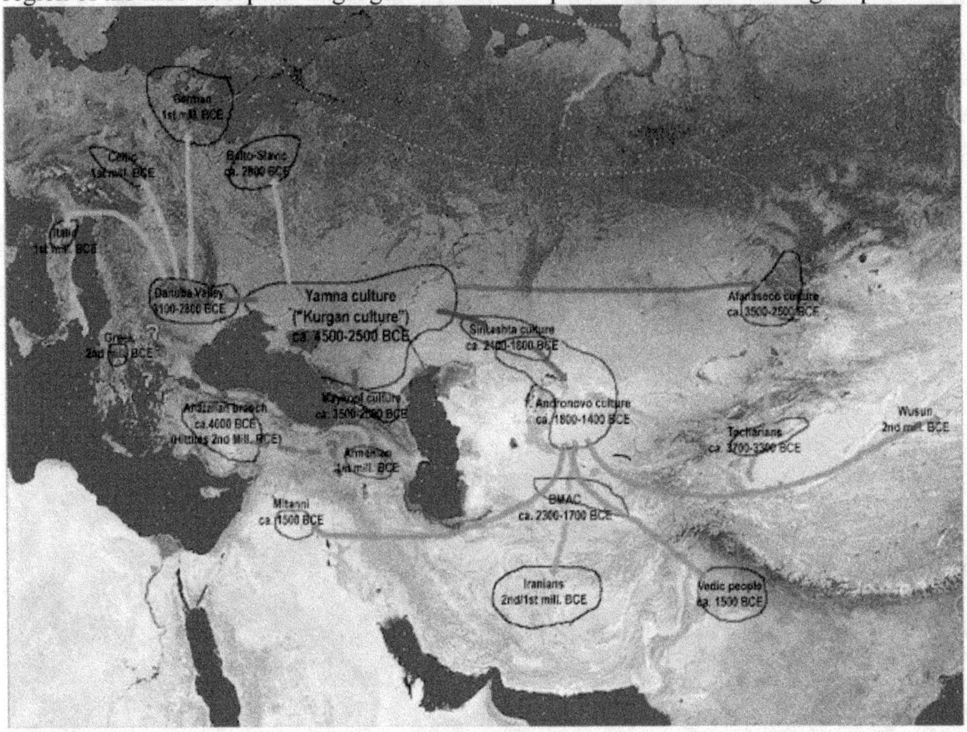

Copper plates of Indus Script and rebus Meluhha readings

Mirror: https://www.academia.edu/8886084/Copper_plates_of_Indus_Script_and_rebus_Meluhha_readings

It is unfortunate that 'fake experts' cry 'fake' the moment a long inscription of 37 hieroglyphs of 'text' PLUS pictorial motifs is evidenced. There are hundreds of inscriptions in Indus corpora which have not been precisely provenienced. This does not automatically make the nine copper plates recently reported as 'blatant fakes'. The blatant appellation comes from those who consider the authors of Indus writing to be illiterates. Massimo Vidale and other archaeologists are convinced that it was a writing system and a number of books have been brought out reading the inscriptions as Meluhha hieroglyphs of metalwork. It is for the criers of wolf or fake to come out with a logical explanation of the purport of the inscriptions which have been found not only in the Sarasvati-Sindhu civilization area but also in the contact areas of Ancient Near East and the Levant (pace two tin ingots found in Haifa with Indus writing inscriptions designating them as tin metal).

Copper tablet (H2000-4498/9889-01) with raised script found in Trench 43. Harappa. (Source: Slide 351. harappa.com) Eight such tablets have been found (HARP, 2005); these were recovered from circular platforms. This example of a uniquely scripted tablet with raised Indus script glyphs shows that copper tablets were also used in Harappa, while hundreds of copper tablets with indus script inscriptions were found in Mohenjo-daro. See also:

The Trench 43 is the same trench which exposed many circular platforms.
Slide 336 harappa.com Overview of Trench 43 in 2000 looking north, showing the HARP-exposed circular platform in the foreground

356. **Detail view** of the **HARP-excavated platform** in **Trench 43** with **Wheeler's platform** to the **east** (**toward** the **top** of the **image**). **Note** the **mud-brick wall foundations** that **surround each platform** to the **east**, **south**, and **west** (the **north walls remain unexposed**). **Traces** of **baked** brick thresholds can be seen on the right (**south**).

J. Mark Kenoyer excavating and sampling the sediments associated with the HARP-excavated platform, which was partly robbed of baked bricks during the Harappan period itself (Trench 43). Pottery found under the platforms permits them to be assigned to Harappa Period 3C, probably toward the middle of

that period (ca. 2100-2000 BC).
https://www.harappa.com/category/slide-photographer/harappa-archaeological-research-project?page=10

To the south of the "granary" or "great hall" at Harappa is an area with numerous circular working platforms that were built inside small rooms or courtyards. These circular working platforms may have been used for husking grain. One of these circular platforms had what may have been a large wooden mortar placed in the center. https://www.harappa.com/indus/16.html

Circular platforms in the southwestern part of Mound F excavated by M.S. Vats in the 1920s and 1930s, as conserved by the Department of Archaeology and Museums, Government of Pakistan.

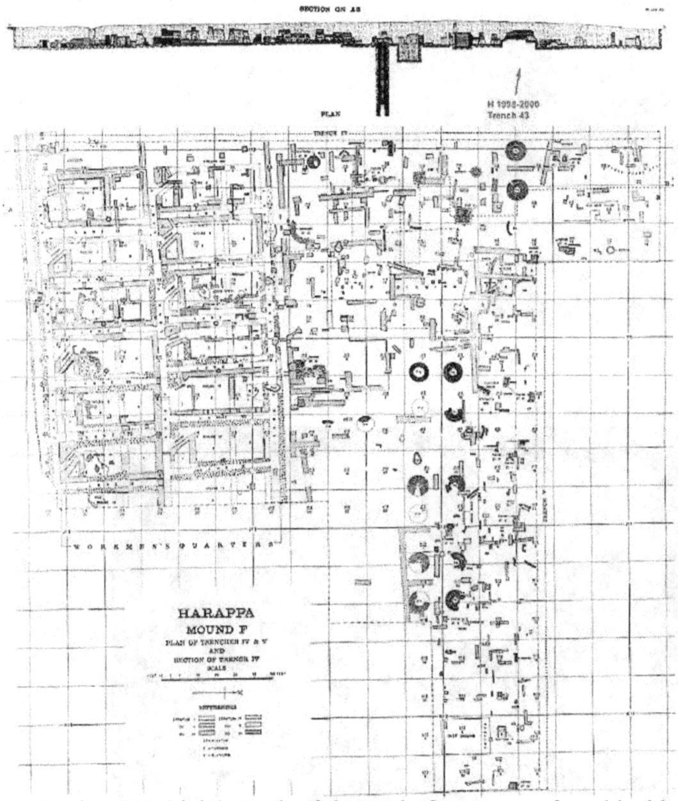

354. Plan of Vats' excavations showing circular platforms. In some cases remnants of the baked brick walls tht probably surrounded each platform can be seen on the plan, although earlier and later walls are also

shown. From MS Vas (1940). *Excavations at Harappa.*

355. The circular platform excavated by Wheeler in 1946 (left) and the one excavated by HARP in 1998 (right). Both of these platforms were found inside small square rooms that originally had baked brick walls, subsequently removed by brick robbers (Trench 43).

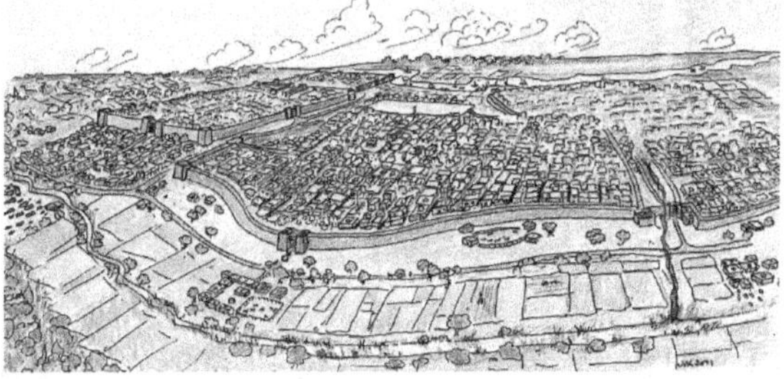

360. Rendition of ancient Harappa as it may have appeared in late Period 3B/early Period 3C, drawn by J. Mark Kenoyer. The granary and working platforms of Mound F are in the northwestern corner of the city (upper left).

<u>An overview of the area on Mound F as seen from the city wall on Mound AB. The circular working platforms are in the background and a row of identical houses that were clearly made all at one time, possibly a housing project of some wealthy merchant or perhaps sponsored by the city council.</u>

m0317 Silver seal

m1199 Silver seal

h381 Bronze dagger

h380 Bronze dagger

Slide 209 Inscribed lead celt

Kalibangan. Inscribed bronze rod (Mahadevan 1977:7)

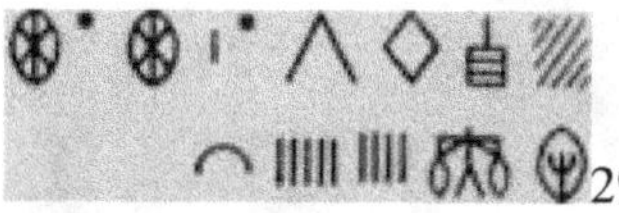

2923 Inscribed bronze implement (MIC Plate CXXVI-3)

2924 Inscribed bronze implement (MIC Plate CXXVI-3)

2925 Inscribed bronze implement (MIC Plate CXXVI-5)

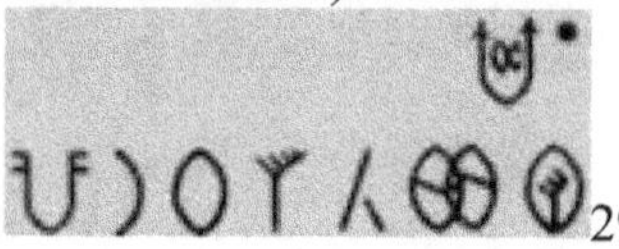

2903 Inscribed copper tablet

Inscribed weapons are further reported from Harappa Vats 1940: 384ss, Pl. CXX, 5,19), Chanhu Daro (Mackay 1943: 178, Pl. LXXIV, 1-1a,8) Chanhu-daro, Pl. LXXIV & Mohenjodaro: copper and bronze tools and utensils (an inscription line mirrored on a zebu seal)

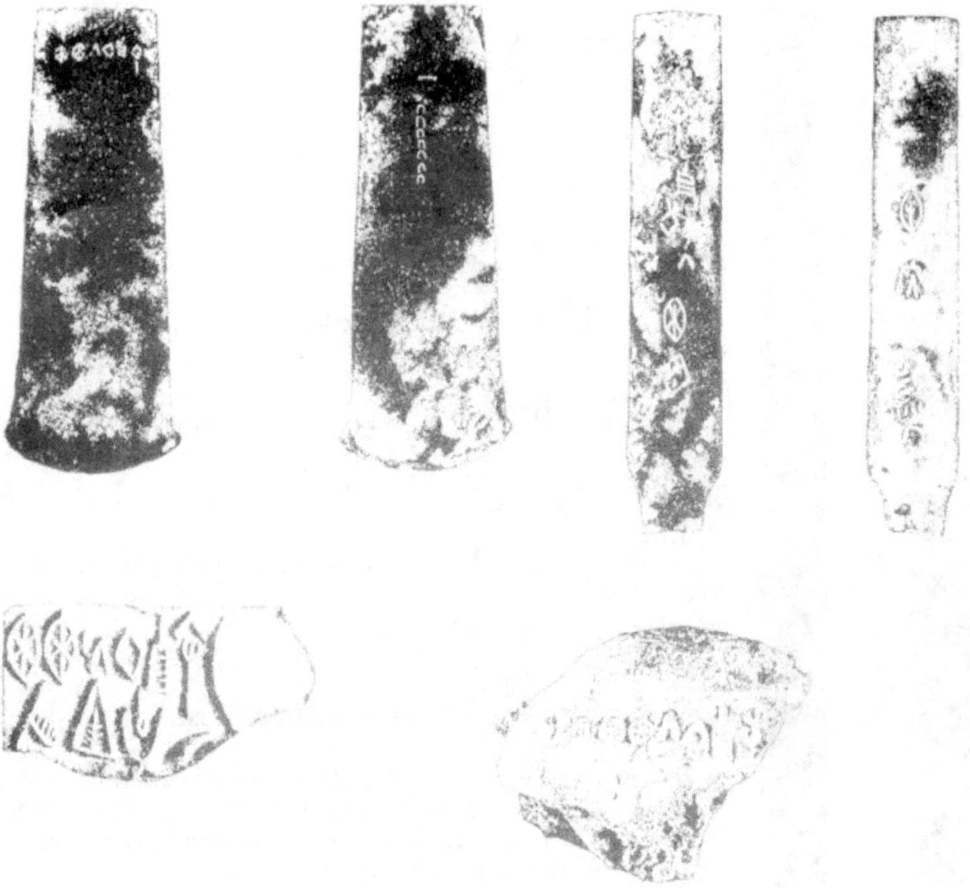

Axe-head of brown schist (L 15 cm) with the head of a leopard or lioness on the butt. From the palace of Mallia, destroyed in LM I B ca. 1450 BCE. After Plate 90 in: Sinclair Hood, 1971, *The Minoans*, New York, Praeger Publishers

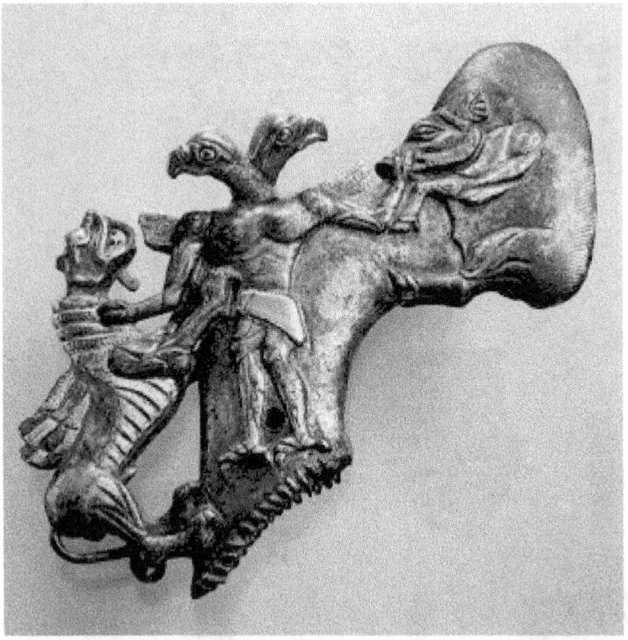

Shaft-hole axhead with a bird-headed demon, boar,and dragon, late 3rd–early 2nd millennium BCE Central Asia (Bactria-Margiana) Silver, gold foil; 5 7/8 in. (15 cm) "Western Central Asia, now known as Turkmenistan, Uzbekistan, and northern Afghanistan, has yielded objects attesting to a highly developed civilization in the late third and early second millennium B.C. Artifacts from the region indicate that there were contacts with Iran to the southwest. Tools and weapons, especially axes, comprise a large portion of the metal objects from this region. This shaft-hole axhead is a masterpiece of three-dimensional and relief sculpture. Expertly cast in silver and gilded with gold foil, it depicts a bird-headed hero grappling with a wild boar and a winged dragon. The idea of the heroic bird-headed creature probably came from western Iran, where it is first documented on a cylinder seal impression. The hero's muscular body is human except for the bird talons that replace the hands and feet. He is represented twice, once on each side of the ax, and consequently appears to have two heads. On one side, he grasps the boar by the belly and on the other, by the tusks. The posture of the boar is contorted so that its bristly back forms the shape of the blade. With his other talon, the bird-headed hero grasps the winged dragon by the neck. The dragon, probably originating in Mesopotamia or Iran, is represented with folded wings, a feline body, and the talons of a bird of prey."

Kuwait gold disc. Al-Sabah Museum.

Kuwait cylinder seal. Gold. Possibly southeastern Iran, mid 3rd millennium BCE. Ht. 2.21 cm. dia. 2.74 cm. Fabricated from gold sheet with chased decoration. Inv. No. LNS 4517J

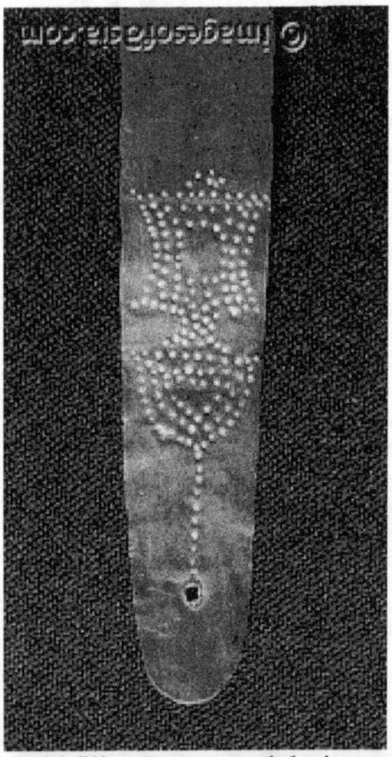

Gold fillet. Punctuated design on both ends.
Mohenjodaro. http://www.imagesofasia.com/html/mohenjodaro/gold-fillet.html

Gold fillet. Punctuated design on both ends.
Mohenjodaro. http://www.imagesofasia.com/html/mohenjodaro/gold-fillet.html

The gold pendant is made from a hollow cylinder with soldered ends and perforated point.

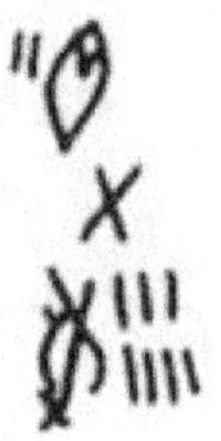

Museum No. MM 1374.50.271; Marshall 1931: 521, pl. CLI, B3. [After Fig. 4.17a, b in: JM Kenoyer, 1998, p. 196]. A fish sign, preceded by seven short numeral strokes, also appears on a gold Golden pendant with inscription from jewelry hoard at Mohenjo-daro. Drawing of inscription that encircles the gold ornament. Needle-like pendant with cylindrical body. Two other examples, one with a different series of incised signs were found together. The pendant is made from a hollow cylinder with soldered ends and perforated point. Museum No. MM 1374.50.271; Marshall 1931: 521, pl. CLI, B3. [After Fig. 4.17a, b in: JM Kenoyer, 1998, p. 196].

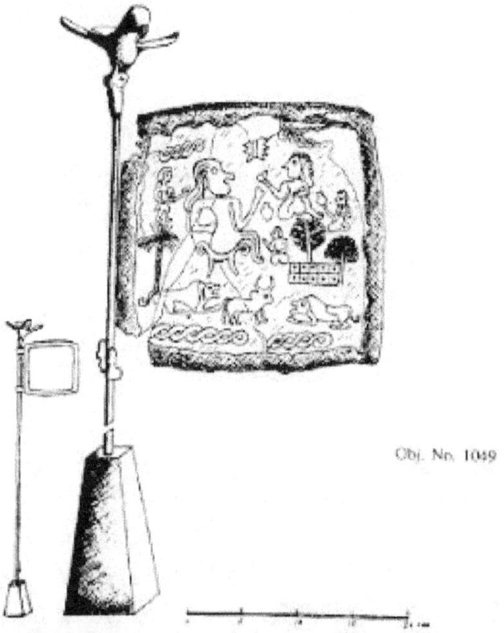

Shahdad Standard. Bronze. Drawing.

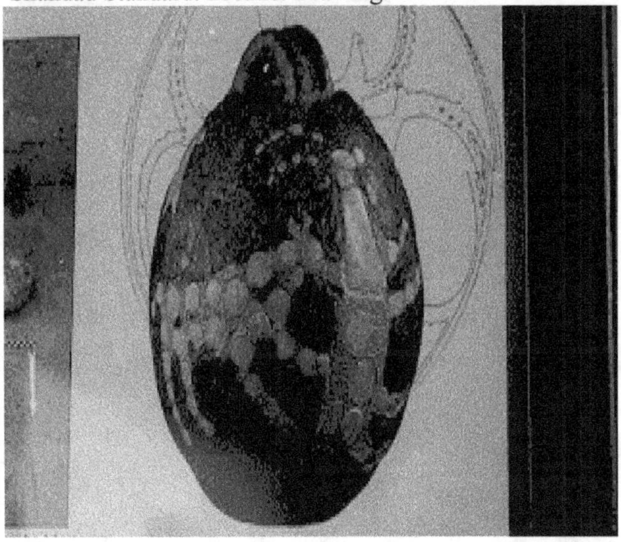

Lead weight. Shahi Tump. Ornamental ball (lead weight) discovered from Shahi Tump, Makran. It is 15 cm high and 15 kg in weight made by pure lead and wrapped in copper using cire perdue technique of casting.

Hieroglyph on obverse of the inscription types A1, A2, A11:

krammara 'look back' (Te.); kamar 'smith' (Santali) PLUS mlekh 'antelope'(Br.); milakkhu 'copper' (Pali). Thus the artisan defines his or her profession as coppersmith.

A1 inscription

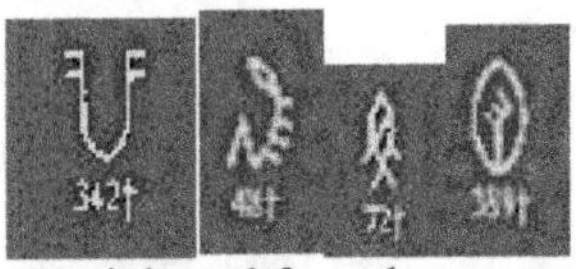

Deciphered from l.: supercargo, large metal (alloy) ingot, ingot for smithy,forge, bharat alloy of copper, zinc and tin

karNika, kanka 'rim of jar' rebus: karNI 'supercargo' karnika 'account, scrobe'
kaṇḍa kanka 'rim of jar' Rebus: *karṇīka* 'account (scribe)'*karṇī*'supercargo'.

aya 'fish' rebus: ayas, aya 'metal, iron' PLUS dhAL 'slanted' Rebus: DhALako 'large ingot'
double parenthesis as circumflex: Oval shaped like a bun ingot; rebus: mũhã 'ingot' PLUS kolmo 'rice-plant' rebus: kolimi 'smithy, forge'.

baraḍo = spine; backbone (Tulu) Rebus: *baran, bharat* 'mixed alloys' (5 copper, 4 zinc and 1 tin) (Punjabi).*baroṭi* 'twelve' *bhārata* 'a factitious alloy of copper, pewter, tin' (Marathi)भरत (p. 603) [bharata] *n* A factitious metal compounded of copper, pewter, tin &c.भरताचें भांडें (p. 603) [bharatācē mbhāṇḍēṃ] *n* A vessel made of the metal भरत. 2 See भरिताचें भांडें.भरती (p. 603) [bharatī] *a* Composed of the metal भरत. (Molesworth Marathi Dictionary).

A2 inscription

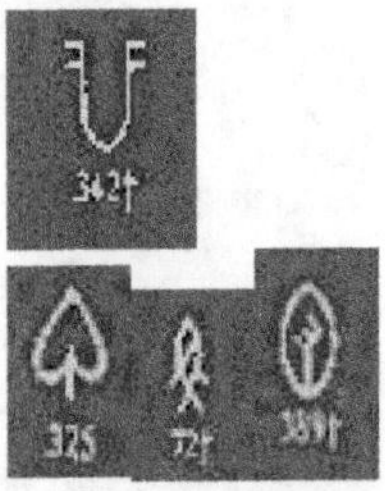

Deciphered from l: As in A1 decipherment but with the replacement of 'spine' hieroglyph with 'ficus' hieroglyph: loa 'ficus' rebus: loh 'copper, metal'.

A4 inscription

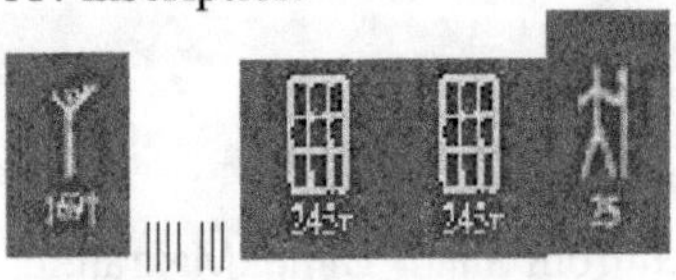

kolmo 'rice-plant' rebus: kolimi 'smithy, forge'
gaNDa 'four' rebus: kanda 'fire-altar' PLUS kolmo 'three' rebus: kolimi 'smithy, forge' (Phonetic determinative of the rice-plant hieroglyph)
khaNDA 'divisions' rebus: khANDa 'implements' PLUS dula 'pair' rebus: 'cast metal', i.e. metal casting implements
med 'body' rebus: meD 'iron' PLUS yupa 'staff, pillar' in Prakritam: Meṇḍa [dial., cp. Prk. mĕṇṭha & miṇṭha: Pischel, *Prk. Gr.* § 293. The Dhtm (156) gives a root meṇḍ (meḍ) in meaning of "koṭilla," i. e. crookedness. (Pali) M. *mẽḍhā* m. ' crook or curved end (of a horn, stick, &c.) (DIAL

10311) Rebus: meD 'iron' (Thus, phonetic determinative of the metal signified by the 'body' hieroglyph.)

A5 inscription

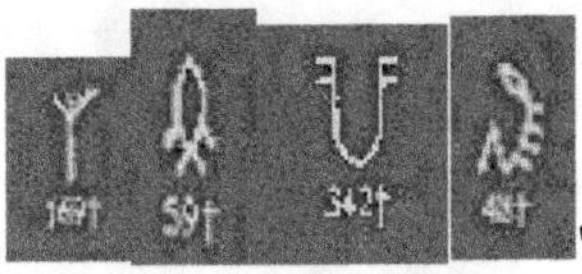" (splinter)(Variant platform) Deciphered from l. to r.:
kolmo 'rice-plant' rebus: kolimi 'smithy, forge'
aya 'fish' rebus: ayas, aya 'metal, iron'

karNika, kanka 'rim of jar' rebus: karNI 'supercargo' karnika 'account, scrobe'

baraḍo = spine; backbone (Tulu) Rebus: *baran, bharat* 'mixed alloys' (5 copper, 4 zinc and 1 tin) (Punjabi).*baroṭi* 'twelve' *bhārata* 'a factitious alloy of copper, pewter, tin' (Marathi)भरत (p. 603) [bharata] *n* A factitious metal compounded of copper, pewter, tin &c.भरताचें भांडें (p. 603) [bharatācē mbhāṇḍēṃ] *n* A vessel made of the metal भरत. 2 See भरिताचें भांडें.भरती (p. 603) [bharatī] *a* Composed of the metal भरत. (Molesworth Marathi Dictionary).

sal 'splinter' rebus: sal 'workshop'

maṇḍa6 ' some sort of framework (?) '. [In *nau -- maṇḍḗ* n. du. ' the two sets of poles rising from the thwarts or the two bamboo covers of a boat (?) ' ŚBr. (as illustrated in BPL p. 42); and in BHSk. and Pa. *bōdhi -- maṇḍa* -- n. perh. ' thatched cover ' rather than ' raised platform ' (BHS ii 402). If so, it may belong to maṇḍapá -- and maṭha --]Ku. *mā̃ṛā* m. pl. ' shed, resthouse ' (CDIAL 9737) Rebus 1: mḗdha m. ' sacrificial oblation ' RV.Pa. *mēdha* -- m. ' sacrifice '(CDIAL 10327) Rebus 2: *meḍ* 'iron' (Mu.Ho.) mẽṛh t iron; ispat m. = steel; dul m. = cast iron (Mu.) meṛed-bica = iron stone ore, in contrast to bali-bica, iron sand ore (Munda) *mẽṛhẽt*'iron'; *mẽṛhẽt icena*'the iron is rusty';*ispat mẽṛhẽt*'steel', *dul mẽṛhẽt*'cast iron'; *mẽṛhẽt khaṇḍa*'iron implements' (Santali) *meḍ.* (Ho.)(Santali.lex.Bodding) *meṛed, mṛed, mṛd* iron; enga meṛed soft iron; *sanḍi meṛed* hard iron;*ispāt meṛed* steel; *dul meṛed* cast iron; *i meṛed* rusty iron, also the iron of which weights are cast; *bica meṛed* iron extracted from stone ore; *bali meṛed* iron extracted from sand ore (Mu.lex.) měď (copper)(Czech) mid′ (copper, cuprum, orichalc)(Ukrainian) med′ (copper, cuprum, Cu), mednyy (copper, cupreous, brassy, brazen, brass), omednyat′ (copper, coppering), sul′fatmedi (Copper), politseyskiy (policeman, constable, peeler, policemen, redcap), pokryvat′ med′yu (copper), payal′nik (soldering iron, copper, soldering pen, soldering-iron), mednyy kotel (copper), medno-krasnyy (copper), mednaya moneta (copper). медь (copper, cuprum, Cu), медный (copper, cupreous, brassy, brazen, brass), омеднять (copper, coppering), Сульфатмеди (Copper), полицейский (policeman, constable, peeler, policemen, redcap), покрывать медью (copper), паяльник (soldering iron, copper, soldering pen, soldering-iron), медный котел (copper), медно-красный (copper), медная монета (copper).(Russian)

A6 inscription

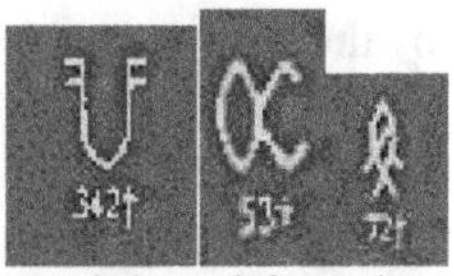

Deciphered from l. to r.:
karNika, kanka 'rim of jar' rebus: karNI 'supercargo' karnika 'account, scrobe'

kamaḍha 'crab' Rebus: *kammaṭa* 'mint, coiner'.*ḍato* = claws of crab (Santali) *ḍato* = claws of crab (Santali) Rebus: *dhātu* 'mineral ore'

aya 'fish' rebus: ayas, aya 'metal, iron' PLUS dhAL 'slanted' Rebus: DhALako 'large ingot' double parenthesis as circumflex: Oval shaped like a bun ingot; rebus: mūhā 'ingot' PLUS kolmo 'rice-plant' rebus: kolimi 'smithy, forge'.

A7 inscription

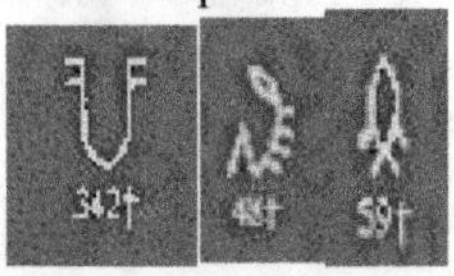
|| (Two long linear strokes)

Deciphered from l. to r.:
karNika, kanka 'rim of jar' rebus: karNI 'supercargo' karnika 'account, scrobe'

baraḍo = spine; backbone (Tulu) Rebus: *baran, bharat* 'mixed alloys' (5 copper, 4 zinc and 1 tin) (Punjabi).*baroṭi* 'twelve' *bhārata* 'a factitious alloy of copper, pewter, tin' (Marathi)भरत (p. 603) [bharata] *n* A factitious metal compounded of copper, pewter, tin &c.भरताचें भांडें (p. 603) [bharatācē mbhāṇḍēṃ] *n* A vessel made of the metal भरत. 2 See भरिताचें भांडें.भरती (p. 603) [bharatī] *a* Composed of the metal भरत. (Molesworth Marathi Dictionary).
aya 'fish' rebus: ayas, aya 'metal, iron'

dula 'two' rebus: dul 'cast metal'

A3a and A3b

Hieroglyph: Endless knot

dhAtu 'strand of rope' Rebus: dhAtu 'mineral, metal, ore'धातु [p= 513,3] *m.* layer , stratum Ka1tyS3r. Kaus3. constituent part , ingredient (esp. [and in RV. only] ifc. , where often = " fold " e.g. त्रि-ध्/आतु , threefold &c ; cf.त्रिविष्टि- , सप्त- , सु-) RV. TS. S3Br. &c (Monier-Williams) dhā´tu *strand of rope ' (cf. *tridhā´tu* -- ' threefold ' RV., *ayugdhātu* -- ' having an uneven number of strands ' KātyŚr.).; S. *dhāī* f. ' wisp of fibres added from time to time to a rope that is being twisted ', L. *dhāī̃* f.(CDIAL 6773) tántu m. ' thread, warp ' RV. [√tan] Pa. *tantu* -- m. ' thread, cord ', Pk. *taṁtu* -- m.; Kho. (Lor.) *ton* ' warp ' < **tand* (whence *tandeni* ' thread between wings of spinning wheel '); S. *tandu* f. ' gold or silver thread '; L. *tand* (pl. °*dū̃*) f. ' yarn, thread being spun, string of the tongue '; P. *tand* m. ' thread ', *tanduā*, °*dūā* m. ' string of the tongue, frenum of glans penis '; A. *tā̃t* ' warp in the loom, cloth being woven '; B. *tā̃t* ' cord '; M. *tā̃tū* m. ' thread '; Si. *tatu*, °*ta* ' string of a lute '; -- with -- *o*, -- *ā* to retain orig. gender: S. *tando* m. ' cord, twine, strand of rope '; N. *tā̃do* ' bowstring '; H. *tā̃tā* m. ' series, line '; G. *tā̃tɔ* m. ' thread '; -- OG. *tāṁtaṇaü* m. ' thread ' < **tāṁtaḍaü*, G.*tā̃tṇɔ* m.(CDIAL 5661)

मेढा [mēḍhā] A twist or tangle arising in thread or cord, a curl or snarl.(Marathi)(CDIAL 10312).L. meṛh f. 'rope tying oxen to each other and to post on threshing floor'(CDIAL 10317) Rebus: *meḍ*'iron'. *mẽṛhet* 'iron' (Mu.Ho.)

Thus, together, a strand and a curl, the hieroglyph-multiplex of endless-knot signifies iron mineral. mRdu dhAtu (iron mineral).

B 19

B19 copper plate epigraph: hunter-blacksmith: कौटिलिकः kauṭilikḥ कौटिलिकः 1 A hunter.-2 A blacksmith. कौटिलिक [p= 315,2] *m.* (fr. कुटिलिका Pa1n2. 4-4 , 18) " deceiving the hunter [or the deer Sch.] by particular movements " , a deer [" a hunter " Sch.] Ka1s3. *f.* (Pa1n2. 4-4 , 18) कुटिलिका crouching , coming stealthily (like a hunter on his prey ; a particular movement on the stage) Vikr. कुटिलिक " using the tool called कुटिलिका " , a blacksmith ib. कुटिलक [p= 288,2] *f.* a tool used by a blacksmith Pa1n2. 4-4 , 18 Ka1s3.*mfn.* bent , curved , crisped Pan5cat.

kamaṭh a crab (Skt.) kamāṭhiyo=archer;kāmaṭhum =a bow; kāmaḍī ,kāmaḍum=a chip of bamboo (G.) kāmaṭhiyo bowman; an archer(Skt.lex.) kamaṛkom= fig leaf (Santali.lex.)kamarmaṛā(Has.), kamaṛkom(Nag.); the petiole or stalk of a leaf (Mundari.lex.)kamaṭha= fig leaf, religiosa(Skt.) dula'tw' Rebus: dul 'cast metal 'Thus, cast loh 'copper casting' infurnace:baṭa= wide-mouthed pot; baṭa= kiln (Te.) kammaṭa=portable furnace(Te.) kampaṭṭam 'coiner,mint' (Tamil) kammaṭa (Malayalam)

Same inscription as on B19 sets of copper plates appears on C6 sets of copper plates but with a distinct hieroglyph-multiplex of ficus PLUS crab (pincers, tongs) on the obverse of the copper plate.

Linked to C! C1 Inscription
Hieroglyph: double-axe

kuṭhāra m. ' **axe** ' R., °*raka* -- m. VarBṛS., °*rī* -- f. lex., °*rikā* -- f. Suśr. [*kuṭhātaṅka* -- m., °*kā* -- f. lex. Prob. ← Drav. and conn. with √kuṭṭ EWA i 223 with lit.]Pa. *kuṭhārī* -- f., Pk. *kuḍhāra* -- m., *kuhāḍa* -- m., °*ḍī* -- f. (for *ṭh* -- *r* ~ *h* -- *ḍ* see piṭhara --), S. *kuhāṛo* m., L. P. *kuhāṛā* m., °*ṛī* f., P. *kulhāṛā* m., °*ṛī* f., WPah. bhal. *kurhāṛi* f., Ku. *kulyāṛo*, gng. *kulyāṛ*, B. *kuṛāl*, °*li*, *kuṛul*, Or. *kuṛāla*, *kurāṛha*, °*ṛhi*, *kurhāṛi*, *kuṛāri*; Bi. *kulhārī* ' large axe for squaring logs '; H. *kulhāṛā* m., °*ṛī* f. ' axe ', G. *kuhāṛɔ* m., °*ṛī* f., *kuvāṛī* f., M. *kurhāḍ*, °*ḍī* f., Si. *keṇeri* Hettiaratchi Indeclinables 6 (connexion, if any, with *keṭeri*,°*ṭēriya* ' long -- handled axe ' is obscure).Addenda: **kuṭhāra --:** WPah.ktg. *khəṛari*, *kəṛari* f. ' axe '.(CDIAL 3244) Rebus: kuThAru 'armourer' **कुठारु [p= 289,1]** an armourer L.

A6 inscription
Elephant hieroglyph
kariba 'trunk of elephant' ibha 'elephant' Rebus: karba 'iron' ib 'iron'
C3, C4a, C4b, Hieroglyph-multiplex

C3 has additional duplicated hieroglyphs: ^^ aduru 'lid' rebus: aduru 'native, unsmelted metal' PLUS dula 'pair' rebus: dul 'cast metal'

kaṇḍa kanka 'rim of jar' Rebus: *karṇīka* 'account (scribe)'*karṇī*'supercargo'.
kaṇḍa 'fire-altar'. Alternative: kanka 'rim of jar' rebus: kanga 'brazier'.

kolom 'three' rebus: kolimi 'smithy, forge' PLUS dula 'pair' rebus: dul 'cast metal' Thus, smithy for metalcasting (perhaps cire perdue (lost-wax) technique is suggested).

Ligaturing element: pair of 'splinters' sal 'splinter' rebus: sal 'workshop' dula 'pair' rebus: dul 'cast meta' Thus metalcasting workshop.

C3 Text

kaṇḍa kanka 'rim of jar' Rebus: *karṇīka* 'account (scribe)'*karṇī*'supercargo'.
kaṇḍa 'fire-altar'. Alternative: kanka 'rim of jar' rebus: kanga 'brazier'.

dATu 'cross' rebus: dhAtu 'mineral'

ankaḍā 'crook, *hook*' rebus: akhāḍā 'comunity'. Thus, mineworker community.

bichā '*scorpion*' (Assamese) Rebus: bica 'stone ore' (Mu.)

aya 'fish' rebus: aya, ayas 'iron, metal' PLUS **खांडा** [*khāṇḍā*] *m* A jag, notch, or indentation (as upon the edge of a tool or weapon)(Marathi). Rebus: *kāṇḍa* 'tools, pots and pans and metal-ware' (Marathi)

C4a Text
kaṇḍa kanka 'rim of jar' Rebus: *karṇīka* 'account (scribe)'*karṇī*'supercargo'.
kaṇḍa 'fire-altar'. Alternative: kanka 'rim of jar' rebus: kanga 'brazier'.

loa ‘ficus’ rebus: loh ‘copper’

aya ‘fish’ rebus: aya, ayas ‘iron, metal’ PLUS dhal ‘slant’ rebus: dhALako ‘large ingot

mũh ‘ingot’ (Santali) PLUS (infixed) kolom 'sprout, rice plant' Rebus: kolimi 'smithy, forge' Thus, ingot smithy

Notes: dula 'pair' Rebus: dul 'cast metal' Ellipse is split into two curves of parenthesis: ( ) Thus, dula 'cast metal' signified by the curves joined into an ellipse.

C4b Text

mũh ‘ingot’ (Santali) PLUS (infixed) kolom 'sprout, rice plant' Rebus: kolimi 'smithy, forge' Thus, ingot smithy

Notes: dula 'pair' Rebus: dul 'cast metal' Ellipse is split into two curves of parenthesis: ( ) Thus, dula 'cast metal' signified by the curves joined into an ellipse.

aya ‘fish’ rebus: aya, ayas ‘iron, metal’ PLUS dhal ‘slant’ rebus: dhALako ‘large ingot

loa ‘ficus’ rebus: loh ‘copper’

kaṇḍa kanka ‘rim of jar’ Rebus: *karṇīka* ‘account (scribe)’*karṇī*‘supercargo’.
kaṇḍa ‘fire-altar’. Alternative: kanka 'rim of jar' rebus: kanga 'brazier'.

c5a Inscription

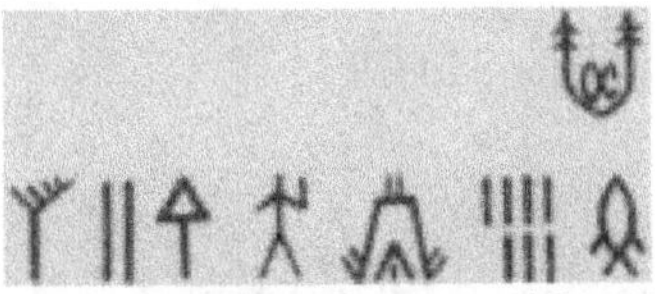

Text on incised copper tablet: Text Number 2901, 2903, 2911 Obverse: markhor These are possibly identical inscriptions on copper plates.

Line 1: Hieroglyph-multiplex

kāṇḍa 'arrow' rebus: khaNDa 'implements' dula 'pair' rebus: dul 'cast metal' PLUS kamaḍha 'crab' rebus: kammaṭa 'mint'. Thus the reading is: mint for cast metal implements.

as shown on c5a, c5b, c6, c9 copper plate types with hieroglyph-multiplex
Variant for Line 1: A pair of ficus leaves as circumflex for crab, claws. loa 'ficus' rebus: loh 'copper' PLUS dula 'pair' rebus: dul 'cast metal'. Thus cast metal infusion of copper.

Line 2: aya 'fish' rebus: aya 'iron' ayas 'metal' PLUS khANDA 'notch' rebus: khaNDa 'implements'. Thus, metal implements.

gaNDa 'four' rebus: khaNDa 'implements' kolmo 'three' rebus: kolimi 'smithy, forge'. Thus forged implements.

koḍa 'sluice'; Rebus: koḍ 'artisan's workshop (Kuwi)

meD 'body' rebus: med 'iron' PLUṢ eṛaka 'upraised arm' (Tamil); rebus: eraka = copper (Kannada). Thus, copper and metal (alloy)

kāṇḍa 'arrowhead' 'arrowhead' Rebus: kaṇḍ 'fire-altar' (Santali) rebus: khANDA kāṇḍa 'tools, pots and pans and metal-ware' (Marathi) 'implements"

dula 'two' rebus: dul 'cast metal'

kolmo 'rice-plant' rebus: kolimi 'smithy, forge'

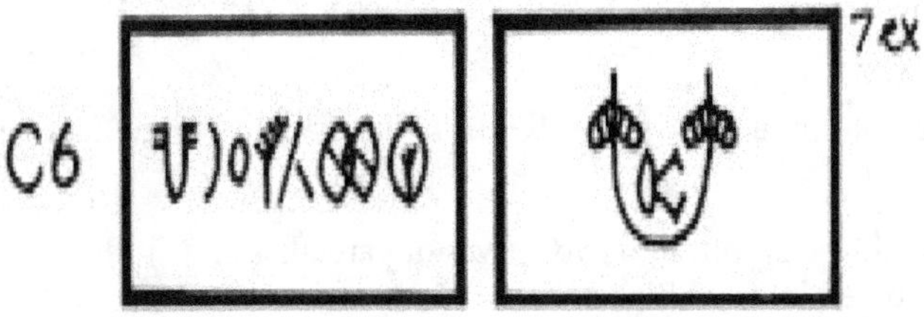

C6 copper plate epigraph: ficus PLUS pincers: metalsmith: लोह--कार [p= 908,3] *m.* a worker in iron , smith , blacksmith R. Hit. Hieroglyph component: *loa* 'ficus glomerata' Rebus: *loha* 'copper, iron' Hieroglyph component: *kāru* pincers, tongs. Rebus: *khār* खार् । लोहकारः 'blacksmith' (Kashmiri)

Since loha signifies 'copper' and kammaTa signifies 'mint' this hieroglyph multiplex on the obverse of C6 set of copper plate inscriptions (ficus PLUS crab+pincers) should more precisely signify semantically: mint-master, coppersmith.

The text of the epigraph common to both sets of copper plates (B16, hunter and C9 ficus+crab/pincers) has hieroglyph-multiplexes

 Inscription message: Supercargo bronze cast metal, ingots (of different shapes), metal implements smithy/forge On C9 set of copper plates, these come from लोहकारः lohakAra kammaTa the mint-master, coppersmith's workshop. On B16 set of copper plates, these come from कौटिलिकः kauṭilikḥ bronze worker's (smithy/forge).

 *mũh* 'ingot' (Santali) PLUS (infixed) kolom 'sprout, rice plant' Rebus: kolimi 'smithy, forge' Thus, ingot smithy

Notes: dula 'pair' Rebus: dul 'cast metal' Ellipse is split into two curves of parenthesis: ( ) Thus, dula 'cast metal' signified by the curves joined into an ellipse.

mũh 'ingot' (Santali) dula 'pair' Rebus: dul 'cast metal' Thus, cast metal ingot.

dula 'pair' Rebus: *dul* 'cast (metal)' PLUS *kana, kanac* = corner (Santali); Rebus: *kañcu* = bronze (Telugu) Thus, cast bronze or bronze casting.

This is a hieroglyph-multiplex: slant PLUS notch: DhAL 'slanted' Rebus: DhALako 'large ingot' PLUS खांडा (p. 202) [khāṇḍā] A jag, notch, or indentation (as upon the edge of a tool or weapon). Rebus: Rebus: *kāṇḍa* 'tools, pots and pans and metal-ware' (Marathi) *khaṇḍa* id. (Santali)

 kolom 'rice-plant, sprout' Rebus: kolimi 'smithy, forge'

 *goṭ* 'seed, rounded object' Rebus: खोट (p. 212) [khōṭa] f A mass of metal (unwrought or of old metal melted down); an ingot or wedge (Marathi) Rebus: *goṭa* 'laterite (ferrite ore))'

 The 'curve' hieroglyph is a splitting of the ellipse. *kuṭila* 'bent' CDIAL 3230 kuṭi— in cmpd. 'curve', *kuṭika*— 'bent' MBh.

Rebus: *kuṭila, katthīl* = bronze (8 parts copper and 2 parts tin) cf. āra-kūṭa, 'brass' Old English *ār* 'brass, copper, bronze' Old Norse *eir* 'brass, copper', German *ehern* 'brassy, bronzen'. kastīra n. ' tin ' lex. 2. *kastilla -- .1. H. *kathīr* m. ' tin, pewter '; G. *kathīr* n. ' pewter '.2. H. (Bhoj.?) *kathīl*, *°lā* m. ' tin, pewter '; M. *kathīl* n. ' tin ', *kathlẽ* n. ' large tin vessel '.(CDIAL 2984)

*kaṇḍa kanka* 'rim of jar' Rebus: *karṇīka* 'account (scribe)' *karṇī* 'supercargo'. *kaṇḍa* 'fire-altar'. Alternative: kanka 'rim of jar' rebus: kanga 'brazier'.

C7

Hieroglyph-multiplex: kolmo 'rice plant' rebus: kolimi 'smithy, forge' ligatured to: *dula* 'pair' Rebus: *dul* 'cast (metal)' PLUS *kana, kanac* = corner (Santali); Rebus: *kañcu* = bronze (Telugu) Thus, cast bronze or bronze casting.

C7 text

kaṇḍa kanka 'rim of jar' Rebus: *karṇīka* 'account (scribe)' *karṇī* 'supercargo'. *kaṇḍa* 'fire-altar'. Alternative: kanka 'rim of jar' rebus: kanga 'brazier'

kolmo 'rice plant' rebus: kolimi 'smithy, forge'

ranku 'liquid measure' rebus: ranku 'tin'

aya 'fish' rebus: aya, ayas 'iron, metal'

kolmo 'three' rebus: kolimi 'smithy, forge'

C8 Hieroglyph: Sting of scorpion:
bichā 'scorpion' (Assamese) Rebus: bica 'stone ore' (Mu.) hematite ore.

C8 text

kaṇḍa kanka 'rim of jar' Rebus: *karṇīka* 'account (scribe)' *karṇī* 'supercargo'. *kaṇḍa* 'fire-altar'. Alternative: kanka 'rim of jar' rebus: kanga 'brazier' bhaTa ‘warrior’ rebus: bhaTa ‘furnace’

dula 'pair' Rebus: dul 'cast metal' Ellipse is split into two curves of parenthesis: ( ) Thus, dula 'cast metal' signified by the curves joined into an ellipse. The 'curve' hieroglyph is a splitting of the ellipse. *kuṭila* ‘bent’ CDIAL 3230 kuṭi— in cmpd. ‘curve’, *kuṭika—* ‘bent’ MBh. Rebus: *kuṭila, katthīl* = bronze (8 parts copper and 2 parts tin) cf. āra-kūṭa, 'brass' Old English *ār* 'brass, copper, bronze' Old Norse *eir* 'brass, copper', German *ehern* 'brassy, bronzen'. kastīra n. ‘ tin ’ lex. 2. *kastilla -- .1. H. *kathīr* m. ‘ tin, pewter ’; G. *kathīr* n. ‘ pewter ’.2. H. (Bhoj.?) *kathīl*, *°lā* m. ‘ tin, pewter ’; M. *kathīl* n. ‘ tin ’, *kathlẽ* n. ‘ large tin vessel ’.(CDIAL 2984)

Sign 34:
muka ‘ladle’ (Tamil)(DEDR 4887) Rebus: *mũh* ‘ingot’ (Santali) *baṭa* = a kind of iron (G.) *baṭa* = rimless pot (Kannada) Thus, iron ingot.+ kāṭi 'body stature; Rebus: fireplace trench. Thus, iron ingot furnace.

aya ‘fish’ rebus: aya, ayas ‘iron, metal’
kamaḍha ‘crab’ Rebus: *kammaṭa* ‘mint, coiner’.*ḍato* = claws of crab (Santali) *ḍato* = claws of crab (Santali) Rebus: *dhātu* ‘mineral ore’

kolom ‘three’ rebus: kolimi ‘smithy, forge’

Sign 34:*muka* ‘ladle’ (Tamil)(DEDR 4887) Rebus: *mũh* ‘ingot’ (Santali) *baṭa* = a kind of iron (G.) *baṭa* = rimless pot (Kannada) Thus, iron ingot.+ kāṭi 'body stature; Rebus: fireplace trench. Thus, iron ingot furnace.

C9 text

khareḍo '*currycomb*' rebus: kharādī 'turner'

kaṇḍa kanka ‘rim of jar’ Rebus: *karṇīka* ‘account (scribe)’*karṇī* ‘supercargo’.
kaṇḍa ‘fire-altar’. Alternative: kanka 'rim of jar' rebus: kanga 'brazier'

bicha ‘scorpion’ rebus: hematite, stone ore.

baTa 'rimless pot' Rebus: bhaTa 'furnace' PLUS muka 'ladle' rebus; mũh 'ingot', quantity of metal got out of a smelter furnace (Santali)

C10

Hieroglyph: Illegible

Text: dula ‘two’ rebus: dul ‘cast metal’

The 'curve' hieroglyph is a splitting of the ellipse. *kuṭila* ‘bent’ CDIAL 3230 kuṭi— in cmpd. ‘curve’, *kuṭika—* ‘bent’ MBh.

Rebus: *kuṭila, katthīl* = bronze (8 parts copper and 2 parts tin) cf. āra-kūṭa, 'brass' Old English *ār* 'brass, copper, bronze' Old Norse *eir* 'brass, copper', German *ehern* 'brassy, bronzen'. kastīra n. ‘ tin ’ lex. 2. *kastilla -- .1. H. *kathīr* m. ‘ tin, pewter ’; G. *kathīr* n. ‘ pewter ’.2. H. (Bhoj.?) *kathīl*, *°lā* m. ‘ tin, pewter ’; M. *kathīl* n. ‘ tin ’, *kathlẽ* n. ‘ large tin vessel ’.(CDIAL 2984)

Deciphered A4 to A11 sets of copper plate inscriptions

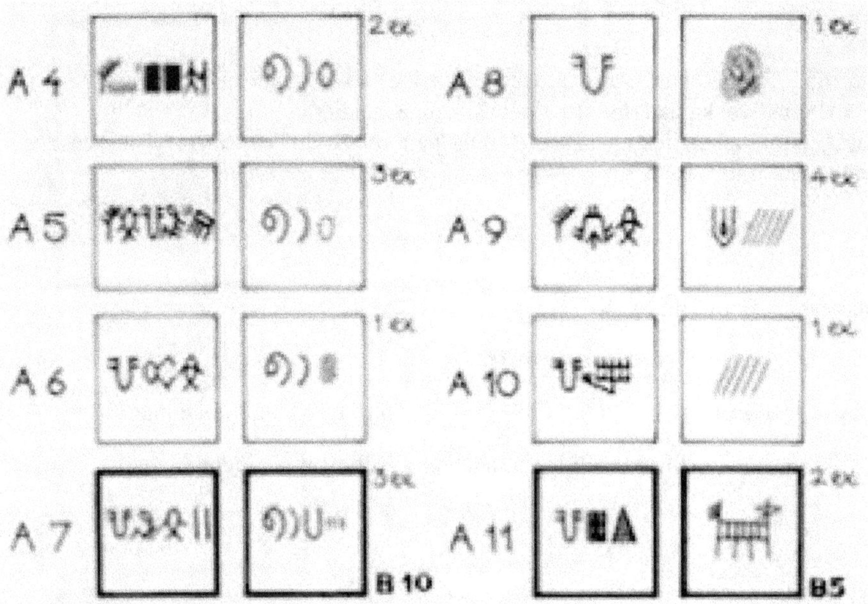

A11

Hieroglyph:

krammara 'look back' (Telugu) rebus: kamar 'blacksmith' mlekh 'goat' rebus: milakkhu, mlecchAs'a 'copper'

*kaṇḍa kanka* 'rim of jar' Rebus: *karṇīka* 'account (scribe)'*karṇī* 'supercargo'. *kaṇḍa* 'fire-altar'. Alternative: kanka 'rim of jar' rebus: kanga 'brazier'.

khaNDA 'dividion' rebus: khANDa 'implements'

Hieroglyph: *Ta.* meṭṭu mound, heap of earth; mēṭu height, eminence, hillock; muṭṭu rising ground, high ground, heap. *Ma.* mēṭu rising ground, hillock; māṭu hillock, raised ground; miṭṭāl rising ground, an alluvial bank; (Tiyya) maṭṭa hill. *Ka.* mēḍu height, rising ground, hillock; miṭṭu rising or high ground, hill; miṭṭe state of being high, rising ground, hill, mass, a large number; (Hav.) muṭṭe heap (as of straw). *Tu.* miṭṭè prominent, protruding; muṭṭe heap. *Te.* meṭṭa raised or high ground, hill; (K.) meṭṭu mound; miṭṭa high ground, hillock, mound; high, elevated, raised, projecting; (*VPK*) mēṭu, mēṭa, mēṭi stack of hay; (Inscr.) meṇṭa-cēnu dry field (cf. meṭṭu-nēla, meṭṭu-vari). *Kol.* (SR.) meṭṭā hill; (Kin.) meṭṭ, (Hislop) met mountain. *Nk.* meṭṭ hill, mountain. *Ga.* (S.3, *LSB* 20.3) meṭṭa high land. *Go.* (Tr. W. Ph.) maṭṭā, (Mu.) maṭṭa mountain; (M. L.) meṭā id., hill; (A. D. Ko.) meṭṭa, (Y. Ma. M.) meṭa hill; (SR.) meṭṭā hillock (*Voc.* 2949). *Koṇḍa* meṭa id. *Kuwi* (S.)metta hill; (Isr.) meṭa sand hill. (DEDR 5058) Rebus: *mẽd, mēd* 'iron'

A10

*kaṇḍa kanka* ‘rim of jar’ Rebus: *karṇīka* ‘account (scribe)’*karṇī*‘supercargo’.
kaṇḍa ‘fire-altar’. Alternative: kanka 'rim of jar' rebus: kanga 'brazier'.
aḍar '*harrow*' rebus: aduru ‘unsmelted metal’PLUS dula 'pair' rebus: dul 'cast metal' Thus, casting of unsmelted metal (meteorite iron?)

A9

kolmo 'rice-plant' rebus: kolimi 'smithy, forge'

koḍa 'sluice'; Rebus: koḍ 'artisan's workshop (Kuwi)

aya ‘fish’ rebus: ayas, aya ‘iron, metal’ PLUS dhAl ‘slope’ rebus: dhALaka ‘large ingot’

baTa ‘rimless pot’ rebus: bhaTa ‘furnace’ PLUS muka '*ladle*' Rebus: mũh 'ingot' (Santali)

A8

*kaṇḍa kanka* ‘rim of jar’ Rebus: *karṇīka* ‘account (scribe)’*karṇī*‘supercargo’.
kaṇḍa ‘fire-altar’. Alternative: kanka 'rim of jar' rebus: kanga 'brazier'.

muh 'ingot' PLUखांडा [khāṇḍā] 'A jag, notch, or indentation (as upon the edge of a tool or weapon)' Rebus: kaNDa 'implements' (Santali)
A4, A5, A6 reverse inscription:

This hieroglyph-multiplex may be an oval as a circumflex with embedded 'notch' hieroglyph. If so, the rebus readings are: muh 'ingot' PLUS खांडा [khāṇḍā] 'A jag, notch, or indentation (as upon the edge of a tool or weapon)' Rebus: kaNDa 'implements' (Santali). Thus, the hypertext signifies ingot (for) metal implements.
O goṭ 'seed, rounded object' Rebus: खोट (p. 212) [khōṭa] f A mass of metal (unwrought or of old metal melted down); an ingot or wedge (Marathi)
) The 'curve' hieroglyph is a splitting of the ellipse. *kuṭila* ‘bent’ CDIAL 3230 kuṭi— in cmpd. ‘curve’, *kuṭika*— ‘bent’ MBh.

Rebus: *kuṭila, katthīl* = bronze (8 parts copper and 2 parts tin)

A7 reverse inscription

muh 'ingot' PLUSखांडा [khāṇḍā] 'A jag, notch, or indentation (as upon the edge of a tool or weapon)' Rebus: kaNDa 'implements' (Santali)

) The 'curve' hieroglyph is a splitting of the ellipse. *kuṭila* ‘bent’ CDIAL 3230 kuṭi— in cmpd. ‘curve’, *kuṭika*— ‘bent’ MBh.

Rebus: *kuṭila, katthīl* = bronze (8 parts copper and 2 parts tin)

U rimless pot: baTa 'rimless pot' Rebus: bhaTa 'furnace'

Numeral 3: kolom 'three' rebus: kolimi 'smithy, forge'.

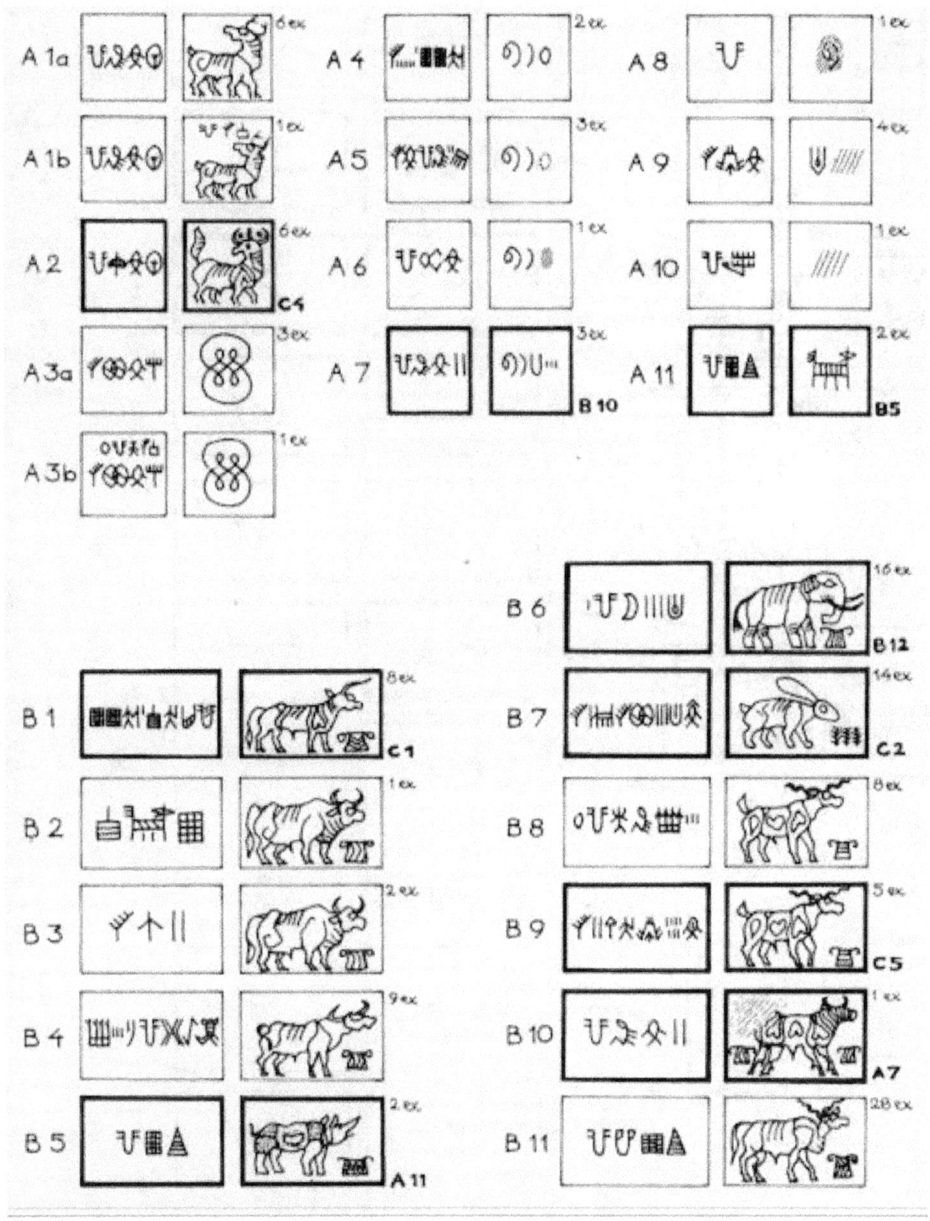

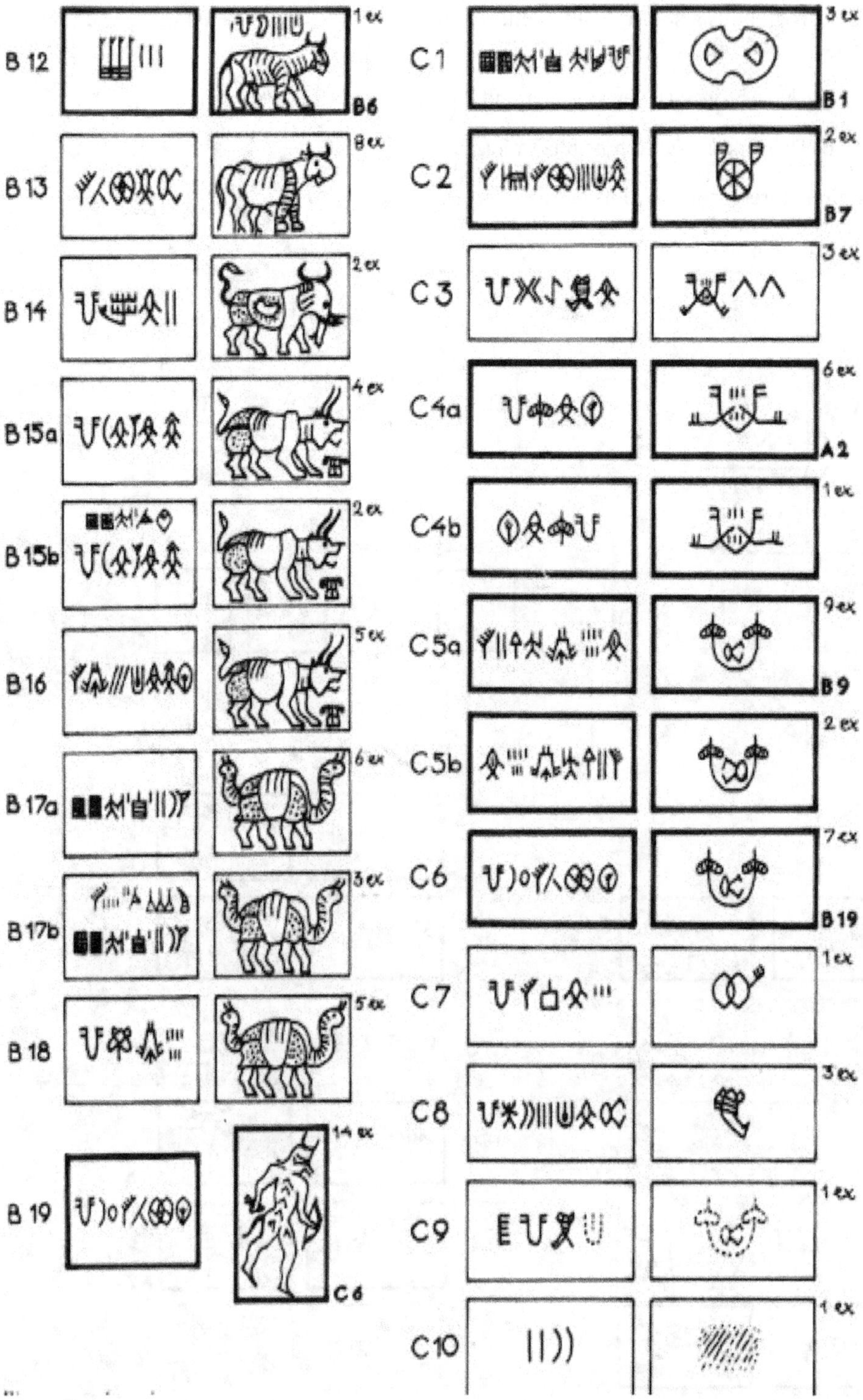
B 12
1 ex
B6
B 13
8 ex
B 14
2 ex
B 15a
4 ex
B 15b
2 ex
B 16
5 ex
B 17a
6 ex
B 17b
3 ex
B 18
5 ex
B 19
14 ex
C6
C 1
3 ex
B1
C 2
2 ex
B7
C 3
3 ex
C 4a
6 ex
A2
C 4b
1 ex
C 5a
9 ex
B9
C 5b
2 ex
C 6
7 ex
B19
C 7
1 ex
C 8
3 ex
C 9
1 ex
C 10
1 ex

B1 inscription

The hieroglyph is bull in front of trough. On C1 the same text has on obverse a double-axe hieroglyph.

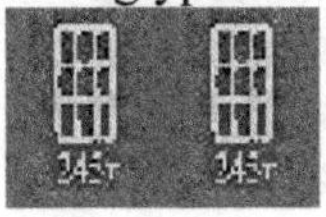

dula 'pair' rebus: dul 'cast metal' khaNDA 'division' rebus: khANDa 'implements', i.e. metal implement castings

mẽd, mēd 'body'; BODY PLUS STAFF is a phonetic determinative: *meḍ(h), meḍhī* f., *meḍhā* ' post, forked stake '; *meṛh* f. ' rope tying oxen to each other and to post on threshing floor ' rebus: *mẽd, mēd* 'iron'

Hieroglyph: notch ' खांडा khāṇḍā] 'A jag, notch, or indentation (as upon the edge of a tool or weapon)' Rebus: kaNDa 'implements' (Santali).

ranku 'liquid measure' rebus: ranku 'tin'

mẽd, mēd 'body'; BODY PLUS 'notch' rebus: *mẽd, mēd* 'iron' PLUS खाडा [kāṇḍā] 'A jag, notch, or indentation (as upon the edge of a tool or weapon)' Rebus: kaNDa 'implements' (Santali).

'hoof': Kumaon. khuṭo 'leg, foot', °ṭī 'goat's leg'; Nepalese. khuṭo 'leg, foot'(CDIAL 3894). S. khuṛī f. 'heel'; WPah. paṅ. khūṛ 'foot'. (CDIAL 3906). Rebus: khũṭ 'community, guild' (Santali)

B1 inscription
Hieroglyph: One horned young bull PLUS pattar 'trough' rebus: pattar 'guild'

What is shown is a bull-calf together with other hieroglyph components: one horn, pannier, rings on neck completing the hieroglyph-multiplex as 'symbolic hypertext' as noted by Dennys Frenez and Massimo Vidale.http://a.harappa.com/sites/g/f... All are hieroglyph components. kodiyum 'rings on neck' kod `horn' (Kuwi); rebus: kod `artisan's workshop' (Gujarati). खोंड [khōṇḍa] m A young bull, a bullcalf.(Marathi) Rebus: kõdā 'to turn in a lathe'(B.) कोंद kōnda 'engraver, lapidary setting or infixing gems' (Marathi). I would like to add two points: 1. Bronze Age discovery of tin-bronzes and ability to produce metal implements necessitated a writing system; and 2. the sources for tin could have extended into the Ancient Far East, the largest mineral tin belt of the world. See evidences at the URL cited in an extensive area from Dong Son to Nahal Mishmar through Shahi

Tump, Nausharo and Mohenjo-daro.

The word for the 'pannier' is: खोंडा [khōṇḍā] m A कांबळा of which one end is formed into a cowl or hood (Marathi). Hence, rebus: kōnda 'engraver, lapidary' (Meluhha. Indian sprachbund). Any one or more Indian languages provide homonymous glosses for the reconstruction of ancient lexis of metalwork, lapidary work expressed in Prakritam, the speech form of the Indian language union called sprachbund in linguistic studies. Mleccha is mispronunciations in speech. Mleccha speakers are attested in most of the janapada's of ancient India..

What is the device in front of the young bull hieroglyph-multiplex? It is also a symbolic hypertext with joined parts: 1. Lathe (gimlet) on top; 2. Portable brazier on bottom; 3. Dotted circles.
The joining of parts is: sãghāṛɔ 'lathe'. 'brazier' (Gujarati) सांगड [sāṅgaḍa] m f (संघट्ट S) f A body formed of two or more (fruits, animals, men) linked or joined together (Marathi). Rebus: sangara 'proclamation'. What is proclaimed in the catalog? Signifying a gimlet creating perforations on beads? kandi 'beads' Rebus: kanda 'fire-altar'.

The fire-altar message is in front of the workshop (koḍ) of कोंद kōnda 'engraver, lapidary (Marathi). This combination ofhieroglyph-multiplexes: 'one-horned young bull with pannier, rings on neck'
PLUS 'lathe, brazier, dotted circles' is thus a proclamation, a catalog of
work performed by a metalworker, engraver. Details of the work and produce are
listed on the top register with four signs: baṭa 'warrior', rebus: bhaṭa 'furnace'; ḍabu 'aniron spoon' Rebus: ḍab, 'lump; kolmo 'paddy plant' Rebus: kolimi 'smithy, forge'; ranku 'liquid measure' Rebus: ranku 'tin'.

The proclamation thus lists how the metallurgical work was done (to produce) tin mineral ingot from furnace and forge. The hypertext cipher stands cracked using words of Indian sprachbund which referred to as Meluhha language on a cylinder seal of Shu-ilishu, who was an Akkadian calling himself eme-bal mel-u-h-ha-ki 'Meluhha translator'.

http://a.harappa.com/content/s.

B2 inscription
Hieroglyph: Bull PLUS trough hieroglyph-multiplex
Hieroglyph: barad, barat 'ox' Rebus: भरत (p. 603) [bharata] *n* A factitious metal compounded of copper, pewter, tin &c.(Marathi) PLUS pattar 'trough' rebus: pattar 'trough'.

B2 text

ranku 'liquid measure' rebus: ranku 'tin'

mlekh 'goat' rebus: milakkhu 'copper'

khaNDa 'division' rebus: khaNDA 'implements'

B3 text

kolmo 'riceplant' rebus: kolimi 'smithy, forge'

kaNDa 'arrow' rebus: khaNDa 'implements'

dula 'two' rebus: dul 'cast metal'

B4 text

rango 'buffalo' rebus: rango 'pewter' PLUS pattar 'trough' rebus: pattar 'guild'

gaNDa 'four' rebus: kanda 'fire-altar' PLUS kolmo 'rice plant' rebus: kolimi 'smithy, forge'

gaNDa 'four' rebus: kanda 'fire-altar' (Phonetic determintive)

notch: khANa 'notch' rebus: khANDA 'implements' PLUS kuṭi = a. *slice*, a bit, a small piece (Santali.lex.Bodding) Rebus: kuṭhi 'iron smelter furnace' (Santali)

karNIka

dATu 'cross' rebus: dhAtu 'mineral'

ankaḍā 'crook, *hook*' rebus: akhāḍā 'comunity'

bichā '*scorpion*' (Assamese) Rebus: bica 'stone ore' (Mu.) .

B5

Hieroglyph: kANDA 'rhinoceros' rebus: khANDA 'implements PLUS pattar 'trough' rebus: pattar 'guild'

kaṇḍa kanka 'rim of jar' Rebus: *karṇīka* 'account (scribe)' *karṇī* 'supercargo'. *kaṇḍa* 'fire-altar'. Alternative: kanka 'rim of jar' rebus: kanga 'brazier'.

khaNDA 'dividion' rebus: khANDa 'implements'

Hieroglyph: *Ta.* meṭṭu mound, heap of earth; mēṭu height, eminence, hillock; muṭṭu rising ground, high ground, heap. *Ma.* mēṭu rising ground, hillock; māṭu hillock, raised ground; miṭṭāl rising ground, an alluvial bank; (Tiyya) maṭṭa hill. *Ka.* mēḍu height, rising ground, hillock; miṭṭu rising or high ground, hill; miṭṭe state of being high, rising ground, hill, mass, a large number; (Hav.) muṭṭe heap (as of straw). *Tu.* miṭṭè prominent, protruding; muṭṭe heap. *Te.* meṭṭa raised or high ground, hill; (K.) meṭṭu mound; miṭṭa high ground, hillock, mound; high, elevated, raised, projecting; (*VPK*) mēṭu, mēṭa, mēṭi stack of hay; (Inscr.) meṇṭa-cēnu dry field (cf. meṭṭu-nēla, meṭṭu-vari). *Kol.* (SR.) meṭṭā hill; (Kin.) meṭṭ, (Hislop) met mountain. *Nk.* meṭṭ hill, mountain. *Ga.* (S.3, *LSB* 20.3) meṭṭa high land. *Go.* (Tr. W. Ph.) maṭṭā, (Mu.) maṭṭa mountain; (M. L.) meṭā id., hill; (A. D. Ko.) meṭṭa, (Y. Ma. M.) meṭa hill; (SR.) meṭṭā hillock (*Voc.* 2949). *Koṇḍa* meṭa id. *Kuwi* (S.)metta hill; (Isr.) meṭa sand hill. (DEDR 5058) Rebus: *mẽd, mēd* 'iron' .

B6 inscription
Hieroglyph: karibha 'trunk of elephant' ibha 'elephant' rebus: karb 'iron' ib 'iron. PLUS pattar 'trough' rebus: pattar 'guild'.

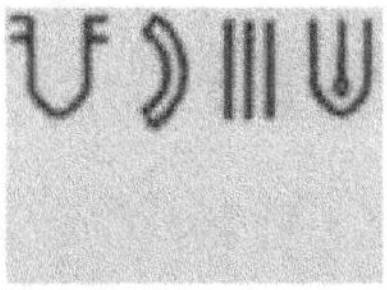

m1486B Text 1711

Obverse: karibha 'trunk of elephant' ibha 'elephant' rebus: kariba 'iron' ib 'iron' khAr 'blacksmith'. Thus, ironsmith.

Reverse: Inscription of hypertext:

baTa 'rimless pot' Rebus: bhaTa 'furnace' PLUS muka 'ladle' rebus; mũh 'ingot', quantity of metal got out of a smelter furnace (Santali)

kolom 'three' Rebus: kolimi 'smithy, forge'

alloy: भरत *bharat*;

bronze: कुटिल *kuṭila, katthīl;*

zinc (pewter): *sattva.*

The lexis entry for bronze is signified by the hieroglyph 'curve' or 'right parenthesis':

 Doubling of this signifies dula 'pair' rebus: dul 'cast metal'. Thus doubling of the right parenthesis results in a hieroglyph-multiplex as shown on the elephant copper plate inscription m1486 text

 This hieroglyph-multiplex is thus read as: *kuṭilika* 'bent, curved' dula 'pair' rebus: *kuṭila, katthīl* = bronze (8 parts copper and 2 parts tin)

 The 'curve' hieroglyph is a splitting of the ellipse. *kuṭila* 'bent' CDIAL 3230 kuṭi— in cmpd. 'curve', *kuṭika*— 'bent' MBh.

Rebus: *kuṭila, katthīl* = bronze (8 parts copper and 2 parts tin) cf. āra-kūṭa, 'brass' Old English *ār* 'brass, copper, bronze' Old Norse *eir* 'brass, copper', German *ehern* 'brassy, bronzen'. kastīra n. ' tin ' lex. 2. *kastilla -- .1. H. *kathīr* m. ' tin, pewter '; G. *kathīr* n. ' pewter '.2. H. (Bhoj.?) *kathīl*, *°lā* m. ' tin, pewter '; M. *kathīl* n. ' tin ', *kathlẽ* n. 'large tin vessel'. (CDIAL 2984)

Hieroglyphs: कौटिलिकः kauṭilikḥ कौटिलिकः 1 A hunter.-2 A blacksmith. कौटिलिक

[p= 315,2] *m.* (fr. कुटिलिका Pa1n2. 4-4 , 18) " deceiving the hunter [or the deer Sch.] by particular movements " , a deer [" a hunter " Sch.] Ka1s3. *f.* (Pa1n2. 4-4 , 18) कुटिलिका crouching , coming stealthily (like a hunter on his prey ; a particular movement on the stage) Vikr. कुटिलिक " using the tool called कुटिलिका " , a blacksmith ib. कुटिलक [p= 288,2] *f.* a tool used by a blacksmith Pa1n2. 4-4 , 18 Ka1s3.*mfn.* bent , curved , crisped Pan5cat.

The hieroglyph-multiplex may be a variant of split ellipse curves paired: dula 'pair' rebus: *dul* 'cast metal' PLUS *mũh* 'ingot' (Paired split ellipse or a pair of right parentheses) -- made of -- *kuṭila, katthīl* = bronze (8 parts copper and 2 parts tin)

karNika 'rim of jar' rebus: karNI 'supercargo'; karNaka 'account'; Alternative: kanka 'rim of jar' rebus: kanga 'brazier'.

Thus, the entire inscription is a metalwork catalog: supercargo of iron, cast bronze metal ingots, our of smithy furnace and forge.

B7

Hieroglyph: kulai 'hare' rebus: kol 'working in iron' kolle 'blacksmith' kolhe 'smelter' PLUS kolmo 'sprout' rebus: kolimi 'smithy, forge'

C2

Hieroglyph: eraka 'nave of wheel' rebus: eraka 'moltencast' 'copper'; Ara 'spoke' rebus: Ara 'brass'

Text:Same as on B7

kolmo 'sprout' rebus: kolimi 'smithy, forge' (for copper): *meḍ(h)*, *meḍhī* f., *meḍhā* ' post, forked stake '; *meṛh* f. ' rope tying oxen to each other and to post on threshing floor ' rebus: *mẽd, mēd* 'iron' PLUS mlekh 'goat' rebus: milakkhu 'copper''

kolmo 'rice plant' rebus: kolimi 'smithy, forge' (for bronze):

gaNDa 'four' rebus: kanda 'fire-altar'

baTa 'rimless pot' rebus: bhaTa 'furnace' PLUS muka 'ladle' rebus: muhA 'ingot'

aya 'fish' rebus: aya, ayas 'iron,metal' PLUS aDaren 'lid' rebus: aduru 'unsmelted metal'

B8

Hieroglyph: meḍho a *ram* rebus: mẽṛhẽt, meḍ 'iron' (Mu.) mRdu 'iron' (Samskritam) PLUS *pattar* 'trough' rebus: *pattar* 'guild' goTa 'round' rebus: goTa 'laterite'

kaṇḍa kanka 'rim of jar' Rebus: *karṇīka* 'account (scribe)' *karṇī* 'supercargo'.
kaṇḍa 'fire-altar'. Alternative: kanka 'rim of jar' rebus: kanga 'brazier'.

bhaTa 'warrior' rebus: bhaTa 'furnace'

baraḍo = spine; backbone (Tulu) Rebus: *baran, bharat* 'mixed alloys' (5 copper, 4 zinc and 1 tin) (Punjabi).*baroṭi* 'twelve' *bhārata* 'a factitious alloy of copper, pewter, tin' (Marathi) भरत (p. 603) [bharata] *n* A factitious metal compounded of copper, pewter, tin &c. भरताचें भांडें (p. 603) [bharatācē mbhāṇḍēṃ] *n* A vessel made of the metal भरत. 2 See भरिताचें भांडें. भरती (p. 603) [bharatī] *a* Composed of the metal भरत. (Molesworth Marathi Dictionary).

gaNDa 'four' rebus: kanda 'fire-altar' PLUS kolmo 'rice plant' rebus: kolimi 'smithy, forge'

kolom 'three' rebus: kolimi 'smithy, forge' (Phonetic determinant)

B9

Hieroglyph: meḍho a *ram* rebus: mẽṛhẽt, meḍ 'iron' (Mu.) mRdu 'iron' (Samskritam) PLUS pattar 'trough' rebus: pattar 'guild'

Text

kolmo 'rice plant' rebus: kolimi 'smithy, forg'

dula 'two' rebus: dul 'cast metal'

mẽd, mēd 'body'; BODY PLUS 'notch' rebus: *mẽd, mēd* 'iron'
PLUS खांडा [khāṇḍā] 'A jag, notch, or indentation (as upon the edge of a tool or weapon)' Rebus: kaNDa 'implements' (Santali).

kaNDa 'arrow' rebus; khaNDa 'implements'

koḍa 'sluice'; Rebus: koḍ 'artisan's workshop (Kuwi)

gaNDa 'four' rebus: kanda 'fire-altar

kolom 'three' rebus: kolimi 'smithy, forge

aya 'fish' rebus: aya, ayas 'iron, metal' PLUS खांडा [khāṇḍā] 'A jag, notch, or indentation (as upon the edge of a tool or weapon)' Rebus: kaNDa 'implements' (Santali).

B10

Hieroglyph: Back-to-back ligatured body of barad, 'ox' rebus: bharata 'aalloy of copper, pewter, tin'

PLUS *pattar* 'trough' rebus: *pattar* 'guild'

It is suggested that the back-to-back duplication of the body of an ox signifies cire perdue cesting technique used to produce metal castings.sangaDa 'joined animals' is a device used in front of the one-horned bull as sangada 'lathe, portable furnace' This technique of sangaDa signifies rebusvajra sanghAta 'damantine glue' to create alloys of metals by the turner.

kaṇḍa 'fire-altar'. Alternative: kanka 'rim of jar' rebus: kanga 'brazier'.

baraḍo = spine; backbone (Tulu) Rebus: *baran, bharat* 'mixed alloys' (5 copper, 4 zinc and 1 tin) (Punjabi).*baroṭi* 'twelve' *bhārata* 'a factitious alloy of copper, pewter, tin' (Marathi)भरत (p. 603) [bharata] *n* A factitious metal compounded of copper, pewter, tin &c.भरताचें भांडें (p. 603) [bharatācē mbhāṇḍēṃ] *n* A vessel made of the metal भरत. 2 See भरिताचें भांडें.भरती (p. 603) [bharatī] *a* Composed of the metal भरत. (Molesworth Marathi Dictionary).

aya 'fish' rebus: aya, ayas 'iron, metal'

dula 'two' rebus: dul 'cast metal'

B11

Hieroglyph: barad 'ox' rebus: bharat 'alloy of copper, pewter, tin' PLUS pattar 'trough' rebus: pattar 'guild'

kaṇḍa kanka 'rim of jar' Rebus: *karṇīka* 'account (scribe)'*karṇī*'supercargo'.

kaṇḍa 'fire-altar'. Alternative: kanka 'rim of jar' rebus: kanga 'brazier'.

baTa 'rimless pot' rebus: bhaTa 'furnace' PLUS dula 'pair' rebus: dul 'cast metal' PLUS koDi 'flag' rebus: koD 'workshop'

khaNDA 'dividion' rebus: khANDa 'implements'

Hieroglyph: *Ta.* meṭṭu mound, heap of earth; mēṭu height, eminence, hillock; muṭṭu rising ground, high ground, heap. *Ma.* mēṭu rising ground, hillock; māṭu hillock, raised ground; miṭṭāl rising ground, an alluvial bank; (Tiyya) maṭṭa hill. *Ka.* mēḍu height, rising ground, hillock; miṭṭu rising or high ground, hill; miṭṭe state of being high, rising ground, hill, mass, a large number; (Hav.) muṭṭe heap (as of straw). *Tu.* miṭṭè prominent, protruding; muṭṭe heap. *Te.* meṭṭa raised or high ground, hill; (K.) meṭṭu mound; miṭṭa high ground, hillock, mound; high, elevated, raised, projecting; (*VPK*) mēṭu, mēṭa, mēṭi stack of hay; (Inscr.) meṇṭa-cēnu dry field (cf. meṭṭu-nēla, meṭṭu-vari). *Kol.* (SR.) meṭṭā hill; (Kin.) meṭṭ, (Hislop) met mountain. *Nk.* meṭṭ hill, mountain. *Ga.* (S.3, *LSB* 20.3) meṭṭa high land. *Go.* (Tr. W. Ph.) maṭṭā, (Mu.) maṭṭa mountain; (M. L.) meṭā id., hill; (A. D. Ko.) meṭṭa, (Y. Ma. M.) meṭa hill; (SR.) meṭṭā hillock (*Voc.* 2949). *Konḍa* meṭa id. *Kuwi* (S.)metta hill; (Isr.) meṭa sand hill. (DEDR 5058) Rebus: *mẽd, mēd* 'iron'

B12

Hieroglyph: kola 'tiger' rebus: kol 'working in iron' kolle 'blacksmith' kolhe 'smelter' kolimi 'smithy, forge'

kaṇḍa kanka 'rim of jar' Rebus: *karṇīka* 'account (scribe)'*karṇī*'supercargo'.
kaṇḍa 'fire-altar'. Alternative: kanka 'rim of jar' rebus: kanga 'brazier'.

kuṭilika 'bent, curved' dula 'pair' rebus: *kuṭila, katthīl* = bronze (8 parts copper and 2 parts tin) dula 'pair' rebus: dul 'cast metal' Thus, bronze casting kolom ‘three’ rebus: kolimi ‘smithy, forge’

baTa ‘rimless pot’ rebus: bhaTa ‘furnace’ PLUS muka 'ladle' rebus; mũh 'ingot', quantity of metal got out of a smelter furnace (Santali)

gaNDa ‘four’ rebus: kanda ‘fire-altar’ PLUS kolmo ‘rice plant’ rebus: kolimi ‘smithy, forge’

kolom 'three' rebus: kolimi 'smithy, forge'

B13

Hieroglyph: kola ‘tiger’ rebus: kol ‘working in iron’ kolle ‘blacksmith’ kolhe ‘smelter’ kolimi ‘smithy, forge’

Text

kolmo ‘rice plant’ rebus: kolimi ‘smithy, forge’

slant PLUS notch: DhAL 'slanted' Rebus: DhALako 'large ingot' PLUS खांडा (p. 202) [khāṇḍā] A jag, notch, or indentation (as upon the edge of a tool or weapon). Rebus: Rebus: *kāṇḍa* ‘tools, pots and pans and metal-ware’ (Marathi) *khaṇḍa* id. (Santali)

mũh ‘ingot’ (Santali) dula 'pair' Rebus: dul 'cast metal' Thus, cast metal ingot.

aya ‘fish’ rebus: aya, ayas ‘iron, metal’ PLUS B. ā̃is ‘ scales of fish ’; Or. āĩsa ‘ flesh, fish, *fish scales* ’ Thus phonetic determinative of ayas ‘metal (alloy)’

ḍato '*claws* or *pincers* of *crab*' (Santali) rebus: dhatu 'ore' (Santali) Vikalpa: erā '*claws*'; Rebus: era 'copper'.PLUS kamaDha ‘crab’ rebus: kammaTa ‘mint, coiner’

B14

Hieroglyph: horned elephant Kariba ‘trunk of elephant’ ibha ‘elephant’ rebus: karb ‘iron’ ib ‘iron’ PLUS koD ‘horn’ rebus: koD ‘workshop’ ibbo ‘merchant

kaṇḍa kanka ‘rim of jar’ Rebus: *karṇīka* ‘account (scribe)’*karṇī*‘supercargo’.
kaṇḍa ‘fire-altar’. Alternative: kanka 'rim of jar' rebus: kanga 'brazier'.

aduru '*harrow*' rebus: aduru 'native metal' PLUS dula ‘pair’ rebus: dul ‘cast metal’ PLUS kolmo ‘sprout’ rebus: kolimi ‘smithy, forge’ Thus smithy/forge for native metal castings

aya ‘fish’ rebus: ayas, aya ‘iron, metal’

dula ‘two’ rebus: dul ‘cast metal’

B15

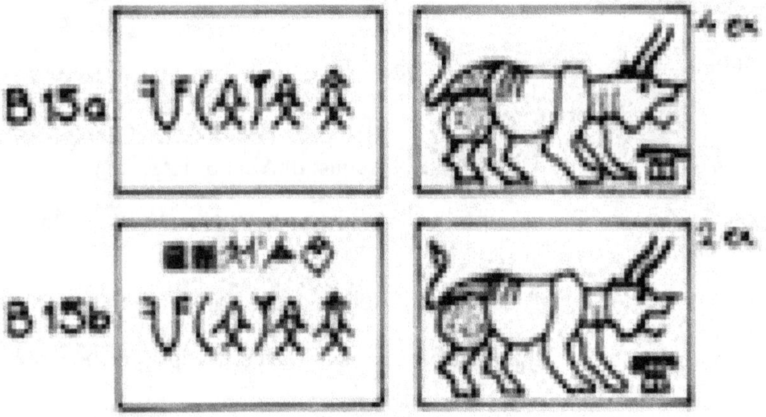

B15a, B15b

Hieroglyph: kaNDa 'rhinoceros' rebus: khANDa 'implement' PLUS pattar 'trough' rebus: pattar 'guild'

Text

Line1 B15b

khaNDa 'division' rebus: khaNDa 'implements' PLUS dula 'pair' rebus: dul 'cast metal'; thus cast metal implements

mẽd, mēd 'body'; BODY PLUS STAFF is a phonetic
determinative: *meḍ(h)*, *meḍhī* f., *meḍhā* ' post, forked stake'; *meṛh* f. ' rope tying oxen to each other and to post on threshing floor ' rebus: *mẽd, mēd* 'iron''

koDi 'flag''rebus: koD 'workshop'

kanac 'corner' rebus: kancu 'bronze'

Line 2 B15b; B15a

kaṇḍa kanka 'rim of jar' Rebus: *karṇīka* 'account (scribe)' *karṇī* 'supercargo'.
kaṇḍa 'fire-altar'. Alternative: kanka 'rim of jar' rebus: kanga 'brazier'

fish PLUS lid: aya 'fish' Rebus: aya 'iron, metal' adaren 'lid' Rebus: aduru 'native unsmelted metal'

fish PLUS notch: खांडा [khāṇḍā] m A jag, **notch** Rebus: ayaskhāṇḍa 'excellent implements: tools, pots and pans, metalware'

aya 'fish' rebus: aya, ayas 'iron, metal' PLUS circumflex of right- and left-parenthesis: kuTilaka 'bronze' PLUS koD 'horn' rebus: koD 'workshop' Thus, bronze, metal workshop.

B16

Hieroglyph: kaNDa 'rhinoceros' rebus: khANDa 'implement' PLUS pattar 'trough' rebus: pattar 'guild'

Text

Kolmo ‘rice plant’ rebus: kolimi ‘smithy, forge’

koḍa 'sluice'; Rebus: koḍ 'artisan's workshop (Kuwi)

kolom ‘three’ rebus: kolimi ‘smithy, forge’ PLUS dhal ‘slant’ rebus: dhALako ‘large ingot’

baTa ‘rimless pot’ rebus: bhaTa ‘furnace’ PLUS muka 'ladle' rebus; mũh 'ingot', quantity of metal got out of a smelter furnace (Santali)

fish PLUS lid: aya 'fish' Rebus: aya 'iron, metal' adaren ‘lid’ Rebus: aduru 'native unsmelted metal'

fish PLUS notch: खांडा [khāṇḍā] m A jag, **notch** Rebus: ayaskhāṇḍa 'excellent implements: tools, pots and pans, metalware'

fish PLUS oval as parenthesis circumscript PLUS horn: aya 'fish' Rebus: aya 'iron, metal' PLUS goTa 'round' Rebus: khoT 'ingot' koD 'horn' Rebus: koD 'workshop'

mũh ‘ingot’ (Santali) PLUS (infixed) kolom 'sprout, rice plant' Rebus: kolimi 'smithy, forge' Thus, ingot smithy

Notes: dula 'pair' Rebus: dul 'cast metal' Ellipse is split into two curves of parenthesis: ( ) Thus, dula 'cast metal' signified by the curves joined into an ellipse.

B17a, B17b, B18

Hieroglyph: two camel heads ligatured to rhinoceros bodies joined back-to-back. Thus, signifying meta casting using cire perdue (lost-wax) technique of creting mirror image metal castings from wax casts

karabhá m. ‘ camel ’ MBh., ‘ young camel ’ Pañcat., ‘ young elephant ’ BhP. 2. kalabhá -- ‘ young elephant or camel ’ Pañcat. [Poss. a non -- aryan *kar* -- ‘ elephant ’ also in karḗṇu -- , karin -- EWA i 165]1. Pk. *karabha* -- m., °*bhī* -- f., *karaha* -- m. ‘ camel ’, S. *karahu*, °*ho* m., P. H. *karhā* m., Marw. *karhau* JRAS 1937, 116, OG. *karahu* m., OM. *karahā*m.; Si. *karaba* ‘ young elephant or camel ’.2. Pa. *kalabha* -- m. ‘ young elephant ’, Pk. *kalabha* -- m., °*bhiā* -- f., *kalaha* -- m.; Ku. *kalṛo* ‘ young calf ’; Or. *kālhuṛi* ‘ young bullock, heifer ’; Si.*kalam̆bayā* ‘ young elephant ’.Addenda: **karabhá -- :** OMarw. *karaha* ‘ **camel** ’.(CDIAL 2797) PLUS dula ‘pair’ rebus: dul ‘cast metal’.

Text Line 1 B17b

kolmo ‘rice plant’ rebus: kolimi ‘smithy, forge’

gaNDA ‘four’ rebus: kanda ‘fire-altar’

sal ‘splinter’ rebus: sal ‘workshop’

koDi ‘flag’ rebus: koD ‘workshop’ (Phonetic determinative)

Three mountain peaks (range): danga ‘mountain range’ rebus: dhangar ‘blacksmith’

koD ‘horn’ rebus: koD ‘workshop’

Text Line 2 B17b, B17a

khaNDa 'division' rebus: khaNDa 'implements' PLUS dula 'pair' rebus: dul 'cast metal'

meD 'body' PLUS meDa 'staff' rebus: meD 'iron'

ranku 'liquid measure' rebus: ranku 'tin'

dula 'two' rebus: dul 'cast metal'

kuTila 'curve' rebus: kuTila 'bronze' PLUS koD 'horn' rebus: koD 'workshop' Thus, bronze workshop.

B18 text

kaṇḍa kanka 'rim of jar' Rebus: *karṇīka* 'account (scribe)'*karṇī* 'supercargo'. *kaṇḍa* 'fire-altar'. Alternative: kanka 'rim of jar' rebus: kanga 'brazier'.

loa 'ficus' rebus: loh 'copper'

koḍa 'sluice'; Rebus: koḍ 'artisan's workshop (Kuwi)

gaNDa 'four' rebus: kanda 'fire-altar' PLUS kolom 'three' rebus: kolimi 'smithy, forge'

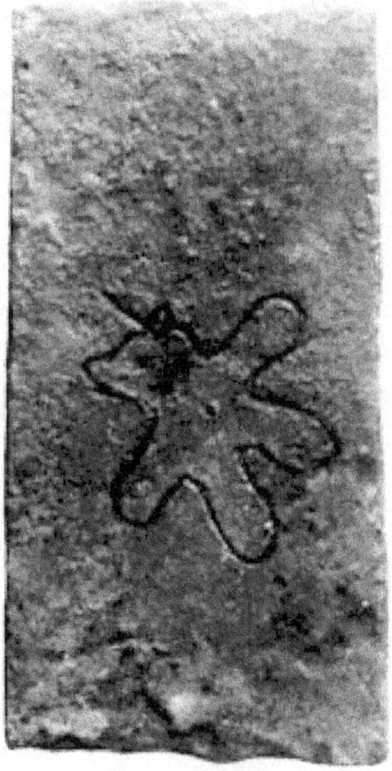

h1018copperobject Head of one-horned bull ligatured with a four-pointed star-fish (Gangetic octopus?).

kodiyum 'rings on neck' kod `horn' (Kuwi); rebus: kod `artisan's workshop' (Gujarati). खोंड [khōṇḍa] m A young bull, a bullcalf.(Marathi) Rebus: kõdā 'to turn in a lathe'(B.) कोंद kōnda 'engraver, lapidary setting or infixing gems' (Marathi). The joined animal is a Gangetic octopus.veṛhā octopus, said to be found in the Indus (Jaṭki lexicon of A. Jukes, 1900) Rebus: . *vēḍa* 'boat'(Prakritam) Alternative:

Rebus: beṛhī 'warehouse';

beṛā building with a courtyard (WPah.)

9308 bēḍā f. ‘ boat ’ lex. 2. vēḍā, *vēṭī* -- f. lex. 3. bhēḍa -- 3 m., *bhēla* -- 1, °*aka* -- m.n. lex.1. Pk. *bēḍa* -- , °*aya* -- m., *bēḍā* -- , °*ḍiyā* -- f. ‘ boat ’, Gy. eur. *bero*, S. *ḇeṛo* m., °*ṛī* ‘ small do. ’; L. *bēṛā* (Ju. *ḇ* --) m. ‘ large cargo boat ’, *bēṛī* f. ‘ boat ’, P. *beṛā* m., °*ṛī* f.; Ku. *beṛo* ‘ boat, raft ’, N. *beṛā*, OAw. *beḍā*, H. *beṛā* m., G. *beṛɔ* m., *beṛi* f., M.*beḍā* m.2. Pk. *vēḍa* -- m. ‘ boat ’.3. Pk. *bhēḍaka* -- , *bhēlaa* -- m., *bhēlī* -- f. ‘ boat ’; B. *bhelā* ‘ raft ’, Or. *bheḷā.*
*bēḍḍa -- , *bēṇḍa -- ‘ defective ’ see *biḍḍa -- .Addenda: bēḍā -- . 1. S.kcch. *beṛī* f. ‘ boat ’, *beṛo* m. ‘ ship ’; WPah.poet. *beṛe* f. ‘ boat ’, J. *beṛī* f.3. bhēḍa -- 3: A. *bhel* ‘ raft ’ (phonet. *bhel*) ‘ raft ’ AFD 89.

h1518copperaxe

beṛhī 'warehouse';

beṛā building with a courtyard (WPah.)

āra 'spokes' rebus: āra 'brass' sal 'splinter' rebus: sal 'workshop'

maṁḍaya -- ‘ adorning ’ (Prakritam) rebus: *mā̃ḍ* m. ‘ array of instruments . (Marathi)(CDIAL 9736) The inscription on the copper axe signifies: array of brass instruments workshop and warehouse.

h2249A Text 3247

baraḍo = spine; backbone (Tulu) Rebus: *baran, bharat* 'mixed alloys' (5 copper, 4 zinc and 1 tin) (Punjabi) *bhārata* 'a factitious alloy of copper, pewter, tin' (Marathi) dula 'pair' Rebus: dul 'cast metal'. The cast metal is pewter.

goTa 'round pebble' rebus: goTa 'laterite ferrous ore'. dula 'pair' rebus: dul 'cast metal'

Thus, the inscription reads rebus: *dul goTa* PLUS *bharat*, i.e., 'cast laterite PLUS pewter'

Mohenjo-daro. Copper seal. National Museum, New Delhi. [Source: Page 18, Fig. 8A in: Deo Prakash Sharma, 2000, *Harappan seals, sealings and copper tablets*, Delhi, National Museum].

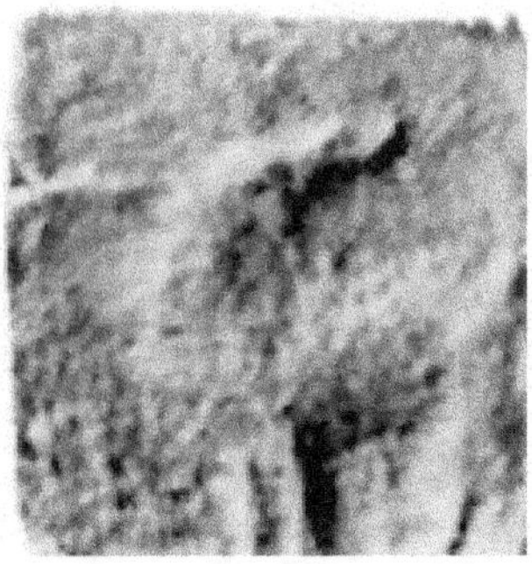

m0438 copper tablet

krammara 'look back' (Telugu) rebus: kamar 'blacksmith' mlekh 'goat' rebus: milakkhu 'copper' mleccha 'copper'. thus, coppersmith.

dhollu 'drummer' (Western Pahari) Rebus: dul 'cast metal'

kola 'tiger' Rebus: kolle 'blacksmith' kol 'working in iron'

kolimi 'smithy, forge' *jasta, dasta 'five' (Kafiri) jasta, sattva 'zinc'*

Zinc (Pewter)

jastaʿh, Pewter, Pl. ئ *ey*. جس *jas*, s.m. (6th) Pewter. Sing. and Pl. See also HI جست *jast*, s.m. (6th) Pewter. Sing. and Pl.(Pashto) These glosses are cognate with jasta 'zinc' (Hindi) *svastika* pewter (Kannada); jasta = zinc (Hindi) yasada (Jaina Prakritam)

hasta 'hand' (Rigveda); Kafiri. **dasta* -- < **jasta* -- is a Meluhha homonym. The semantics 'hand' and 'five' are meanings signified by *hath*, *ath* ' hand, five '(Gypsy). Thus, it is reasonably deduced that Proto-Prakritam (Meluhha) *jasta* signified numeral 'five'.

I suggest that it reads *sattva*. Its rebus rendering and meaning is *zastas* 'spelter or sphalerite or sulphate of zinc.'

Zinc occurs in sphalerite, or sulphate of zinc in five colours.

The Meluhha gloss for 'five' is: *taṭṭal* Homonym is: ṭhaṭṭha 'brass'(i.e. alloy of copper + zinc).

Copper plate m1457 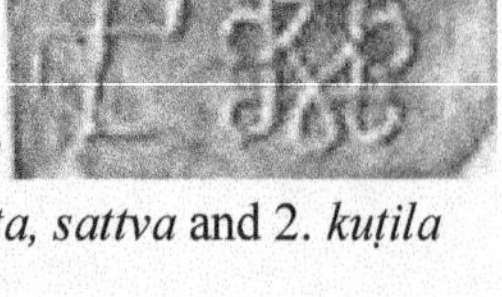 The set of hieroglyphs deciphered as: 1. zinc-pewter and 2. bronze:1. *jasta, sattva* and 2. *kuṭila*

Hieroglyph: *sattva* 'svastika hieroglyph'; *jasta, dasta 'five'* (Kafiri) Rebus: *jasta, sattva 'zinc'*

Hieroglyph: *kuṛuk* 'coil' Rebus: *kuṭila, katthīl* = bronze (8 parts copper and 2 parts tin) cf. āra-kūṭa, 'brass' Old English *ār* 'brass, copper, bronze' Old Norse *eir* 'brass, copper', German *ehern* 'brassy, bronzen'. kastīra n. ' tin ' lex. 2. *kastilla -- .1. H. *kathīr* m. ' tin, pewter '; G. *kathīr* n. ' pewter '.2. H. (Bhoj.?) *kathīl*, °*lā* m. ' tin, pewter '; M. *kathīl* n. ' tin ', *kathlẽ* n. ' large tin vessel '.(CDIAL 2984)

Hieroglyph: kuṭi in cmpd. ' curve ', *kuṭika* -- ' bent ' MBh. [√kuṭ1]
Ext. in H. *kuṛuk* f. ' coil of string or rope '; M. *kuḍċā* m. ' palm contracted and hollowed ', *kuḍapṇẽ* ' to curl over, crisp, contract '. (CDIAL 3230)

kuṭilá ' bent, crooked ' KātyŚr., °*aka* -- Pañcat., n. ' a partic. plant ' lex. [√kuṭ1]
Pa. *kuṭila* -- ' bent ', n. ' bend '; Pk. *kuḍila* -- ' crooked ', °*illa* -- ' humpbacked ', °*illaya* -- ' bent '(CDIAL 3231) kauṭilya n. ' crookedness ' Pāṇ., ' falsehood ' Pañcat. 2. *kauṭiliya -- . [kuṭilá --]

1. Pa. *kōṭilla* -- n. ' crookedness '; Pk. *kōḍilla* -- m. ' backbiter '.2. Pa. *kōṭilya* -- n. ' crookedness '; Si. *keḷilla*, st. °*ili*<-> ' bending of the knees ', °*illen iňdinavā* ' to squat '.(CDIAL 3557)

Ficus, crab multiplex, archer Indus Script hieroglyph connote distinct details of mintwork catalogs

Decipherment of two copper tablet inscriptions are compared to provide data mining of significantly distinct details of archaeometallurgical advances and documentation of work in a mint, or coinage work by ancient coiners of the Bronze Age ca 3rd millennium BCE.

kamaṭh a crab (Samskritam kamāṭhiyo=archer;kāmaṭhum =a bow; kāmaḍī ,kāmaḍum=a chip of bamboo (G.) kamaṛkom= fig leaf (Santali.lex.)kamarmaṛā(Has.), kamaṛkom(Nag.); the petiole or stalk of a leaf (Mundari.lex.) dula'two' Rebus: dul 'cast metal 'Thus, cast loh 'copper casting' infurnace:baṭa= wide-mouthed pot; baṭa= kiln (Te.) kammaṭa=portable furnace(Te.) kampaṭṭam 'coiner,mint' (Tamil) kammaṭa (Malayalam)

as shown on c5a, c5b, c6, c9 copper plate types with hieroglyph-multiplex kamaṭha= fig leaf, religiosa(Samskritam)dula 'two' Rebus: dul 'cast metal 'Thus, cast loh 'copper casting' in furnace:baṭa= wide-mouthed pot; baṭa= kiln (Te.) kammaṭa=portable furnace(Te.) kampaṭṭam 'coiner,mint' (Tamil) kammaṭa (Malayalam) loa 'ficus' rebus: loh 'copper'

Thus, the hieroglyph-multiplexes (Signs 362, 363, 364 variants) signify: cast copper mint. Thus the multiplex as hypertext is an example of data mining technique to precisely delineate the processes involved and ancient professions of metalwork delineated.

Yes, the two copper tablets m1563 (with ficus leaves, crab) and m1540 (archer) together with identical text messages convey the metalwork catalog of 1) a cast copper mint and 2) a mint, coiner respectively.

Thus, the two messages are NOT identical (allographs) but connote elaborations of data sets with the degrees of freedom provided by the choice of hieroglyphs to signify rebus metalwork processes.

kāmaṭhiyo bowman; an archer (Gujarati.Samskritam) Rebus: kampaṭṭam 'coiner,mint' (Tamil) kammaṭa, kammaṭi (Malayalam. Kannada)

The hieroglyph of 'archer' signifies: coiner, mint.

m1540b Obverse. Copper plate inscription. Mohenjo-daro

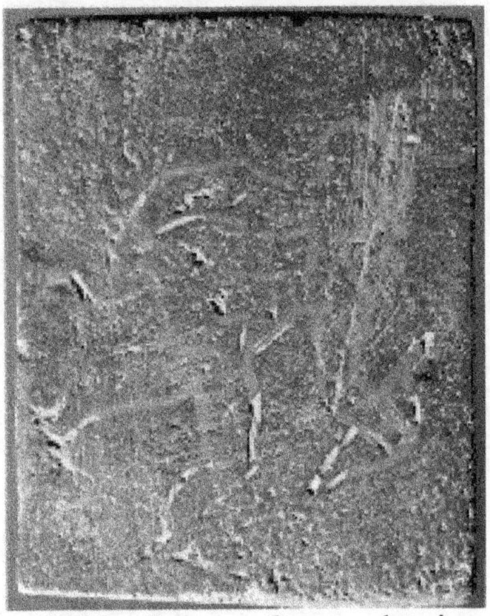

m1540Act Reverse. Copper plate inscription. Mohenjo-daro

2903 text

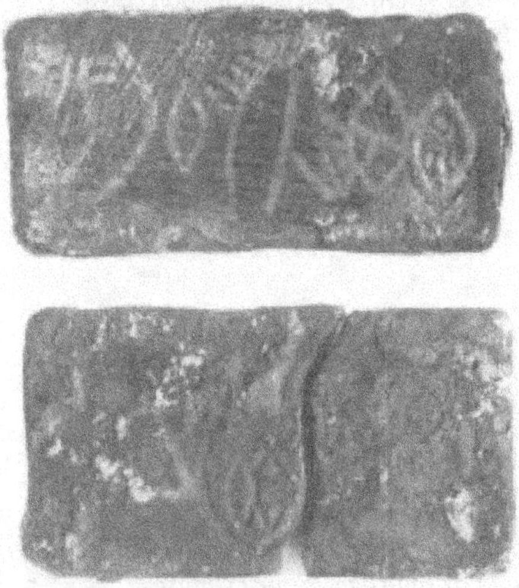

m1563Actm1563Bct

A line drawing rendering of the hieroglyph as Pict-89 pictorial motif on Mahadevan concordance.

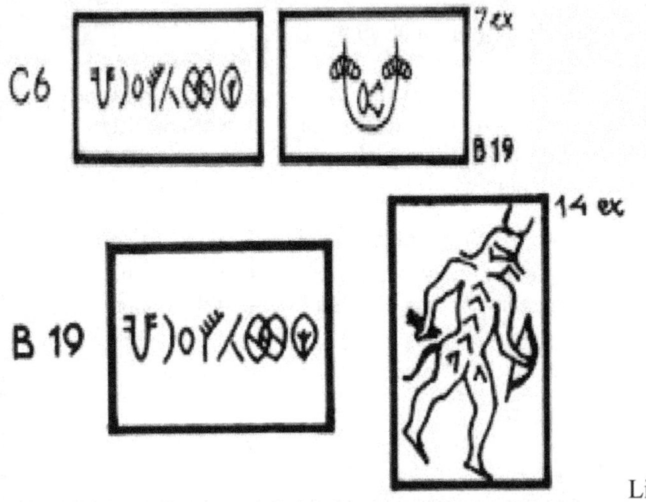

Line drawing of the copper tablet m1540 (pace Asko Parpola, BM Pande).

kammaṭa 'coiner, mint' signified by hieroglyph: *kamāṭhiyo* 'archer' evolves as an iconic metaphor of the aniconic ekamukhalinga on Batesvar sculptural frieze shown atop a smelter together with a tree in the background: kuTi 'tree' rebus: kuThi 'smelter', thus reinforcing the association of Yupa Skambha as a fiery pillar of light as a metaphor for the smelting processes transmuting mere earth and stone into metal heralding the inexorable processes of creation, destruction and rebirth exemplified by the Supreme divine -- a transformation from Being tio Becoming exemplified by the Cosmic Dancer emerging out of the Sivalinga. The process is mentioned as *gangga sudhi* on Candi Sukuh inscription on a linga signifying sudhi, 'purification' by *kanga* 'brazier'.

Indus Script hieroglyph multiplexes signify mint; scorpion, ficus glomerata, fish signify bica 'hematite ore', loa 'copper ore', ayas 'native metal'

meRed bica 'iron stone ore', lo 'copper ore'

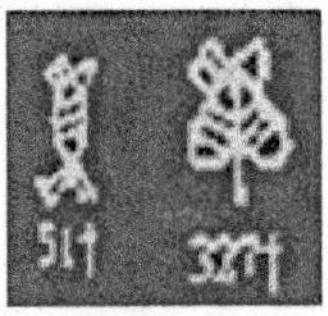

These are two glyphs of the script with unique superscripted ligatures; this pair of ligatures does not occur on any other ligatured glyph in the entire corpus of Indus script inscriptions. Orthographically, Sign 51 glyph is a 'scorpion'; Sign 327 glyph is a 'ficus glomerata leaf'. The glosses for the 'sound values' are, respectively: bica 'scorpion' (Santali), lo 'ficus' (Santali).

It is assumed that locks of hair are superscripted on the scorpion hieroglyhph. Hieroglyph: *mēṇḍhī ' lock of hair, curl '. [Cf. **mēṇḍha* -- 1 s.v. *miḍḍa --]S. *mī̃ḍhī* f., *°ḍho* m. ' braid in a woman's hair ', L. *mẽḍhī* f.; G. *mī̃ḍlɔ, miḍ°* m. ' braid of hair on a girl's forehead '; M. *meḍhā* m. ' curl, snarl, twist or tangle in cord or thread '.(CDIAL 10312). Thus, the message is : *meṛed-bica* = 'iron (hematite) stone ore'. Hieroglyph: Superscript of a curl to the scorpion hieroglyph: मेढा (p. 665) [mēḍhā] A twist or tangle arising in thread or cord, a curl or snarl.(Marathi) Rebus: *mẽṛhẽt, meḍ* 'iron' (Mu.Ho.)

Hook hieroglyph which sometimes follows the 'scorpion' hieroglyhph:

M. *mẽḍhā* m. ' crook or curved end (of a horn, stick, &c.) '.Thus, the 'crook' hieroglyph is a semantic determinant of the hieroglyph-multiplex composed of the 'curl PLUS crook PLUS scorpion'. Hence, Rebus: *mẽṛhẽt, meḍ* 'iron' (Mu.Ho.) PLUS bicha; that is, the compound phrase *meṛed-bica* = 'iron (hematite) stone ore' (Santali)

Similarly, the ligature superscript on 'ficus' hieroglyph is a determinative of 'metal, mineral': मेढा (p. 665) [mēḍhā] A twist or tangle arising in thread or cord, a curl or snarl.(Marathi) Rebus: *mẽṛhẽt, meḍ* 'iron' (Mu.Ho.) Thus, it appears that the metallic nature of the copper was signified by a gloss which signified a ferrite ore.

The inscription on the seal starts with 'scorpion' hieroglyph on modern impression of seal M-414 from Mohenjo-daro. After CISI 1:100. This sign is followed by a hieroglyph multiplex signifyinjg: rimledss pot PLUS ficus leaves PLUS infixed crab hieroglyphs. The terminal sign is 'fish' hieroglyph.

Rebus-metonymy readings in Meluhha cipher (mlecchita vikalpa) are of the three sets of hieroglyph multipexes: 1. *meṛed-bica* 'iron (hematite) stone ore' 2. *bhaTa loh kammaṭa* 'furnace copper mint, coiner' 3. *aya* 'alloy metal'.

Note: The 'ficus' hieroglyph is signified by two glosses: *vaTa* 'banyan' *loa* 'ficus glomerata'. Rebus: bhaTa 'furnace' loha 'copper, iron'.

m-857 Seal. Mohenjo-daro The four hieroglyph multiplex on Mohenjo-daro seal m-857 signifies: 1. *meṛed-bica* = 'iron (hematite) stone ore' 2. *dhatu karava karNI* 'supercargo of mineral ore', scribed. (The one-horned young bull PLUS standard device is deciphered as: kondh 'young bull' Rebus: kondh 'turner'; koD 'horn' Rebus: koD 'workshop'; sangaDa 'lathe' Rebus: sangAta 'collection of materials, i.e. consignment or boat load.

On Mohenjo-daro seal m-414, the 'scorpion' sign is followed by a hieroglyph multiplex which is explained by Asko Parpola:

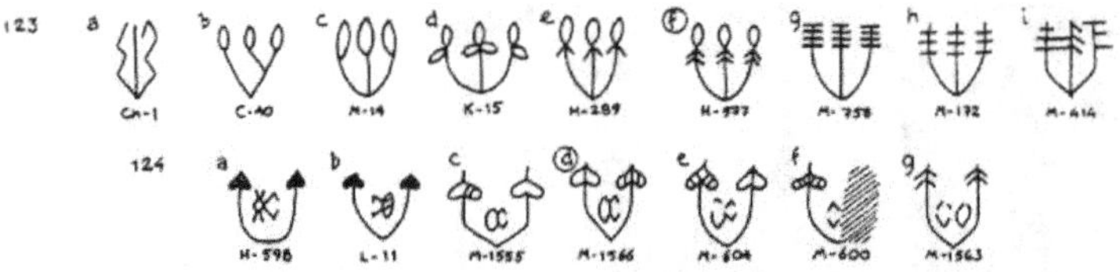

Many variants of Sign 123 (Parpola corpus) are identified signifying, according to Parpola [quote] a three-branched 'fig-tree' and of its ligature with the 'crab' sign, where the middlemost branch has been omitted to accommodate the inserted 'crab' sign. (After Parpola, Asko, 1994, Deciphering the Indus Script, Cambridge, Cambridge University Press: 235).

Parpola illustrates the 'crab' hieroglyhph with the following examples from copper plate inscriptions (Note: there are 240 copper plates with inscriptions from Mohenjo-daro):

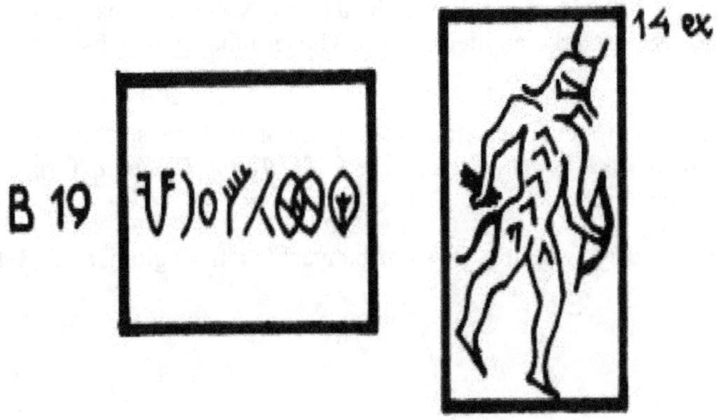

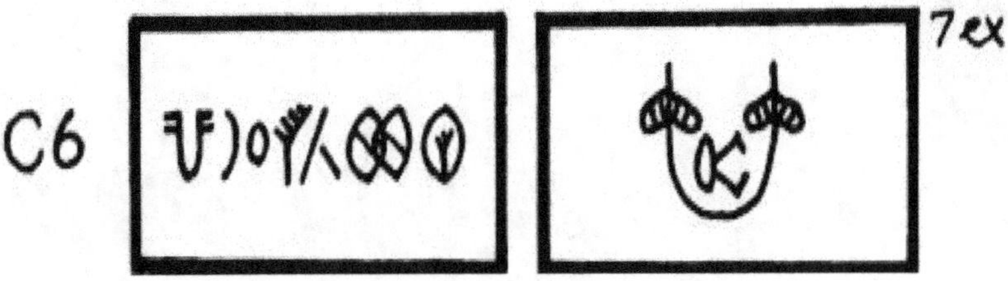

Copper tablets from Mohenjo-daro providing a 'pictorial translation' of the Indus sign 'crab inside fig tree' (After Parpola 1994: 234, fig. 13.13)

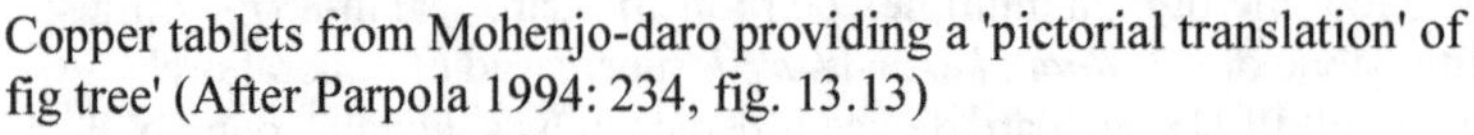

Variants of 'crab' hieroglyph (After Parpola 1994: 232, cf. 71-72)

The hieroglyph-multiplex, thus orthographically signifies two ficus leaves ligatured to the top edge of a wide rimless pot and a crab hieroglyph is inscripted. In this hieroglyph-multiplex three hieroglyph components are signified: 1. rimless pot, 2. two ficus leaves, 3. crab. baTa 'rimless pot'

Rebus: bhaTa 'furnace'; loa 'ficus' Rebus: loha 'copper, iron'; kamaDha 'crab' Rebus: kammaTa 'coiner, mint'.

Examples are:

Modern impression of Harappa Seal h-598

Modern impression of seal L-11 Lothal

The third sign is a 'fish' hieroglyph.

(http://www.harappa.com/script/script-indus-parpola.pdf Asko Parpola, 2009k,'Hind leg' + 'fish': towards further understanding of the Indus Script, in: SCRIPTA, volume 1 (September 2009): 37-76, The Hummn Jeongeum Society)

Annex A: loa 'ficus glomerata' Rebus: loha 'copper, iron'

Parpola also presents a figure of a pot with ficus leaves hieroglyph. A painted goblet with the 'three-branched fig tree' motif from Nausharo I D, transitional phase between the Early and Mature Harappan periods (c. 2600-2550 BCE) (After Samzun 1992: 250, fig.29.4 no.2)

vaṭa1 m. ' the banyan Ficus indica ' MBh. Pa. *vaṭa* -- m. ' banyan ', Pk. *vaḍa* -- , °*aga* -- m., K. *war* in *war* -- *kulu* m., S. *baṛu* m. (← E); P. *vaṛ*, *baṛ* m., *vohṛ*, *bohṛ* f. ' banyan ', *vaṛoṭā, ba*° m. ' young banyan ' (+?); N. A. *bar* ' banyan ', B. *baṛ*, Bi. *bar* (→ Or. *bara*), H. *baṛ* m. (→ Bhoj. Mth. *baṛ*), G. *vaṛ* m., M. *vaḍ* m., Ko. *vaḍu.* *vaṭapadra -- , *vaṭapātikā -- .Addenda: vaṭa -- 1: Garh. *baṛ* ' fig tree '. 11215 *vaṭapātikā ' falling from banyan '. [vaṭa -- 1, pāta --] G. *vaṛvāī* f. ' hanging root of banyan tree '. (CDIAL 11211)

Allograph: vaṭa 'string': vaṭa2 ' string ' lex. [Prob. ← Drav. Tam. *vaṭam*, Kan. *vaṭi*, *vaṭara*, &c. DED 4268] N. *bariyo* ' cord, rope '; Bi. *barah* ' rope working irrigation lever ', *barhā* ' thick well -- rope ', Mth. *barahā* ' rope '.vaṭāraka -- , *varāṭaka* -- m. ' string ' MBh. [vaṭa -- 2]Pa. *sa* -- *vaṭākara* -- ' having a cable '; Bi. *baral* -- *rassī* ' twisted string '; H. *barrā* m. ' rope ', *barārā* m. ' thong '. (CDIAL 11212, 11217)

lo 'nine', loa 'ficus religiosa' Rebus: loh 'copper'; kunda 'young bull' Rebus: kundār, kũdār 'turner'; firs hieroglph from r. on the text: eraka 'nave of wheel' Rebus: eraka 'moltencast'; arA 'spoke' Rebus: Ara 'brass'; kanac 'corner' Rebus: kancu 'bronze'.

lo = nine (Santali) [Note the count of nine fig leaves on m0296]

loa = a species of fig tree, ficus glomerata, the fruit of ficus glomerata (Santali.lex.)

loha lut.i = iron utensils and implements (Santali.lex.)

lauha = made of copper or iron (Gr.S'r.); metal, iron (Skt.); lo_haka_ra = coppersmith, ironsmith (Pali); lo_ha_ra = blacksmith (Pt.); lohal.a (Or.); lo_ha = metal, esp. copper or bronze (Pali); copper (VS.); loho, lo_ = metal, ore, iron (Si.)

Ficus glomerata: loa, kamat.ha = ficus glomerata (Santali); rebus: loha = iron, metal (Skt.) kamat.amu, kammat.amu = portable furnace for melting precious metals (Te.) kammat.i_d.u = a goldsmith, a silversmith (Te.) kampat.t.tam coinage coin (Ta.);*kammat.t.am kammit.t.am* coinage, mint (Ma.); *kammat.a* id.; *kammat.i* a coiner (Ka.)(DEDR 1236)

Sumerian cylinder seal showing flanking goats with hooves on tree and/or mountain. Uruk period. (After Joyce Burstein in: Katherine Anne Harper, Robert L. Brown, 2002, The roots of tantra, SUNY Press, p.100)Hence, two goats + mountain glyph reads rebus: meḍ kundār 'iron turner'. Leaf

on mountain: kamaṛkom 'petiole of leaf'; rebus: kampaṭṭam 'mint'. loa = a species of fig tree, ficus glomerata, the fruit of ficus glomerata (Santali) Rebus: lo ‘iron’ (Assamese, Bengali); loa ‘iron’ (Gypsy). The glyphic composition is read rebus: meḍ loa kundār 'iron turner mint'. kundavum = manger, a hayrick (G.) Rebus: kundār turner (A.); kũdār, kũdāri (B.); kundāru (Or.); kundau to turn on a lathe, to carve, to chase; kundau dhiri = a hewn stone; kundau murhut = a graven image (Santali) kunda a turner's lathe (Skt.)(CDIAL 3295) This rebus reading may explain the hayrick glyph shown on the sodagor 'merchant, trader' seal surrounded by four animals.Two antelopes are put next to the hayrick on the platform of the seal on which the horned person is seated. mlekh 'goat' (Br.); rebus: milakku 'copper' (Pali); mleccha 'copper' (Skt.) Thus, the composition of glyphs on the platform: pair of antelopes + pair of hayricks read rebus: milakku kundār 'copper turner'. Thus the seal is a framework of glyphic compositions to describe the repertoire of a brazier-mint, 'one who works in brass or makes brass articles' and 'a mint'.

Ta. meṭṭu mound, heap of earth; mēṭu height, eminence, hillock; muṭṭu rising ground, high ground, heap. Ma. mēṭu rising ground, hillock; māṭu hillock, raised ground; miṭṭāl rising ground, an alluvial bank; (Tiyya) maṭṭa hill. Ka. mēḍu height, rising ground, hillock; miṭṭu rising or high ground, hill; miṭṭe state of being high, rising ground, hill, mass, a large number; (Hav.) muṭṭe heap (as of straw). Tu. miṭṭè prominent, protruding; muṭṭe heap. Te. meṭṭa raised or high ground, hill; (K.) meṭṭu mound; miṭṭa high ground, hillock, mound; high, elevated, raised, projecting; (VPK) mēṭu, mēṭa, mēṭi stack of hay; (Inscr.) meṇṭa-cēnu dry field (cf. meṭṭu-nēla, meṭṭu-vari). Kol. (SR.) meṭṭā hill; (Kin.) meṭṭ, (Hislop) met mountain. Nk. meṭṭ hill, mountain. Ga. (S.3, LSB 20.3) meṭṭa high land. Go. (Tr. W. Ph.) maṭṭā, (Mu.) maṭṭa mountain; (M. L.) meṭā id., hill; (A. D. Ko.) meṭṭa, (Y. Ma. M.) meṭa hill; (SR.) meṭṭā hillock (Voc. 2949). Koṇḍa meṭa id. Kuwi (S.) metta hill; (Isr.) meṭa sand hill. (DEDR 5058) kamaṛkom = fig leaf (Santali.lex.) kamarmaṛā (Has.), kamaṛkom (Nag.); the petiole or stalk of a leaf (Mundari.lex.)Rebus: kampaṭṭam coinage, coin (Ta.)(DEDR 1236) kampaṭṭa- muḷai die, coining stamp (Ta.) Vikalpa: lo ‘iron’ (Assamese, Bengali); loa ‘iron’ (Gypsy)

Etyma from Indo-Aryan languages: lōhá 'copper, iron'

11158 lōhá ‘ red, copper -- coloured ’ ŚrS., ‘ made of copper ’ ŚBr., m.n. ‘ copper ’ VS., ‘ iron ’ MBh. [*rudh --] Pa. *lōha* -- m. ‘ metal, esp. copper or bronze ’; Pk. *lōha* -- m. ‘ iron ’, Gy. pal. *li°*, *lihi*, obl. *elhás*, as. *loa* JGLS new ser. ii 258; Wg. (Lumsden) "*loa*" ‘ steel ’; Kho. *loh* ‘ copper ’; S. *lohu* m. ‘ iron ’, L. *lohā* m., awāṇ. *lō`ā*, P. *lohā* m. (→ K.rām. ḍoḍ. *lohā*),

WPah.bhad. *lɔ̄u* n., bhal. *lòtilde;* n., pāḍ. jaun. *lōh*, paṅ. *luhā*, cur. cam. *lohā*, Ku. *luwā*, N. *lohu*, *°hā*, A. *lo*, B. *lo*, *no*, Or. *lohā*, *luhā*, Mth. *loh*, Bhoj. *lohā*, Aw.lakh. *lōh*, H. *loh*, *lohā* m., G. M. *loh* n.; Si. *loho*, *lō* ' metal, ore, iron '; Md. *ratu -- lō* ' copper '. *lōhala -- , *lōhila -- , *lōhiṣṭha -- , lōhī -- , laúha -- ; lōhakāra -- , *lōhaghaṭa -- , *lōhaśālā -- , *lōhahaṭṭika -- , *lōhōpaskara -- ; vartalōha -- .Addenda: lōhá -- : WPah.kṭg. (kc.) *lóɔ* ' iron ', J. *lohā* m., Garh. *loho*; Md. *lō* ' metal '.†*lōhaphāla -- or †*lōhahala -- . lōhakāra 11159 lōhakāra m. ' iron -- worker ', *°rī* -- f., *°raka* -- m. lex., *lauhakāra* -- m. Hit. [lōhá -- , kāra -- 1] Pa. *lōhakāra* -- m. ' coppersmith, ironsmith '; Pk. *lōhāra* -- m. ' blacksmith ', S. *luhā̆ru* m., L. *lohār* m., *°rī* f., awāṇ. *luhār*, P. WPah.khaś. bhal. *luhār* m., Ku. *lwār*, N. B. *lohār*, Or. *lohaḷa*, Bi.Bhoj. Aw.lakh. *lohār*, H. *lohār*, *luh°* m., G. *lavār* m., M. *lohār* m.; Si. *lōvaru* ' coppersmith '. Addenda: lōhakāra -- : WPah.kṭg. (kc.) *lhwā`r* m. ' blacksmith ', *lhwàri* f. ' his wife ', Garh. *lwār* m.

lōhaghaṭa 11160 *lōhaghaṭa ' iron pot '. [lōhá -- , ghaṭa -- 1]
Bi. *lohrā*, *°rī* ' small iron pan '. 11160a †*lōhaphāla -- ' ploughshare '. [lōhá -- , phā'la -- 1] WPah.kṭg. *lhwā`ḷ* m. ' ploughshare ', J. *lohāl* m. ' an agricultural implement ' Him.I 197; -- or < †*lōhahala -- . lōhala 11161 lōhala ' made of iron ' W. [lōhá --] G. *lohar*, *lohariyɔ* m. ' selfwilled and unyielding man '.

lōhaśālā 11162 *lōhaśālā ' smithy '. [lōhá -- , śā'lā --]
Bi. *lohsārī* ' smithy '. lōhahaṭṭika 11163 *lōhahaṭṭika ' ironmonger '. [lōhá -- , haṭṭa --] P.ludh. *lōhṭiyā* m. ' ironmonger '. 11163a †*lōhahala -- ' ploughshare '. [lōhá -- , halá --] WPah.kṭg. *lhwā`ḷ* m. ' ploughshare ', J. *lohāl* ' an agricultural instrument '; rather < †*lōhaphāla -- . lōhi 11164 lōhi ' *red, blood ' (n. ' a kind of borax ' lex.). [~ rṓhi -- . -- *rudh --] Kho. *lei* ' blood ' (BelvalkarVol 92 < **lōhika* --), Kal.rumb. *lū˘i*, urt. *lhɔ̄̃i*. lṓhita 11165 lṓhita ' red ' AV., n. ' any red substance ' ŚBr., ' blood ' VS. [< rṓhita -- . -- *rudh --] Pa. *lōhita* -- in cmpds. ' red ', n. ' blood ', *°aka* -- ' red '; Pk. *lōhia* -- ' red ', n. ' blood '; Gy. eur. *lolo* ' red ', arm. *nəxul* ' blood, wound ', pal. *lúḥră* ' red ', *inhī'r* ' blood ', as. *lur* ' blood ', *lohri* ' red ' Miklosich Mund viii 8; Ḍ. *lōya* ' red '; Ash. *leu* ' blood ', Wg. *läi*, Kt. *lūi*, Dm. *lōi*; Tir. *ləwī*, (Leech) *luhī* ' red ', *lṑi* ' blood '; Paš. *lū* f. ' blood ', Shum. *lúī*, Gmb. *lūi*, Gaw. *lō*; Bshk. *lōu* ' red ' (AO xviii 241 < **lohuta* --); S. *lohū* m. ' blood ', L. *lahū* m., awāṇ. *làū*; P. *lohī* ' red ', *lohū*, *lahū* m. ' blood '; WPah.jaun. *loī* ' blood ', Ku. *loi*, *lwe*, B. *lau*, Or. *lohu*, *nohu*, *la*(*h*)*u*, *na*(*h*)*u*, *laa*, Mth. *lehū*, OAw. *lohū* m., H. *lohū*, *lahū*, *lehū* m., G. *lohī* n.; OM.*lohivā* ' red ' Panse Jñān 536; Si. *lehe*, *lē* ' blood ', *le* ' red ' SigGr ii 460; Md. *lē* ' blood '. -- Sh. *lēl* m. ' blood ', *lōlyŭ* ' red ' rather < *lōhila -- . lōhitaka -- . Addenda: lṓhita -- : Kho. *lei* ' blood ' BKhoT 70, WPah.kṭg. *lóu* m., Garh. *loi*, Md. *lei*, *lē.*

lōhitaka 11166 lōhitaka ' reddish ' Āpast., n. ' calx of brass, bell- metal ' lex. [lṓhita --] K. *lŏy* f. ' white copper, bell -- metal '. lōhittara 11167 *lōhittara ' reddish '. [Comp. of **lōhit* -- ~ rōhít -- . -- *rudh --] Woṭ. *latúr* ' red ', Gaw. *luturá*: very doubtful (see úparakta --) lōhila 11168 *lōhila ' red '. [lōhá --] Wg. *lailäi -- štä* ' red '; Paš.chil. *lēle -- šiṓl* ' fox '; Sv. *lohīló* ' red ', Phal. *lohílu*, *ləhōilo*; Sh.gil. jij. *lēl* m. ' blood ', gil. *lōlyŭ*, (Lor.)*loilo* ' red, bay (of horse or cow) ', pales. *lēlo swā̃rə* ' (red) gold '. -- X nī'la -- : Sh.gil. *līlo* ' violet ', koh. *līlu̯*, pales. *lī'lo* ' red '. -- Si. *luhul*, *lūlā* ' the dark -- coloured river fish Ophiocephalus striatus '? -- Tor. *lohūr*, *laūr*, f. *lihīr* ' red ' < **lōhuṭa*<-> AO xviii 241? lōhiṣṭha 11169 *lōhiṣṭha ' very red '. [lōhá --] Kal.rumb. *lohíṣṭ*, urt. *liūṣṭ* ' male of Himalayan pheasant ', Phal. *lōwīṣṭ* (f. *šām* s.v. śyāmá --); Bshk. *lōī'ṭ* ' id., golden oriole '; Tor.*lawēṭ* ' male golden oriole ', Sh.pales. *lēṭh.*

lōhī 11170 lōhī f. ' any object made of iron ' Kāv., ' pot ' Divyāv., *lōhikā* -- f. ' large shallow wooden bowl bound with iron ',*lauhā* -- f. ' iron pot ' lex. [lōhá --]

Pk. *lōhī* -- f. ' iron pot '; P. *loh* f. ' large baking iron '; A. *luhiyā* ' iron pan '; Bi. *lohiyā* ' iron or brass shallow pan with handles '; G.*lohiyũ* n. ' frying pan '.

lōhōpaskara 11171 *lōhōpaskara ' iron tools '. [lōhá -- , upaskara -- 1]
N. *lokhar* ' bag in which a barber keeps his tools '; H. *lokhar* m. ' iron tools, pots and pans '; --
X lauhabhāṇḍa -- : Ku. *lokhaṛ* ' iron tools '; H. *lokhaṇḍ* m. ' iron tools, pots and pans ';
G. *lokhãḍ* n. ' tools, iron, ironware '; M. *lokhãḍ* n. ' iron ' (LM 400 < -- *khaṇḍa* --). laúkika -- , laukyá -- see *lōkíya -- . laulāha 11172 laulāha m. ' name of a place ' Stein RājatTrans ii 487.

K. *lōlav* ' name of a Pargana and valley west of Wular Lake '.

11172a laúha -- ' made of copper or iron ' GṛŚr., ' red ' MBh., n. ' iron, metal ' Bhaṭṭ. [lōhá --] Pk. *lōha* -- ' made of iron '; L. *lohā* ' iron -- coloured, reddish '; P. *lohā* ' reddish -- brown (of cattle) '. lauhabhāṇḍa -- , *lauhāṅga -- .
lauhakāra -- see lōhakāra -- . Addenda: laúha -- [Dial. *au* ~ *ō* (in *lōhá* --) < IE. *ou* T. Burrow BSOAS xxxviii 74]

lauhabhāṇḍa 11173 lauhabhāṇḍa n. ' iron pot, iron mortar ' lex. [laúha -- , bhāṇḍa -- 1] Pa. *lōhabhaṇḍa* -- n. ' copper or brass ware '; S. *luhãḏiṛī* f. ' iron pot ', L.awāṇ. *luhãḍā*;
P. *luhãḍā, lohṇḍā*, ludh. *lõhḍā* m. ' frying pan '; N. *luhũṛe* ' iron cooking pot '; A. *lohorā* ' iron pan '; Bi. *lohãṛā* ' iron vessel for drawing water for irrigation '; H. *lohaṇḍā, luh°* m. ' iron pot ';
G. *loḍhũ* n. ' iron, razor ', pl. ' car<-> penter's tools ', *loḍhī* f. ' iron pan '. -- X *lōhōpaskara<-> q.v.

lauhāṅgika 11174 *lauhāṅgika ' iron -- bodied '. [láuha -- , áṅga -- 1]
P. *luhãgī* f. ' staff set with iron rings ', H. *lohãgī* f., M. *lohãgī, lavh°, lohãgī* f.; --
Bi. *lohãgā, lahaũgā* ' cobbler's iron pounder ', Mth.*lehõgā.*

A variant orthography for *sãghāṛɔ* 'lathe' is displayed on m0296 Mohenjo-daro seal.

m0296 Decoding of a very remarkable set of glyphs and a 5-sign epigraph on a seal, m0296, together with a review of few other pictographs used in the writing system of Indus script. This seal virtually defines and prefaces the entire corpus of inscriptions of mleccha (cognate meluhha) artisans of smithy guild, caravan of Sarasvati-Sindhu civilization. The center-piece of the orthography is a stylized representation of a 'lathe' which normally is shown in front of a one-horned young bull on hundreds of seals of Indus Script Corpora. This stylized sãghāṛɔ 'lathe' is a layered rebus-metonymy to denote 'collection of implements': sangāṭh संगाठ् । सामग्री m. (sg. dat. sangāṭas संगाटस्), a collection (of implements, tools, materials, for any object), apparatus, furniture, a collection of the things wanted on a journey, luggage, and so on. This device of a stylized 'lathe' is ligatured with a circular grapheme enclosing 'protuberances' from which emanate a pair of 'chain-links'. These hieroglyphs are also read as rebus-metonymy layers to represent a specific form of lapidary or metalwork: *goṭī 'lump of* silver' (Gujarati); *goṭa* m. ' edging of gold braid '(Kashmiri). Thus, a collection of hieroglyphs are deployed as rebus-metonymy layered encryptions, to convey a message in Meluhha (mleccha) speech form.

Hieroglyph: gö̃ṭh 1 अर्गलम्, चिन्हितग्रन्थिः f. (sg. dat. gö̃ṭhi गॉ&above;ठि), a bolt, door-chain; a method of tying up a parcel with a special knot marked or sealed so that it cannot be opened by an unauthorized person. Cf. gā̃ṭh and gö̃ṭhü. -- dyunu -- m.inf. to knot, fasten; to bolt, fasten (a door) (K.Pr. 76). *gōṭṭa ' something round '. [Cf. guḍá -- 1. -- In sense ' fruit, kernel ' cert. ← Drav., cf. Tam. *koṭṭai* ' nut, kernel ', Kan. *goraṭe* &c. listed DED 1722] K. *goṭh* f., dat. *°ṭi* f. ' chequer or chess or dice board '; S. *goṭu* m. ' large ball of tobacco ready for hookah ', *°ṭī* f. ' small do. '; P. *goṭ* f. ' spool on which gold or silver wire is wound, piece on a chequer board '; N. *goṭo* ' piece ', *goṭi* ' chess piece '; A. *goṭ* ' a fruit, whole piece ', *°ṭā* ' globular, solid ', *guṭi* ' small ball, seed, kernel '; B. *goṭā* ' seed, bean, whole '; Or. *goṭā* ' whole, undivided ', *goṭi* ' small ball, cocoon ', *goṭāli* ' small round piece of chalk '; Bi. *goṭā* ' seed '; Mth. *goṭa* ' numerative particle '; H.*goṭ* f. ' piece (at chess &c.) '; G. *goṭ* m. ' cloud of smoke ', *°ṭɔ* m. ' kernel of coconut, nosegay ', *°ṭī* f. ' lump of silver, clot of blood ', *°ṭilɔ* m. ' hard ball of cloth '; M. *goṭā*m. ' roundish stone ', *°ṭī* f. ' a marble ', *goṭuḷā* ' spherical '; Si. *guṭiya* ' lump, ball '; -- prob. also P. *goṭṭā* ' gold or silver lace ', H. *goṭā* m. ' edging of such ' (→ K. *goṭa* m. ' edging of gold braid ', S. *goṭo* m. ' gold or silver lace '); M. *goṭ* ' hem of a garment, metal wristlet '. Rebus: *°ṭī* f. ' lump of silver*gōḍḍ -- ' dig ' see *khōdd -- .Ko. *gōṭu* ' silver or gold braid '.(CDIAL 4271).Rebus: *goṭī* f. ' lump of silver (Gujarati).

Hieroglyph: kaḍī a chain; a hook; a link (G.); kaḍum a bracelet, a ring (G.) Rebus: kaḍiyo [Hem. Des. kaḍaio = Skt. sthapati a mason] a bricklayer; a mason; kaḍiyaṇa, kaḍiyeṇa a woman of the bricklayer caste; a wife of a bricklayer (Gujarati)

Why nine leaves? lo = nine (Santali); no = nine (Bengali) [Note the count of nine 'ficus' leaves depicted on the epigraph.]
lo, no 'nine' phonetic reinforcement of Hieroglyph: *loa* 'ficus' *loa* = a species of fig tree, ficus glomerata (Santali) Rebus*: lo* 'copper' (Samskritam) loha lut.i = iron utensils and implements (Santali) lauha = made of copper or iron (Gr.S'r.); metal, iron (Skt.); lo_haka_ra = coppersmith, ironsmith (Pali); lo_ha_ra = blacksmith (Pt.); lohal.a (Or.); lo_ha = metal, esp. copper or bronze (Pali); copper (VS.); loho, lo_ = metal, ore, iron (Si.)

Interlocking bodies: ca_li (IL 3872); rebus: s'lika (IL) village of artisans. [cf. sala_yisu = joining of metal (Ka.)]
kamaḍha = *ficus religiosa* (Skt.); kamar.kom 'ficus' (Santali) rebus: kamaṭa = portable furnace for melting precious metals (Te.); kampaṭṭam = mint (Ta.) Vikalpa: Fig leaf 'loa'; rebus: loh '(copper) metal'. loha-kāra 'metalsmith' (Sanskrit). *loa* 'fig leaf; Rebus: loh '(copper) metal' The unique ligatures on the 'leaf' hieroglyph may be explained as a professional designation: *loha-kāra* 'metalsmith'; *kāruvu* [Skt.] n. 'An artist, artificer. An agent'.(Telugu).

sãghāṛɔ 'lathe' is a signifier and the signified is: सं-घात sãghāta 'caravan consignment' [an assemblage, aggregate of metalwork objects (of the turner in workshop): metals, alloys]. sangāṭh संगाठ् । सामग्री m. (sg. dat. sangāṭas संगाटस्), a collection (of implements, tools, materials, for any object), apparatus, furniture, a collection of the things wanted on a journey, luggage, and so on. -- karun -- करुन् । सामग्रीसंग्रहः m.inf. to collect the ab. (L.V. 17).(Kashmiri).
Hieroglyph: one-horned young bull: खोंड (p. 216) [khōṇḍa] m A young bull, a bullcalf. Rebus: कोंद kōnda 'engraver, lapidary setting or infixing gems' (Marathi)
kot.iyum = a wooden circle put round the neck of an animal; kot. = neck (G.lex.) [cf. the orthography of rings on the neck of one-horned young bull]. ko_d.iya, ko_d.e = young bull; ko_d.elu = plump young bull; ko_d.e = a. male as in: ko_d.e du_d.a = bull calf; young, youthful (Te.lex.)

Glyph: ko_t.u = horns (Ta.) ko_r (obl. ko_t-, pl. ko_hk) horn of cattle or wild animals (Go.); ko_r (pl. ko_hk), ko_r.u (pl. ko_hku) horn (Go.); kogoo a horn (Go.); ko_ju (pl. ko_ska) horn, antler (Kui)(DEDR 2200). Homonyms: kohk (Go.), gopka_ = branches (Kui), kob = branch (Ko.) gorka, gohka spear (Go.) gorka (Go)(DEDR 2126).
kod. = place where artisans work (Gujarati) kod. = a cow-pen; a cattlepen; a byre (G.lex.) gor.a = a cow-shed; a cattleshed; gor.a orak = byre (Santali.lex.) got.ho [Skt. kos.t.ha the inner part] a warehouse; an earthen
Rebus: kõdā'to turn in a lathe'(B.) कोंद kōnda 'engraver, lapidary setting or infixing gems' (Marathi) koḍ 'artisan's workshop' (Kuwi) koḍ = place where artisans work (G.) ācāri koṭṭya 'smithy' (Tu.) कोंडण [kōṇḍaṇa] f A fold or pen. (Marathi) B. kõdā 'to turn in a lathe'; Or.kū̃nda 'lathe', kū̃dibā, kū̃d 'to turn' (→ Drav. Kur. Kū̃d ' lathe') (CDIAL 3295) A. kundār, B. kū̃dār, ri, Or.Kundāru; H. kū̃derā m. 'one who works a lathe, one who scrapes', rī f., kū̃dernā 'to scrape, plane, round on a lathe'; kundakara—m. 'turner' (Skt.)(CDIAL 3297). कोंदण [kōndaṇa] n (कोंदणें) Setting or infixing of gems.(Marathi) খোদকার [khōdakāra] n an engraver; a carver. খোদকারি n. engraving; carving; interference in other's work. খোদাই [khōdāi] n engraving; carving. খোদাই করা v. to engrave; to carve. খোদানো v. & n. en graving; carving. খোদিত [khōdita] a engraved. (Bengali) खोदकाम [khōdakāma] n Sculpture; carved work or work for the carver. खोदगिरी [khōdagirī] f Sculpture, carving, engraving: also sculptured or carved work. खोदणावळ [khōdaṇāvaḷa] f (खोदणें) The price or cost of sculpture or carving. खोदणी [khōdaṇī] f (Verbal of खोदणें) Digging, engraving &c. 2 fig. An exacting of money by importunity. V लाव, मांड. 3 An instrument to scoop out and cut flowers and figures from paper. 4 A goldsmith's die. खोदणें [khōdaṇēṃ] v c & i (H) To dig. 2 To engrave. खोद खोदून विचारणें or –पुसणें To question minutely and searchingly, to probe. खोदाई [khōdāī] f (H.) Price or cost of digging or of sculpture or carving. खोदींव [khōdīṃva] p of खोदणें Dug. 2 Engraved, carved, sculptured. (Marathi)

A more precise understanding of the gloss 'ayas' comes from the frequent use of a hieroglyph on Indus Script inscriptions.

A Munda gloss for fish is 'aya'. Read rebus: *aya* 'iron' (Gujarati) *ayas* 'metal' (Vedic).

The script inscriptions indicate a set of modifiers or ligatures to the hieroglyph indicating that the metal, *aya*, was worked on during the early Bronze Age metallurgical processes -- to produce *aya* ingots, *aya* metalware,*aya* hard alloys.

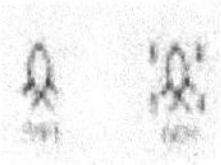

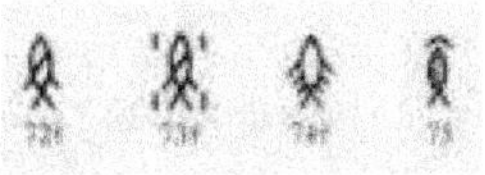

Fish hieroglyph in its vivid orthographic form is shown in a Susa pot which contained metalware -- weapons and vessels.

Context for use of 'fish' glyph. This photograph of a fish and the 'fish' glyph on Susa pot are comparable to the 'fish' glyph on Indus inscriptions.

The modifiers to the 'fish' hieroglyph which commonly occur together are: slanted stroke, notch, fins, lid-of-pot ligatured as superfix: 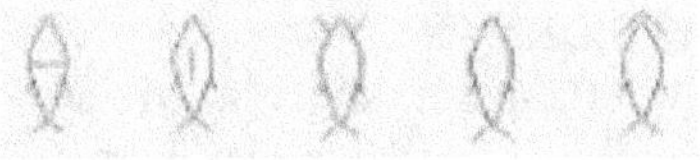 For determining the semantics of the messages conveyed by the script. Positional analysis of 'fish' glyphs has also been presented in: *The Indus Script: A Positional-statistical Approach* By Michael Korvink, 2007, Gilund Press.

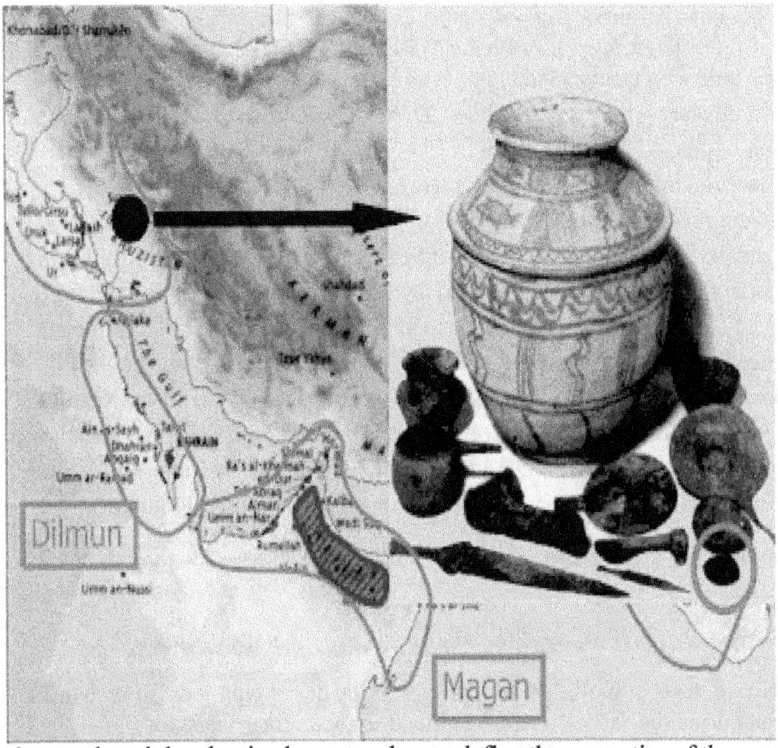

Table from: The Indus Script: A Positional-statistical Approach By Michael Korvink, 2007, Gilund Press. Mahadevan notes (Para 6.5 opcit.) that 'a unique feature of the FISH signs is their tendency to form clusters, often as pairs, and rarely as triplets also. This pattern has fascinated and baffled scholars from the days of Hunter posing problems in interpretation.' One way to resolve the problem is to interpret the glyptic elements creating ligatured fish signs and read the glyptic elements rebus to define the semantics of the message of an inscription.

karaṇḍa 'duck' (Sanskrit) *karaṛa* 'a very large aquatic bird' (Sindhi) Rebus: करडा [*karaḍā]* Hard from alloy--iron, silver &c. (Marathi) Rebus: fire-god: @B27990. #16671. Remo <*karandi*>E155 {N} ``^fire-^god".(Munda) Rebus:. *kharādī* ' turner' (Gujarati)

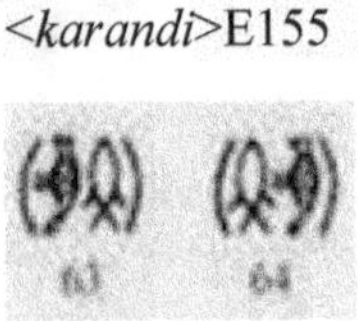

The 'parenthesis' modifier is a circumfix for both 'fish' and 'duck' hieroglyphs, the semantics of () two parenthetical modifiers are: kuṭilá— 'bent, crooked' KātyŚr., °*aka*— Pañcat., n. 'a partic. plant' [√kuṭ 1] Pa. *kuṭila*— 'bent', n. 'bend'; Pk. *kuḍila*— 'crooked', °*illa*— 'humpbacked', °*illaya*— 'bent'DEDR 2054 *(a) Ta.* koṭu curved, bent, crooked; koṭumai crookedness, obliquity; koṭukki hooked bar for fastening doors, clasp of an ornament. A pair of curved lines: *dol* 'likeness, picture, form' [e.g., two tigers, two bulls, sign-pair.] Kashmiri. dula दुल । युग्मम् m. a pair, a couple, esp. of two similar things (Rām. 966). Rebus: dul meṛeḍ cast iron (Mundari. Santali) *dul* 'to cast metal in a mould' (Santali) pasra meṛed, pasāra meṛed = syn. of koṭe meṛed = forged iron, in contrast to dul meṛed, cast iron (Mundari.) Thus, *dul kuṭila* 'cast bronze'.

The parenthetically ligatured fish+duck hieroglyphs thus read rebus: *dul kuṭila ayas karaḍā* 'cast bronze *ayas*or cast alloy metal with *ayas* as component to create *karaḍā* ''hard alloy with *ayas*'.

Ligatures to fish: parentheses + snout *dul kuṭila ayas* 'cast bronze *ayas* alloy with *tuttha*, copper sulphate'

Modifier hieroglyph: 'snout' Hieroglyph: WPah.kṭg. *ṭōṭ* ' mouth '.WPah.kṭg. *thóttì* f., *thótthər* m. ' snout, mouth ', A. *ṭhõt*(phonet. *thõt*) (CDIAL 5853). Semantics, Rebus:

tutthá n. (m. lex.), *tutthaka* -- n. ' blue vitriol (used as an eye ointment) ' Suśr., *tūtaka* -- lex. 2. *thōttha -- 4. 3. *tūtta -- . 4. *tōtta -- 2. [Prob. ← Drav. T. Burrow BSOAS xii 381; cf. *dhūrta* -- 2 n. ' iron filings ' lex.]1. N. *tutho* ' blue vitriol or sulphate of copper ', B. *tuth*.2. K. *thŏth*, dat. °*thas* m., P. *thothā* m.3. S.*tūtio* m., A. *tutiyā*, B. *tũte*, Or. *tutiā*, H. *tūtā*, *tūtiyā* m., M. *tutiyā* m. 4. M. *totā* m.(CDIAL 5855) *Ka.* tukku rust of iron; tutta, tuttu, tutte blue vitriol. *Tu.* tukků rust; mair(ů)suttu, (*Eng.-Tu. Dict.*) mairůtuttu blue vitriol. *Te.* t(r)uppu rust; (*SAN*) trukku id., verdigris. / Cf. Skt. tuttha- blue vitriol (DEDR 3343).

Fish + corner, *aya koṇḍa*, 'metal turned or forged'

Fish, *aya* 'metal'

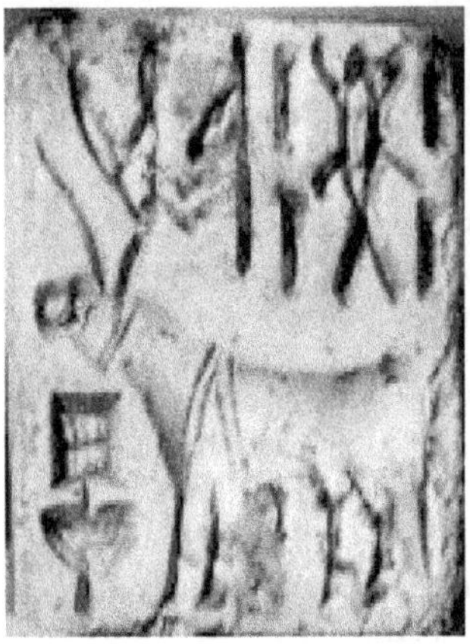

Binjor seal. Fish + scales, *aya ā̃s (amśu)* 'metallic stalks of stone ore'. Vikalpa: *badhoṛ* 'a species of fish with many bones' (Santali) Rebus: *baḍhoe* 'a carpenter, worker in wood'; *badhoria* 'expert in working in wood'(Santali) It is possible that the orthography signifies Fish + fins. The gloss for fins is ***skambha**2 ' shoulder -- blade, wing, plumage '. [Cf. **skapa* -- s.v. *khavaka --]
S. *khambhu*, °*bho* m. ' plumage ', *khambhuṛi* f. ' wing ';
L. *khabbh* m., mult. ***khambh*** m. ' shoulder -- blade, wing, feather ', khet. *khamb* ' wing ', mult. *khambhaṛā* m. ' fin '; P. *khambh* m. ' wing, feather '; G. *khā̆m* f., *khabhɔ* m. ' shoulder '.(CDIAL 13640)
It is significant that this ligatured fish hieroglyph-multiplex is used on Binjor seal associated with the performance of Soma Yaga (signified by the octagonal yupa on the yajna kunda).

Aya 'fish' rebus: aya, ayas 'iron metal' PLUS *khambhaṛā* m. ' fin ' (Lahnda) rebus: kammaTa 'mint, coiner'. Thus, this unique fish ligature is seen to signify metal used by the coiner in a mint.

Fish + splinter, *aya aduru* 'smelted native metal'

Fish + sloping stroke, *aya ḍhāḷ* 'metal ingot'

Fish + arrow or allograph, Fish + circumscribed four short strokes

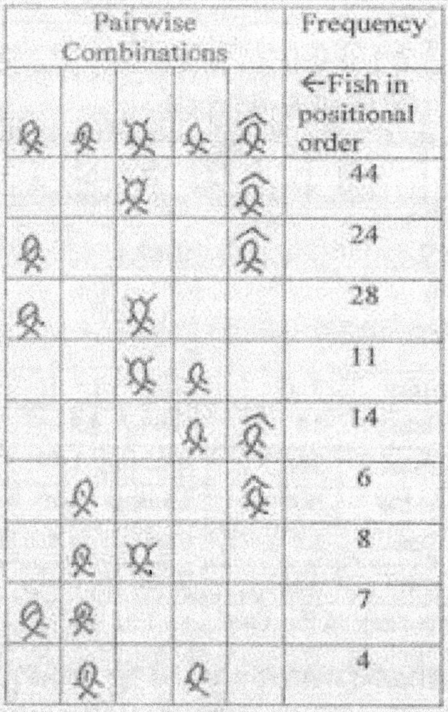
Pairwise Combinations
Frequency
←Fish in positional order
44
24
28
11
14
6
8
7
4

Figure 20: Positional Order of the "Fish" Signs

This indication of the occurrence, together, of two or more 'fish' hieroglyphs with modifiers is an assurance that the modifiers ar semantic indicators of how aya 'metal' is worked on by the artisans.

ayakāṇḍa ''large quantity of stone (ore) metal' or *aya kaṇḍa,* 'metal fire-altar'. *ayo, hako* 'fish'; *ã̄s* = scales of fish (Santali); rebus: *aya* 'metal, iron' (G.); *ayah, ayas* = metal (Skt.) Santali lexeme, *hako* 'fish' is concordant with a proto-Indic form which can be identified as *ayo* in many glosses, Munda, Sora glosses in particular, of the Indian linguistic area.

beḍa hako (ayo) 'fish' (Santali); *beḍa* 'either of the sides of a hearth' (G.) Munda: So. *ayo* `fish'. Go. ayu `fish'. Go <ayu> (Z), <ayu?u> (Z),, <ayu?> (A) {N} ``^fish". Kh. kaDOG `fish'. Sa. Hako `fish'. Mu. hai (H) ~ haku(N) ~ haikO(M) `fish'. Ho haku `fish'. Bj. hai `fish'. Bh.haku `fish'. KW haiku ~ hakO |Analyzed hai-kO, ha-kO (RDM). Ku. Kaku`fish'.@(V064,M106) Mu. ha-i, haku `fish' (HJP). @(V341) ayu>(Z), <ayu?u> (Z) <ayu?>(A) {N} ``^fish". #1370. <yO>\\<AyO>(L) {N} ``^fish". #3612. <kukkulEyO>,,<kukkuli-yO>(LMD) {N} ``prawn". !Serango dialect. #32612. <sArjAjyO>,,<sArjAj>(D) {N} ``prawn". #32622. <magur-yO>(ZL) {N} ``a kind of ^fish". *Or.<>. #32632. <ur+GOl-Da-yO>(LL) {N} ``a kind of ^fish". #32642.<bal.bal-yO>(DL) {N} ``smoked fish". #15163. Vikalpa: Munda: <aDara>(L) {N} ``^scales of a fish, sharp bark of a tree".#10171. So<aDara>(L) {N} ``^scales of a fish, sharp bark of a tree".

Indian mackerel Ta. *ayirai, acarai, acalai* loach, sandy colour, *Cobitis thermalis*; *ayilai* a kind of fish. Ma.*ayala* a fish, mackerel, scomber; *aila, ayila* a fish; *ayira* a kind of small fish, loach (DEDR 191) aduru native metal (Ka.); ayil iron (Ta.) ayir, ayiram any ore (Ma.); ajirda karba very hard iron (Tu.)(DEDR 192). Ta. ayil javelin, lance, surgical knife, lancet.Ma. ayil javelin, lance; ayiri surgical knife, lancet. (DEDR 193). aduru = gan.iyinda tegadu karagade iruva aduru = ore taken from the mine and not subjected to melting in a furnace (Ka. Siddhānti Subrahmaṇya' Śastri's new interpretation of the AmarakoŚa, Bangalore, Vicaradarpana Press, 1872, p.330); adar = fine sand (Ta.); ayir – iron dust, any ore (Ma.) Kur. adar the waste of pounded rice, broken grains, etc. Malt. adru broken grain (DEDR 134). Ma. aśu thin, slender;ayir, ayiram iron dust.Ta. ayir subtlety, fineness, fine sand, candied sugar; ? atar fine sand, dust. அய.ர[3] ayir, n. 1. Subtlety, fineness; நணசம. (த_வ_.) 2. [M. ayir.] Fine sand; நணமணல. (மலசலப. 92.) ayiram, n. Candied sugar; ayil, n. cf. ayas. 1. Iron; 2. Surgical knife, lancet; Javelin, lance; ayilavaṉ, Skanda, as bearing a javelin (DEDR 341).Tu. gadarů a lump (DEDR 1196)

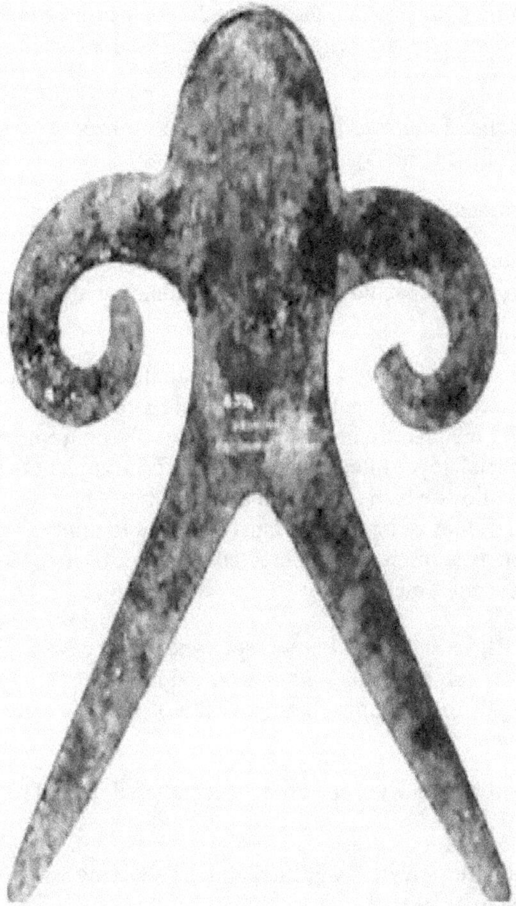

kadara— m. ‘iron goad for guiding an elephant’ lex. (CDIAL 2711). अयोगूः A blacksmith; Vāj.3.5. अयस् a. [इ-गतौ-असुन्] Going, moving; nimble. n. (-यः) 1 Iron

(एति चलति अयस्कान्तसंनिकर्षं इति तथात्वम्; नायसोल्लिख्यते रत्नम् Śukra 4.169. अभितप्तमयो$पि मार्दवं भजते कैव कथा शरीरिषु R.8.43. -2 Steel. -3 Gold. -4 A metal in general. ayaskāṇḍa 1 an iron-arrow. -2 excellent iron. -3 a large quantity of iron. -क_नत_(अयसक_नत_) 1 'beloved of iron', a magnet, load-stone; 2 a precious stone; °मजण_ a loadstone; ayaskāra 1 an iron-smith, blacksmith (Skt.Apte) ayas-kāntamu. [Skt.] n. The load-stone, a magnet. ayaskāruḍu. n. A black smith, one who works in iron. ayassu. n. ayō-mayamu. [Skt.] adj. made of iron (Te.) áyas— n. ‘metal, iron’ RV. Pa. ayō nom. sg. n. and m., aya— n. ‘iron’, Pk. aya— n., Si. ya. AYAŚCŪRṆA—, AYASKĀṆḌA—, *AYASKŪṬA—. Addenda: áyas—: Md. da ‘iron’, dafat ‘piece of iron’. ayaskāṇḍa— m.n. ‘a quantity of iron, excellent iron’ Pāṇ. gaṇ. viii.3.48 [ÁYAS—, KAA ́ṆḌA—]Si.yakaḍa ‘iron’.*ayaskūṭa— ‘iron hammer’. [ÁYAS—, KUU ́ṬA—1] Pa. ayōkūṭa—, ayak m.; Si. yakuḷa‘sledge —hammer’, yavuḷa (< ayōkūṭa) (CDIAL 590, 591, 592). cf. Lat. aes , aer-is for as-is ; Goth. ais , Thema aisa; Old Germ. e7r , iron ;Goth. eisarn ; Mod. Germ. Eisen.

Note on *(amśu)* ‘metallic stalks of stone ore’. An uncertain meaning of *soma* in Rigveda though the entire samhita holds the processing of soma in a nutshell, can be resolved in the context of modifers to 'fish' hieroglyph to denote 'fins or scales'.

The vedic texts provide an intimation treating *amśu* as a synonym of *soma.*

George Pinault has found a cognate word in Tocharian, *ancu* which means 'iron'. I have argued in my book, *Indian alchemy, soma in the Veda*, that *Soma* was an allegory, 'electrum' (gold-silver compound).

The link with the Tocharian word is intriguing because *Soma* was supposed to come from Mt. Mujavant. A cognate of Mujavant is Mustagh Ata of the Himalayan ranges in Kyrgystan.

Is it possible that the *ancu* of Tocharian from this mountain was indeed *Soma*?

The referemces to *Anzu* in ancient Mesopotamian tradition parallels the legends of *śyena* 'falcon' which is used in Vedic tradition of *Soma yajña* attested archaeologically in Uttarakhand with a *śyenaciti*, 'falcon-shaped' fire-altar.

Comparing the allegory of soma and the legend of Anzu, the bird which stole the tablets of destiny, I posit a hypothesis that the tablets of destiny are paralleled by the Indus writing corpora which constitute a veritable catalog of stone-, mineral- and metal-ware in the bronze age evolving from the chalcolithic phase of what constituted an 'industrial' revolution of ancient times creating ingots of metal alloys and weapons and tools using metal alloys which transformed the relation of communities with nature and resulted in the life-activities of lapidaries transforming into miners, smiths and traders of metal artefacts. I suggest that ayas of bronze age created a revolutionary transformation in the lives of people of these bronze age times.

Maybe, Tocharian ancu had the same meaning as Rigvedic gloss, *amśu.* If so, *ancu* might have denoted electrum, 'gold-silver compound' which was subjected to reduction, by oxidation of impurities, by incessant firing for five days and nights to create the shining wealth of gold. The old Egyptian gloss for electrum was*assem*, cognate *soma.*

Indus Script hieroglyph 'twisted rope' on 14 Ancient Near East seals/artifacts deciphered, linked to Dhărvăḍ iron-ore town Karnataka, India

'Twisted rope' which is identified as an Indus Script hieroglyph is signified on the following 14 artifacts of Ancient Near East, dated from ca. 2400 to 1650 BCE:

Fig. 1 First cylinder seal-impressed jar from Taip 1, Turkmenistan
Fig. 2 Hematite cylinder seal of Old Syria ca. 1820-1730 BCE
Fig. 3 Hematite seal. Old Syria. ca. 1720-1650 BCE
Fig. 4 Cylinder seal modern impression. Mitanni. 2nd millennium BCE
Fig. 5 Cylinder seal modern impression. Old Syria. ca. 1720-1650 BCE
Fig. 6 Cylinder seal. Mitanni. 2nd millennium BCE
Fig. 7 Stone cylinder seal. Old Syria ca. 1720-1650 BCE
Fig. 8 Hematite cylinder seal. Old Syria. ca. early 2nd millennium BCE
Fig. 9 Fragment of an Iranian Chlorite Vase. 2500-2400 BCE
Fig.10 Shahdad standard. ca. 2400 BCE Line drawing
Fig.11 Cylinder seal. 2 seated lions. Twisted rope. Louvre AO7296
Fig.12 Cylinder seal. Sumerian. 18th cent. BCE. Louvre AO 22366
Fig.13 Bogazkoy Seal impression ca. 18th cent. BCE
Fig.14 Dudu plaque.Votive bas-relief of Dudu, priest of Ningirsu in the time of Entemena, prince of Lagash, ca. 2400 BCE Tello (ancient Girsu)
The orthography of the 'twisted rope' is characterised by an endless twist, sometimes signified with three strands of the rope.

Meluhha rebus-metonymy Indus Script cipher on all the 14 seals/artifacts is: Hieroglyph: *ti-dhAtu* 'three strands' Rebus: *ti-dhAtu* 'three red stone ores: magnetite, hematite, laterite'. The three ores are: *poLa* 'magnetite', *bica* 'hematite', *goTa* 'laterite'. The hieroglyphs signifying these mineral ores are: *poLa* 'zebu', *bica* 'scorpion' *goTa* 'round object or seed'.

Some associated hieroglyphs on the 14 seals/artifacts are:

Hieroglyph: *poLa* 'zebu' Rebus: *poLa* 'magnetite' (Fig.1)
Hieroglyph: *bica* 'scorpion' Rebus: *bica* 'hematite' (Fig.4)
Hieroglyph: *karaNDava* 'aquatic bird' Rebus: *karaDa* 'hard alloy'. (Fig.7)
Hieroglyph: *kuThAru* 'monkey' Rebus: *kuThAru* 'armourer'. (Fig.2)
Hieroglyph: *arye* 'lion' (Akkadian) Rebus: *arA* 'brass'. (Fig.2)
Hieroglyph: *eruvai* 'kite' Rebus: *eruvai* 'copper'. (Fig.13)
Hieroglyph: *eraka* 'wing' Rebus: *eraka* 'moltencast copper'. (Fig.14)
Hieroglyph: *dhangar* 'bull' Rebus: *dhangar* 'blacksmith' (Fig.2)
Hieroglyph: *ranku* 'antelope' Rebus: *ranku* 'tin'. (Fig.4)
Hieroglyph: *kolmo* 'rice plant' Rebus: *kolimi* 'smithy/forge' (Fig.1)

Hieroglyph: *dula* 'pair' Rebus: *dul* 'cast metal'. (Fig.3)

The semantic elaboration of *dhāv* 'a red stone ore' is identified in the gloss: *dhǎ̄vaḍ* '(Guild of) iron-smelters'. There is a place-name in Karnataka called *dhǎrvǎ̄ḍ*

The suffix *-vǎ̄ḍ* in the place-name is also explained in the context of 'rope' hieroglyph: vaṭa2 ' string ' lex. [Prob. ← Drav. Tam. *vaṭam*, Kan. *vaṭi, vaṭara*, &c. DED 4268] N. *bariyo* ' cord, rope '; Bi. *barah* ' rope working irrigation lever ', *barhā* ' thick well -- rope ', Mth. *barahā* ' rope '.(CDIAL 11212) *Ta.* vaṭam cable, large rope, cord, bowstring, strands of a garland, chains of a necklace; vaṭi rope; vaṭṭi (-pp-, -tt-) to tie. *Ma.* vaṭam rope, a rope of cowhide (in plough), dancing rope, thick rope for dragging timber. *Ka.* vaṭa, vaṭara, vaṭi string, rope, tie. *Te.* vaṭi rope, cord. *Go.* (Mu.) vaṭiya strong rope made of paddy straw (*Voc.* 3150). Cf. 3184 Ta. tāṟvaṭam. / Cf. Skt. vaṭa- string, rope, tie; vaṭāraka-, vaṭākara-, varāṭaka- cord, string(DEDR 5220).

Dhǎrvǎ̄ḍ is an ancient major trading down dealing -- even today -- with iron ore and mineral-belt of Sahyadri mountain ranges in western Karnataka. The word *dhāv* is derived from *dhātu* which has two meanings: 'strand of rope' (Rigveda)(hieroglyph) and 'mineral' (metalwork ciphertext of Indian *sprachbund*.)

I suggest that Shahdad which has a standard of ca. 2400 BCE with the 'twisted rope' hieroglyph -- and hence dealing with ferrote ores (magnetite, hematite, laterite) -- should be recognized as a twin iron-ore town of *Dhǎrvǎ̄ḍ* It is hypothesised that further archaeometallurgical researchers into ancient iron ore mines of *Dhǎrvǎ̄ḍ* region are likely to show possible with an archaeological settlement of Sarasvati_Sindhu civilization: Daimabad from where a seal was discovered showing the most-frequently used Indus Script hieroglyph: rim of jar.

Daimabad seal. Rim of jar hieroglyph. karNI 'rim of jar' Rebus: karNI 'supercargo', karNIka 'scribe'.

dhāī wisp of fibers added to a rope (Sindhi) Rebus: *dhātu* 'mineral ore' (Samskritam) *dhāū, dhāv* m.f. 'a partic. soft red stone' (whence *dhā̆vaḍ* m. ' a caste of iron -- smelters ', *dhāvḍī* ' composed of or relating to iron '(Marathi)

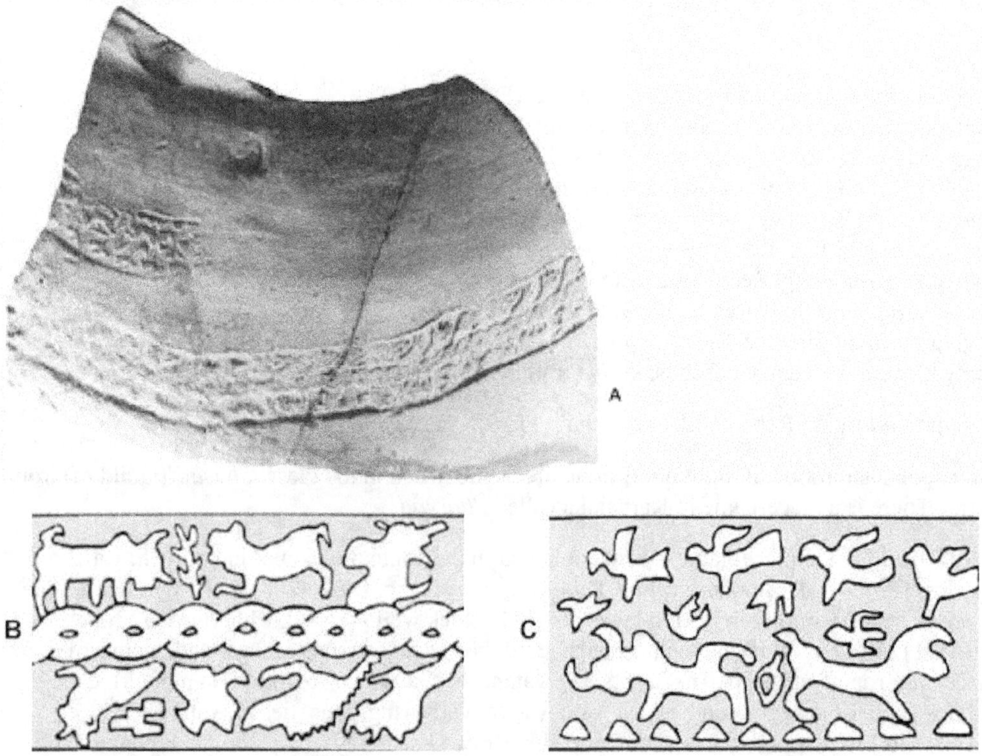

Fig. 1 First cylinder seal-impressed jar from Taip 1, Turkmenistan

(Photo: Kohl 1984: Pl. 15c; drawings after Collon 1987: nos. 600, 599. (After Fig. 5 Eric Olijdam, 2008, A possible central Asian origin for seal-impressed jar from the 'Temple Tower' at Failaka, in: Eric Olijdam and Richard H. Spoor, eds., 2008, *Intercultural relations between south and southwest Asia, Studies in commemoration of ECL During Caspers (1934-1996),* Society for Arabian Studies Monographs No. 7 [eds. D. Kennet & St J. Simpson], BAR International Series 1826 pp. 268-287). https://www.academia.edu/403945/A_Possible_Central_Asian_Origin_for_the_Seal-Impressed_Jar_from_the_Temple_Tower_at_Failaka

Decipherment of Indus Script hieroglyphs:

Hieroglyphs on the cylinder impression of the jar are: zebu, stalk (tree?), one-horned young bull (?), twisted rope, birds in flight, mountain-range *dhāī* wisp of fibers added to a rope (Sindhi) Rebus: *dhātu* 'mineral ore' (Samskritam) *dhāū, dhāv* m.f. 'a partic. soft red stone' (whence *dhā̆vaḍ* m. ' a caste of iron -- smelters ', *dhāvḍī* ' composed of or relating to iron '(Marathi)

poLa 'zebu' Rebus: poLa 'magnetite ore'

kōḍe, kōḍiya. [Tel.] n. A bullcalf. Rebus: koḍ artisan's workshop (Kuwi) kunda 'turner' kundār turner (Assamese)

kolmo 'rice plant' Rebus: kolimi 'smithy, forge'

eruvai 'eagle' Rebus: eruvai 'copper (red)'

dAng 'mountain-range' Rebus: dhangar 'blacksmith'

Thus, the storage jar contents are the message conveyed by the hieroglyph-multiplex: copper smithy workshop magnetite ore, iron castings.

Fig. 2 Hematite cylinder seal of Old Syria ca. 1820-1730 BCE

Period: Old Syrian

Date: ca. 1820–1730 B.C.E

Geography: Syria

Medium: Hematite

Dimensions: H. 1 1/16 in. (2.7 cm); Diam. 1/2 in. (1.2 cm)

Classification: Stone-Cylinder Seals

Credit Line: Gift of Nanette B. Kelekian, in memory of Charles Dikran and Beatrice Kelekian, 1999

Accession Number: 1999.325.142 Metmuseum

Fig. 3 Hematite seal. Old Syria. ca. 1720-1650 BCE

Period: Old Syrian

Date: ca. 1720–1650 B.C.E

Geography: Syria

Medium: Hematite

Dimensions: H. 15/16 in. (2.4 cm); Diam. 3/8 in. (1 cm)

Classification: Stone-Cylinder Seals

Credit Line: Gift of Nanette B. Kelekian, in memory of Charles Dikran and Beatrice Kelekian, 1999

Accession Number: 1999.325.155 Metmuseum

Fig. 4 Cylinder seal modern impression. Mitanni. 2nd millennium BCE

(male and griffin demon slaying animal; terminal: animal attack scenes, guilloche)

Period: Mitanni

Date: 2nd millennium B.C.E

Geography: Mesopotamia or Syria

Culture: Mitanni

Medium: Hematite

Dimensions: H. 13/16 in. (2 cm); Diam. 7/16 in. (1.1 cm)

Classification: Stone-Cylinder Seals

Credit Line: Gift of Nanette B. Kelekian, in memory of Charles Dikran and Beatrice Kelekian, 1999

Accession Number: 1999.325.165 Metmuseum

Fig. 5 Cylinder seal modern impression. Old Syria. ca. 1720-1650 BCE

(royal figures approaching weather god; divinities)

Period: Old Syrian

Date: ca. 1720–1650 B.C.E

Geography: Syria

Medium: Hematite

Dimensions: H, 1 1/8 in. (2.9 cm); Diam. 7/16 in. (1.1 cm)

Classification: Stone-Cylinder Seals

Credit Line: Gift of Nanette B. Kelekian, in memory of Charles Dikran and Beatrice Kelekian, 1999

Accession Number: 1999.325.147 Metmuseum

Fig. 6 Cylinder seal. Mitanni. 2nd millennium BCE

Period: Mitanni

Date: ca. late 2nd millennium B.C.E

Geography: Mesopotamia or Syria

Culture: Mitanni

Medium: Hematite

Dimensions: H. 1 in. (2.6 cm); Diam. 1/2 in. (1.2 cm)

Classification: Stone-Cylinder Seals

Credit Line: Gift of Nanette B. Kelekian, in memory of Charles Dikran and Beatrice Kelekian, 1999

Accession Number: 1999.325.190 Metmuseum

Fig. 7 Stone cylinder seal. Old Syria ca. 1720-1650 BCE

Period: Old Syrian

Date: ca. 1720–1650 B.C.

Geography: Syria

Medium: Stone

Dimensions: H. 1.9 cm x Diam. 1.1 cm

Classification: Stone-Cylinder Seals

Credit Line: Bequest of W. Gedney Beatty, 1941

Accession Number: 41.160.189 Metmuseum

Fig. 8 Hematite cylinder seal. Old Syria. ca. early 2nd millennium BCE

Period: Old Syrian

Date: ca. early 2nd millennium B.C.E

Geography: Syria

Medium: Hematite

Dimensions: H. 11/16 in. (1.7 cm); Diam. 5/16 in. (0.8 cm)

Classification: Stone-Cylinder Seals

Credit Line: Gift of Nanette B. Kelekian, in memory of Charles Dikran and Beatrice Kelekian, 1999

Accession Number: 1999.325.161 Metmuseum

- Fig. 9 Fragment of an Iranian Chlorite Vase. 2500-2400 BCE
- Decorated with the lion headed eagle (Imdugud) found in the temple of Ishtar during the 1933 - 1934 fieldwork by Parrot. Dated 2500 - 2400 BCE. Louvre Museum collection AO 17553.

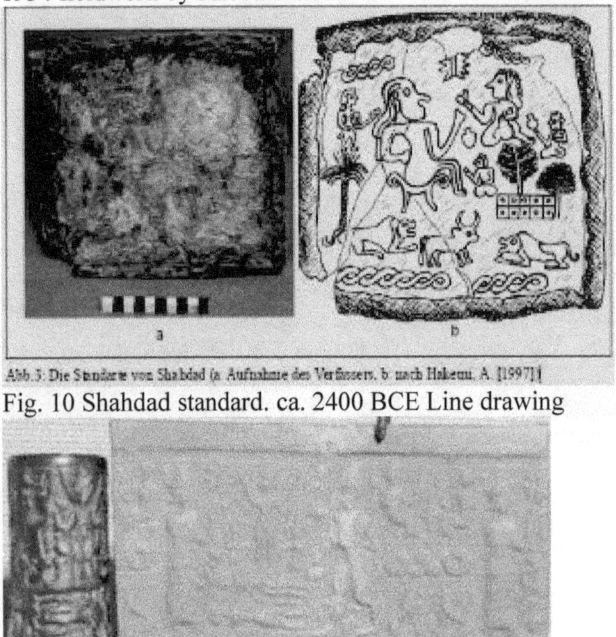
a
b
Abb.3: Die Standarte von Shahdad (a: Aufnahme des Verfassers, b: nach Hakemi, A. [1997])

Fig. 10 Shahdad standard. ca. 2400 BCE Line drawing

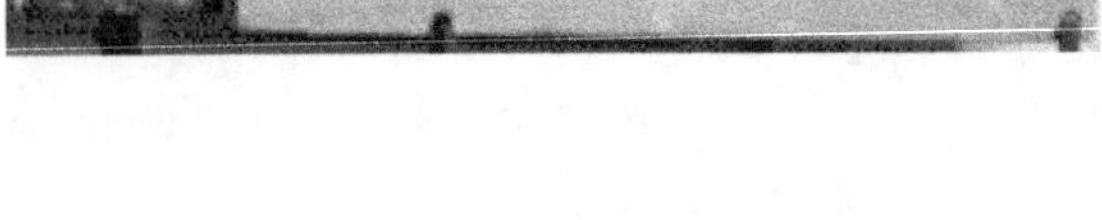

Fig. 11 Cylinder seal. 2 seated lions.

Twisted rope. Louvre AO7296
http://www.bibliotecapleyades.net/sumer_anunnaki/anunnaki3a/Louvre%20Dec%201%202002%20192.html

Fig.12 Cylinder seal. Sumerian. 18th cent. BCE. Louvre AO 22366

http://www.bibliotecapleyades.net/sumer_anunnaki/anunnaki3a/Louvre%20Dec%201%202002%20181.html

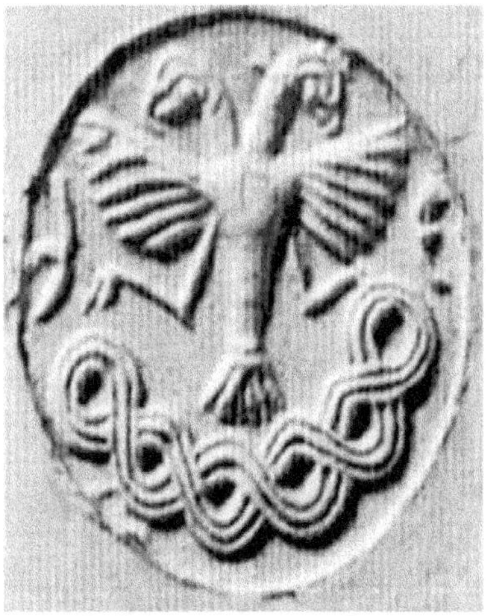

Fig. 13 Bogazkoy Seal impression ca. 18th cent. BCE

(Two-headed eagle, a twisted cord below. From Bogazköy . 18th c. BCE (Museum Ankara).

Bogazkoy Seal impression Decipherment:

eruvai 'kite' Rebus: *eruvai* 'copper' *dhAtu* 'strands of rope' Rebus: *dhAtu* 'mineral' (Note the three strands of the rope hieroglyph on the seal impression from Bogazkoy; it is read: tridhAtu 'three mineral elements'). It signifies copper compound of three minerals; maybe, arsenic copper? or arsenic bronze, as distinct from tin bronze?*eruvai* 'kite' *dula* 'pair' *eraka* 'wing' Rebus: *eruvai dul* 'copper cast metal' *eraka* 'moltencast' PLUS *dhāu* 'strand of rope' Rebus: *dhāv* 'red ore' (ferrite) ti-*dhāu* 'three strands' Rebus: *ti-dhāv* 'three ferrite ores: magnetite, hematite, laterite'.

Copper and arsenic ores

Ore name	Chemical formula
Arsenopyrite	$FeAsS$
Enargite	Cu_3AsS_4
Olivenite	$Cu_2(AsO_4)OH$
Tennantite	$Cu_{12}As_4S_{13}$
Malachite	$Cu_2(OH)_2CO_3$
Azurite	$Cu_3(OH)_2(CO_3)_2$

Sulfide deposits frequently are a mix of different metal sulfides, such as copper, zinc, silver, lead, arsenic and other metals. (Sphalerite (ZnS2), for example, is not uncommon in copper sulfide deposits, and the metal smelted would be brass, which is both harder and more durable than bronze.)The metals could theoretically be separated out, but the alloys resulting were typically much stronger than the metals individually.

Dudu plaque ca. 2400 BCE signifies *sanga* of Ningirsu.

Shahdad standard ca. 2400 BCE signifies *dhāvaḍ* 'iron-smelters'. (Note: the gloss explains the place name *Dharwar* close to the iron ore mines in Deccan Plateau of India).

The continuum of Sarasvati-Sindhu civilization in an extensive civilizational contact area from 3rd millennium BCE and the metalwork competence of *Bhāratam Janam* is explained by this link of Dharwar city of Karnataka to the artifacts of over 4000 years Before Present found in Ancient Near East (Sumer/Elam/Mesopotamia). This is a moment for celebration of Dharwar and Shahdad as twin cities from ancient Bronze Age times.

Both artifacts -- Dudu plaque and Shahdad standard -- signify a three-stranded twisted rope hieroglyph, (together with other metalwork signifying hieroglyphs). The hieroglyph-multiplexes on both artifacts signify workers with *tridhātu* 'three minerals (metals of soft red stones)'.

These inscribed artifacts herald a Bronze Age advance into the Iron Age of Ancient Iran.
The language used to render the Indus Script cipher is Proto-Prakritam. No wonder, speakers of Proto-Prakritam were present in Ancient Iran.

sanga 'priest' is a loanword in Sumerian/Akkadian. The presence of such a sanga may also explain Gudea as an Assur, in the tradition of ancient metalworkers speaking Proto-Prakritam of Indian sprachbund.
The Sumerian/Akkadian word *sanga*, is a loan from Proto-Prakritam or Meluhha of Indian *sprachbund.* **saṁghapati** m. ' chief of a brotherhood ' Śatr. [saṁghá -- , páti --]G. ***saṅghvī*** m. ' leader of a body of pilgrims, a partic. surname '.(CDIAL 12857) **saṁghá** m. ' association, a community ' Mn. [√han1]
Pa. *saṅgha* -- m. ' assembly, the priesthood '; Aś. *saṁgha* -- m. ' the Buddhist community '; Pk. *saṁgha* -- m. ' assembly, collection '; OSi. (Brāhmī inscr.) *saga*, Si. *saňga* ' crowd, collection '. -- Rather < saṅga -- : S. *saṅgu* m. ' body of pilgrims ' (whence *sãgo* m. ' caravan '), L. P. *saṅg* m. (CDIAL 12854).

dhātu (f.) [Sk. dhātu to dadhāti, Idg. ***dhē**, cp. Gr. ti/qhmi, a)na/ -- qhma, Sk. dhāman, dhāṭr (=Lat. conditor); Goth. gadēds; Ohg. tāt, tuom (in meaning -- °=dhātu, cp. E. serf -- dom "condition of . . .") tuon=E. to do; & with k -- suffix Lat. facio, Gr. (e)/)qhk(a), Sk. dhāka; see also dhamma] element... -- **kusala** skilled in the elements M iii.62; °kusalatā proficiency in the (18) elements D iii.212; Dhs 1333; -- **ghara** "house for a relic," a dagoba SnA 194. -- **cetiya** a shrine over a relic **DhA** iii.29 (Pali)

Ti° [Vedic tris, Av. priś, Gr. tri/s, Lat. ter (fr. ters>*tris, cp. testis>*tristo, trecenti>*tricenti), Icl. prisvar, Ohg. driror] base of numeral three in compn; consisting of three, threefold; in numerical cpds. also= three (3 times)...-- **vidha** 3 fold, of sacrifice (yañña) D i.128, 134, 143; of aggi (fire) J i.4 & Miln 97; Vism 147 (°kalyāṇatā). (Pali)

Hieroglyph: 'three strands of rope': *tridhā'tu* -- ' threefold ' RV (CDIAL 6283) *ti-dhātu* (Proto-Prakritam, Meluhha) signifies three elements (minerals of 'soft red stones').The Meluhha glosses: *dhāū*, *dhāv* connote a soft red stone. (See cognate etyma of Indian *sprachbund* appended).

I suggest that the 'twist' hieroglyphs on Dudu plaque and on Shahdad standard signify *ti-dhātu* 'three strands of rope' Rebus: *ti-dhātu* 'three minerals'. The *dhā-* suffix signifies 'elements, minerals': *dhāvaḍ* 'iron-smelters'. *dhāvḍī* 'composed of or relating to iron'. Thus, the hieroglyph 'twist' is signified by the Proto-Prakritam gloss: *ti-dhātu* semantically 'three metal/mineral elements.' Thus Dudu, sanga of Ningirsu and the sanga 'priest' shown on Shahdad standard can be identified as *dhāvaḍ* 'iron (metal)-smelters'.

This decipherment is consistent with other hieroglyphs shown the Dudu plaque and on Shahdad standard.

Shahdad standard: Meluhha smithy catalog of Shahdad, Marhashi

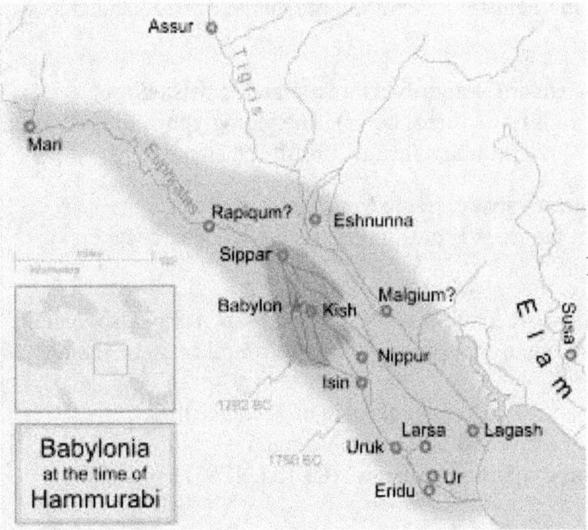

Location of Lagash. At the time of **Hammurabi**, Lagash was located near the shoreline of the gulf.

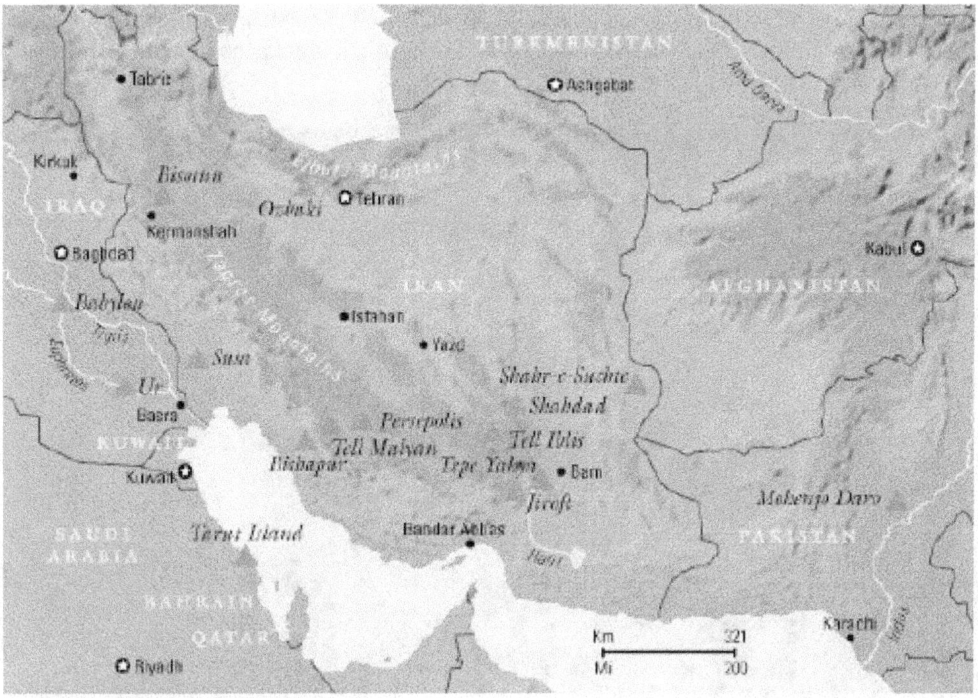

Location of Shahdad

Oldest standard in the world. Shahdad standard, 2400 BCE

(Prof. Mahmoud Rexa Maheri, Prof. Dept. of Civil Engineering, Shiraz University, dates this to ca. 3000 BCE Oct. 15, 2015 "Following an archeological survey of the South-East Iran in 1930's by Sir Auriel Stein, in 1960's and 1970's a number of archeological expeditions spent a few seasons digging at different locations through theKerman province. Of these, three teams are worthy of mention; one team from Harvard University lead by Professor Lamberg-Karlovsky focused on different layers of the 7000 years old Tape-Yahya at Sogan valley; another team from Illinois University lead by Professor Joseph Caldwell worked on the remains of Tal-i-Iblis, another 7000 years old settlement and a third team by Iranian Department of Archaeology, lead by Mr Hakemi, dug the rich graveyards of the 6000 years old Shahdad near the great Lut desert. The wealth of discoveries though great, went almost unnoticed by the public in the pursuant academic research in the form of Doctorate theses and expedition reports and scientific journal papers. Little attempt was also made to correlate the findings at different sites." http://www.mrmaheri.com/page.php?id=1-5-1)

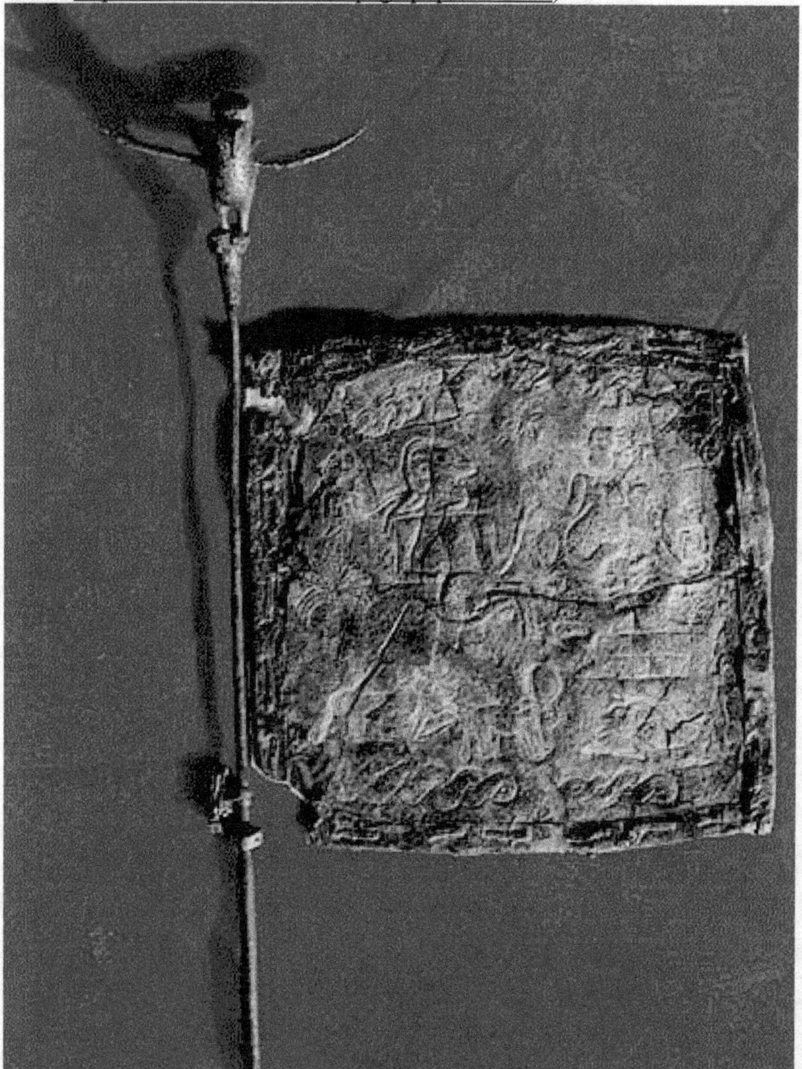

Source: http://www.cais-soas.com/CAIS/Images2/Pre-Median/Shahdad_Standard.jpg "The discovered standard in Shahdad is consisted of a squared metal piece, 23.4 in 23.4 centimetres in size, mounted on a 128-centimeter metal axle which the flag can turn over it. An eagle with opened wings which is in a landing position can be seen on top of the axle. The flag is engraved with some designs which depicting requesting water from rein goddess, which reveal irrigation method which was practiced during the third and fourth millennia BCE in Shahdad." http://www.cais-soas.com/News/2007/May2007/14-05-iran.htm

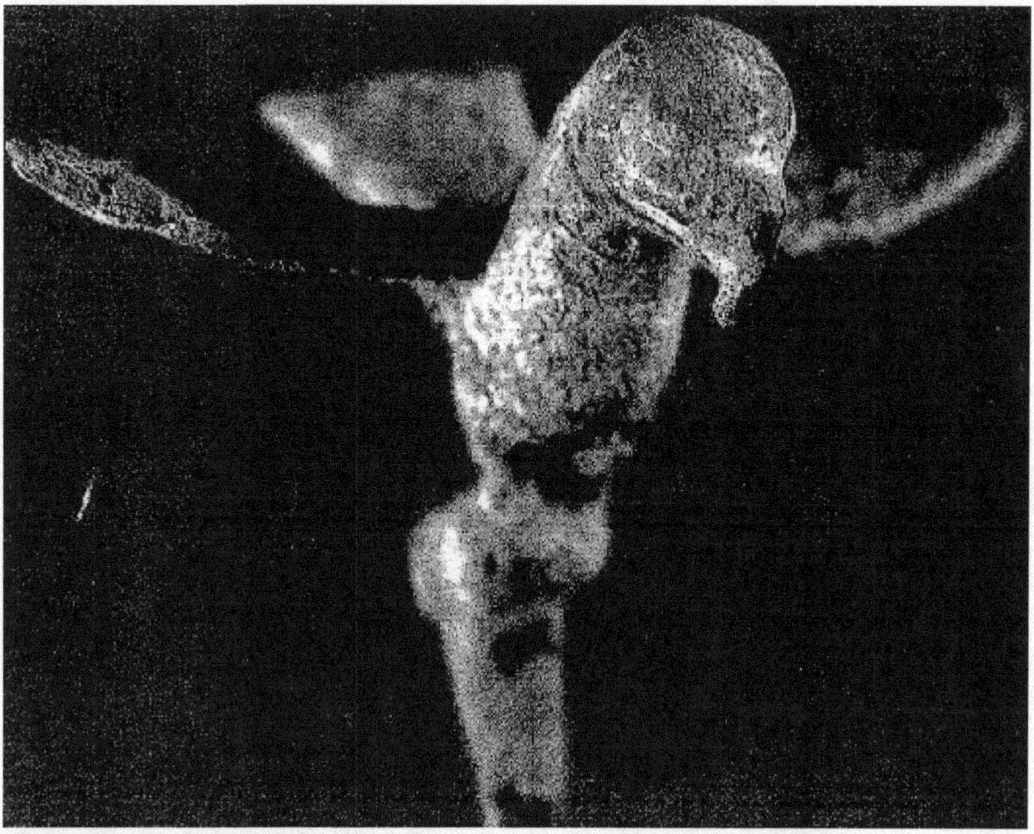
The upper section of the Shahdad Standard, grave No. 114, Object No. 1049 (p.24)

Obj. No. 1049

Three pots are shown of three sizes in the context of kneeling adorants seated in front of the person seated on a stool. meṇḍā 'kneeling position' (Gondi) Rebus: meḍ 'iron' (Munda)

eruvai 'kite' Rebus:eruvai 'copper'

dula 'pair' Rebus: dul 'cast metal'

arya 'lion' (Akkadian) Rebus: Ara 'brass'

kul, kOla 'tiger' Rebus: kol 'working in iron'

poLa 'zebu' Rebus: poLa 'magnetite'

kōla = woman (Nahali) Rebus: kol 'furnace, forge' (Kuwi) kol 'alloy of five

metals, pañcaloha' (Tamil) kol 'working in iron' (Tamil)

kaṇḍō a stool. Malt. Kanḍo stool, seat. (DEDR 1179) Rebus: kaṇḍ = a furnace, altar (Santali)

If the date palm denotes tamar (Hebrew language), 'palm tree, date palm' the rebus reading would be: tam(b)ra, 'copper' (Pkt.)

kuṭi 'tree'. Rebus: kuṭhi 'smelter' (Santali). The two trees are shown ligatured to a rectangle with ten square divisions and a dot in each square. The dot may denote an ingot in a furnace mould.

Hieroglyph: BHSk. *gaṇḍa* -- m. ' piece, part '(CDIAL 3791)

Hieroglyph: Paš. lauṛ. *khaṇḍā* ' cultivated field ', °*ḍī* ' small do. ' (→ Par. *kheṇ* ' field ' IIFL i 265); Gaw. *khaṇḍa* ' hill pasture ' (see also bel)(CDIAL 3792)

Rebus: *khaṇḍa* 'implements'

Mĕrhĕt̓. Iron.
Mĕṛhĕt̓ iċena. The iron is rusty.
Ispat mĕṛhĕt̓. Steel.
Dul mĕṛhĕt̓. Cast iron.
Mĕṛhĕt̓ khanḍa. Iron implements. Santali glosses See: mRdu 'iron' (Samskritam)

मृदुकृष्णायसं, क्ली, (मृदु च
तत् कृष्णायसं चेति ।)

सीसकम् । इति
राजनिर्घण्टः ॥ Source: Sabdakalpadruma which signifies mRdu, mRdukRSNAyasam as 'iron (soft, black iron) PLUS *sīsa* 'lead'.

Glyph of rectangle with divisions: *baṭai* = to divide, share (Santali) [Note the glyphs of nine rectangles divided.] Rebus: *bhaṭa* = an oven, kiln, furnace (Santali)

ḍāḷ= a branch of a tree (G.) Rebus: *ḍhāḷako* = a large ingot (G.) ḍhāḷakī = a metal heated and poured into a mould; a solid piece of metal; an ingot (G.)

Three sets of entwined 'glyphs (like twisted ropes) are shown around the entire narrative of the Shahdad standard.

Twisted rope as hieroglyph:

Rebus: dhā́tu n. ' substance ' RV., m. ' element ' MBh., ' metal, mineral, ore (esp. of a red colour) ' Mn.Pk. dhāu -- m. ' metal, red chalk '; N. dhāu ' ore (esp. of copper) '; Or. ḍhāu ' red chalk, red ochre ' (whence ḍhāuā ' reddish '; M. dhāū, dhāv m.f. ' a partic. soft red stone ' (whence dhā̆vaḍ m. ' a caste of iron -- smelters ', dhāvḍī ' composed of or relating to iron ')(CDIAL 6773).

- Votive relief of Dudu, priest of Ningirsu, in the days of King Entemena of Lagash.
- Mésopotamie, room 1a: La Mésopotamie du Néolithique à l'époque des Dynasties archaïques de Sumer. Richelieu, ground floor.
  This work is part of the collections of the Louvre (Department of Near Eastern Antiquities).Louvre Museum1881: excavated by Ernest de Sarzec. Place: Girsu (modern city of Telloh, Iraq). Musée du Louvre, Atlas database: entry 11378 Votive relief of Dudu, priest of Ningirsu, in the days of King Entemena of Lagash. Oil shale, ca. 2400 BC. Found in Telloh, ancient city of Girsu. |H. 25 cm (9 ¾ in.), W. 23 cm (9 in.), D. 8 cm (3 in.)

Votive bas-relief of Dudu, priest of Ningirsu in the time of Entemena, prince of Lagash C. 2400 BCE Tello (ancient Girsu) Bituminous stone H. 25 cm; W. 23 cm; Th. 8 cm De Sarzec excavations, 1881 AO 2354

- Hieroglyph: dhA 'rope strand' Rebus: dhAtu 'mineral element' Alternative: मेढा [*mēḍhā*] 'a curl or snarl; twist in thread' (Marathi) Rebus: *mẽṛhẽt, meḍ* 'iron' (Mu.Ho.) *eruvai* 'eagle'
- Rebus: *eruvai* 'copper'.
-
- eraka 'wing' Rebus: erako 'moltencast copper'.
-
- Plaques perforated in the center and decorated with scenes incised or carved in relief were particularly widespread in the 2nd and 3rd Early Dynastic Periods (2800-2340 BC), and have been found at many sites in Mesopotamian and more rarely in Syria or Iran. The perforated plaque of Dudu, high priest of Ningirsu in the reign of Entemena, prince of Lagash (c.2450 BC), belongs to this tradition. It has some distinctive features, however, such as being made of bitumen.

Dudu, priest of Ningirsu

The bas-relief is perforated in the middle and divided into four unequal sections. A figure occupying the height of two registers faces right, leaning on what appears to be a long staff. He is dressed in the kaunakes, a skirt of sheepskin or other material tufted in imitation of it. His name is inscribed alongside: Dudu, rendered by the pictograph for the foot, "du," repeated. Dudu was high priest of the god Ningirsu at the time of Entemena, prince of Lagash (c.2450 BC). Incised to his left is the lion-headed eagle, symbol of the god Ningirsu and emblem of Lagash, as found in other perforated plaques from Telloh, as well as on other objects such as the mace head of Mesilim, king of Kish, and the silver vase of Entemena, king of Lagash. On this plaque, however, the two lions, usually impassive, are reaching up to bite the wings of the lion-headed eagle. Lower down is a calf, lying in the same position as the heifers on Entemena's vase. The lower register is decorated with a plait-like motif, according to some scholars a symbol of running water.

Perforated plaques

This plaque belongs to the category of perforated plaques, widespread throughout Phases I and II of the Early Dynastic Period, c.2800-2340 BCE, and found at many sites in Mesopotamia (especially in the Diyala region), and more rarely in Syria (Mari) and Iran (Susa). Some 120 examples are known, of which about 50 come from religious buildings. These plaques are usually rectangular in form, perforated in the middle and decorated with scenes incised or carved in relief. They are most commonly of limestone or gypsum: this plaque, being of bitumen, is an exception to the rule.

Bibliography

André B, Naissance de l'écriture : cunéiformes et hiéroglyphes, (notice), Paris, Exposition du Grand Palais, 7 mai au 9 août 1982, Paris, Editions de la Réunion des musées nationaux, 1982, p. 85, n 42.Contenau G., Manuel d'archéologie orientale, Paris, Picard, 1927, p. 487, fig. 357.Heuzey L., Les Antiquités chaldéennes, Paris, Librairie des Imprimeries Réunies, 1902, n 12.Orthmann W., Der Alte Orient, Berlin, Propylaën (14), 1975, pl. 88. Sarzec É., Découvertes en Chaldée, Paris, Leroux, 1884-1912, pp. 204-209.Thureau-Dangin, Les inscriptions de Sumer et d'Akkad, Paris, Leroux, 1905, p. 59.

- The image may be read as a series of rebuses or ideograms. A priest dedicates an object to his god, represented by his symbol, and flanked perhaps by representations of sacrificial offerings: an animal for slaughter and a libation of running water. The dedicatory inscription, confined to the area left free by the image in the upper part , runs over the body of the calf: "For Ningirsu of the Eninnu, Dudu, priest of Ningirsu ... brought [this material] and fashioned it as a mace stand." See alternative readings provided for the 'twist' hieroglyph. Maybe, the calf is NOT an animal for slaughter but a gloss which sounds similar to the name of the sanga, 'priest': Dudu. The calf is called dUDa (Indian *sprachbund*). It may also have sounded: *dāmuri* 'calf' evoking the rebus of dAv 'strands of rope' rebus: dhAtu 'mineral elements'.

- The precise function of such plaques is unknown, and the purpose of the central perforation remains a mystery. The inscription here at first led scholars to consider them as mace stands, which seems unlikely. Some have thought they were to be hung on a wall, the hole in the center taking a large nail or peg. Others have suggested they might be part of a door-closing mechanism. Perforated plaques such as this are most commonly organized in horizontal registers, showing various ceremonies, banquets (particularly in the Diyala), the construction of buildings (as in the perforated plaque of Ur-Nanshe), and scenes of cultic rituals (as in the perforated plaque showing "the Libation to the Goddess of Fertility"). The iconography is often standardized, almost certainly an indication that they represent a common culture covering the whole of Mesopotamia, and that they had a specific significance understood by all." http://www.louvre.fr/en/oeuvre-notices/perforated-plaque-dudu
- Perforated plaque of Dudu with 'twisted rope' and other Indus Script hieroglyphs

I suggest that the hieroglyphs on the Dudu plaque are: eagle, pair of lions, twisted rope, calf

Hieroglyph: eruvai 'kite' Rebus: eruvai 'copper'

Hieroglyph: arye 'lion' (Akkadian) Rebus: Ara 'brass'

Hieroglyph: *dām* m. 'young ungelt ox': damya 'tameable', m. 'young bullock to be tamed' Mn. [~ *dāmiya -- . -- √dam]Pa. *damma* -- 'to be tamed (esp. of a young bullock)'; Pk. *damma* -- ' to be tamed '; S. *ḏamu* ' tamed '; -- ext. -- *ḍa* -- : A. *damrā* ' young bull ', *dāmuri* ' calf '; B.*dāmṛā* ' castrated bullock '; Or. *dāmaṛī* 'heifer', *dāmaṛiā* 'bullcalf, young castrated bullock', *dāmuṛ*, °*ṛi* 'young bullock'.Addenda: damya -- : WPah.kṭg. *dām* m. 'young ungelt ox'.(CDIAL 6184). This is a phonetic determinative of the 'twisted rope' hieroglyph: *dhāī̃* f. dā́man1 'rope' (Rigveda)

- Dudu, sanga priest of Ningirsu, dedicatory plaque with image of Anzud (Imdugud)

Fig. 14 Dudu plaque. Votive bas-relief of Dudu, priest of Ningirsu in the time of Entemena, prince of Lagash, ca. 2400 BCE Tello (ancient Girsu)

- Bituminous stone

  H. 25 cm; W. 23 cm; Th. 8 cm

- De Sarzec excavations, 1881 , 1881

AO 2354

- Anzud with two lions.
- Hieroglyph: endless knot motif

After Fig. 52, p.85 in Prudence Hopper opcit. Plaque with male figures, serpents and quadruped. Bitumen compound. H. 9 7/8 in (25 cm); w. 8 ½ in. (21.5 cm); d. 3 3/8 in. (8.5 cm). ca. 2600-2500 BCE. Acropole, temple of Ninhursag Sb 2724. The scene is described: "Two beardless, long-haired, nude male figures, their heads in profile and their bodies in three-quarter view, face the center of the composition…upper centre, where two intertwined serpents with their tails in their mouths appear above the upraised hands. At the base of the plaque, between the feet of the two figures, a small calf or lamb strides to the right. An irregular oblong cavity or break was made in the centre of the scene at a later date."

The hieroglyphs on this plaque are: kid and endless-knot motif (or three strands of rope twisted).

Hieroglyph: 'kid': करडूं or करडें (p. 137) [karaḍū or ṅkaraḍēṃ] *n* A kid. कराडूं (p. 137) [karāḍūṃ] *n* (Commonly करडूं) A kid. Rebus: करडा (p. 137) [karaḍā] Hard from alloy--iron, silver &c.(Marathi)

I suggest that the center of the composition is NOT set of intertwined serpents, but an endless knot motif signifying a coiled rope being twisted from three strands of fibre.

Twisted rope as hieroglyph on a plaque.

Alternative hieroglyph: मेढा [mēḍhā] 'a curl or snarl; twist in thread' (Marathi) Rebus: mẽṛhẽt, meḍ 'iron' (Mu.Ho.) *eruvai* 'eagle' Rebus: *eruvai* 'copper'. kōḍe, kōḍiya. [Tel.] n. A bullcalf.

Rebus: *koḍ* artisan's workshop (Kuwi) *kunda* 'turner' *kundār* turner (Assamese) मेढा [mēḍhā] A twist or tangle arising in thread or cord, a curl or snarl.(Marathi)(CDIAL 10312).L. meṛh f. 'rope tying oxen to each other and to post on threshing floor'(CDIAL 10317) Rebus: mẽṛhẽt, meḍ 'iron' (Mu.Ho.)

This hieroglyph-multiplex seen on a cylinder seal is deciphered: Hieroglyph: *ti-dhātu* 'three-strands of rope' Rebus: *ti-dhāū*, ti-*dhāv; dula 'pair'* Rebus: *dul* "cast metal' PLUS *arye* 'lion' Rebus: *Ara* 'brass' (which may be an alloy of copper, zinc and tin minerals and/or arsenopyrites including ferrous ore elements). Thus, the hieoglyph-multiplex composition signifies *dul Ara* 'cast brass alloy' of *ti-dhātu* 'three minerals'.

A stranded rope as a hieroglyph signifies dhAtu rebus metal, mineral, ore. This occurs on Ancient Near East objects with hieroglyphs such as votive bas-relief of Dudu, priest of Ningirsu in the time of Entemena, prince of Lagash C. 2400 BCE Tello (ancient Girsu), eagle and stranded rope from Bogazhkoy. Indus Script decipherment of these hieroglyph-multiplexes confirms the underlying Prakritam as an Indo-European language and Indus Script Corpora is emphatically catalogus catalogorum of metalwork of the Bronze Age in Ancient Near East.

m1406 Seal using three-stranded rope: dhAtu Rebus: iron ore.

Hieroglyph: धातु [p= <u>513</u>,3] *m.* layer , stratum <u>Ka1tyS3r. Kaus3.</u> constituent part , ingredient (esp. [and in <u>RV.</u> only] ifc. , where often = " fold " e.g. त्रि-धृ/आतु , threefold &c ; cf.त्रिविष्टि- , सप्त- , सु-) <u>RV. TS. S3Br.</u> &c (Monier-Williams) dhā́tu *strand of rope ' (cf. *tridhā́tu* -- ' threefold ' RV., *ayugdhātu* -- ' having an uneven number of strands ' KātyŚr.).; S. *dhāī* f. ' wisp of fibres added from time to time to a rope that is being twisted ', L. *dhāī̃* f.(CDIAL 6773)

Rebus: M. *dhāū*, *dhāv* m.f. ' a partic. soft red stone ' (whence *dhāvaḍ* m. ' a caste of iron -- smelters ', *dhāvḍī* ' composed of or relating to iron '); dhā́tu n. ' substance ' RV., m. ' element ' MBh., ' metal, mineral, ore (esp. of a red colour) '; Pk. *dhāu* -- m. ' metal, red chalk '; N. *dhāu* ' ore (esp. of copper) '; Or. *ḍhāu* ' red chalk, red ochre ' (whence *ḍhāuā* ' reddish '; (CDIAL 6773) धातु primary element of the earth i.e. metal , mineral, ore (esp. a mineral of a red colour) <u>Mn. MBh.</u> &c element of words i.e. grammatical or verbal root or stem <u>Nir. Pra1t. MBh.</u> &c (with the southern Buddhists धातु means either the 6 elements [see above] <u>Dharmas.</u> xxv ; or the 18 elementary spheres [धातु-लोक] ib. lviii ; or the ashes of the body , relics <u>L.</u> [cf. -गर्भ]) (Monier-Williams. Samskritam)

Indus script hieroglyphs signify dhAtu 'iron ore', Dharwar, Ib names of places in India in the iron ore belt.

There are two Railway stations in India called Dharwad and Ib. Both are related to Prakritam words with the semantic significance: iron worker, iron ore.

dhăvaḍ m. ‘ a caste of iron -- smelters ’, *dhāvḍī* ‘ composed of or relating to iron ’ (Marathi)(CDIAL 6773)

ib 'iron' (Santali) karba 'iron'; ajirda karba 'native metal iron' (Tulu) karabha 'trunk of elephant' Rebus: karba 'iron' ibha 'elephant' Rebus: ib 'iron ore' (Santali) The gloss ajirda (Tulu) is cognate with aduru, ayas. Hence, it is likely that the gloss ayas of Rigveda signifies native, unsmelted metal of iron ore.

642

Glazed steatite . Cylinder seal. 3.4cm high; imported from Indus valley. Rhinoceros, elephant, crocodile (lizard?).Tell Asmar (Eshnunna), Iraq. Elephant, rhinoceros, crocodile hieroglyphs: ib 'elephant' Rebus: ib 'iron' kANDa 'rhinoceros' Rebus: kANDa 'iron implements' karA 'crocodile' Rebus: khAr 'blacksmith' (Kashmiri)

Located on the Map of India are regions with Fe (Iron ore) mines: the locations include Dharwad and Ib.

Prakritam glosses: Dhavad is a smelter. Ib is iron.

INDIA

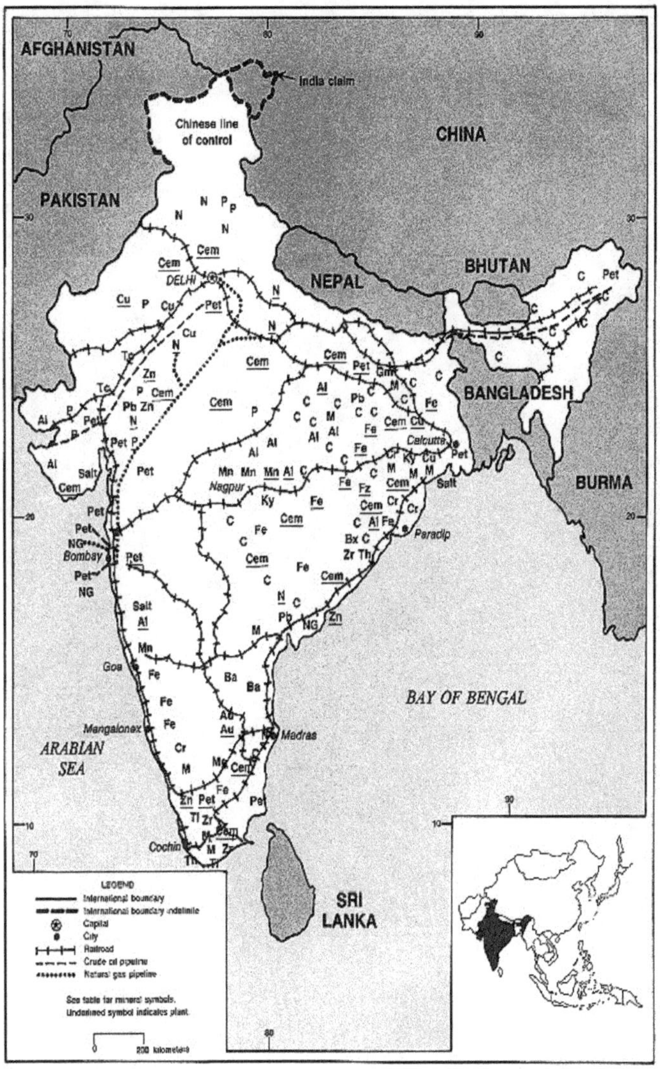

Dharwad is the district headquarters of Dharwad district in the state of Karnataka, India. It was merged with the city of Hubli in 1961 to form the twin cities of Hubli-Dharwad. It covers an area of 200.23 km² and is located 425 km northwest of Bengaluru, onNH 4,
between Bengaluru and Pune...The word "Dharwad" means a place of rest in a long travel or a small habitation. For centuries, Dharwad acted as a gateway between the Malenaadu (western mountains) and the Bayalu seeme (plains) and it became a resting place for travellers. Inscriptions found near Durga Devi temple in Narendra (a nearby village) and RLS High School date back to the 12th century and have references to Dharwad. This makes Dharwad at least 900 years

old. https://en.wikipedia.org/wiki/Dharwad The place is located in the region of hematite (iron ore) -- e.g. Sandur taluk

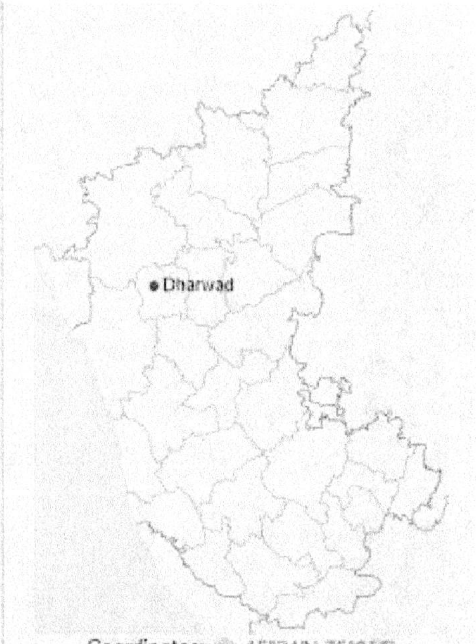

Coordinates: 15°21'N 75°05'E

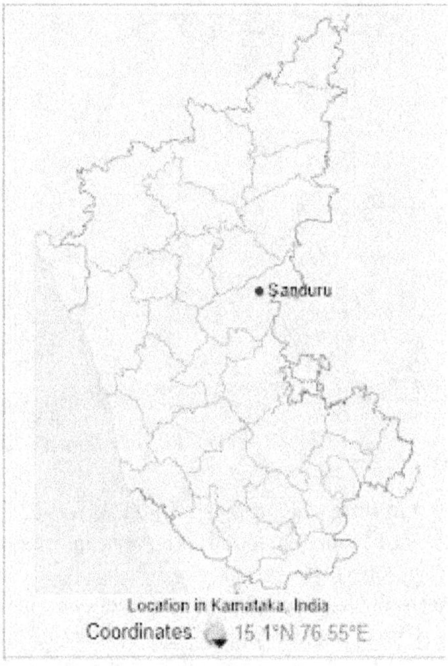

Location in Karnataka, India

Coordinates: 15.1°N 76.55°E

The station derives its name from Ib River flowing nearby. Ib railway station came up with the opening of the Nagpur-Asansol main line of Bengal Nagpur Railway in 1891. It became a station on the crosscountry Howrah-Nagpur-Mumbai line in 1900 In 1900, when Bengal Nagpur Railway was building a bridge across the Ib River, coal was accidentally discovered in what later became Ib Valley Coalfield. https://en.wikipedia.org/wiki/Ib_railway_station

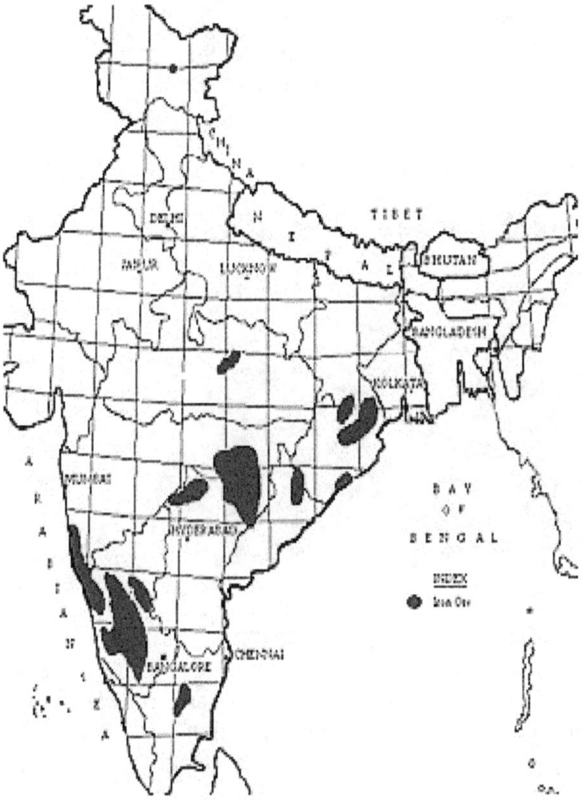

Iron Ore Deposits of India

dhAtu is a gloss which signifies metal, mineral, ore. It is likely that in early Bronze Age, the mineral specifically referred to is iron ore or meteoric iron as naturally occurring native, unsmelted metal called aduru, ayas. A gloss *dhāvaḍ* has the meaning: iron smelters. This gloss derived rom dhAtu can be explained in an archaeometallurgical context with evidences from Indus Script Corpora.

This suggestion is premised on a Marathi gloss (Prakritam, Meluhha pronunciation) cognate with dhAtu: *dhāū, dhāv* m.f. 'a partic. soft red stone' (Marathi)

This note suggests that the place names in India of Dharwad and Ib are related to nearby iron ore regions and lived in by iron workers. The names are derived from two etyma streams:
1 *dhāū, dhāv* m.f. ' a partic. soft red stone '

(whence *dhā̆vaḍ* m. 'a caste of iron -- smelters', *dhāvḍī* ' composed of or relating to iron '); dhātu n. ' substance ' RV., m. ' element ' 2. ib 'iron' kara +iba, karba 'iron'. For example, the place name Dharwad is relatable to *dhāvaḍ* 'iron-smelters'. Archaeological explorations near Dharwad and Ib may indicate evidences for iron smelting.

ಢಾಳ ḍhâḷa. (Śmd. 24 Mḍb., o. r. ಅಢಾಳ). A tall banner (= ಢಾಳ, My.).
ಢಾಳು ḍhâḷu. Cast, mould; way, style (Mhr. ಢಾಳ). — ಢಾಳ-ಆ 3. A clever fellow (Bh. 8, 26, 32).

This etymon indicates the possible reading of the tall flagpost carried by kneeling persons with six locks of hair: baTa 'six' Rebus: bhaTa 'furnace'. Associated with nAga 'serpent' Rebus: nAga 'lead'

The banner flagpost carried by four flag-bearers includes a banner associated with fish. aya 'fish' Rebus: aya 'iron' (Gujarati) ayas 'metal' (Rigveda)

Red jasper H. 1 1/8 in. (2.8 cm), Diam. 5/8 in. (1.6 cm) cylinder Seal with four hieroglyphs and four kneeling persons (with six curls on their hair) holding flagposts, c. 2220-2159 B.C.E., Akkadian (Metropolitan Museum of Art) Cylinder Seal (with modern impression). The four hieroglyphs are: from l. to r. 1. crucible PLUS storage pot of ingots, 2. sun, 3. narrow-necked pot with overflowing water, 4. fish A hooded snake is on the edge of the composition. (The dark red color of jasper reinforces the semantics: eruvai 'dark red, copper' Hieroglyph: eruvai 'reed'; see four reedposts held.

If the hieroglyph on the leftmost is moon, a possible rebus reading: قمر ḳamar

A قمر *ḳamar*, s.m. (9th) The moon. Sing. and Pl. See سپوږمي or سپوگمي (Pashto) Rebus: kamar 'blacksmith

Situated at the end of a small delta on a dry plain, Shahdad was excavated by an Iranian team in the 1970s. (Courtesy Maurizio Tosi)

[Quote]An Iranian-Italian team, including archaeologist Massimo Vidale (right), surveyed the site in 2009. (Courtesy Massimo Vidale) The peripatetic English explorer Sir Aurel Stein, famous for his archaeological work surveying large swaths of Central Asia and the Middle East, slipped into Persia at the end of 1915 and found the first hints of eastern Iran's lost cities. Stein traversed what he described as "a big stretch of gravel and sandy desert" and encountered "the usual...robber bands from across the Afghan border, without any exciting incident." What did excite Stein was the discovery of what he called "the most surprising prehistoric site" on the eastern edge of the Dasht-e Lut. Locals called it Shahr-i-Sokhta ("Burnt City") because of signs of ancient destruction. It wasn't until a half-century later that Tosi and his team hacked their way through the thick salt crust and discovered a metropolis rivaling those of the first great urban centers in Mesopotamia and the Indus. Radiocarbon data showed that the site was founded around 3200 B.C., just as the first substantial cities in Mesopotamia were being built, and flourished for more than a thousand years. During its heyday in the middle of the third millennium B.C., the city covered more than 150 hectares and may have been home to more than 20,000 people, perhaps as populous as the large cities of Umma in Mesopotamia and Mohenjo-Daro on the Indus River. A vast shallow lake and wells likely provided the necessary water, allowing for cultivated fields and grazing for animals. Built of mudbrick, the city boasted a large palace, separate neighborhoods for pottery-making, metalworking, and other industrial activities, and distinct areas for the production of local goods. Most residents lived in modest one-room houses, though some were larger compounds with six to eight rooms. Bags of goods and storerooms were often "locked" with stamp seals, a procedure common in Mesopotamia in the era. Shahr-i-Sokhta boomed as the demand for precious goods among elites in the region and elsewhere grew. Though situated in inhospitable terrain, the city was close to tin, copper, and turquoise mines, and lay on the route bringing lapis lazuli from Afghanistan to the west. Craftsmen worked shells from the Persian Gulf, carnelian from India, and local metals such as tin and copper. Some they made into finished products, and others were exported in unfinished form. Lapis blocks brought from the Hindu Kush mountains, for example, were cut into smaller chunks and sent on to Mesopotamia and as far west as Syria. Unworked blocks of lapis weighing more than 100 pounds in total were unearthed in the ruined palace of Ebla, close to the Mediterranean Sea. Archaeologist Massimo Vidale of the University of Padua says that the elites in eastern Iranian cities like Shahr-i-Sokhta were not simply slaves to Mesopotamian markets. They apparently kept the best-quality lapis for themselves, and sent west what they did not want. Lapis beads found in the royal tombs of Ur, for example, are intricately carved, but of generally low-quality stone compared to those of Shahr-i-Sokhta. Pottery was produced on a massive scale. Nearly 100 kilns were clustered in one part of town and the craftspeople also had a thriving textile industry. Hundreds of wooden spindle whorls and combs were uncovered, as were well-preserved textile fragments made of goat hair and wool that show a wide variation in their weave. According to Irene Good, a specialist in ancient textiles at Oxford University, this group of textile fragments constitutes one of the most important in the world, given their great antiquity and the insight they provide into an early stage of the evolution of wool production. Textiles were big business in the third millennium B.C., according to Mesopotamian texts, but actual textiles from this era had never before been found.A metal flag found at Shahdad, one of eastern Iran's early urban sites, dates to around 2400 B.C. The flag depicts a man and woman facing each other, one of the recurrent themes in the region's art at this time. (Courtesy Maurizio Tosi)

This plain ceramic jar, found recently at Shahdad, contains residue of a white cosmetic whose complex formula is evidence for an extensive knowledge of chemistry among the city's ancient inhabitants. (Courtesy Massimo Vidale) The artifacts also show the breadth of Shahr-i-Sokhta's connections. Some excavated red-and-black ceramics share traits with those found in the hills and steppes of distant Turkmenistan to the north, while others are similar to pots made in Pakistan to the east, then home to the Indus civilization. Tosi's team found a clay tablet written in a script called Proto-Elamite, which emerged at the end of the fourth millennium B.C., just after the advent of the first known writing system, cuneiform, which evolved in Mesopotamia. Other such tablets and sealings with Proto-Elamite signs have also been found in eastern Iran, such as at Tepe Yahya. This script was used for only a few centuries starting around 3200 B.C. and may have emerged in Susa, just east of Mesopotamia. By the middle of the third millennium B.C., however, it was no longer in use. Most of the eastern Iranian tablets record simple transactions involving sheep, goats, and grain and could have been used to keep track of goods in large households. While Tosi's team was digging at Shahr-i-Sokhta, Iranian archaeologist Ali Hakemi was working at another site, Shahdad, on the western side of the Dasht-e Lut. This settlement emerged as early as the fifth millennium B.C. on a delta at the edge of the desert. By the early third millennium B.C., Shahdad began to grow quickly as international trade with Mesopotamia expanded. Tomb excavations revealed spectacular artifacts amid stone blocks once painted in vibrant colors. These include several extraordinary, nearly life-size clay statues placed with the dead. The city's artisans worked lapis lazuli, silver, lead, turquoise, and other materials imported from as far away as eastern Afghanistan, as well as shells from the distant Persian Gulf and Indian Ocean. Evidence shows that ancient Shahdad had a large metalworking industry by this time. During a recent survey, a new generation of archaeologists found a vast hill—nearly 300 feet by 300 feet—covered with slag from smelting copper. Vidale says that analysis of the copper ore suggests that the smiths were savvy enough to add a small amount of arsenic in the later stages of the process to strengthen the final product. Shahdad's metalworkers also created such remarkable artifacts as a metal flag dating to about 2400 B.C. Mounted on a copper pole topped with a bird, perhaps an eagle, the squared flag depicts two figures facing one another on a rich background of animals, plants, and goddesses. The flag has no parallels and its use is unknown. Vidale has also found evidence of a sweet-smelling nature. During a spring 2009 visit to Shahdad, he discovered a small stone container lying on the ground. The vessel, which appears to date to the late fourth millennium B.C., was made of chlorite, a dark soft stone favored by ancient artisans in southeast Iran. Using X-ray diffraction at an Iranian lab, he discovered lead carbonate—used as a white cosmetic—sealed in the bottom of the jar. He identified fatty material that likely was added as a binder, as well as traces of coumarin, a fragrant chemical compound found in plants and used in some perfumes. Further analysis showed small traces of copper, possibly the result of a user dipping a small metal applicator into the container. Other sites in eastern Iran are only now being investigated. For the past two years, Iranian archaeologists Hassan Fazeli Nashli and Hassain Ali Kavosh from the University of Tehran have been digging in a small settlement a few miles east of Shahdad called Tepe Graziani, named for the Italian archaeologist who first surveyed the site. They are trying to understand the role of the city's outer settlements by examining this ancient mound, which is 30 feet high, 525 feet wide, and 720 feet long. Excavators have uncovered a wealth of artifacts including a variety of small sculptures depicting crude human figures, humped bulls, and a Bactrian camel dating to approximately 2900 B.C. A bronze mirror, fishhooks, daggers, and pins are among the metal finds. There are also wooden combs that survived in the arid climate. "The site is small but very rich," says Fazeli, adding that it may have been a prosperous suburban production center for Shahdad. Sites such as Shahdad and Shahr-i-Sokhta and their suburbs were not simply islands of settlements in what otherwise was empty desert. Fazeli adds that some 900 Bronze Age sites have been found on the Sistan plain, which borders Afghanistan and Pakistan. Mortazavi, meanwhile, has been examining the area around the Bampur Valley, in Iran's extreme southeast. This area was a corridor between the Iranian plateau and the Indus Valley, as well as between Shahr-i-Sokhta to the north and the Persian Gulf to the south. A 2006 survey along the Damin River identified 19 Bronze Age sites in an area of less than 20 square miles. That river periodically vanishes, and farmers depend on underground channels called qanats to transport water. Despite the lack of large rivers, ancient eastern Iranians were very savvy in marshaling their few water resources. Using satellite remote sensing data, Vidale has found remains of what might be ancient canals or qanats around Shahdad, but more work is necessary to understand how inhabitants supported themselves in this harsh climate 5,000 years ago, as they still do today. [unquote]

http://www.archaeology.org/1111/features/iran_burial_goods.html

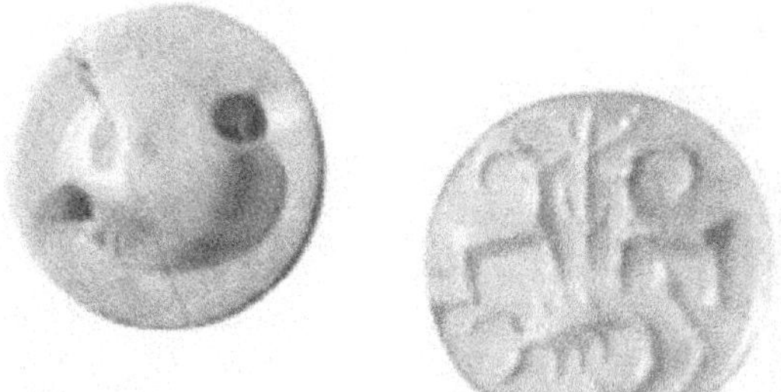

c

A Proto-Dilmun seal?
Source: https://www.academia.edu/7837834/From_rags_to_riches_three_crucial_steps_in_Dilmun_s_rise_to_fame_poster_-_HIGH_RESOLUTION_FIGS._1-4

kolmo 'rice-plant' Rebus: kolimi 'smithy, forge' melh 'goat' Rebus: milakkhu 'copper' bica 'scorpion' Rebus: bica 'laterite' kulA 'hooded serpent' Rebus: kolhe 'smelter'.

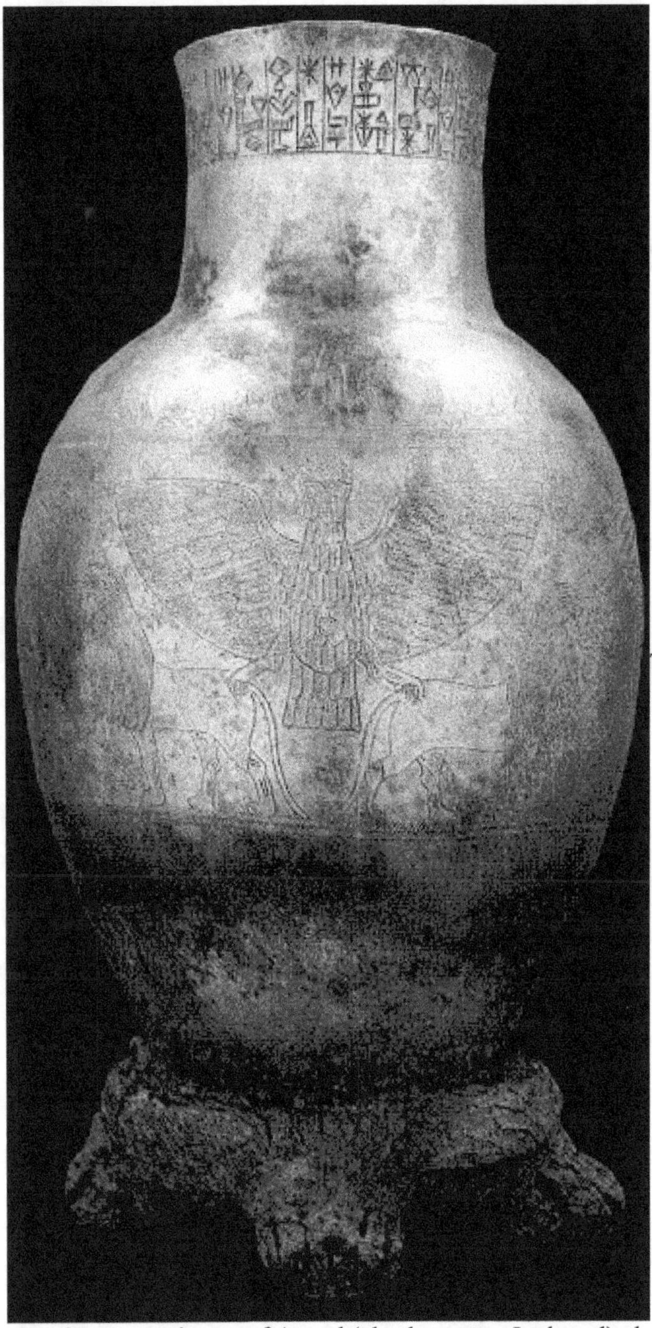
The legs are made of copper. The vase features an image of Anzud (also known as Imdugud), the lion-headed eagle, grasping two lions with his talons.

Detail drawing of the Enmetena vase. Lions kisse the antelopes.

Inscribed vase of silver and copper of Entemena, king of Lagash, with dedication to the god Ningirsu, around 2400 BC, Musée du Louvre, Paris. Found in Telloh, ancient city of Girsu.

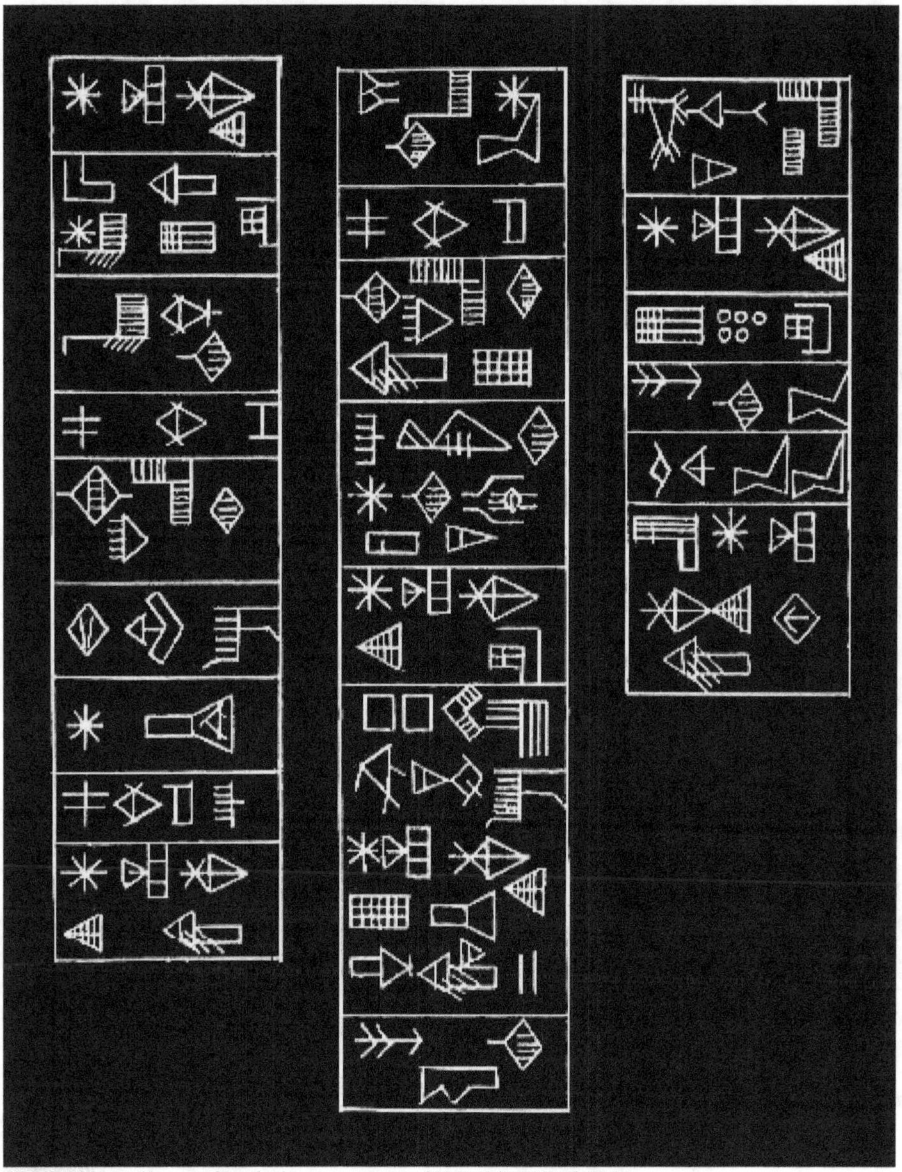

Source: http://sumerianshakespeare.com/70701/74901.html
The dedicatory inscriptions wrap around the neck of the vase:

Translation of the inscriptions from the CDLI (**P222539**):

For Ningirsu, the hero of Enlil,
Enmetena, ruler of Lagash,
chosen by the heart of Nanshe,
chief ruler of Ningirsu,
son of Enannatum, ruler of Lagash,
for the king who loved him, Ningirsu,
(this) gurgur-vessel of refined silver,
from which Ningirsu will consume the monthly oil (offering),
he had fashioned for him.
For his life, before Ningirsu of the Eninnu (temple)
he had it set up.
At that time Dudu
was the temple administrator of Ningirsu.

Votive relief of Ur-Nanshe, king of Lagash. Limestone, Early Dynastic III (2550–2500 BC). Found in Telloh (ancient city of Girsu).Louvre AO2344 At the top he creates the foundation for a shrine, at the bottom he presides over the dedication (Louvre). https://en.wikipedia.org/wiki/Lagash#/media/File:Relief_Ur-Nanshe_Louvre_AO2344.jpg Inscription: "Ur-Nanshe, king of Lagash, son of Gunidu, built the temple of Ningirsu; he built the temple of Nanshe; he built Apsubanda...boats from the (distant) land of Dilmun carried the wood (for him)". This is the oldest known written record of Dilmun and importation of goods intoMesopotamia. (Pouysségur, Patrick , ed. "Perforated Relief of King Ur-Nanshe." Lourve Museum. Louvre Museum). http://cdli.ox.ac.uk/wiki/doku.php?id=ur-nanshe

Votive relief of Ur-Nanshe, king of Lagash, representing the bird-god Anzu (or Im-dugud) as a lion-headed eagle. Alabaster, Early Dynastic III (2550–2500 BC). Found in Telloh, ancient city of Girsu https://en.wikipedia.org/wiki/Ur-Nanshe#/media/File:Relief_Im-dugud_Louvre_AO2783.jpg

Decipherment:

Hieroglyph: eraka 'wing' Rebus: eraka 'moltencast copper'; kola 'tiger' Rebus: kolhe 'smelter' kol 'working in iron'; arya 'lion' Rebus: Ara 'brass' dula 'pair' Rebus: dul 'cast metal'.

Etyma: Indian *sprachbund*
kul ‘tiger’ (Santali); kōlu id. (Te.) kōlupuli = Bengal tiger (Te.)Pk. Kolhuya -- , kulha — m. ‘ jackal ’ < *kōḍhu -- ; H.kolhā, °lā m. ‘ jackal ’, adj. ‘ crafty ’; G. kohlũ, °lũ n. ‘ jackal ’, M. kolhā, °lā m. krōṣṭṛ̊ ‘ crying ’ BhP., m. ‘ jackal ’ RV. = krṓṣṭu — m. Pāṇ. [√kruś] Pa. koṭṭhu -- , °uka — and kotthu -- , °uka — m. ‘ jackal ’, Pk. Koṭṭhu — m.; Si. Koṭa ‘ jackal ’, koṭiya ‘ leopard ’ GS 42 (CDIAL 3615). कोल्हा [kōlhā] कोल्हें [kōlhēṃ] A jackal (Marathi) Rebus: kol ‘furnace, forge’ (Kuwi) kol ‘alloy of five metals, pañcaloha’ (Ta.)

meṛhao = v.a.m. entwine itself; wind round, wrap round roll up (Santali); maṛhnā cover, encase (Hindi) (Santali.lex.Bodding) Rebus: *meḍ* ‘iron’ (Mu.Ho.) mẽṛh t iron; ispat m. = steel; dul m. = cast iron (Mu.) meṛed-bica = iron stone ore, in contrast to bali-bica, iron sand ore (Munda) *mẽṛhẽt* ‘iron’; *mẽṛhẽt icena* ‘the iron is rusty’; *ispat mẽṛhẽt* ‘steel’, *dul mẽṛhẽt* ‘cast iron’;*mẽṛhẽt khaṇḍa* ‘iron implements’
(Santali) *meḍ.* (Ho.)(Santali.lex.Bodding) *meṛed, mṛed, mṛd*iron; enga meṛed soft iron; *saṇḍi meṛed* hard iron; *ispāt meṛed* steel; *dul meṛed* cast iron; *i meṛed* rusty iron, also the iron of which weights are cast; *bica meṛed* iron extracted from stone ore; *bali meṛed* iron extracted from sand ore

(Mu.lex.)

mĕď (copper)(Czech) mid′ (copper, cuprum, orichalc)(Ukrainian) med′ (copper, cuprum, Cu), mednyy (copper, cupreous, brassy, brazen, brass), omednyat′ (copper, coppering), sul′fatmedi (Copper), politseyskiy (policeman, constable, peeler, policemen, redcap), pokryvat′ med′yu (copper), payal′nik (soldering iron, copper, soldering pen, soldering-iron), mednyy kotel (copper), medno-krasnyy (copper), mednaya moneta (copper). медь (copper, cuprum, Cu), медный (copper, cupreous, brassy, brazen, brass), омеднять (copper, coppering), Сульфатмеди (Copper), полицейский (policeman, constable, peeler, policemen, redcap), покрывать медью (copper), паяльник (soldering iron, copper, soldering pen, soldering-iron), медный котел (copper), медно-красный (copper), медная монета (copper).(**Russian**)

పోలడు [pōlaḍu] , పోలిగాడు or దూడలపోలడు *pōlaḍu*. [Tel.] n. An eagle. పసులపోలిగాడు the bird called the Black Drongo. *Dicrurus ater*. (F.B.I.)

Te. dūḍa a calf. *Go.* (ASu.) ḍuḍḍe female young of buffalo. *Konḍa* dūṛa calf (< Te.). (DEDR 3378) దూడ (p. 0604) [dūḍa] *dūḍa*. [Tel.] n. A calf. దూడలు అరిచినవి the calves were bleating. దూడలగొట్టిగాడు *dūḍala-goṭṭi-gāḍu*. n. The bird called an Adjutant, *Leptoptilus dubius* (F.B.I.) దూడలపోలిగాడు *dūḍala-pōligāḍu*. n. An eagle. *Te.* kōḍiya, kōḍe young bull; *adj.* male (e.g. kōḍe dūḍa bull calf), young, youthful; kōḍekā̃ḍu a young man. *Kol.*(Haig) kōḍē bull. *Nk.* khoṛe male calf. *Konḍa* kōḍi cow; kōṛe young bullock. *Pe.* kōḍi cow. *Manḍ.* kūḍi id. *Kui* kōḍi id., ox.*Kuwi* (F.) kōdi cow; (S.) kajja kōḍi bull; (Su. P.) kōḍi cow(DEDR 2199)

Ta. eruvai blood, (?) copper. *Ka.* ere a dark-red or dark-brown colour, a dark or dusky colour; (Badaga) erande sp. fruit, red in colour. *Te.* rēcu, rēcu-kukka a sort of ounce or lynx said to climb trees and to destroy tigers; (B.) a hound or wild dog.*Kol.* resn a·te wild dog (i.e. *res na·te; see 3650). *Pa.* iric netta id. *Ga.* (S.3) rēs nete hunting dog, hound. *Go.* (Ma.) erm ney, (D.) erom nay, (Mu.) arm/aṛm nay wild dog (*Voc.* 353); (M.) rac nāī, (Ko.) rasi ney id. (*Voc.* 3010). For 'wild dog', cf. 1931 Ta. ce- red, esp. the items for 'red dog, wild dog'. (DEDR 817)

Ta. eruvai a kind of kite whose head is white and whose body is brown; eagle. *Ma.* eruva eagle, kite.(DEDR 818)

Ta. eruvai European bamboo reed; a species of Cyperus; straight sedge tuber. *Ma.* eruva a kind of grass.(DEDR 819)
dhā́tu ' *strand of rope ' (cf.*tridhā́tu* -- ' threefold ' RV., *ayugdhātu* -- ' having an uneven number of strands ' KātyŚr.).S. *dhāī* f. ' wisp of fibres added from time to time to a rope that is being twisted ', L. *dhāī̃* f. (CDIAL 6773)

Dāma (nt.) [Sk. dāman to dyati to bind (Gr. di/dhmi), *dē, as in Gr. de/sma (rope), dia/dhma (diadem), u(po/dhma (sandal)] a bond, fetter, rope; chain, wreath, garland S iv.163 (read dāmena for damena), 282, (id.); A iii.393 (dāmena baddho); Sn 28 (=vacchakānaŋ bandhanatthāya katā ganthitā nandhipasayuttā rajjubandhanavisesā); Vism 108. Usually -- °, viz. anoja -- puppha° J i.9; vi.227; olambaka° VvA 32; kusuma° J iii.394; gandha° J i.178; VvA 173, 198; puppha° Ji.397; VvA 198; mālā° J ii.104; rajata° J i.50; iii.184; iv.91; rattapuppha° J iii.30; sumana° J iv.455. (Pali) दामन् *n.* [दो-मनिन्] 1 A string, thread, fillet, rope. -2 A chaplet, a garland in general; आद्ये बद्धा विरहदिवसे या शिखा दाम हित्वा Me.93; कनकचम्पकदामगौरीम् Ch. P.1; Śi.4.5. **-3** A line,

streak (as of lightning); वुद्‌युद्- दाम्ना हेमराजीव विन्ध्यम् M.3.2; Me.27. **-4** A large bandage. **-5** Ved. A gift. **-6** A portion, share. **-7** A girdle. **-Comp. -अञ्चलम्, -अञ्जनम्** a foot-rope for horses, &c.; ससुः सरोषपरिचारकवार्यमाणा दामाञ्चलस्खलितलोलपदं तुरङ्गाः Śi.5.61. **-उदरः** an epithet of Kṛiṣṇa. dāmanī दामनी A foot-rope. dāmā दामा A string, cord. धामन् dhāman A fetter. **dā´man**1 ' **rope** ' RV. 2. ***dāmana -- ,** *dāmanī* -- f. ' long rope to which calves are tethered ' Hariv. 3. ***dāmara -- .** [**dāmara* -- is der. fr. *n*/*r* n. stem. -- √dā2]1. Pa. *dāma* -- , inst. °*mēna* n. ' rope, fetter, garland ', Pk. *dāma* -- n.; Wg. *dām* ' rope, thread, bandage '; Tir. *dām* ' rope '; Paš.lauṛ. *dām* ' thick thread ', gul. *dūm* ' net snare ' (IIFL iii 3, 54 ← Ind. or Pers.); Shum. *dām* ' rope '; Sh.gil. (Lor.) *dōmo* ' twine, short bit of goat's hair cord ', gur. *dōm* m. ' thread ' (→ Ḍ. *dōṅ* ' thread '); K. *gu* -- *dômu* m. ' cow's tethering rope '; P. *dā̃u*, *dāvā̃* m. ' hobble for a horse '; WPah.bhad. *daũ* n. ' rope to tie cattle ', bhal. *daõ* m., jaun. *dā̃w;* A. *dāmā* ' peg to tie a buffalo -- calf to '; B. *dām, dāmā* ' cord '; Or. *duā̃* ' tether ', *dāī̃* ' long tether to which many beasts are tied '; H. *dām* m.f. ' rope, string, fetter ', *dāmā* m. ' id., garland '; G. *dām* n. ' tether ', M. *dāvẽ* n.; Si. *dama* ' chain, rope ', (SigGr) *dam* ' garland '. -- Ext. in Paš.dar. *damaṭā´*, °*ṭī´*, nir. weg. *damaṭék* ' rope ', Shum.*ḍamaṭik*, Woṭ. *damṓṛ* m., Sv. *dåmoṛī´*; -- with -- *ll* -- : N. *dāmlo* ' tether for cow ', *dā̃wali, dāũli, dāmli* ' bird -- trap of string ', *dā̃wal, dāmal* ' coeval ' (< ' tied together '?); M. *dā̃vlī* f. ' small tie -- rope '.2. Pk. *dāvaṇa* -- n., *dāmaṇī* -- f. ' tethering rope '; S. *ḍāvaṇu, ḍāṇu* m. ' forefeet shackles ', *ḍāviṇī, ḍāṇī* f. ' guard to support nose -- ring '; L. *ḍā̃vaṇ* m., *ḍā̃vaṇī, ḍāuṇī*(Ju. *ḍ* --) f. ' hobble ', *dāuṇī* f. ' strip at foot of bed, triple cord of silk worn by women on head ', awāṇ. *dāvuṇ* ' picket rope '; P. *dāuṇ, dauṇ*, ludh. *daun* f. m. ' string for bedstead, hobble for horse ', *dāuṇī* f. ' gold ornament worn on woman's forehead '; Ku. *dauṇo* m., °*ṇī* f. ' peg for tying cattle to ', gng. *dɔ̃ṛ* ' place for keeping cattle, bedding for cattle '; A. *dan* ' long cord on which a net or screen is stretched, thong ', *danā* ' bridle '; B. *dāmni* ' rope '; Or. *daaṇa* ' string at the fringe of a casting net on which pebbles are strung ', *dāuṇi* ' rope for tying bullocks together when threshing '; H. *dāwan* m. ' girdle ', *dāwanī* f. ' rope ', *dā̃wanī* f. ' a woman's orna<-> ment '; G. *dāmaṇ, ḍā*° n. ' tether, hobble ', *dāmṇũ* n. ' thin rope, string ', *dāmṇī* f. ' rope, woman's head -- ornament '; M. *dāvaṇ* f. ' picket -- rope '. -- Words denoting the act of driving animals to tread out corn are poss. nomina actionis from *dāmayati2.
3. L. *ḍā̃varāvaṇ*, (Ju.) *ḍā̃v*° ' to hobble '; A. *dāmri* ' long rope for tying several buffalo -- calves together ', Or. *daũrā, daürā* ' rope '; Bi. *daũrī* ' rope to which threshing bullocks are tied, the act of treading out the grain ', Mth. *dā̃mar, daũraṛ* ' rope to which the bullocks are tied '; H. *dā̃wrī* f. ' id., rope, string ', *dā̃wrī* f. ' the act of driving bullocks round to tread out the corn '. -- X *dhāgga<-> q.v.*dāmayati2; *dāmakara -- , *dāmadhāra -- ; uddāma -- , prōddāma -- ; *antadāmanī -- , *galadāman -- , *galadāmana -- , *gōḍḍadāman -- , *gōḍḍadāmana -- , *gōḍḍadāmara -- **.dāmán** -- 2 m. (f.?) ' gift ' RV. [√dā1]. See dā´tu -- .***dāmana --** ' rope ' see dā´man -- 1.Addenda: **dā´man** -- 1. 1. Brj. *dā̃u* m. ' tying '.3. ***dāmara -- :** Brj. *dā̃wrī* f. ' rope '.(CDIAL 6283)
धातुः [**धा**-आधारे तुन्] **-कुशल** *a.* skilful in working in metals, metallurgist.

धम dhama *a.* (-मा, -मी *f.*) [धम् ध्माने-अच्] (Usually at the end of comp.)
1 Blowing; अग्निंधम, नाडिंधम. -2 Melting, fusing. **-मः** 1 The moon. -2 An epithet of Kṛiṣṇa. -3 Of Yama, the god of death. -4 Of Brahmā.धमकः dhamakḥ A blacksmith. धमनिः नी *f.* 1 A reed, blow-pipe; वेणुधमन्या प्रबोध्य Vaiśvadeva. धामनिका धामनी See धमनी.

dhā´tu n. ' substance ' RV., m. ' element ' MBh., ' metal, mineral, ore (esp. of a red colour) ' Mn., ' ashes of the dead ' lex., [√dhā]Pa. *dhātu* -- m. ' element, ashes of the dead, relic '; KharI. *dhatu* ' relic '; Pk. *dhāu* -- m. ' metal, red chalk '; N. *dhāu* ' ore (esp. of copper) '; Or. *ḍhāu* ' red chalk, red ochre ' (whence *ḍhāuā* ' reddish '; M. *dhāū, dhāv* m.f. ' a partic. soft red stone ' (whence *dhăvaḍ* m. ' a caste of iron -- smelters ', *dhāvḍī* ' composed of or relating to iron '); -- Si. *dā* ' relic '; -- (CDIAL 6773)

dhākḥ धाकः [धा-उणा ° क तस्य नेत्वम्] **1** An ox. **-2** A receptacle, reservoir. **-3** Food, boiled rice. **-4** A post, pillar, column. **-5** Brahman. **-6** A supporter.

Data mining of Indus Script Corpora ranku 'antelope' rebus 'tin' करडूं karaḍū 'kid' rebus karaḍā 'hard alloy'

Antelope is a hieroglyph pictorial motif. The pictorial depiction also highlights the short tail with three short strokes. Orthographic styles used in the corpora seem to indicate that a distinction is made between an antelope and a kid (young antelope or goat). It is suggested that the two are distinct signifiers of two distinct rebus readings to signify specific advances in archaeo-metallurgy, related to the hardening of copper mineral by adding other minerals (such as tin) to produce metal alloys.

Hieroglyph: Kur. xolā **tail**. Malt. qoli id. (DEDR 2135) Rebus: **kol** 'working in iron' kolhe 'smelters' kolle 'blacksmith'

This pictorial representation also is recognized as a 'sign' on some concordance lists of the Indus Script Corpora.

Antelope hieroglyph occurs in the context of smithy-forge implement cluster from out of 240 copper tablets:

Smithy-forge Implements cluster associated with typical hieroglyphs (both pictorial motifs and signs):

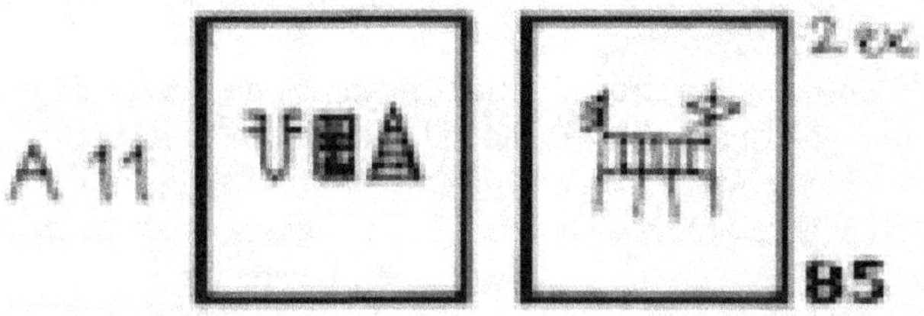

B5

A11

Hieroglyph:
krammara 'look back' (Telugu) rebus: kamar 'blacksmith' mlekh 'goat' rebus: milakkhu, mlecchAs'a 'copper'

*kaṇḍa kanka* ‘rim of jar’ Rebus: *karṇīka* ‘account (scribe)’*karṇī*‘supercargo’. *kaṇḍa* ‘fire-altar’. Alternative: kanka 'rim of jar' rebus: kanga 'brazier'.

khaNDA 'dividion' rebus: khANDa 'implements'

Hieroglyph: *Ta.* meṭṭu mound, heap of earth; mēṭu height, eminence, hillock; muṭṭu rising ground, high ground, heap. *Ma.* mēṭu rising ground, hillock; māṭu hillock, raised ground; miṭṭāl rising ground, an alluvial bank; (Tiyya) maṭṭa hill. *Ka.* mēḍu height, rising ground, hillock; miṭṭu rising or high ground, hill; miṭṭe state of being high, rising ground, hill, mass, a large number; (Hav.) muṭṭe heap (as of straw). *Tu.* miṭṭè prominent, protruding; muṭṭe heap. *Te.* meṭṭa raised or high ground, hill; (K.) meṭṭu mound; miṭṭa high ground, hillock, mound; high, elevated, raised, projecting; (*VPK*) mēṭu, mēṭa, mēṭi stack of hay; (Inscr.) meṇṭa-cēnu dry field (cf. meṭṭu-nēla, meṭṭu-vari). *Kol.* (SR.) meṭṭā hill; (Kin.) meṭṭ, (Hislop) met mountain. *Nk.* meṭṭ hill, mountain. *Ga.* (S.3, *LSB* 20.3) meṭṭa high land. *Go.* (Tr. W. Ph.) maṭṭā, (Mu.) maṭṭa mountain; (M. L.) meṭā id., hill; (A. D. Ko.) meṭṭa, (Y. Ma. M.) meṭa hill; (SR.) meṭṭā hillock (*Voc.* 2949). *Konḍa* meṭa id. *Kuwi* (S.)metta hill; (Isr.) meṭa sand hill. (DEDR 5058) Rebus: *mẽd, mēd* 'iron'

Link to B5: Hieroglyph: kANDA ‘rhinoceros’ rebus: khANDA ‘implements PLUS pattar 'trough' rebus: pattar 'guild'

*kaṇḍa kanka* ‘rim of jar’ Rebus: *karṇīka* ‘account (scribe)’*karṇī*‘supercargo’. *kaṇḍa* ‘fire-altar’. Alternative: kanka 'rim of jar' rebus: kanga 'brazier'.

khaNDA 'dividion' rebus: khANDa 'implements'

Hieroglyph: *Ta.* meṭṭu mound, heap of earth; mēṭu height, eminence, hillock; muṭṭu rising ground, high ground, heap. *Ma.* mēṭu rising ground, hillock; māṭu hillock, raised ground; miṭṭāl rising ground, an alluvial bank; (Tiyya) maṭṭa hill. *Ka.* mēḍu height, rising ground, hillock; miṭṭu rising or high ground, hill; miṭṭe state of being high, rising ground, hill, mass, a large number; (Hav.) muṭṭe heap (as of straw). *Tu.* miṭṭè prominent, protruding; muṭṭe heap. *Te.* meṭṭa raised or high ground, hill; (K.) meṭṭu mound; miṭṭa high ground, hillock, mound; high, elevated, raised, projecting; (*VPK*) mēṭu, mēṭa, mēṭi stack of hay; (Inscr.) meṇṭa-cēnu dry field (cf. meṭṭu-nēla, meṭṭu-vari). *Kol.* (SR.) meṭṭā hill; (Kin.) meṭṭ, (Hislop) met mountain. *Nk.* meṭṭ hill, mountain. *Ga.* (S.3, *LSB* 20.3) meṭṭa high land. *Go.* (Tr. W. Ph.) maṭṭā, (Mu.) maṭṭa mountain; (M. L.) meṭā id., hill; (A. D. Ko.) meṭṭa, (Y. Ma. M.) meṭa hill; (SR.) meṭṭā hillock (*Voc.* 2949). *Konḍa* meṭa id. *Kuwi* (S.)metta hill; (Isr.) meṭa sand hill. (DEDR 5058) Rebus: *mẽd, mēd* 'iron' .

Signs 182, 183, 184 Mahadevan Concordance

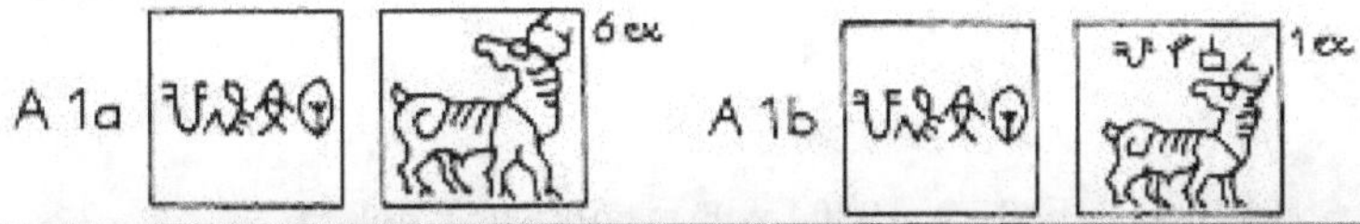

m516B Copper tablet

m0516Atm0516Bt 3398 [Copper tablet; side B perhaps is a graphemic representation of an antelope; note the ligatured tail comparable to the tail on m273, b012 and k037] *rīṛ* high mountain (WPah.)(CDIAL 10749a) Rebus: *rīti* 'yellow brass, bell metal': rīti2 f. ' yellow brass, bell metal ' Kathās., *rītika* -- n. ' calx of brass ', °*kā* -- f. ' brass ' lex. 2. rīrī -- , *rirī* -- f. ' yellow brass ' lex. [Ac. to AO xviii 248 Dard. forms < *raktikā -- 2] 1. Dm. *rit* ' copper ', Gaw. *rīt* (→ Sv. *rīda* NoPhal 49); Bshk. *rīd* ' brass ', Tor. *žit* f. 2. Pk. *rīrī* -- f. ' brass '; Sh. *rīl* m. ' brass, bronze, copper '.(CDIAL 10752).

கண்டம்³ kaṇṭam , *n.* < *khaṇḍa.* Piece, cut or broken off; fragment, slice, cutting, chop, parcel, portion, slip; துண்டம். செந்தயிர்க் கண்டம் (கம்பரா. நாட்டுப். 19).Rebus: *khaṇḍa* 'tools, pots and pans and metal-ware'.

kanka, karṇaka 'rim of jar' Rebus: ***karṇaka*** 'account scribe'.

The pictograph on m516 B (antelope) appears on a tin ingot found in Haifa, Israel. T**he antelope may be connoted by *ranku*, deer. Rebus: *ranga* = tin.** Kur. *xolā* tail. Malt. *qoli* id. (DEDR 2135). Rebus: *kol* 'working in iron' (Tamil)

B009 markhor (*capra falconeri heptneri*).

Banawali10 9204 xolā = tail (Kur.); qoli id. (Malt.)(DEDR 2135). Rebus: kol 'pañcalōha' (Ta.) கொல் kol, n. Iron. (Tamil) Dm. *mraṅ* m. 'markhor' *Wkh. merg f. 'ibex'* (CDIAL 9885) Tor. *miṇḍ* 'ram', *miṇḍā́l* 'markhor' (CDIAL 10310) Rebus: meḍ 'iron' (Ho.) kolom 'sprout' Rebus: kolami 'smithy/forge'. eae 'seven' (Santali); rebus: eh-ku 'steel' (Ta.) gaṇḍa 'four' (Santali) Rebus: kaṇḍ fire-altar, furnace' (Santali) tagaraka 'tabernae montana' Rebus: tagaram 'tin'.

Courtyard with turners' workshops

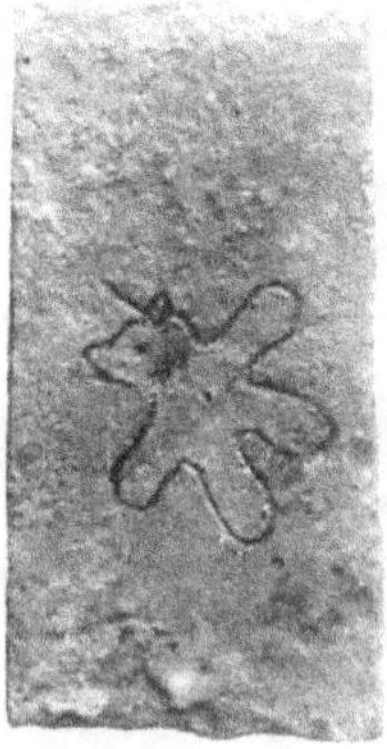

h1018 copper plate. Star-fish? Gangetic octopus?

m297a. seal. 2641

veṛhā octopus, said to be found in the Indus (Jaṭki lexicon of A. Jukes, 1900) Rebus: L. *veṛh, vehṛ* m. fencing; Mth. *beṛhī* granary; L. *veṛhā, vehṛā* enclosure containing many houses; *beṛā* building with a courtyard (WPah.) (CDIAL 12130)

koḍ 'horn' Rebus: koḍ = artisan's workshop (Kuwi)

खोंड [khōṇḍa] m A young bull, a bullcalf (Marathi) Rebus: *kõdār* 'turner' (Bengali)

मेड [mēḍa] *f* (Usually मेढ q. v.) मेडका *m* A stake (Marathi) meḍa 'pillar' (Go.) Rebus: meḍ 'iron' (Ho.)

kāṭhī = body, person; *kāṭhī* the make of the body; the stature of a man (Gujarati) Rebus: *khātī* 'wheelwright' (H.)

Epigraphs in the corpora are related to stone-, mineral-, metal-ware catalogs, continuing the bullae-tokens tradition of account-keeping in bronze-age. Almost all glyphs are remarkably unambiguous and vivid with specific orthographic features, including those glyphs which are referred to as geometric designs or dotted circles or svastika or ligatured composite animals (with glyptic elements such as ‘human face’, ‘trunk of elephant’, ‘forelegs of a bovine’, ‘hindlegs of a feline’) or ligatured signs (such as a a ‘rim-of-jar’ glyph ligatured to a ‘water-carrier’ glyph).

117 antelope; sun motif. Dholavira seal impression. arka 'sun' Rebus: araka, eraka 'copper, moltencast' PLUS करडूं karaḍū 'kid' Rebus: karaḍā 'hard alloy'. Thus, together, the rebus message: hard alloy of copper.

On arka in compound expressions: *அருக்கம்[1] arukkam, n.* < ***arka***. (நாநார்த்த.) 1. Copper; செம்பு (Tamil) అగసాలి (p. 0023) [agasāli] or **అగసాలెవాడు** *agasāli*. [Tel.] n. A goldsmith. కంసాలివాడు.(Telugu) Kannada (Kittel lexicon):

ಅಕಸಾಲ aka2-sâla. = ಅಕ್ಕಸಾಲ, ಅಗಸಾಲ. A gold or silver smith (C.).

ಅಕಸಾಲಿಕೆ aka2-sâlikĕ. = ಅಕ್ಕಸಾಲಿಕೆ. The business of a gold or silver smith (C.).

ಅಕಸಾಲಿಗ aka2-sâliga. = ಅಕ್ಕಸಾಲಿಗ, ಅಗಸಾಲಿಗ. A gold or silver smith (C.).

ಅಕಸಾಲೆ aka-sâlĕ. = ಅಕ್ಕಸಾಲೆ q. v., ಅಗಸಾಲೆ. The workshop of a goldsmith. 2, a goldsmith (C.).

Bet Dwaraka turbinella pyrum seal. करडूं karaḍū 'kid' Rebus: karaḍā 'hard alloy'. barad 'ox' Rebus: bharata 'alloy of copper, pewter, tin' khond 'young bull' koD 'horn' Rebus: khond 'turner' koD 'workshop'. Thus workshop of hard alloys of copper, pewter, tin.

Bhirrrna seal. ASI karNika 'rim of jar' rebus: karNI 'supercargo'; karNaka 'account'; Alternative: kanka 'rim of jar' rebus: kanga 'brazier'. A variant of Signs is seen on the

Bhirrana seal: 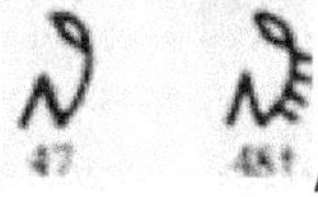 *karaṁḍa* -- m.n. ' bone shaped like a bamboo ', *karaṁḍuya* -- n. ' backbone ' (Prakrit) Rebus: करडा [*karaḍā*] Hard from alloy--iron, silver &c. (Marathi)

40 Three-headed animal, plant; sun motifDholavira. Seal. Readings as above. PLUS kolmo 'rice plant' Rebus: kolami 'smithy, forge'. Thus, the message of the hieroglyph-multiplex is: smithy/forge for moltencast coper and hard alloys of copper, pewter, tin.

Hieroglyph: करडूं or करडें (p. 137) [karaḍū or karaḍēṃ] *n* A kid. कराडूं (p. 137) [karāḍūṃ] *n* (Commonly करडूं) A kid. (Marathi) Rebus: करडा (p. 137) [karaḍā] Hard from alloy--iron, silver &c. (Marathi. Molesworth).

 Lothal 070  Lothal123A 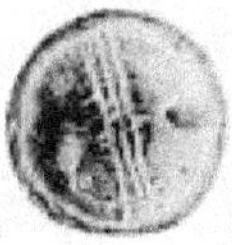 Lothal123B Glyph: svastika; rebus: jasta 'zinc' (Kashmiri). Svastika: sathiyā (H.), sāthiyo (G.); satthia, sotthia (Pkt.) Rebus: svastika pewter (Kannada)

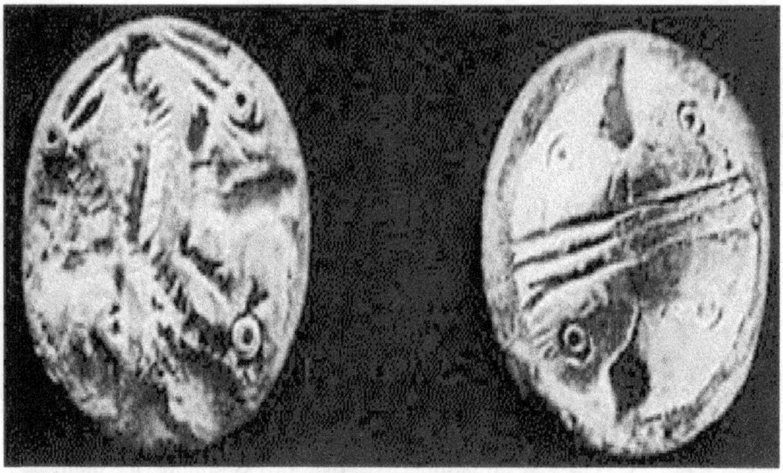

Circular seal, of steatite, from Bahrein, found at

Lothal. A Stamp seal and its impression from the Harappan site of Lothal north of Bombay, of the type also found in the contemporary cultures of southern Iraq and the Persian Gulf Area. http://www.penn.museum/sites/expedition/archaeology-in-india/

http://www.penn.museum/sites/expedition/shipping-and-maritime-trade-of-the-indus-people/

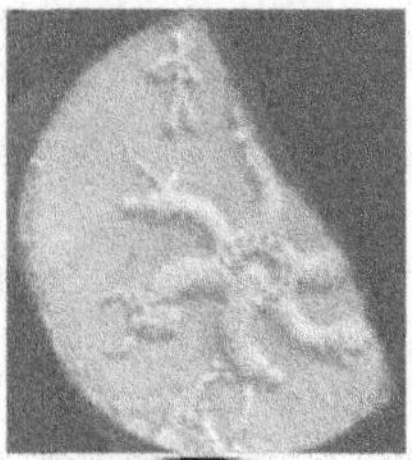

ranku 'antelope' Rebus: ranku 'tin'

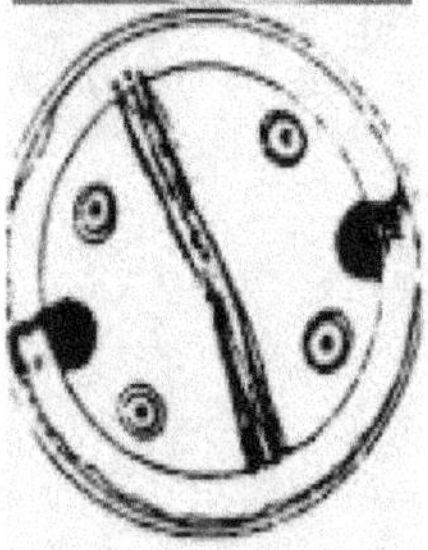

m417 Glyph: ‘ladder’: H. sainī, senī f. ‘ ladder ’ Rebus: Pa. sēṇi -- f. ‘ guild, division of army ’; Pk. sēṇi -- f. ‘ row, collection ’; śrḗṇi (metr. often śrayaṇi --) f. ‘ line, row, troop ’ RV. The lexeme in Tamil means: Limit, boundary; எல்லை. நளியிரு முந்நீரேணி யாக (புறநா. 35, 1). Country, territory.

The glyphics are:
Semantics: ‘group of animals/quadrupeds’: paśu ‘animal’ (RV), pasaramu, pasalamu = an animal, a beast, a brute, quadruped (Te.) Rebus: pasra ‘smithy’ (Santali)

Glyph: ‘six’: bhaṭa ‘six’. Rebus: bhaṭa ‘furnace’.
Glyph (the only inscription on the Mohenjo-daro seal m417): ‘warrior’: bhaṭa. Rebus: bhaṭa ‘furnace’. Thus, this glyph is a semantic determinant of the message: ‘furnace’. It appears that the six heads of ‘animal’ glyphs are related to ‘furnace’ work.
This guild, community of smiths and masons evolves into Harosheth Hagoyim, ‘a smithy of nations’.

It appears that the Meluhhans were in contact with many interaction areas, Dilmun and Susa (elam) in particular. There is evidence for Meluhhan settlements outside of Meluhha. It is a reasonable inference that the Meluhhans with bronze-age expertise of creating arsenical and bronze alloys and working with other metals constituted the ‘smithy of nations’, Harosheth Hagoyim.

Dilmun seal from Barbar; six heads of antelope radiating from a circle; similar to animal protomes in Failaka, Anatolia and Indus. Obverse of the seal shows four dotted circles. [Poul Kjaerum, The Dilmun Seals as evidence of long distance relations in the early second millennium BC, pp. 269-277.] A tree is shown on this Dilmun seal.

Glyph: 'tree': kuṭi 'tree'. Rebus: kuṭhi 'smelter furnace' (Santali).

baTa 'six' Rebus: bhaTa 'furnace' ranku 'antelope' Rebus: ranku 'tin'

Izzat Allah Nigahban, 1991, Excavations at Haft Tepe, Iran, The University Museum, UPenn, p. 97. furnace' Fig.96a.

There is a possibility that this seal impression from Haft Tepe had some connections with Indian hieroglyphs. This requires further investigation. "From Haft Tepe (Middle Elamite period, ca. 13th century) in Ḵūzestān an unusual pyrotechnological installation was associated with a craft workroom containing such materials as mosaics of colored stones framed in bronze, a dismembered elephant skeleton used in manufacture of bone tools, and several hundred bronze arrowpoints and small tools. "Situated in a courtyard directly in front of this workroom is a most unusual kiln. This kiln is very large, about 8 m long and 2 and one half m wide, and contains two long compartments with chimneys at each end, separated by a fuel chamber in the middle. Although the roof of the kiln had collapsed, it is evident from the slight inturning of the walls which remain in situ that it was barrel vaulted like the roofs of the tombs. Each of the two long heating chambers is divided into eight sections by partition walls. The southern heating chamber contained metallic slag, and was apparently used for making bronze objects. The northern heating chamber contained pieces of broken pottery and other material, and thus was apparently used for baking clay objects including tablets . . ." (loc.cit. Bronze in pre-Islamic Iran, Encyclopaedia Iranica, http://www.iranicaonline.org/articles/bronze-i Negahban, 1977; and forthcoming).

Many of the bronze-age manufactured or industrial goods were surplus to the needs of the producing community and had to be traded, together with a record of types of goods and types of processes such as native metal or minerals, smelting of minerals, alloying of metals using two or more minerals, casting ingots, forging and turning metal into shapes such as plates or vessels, using anvils, cire perdue technique for creating bronze statues – in addition to the production of artifacts such as bangles and ornaments made of śankha or shell (turbinella pyrum), semi-precious stones, gold or silver beads. Thus writing was invented to maintain production-cum-trade accounts, to cope with the economic imperative of bronze age technological advances to take the artisans of guilds into the stage of an industrial production-cum-trading community.

Tablets and seals inscribed with hieroglyphs, together with the process of creating seal impressions took inventory lists to the next stage of trading property items using bills of lading of trade loads of industrial goods. Such bills of lading describing trade loads were created using tablets and seals with the invention of writing based on phonetics and semantics of language – the hallmark of Indian hieroglyphs.

Indus Script Hieroglyph-multiplex hypertext on al-Sabah Kuwait gold disc Meluhha brassworker's artisanal repertoire

Thanks to Benoy Behl for disseminating the photograph of an exquisite gold disc now in al-Sabah collection of Kuwait National Museum. This gold disc is a veritable metalwork catalog, consistent with the entire Indus Script Corpora as catalogus catalogorum of metalwork. The uniqueness of the collection of hieroglyph-multiplexs on this gold disc is that a large number of metalwork catalog items (more than 12) have been presented on a circular space with 9.6 cm diameter validating the Maritime Tin Route which linked Hanoi to Haifa through the Persian Gulf.

"Gold disc. al-Sabah Collection, Kuwait National Museum. 9.6 cm diameter, which was obviously from the Indus Valley period in India. Typical of that period, it depicts zebu, bulls, human attendants, ibex, fish, partridges, bees, pipal free an animal-headed standard." Benoy K. Behl https://www.facebook.com/BenoyKBehlArtCulture

The hieroglyphs on the Kuwait Museum gold disc can be read rebus:

1. A pair of *tabernae montana* flowers *tagara* 'tabernae montana' flower; rebus: *tagara* 'tin'

2. A pair of rams *tagara* 'ram'; rebus: *damgar* 'merchant' (Akkadian) Next to one ram: kuTi 'tree' Rebus: kuThi 'smelter' Alternative: kolmo 'rice plant' Rebus: kolimi 'smithy, forge'.

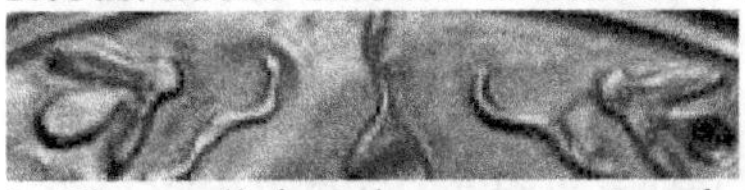

3. Ficus religiosa leaves on a tree branch (5) *loa* 'ficus leaf'; rebus: *loh* 'metal'. *kol* in Tamil means *pancaloha*'alloy of five metals'. PLUS flanking pair of lotus flowers: tAmarasa 'lotus' Rebus: tAmra 'copper' dula 'pair' Rebus: dul 'cast metal' thus, denoting copper castings.

4. A pair of bulls tethered to the tree branch: barad, barat 'ox' Rebus: bharata 'alloy of copper, pewter, tin' (Marathi) PLUS kola 'man' Rebus: kolhe 'smelter' kur.i 'woman' Rebus: kol 'working in iron' Alternative: *ḍhangar* 'bull'; rebus *ḍhangar* 'blacksmith' poLa 'zebu' Rebus: poLa 'magnetite'. Two persons touch the two bulls: *meḍ* 'body' (Mu.) Rebus: *meḍ* 'iron' (Ho.) Thus, the hieroglyph composition denotes ironsmiths.
5. A pair of antelopes looking back: *krammara* 'look back'; rebus: *kamar* 'smith' (Santali); *tagara* 'antelope'; rebus: *damgar* 'merchant' (Akkadian) Alternative: *melh, mr..eka* 'goat' (Brahui. Telugu) Rebus: milakkhu 'copper' (Pali), mleccha-mukha 'copper' (Samskritam)
6. A pair of antelopes *mẽḍh* 'antelope, ram'; rebus: *mẽḍ 'iron' (Mu.)*
7. A pair of combs *kāṅga* 'comb' Rebus: *kanga* 'brazier, fireplace'

Phal. *kāṅga* ' combing ' in *ṣiṣ k° dūm* 'I comb my hair' *khyḗṅgia, kēṅgī* f.; *kaṅghā* m. ' large comb (Punjabi) káṅkata m. ' comb ' AV., n. lex., °*tī* -- , °*tikā* -- f. lex. 2. *kaṅkaṭa -- 2. 3. *kaṅkaśa -- . [Of doubtful IE. origin WP i 335, EWA i 137: aberrant -- *uta* -- as well as -- *aśa* -- replacing -- *ata* -- in MIA. and NIA.]1. Pk. *kaṁkaya* -- m. ' comb ', *kaṁkaya* -- , °*kaï* -- m. ' name of a tree '; Gy. eur. *kangli* f.; Wg. *kuṇi* -- *přũ* ' man's comb ' (for *kuṇi* -- cf. *kuṇälík* beside *kuṅälíks*.v. kr̥muka -- ; -- *přũ* see prapavaṇa --); Bshk. *kēṅg* ' comb ', Gaw. *khēṅgī´*, Sv. *khḗṅgiā*, Tor. *kyäṅg* ' comb ' (Dard. forms, esp. Gaw., Sv., Phal. but not Sh., prob. ← L. P. type < **kaṅgahiā* -- , see 3 below); Sh. *kōṅyi̯* f. (→ Ḍ. *k*lni* f.), gil. (Lor.) *kōī̃* f. ' man's comb ', *kōũ* m. ' woman's comb ', pales. *kōgō* m. ' comb '; K. *kanguwu* m. ' man's comb ', *kangañ* f. ' woman's '; WPah. bhad. *kā̃´kei* ' a comb -- like fern ', bhal. *kā̃kei* f. ' comb, plant with comb -- like leaves '; N. *kāṅiyo, kāĩyo* ' comb ', A. *kā̃kai*, B. *kā̃kui;* Or. *kaṅkāi, kaṅkuā* ' comb ', *kakuā* ' ladder -- like bier for carrying corpse to the burning -- ghat '; Bi. *kakwā* ' comb ', *kakahā*, °*hī*, Mth. *kakwā*, Aw. lakh. *kakawā*, Bhoj. *kakahī* f.; H. *kakaiyā* ' shaped like a comb (of a brick) '; G. (non -- Aryan tribes of Dharampur)*kākhāī* f. ' comb '; M. *kaṅkvā* m. ' comb ', *kā̃kaī* f. ' a partic. shell fish and its shell '; -- S. *kaṅgu* m. ' a partic. kind of small fish ' < **kaṅkuta* -- ? -- Ext. with --*l* -- in Ku. *kā̃gilo, kāĩlo* ' comb '.2. G. (Soraṭh) *kā̃gaṛ* m. ' a weaver's instrument '?3. L. *kaṅghī* f. ' comb, a fish of the perch family ', awāṇ. *kaghī* ' comb '; P. *kaṅghā* m. ' large comb ', °*ghī* f. ' small comb for men, large one for women ' (→ H. *kaṅghā* m. ' man's comb ', °*gahī*, °*ghī* f. ' woman's ', *kaṅghuā* m. ' rake or harrow '; Bi. *kā̃gahī* ' comb ', Or. *kaṅgei*, M. *kaṅgvā*); -- G. *kā̃gsī* f. ' comb ', with metath. *kā̃sko* m., °*kī* f.; WPah. khaś. *kāgśī*, śeu. *kā̃śkī* ' a comblike fern ' or < **kaṅkataśikha* -- .WPah.ktg. *kaṅgi* f. ' comb '; J. *kā̃gṛu* m. ' small comb '.(CDIAL 2598)

Rebus: large furnace, fireplace: kang कंग् । आवसथ्यो &1;ग्निः m. the fire-receptacle or fire-place, kept burning in former times in the courtyard of a Kāshmīrī house for the benefit of guests, etc., and distinct from the three religious domestic fires of a Hindū; (at the present day) a fire-place or brazier lit in the open air on mountain sides, etc., for the sake of warmth or for keeping off wild beasts. nāra-kang, a fire-receptacle; hence, met. a shower of sparks (falling on a person) (Rām. 182). kan:gar `portable furnace' (Kashmiri)Cf. kā̃gürü, which is the fem. of this word in a dim. sense (Gr.Gr. 33, 7). kā̃gürü काँग्ुरु or kā̃gürü काँग or kā̃gar काँग्ुर्ु । हसब्तिका f. (sg. dat. kā̃grĕ काँग्र्य or kā̃garĕ काँगर्य, abl. kā̃gri काँग्रि), the portable brazier, or *kāngrī,* much used in Kashmīr (K.Pr. *kángár,* 129, 131, 178; *káṅgrí,* 5, 128, 129). For particulars see El. s.v. *kángri;* L. 7, 25, *kangar;*and K.Pr. 129. The word is a fem. dim. of kang, q.v. (Gr.Gr. 37). kā̃gri-khŏphürükā̃gri-khŏphürü काँग्रि-ख्वफ्ु&above;रू&below; । भग्ना काष्ठाङ्गारिका f. a worn-out brazier. -khôru -खोरु&below; । काष्ठाङ्गारिका<-> र्धभाग: m. the outer half (made of woven twigs) of a brazier, remaining after the inner earthenware bowl has been broken or removed; see khôru. -kŏnḍolu -कंड । हसन्तिकापात्रम् m. the circular earthenware bowl of a brazier, which contains the burning fuel. -kōñü -का&above;ञू&below; । हसन्तिकालता f. the covering of woven twigs outside the earthenware bowl of a brazier.

It is an archaeometallurgical challenge to trace the Maritime Tin Route from the tin belt of the world on Mekong River delta in the Far East and trace the contributions made by seafaring merchants of Meluhha in reaching the tin mineral resource to sustain the Tin-Bronze Age which was a revolution unleashed ca. 5th millennium BCE

8. A pair of fishes ayo 'fish' (Mu.); rebus: ayo 'metal, iron' (Gujarati); ayas 'metal' (Sanskrit)
9.A pair of buffaloes tethered to a post-standard kāṛā 'buffalo' கண்டி kaṇṭi buffalo bull (Tamil); rebus: *kaṇd* 'stone ore'; *kāṇḍa* 'tools, pots and pans and metal-ware'; *kaṇḍ* 'furnace, fire-altar, consecrated fire'.
10. A pair of birds Rebus 1: *kōḍi.* [Tel.] n. A fowl, a bird. (Telugu) Rebus: *khōṭ* 'alloyed ingots'. Rebus 2: *kol* 'the name of a bird, the Indian cuckoo' (Santali) *kol* 'iron, smithy, forge'. Rebus 3: baṭa = quail (Santali) Rebus: baṭa = furnace, kiln (Santali) bhrāṣṭra = furnace (Skt.) baṭa = a kind of iron (G.) bhaṭa 'furnace' (Gujarati)
11. The buffaloes, birds flank a post-standard with curved horns on top of a stylized 'eye' PLUS 'eyebrows' with one-horn on either side of two faces

mũh 'face'; rebus: *mũh* 'ingot' (Mu.)

ṭhaṭera 'buffalo horns'. *ṭhaṭerā* 'brass worker' (Punjabi)
Pe. kaṇga (*pl.* -ŋ, kaṇku) eye. Rebus: kanga ' large portable brazier, fire-place' (Kashmiri). Thus the stylized standard is read rebus: Hieroglyph components:*kanga* + *ṭhaṭerā* 'one eye + buffalo horn' Rebus: *kanga* 'large portable barzier' (Kashmiri) + *ṭhaṭerā* 'brass worker' (Punjabi)

Ta. kaṇ eye, aperture, orifice, star of a peacock's tail. *Ma.* kaṇ, kaṇṇu eye, nipple, star in peacock's tail, bud. *Ko.* kaṇ eye. *To.* koṇ eye, loop in string.*Ka.* kaṇ eye, small hole, orifice. *Koḍ.* kaṇṇï id. *Tu.* kaṇṇů eye, nipple, star in peacock's feather, rent, tear. *Te.* kanu, kannu eye, small hole, orifice, mesh of net, eye in peacock's feather. *Kol.* kan (*pl.* kanḍl) eye, small hole in ground, cave. *Nk.* kan (*pl.* kanḍl) eye, spot in peacock's tail. *Nk. (Ch.)* kan (*pl.* -l) eye. *Pa.*(S. only) kan (*pl.* kanul) eye. *Ga.* (Oll.) kaṇ (*pl.* kaṇkul) id.; kaṇul maṭṭa eyebrow; kaṇa (*pl.* kaṇul) hole; (S.) kanu (*pl.* kankul) eye. *Go.* (Tr.) kan (*pl.*kank) id.; (A.) kaṛ (*pl.* kaṛk) id. *Konḍa* kaṇ id. *Pe.* kaṇga (*pl.* -ŋ, kaṇku) id. *Manḍ.* kan (*pl.* -ke) id. *Kui* kanu (*pl.* kan-ga), (K.) kanu (*pl.* kaṛka) id. *Kuwi*(F.) kannū (*pl.* kar&nangle;ka), (S.) kannu (*pl.* kanka), (Su. P. Isr.) kanu (*pl.* kaṇka) id. *Kur.* xann eye, eye of tuber; xannērnā (of newly born babies or animals) to begin to see, have the use of one's eyesight (for ērnā, see 903). *Malt.* qanu eye. *Br.* xan id., bud. (DEDR 1159) kāṇá ' one -- eyed ' RV. Pa. Pk. *kāṇa* -- ' blind of one eye, blind '; Ash. *kā̃ṛa, °ṛī* f. ' blind ', Kt. *kā̃ŕ*, Wg. *kŕā̃macrdotdot;*, Pr. *k&schwatildemacr;*, Tir. *kā´na*, Kho. *kāṇu* NTS ii 260,*kánu* BelvalkarVol 91; K. *kônu* ' one -- eyed ', S. *kāṇo*, L. P. *kāṇā̃*; WPah. rudh. śeu. *kāṇā* ' blind '; Ku. *kāṇo*, gng. *kā̃&rtodtilde;* ' blind of one eye ', N. *kānu;*A. *kanā* ' blind '; B. *kāṇā* ' one -- eyed, blind '; Or. *kaṇā*, f. *kāṇī* ' one -- eyed ', Mth. *kān*, *°nā*, *kanahā*, Bhoj. *kān*, f. *°ni*, *kanwā* m. ' one -- eyed man ', H. *kān,°nā*, G. *kāṇũ*; M. *kāṇā* ' one -- eyed, squint -- eyed '; Si. *kaṇa* ' one -- eyed, blind '. -- Pk. *kāṇa* -- ' full of holes ', G. *kāṇũ* ' full of holes ', n. ' hole ' (< ' empty eyehole '? Cf. *ā̃dhḷũ* n. ' hole ' < andhala --).S.kcch. *kāṇī* f.adj. ' one -- eyed '; WPah.kṭg. *kaṇɔ* ' blind in one eye ', J. *kāṇā*; Md. *kanu* ' blind '.(CDIAL 3019) Ko. *kāṇso* ' squint -- eyed '.(Konkani)

Paš. ainċ -- gánik ' eyelid '(CDIAL 3999) Phonetic reinforcement of the gloss: *Pe.* kaṇga (*pl.* -ŋ, kaṇku) eye.

See also: *nimišta kanag* 'to write' (SBal): *nipēśayati ' writes '. [√piś] Very doubtful: Kal.rumb. Kho. nivḗš -- ' to write ' more prob. ← EPers. Morgenstierne BSOS viii 659. <-> Ir. pres. st. *nipaiš -- (for *nipais -- after past *nipišta --) in Yid. nuviš -- , Mj. nuvuš -- , Sang. Wkh. nəviš -- ; -- Aś. nipista<-> ← Ir. *nipista -- (for *nipišta -- after pres. *nipais --) in SBal. novīsta or nimišta kanag ' to write '.(CDIAL 7220)
Alternative: dol 'eye'; Rebus: *dul* 'to cast metal in a mould' (Santali)*Alternative: kandi* 'hole, opening' (Ka.)[Note the eye shown as a dotted circle on many Dilmun seals.]; *kan* 'eye' (Ka.); rebus: *kandi* (pl. –l) necklace, beads (Pa.);*kanḍ* 'stone ore' Alternative: *kā̃gsī* f. 'comb' (Gujarati); rebus 1: *kangar* 'portable furnace' (Kashmiri); rebus 2: *kamsa* 'bronze'.
khunḍ 'tethering peg or post' (Western Pahari) Rebus: *kūṭa* 'workshop'; *kuṭi*= smelter furnace (Santali); Rebus 2: *kunḍ 'fire-altar'*

Why are animals shown in pairs?

dula 'pair' (Kashmiri); rebus: dul 'cast metal' (Mu.)
Thus, all the hieroglyphs on the gold disc can be read as Indus writing related to one bronze-age artifact category: metalware catalog entries.

Data mining of Indus Script hieroglyph clusters names Bronze Age professionals: *damgar* 'merchant, *khār* 'smith', *ṭhākur* 'blacksmith' খোন্দকার 'farmer' in कोंड 'hamlets'

Data mining of Indus Script hieroglyph clusters names Bronze Age professionals: *damgar* 'merchant, *khār* 'smith', *ṭhākur* 'blacksmith' খোন্দকার 'farmer' in कोंड 'hamlets'. The composite anthropomorph of a crocodile, ram, one-horned young bull signifies this combined professionalism of farming, metalwork and seafaring trade (boatman). [A synonym for ram is *meDha* 'ram' rebus: *med* 'drummer, boatman, basketmaker'; meD 'iron' med 'copper' (Slavic languages)].**mēda** m. ‘ a mixed caste, any one living by a degrading occupation ’ Mn. [→ Bal. *mēd* ‘ boatman, fisher- man ’. -- Cf. Tam. *metavar* ‘ **basket** -- maker ’ &c. DED 4178]Pk. *mēa* -- m., *mēī* -- f. ‘ member of a non -- Aryan tribe ’; S. *meu* m. ‘ fisherman ’ (whence *miā̃ṇī* f. ‘ a fishery ’), L. *mē̃* m.; P. *meũ* m., f. *meuṇī* ‘ boatman ’. -- Prob. separate from S. *muhā̃ṇo* m. ‘ member of a class of Moslem boatmen ’, L. *mohā̃ṇā* m., °*ṇī* f.: see *mr̥gahanaka -- . (CDIAL 10320).

An important official named in a cuneiform text was 'chief of **merchants**' (LU rab **tamkaru**). (Jonas Carl Greenfield, Ziony Zevit, Seymour Gitin, Michael Sokoloff, 1995, *Solving Riddles and Untying Knots: Biblical, Epigraphic, and Semitic Studies in Honor of Jonas C. Greenfield*, Eisenbrauns, p. 527). The gloss tamkaru is cognte damgar (Akkadian) and also *ṭhākur* ‘blacksmith’.)

These professionals constitute the bhāratam janam blessed by Rishi Visvamitra in Rigveda (RV 3.53.12). They are Sarasvati's children since 80# of the archaeological sites of the civilization which are a continuum of Vedic culture signified by yupa (see octagonal yupa found in Binjore Soma Yaga yajna kunda) are found in Vedic River Sarasvati Basin in Northwest Bharatam.

Wheat chaff on Yupa as caSAla: ***kuṇḍaka** ‘ husks, bran ’.Pa. *kuṇḍaka* -- m. ‘ red powder of rice husks ’; Pk. *kuṁḍaga* -- m. ‘ chaff ’; N. *kũṛo* ‘ boiled grain given as fodder to buffaloes ’, *kunāuro* ‘ husk of lentils ’ (for ending cf.*kusāuro* ‘chaff of mustard’); B. *kũṛā* ‘rice dust’; Or. *kuṇḍā* ‘rice bran’; M. *kũḍā*, *kõ°* m. ‘bran’; Si. *kuḍu* ‘powder of paddy’ &c.(CDIAL 3267) Rebus: *kuṇḍa* 'vedic altar, fire place, yagashala'.

Two professionals are signified by a composite hieroglyph-multiplex signified on a bronze artifact as a composite anthropomorphic metaphor with hieroglyphs: crocodile, ram, one-horned young bull. Each hieroglyph component in the multiplex has a history in Indus Script Corpora signifying metalwork catalogs.

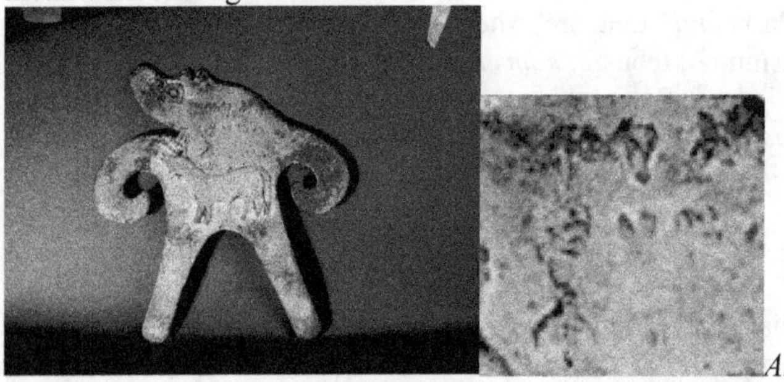

An animal-headed anthropomorph. A clipped enlargement of the Indus Script 'inscription' from the photograph. http://www.business-standard.com/article/specials/naman-

1. Smith, turner, engraver, merchant

kāru 'crocodile' (Telugu) Rebus: *kāruvu* 'artisan' (Telugu) *khār* 'blacksmith' (Kashmiri) *tagara* 'ram' (Kannada) Rebus: *damgar* 'merchant' (Akkadian) *tagara* 'tin' (Kannada) The semantics of damana 'blowing with bellows' links with the dam- prefix in: damgar 'merchant' (Akkadian), perhaps a merchant of products out of the furnace/smelter.

2. Farmer, producer of crops, who live in circular hamlets कोंड [*kōṇḍa*] (Marathi) *kɔṛi* f. ' cowpen' (Gondi)

Hieroglyph: *khoṇḍ, kõda* 'young bull-calf' Rebus 1: *kũdār* 'turner'. **कोंद** *kōnda* 'engraver, lapidary setting or infixing gems' (Marathi) Rebus 2: **kuḍu** śūdra, **farmer (Kannada);** n crop (রবিখন্দ).˜**কার, খোন্দকার** *n.* a producer of crops, a farmer; a (Mus lim) title of honour awarded to wealthy farmers.**kara, khondakara** *n.* a producer of crops, a farmer; a (Mus lim) title of honour awarded to wealthy farmers (Bengali).कोंड [*kōṇḍa*] A circular hamlet; a division of a मौजा or village, composed generally of the huts of one caste.

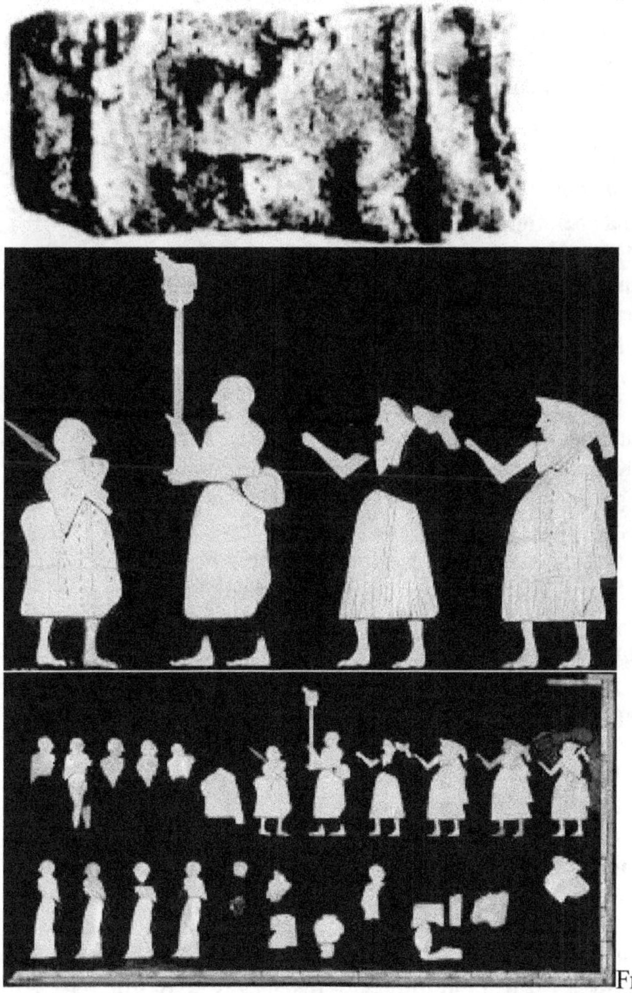

Frieze of a mosaic panel Circa 2500-2400 BCE Temple of Ishtar, Mari (Tell Hariri), Syria Shell and shale André Parrot excavations, 1934-36 AO 19820

These inlaid mosaics, composed of figures carved in mother-of-pearl, against a background of small blocks of lapis lazuli or pink limestone, set in bitumen, are among the most original and attractive examples of Mesopotamian art. It was at Mari that a large number of these mosaic pieces were discovered. Here they depict a victory scene: soldiers lead defeated enemy captives, naked and in chains, before four dignitaries.

A person is a standard bearer of a banner holding aloft the one-horned young bull which is the signature glyph of Indus writing. The banner is comparable to the banner shown on two Mohenjo-daro tablets of standards held up on a procession including a standard signifying a one-horned young bull.

mēda 10320 **mēda** m. ' a mixed caste, any one living by a degrading occupation ' Mn. [→ Bal. *mēd* ' boatman, fisher- man '. -- Cf. Tam. *metavar* ' **basket** -- maker ' &c. DED 4178] Pk. *mēa* -- m., *mēī* -- f. ' member of a non -- Aryan tribe '; S. *meu* m. ' fisherman ' (whence *miāṇī* f. ' a fishery '), L. *mē* m.; P. *meũ* m., f. *meuṇī* ' boatman '. -- Prob. separate from S. *muhāṇo* m. ' member of a class of Moslem boatmen ', L. *mohāṇā* m., °*ṇī* f.: see *mr̥gahanaka -- .

మేడము (p. 1034) [mēḍamu] *mēḍamu*. [Tel.] n. Joining,union, కూడిక. A fight, battle, యుద్ధము. **మేడము పొడుచు** *mēdamu-poḍuṭsu*. v. n. To fight a battle. యుద్ధముచేయు, కోడిమేడము a cock fight.

1655 ***Ta.*** **kuṭi** house, abode, home, family, lineage, town, tenants; **kuṭikai** hut made of leaves, temple; **kuṭical** hut; **kuṭicai, kuṭiñai** small hut, cottage; **kuṭimai** family, lineage, allegiance (as of subjects to their sovereign), servitude; **kuṭiy-āḷ** tenant; **kuṭiyilār** tenants; **kuṭil** hut, shed, abode; **kuṭaṅkar** hut, cottage; **kaṭumpu** relations. ***Ma.*kuṭi** house, hut, family, wife, tribe; **kuṭima** the body of landholders, tenantry; **kuṭiyan** slaves (e.g. in Coorg); **kuṭiyān** inhabitant, subject, tenant; **kuṭiññil** hut, thatch;**kuṭil** hut, outhouse near palace for menials. ***Ko.*** **kuṛjl** shed, bathroom of Kota house; **kuṛm** family; **kuḍḷ** front room of house; **kuṛḷ** hut; **guṛy** temple. ***To.*** **kwïṣ** shed for small calves; **kuṣ** room (in dairy or house); **kuḍṣ** outer room of dairy, in: **kuḍṣ waṣ** fireplace in outer room of lowest grade of dairies (cf. 2857), **kuḍṣ moṇy** bell(s) in outer section of ti· dairy, used on non-sacred buffaloes (cf. 4672); **kuṛy** Hindu temple; ? **kwïḍy** a family of children. ***Ka.*** **kuḍiya, kuḍu** śūdra, **farmer; guḍi** house, temple; **guḍil, guḍalu, guḍisalu, guḍasalu, guḍasala**, etc. hut with a thatched roof. ***Koḍ.*** **kuḍi** family of servants living in one hut; **kuḍië** man of toddy-tapper caste. ***Tu.*guḍi** small pagoda or shrine; **guḍisalů, guḍisilů, guḍsilů, guḍicilů** hut, shed. ***Te.*** **koṭika** hamlet; **guḍi** temple; **guḍise** hut, cottage, hovel. ***Kol.*** (SR) **guḍī** temple. ***Pa.*** **guḍi**temple, village resthouse. *Ga.* (Oll.) **guḍi** temple. *Go.* (Ko.) **kuṛma** hut, outhouse; (Ma.) **kurma** menstruation; (Grigson) **kurma lon** menstruation hut (*Voc.* 782, 800); (SR.) **guḍi**, (Mu.) **guḍḍi**, (S. Ko.) **guṛi** temple; **guḍḍī** (Ph.) temple, (Tr.) tomb (*Voc.* 1113). ***Kui*** **guḍi** central room of house, living room. / Cf. Skt. **kūˇṭa-, kuṭi-, kūˇṭī-** (whence Ga. (P.) **kuṛe** hut; **Kui kūṛi** hut made of boughs, etc.; Kur. **kuṛyā** small shed or outhouse; Malt. **kuṛya** hut in the fields; Br. **kuḍ(ḍ)ī** hut, small house, wife), **kuṭīkā-, kuṭīra-, kuṭuṅgaka-, kuṭīcaka-, koṭa-** hut;**kuṭumba-** household (whence Ta. Ma. **kuṭumpam** id.; Ko. **kuṛmb** [? also **kuṛm** above]; To. **kwïḍb, kwïḍbïl [-ïl** from **wïkïl**, s.v. 925 Ta. **okkal]**; Ka., Koḍ., Tu.**kuṭumba**; Tu. **kuḍuma**; Te. **kuṭumbamu**; ? Kui **kumbu** house [balance word of **iḍu**, see s.v. 494 Ta. **il]**). See Turner, *CDIAL*, no. 3232, **kuṭī-**, no. 3493, **kōṭa-**, no. 3233, **kuṭumba-**, for most of the Skt. forms; Burrow, *BSOAS* 11.137. **kōṭa**3 m. ' hut, shed ' lex. [← Drav. T. Burrow TPS 1945, 95: cf. kuṭī --]G. *kɔṛi* f. ' cowpen '.(CDIAL 3493)

Ta.* koṭi** banner, **flag**, streamer; **kōṭu** summit of a hill, peak, mountain; **kōṭai** mountain; **kōṭar** peak, summit of a tower; **kuvaṭu** mountain, hill, peak; **kuṭumi**summit of a mountain, top of a building, crown of the head, bird's crest, tuft of hair (esp. of men), crown, projecting corners on which a door swings. ***Ma.* koṭi** top, extremity, flag, banner, sprout; **kōṭu** end; **kuvaṭu** hill, mountain-top; **kuṭuma, kuṭumma** narrow point, bird's crest, pivot of door used as hinge, lock of hair worn as caste distinction; **koṭṭu** head of a bone. ***Ko.* koṛy** flag on temple; **koṭ** top tuft of hair (of Kota boy, brahman), crest of bird; **kuṭ** clitoris. ***To.* kwïṭ** tip, nipple, child's back lock of hair. ***Ka.* kuḍi** pointed end, point, extreme tip of a creeper, sprout, end, top, flag, banner; **guḍi** point, flag, banner; **kuḍilu** sprout, shoot; **kōḍu** a point, the peak or top of a hill; **koṭṭu** a point, nipple, crest, gold ornament worn by women in their plaited hair; **koṭṭa** state of being extreme; **koṭṭa-kone** the extreme point; (Hav.) **koḍi** sprout; ***Koḍ.*koḍi** top (of mountain, tree, rock, table), rim of pit or tank, flag. ***Tu.* koḍi** point, end, extremity, sprout, flag; **koḍipuni** to bud, germinate; (B-K.) **koḍipu, koḍipelů** a sprout; **koḍirè** the top-leaf; **koṭṭu** cock's comb, peacock's tuft. ***Te.* koḍi** tip, top, end or point of a flame; **koṭṭa-kona** the very end or extremity. ***Kol. (Kin.) **koṛi** point. ***Pa.*kūṭor** cock's comb. ***Go.*** (Tr.) **koḍḍī** tender tip or shoot of a plant or tree; **koḍḍi** (S.) end, tip, (Mu.) tip of bow; (A.) **koḍi** point (***Voc.*** 891). ***Malt.* qoṛgo** comb of a cock; ?**qóru** the end, the top (as of a tree). Cf. 2081 Ta. **koṇṭai** and 2200 Ta. **kōṭu**.(DEDR 2049).

***Ta.* koṇṭai** tuft, dressing of hair in large coil on the head, crest of a bird, head (as of a nail), knob (as of a cane), round top. ***Ma.* koṇṭa** tuft of hair. ***Ko.* goṇḍ** knob on end of walking-stick, head of pin; **koṇḍ** knot of hair at back of head. ***To.* kwïḍy** Badaga woman's knot of hair at back of head (< Badaga **koṇḍe). *Ka.* koṇḍe, goṇḍe** tuft, tassel, cluster. ***Koḍ.* koṇḍe** tassels of sash, knob-like foot of cane-stem. ***Tu.* goṇḍè** topknot, tassel, cluster. ***Te.* koṇḍe**, (K. also) **koṇḍi** knot of hair on the crown of the head. Cf. 2049 Ta. **koṭi**. / Cf. Skt. **kuṇḍa-** clump (e.g. **darbha-kuṇḍa-**), Pkt. (*DNM*) **goṇḍī- = mañjarī-**; Turner, *CDIAL*, no. 3266; cf. also Mar. **gōḍā** cluster, tuft.
3266 kuṇḍa3 n. ' clump ' e.g. *darbha -- kuṇḍa* -- Pāṇ. [← Drav. (Tam. *koṇṭai* ' tuft of hair ', Kan. *goṇḍe* ' cluster ', &c.) T. Burrow BSOAS xii 374](DEDR 2081)
Pk. *kuṁḍa* -- n. ' heap of crushed sugarcane stalks '; WPah. bhal. *kunnū* m. ' large heap of a mown crop '; N. *kunyũ* ' large heap of grain or straw ', *baṛ -- kũṛo* ' cluster of berries '.
3267 ***kuṇḍaka** ' husks, bran '.
Pa. *kuṇḍaka* -- m. ' red powder of rice husks '; Pk. *kuṁḍaga* -- m. ' chaff '; N. *kũṛo* ' boiled grain given as fodder to buffaloes ', *kunāuro* ' husk of lentils ' (for ending cf.*kusāuro* ' chaff of mustard '); B. *kũṛā* ' rice dust '; Or. *kuṇḍā* ' rice bran '; M. *kũḍā, kõ°* m. ' bran '; Si. *kuḍu* ' powder of paddy &c. '
Addenda: kuṇḍaka -- in cmpd. *kaṇa -- kuṇḍaka* -- Arthaś.
Te. kōḍiya, kōḍe young bull; *adj.* male (e.g. kōḍe dūḍa bull calf), young, youthful; kōḍekā̃ḍu a young man. *Kol.* (Haig) kōḍē bull. *Nk.* khoṛe male calf. *Konḍa*kōḍi cow; kōṛe young bullock. *Pe.* kōḍi cow. *Manḍ.* kūḍi id. *Kui* kōḍi id., ox. *Kuwi* (F.) kōdi cow; (S.) kajja kōḍi bull; (Su. P.) kōḍi cow. (DEDR 2199)
खाण्डव [p= 339,1] N. of a forest in कुरु-क्षेत्र (sacred to इन्द्र and burnt by the god of fire aided by अर्जुन and कृष्ण MBh. Hariv. BhP. i , 15 , 8 Kathals.)Taln2d2yaBr. xxv , 3 TA1r.
ఖాండవము (p. 0344) [khāṇḍavamu] *khāṇḍavamu*. [Skt.] n. The name of a grove sacred to Indra. ఇంద్రునియొక్క ఒకానొక వనము.
n crop (রবিখন্দ).˜কার, খোন্দকার *n.* a producer of crops, a farmer; a (Mus lim) title of honour awarded to wealthy farmers.kara, khondakara *n.* a producer of crops, a farmer; a (Mus lim) title of honour awarded to wealthy farmers.

khōdd 3934 *khōdd ' dig '. 2. *khōḍḍ -- . 3. *kōḍḍ -- . 4. *gōdd -- . 5. *gōḍḍ -- . 6. *guḍḍ -- . [Poss. conn. with *khudáti* ' thrusts (penis) into ' RV., *prákhudati* ' futuit ' AV.; cf. also *khōtr -- , *kōtr --]
1. P. *khodṇā* ' to dig, carve ', *khudṇā* ' to be dug '; Ku. *khodṇo* ' to dig, carve ', N. *khodnu*, B. *khodā, khudā*, Or. *khodibā, khud°*; Bi. mag. *khudnī* ' a kind of spade '; H. *khodnā* ' to dig, carve, search ', *khudnā* ' to be dug '; Marw. *khodṇo* ' to dig '; G. *khodvũ* ' to dig, carve ', M. *khodṇẽ* (also X khānayati q.v.). -- N. *khodalnu* ' to search for ' cf. **khuddati* s.v. *khōjja -- ?
2. B. *khõṛā* ' to dig ' or < **khōṭayati* s.v. *khuṭati.
3. B. *koṛā, kõṛā* ' to dig, pierce ', Or. *koṛibā* ' to cut clods of earth with a spade, beat '; Mth. *koṛab* ' to dig ', H. *koṛnā.*
4. K. *godu* m. ' hole ', *g° karun* ' to pierce '; N. *godnu* ' to pierce '; H. *godnā* ' to pierce, hoe ', *gudnā* ' to be pierced '; G. *godɔ* m. ' a push '; M. *godṇẽ* ' to tattoo '.
5. L. *goḍaṇ* ' to hoe ', P. *goḍṇā, goḍḍī* f. ' hoeings '; N. *goṛnu* ' to hoe, weed '; H. *goṛnā* ' to hoe up, scrape ', *goṛhnā* (X *kāṛhnā*?); G. *goḍvũ* ' to loosen earth round roots of a plant '.
6. S. *guḍaṇu* ' to pound, thrash '; P. *guḍḍṇā* ' to beat, pelt, hoe, weed '.
Addenda: *khōdd -- . 1. S.kcch. *khodhṇũ* ' to dig ', WPah.kṭg. (Wkc.) *khóḍṇõ*, J. *khodṇu.*
2. *khōḍḍ -- : WPah.kc. *khoḍṇo* ' to dig '; -- kṭg. *khoṛnõ* id. see *khuṭati Add2.
Composite copper alloy anthropomorphic Meluhha hieroglyphs of Haryana and Sheorajpur: fish, markhor, crocodile, one-horned young bull

Mirror: https://www.academia.edu/12200059/Composite_copper_alloy_anthropomorphic_Meluhha_hieroglyphs_of_Haryana_and_Sheorajpur_fish_markhor_crocodile_one-horned_young_bull

Oxford English Dictionary defines anthropomorphic: "a. treating the deity as anthropomorphous, or as having a human form and character; b. attributing a human personality to anything impersonal or irrational."

The copper anthropomorph of Haryana is comparable to and an elaboration of a copper anthropomorph of Sheorajpur, Uttar Pradesh. Both deploy Meluhha hieroglyphs using rebus-metonymy layered cipher of Indus writing.

The hieroglyhs of the anthropomorphs are a remarkable archaeological evidence attesting to the evidence of an ancient Samskritam text, *Baudhāyana śrautasūtra.*

Baudhāyana śrautasūtra 18.44 which documents migrations of Āyu and Amavasu from a central region:

pran Ayuh pravavraja. tasyaite Kuru-Pancalah Kasi-Videha ity. etad Ayavam pravrajam. pratyan amavasus. tasyaite Gandharvarayas Parsavo 'ratta ity. etad Amavasavam

Trans. Ayu went east, his is the Yamuna-Ganga region (Kuru-Pancala, Kasi-Videha). Amavasu went west, his is Gandhara, Parsu and Araṭṭa.

Ayu went east from Kurukshetra to Kuru-Pancala, Kasi-Videha. The migratory path of Meluhha artisand in the lineage of Ayu of the Rigvedic tradition, to Kasi-Videha certainly included the very ancient temple town of Sheorajpur of Dist. Etawah (Kanpur), Uttar Pradesh.

Haryana anthropormorph (in the Kurukshetra region on the banks of Vedic River Sarasvati) deploys hieroglyphs of markhor (horns), crocodile and one-horned young bull together with an inscription text using Indus Script hieroglyphs. The Sheorajpur anthropomorph deploys hieroglyphs of markhor (horns) and fish. The astonishing continuity of archaeo-metallurgical tradition of Sarasvati-Sindhu (Hindu) civilization is evident from a temple in Sheorajpur on the banks of Sacred River Ganga. This temple dedicated to Siva has metalwork ceilings !!!

Both anthropomorph artefacts in copper alloy are metalwork catalogs of *dhokara kamar 'cire perdue*(lost-wax) metal casters'.

Hieroglyhph: *eraka* 'wing' Rebus: *eraka, arka* 'copper'.In 2003, Paul Yule wrote a remarkable article on metallic anthropomorphic figures derived from Magan/Makkan, i.e. from an Umm an-Nar period context in al-Aqir/Bahla' in the south-western piedmont of the western Hajjar chain. "These artefacts are compared with those from northern Indian in terms of their origin and/or dating. They are particularly interesting owing to a secure provenance in middle Oman...The anthropomorphic artefacts dealt with...are all the more interesting as documents of an ever-growing body of information on prehistoric international contact/influence bridging the void between south-eastern Arabia and South Asia...Gerd Weisgerber recounts that in winter of 1983/4...al-Aqir near Bahla' in the al-Zahirah Wilaya delivered prehistoric planoconvex 'bun' ingots and other metallic artefacts from the same find complex..."

In the following plate, Figs. 1 to 5 are anthropomorphs, with 'winged' attributes. The metal finds from the al-Aqir wall include ingots, figures, an axe blade, a hoe, and a cleaver (see fig. 1, 1-8), all in copper alloy.

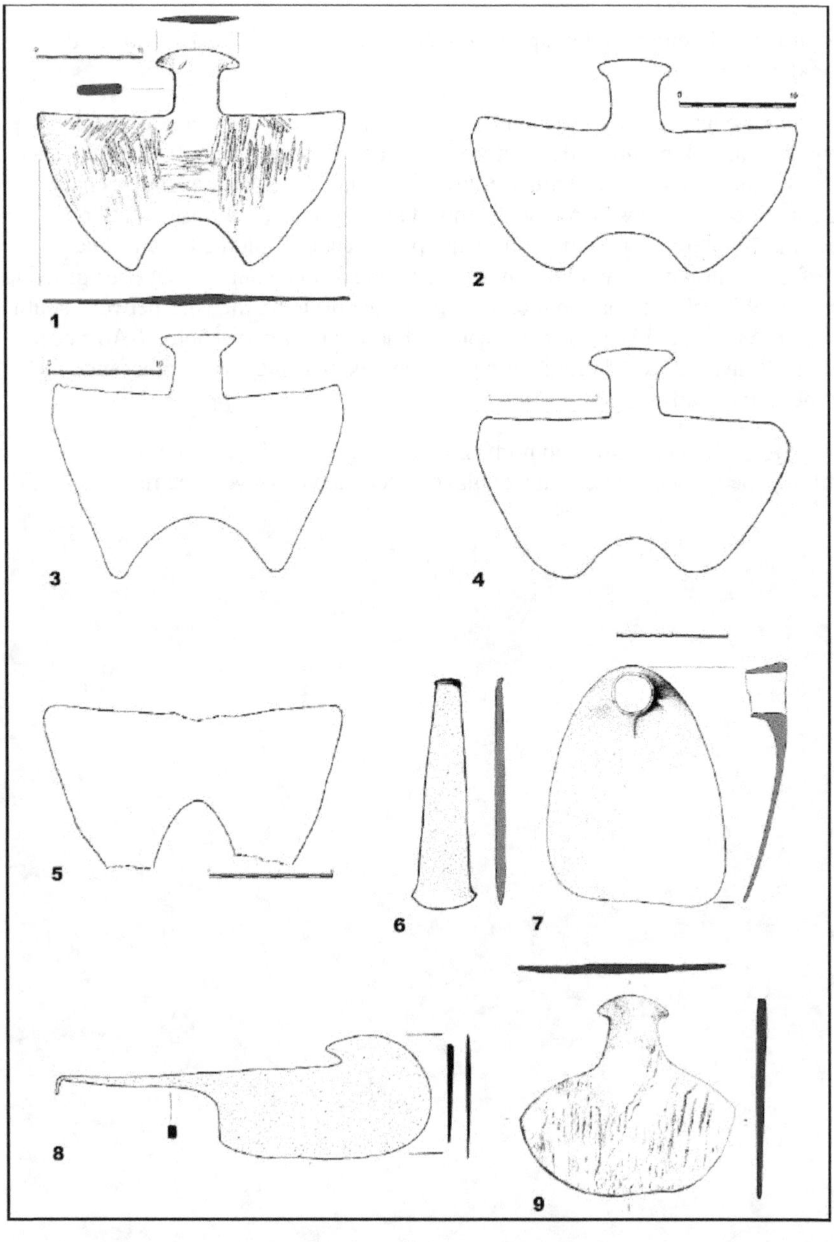

Fig. 1: Prehistoric metallic artefacts from the Sultanate of Oman: 1-8 al-Aqir/Bahla'; 9 Ra's al-Jins 2, building vii, room 2, period 3 (DA 11961) "The cleaver no. 8 is unparalleled in the prehistory of the entire Near East. Its form resembles an iron coco-nut knife from a reportedly subrecent context in Gudevella (near Kharligarh, Dist. Balangir, Orissa) which the author examined some years ago in India...The dating of the figures, which command our immediate attention, depends on two strands of thought. First, the Umm an-Nar Period/Culture dating mentioned above, en-compasses a time-space from 2500 to 1800 BC. In any case, the presence of "bun" ingots among the finds by

nomeans contradicts a dating for the anthropomorphic figures toward the end of the second millennium BC. Since these are a product of a simple form of copper production, they existed with the beginning of smelting in Oman. The earliest dated examples predate this, i.e. the Umm an-NarPeriod. Thereafter, copper continues to be produced intothe medieval period. Anthropomorphic figures from the Ganges-Yamuna Doab which resemble significantly theal-Aqir artefacts (fig. 2,10-15) form a second line of evidence for the dating. To date, some 21 anthropomorphsfrom northern India have been published." (p. 539; cf. Yule, 1985, 128: Yule et al. 1989 (1992) 274: Yule et al 2002. More are known to exist, particularly from a large hoard deriving from Madarpur.)

Prehistoric metallic artefacts from al-Aqir (excepting ingots)

No.	cm	Inventory No.	description
1	29.5 x 19.5 x 0,9	DA 15499	anthropomorph
2	29.0 x 20.3	DA 15496	anthropomorph
3	27.7 x 17.4	DA 15497	anthropomorph
4	26.1 x 20.4	DA 15495	anthropomorph
5	30.1 x 15.2 (pres.)	DA 15713	anthropomorph
6	5.4 x 18.7 x 0.9	DA 11783	palstave
7	16.5 x 21.0 x 3.8	DA 11782	hoe
8	40.0 x 12.2 x 0.4	DA 15498	cleaver

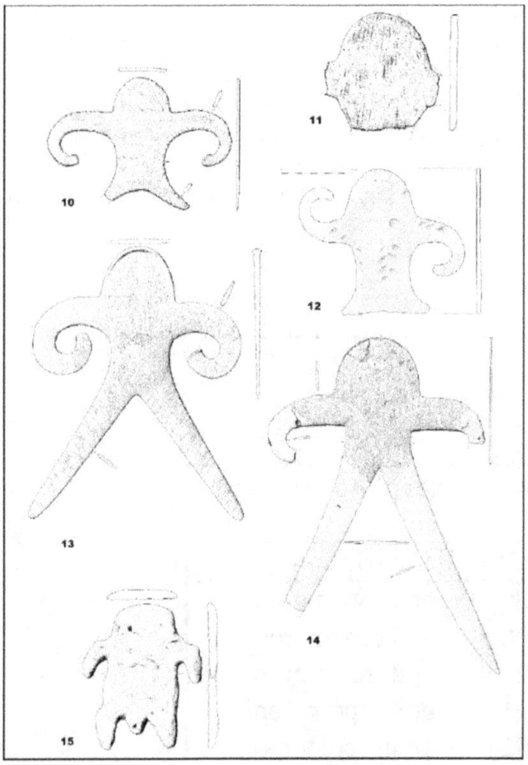

Fig. 2: Anthropomorphic figures from the Indian Subcontinent. 10 type I, Saipai, Dist. Etawah, U.P.; 11 type I, Lothal, Dist. Ahmedabad,Guj.; 12 type I variant, Madarpur, Dist. Moradabad, U.P.; 13 type II, Sheorajpur, Dist. Kanpur, U.P.; 14 miscellaneous type, Fathgarh,
Fig. 2: Anthropomorphic figures from the Indian Subcontinent. 10 type I, Saipai, Dist. Etawah, U.P.; 11 type I, Lothal, Dist. Ahmedabad,Guj.; 12 type I variant, Madarpur, Dist. Moradabad, U.P.; 13 type II, Sheorajpur, Dist. Kanpur, U.P.; 14 miscellaneous type, Fathgarh,Dist. Farrukhabad, U.P.; 15 miscellaneous type, Dist. Manbhum, Bihar.

The anthropomorph from Lothal/Gujarat (fig. 2,11), from a layer which its excavator dates to the 19 th century BCE. Lothal, phase 4 of period A, type 1. Some anthropomorphs were found stratified together with Ochre-Coloured Pottery, dated to ca. 2nd millennium BCE. Anthropomorph of Ra's al-Jins (Fig. 1,9) clearly reinforces the fact that South Asians travelled to and stayed at the site of Ra's al-Jins. "The excavators date the context from which the Ra's al-Jins copper artefact derived to their period III, i.e. 2300-2200 BCE (Cleuziou & Tosi 1997, 57), which falls within thesame time as at least some of the copper ingots which are represented at al-Aqir, and for example also in contextfrom al-Maysar site M01...the Franco-Italian teamhas emphasized the presence of a settled Harappan-Peri-od population and lively trade with South Asia at Ra's al-Jins in coastal Arabia. (Cleuziou, S. & Tosi, M., 1997, Evidence for the use of aromatics in the early Bronze Age of Oman, in: A. Avanzini, ed., *Profumi d'Arabia*, Rome 57-81)."

"In the late third-early second millennium, given the presence of a textually documented 'Meluhha village' in Lagash (southern Mesopotamia), one cannot be too surprised that such colonies existed 'east of Eden' in south-eastern Arabia juxtaposed with South Asia. In any case, here we encounter yet again evidence for contact between the two regions -- a contact of greater intimacy and importance than for the other areas of the Gulf."(Paul Yule, 2003, Beyond the pale of near Eastern Archaeology: Anthropomorphic figures from al-Aqir near Bahla' In: Stöllner, T. (Hrsg.): Mensch und Bergbau Studies in Honour of Gerd Weisgerber on Occasion of his 65th Birthday. Bochum 2003, pp. 537-542).

https://www.academia.edu/1043347/Beyond_the_Pale_of_Near_Eastern_Archaeology_Anthropomorphic_Figures_from_al-Aqir_near_Bahl%C4%81_Sultanate_of_Oman)

See: Weisgerber, G., 1988, Oman: A bronze-producing centre during the 1st half of the 1st millennium BCE, in: J. Curtis, ed., *Bronze-working centres of western Asia*, c. 1000-539 BCE, London, 285-295.

With curved horns, the 'anthropomorph' is a ligature of a mountain goat or *markhor* (makara) and a fish incised between the horns. Typical find of Gangetic Copper Hoards. At Sheorajpur, three anthropomorphs in metal were found. (Sheorajpur, Dt. Kanpur. Three anthropomorphic figures of copper. *AI*, 7, 1951, pp. 20, 29).

One anthropomorph had fish hieroglyph incised on the chest of the copper object, Sheorajpur, upper Ganges valley, ca. 2nd millennium BCE, 4 kg; 47.7 X 39 X 2.1 cm. State Museum, Lucknow (O.37) Typical find of Gangetic Copper Hoards. miṇḍāl markhor (Tor.wali) meḍho a ram, a sheep (G.)(CDIAL 10120) Rebus: meḍh 'helper of merchant' (Gujarati) meḍ iron (Ho.) meṛed-bica = iron stone ore, in contrast to bali-bica, iron sand ore (Munda) ayo 'fish' Rebus: ayo, ayas 'metal. Thus, together read rebus: *ayo meḍh* 'iron stone ore, metal merchant.'

A remarkable legacy of the civilization occurs in the use of 'fish' sign on a

copper anthropomorph found in a copper hoard. This is an apparent link of the 'fish' broadly with the profession of 'metal-work'. The 'fish' sign is apparently related to the copper object which seems to depict a 'fighting ram' symbolized by its in-curving horns. The 'fish' sign may relate to a copper furnace. The underlying imagery defined by the style of the copper casting is the pair of curving horns of a fighting ram ligatured into the outspread legs (of a warrior).

The center-piece of the makara symbolism is that it is a big jhasa, big fish, but with ligatured components (alligator snout, elephant trunk, elephant legs and antelope face). Each of these components can be explained (alligator: manger; elephant trunk: sunda; elephant: ibha; antelope: ranku; rebus: mangar 'smith'; sunda 'furnace'; ib 'iron'; ranku 'tin'); thus the makara jhasa or the big composite fish is a complex of metallurgical repertoire.)

One nidhi was makara (syn. Kohl, antimony); the second was makara (or, jhasa, fish) [bed.a hako (ayo)(syn. bhed.a 'furnace'; med. 'iron'; ayas 'metal')]; the third was kharva (syn. karba, iron).

Title / Object:	anthropomorphic sheorajpur
Fund context:	Saipai, Dist. Kanpur

Time of admission: 1981

Pool: SAI South Asian Archaeology

Image ID: 213 101

Copyright: Dr Paul Yule, Heidelberg

Photo credit: Yule, Metalwork of the Bronze in India, Pl 23 348 (dwg)

Saipal, Dist. Etawah, UP. Anthropomorph, type I. 24.1x27.04x0.76 cm., 1270 gm., both sides show a chevron patterning, left arm broken off (Pl. 22, 337). Purana Qila Coll. Delhi (74.12/4) -- Lal, BB, 1972, 285 fig. 2d pl. 43d

http://heidicon.ub.uni-heidelberg.de/heidicon/239/213101.html

http://katalog.ub.uni-heidelberg.de/cgi-bin/titel.cgi?katkey=900213101

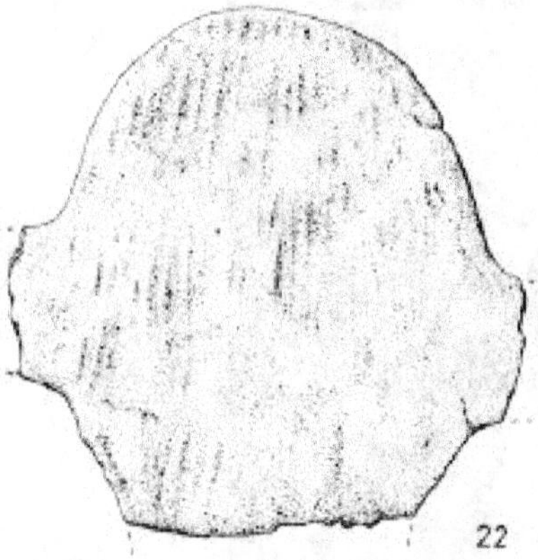

22

From Lothal was reported a fragmentary Type 1 anthropomorph (13.0 pres. X 12.8 pres. X c. 0.08 cm, Cu 97.27%, Pb 2.51% (Rao), surface ptterning runs lengthwise, lower portion slightly thicker than the edge of the head, 'arms' and 'legs' broken off (Pl. 1, 22)-- ASI Ahmedabad (10918 -- Rao, SR, 1958, 13 pl. 21A)

The extraordinary presence of a Lothal anthropomorph of the type found on the banks of River Ganga in Sheorajpur (Uttar Pradesh) makes it apposite to discuss the anthropomorph as a Meluhha hieroglyph, since Lothal is reportedly a mature site of the civilization which has produced nearly 7000 inscriptions (what may be called Meluhha epigraphs, almost all of which are relatable to the bronze age metalwork of India).

"Anthropomorphs occur in a variety of shapes and sizes (Plate A). The two basic types dominate, as defined by the proportions in combination with certain morphological features. All show processes suggestive of a human head, arms and legs. With one exception (no. 539) all are highly geometricising and flat. Fashioned from thick metal sheeting, these artifacts have stocky proportions and are patterned on both sides with elongated gouches or dents which usually are lengthwise oriented. Sometimes, however, the patterning is chevroned or cross-hatched. Significantly, the upper edge of the 'head' shows no thickening, as is the case of type H anthropomorphs. Examples have come to light at mid doab and a broken anthropomorph from distant Lothal as well. The only stratified example derives from Lothal, level IV. height range. 23.2-24.1cm; L/W: 0.65 - 0.88: 1; weight mean: 1260 gm." (Yule, Paul, pp.51-52). "Conclusions..."To the west at Harappa Lothal in Gujarat the presence of a fragmentary import type I anthropomorph suggests contact with the doab." "(p.92)

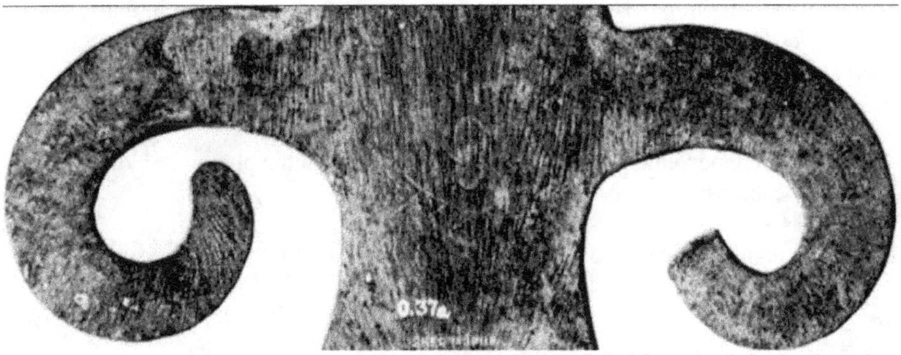

The Sheorajpur anthropomorph (348 on Plate A) has a 'fish' hieroglyph incised on the chest

Hieroglyphs: t*agara* 'ram' (Kannada) Rebus: *damgar* 'merchant' (Akk.) Rebus: *tagara* 'tin' (Kannada)

Ta. *takar* sheep, ram, goat, male of certain other animals (yāḷi, elephant, shark). பொருநகர் தாக்கற்குப் பேருந் தகைத்து (குறள், 486).Ma. *takaran* huge, powerful as a man, bear, etc. Ka. *tagar, ṭagaru, ṭagara, ṭegaru* ram. Tu. *tagaru, ṭagarů* id. Te. *tagaramu, tagaru* id. / Cf. Mar. *tagar* id. (DEDR 3000). Rebus 1:*tagromi* 'tin, metal alloy' (Kuwi) *takaram* tin, white lead, metal sheet, coated with tin (Ta.); tin, tinned iron plate (Ma.); tagarm tin (Ko.); tagara, tamara, tavara id. (Ka.) tamaru, tamara, tavara id. (Ta.): tagaramu, tamaramu, tavaramu id. (Te.); ṭagromi tin metal, alloy (Kuwi); tamara id. (Skt.)(DEDR 3001). trapu tin (AV.); tipu (Pali); tau, taua lead

(Pkt.); *tū̃* tin (P.); ṭau zinc, pewter (Or.); tarūaum lead (OG.);*tarvū̃* (G.); tumba lead (Si.)(CDIAL 5992). Rebus 2: *damgar* 'merchant'.

ṭhākur 'blacksmith': ṭhakkura m. ' idol, deity (cf. *ḍhakkārī* --), ' lex., ' title ' Rājat. [Dis- cussion with lit. by W. Wüst RM 3, 13 ff. Prob. orig. a tribal name EWA i 459, which Wüst considers nonAryan borrowing of *śākvará* -- : very doubtful]Pk. *ṭhakkura* -- m. ' Rajput, chief man of a village '; Kho. (Lor.) *takur* ' barber ' (= *ṭ*° ← Ind.?), Sh. *ṭhăkŭr* m.; K. *ṭhôkur* m. ' idol ' (← Ind.?); S. *ṭhakuru* m. ' fakir, term of address between fathers of a husband and wife '; P. *ṭhākar* m. ' landholder ', ludh. *ṭhaukar* m. ' lord '; Ku. ***ṭhākur*** m. ' master, title of a Rajput '; N. *ṭhākur* ' term of address from slave to master ' (f. *ṭhakurāni*), *ṭhakuri* ' a clan of Chetris ' (f. *ṭhakurni*);
A. *ṭhākur* ' a Brahman ', *ṭhākurānī* ' goddess '; B. *ṭhākurāni*, *ṭhākrān*, °*run* ' honoured lady, goddess '; Or. *ṭhākura* ' term of address to a Brahman, god, idol ', *ṭhākurāṇī* ' goddess ';
Bi. *ṭhākur* ' barber '; Mth. *ṭhākur* ' blacksmith '; Bhoj. Aw.lakh.*ṭhākur* ' lord, master ';
H. *ṭhākur* m. ' master, landlord, god, idol ', *ṭhākurāin*, *ṭhā̆kurānī* f. ' mistress, goddess ';
G. *ṭhākor*, °*kar* m. ' member of a clan of Rajputs ',*ṭhakrāṇī* f. ' his wife ', *ṭhākor* ' god, idol ';
M. *ṭhākur* m. ' jungle tribe in North Konkan, family priest, god, idol '; Si. mald. "*tacourou*" ' title added to names of noblemen ' (HJ 915) prob. ← Ind.
Addenda: ṭhakkura -- **:** Garh. *ṭhākur* ' master '; A. *ṭhākur* also ' idol '(CDIAL 5488)

Hieroglyphs, allographs: ram, tabernae montana coronaria flower: तगर [tagara] *f* A flowering shrub, Tabernæ montana coronaria. 2 *n* C The flower of it. 3 *m* P A ram. (Marathi)

*tagga ' mud '. [Cf. Bur. *t**lg*ḷy* ' mud '] Kho. (Lor.) *toq* ' mud, quagmire '; Sh. *tăgā′* ' mud ';
K. *tagöri* m. ' a man who makes mud or plaster '; Ku. *tāgaṛ* ' mortar '; B. *tāgāṛ* ' mortar, pit in which it is prepared '.(CDIAL 5626). (Note: making of mud or plaster is a key step in dhokra kamar's work of *cire perdue* (lost-wax) casting.)
krəm back'(Kho.) karmāra 'smith, artisan' (Skt.) kamar 'smith' (Santali)

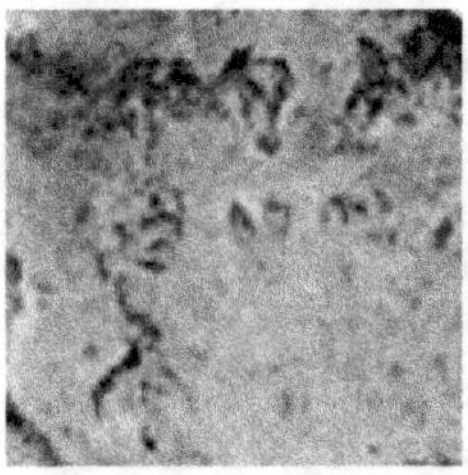

A clipped enlargement of the 'inscription' from the photograph of composite anthropomorph

It appears that the inscription is composed of Indus Script hieroglyphs and no Brahmi letters can be discerned. Hopefully, Prof. Naman Ahuja's response to my request will provide for a transcript with sharper visibility.

According to the curaorf, Naman Ahuja, the inscription in Brahmi reads "*King/Ki Ma Jhi* [name of king]/ *Sha Da Ya* [form of god]" and according to the curator, "looks unmistakably like the Hindu god Varaha". The Uttar Pradesh archaeological department has accepted this as an antique piece and dates it to the second to the first millennium BCE.

The hieroglyphs of the inscription include the following, possible metalwork catalog:

Hieroglyph: baraḍo = spine; backbone (Tulu) Rebus: baran, bharat 'mixed alloys' (5 copper, 4 zinc and 1 tin) (Punjabi)

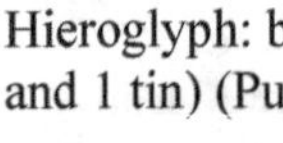

<u>Rim-of-jar hieroglyph: karNIka 'rim of jar' (Samskritam); kanka 'rim of jar' (Santali) Rebus: karṇaka'scribe' (Skt.) Alternative: khanaka 'mineworker' (Sanskrit) Rebus: karNI 'supercargo'.</u>

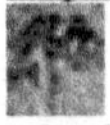

The hieroglyph appears to be two cartwheels and axle rod of the cart-frame. Hieroglyph: sal = wedge joining the parts of a solid **cart wheel** (Santali) Rebus: sal 'workshop' (Santali)

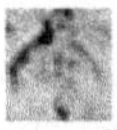

loa 'fig leaf; Rebus: loh '(copper)

Image from *The Art Newspaper*
The remarkable artifact 30 cm tall, 2 kg., *is said to have been* found under the foundation of a home in Haryana. It was in display in Brussels and later in Delhi in September 2014.

Description which appeared in *The Art Newspaper reads:* "The figure has a cast relief on its chest of a unicorn-like animal, similar to motifs found on seals of the Harappa culture, which thrived until around 1900 BCE."

The inscription above this creature; according to the curator Naman Ahuja the inscription represents "a combination of Harappan signs and Brahmi letters."

अमृत -इष्टका and hurling the चषाल caṣāla, 'thunderbolt' from the yupa after reaching heaven, gaining the अमृत, 'ambrosia'

अ-मृत [p= 82,2]*n.* world of immortality , heaven , eternity RV. VS. AV.
(also आनि *n.* pl. RV. i , 72 , 1 and iii , 38 , 4); food, property, gold. splendour, light. [cf. Gr. *ambrotos, ambrosia;* L. *immortalis*]. cf. अमृतं वारि सुरयोर्निर्वाणे चातिसुन्दरे । अयाचिते यज्ञशेषे पुंसि धन्वन्तरे$पि च । पीयूषे च धृते दीप्तावाचार्ये विबुधे$पि च । हरीतक्यामाम- लक्यां गलूच्यामपि तत्स्त्रियाम् । An expression is significant, linking the amRtatva 'immortality' to process the yajna using *amṛta-iSTakA*
अमृत **-इष्टका** a kind of sacrificial brick shaped like the golden head of men, beasts &c. (पशुशीर्षाणि). ఇటిక [iṭika] or ఇటికె or ఇటుక *iṭika.* [Tel.] n.
Brick. ఇటికెలుకోయు or ఇటుకచేయు to make bricks. వెయ్యి యిటుక కాల్చిరి they burnt 1000 bricks. ఇటుక [iṭuka] See ఇటిక.

The process of reaching to heaven (which may be elaborated by a metaphor of obtaining amRtatva as in RV 1.72.1 and RV 3.38.4) is paralleled by the processing of a yajna as detailed in the Satapatha Brahmana:

SBr. ३.७.१.[१८] अथ चषालमुदीक्षते । तद्विष्णोः परमं पदं सदा पश्यन्ति सूरयः दिवीव चक्षुराततमिति वज्रं वा एष प्राहार्षीद्यो यूपमुदशिश्रियत्ता विष्णोर्विजितिम्पश्यतेत्येवैतदाह यदाह तद्विष्णोः परमं पदं सदा पश्यन्ति सूरयः दिवीव चक्षुराततमिति

Translation of Eggeling is as follows:
18. He then looks up at the top-ring with (Vāj. S. VI, 5; Rig-veda I, 22, 20), 'The wise ever behold that highest step of Viṣṇu, fixed like an eye in the heaven.' For he who has set up the sacrificial stake has hurled the thunderbolt: 'See ye that conquest of Viṣṇu!' he means to say when he says, 'The wise ever behold that highest step of Viṣṇu, fixed like an eye in the heaven.'

A horizontally placed vishnu cakra is also a substitute for caSAla. But the key in archaeometallurgical terms is wheat straw, which is a carburization mediation to harden wrought iron into steel. Thus, climbing up to the entire top portion of the Yupa as a metaphor is the attainment of immortality. This amRtatva in materialistic terms is the acquisition of ***muhã̄***, 'quantity of iron produced from a smelter'. Hence the *mukha, mũh* 'face' ligatured to the sivalinga atop the smelting structure shown on Bhutesvar sculptural frieze.*kuTi* 'tree' rebus: *kuThi* 'smelter'

Relief with Ekamukha linga. Mathura. 1st cent. CE (Fig. 6.2)

The linga emerges out of the roof of the brick kiln, a furnace or smelter and is accompanied by gaNa, dwarfs with a tree in the background: The background pictorial motif ligaturing a 'tree' is a semantic determinant of the function of the brick-kiln': *kuṭi* 'tree'
Rebus: *kuṭhi* 'smelter': *mũh* 'face'
(Hindi) rebus: *mũhe* 'ingot' (Santali) *mũhã̄* = the quantity of iron produced at one time in a native smelting furnace of the Kolhes; iron produced by the Kolhes and formed like a four-cornered piece a little pointed at each end; mũhã mẽṛhẽt = iron smelted by the Kolhes and formed into an equilateral lump a little pointed at each of four ends;*kolhe tehen mẽṛhẽt ko mũhã akata* = the Kolhes have to-day produced pig iron (Santali);

Linga worship relief. Bhutesvara, Mathura. 1st cent. BCE

I have suggested that the weapon hurled is the vajra which is the wheat straw which constitutes the चषाल caṣāla. Yupa is the अमृत -इष्टका as shown on Bhutesvar sculptural friezes.

गो-धूम 'wheat, earth-smoke' of चषालः *caṣāla* of *Yupa* yields soma in Vajapeya, *amṛtā abhūmeti* 'we have become immortal'

शत-पथ-ब्राह्मण vividly, metaphirically describes Vajapeya ascent on the Yupa to heaven (*amṛtā abhūmeti* 'we have become immortal') with metaphors of गो 'thunderbolt' गो-धूम 'wheat' rebus: 'earth-smoke'. The expression गो-धूम can be explained as composed of गो and धूम Attainment of immortality is a metaphor for the successful processing of Soma yaga yielding Soma, molten metal (hence, the metaphor of Vajapeya, 'drink of strength or battle'. Hence, the metaphor of vajra, thunderbolt weapon.

गो or गो-धूम is the thunderbolt weapon of Indra. It is चषालः caṣāla and **वज्र** vajra. धूम is smoke , vapour, mist which emanates from the yupa as a fiery pillar of light during the Vajapeya yajna or Soma processing or smelting process. Orthographically, the चषालः caṣāla is denoted as an अष्टाश्रि octagonal thunderbolt weapon carried by Vajrapani. Rudra is also VajrabAho.
On nirvana of the Buddha, Vajrapani lets fall the vajra in depair. It is shaped like an octagonal hour-glass. It is also made of wheat

Vajra with octagonal bases. Relief fragment. Dipamkara Jataka with Buddha & Vajrapani. Butkara, Swat, 1st-2nd cent. CE c., Museo Nazionale d'Arte Orientale 'Giuseppe Tucci', Roma, dep. IsIAO, Inv. MNAOR 1127, MAI B 65;79 (after Bussagli, M.,1984, L'Arte del Gandhara, Torino, p.146) Note: Vajrapani holds a Vajra of eight-angles.

During pyrolysis/carburizing process iron absorbs carbon liberated when the metal is heated in the presence of a carbon bearing material, the wheat chaff.

अथ य इमे ग्राम इष्टापूर्ते दत्तमित्युपासते ते
धूममभिसम्भवन्ति धूमाद्रात्रिꣳ
रात्रेरपरपक्षमपरपक्षाद्यान्षड्दक्षिणैति
मासाꣳस्तान्नैते संवत्सरमभिप्राप्नुवन्ति ॥ ५.१०.३॥
मासेभ्यः पितृलोकं पितृलोकादाकाशमाकाशाच्चन्द्रमसमेष

"They who perform pious deeds in their village enter the smoke, . . . and then they go from the sky to the moon planet."

सोमो राजा तद्देवानामन्नं तं देवा भक्षयन्ति ॥ ५.१०.४॥

Chandogya Upanishad (5.10.3-4) explains the ascent of the yajnika (Vajapeya soma yaga) to heaven. Here the metaphor is reaching the moon planet.

The reaching of heaven is recognized by declaring Soma, the king and the way Soma is processed as food by the divinities. This metaphor signifies an archaeometallurgical process of attaining Soma using bhũ 'wheat chaff' as annam in smelting. In iconographic rendering this bhũ 'wheat chaff' is signified by the rebus hieroglyph: bhũĩ 'earth' as bhudevi 'mother earth'.

The structure of the octagonal yupa signifying Vajapeya Soma yaga includes an octagonal चषालः caṣāla signified by the hour-glass-shaped vajra as shown in the iconography of Vajrapani and in the cylinder seal rendering in Jasper Cylinder seal showing flagstaff-carriers with six-locks of hair (baTa 'six' rebus: bhaTa 'furnace) and signifying the flagstaff with an hour-glass-shaped top vajra 'thunderbolt weapon' as चषालः caṣāla. The signified are metalworkers smelting working with furnaces to produce metallic weapons. Four specific metal artifacs are signified on the cylinder seal:

Cylinder seal with kneeling nude heroes, ca. 2220–2159 b.c.; Akkadian Mesopotamia Red jasper H. 1 1/8 in. (2.8 cm), Diam. 5/8 in. (1.6 cm) Metropolitan Museum of Art - USA

Yupa as flagpost, Indus Script evidences of proclamation from Girsu, Ancient Near East to Candi Sukuh, Ancient Far East

I suggest that yupa inscriptions and yupa found in archaeological sites of Kalibangan and Binjor (in fact, in almost every single site of the civilization) are flags hoisted as proclamations of metalwork signified by Somayaga in the Vedic tradition.

This Vedic tradition exemplified by flasposts is seen in an extensive civilizational contact area from Haifa, Israel to Hanoi, Vietnam which is, in effect, the Ancient Maritime Tin Road which preceded by 2 millennia, the Ancient Silk Road. The Tin Road linked the tin belt of the world with the regions which demanded tin to create tin-bronzes during the urban revolution unleashed by the Bronze Age.

A flagpost is proclamation. sangaDa 'lathe' 'portable furnace' as a device in front of the one-horned young bull is also sangara 'proclamation'.

The significance of the yupa with caSAla in a somayaga gets replicated, as an abiding Indus Script hieroglyph-multiplex hypertext, on many artifacts from an extensive contact zone from the Ancient Near East to Ancient Far East.

The tradition of processions of flagposts with hieroglyphs atop continued in Sumer/ Mesopotamia as may be seen from the following example:

Cylinder seal with kneeling nude heroes, ca. 2220–2159B.C.; Akkadian
Mesopotamia Red jasper; H. 1 1/8 in. (2.8 cm), Diam. 5/8 in. (1.6 cm) (L.1992.23.5)

"Four representations of a nude hero with six sidelocks of hair appear on this cylinder seal. Each wears a three-strand belt with a tassel. In all cases, the hero kneels on one knee and with both hands holds up a gatepost standard in front of his raised leg. Two vertical lines of inscription, one placed before a hero and another placed behind a second hero, give the name as Shatpum, son of Shallum, but do not provide an official title. Placed vertically in the field, a serpent appears behind one hero. In the spaces between the tops of the standards are four symbols: a sun disk, a lunar crescent, a fish, and a vase with flowing streams of water."

http://www.metmuseum.org/toah/works-of-art/L.1992.23.5

The heroes carrying the standard are signified by six curls on hair.

baTa 'six' rebus: bhaTa 'furnace' meDh 'curl' rebus: meD 'iron (metal)'.

Cylinder seal with kneeling nude heroes, ca. 2220–2159 b.c.; Akkadian Mesopotamia Red jasper H. 1 1/8 in. (2.8 cm), Diam. 5/8 in. (1.6 cm) Metropolitan Museum of Art - USA

Four flag-posts(reeds) with rings on top held by the kneeling persons define the four components of the iron smithy/forge.

The key hieroglyph is the hood of a snake seen as the left-most hieroglyph on this rolled out cylinder seal impression. I suggest that this denotes the following Meluhha gloss:

Hierogyph: A. kulā 'hood of serpent' Rebus: kolle 'blacksmith'; kolhe 'smelter' kol 'working in iron'

Alternative: *paṭam* , *n.* < *phaṭa.* ‘cobra's hood’ phaṭa n. ‘ expanded hood of snake ’ MBh. 2. *phēṭṭa -- 2. [Cf. *phuṭa* -- m., *°ṭā* -- f., *sphuṭa* -- m. lex., *°ṭā* -- f. Pañcat. (Pk. *phuḍā* -- f.), *sphaṭa* -- m., *°ṭā*-- f., *sphōṭā* -- f. lex. and phaṇa -- 1. Conn. words in Drav. T. Burrow BSOAS xii 386]1. Pk. *phaḍa* -- m.n. ‘ snake's hood ’, *°ḍā* -- f., M. *phaḍā* m., *°ḍī* f.2. A. *pheṭ, phẽṭ.* (CDIAL 9040). Rebus: ‘sharpness of iron’: *padm* (obl.*padt-*) temper of iron (Kota)(DEDR 3907); *paṭam* ‘sharpness, as of the edge of a knife’ (Tamil) Alternative complementary reading: <naG bubuD>(Z) {N} ``^cobra''. |<naG> `?'. ^snake. *IA<naG>. ??is IA form <naG> or <nag>? #23502. **nāgá**1 m. ‘ snake ’ ŚBr. 2. ‘ elephant ’ BhP. [As ‘ ele- phant ’ shortened form of **nāga* -- *hasta* -- EWA ii 150 with lit. or extracted from *nāga* -- *danta* -- ‘ elephant tusk, ivory ’ < ‘ snake -- shaped tusk ’].
1. Pa. *nāga* -- m. ‘ snake ’, NiDoc. *nāǵa* F. W. Thomas AO xii 40, Pk. *ṇāya* -- m., Gy. as. *nâ* JGLS new ser. ii 259; Or. *naa* ‘ euphem. term for snake ’; Si. *nay, nā,nayā* ‘ snake ’. -- With early nasalization **nāṅga* -- : Bshk. *nāṅg* ‘ snake ’. -- Kt. Pr. *noṅ*, Kal. *nhoṅ* ‘ name of a god < *nā´ga* -- or ← Pers. *nahang* NTS xv 283. 2. Pa. *nāga* -- m. ‘ elephant ’, Pk. *ṇāya* -- m., Si. *nā.* śiśunāka -- . (CDIAL 7039) Rebus: **nāga**2 n. ‘ lead ’ Bhpr. [Cf. raṅga -- 3] Sh. *naṅ* m. ‘ lead ’ (< **nāṅga* -- ?), K. ***nāg*** m. (< **nāgga* -- ?).(CDIAL 7040) cf. annaku, anakku 'tin' (Akkadian) நாகம் nākam Black **lead;** காரீயம். (பிங்.) 9. Zinc; துத்தநாகம். (பிங்.) 10. A prepared arsenic; பாஷாணவகை (Tamil).
There is a possibility that the hieroglyph was intended to convey the message of an alloying metal like lead or tin or zinc which had revolutionised the bronze age with tin-bronzes, zinc-copper brass and other alloys to substitute for arsenical copper to make hard weapons and tools. It is instructive that zinc was called *tuthunāg **which might have referred to the*** sublimate of **zinc** and calamine collected in the furnaces in Zawar.

The leftmost hieroglyph shows ingots in a conical-bottom storage jar (similar to the jar shown on Warka vase, delivering the ingots to the temple of Inanna). Third from left, the overflowing pot is similar to the hieroglyph shown on Gudea statues. Fourth from left, the fish hieroglyph is similar to the one shown on a Susa pot containing metal tools and weapons. (Picture credit for the Susa pot with 'fish' hieroglyph: Maurizio Tosi).

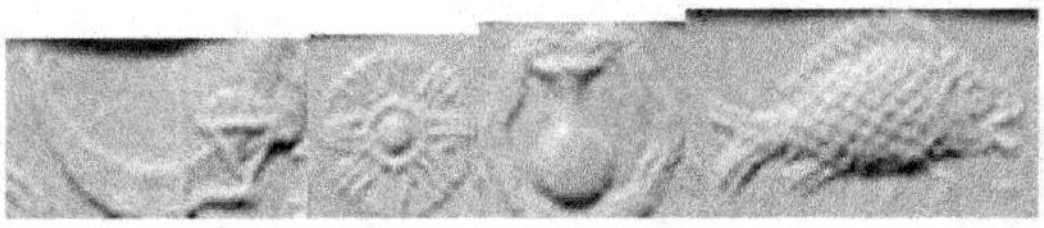

The leftmost hieroglyph shows ingots in a conical-bottom storage jar (similar to the jar shown on Warka vase (See Annex: Warka vase), delivering the ingots to the temple of Inanna). Third from left, the overflowing pot is similar to the hieroglyph shown on Gudea statues. Fourth from left, the fish hieroglyph is similar to the one shown on a Susa pot containing metal tools and weapons. (See Susa pot hieroglyphs of bird and fish: Louvre Museum) Hieroglyph: ***meṇḍā*** 'lump, clot' (Oriya) On mED 'copper' in Eurasian languages see Annex A: Warka vase).

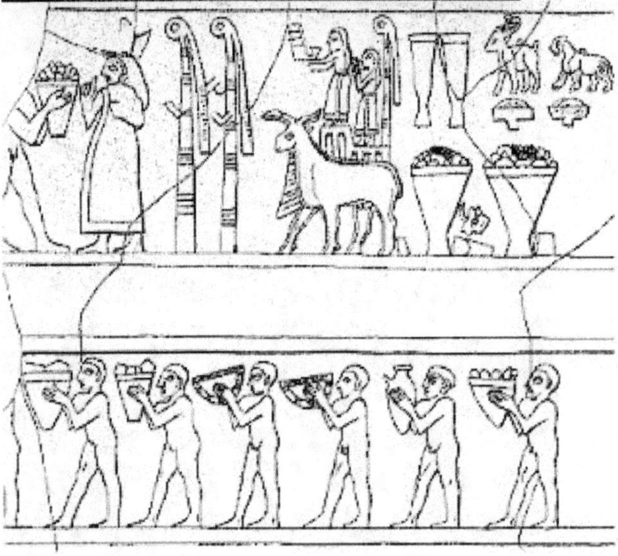

The leftmost hieroglyph shows ingots in a conical-bottom storage jar (similar to the jar shown on Warka vase (See Annex: Warka vase), delivering the ingots to the temple of Inanna). Third from left, the overflowing pot is similar to the hieroglyph shown on Gudea statues. Fourth from left, the fish hieroglyph is similar to the one shown on a Susa pot containing metal tools and weapons. (See Susa pot hieroglyphs of bird and fish: Louvre Museum) Hieroglyph: ***meṇḍā*** 'lump, clot' (Oriya)

On mED 'copper' in Eurasian languages:

Wilhelm von Hevesy wrote about the Finno-Ugric-Munda kinship, like "Munda-Magyar-Maori, an Indian link between the antipodes new tracks of Hungarian origins" and "Finnisch-Ugrisches aus

Indien". (DRIEM, George van: Languages of the Himalayas: an ethnolinguistic handbook. 1997. p.161-162.) Sumerian-Ural-Altaic language affinities have been noted. Given the presence of Meluhha settlements in Sumer, some Meluhha glosses might have been adapted in these languages. One etyma cluster refers to 'iron' exemplified by meD (Ho.). The alternative suggestion for the origin of the gloss med 'copper' in Uralic languages may be explained by the word meD (Ho.) of Munda family of Meluhha language stream:

Sa. <i>mE~R~hE~'d</i> `iron'. ! <i>mE~RhE~d</i>(M).

Ma. <i>mErhE'd</i> `iron'.

Mu. <i>mERE'd</i> `iron'.

~ <i>mE~R~E~'d</i> `iron'. ! <i>mENhEd</i>(M).

Ho <i>meD</i> `iron'.

Bj. <i>merhd</i>(Hunter) `iron'.

KW <i>mENhEd</i>

@(V168,M080)

http://www.ling.hawaii.edu/austroasiatic/AA/Munda/ETYM/Pinnow&Munda

— Slavic glosses for 'copper'

Мед [Med]Bulgarian

Bakar Bosnian

Медзь [medz']Belarusian

Měď Czech

Bakar Croatian

KòperKashubian

Бакар [Bakar]Macedonian

Miedź Polish

Медь [Med']Russian

Meď Slovak

BakerSlovenian

Бакар [Bakar]Serbian

Мідь [mid'] Ukrainian[unquote]

http://www.vanderkrogt.net/elements/element.php?sym=Cu

Miedź, med' (Northern Slavic, Altaic) 'copper'.

One suggestion is that corruptions from the German "Schmied", "Geschmeide" = jewelry. Schmied, a smith (of tin, gold, silver, or other metal)(German) result in med 'copper'.

Four flag-posts(reeds) with rings on top held by the kneeling persons define the four components of the iron smithy/forge.

Hieroglyph: staff: మేడెము [mēḍemu] or మేడియము *mēḍemu*. [Tel.] n. A spear or dagger. ఈటె, బాకు. The rim of a bell-shaped earring, set with gems. రాళ్లుచెక్కిన□మికీ అంచుయొక్క పనితరము. "క ఒడితినన్నన్ వారక మేడెముపొడుతురె." BD. vi. 116.

Hieroglyph: meṇḍa 'bending on one knee': మండి [maṇḍi] or మండీ *manḍi*. [Tel.] n. Kneeling down with one leg, an attitude in archery, ఒక కాలితో నేలమీద మోకరించుట, ఆలీఢపాదము.

मेट [mēṭa] *n* (मिटणें) The knee-joint or the bend of the knee. मेटेंखुंटीस बसणें To kneel down. *Ta.* maṇṭi kneeling, kneeling on one knee as an archer. *Ma.* maṇṭuka to be seated on the heels. *Ka.* maṇḍi what is bent, the knee. *Tu.* maṇḍi knee. *Te.* maṇḍī kneeling on one knee. *Pa.* maḍtel knee; maḍi kuḍtel kneeling position. *Go.* (L.) meṇḍā, (G. Mu. Ma.) minḍa knee (*Voc.* 2827). *Konḍa* (BB) meḍa,
meṇḍa id. *Pe.* menḍa id. *Manḍ.* menḍe id. *Kui* menḍa id. *Kuwi* (F.) menda, (S. Su. P.) menḍa, (Isr.) meṇḍa id. Cf. 4645 Ta. maṭaṅku (maṇi-forms). / ? Cf. Skt. maṇḍūkī- part of an elephant's hind leg; Mar. meṭ knee-joint. (DEDR 4677) Rebus: mẽṛhẽt, meḍ 'iron' (Mu.Ho.) [See the dance step of Ganes'a on Candi Sukuh sculptural frieze.]

Hieroglyph: எருவை eruvai European bamboo reed. See கொறுக்கச்சி. (குறிஞ்சிப்.) Rebus: 817 ***Ta.* eruvai** blood, (?) copper. ***Ka.* ere** a dark-red or dark-brown colour, a dark or dusky colour; (Badaga) **erande** sp. fruit, red in colour. ***Te.* rēcu, rēcu-kukka**a sort of ounce or lynx said to climb trees and to destroy tigers; (B.) a hound or wild dog. ***Kol.* resn a·te** wild dog (i.e. ***res na·te**; see 3650). ***Pa.* iric netta** id. ***Ga.***(S.3) **rēs nete** hunting dog, hound. ***Go.*** (Ma.) **erm ney**, (D.) **erom nay**, (Mu.) **arm/aṛm nay** wild dog (***Voc.*** 353); (M.) **rac nāī**, (Ko.) **rasi ney** id. (***Voc.*** 3010). For 'wild dog', cf. 1931 Ta. **ce-** red, esp. the items for 'red dog, wild dog'.

patākā f. ' flag ' MBh. 2. **paṭākā** -- f. lex. 3. ***phaṭākā** -- **.** [Prob. ← a non -- Aryan word containing *p(h)aṭ* aryanized with *t* EWA ii 200] 1. Pa. *patākā* -- f. ' flag '. 2. Pa. *paṭāka* -- n., Pk. *paḍāga* -- m., *paḍāyā* -- , *paḍāiā* -- f., mh. *paḍāha* -- m.; G. *paṛāi* f. ' paper kite '. 3. Kal.rumb. *phṛā* ' flag '; Or. *phaṛkā* (perh. influenced by Or. *phaṛa -- phaṛa* ' with a sudden movement ' s.v. *phaṭ --). Addenda: **patākā** -- . 2. **paṭākā** -- **:** S.kcch. *paṛāī* f. ' paper kite '.(CDIAL 7726)

mūhā mẽṛhẽt 'iron smelted by the Kolhes and formed into an equilateral lump a little pointed at each of four ends.' (Note ingots in storage pot superfixed on the crucible hieroglyph).

paTam 'snake hood' Rebus: padm 'sharpness' *paṭa* 'hood of snake'. *Rebus: padm* 'tempered, sharpness (metal)'. nāga 'serpent' Rebus: nāga 'lead (alloy)'

Ta. paṭam instep. *Ma.* paṭam flat part of the hand or foot. *Pe.* paṭa key palm of hand. *Manḍ.* paṭa kiy id.; paṭa kāl sole of foot. *Kuwi.* (Su.) paṭa nakipalm of hand. (DEDR 3843)

పదును (p. 0710) [padunu] or పదను *padunu*. [Tel. పది+ఉను.] Temper, sharpness, whetting, *Go.* (ASu.) padnā sharpness. *Koṇḍa* padnu being ready for use (as oilseed being preparèd for pressing), sharpening (of knife by heating and hammering). *Ta.* patamsharpness (as of the edge of a knife),*Ko.* padm (*obl.* padt-) temper of iron.(DEDR 3907)

Ta. patam cobra's hood. *Ma.* paṭam id. *Ka.* peḍe id. *Te.* paḍaga id. *Go.* (S.) paṛge, (Mu.) baṛak, (Ma .) baṛki, (F-H.) biṛki hood of serpent (*Voc.* 2154). / Turner, *CDIAL*, no. 9040, Skt. (s)phaṭa-, sphaṭā- a serpent's expanded hood, Pkt. phaḍā- id. For IE etymology, see Burrow, *The Problem of Shwa in Sanskrit*, p. 45.(DEDR 45 Appendix) phaṭa n. ' expanded hood of snake ' MBh. 2. *phēṭṭa -- 2. [Cf. *phuṭa* -- m., °*ṭā* -- f., *sphuṭa* -- m. lex., °*ṭā* -- f. Pañcat. (Pk. *phuḍā* -- f.), *sphaṭa* -- m., °*ṭā* -- f., *sphōṭā* -- f. lex. and phaṇa -- 1. Conn. words in Drav. T. Burrow BSOAS xii 386] 1. Pk. *phaḍa* -- m.n. ' snake's hood ', °*ḍā* -- f., M. *phaḍā* m., °*ḍī* f. 2. A. *pheṭ, phẽṭ.*(CDIAL 9040)

Hieroglyph: मेढा (p. 665) [mēḍhā] A twist or tangle arising in thread or cord, a curl or snarl.(Marathi. Molesworth)Rebus: mẽṛhẽt, meḍ 'iron' (Mu.Ho.)

The top of each of the four posts is signified by an 'octagonal' (?) vajra rebus: 'thunderbolt weapon'. The flagpost also has a ring comparable to the ring described for a Somayaga Yupa in Satapatha Brahmana. Somayaga is a Soma सं- √ स्था a [p=1121,2]*A1.* -तिष्ठते (Pa1n2. 1-3 , 22 ; ep. and mc. also *P.* -तिष्ठति ; Ved. inf. -स्थातोस् A1pS3r.) , to stand together , hold together (pf. p. du. -तस्थान्/ए , said of heaven and earth) RV. ; to build (a town) Hariv. ; to heap , store up (goods) VarBr2S. occupation , business , profession W.

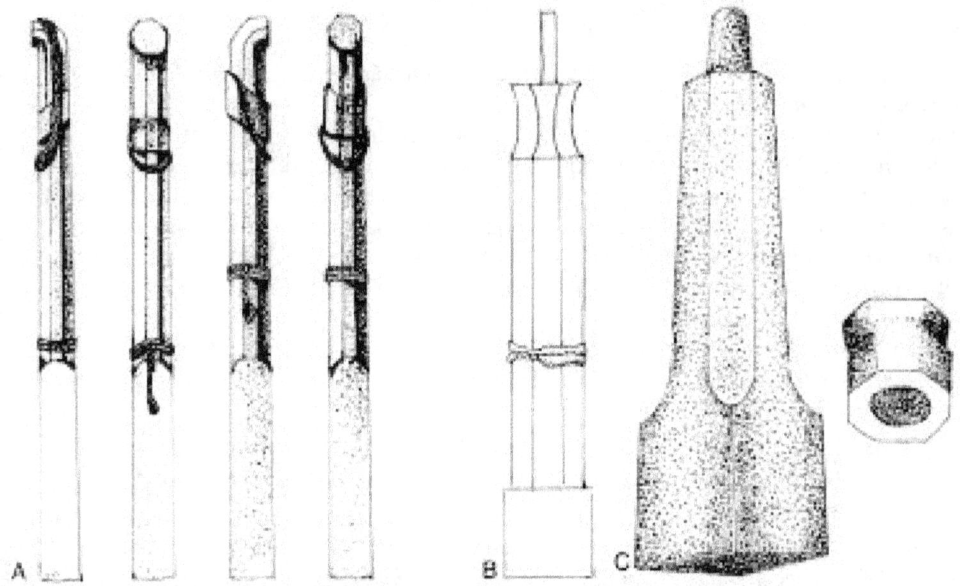

Shapes of Yupa: A. Commemorative stone yupa, Isapur – from Vogel, 1910-11, plate 23; drawing based on Vedic texts – from Madeleine Biardeau, 1988, 108, fig. 1; cf. 1989, fig. 2); C. Miniature wooden yupa and caSAla from Vaidika Samsodana Mandala Museum of Vedic sacrificial utensils – from Dharmadhikari 1989, 70) (After Fig. 5 in Alf Hiltebeitel, 1988, The Cult of Draupadi, Vol. 2, Univ. of Chicago Press, p.22)

Isapur Yupa inscription (102 CE, dated in year 24 in Kushana king Vasishka's reign) indicates performance of a sattra (yajna) of dvadasarAtra, 'twelve nights'. (Vogel, JP, The sacrificial posts of Isapur, *Annual Report of the Archaeological Survey of India, 1910-11*: 40-8).The Isapur yupa is comparable to the ring and vajra atop the flagpost of Jasper cylinder seal. (See the comparable orthography of the vajra carried by Vajrapani on a sculptural frieze from Peshawar).

Relief narrating the visit of Buddha and Vajrapani to an ascetic. From Hoti Mardan Guide Mess, Peshawar, n. 2066, 2nd-3rd cent. CE

This is an announcement of four shops, पेढी (Gujarati. Marathi). पेंढें 'rings' Rebus: पेढी 'shop'.āra 'serpent' Rebus; āra 'brass'. *karaḍa* 'double-drum' *Rebus: karaḍa* 'hard alloy'.

Specific materials offered for sale/exchange in the shop are: hard alloy brass metal (*ayo*, fish); *lokhaṇḍ*(overflowing pot) 'metal tools, pots and pans, metalware'; *arka/erka* 'copper' ; *kammaṭa* (a portable furnace for melting precious metals) 'coiner, mint' Thus, the four shops are: 1. brass alloys, 2. metalware, 3. copper and 4. mint (services).

erãguḍu bowing, salutation (Telugu) *iṟai* (-v-, -nt-) to bow before (as in salutation), worship (Tamil)(DEDR 516). Rebus: *eraka, eṟaka* any metal infusion (Kannada.Tulu) *eruvai* 'copper' (Tamil); *ere* dark red (Kannada)(DEDR 446).

puṭa Anything folded or doubled so as to form a cup or concavity; crucible. Alternative: *ḍhālako* = a large metal ingot (G.) *ḍhālakī* = a metal heated and poured into a mould; a solid piece of metal; an ingot (Gujarati)

Allograph: ढाल [ḍhāla] *f* (S through H) The grand flag of an army directing its march and encampments: also the standard or banner of a chieftain: also a flag flying on forts &c. ढालकाठी [ḍhālakāṭhī] *f* ढालखांब *m* A flagstaff; esp.the pole for a grand flag or standard. 2 fig. The leading and sustaining member of a household or other commonwealth. 5583 ḍhāla n. ' shield ' lex. 2. *ḍhāllā -- . 1. Tir. (Leech) "*dàl*" ' shield ', Bshk. *ḍāl*, Ku. *ḍhāl*, gng. *ḍhāw*, N. A. B. *ḍhāl*, Or. *ḍhāḷa*, Mth. H. *ḍhāl* m.2. Sh. *ḍal* (pl. °*lẹ*) f., K. *ḍāl* f., S. *ḍhāla*, L. *ḍhāl* (pl. °*lā̃*) f., P. *ḍhāl* f., G. M. *ḍhāl* f. WPah.kṭg. (kc.) *ḍhā`l* f. (obl. -- *a*) ' shield ' (a word used in salutation), J. *ḍhāl* f. (CDIAL 5583).

They are four Glyphs: *paṭākā* 'flag' Rebus: *pāṭaka,* four quarters of the village.

kā̃ḍ reed Rebus: *kāṇḍa* 'tools, pots and pans, metal-ware'.
1. Pk. *kamaḍha* -- , °*aya* -- m. ' bamboo '; Bhoj. *kōro* ' bamboo poles '. 2. N. *kāmro* ' bamboo, lath, piece of wood ', OAw. *kāṁvari* ' bamboo pole with slings at each end for carrying things ', H. *kā̃waṛ*, °*ar*, *kāwaṛ*, °*ar* f., G. *kāvaṛ*f., M. *kāvaḍ* f.; -- deriv. Pk. *kāvaḍia* -- , *kavvāḍia* -- m. ' one who carries a yoke ', H. *kā̃waṛī*, °*ṛiyā* m., G. *kāvaṛiyɔ* m. 3. S. *kāvāṭhī* f. ' carrying pole ', *kāvāṭhyo* m. ' the man who carries it '. 4. Or. *kāmaṛā*, °*muṛā* ' rafters of a thatched house '; G. *kāmṛũ* n., °*ṛī* f. ' chip of bamboo ', *kāmaṛ -- koṭiyũ* n. ' bamboo hut '. 5. B. *kāmṭhā* ' bow ', G. *kāmṭhũ* n., °*ṭhī* f. ' bow '; M. *kamṭhā*, °*ṭā* m. ' bow of bamboo or horn '; -- deriv. G. *kāmṭhiyɔ* m. ' archer '. 6. A. *kabāri* ' flat piece of bamboo used in smoothing an earthen image '.
7. *kā̃bīṭ*, °*baṭ*, °*bṭī*, *kāmīṭ*, °*maṭ*, °*mṭī*, *kāmṭhī*, *kāmāṭhī* f. ' split piece of bamboo &c., lath '.(CDIAL 2760). kambi f. ' branch or shoot of bamboo ' lex. Pk. *kaṁbi* -- , °*bī* -- , °*bā* -- f. ' stick, twig ', OG. *kāṁba*; M. *kā̃b* f. ' longitudinal division of a bamboo &c., bar of iron or other metal '. (CDIAL 2774).
कंबडी [kambaḍī] *f* A slip or split piece (of a bamboo &c.)(Marathi)
The rings atop the reed standard: पेंढें [pēṇḍhēṃ] पेंडकें [pēṇḍakēṃ] n Weaver's term. A cord-loop or metal ring (as attached to the गुलडा of the बैली and to certain other fixtures). पेंडें [pēṇḍēṃ] n (पेड) A necklace composed of strings of pearls. 2 A loop or ring. Rebus: पेढी (Gujaráthí word.) A shop (Marathi)Alternative: *koṭiyum* [*koṭ, koṭī* neck] a wooden circle put round the neck of an animal (Gujarati) Rebus:*ācāri koṭṭya* = forge, *kammārasāle* (Tulu)

Six curls shown on the hairstyle of carriers of flagposts:
Allograph: The six curls on the kneeling person's head denote an copper-brass smelter:

erugu = to bow, to salute or make obeisance (Telugu) Rebus: eraka 'copper'.
Glyphs: six (numeral) + ring of hair: आर [āra] A term in the play of इटीदांडू,--the number six. (Marathi) आर [āra] A tuft or ring of hair on the body. (Marathi) Rebus: arā 'brass'.

मेढा mēḍhā A twist or tangle arising in thread or cord, a curl or snarl. (Marathi) Rebus: meḍ 'iron' (Ho.)*bhaṭa* 'six (hair-curls)' Rebus: *bhaṭa* 'furnace'.

saman = to offer an offering, to place in front of; front, to front or face (Santali) Rebus: *samṛobica*, stones containing gold (Mundari) samanom = an obsolete name for gold (Santali) [*bica* 'stone ore' (Munda):*meṛed-bica* = iron stone ore, in contrast to *bali-bica*, iron sand ore (Munda]
"... head and torso of a human but the horns, lower body and legs of a bull...Baked clay plaques like this were mass-produced using moulds in southern Mesopotamia from the second millennium BCE. British Museum. WCO2652. Bull-manTerracotta plaque. Bull-man holding a post. Mesopotamia, ca. 2000-1600 BCE."
Terracotta. This plaque depicts a creature with the head and torso of a human but the horns, lower body and legs of a bull. Though similar figures are depicted earlier in Iran, they are first seen in

Mesopotamian art around 2500 BC, most commonly on cylinder seals, and are associated with the sun-god Shamash. The bull-man was usually shown in profile, with a single visible horn projecting forward. However, here he is depicted in a less common form; his whole body above the waist, shown in frontal view, shows that he was intended to be double-horned. He may be supporting a divine emblem and thus acting as a protective deity.

Old Babylonian, about 2000-1600 BCE From Mesopotamia Length: 12.8 cm Width: 7cm ME 103225 Room 56: Mesopotamia

Baked clay plaques like this were mass-produced using moulds in southern Mesopotamia from the second millennium BCE. While many show informal scenes and reflect the private face of life, this example clearly has magical or religious significance.

Hieroglyph carried on a flagpost by the blacksmith (bull ligatured man: Dhangar 'bull' Rebus: blacksmith'): karava 'pot with narrow neck' karNaka 'rim of jar' Rebus: kharva 'nidhi, wealth, karba 'iron'; karNI 'supercargo' karNIka 'scribe'.

http://www.britishmuseum.org/explore/highlights/highlight_objects/me/t/terracotta_plaque,_bull-man.aspx

Archaeologically attested yupa.
Girsu (Tlloh) archaeological find. 11 ft. tall copper plated flagpost. This may relate to a period when

Girsu (ca. 2900-2335 BCE) was the capital of Lagash at the time of Gudea

A soldier and a Mari dignitary who carries the standard of Mari. Detail of a victory parade, from the Ishtar temple, Mari, Syria. 2400 BCE Schist panel inlaid with mother of pearl plaques. Louvre Museum.

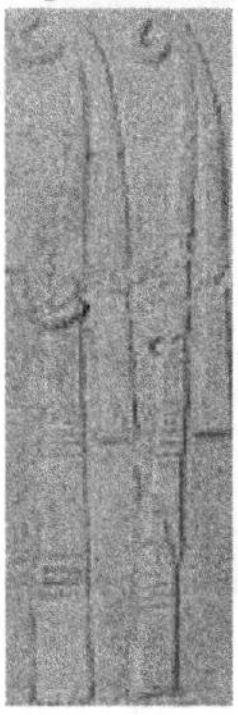

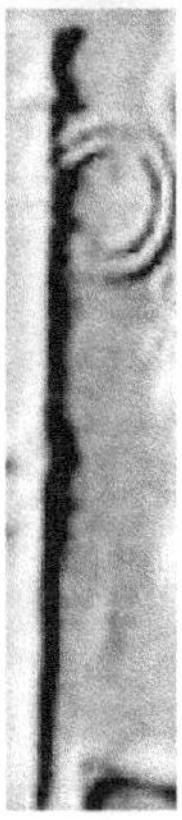

One reedpost has a 'scarf' hieroglyph ligatured at the top (the context of metalwork is seen from a 'fish' hieroglyph: aya 'fish' Rebus: aya 'metal'). This reedost is seen on Warka vase._Another reedpost has a 'ring' hieroglyph ligatured at the top. This flagpost is seen on a jasper cylinder seal.

Such a flagpost is seen on a Gudea cup, held by Mus-hussu (dragon):

On this cylinder seal, the flagposts with rings are shown together with hieroglyphs of: a person carrying an antelope (like the hioeroglyph shown on Shu-ilishu Meluhha translator cylinder seal), overflowing water, fishes, crucible, mountain range, sun (Source: http://enenuru.net/html/gal/urukprocexpl.htm)

The context of metalwork is seen from the 'scarf' hieroglyph: dhatu 'scarf' Rebus: dhatu 'mineral'.

The context of a smithy/forge is seen from the 'ring' hieroglyph: *koṭiyum* [*koṭ, koṭī* neck] a wooden circle put round the neck of an animal (Gujarati) Rebus: *ācāri koṭṭya* = forge, *kammārasāle* (Tulu)

Two types of flagposts are seen in some Ancient Near East artifacts in the context of metalwork: 1. reedpost with scarf; and 2. reedpost with ring.

Hieroglyph: *Ta.* eruvai European bamboo reed; a species of Cyperus; straight sedge tuber. *Ma.* eruva a kind of grass.(DEDR 819) Rebus: *Ta.* eruvai blood, (?) copper. *Ka.* ere a dark-red or dark-brown colour, a dark or dusky colour (DEDR 817)

The reedpost with scarf occurs in a pair: dula 'pair' Rebus: dul 'cast metal' and denotes the warehouse which receives ingots of cast metal.

The reedpost with ring occurs on a jasper cylinder seal with four holders of four reedposts. The holders have six locks of hair as semantic determinatives. Hieroglyph: पेंडें [pēṇḍēṃ] n (पेड) A loop or ring.Rebus: पेठ or पेंठ (p. 527) [pēṭha or pēṇṭha] f (H) A manufacturing or trading town, an emporium, a mart: also a markettown. pēṭhpēṭaka 'caravanserai'. The hieroglyph multiplexed signify a caravensarai from a trading emporium or trading town of copper, metal implements and products from smithy/forge.

Hieroglyph: baTa 'six' Rebus: bhaTa 'furnace'.

Hieroglyph: मेढा (p. 665) [mēḍhā] A twist or tangle arising in thread or cord, a curl or snarl.(Marathi. Molesworth)Rebus: mẽṛhẽt, meḍ 'iron' (Mu.Ho.). Thus the hieroglyph multiplex signifies iron furnace.

On the jasper cylinder seal the four reedpost holders (with six hair curls) are signified by semantic determinatives of four hieroglyphs: 1. crucible PLUS storage pot of ingots, 2. sun, 3. narrow-necked pot with overflowing water, 4. fish

A hooded snake is on the edge of the composition. (The dark red color of jasper reinforces the semantics: eruvai 'dark red, copper' Hieroglyph: eruvai 'reed'; see four reedposts held.

1. Hieroglyph: OP. *koṭhārī* f. ' **crucible** '(CDIAL 3546) Rebus: *koṭhār* 'treasury, warehouse'
2. Hieroglyph: arka 'sun' (Kannada) Rebus: arka, eraka 'copper'
3. Hieroglyph: overflowing pot: lokhaNDa 'overflowing pot' Rebus: lokhANDa 'metalware, pots and pans of metal, metal implements'
4. Hieroglyph: aya 'fish' Rebus: aya 'iron' ayas 'metal' (Rigveda)

Thus, the four holders of four reedposts with attached ring display metalwork of a smithy/forge announcing metal implements, iron, copper and iron.

On many hierolyph multiplexes, water-buffalo (*rã̄go*) is associated with kANDa 'overflowing water'. The rebus renderings are: rāṅgā khaNDA 'zinc alloy implements'. The semantics of khaNDa 'implements' is attested in Santali: me~r.he~t khaNDa 'iron implements'.

Mẽrhẽt. Iron.
Mẽṛhẽt icena. The iron is rusty.
Ispat mẽṛhẽt. Steel.
Dul mẽṛhẽt. Cast iron.
Mẽṛhẽt khanḍa. Iron implements. Santali glosses

A lexicon suggests the semantics of Panini's compound अयस्--काण्ड [p= 85,1] *m. n.* " a quantity of iron " or " excellent iron " , (g. कस्का*दि q.v.)(Pa1n2. 8-3 , 48)(Monier-Williams).

From the example of a compound gloss in Santali, I suggest that the suffix -kANDa in Samskritam should have referred to 'implements'. Indus Script hieroglyphs as hypertext components to signify kANDa 'implements' are: kANTa, 'overflowing water' kANDa, 'arrow' gaNDa, 'four short circumscript strokes'.
Hieroglyph: kāṇḍam காண்டம்² kāṇṭam, n. < kāṇḍa. 1. Water; sacred water; நீர். துருத்திவா யதுக்கிய குங்குமக் காண் டமும் (கல்லா. 49, 16). Rebus: khāṇḍā 'metal tools, pots and pans' (Marathi)

Hieroglyhph: <lo->(B) {V} ``(pot, etc.) to ^overflow''. See <lo-> `to be left over'. @B24310. #20851. <lo->(B) {V} ``to be ^left over, to be ^saved''. Caus. <o-lo->. @B24300. #20861.(Munda etyma)

Rebus: loh 'copper' (Hindi)

The hieroglyph multiplex clearly refers to the metal tools, pots and pans of copper. लोहोलोखंड [lōhōlōkhaṇḍa] *n* (लोह & लोखंड) Iron tools, vessels, or articles in general.रुपेशाई लोखंड [rupēśāī lōkhaṇḍa] *n* A kind of iron. It is of inferior quality to शिक्केशाई. लोखंड [lōkhaṇḍa] *n* (लोह S) Iron. लोखंडाचे चणे खाववणें or चारणें To oppress grievously. लोखंडकाम [lōkhaṇḍakāma] *n* Iron work; that portion (of a building, machine &c.) which consists of iron. 2 The business of an ironsmith. लोखंडी [lōkhaṇḍī] *a* (लोखंड) Composed of iron; relating to iron. 2 fig. Hardy or hard--a constitution or a frame of body, one's हाड or natal bone or parental stock. 3 Close and hard;--used of kinds of wood. 4 Ardent and unyielding--a fever. 5 लोखंडी, in the sense Hard and coarse or in the sense Strong or enduring, is freely applied as a term of distinction or designation. Examples follow. लोखंडी [lōkhaṇḍī] *f* (लोखंड) An iron boiler or other vessel. लोखंडी जर [lōkhaṇḍī jara] *m* (लोखंड & जर) False brocade or lace; lace &c. made of iron.लोखंडी रस्ता [lōkhaṇḍī rastā] *m* लोखंडी सडक *f* (Iron-road.) A railroad.

Alternative: *ḍhālako* = a large metal ingot (G.) *ḍhālakī* = a metal heated and poured into a mould; a solid piece of metal; an ingot (Gujarati)
Allograph: ढाल [ḍhāla] *f* (S through H) The grand flag of an army directing its march and encampments: also the standard or banner of a chieftain: also a flag flying on forts &c. ढालकाठी [ḍhālakāṭhī] *f* ढालखांब *m* A flagstaff; esp.the pole for a grand flag or standard. 2 fig. The leading and sustaining member of a household or other commonwealth. 5583 ḍhāla n. ' shield ' lex. 2. *ḍhāllā -- . 1. Tir. (Leech) "*dàl*" ' shield ', Bshk. *ḍāl*, Ku. *ḍhāl*, gng. *ḍhāw*, N. A. B. *ḍhāl*, Or. *ḍhāḷa*, Mth. H. *ḍhāl* m.2. Sh. *ḍal* (pl. °*lẹ*) f., K. *ḍāl* f., S. *ḍhāla*, L. *ḍhāl* (pl. °*lā̃*) f., P. *ḍhāl* f., G. M. *ḍhāl* f. WPah.kṭg. (kc.) *ḍhā`l* f. (obl. -- *a*) ' shield ' (a word used in salutation), J. *ḍhāl* f. (CDIAL 5583).

The yupa shown next to the dancing Ganesa on Candi Sukuh frieze is also comparable to the Yupa held on Jasper cylinder seal. Hieroglyph: meD 'dance step' rebus: meD 'iron'

Spoked-wheel standard, safflower hierolyph. Fire-altar pedestal of Tukulti-Ninurta I, 1243-1208 BCE Ishtar temple, Assur. Shows the king standing flanked by two standard-bearers; the standard has a spoked-wheel hieroglyph on the top of the staffs and also on the volutes of the altar frieze

करंडा [*karaṇḍā*] A clump, chump, or block of wood. 4 The stock or fixed portion of the staff of the large leaf-covered summerhead or umbrella. करांडा [karāṇḍā] *m* C A cylindrical piece as sawn or chopped off the trunk or a bough of a tree; a clump, chump, or block.

करडी [*karaḍī*] *f* (See करडई) Safflower: also its seed.

Rebus: karaḍa 'hard alloy' of arka 'copper'. Rebus: fire-god: @B27990. #16671. Remo <karandi>E155 {N} ``^fire-^god".(Munda)

Glyphic element: erako nave; era = knave of wheel. Glyphic element: āra 'spokes'. Rebus: āra 'brass' as in ārakūṭa (Skt.) Rebus: Tu. eraka molten, cast (as metal); eraguni to melt (DEDR 866) erka = ekke (Tbh. of arka) aka (Tbh. of arka) copper (metal); crystal (Ka.lex.) cf. eruvai = copper (Ta.lex.) eraka, er-aka = any metal infusion (Ka.Tu.); erako molten cast (Tu.lex.) Glyphic element: kund opening in the nave or hub of a wheel to admit the axle (Santali) Rebus: kunda 'turner' kundār turner (A.); kũdār, kũdāri (B.); kundāru (Or.); kundau to turn on a lathe, to carve, to chase; kundau dhiri = a hewn stone; kundau murhut = a graven image (Santali) kunda a turner's lathe (Skt.)(CDIAL 3295).

arká1 m. ' flash, ray, sun ' RV. [√arc] Pa. Pk. *akka* -- m. ' sun ', Mth. *āk;* Si. *aka* ' lightning ', inscr. *vid -- äki* ' lightning flash '.(CDIAL 624) *அருக்கன் arukkaṉ, n. < arka. Sun; சூரியன். அருக்க னணிநிறமுங் கண்டேன் (திவ். இயற். 3, 1).*(Tamil) agasāle 'goldsmithy' (Kannada) అగసాలి [agasāli] or అగసాలెవాడు *agasāli*. n. A goldsmith. కంసాలివాడు. (Telugu) erka = ekke (Tbh. of arka) aka (Tbh. of arka) copper (metal); crystal (Kannada) cf. eruvai = copper

(Tamil) eraka, er-aka = any metal infusion (Ka.Tu.); erako molten cast (Tulu) Rebus: eraka = copper (Ka.) eruvai = copper (Ta.); ere - a dark-red colour (Ka.)(DEDR 817). eraka, era, er-a = syn. erka, copper, weapons (Ka.) erka = ekke (Tbh. of arka) aka (Tbh. of arka) copper (metal); crystal (Kannada) akka, aka (Tadbhava of arka) metal; akka metal (Te.) arka = copper (Skt.) erako molten cast (Tulu)

At the head of each nome was a nomarch. Each ruler Menes claims unification of nomes demonstrated on standards carried in processions holding aloft hieroglyphs on flagposts.

m0490, m0491

Stone-smithy guild on a Meluhha standard

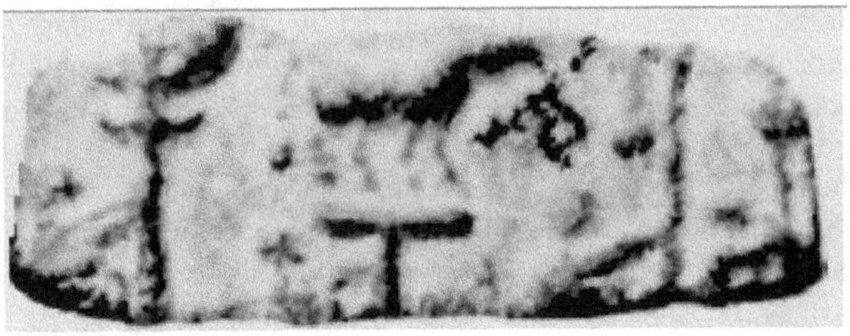

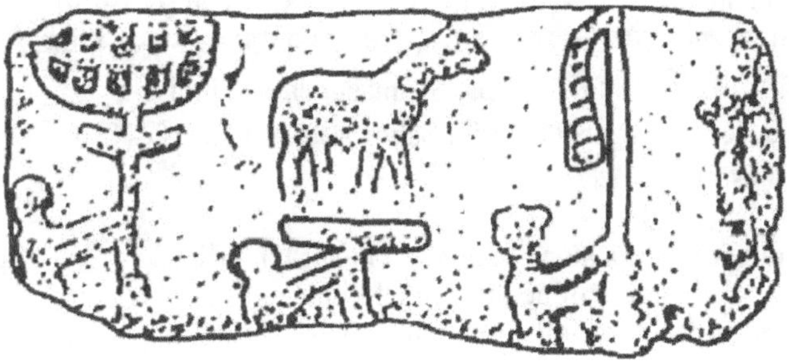

Harappa Tablet. Pict-91 (Mahadevan) m0490At m0490B Mohenjodaro Tablet showing Meluhha combined standard of three standards carried in a procession, comparable to Tablet m0491.

'Raised hand' hieroglyph on Pict-91 Harappa tablet: er-aka 'upraised hand' (Tamil) Rebus: eraka 'copper'.

m0491 Tablet. Line drawing (right). This tablet showing three hieroglyphs may be called the Meluhha standard.Combined reading for the joined or ligatured glyphs

Rebus reading is: dhatu kõdā sangaḍa 'mineral, turner, stone-smithy guild'.

Dawn of the bronze age is best exemplified by this Mohenjo-daro tablet which shows a procession of three hieroglyphs carried on the shoulders of three persons. The hieroglyphs are: 1. Scarf carried on a pole (dhatu Rebus: mineral ore); 2. A young bull carried on a stand kõdā Rebus: turner; 3. Portable standard device (Top part: lathe-gimlet; Bottom part: portable furnace sãgāḍ Rebus: stone-cutter sangatarāśū). sanghāḍo (Gujarati) cutting stone, gilding (Gujarati); sangsāru karaṇu = to stone (Sindhi) sanghāḍiyo, a worker on a lathe (Gujarati) sangataras. संगतराश lit. 'to collect stones, stone-cutter, mason.' संगतराश संज्ञा पुं० [फ़ा०] पत्थर काटने या गढ़नेवाला मजदूर । पत्थरकट । २. एक औजार जो पत्थर काटने के काम में आता है । (Dasa, Syamasundara. Hindi sabdasagara. Navina samskarana. 2nd ed. Kasi : Nagari Pracarini Sabha, 1965-1975.) पत्थर या लकडी पर नकाशी करनेवाला, संगतराश, 'mason'.

The procession is a celebration of the graduation of a stone-cutter as a metal-turner in a smithy/forge. A sangatarāśū 'stone-cutter' or lapidary of neolithic/chalolithic age had graduated into a metal turner's workshop (koḍ), working with metallic minerals (dhatu) of the bronze age.

Three professions are described by four standards; three of these standards are three hieroglyphs: scarf, young bull, standard device dhatu kõdāsãgāḍī Rebus words denote: ' mineral worker; metals turner-joiner (forge); worker on a lathe' – associates (guild).

On this tablet, the standard which is also a hieroglyph on the very front is not clear. It is surmised that this standard, the first hieroglyph of four hieroglyphs carried on the procession may be comparable to the standard shown on Tukulti-Ninurta I altar discovered in the Ashur temple.

This fourth standard could be compared with this hieroglyph of the Tukulti-Ninurta altar:

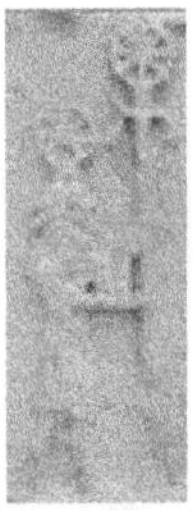

A spoked wheel is shown atop on the standard and the hieroglyph is also reinforced by depicting the hieroglyph on the top of the standard-bearer's head. This Meluhha hieroglyph is read rebus: eraka'knave of wheel' Rebus: 'moltencast copper'; āra 'spokes' Rebus: āra 'brass'.

Thus, the fourth profession is depicted as the smith working with metal alloys.

Thus, together the four professions depicted on the Mohenjodaro-standard showing four hieroglyphs in procession are read rebus:

Hieroglyph: dhatu 'scarf' Rebus: dhatu 'mineral'

Hieroglyph: kõdā 'young bull calf' Rebus: kõdā 'turner-joiner' (forge), worker on a lathe

Hieroglyph: sā̃gāḍī 'lathe (gimlet), portable furnace' Rebus: sā̃gāḍī 'metalsmith associates (guild)'

Hieroglyph eraka āra 'knave of wheel', 'spokes of wheel' Rebus: eraka āra 'copper alloy brass'

Thus Rebus readings of the four hieroglyphs denote: ' mineral worker; metals turner-joiner (forge); worker on a lathe' – associates (guild), copper alloy brass.

dhatu kõdā sā̃gāḍī eraka āra

Safflower hieroglyph adorns one side of Tukulti-Ninurta I altar: करडी [karaḍī] f (See करडई) Safflower: also its seed. Rebus: karaḍa 'hard alloy' of arka 'copper'. Rebus: fire-god: @B27990. #16671. Remo <karandi>E155 {N} ``^fire-^god".(Munda).

Rebus Meluhha reading of safflower karaḍī as fire-god karandi renders the hieroglyph sacred and could well have denoted sacredness of the effulgent sun divinity.

A bracelet with the face of a bull. ḍangar 'bull' Rebus: ḍangar 'blacksmith' (Hindi)

Nahal Mishmar arsenical-copper artifacts (with hieroglyphs), 4th millennium BCE.

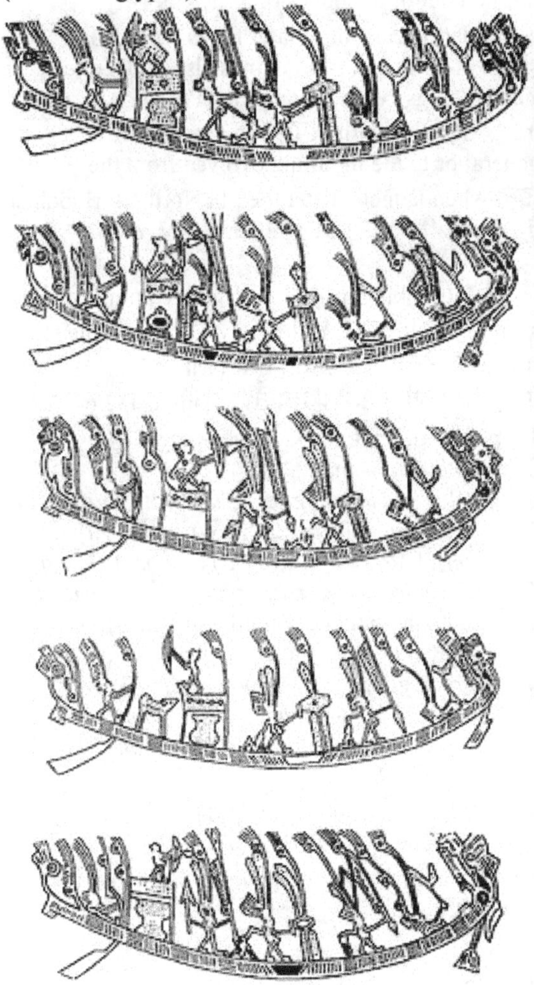

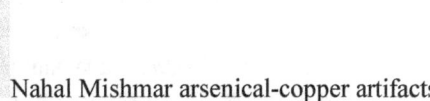

Flagposts on boat. Dong Son bronze drum hieroglyphs.

Processions with flagposts was a signature tune of the metalworkers of the Bronze Age in an extensive area stretching from Haifa, Israel to Hanoi, Vietnam.

वज्र vajra *mn. m.* a kind of column or pillar VarBr2S.; *m.* a kind of hard mortar or cement (कल्क) VarBr2S. (cf. -लेप); *mfn.* adamantine , hard , impenetrable W.; *mfn.* shaped like a kind of cross (cf. above) , forked , zigzag ib. [cf. Zd. vazra , " a club. "]; " the hard or mighty one " , a thunderbolt (esp. that of इन्द्र , said to have been formed out of the bones of the ऋषि दधीच or दधीचि [q.v.] , and shaped like a circular discus , or in later times regarded as having the form of two transverse bolts crossing each other thus x ; sometimes also applied to similar weapons used by various gods or superhuman beings , or to any mythical weapon destructive of spells or charms , also to मन्यु, " wrath " RV. or [with अपाम्] to a jet of water AV. &c ; also applied to a thunderbolt in general or to the lightning evolved from the centrifugal energy of the circular thunderbolt of इन्द्र when launched at a foe ; in Northern Buddhist countries it is shaped like a dumb-bell and called Dorje ;» MWB. 201 ; 322 &c) RV. &c

gō गो *m. f.* (*Nom.* गौः) [गच्छत्यनेन, गम् करणे डो Tv.] **1** Cattle, kine (pl.) **-2** Anything coming from a cow; such as milk, flesh, leather &c. **-3** The stars; वि रश्मिभिः ससृजे सूर्यो गाः Rv.7.36.1. **-4** The sky. **-5** The thunder- bolt of Indra; Ki.8.1. **-6** A ray of light; नान्यस्तप्ता विद्यते गोषु देव Mb.1.232.11; बालोऽयं गिरिशिखरेषु चारयन् गाः त्रैलोक्यं तिमिरभरेण दुष्टमेतत् (रविः नैर्मल्यं नयति) I Rām. Ch. 7.6. **-7** A diamond. **-8** Heaven. **-9** An arrow. **-धुमः, -धूमः 1** wheat; Bṛi. Up.6.3.13. **-2** the orange. °चूर्णम् wheat flour **gōdhū´ma** (usu. pl.) m. ' wheat ' VS.Pa. *gōdhūma* -- m., NiDoc. ***goduma***, *gohomi*, *goma*, Pk. *gōhūma* -- m., Gy. kar. *gišu*, pal. *gḗsū*, *gēsū́wi*, arm. *gihu*, *giu*, eur. *giv* m. ' wheat, rye '; Ash. *gōm*, *gūm*, Kt. *gūm* (→ Pr. *umū´* NTS xv 248), Wg. *gə̄̃m*, *gū˜m*, Pr. *ulyúm* ' growing wheat ' (Brah. *xōlum* ← IA. **gōlūm*); Dm.*gɔ̄̃m* ' wheat ', Tir. *gə̄̃m*, Paš. *gūm*, Niṅg. Shum. *gōom*, Woṭ. *guōmə*, Gaw. *gə̄̃m*, *g'ū˜m*, Kal. rumb. *gū´hum*, urt. *ghɔ̄̃m*, Kho. *góm*, Bshk.*gɔ̄̃m*, Tor. *ghomū*, Mai. *gōm*, Gau. *gū̃*, Sv. *ghuma*, Phal. *ghōm* m., Sh gil. *gūmị* m. pl., gur. *gūm* m., koh. pales. *ghūm* (older **gōm* → Ḍ.*gōmu*), K. *guyu* (← Ind.?), S. *gehū̃* m., WPah. bhad. *gahū̃*, paṅ. *giū̃h*, bhal. *geùtilde;* m., Ku. *gyū̃*, N. *gahū̃*, *gaū̃*, A. *ghẽh*, Or. *gahū̃*, WBi.*gohū̃*, Bhoj. Aw. lakh. *gōhū̃*, H. *gohū̃*, *gehū̃*, *gahū̃* m., G. *gahū̃*, *ghaū̃* m., M. *gahū̃* m., Ko. *gaṁv* m.; Si. *goyama* ' growing corn '; -- with unexpl. -- *m* -- : A. *gomdhān* ' maize '; B. *gom*, *gam* ' wheat ', Or. *gahama*, EBi. *gahum*, (S of Gaya) *gohum*, Mth. *gohum*, *gahūm*.

Addenda: **gōdhū´ma -- :** WPah.kṭg. (kc.) *gíū̃* m.pl. ' wheat ', J. *gī˜ū̃* m., Garh. *gewū̃*, A. also *ghẽhu* AFD 194; -- Md. *godan* (+ *dan* <dhānyà --) ' wheat '(CDIAL 4287).धूम [p= 518,1]*m.* (√धू or 1. ध्वन्) smoke , vapour , mist RV. &c; wheat L. *Godhūma* **wheat** (usually mentioned with yava, spelt) Miln 267; DA i.163; SnA 323.(Pali)

वाजपेय is a सोमः-संस्था, a Soma storing up, occupation.

सोमः sōmḥ -संस्था a form of the Soma-sacrifice; (these are seven:- अग्निष्टोम, अत्यग्निष्टोम, उक्थ, षोढशी, अतिरात्र, आप्तोर्याम and **वाजपेय). वाज--पेय [p=938,1]** *mn.* " the drink of strength or of battle " , N. of one of the seven forms of the सोम-sacrifice (offered by kings or Brahmans aspiring to the highest position , and preceding the राज-su1ya and the बृहस्पति-sava) AV. Br. S3rS. MBh.

R. Pur. N. of the 6th book of the शतपथ-ब्राह्मण in the काण्व-शाखा *m.* = वाजपेये भवो मन्त्रः , or वाजपेयस्य व्याख्यानं कल्पः Pat. on Pa1n2. 4-3 , 66 Va1rtt. 5 &c **सं- √ स्था a [p=1121,2]** *A1.* -तिष्ठते (Pa1n2. 1-3 , 22 ; ep. and mc. also *P.* -तिष्ठति ; Ved. inf. -स्थातोस् A1pS3r.) , to stand together , hold together (pf. p.du. -तस्थान्/ए , said of heaven and earth) RV. ; to fix or place upon or in (loc.) Kaus3. MBh. &c to build (a town) Hariv. ; to heap , store up (goods) VarBr2S. ; to found , establish , fix , settle , introduce , set a foot MBh. R. Ra1jat. ; occupation , business , profession W.

शत--पथ---ब्राह्मण [p=1049,2] *n.* " the ब्राह्मण with a hundred paths or sections " N. of a well-known ब्राह्मण attached to the वाजसनेयि-संहिता or White यजुर्-वेद , (like the संहिता , this ब्राह्मणis ascribed to the ऋषि याज्ञवल्क्य ; it is perhaps the most modern of the ब्राह्मणs , and is preserved in two शाखाs or schools , माध्यंदिन and काण्व ; the version belonging to the former is best known , and is divided into fourteen काण्डs or books which contain one hundred अध्यायs or lectures [or according to another arrangement into sixty-eight प्रपाठकs] ; the whole work is regarded as the most systematic and interesting of all the ब्राह्मणs , and though intended mainly for ritual and sacrificial purposes , is full of curious mythological details and legends ; cf. यजुर्-वेद , विजसनेयिसंहिता ,ब्राह्मण) IW. 25 &c

गो--धूम a [p= 365,1] *m.* (√गुध् Un2.) " earth-smoke " , wheat (generally pl.) VS. TBr. i S3Br. v (sg.) , xii , xiv S3a1n3khS3r. Mn. &c **गो--धूमी***f.* = -लोमिका L. **गो** *mf.* the thunderbolt Sa1y. on RV. v , 30 , 7

amṛtā abhūmeti 'we have become immortal'

--Satapatha Brahmana elucidates the process using wheat chaff as चषालः caṣāla, the metaphor is ascent on Yupa to heaven.

5.2.1.[9]

atha niśrayaṇo niśrayati | sa dakṣiṇata udaṅ roheduttarato vā dakṣiṇā dakṣiṇatastvevodaṅ rohettathā hyudagbhavati

5:2:1:99. He then leans a ladder (against the post). He may ascend either from the south northwards, or from the north southwards; but let him rather ascend from the south northwards (udak), for thus it goes upwards (udak).

5.2.1.[10]

sa rokṣyanjāyāmāmantrayate | jāya ehi svo rohāveti rohāvetyāha jāyā tadyajjāyāmāmantrayate 'rdho ha vā eṣa ātmano yajjāyā tasmādyāvajjāyāṃ na vindate naiva tāvatprajāyate 'sarvo hi tāvadbhavatyatha yadaiva jāyāṃ vindate 'tha prajāyate tarhi hi sarvo

bhavati sarva etāṃ gatiṃ gacānīti tasmājjāyāmāmantrayate

5:2:1:1010. Being about to ascend, he (the Sacrificer) addresses his wife, 'Come, wife, ascend we the sky!'--'Ascend we!' says the wife. Now as to why he addresses his wife: she, the wife, in sooth is one half of his own self; hence, as long as he does not obtain her, so long he is not regenerated, for so long he is incomplete. But as soon as he obtains her he is regenerated, for then he is complete. 'Complete I want to go to that supreme goal,' thus (he thinks) and therefore he addresses his wife.

5.2.1.[11]

sa rohati | prajāpateḥ prajā abhūmeti prajāpaterhyeṣa prajā bhavati yo vājapeyena yajate

5:2:1:1111. He ascends, with, 'We have become Pra*j*âpati's children;' for he who offers the Vâgapeya indeed becomes Pra*j*âpati's child:

5.2.1.[12]

atha godhūmānupaspṛśati | svardevā aganmeti svarhyeṣa gacati yo vājapeyena yajate

5:2:1:1212. He then touches the wheat (top-piece) 2, with, 'We have gone to the light, O ye gods!' for he who offers the Vâgapeya, indeed goes to the light.

5.2.1.[13]

tadyadgodhūmānupaspṛśati | annaṃ vai godhūmā annaṃ vā eṣa ujjayati yo vājapeyena yajate 'nnapeyaṃ ha vai nāmaitadyadvājapeyaṃ tadyadevaitadannamudajaiṣīttenaivaitadetāṃ gatiṃ gatvā saṃspṛśate tadātmankurute tasmādgodhūmānupaspṛśati

5:2:1:1313. And as to why he touches the wheat: wheat is food, and he who offers the Vâgapeya, wins food, for vâga-peya is the same as anna-peya (food and drink): thus whatever food he has thereby won, therewith now that he has gone to that supreme goal, he puts himself in contact, and possesses himself of it,--therefore he touches the wheat (top-piece).

5.2.1.[14]

atha śīrṣṇā yūpamatyujjihīte | amṛtā abhūmeti devalokamevaitenojjayati

5:2:1:1414. He then rises by (the measure of) his head over the post, with, 'We have become immortal!' whereby he wins the world of the gods.

5.2.1.[15]

atha diśo 'nuvīkṣamāṇo japati | asme vo astvindriyamasme nṛmṇamuta kraturasme varcāṃsi santu va iti sarvaṃ vā eṣa idamujjayati yo vājapeyena yajate prajāpatiṃ hyujjayati sarvamu hyevedam prajāpatiḥ so 'sya sarvasya yaśa indriyaṃ vīryaṃ saṃvṛjya tadātmandhatte tadātmankurute tasmāddiśo 'nuvīkṣamāṇo japati

5:2:1:1515. Thereupon, while looking in the different directions, he mutters (Vâg. S. IX, 22), 'Ours be your power, ours your manhood and intelligence ours be your energies!' For he who offers the Vâgapeya wins everything here, winning as he does Pra*j*âpati, and Pra*j*âpati being everything here;--having appropriated to himself the glory, the power, and the strength of this All, he now lays them within himself, makes them his own: that is why he mutters, while looking in the different directions.

5.2.1.[16]

athainamūṣapuṭairanūdasyanti | paśavo vā ūṣā annaṃ vai paśavo 'nnaṃ vā eṣa ujjayati yo vājapeyena yajate 'nnapeyaṃ ha vai nāmaitadyadvājapeyaṃ tadyadevaitadannamudajaiṣīttenaivaitadetāṃ gatiṃ gatvā saṃspṛśate tadātmankurute tasmādenamūṣapuṭairanūdasyanti

5:2:1:1616. They throw up to him bags of salt; for salt means cattle, and cattle is food; and he who offers the Vâgapeya wins food, for vâga-peya is the same as anna-peya: thus whatever food he thereby has gained, therewith now that he has gone to the supreme goal, he puts himself in contact, and makes it his own,--therefore they throw bags of salt up to him.

5.2.1.[17]

āśvattheṣu palāśeṣūpanaddhā bhavanti | sa yadevādo 'śvatthe tiṣṭhata indro maruta upāmantrayata tasmādāśvattheṣu palāśeṣūpanaddhā bhavanti viśo 'nūdasyanti viśo vai maruto 'nnaṃ viśastasmādviśo 'nūdasyanti saptadaśa bhavanti saptadaśo vai prajāpatistatprajāpatimujjayati

5:2:1:1717. They (the pieces of salt) are done up in a*s*vattha (ficus religiosa) leaves: because Indra on that (former) occasion called upon the Maruts staying on the A*s*vattha tree 1, therefore they are done up in a*s*vattha leaves. Peasants (vi*s*) throw them up to him, for the Maruts are the peasants, and the peasants are food (for the nobleman): hence peasants throw them up. There are seventeen (bags), for Pra*j*âpati is seventeenfold: he thus wins Pra*j*âpati.

5.2.1.[18]

athemāmupāvekṣamāṇo japati | namo mātre pṛthivyai namo mātre pṛthivyā iti bṛhaspaterha vā abhiṣiṣicānātpṛthivī bibhayāṃ cakāra mahadvā ayamabhūdyo 'bhyaṣeci yadvai māyaṃ nāvadṛṇīyāditi bṛhaspatirha pṛthivyai bibhayāṃ cakāra yadvai meyaṃ nāvadhūnvīteti tadanayaivaitanmitradheyamakuruta na hi mātā putraṃ hinasti na putro mātaram

5:2:1:1818. Thereupon; while looking down upon this (earth), he mutters, Homage be to the mother Earth! homage be to the mother Earth!' For when B*ri*haspati had been consecrated, the Earth was afraid of him, thinking, 'Something great surely has he become now that he has been consecrated: I fear lest he may rend me asunder 2!' And B*ri*haspati also was afraid of the Earth, thinking, 'I fear lest she may shake me off!' Hence by that (formula) he entered into a friendly relation with her; for a mother does not hurt her son, nor does a son hurt his mother.

5.2.1.[19]

bṛhaspatisavo vā eṣa yadvājapeyam | pṛthivyu haitasmādbibheti mahadvā

ayamabhūdyo 'bhyaṣeci yadvai māyaṃ nāvadṛṇīyādityeṣa u hāsyai bibheti yadvai meyaṃ nāvadhūnvīteti tadanayaivaitanmitradheyaṃ kurute na hi mātā putraṃ hinasti na putro mātaram

5:2:1:1919. Now the Brihaspati consecration 3 is the same as the Vâgapeya; and the earth in truth is afraid of that (Sacrificer), thinking, 'Something great
surely has he become now that he has been consecrated: I fear lest he may rend me asunder!' And he himself is afraid of her, thinking, 'I fear lest she may shake me off!' Hence he thereby enters into a friendly relation with her, for a mother does not hurt her son; neither does a son hurt his mother.

5.2.1.[20]

atha hiraṇyamabhyavarohati | amṛtamāyurhiraṇyaṃ tadamṛta āyuṣi pratitiṣṭhati

5:2:1:2020. He then descends (and treads) upon a piece of gold;--gold is immortal life: he thus takes his stand on life immortal.

5.2.1.[21]

athājarṣabhasyājinamupastṛṇāti | tadupariṣṭādrukmaṃ nidadhāti tamabhyavarohatīmāṃ vaiva

5:2:1:2121. Now (in the first place) he (the Adhvaryu) spreads out the skin of a he-goat, and lays a (small) gold plate thereon: upon that--or indeed upon this (earth) itself--he (the Sacrificer) steps.

5.2.1.[22]

athāsmā āsandīmāharanti | uparisadyaṃ vā eṣa jayati yo jayatyantarikṣasadyaṃ tadenamuparyāsīnamadhastādimāḥ prajā upāsate tasmādasmā āsandīmāharanti

5:2:1:2222. They then bring a throne-seat for him; for truly he who gains a seat in the air 1, gains a seat above (others): thus these subjects of his sit below him who is seated above,--this is why they bring him a throne-seat.

5.2.1.[23]

audumbarī bhavati | annaṃ vā ūrgudumbara ūrjo 'nnādyasyāvaruddhyai tasmādaudumbarī bhavati tāmagreṇa havirdhāne jaghanenāhavanīyaṃ nidadhāti

5:2:1:2323. It is made of udumbara wood,--the Udumbara tree being sustenance, (that is) food,--for his obtainment of sustenance, food: therefore it is made of udumbara wood. They set it down in front of the Havirdhâna (cart-shed), behind the Âhavanîya (fire).

5.2.1.[24]

athājarṣabhasyājinamāstṛṇāti | prajāpatirvā eṣa yadajarṣabha etā vai prajāpateḥ pratyakṣatamāṃ yadajāstasmādetāstriḥ saṃvatsarasya vijāyamānā dvau trīniti janayanti tatprajāpatimevaitatkaroti tasmādajarṣabas yājinamāstṛṇāti

5:2:1:2424. He then spreads the goat-skin thereon; for truly the he-goat is no other than Pra/âpati, for they, the goats, are most clearly of Pra/âpati (the lord of generation or creatures);--whence, bringing forth thrice in a year, they produce two or three 2: thus he thereby makes him (the Sacrificer) to be Pra/âpati himself,--this is why he spreads the goat-skin thereon.

5.2.1.[25]

sa āstṛṇāti | iyaṃ te rāḍiti rājyamevāsminnetaddadhātyathainamāsādayati yantāsi yamana iti yantāramevainametadyamanamāsām prajānāṃ karoti dhruvo 'si dharuṇa iti dhruvamevainametaddharuṇamasmiṃloke karoti kṛṣyai tvā kṣemāya tvā rayyai tvā poṣāya tveti sādhave tvetyevaitadāha

5:2:1:2525. He spreads it, with, 'This is thy kingship 1!' whereby he endows him with royal power. He then makes him sit down, with, Thou art the ruler, the ruling lord!' whereby he makes him the ruler, ruling over those subjects of his Thou art firm, and steadfast!' whereby he makes him firm and stedfast in this world;--'Thee for the tilling!--Thee for peaceful dwelling!--Thee for wealth!--Thee for thrift!' whereby he means to say, '(here I seat) thee for the welfare (of the people).'

http://gretil.sub.uni-goettingen.de/gretil/1_sanskr/1_veda/2_bra/satapath/sb_05_u.htm (Text)

http://www.sacred-texts.com/hin//sbr/sbe41/sbe4108.htm (Translation)

चषालः *caṣāla* on octagonal Sivalinga -- as *Yupa*, fiery pillar of light in a smelting process

In continuation of the following references attesting yupa in sama yaga, the cognate shapes of octagonal sivalinga are presented juxtaposed to the archaeological evidence of a fire-altar from Binjor together with an octagonal brick:

Galagesvara temple of Galaganatha. An octagonal pillar -- Yupa.

PLAN OF SACRIFICIAL GROUND.

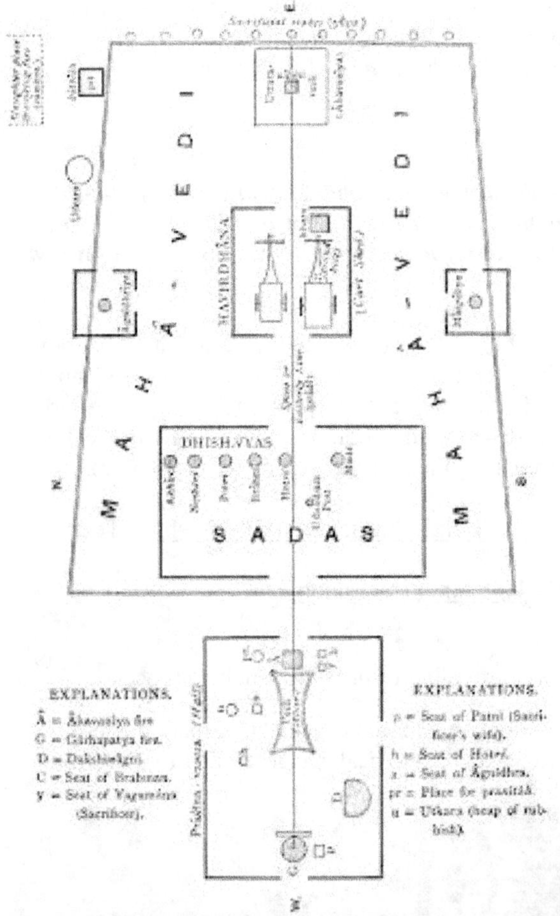

http://www.wisdomlib.org/hinduism/book/the-%C5%9Batapatha-br%C4%81hma%E1%B9%87a-part-ii/d/doc63259.html

Syena-citi: A Monument of Uttarkashi The first layer of one kind of śyenaciti or falcon altar described in the Śulbasūtras, made of 200 bricks of six shapes or sizes, all of them adding up to a specified total area.

Distt.EXCAVATED SITE -PUROLA Geo-Coordinates-Lat. 30° 52'54" N Long. 77° 05'33" E Notification No& Date;2742/-/16-09/1996The ancient site at Purola is located on the left bank of river Kamal. The excavation yielded the remains of Painted Grey Ware (PGW) from the earliest level alongwith other associated materials include terracotta figurines, beads, potter-stamp, the dental and femur portions of domesticated horse (Equas Cabalus Linn). The most important finding from the site is a brick alter identified as Syenachiti by the excavator. The structure is in the shape of a flying eagle Garuda, head facing east with outstretched wings. In the center of the structure is the chiti is a square chamber yielded remains of pottery assignable to circa first century B.C. to second century AD. In addition copper coin of Kuninda and other material i.e. ash, bone pieces etc and a thin gold leaf impressed with a human figure tentatively identified as Agni have also been recovered from the central chamber. http://asidehraduncircle.in/uttarkashi.html

Relief with Ekamukha linga. Mathura. 1st cent. CE (Fig. 6.2). This is the most emphatic representation of linga as a pillar of fire. The pillar is embedded within a brick-kiln with an angular roof and is ligatured to a tree. Hieroglyph: kuTi 'tree' rebus: kuThi 'smelter'. In this composition, the artists is depicting the smelter used for smelting to create *mũh* 'face' (Hindi) rebus: *mũhe* 'ingot' (Santali) of *mēḍha* 'stake' rebus: *meḍ* 'iron, metal' (Ho. Munda). मेड (p. 662) [mēḍa] *f* (Usually **मेढ** q. v.) **मेडका** *m* A stake, esp. as bifurcated. मेढ (p. 662) [mēḍha] *f* A forked stake. Used as a post. Hence a short post generally whether forked or not. मेढा (p. 665) [mēḍhā] *m* A stake, esp. as forked. 2 A dense arrangement of stakes, a palisade, a paling. मेढी (p. 665) [mēḍhī] *f* (Dim. of **मेढ**) A small bifurcated stake: also a small stake, with or without furcation, used as a post to support a cross piece. मेढ्या (p. 665) [mēḍhyā] *a* (**मेढ** Stake or post.) A term for a person considered as the pillar, prop, or support (of a household, army, or other body), the *staff* or *stay*. मेढेजोशी (p. 665) [mēḍhējōśī] *m* A stake-**जोशी**; a **जोशी** who keeps account of the **तिथि** &c., by driving stakes into the ground: also a class, or an individual of it, of fortune-tellers, diviners, presagers, seasonannouncers, almanack-makers &c. They are Shúdras and followers of the **मेढेमत** q. v. 2 Jocosely. The hereditary or settled (quasi fixed as a stake) **जोशी** of a

village.मेंधला (p. 665) [mēndhalā] *m* In architecture. A common term for the two upper arms of a double **चौकठ** (door-frame) connecting the two. Called also **मेंढरी** & **घोडा**. It answers to **छिली** the name of the two lower arms or connections. (Marathi)

मेंढा [*mēṇḍhā*] A crook or curved end rebus: *meḍ* 'iron, metal' (Ho. Munda)

A terracotta cake is a *piṇḍa* पिण्ड [p=625,2] m. (rarely n.) any round or roundish mass or heap , a ball , globe , knob , button , clod , lump , piece (cf. अयः-. , मांस- &c) RV. (only i , 162 , 19 and here applied to lumps of flesh) TS. S3Br.&c; n. (L.) iron; steel (Monier-Williams. Samskritam). What archaeometallurgical functions were served by the terracotta cakes offered as *piṇḍa* पिण्ड in fire-altars? One possibility is that the terracotta cakes (of circular and triangular shapes) served the functions of *piṇḍika*a which is a support base for the Sivalinga which is a divine impeller of the cosmic dance of transmutation occurring in a fire-altar . A skambha linking heaven and earth, a fiery pillar of light. The following three ricas of Rigveda also refer to and explain the metaphor of skambha as a prop which upholds heaven and earth; RV 9.89.6 places it in the context of purification of Soma, reinforcing the possibility that the Skambha signified the impeller of the purification process of yajna -- a process which is replicated in the purification of metals in a smelter/funace/fire-altar:

इन्द्रो॑ः दि॒वः प्र॑ति॒मानं॑ पृथि॒व्या विश्वा॑ वेद॒ सव॑ना॒ हन्ति॒ शुष्ण॑म् ।
म॒हीं चि॒द्द्यामात॑नो॒त्सूर्ये॑ण चा॒स्कम्भ॑ चि॒त्कम्भ॑नेन॒ स्कभी॑यान् ॥ 5 ॥

10.111.05 Indra, the counterpart of heaven and earth, is cognizant of all sacrifices, he is the slayer of S'us.n.a; he spread out the spacious heaven with the sun (to light it up); best of proppers, he propped up (the heaven) with a prop. [Propped up the heaven with a prop: Satyata_ta_ = that which is stretched out by the true ones, the gods; or, ta_ti as a suffix, that which is true, i.e.,
heaven].

दि॒वो यः स्क॒म्भो ध॒रुणः॒ स्वा॑तत॒ आपू॑र्णो अं॒शुः प॒र्येति॑ वि॒श्वतः॑ ।
सेमे म॒ही रोद॑सी यक्षदा॒वृता॑ समीची॒ने दा॑धार॒ समिषः॑ क॒विः ॥ 2 ॥

9.074.02 The supporter of heaven, the prop (of the earth), the Soma-juice who, widely spreading, filling (the vessels), flows in all directions-- may he unite the two great worlds by his own strength; he has upheld them combined; (may he) the sage (bestow) food upon (his worshippers). [The prop of the earth: cf. RV. 9.089.06; may he unite: yaks.at = sam.yojayatu; a_vr.ta = by its own unaided strength].

वि॒ष्ट॒म्भो दि॒वो ध॒रुणः॑ पृथि॒व्या विश्वा॑ उ॒त क्षि॒तयो॒ हस्ते॑ अस्य ।
अस॑त्त॒ उत्सो॑ गृण॒ते नि॒यत्वा॒न्मध्वो॑ अं॒शुः प॑वत इन्द्रि॒याय॑ ॥ 6 ॥

9.089.06 The prop of heaven, the support of earth-- all beings (are) in his hands; may (Soma) the fountain (of desires) be possessed of horses for you (his) adorer; the filament of the sweet-flavoured (Soma) is purified for (the sake of winning) strength.

Linga with One Face of Shiva (Ekamukhalinga), Mon–Dvaravati period, 7th–early 8th century. Thailand (Phetchabun Province, Si Thep) Stone; H. 55 1/8 in. Octagonal form of ViSNubhAga and the occurrence of pancamukhalinga is consistent with the tradition of *pancaloha* 'five dhAtu or five mineral alloy' images as utsavaberas.

Ekamukhalinga from JaiyA, National Museum, Bangkok. The shape is as described in Satapatha Brahmana,

quadrangular base, octagonal middle, caSAla at the top (made of wheat straw paste).

Ekamukhalinga from Vat Sak Sampou

"The JaiyA ekamukhalinga is divided into three parts in accordance with the prescriptions in the Siva Agamas. The base, BrahmabhAga, is cubic in form and is 47.8 cms. High. The middle section, the ViSNubhAga, is octagonal in shape and is approximately 43 cm. High. The topmost section, the RudrabhAga, is cylindrical and is approximately 51 cms high, while the superimposed face measures 29.5 cms from the bottom of the chin to the top of the jaTA. The two lower sections

of the linga would not normally be visible, since they would be enclosed in the pedestal (pIThikA)...One of the singular features of these pre-Angkorian mukhalingas is the fusing of the jaTA with the filet on the gland of the RudrabhAga (fig.2)...There is, however, an ekamukhalinga from Vat Sak Sampou (fig. 3) which displays a coiffure which is very muh like that worn on the JaiyA linga." (O'Connor, SJ, 1961, *An ekamukhalinga from Peninsular Siam, The Journal of the Siam Society*. The Siam Society. pp. 43-49).
http://www.siameseheritage.org/jsspdf/1961/JSS_054_1e_OConnor_EkamukhalingaFromPeninsularSiam.pdf

Clay sealing

Malwa, clay sealing

Weight: 4.48 gm., Dimensions: 20x15 mm.
Railed yupa (sacrificial post) with side decorations and

a Brahmi legend below reading khadasa
Reference: Pieper collection

Thanks to Shailendra Bhandare for the correct reading. According to Bhandare the legend refers to the worship of Skanda; similar objects pertaining to the Skanda cult have been reported from regions of Malwa, Vidarbha and the Deccan.

http://coinindia.com/galleries-eran2.html

The coin hieroglyphs signify iron ore smelting in a mint.

Pa. kandi (pl. -l) necklace, beads. Ga. (P.) kandi (pl. -l) bead, (pl.) necklace; (S.2) kandiṭ bead. (DEDR 1215) Rebus: Tu. kandůka, kandaka ditch, trench. Te. kandakamu id. Koṇḍa kanda trench made as a fireplace during weddings. Pe. kandafire trench. Kui kanda small trench for fireplace. Malt. kandri a pit. (DEDR 1214)

Dotted circle is a cross-section of a strand of rope: S. *dhāī* f. ' wisp of fibres added from time to time to a rope that is being twisted ', L. *dhāī̃* f. Rebus: dhā́tu n. 'substance ' RV., m. ' element ' MBh., ' metal, mineral, ore (esp. of a red colour)'; *dhāū*, ***dhāv*** m.f. ' a partic. soft red stone '(Marathi) धवड (p. 436) [dhavaḍa] *m* (Or **धावड**) A class or an individual of it. They are smelters of iron (Marathi) gaNDa 'four' *(DEDR 1215)* Rebus: kanda 'fire-altar'. Thus, the Ujjain hieroglyph of four joined dotted circles signifies a fire-altar for mineral ore. poLa 'zebu' Rebus: poLa 'magnetite ore' sangaDa 'lathe, portabe furnace' Rebus: sanghAta 'adamantine glue', sangara 'proclamation'; mēḍhā *m* A stake, esp. as forked. Rebus: mẽṛhẽt, meḍ 'iron' (Munda.Ho.) med 'copper' (Slavic languages)

- File:ചിതിയുടെയും-ഉപകരണങ്ങളുടെയും മാതൃക.jpg
- Uploaded by Sreejithk2000
- Created: 11 April 2011

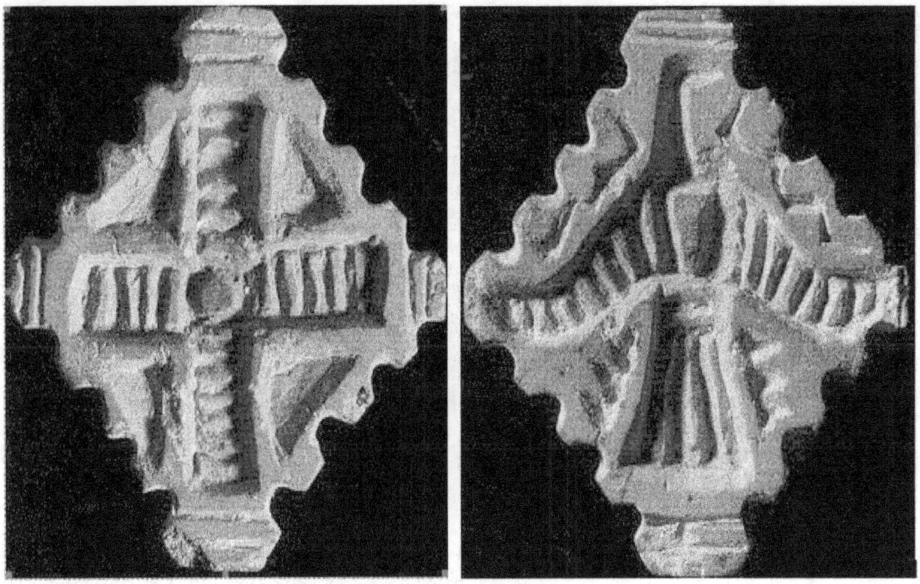

Syenaciti. Fire-altar. **sēṇa 'eagle'** rebus: sena 'thunderbolt' (weapon)

Procedure fo vājapeya soma yaga

SBr. 5.1.2.12-18

12. He then touches the wheat (top-piece)[8], with,
[Page 33] 'We have gone to the light, O ye gods!' for he who offers the Vājapeya, indeed goes to the light.
13. And as to why he touches the wheat: wheat is food, and he who offers the Vājapeya, wins food, for vāja-peya is the same as anna-peya (food and drink): thus whatever food he has thereby won, therewith now that he has gone to that supreme goal, he puts himself in contact, and possesses himself of it,--therefore he touches the wheat (top-piece).

14. He then rises by (the measure of) his head over the post, with, 'We have become immortal!' whereby he wins the world of the gods.
15. Thereupon, while looking in the different directions, he mutters (Vāj. S. IX, 22), 'Ours be your power, ours your manhood and intelligence ours be your energies!' For he who offers the Vājapeya wins everything here, winning as he does Prajāpati, and Prajāpati being everything here;--having appropriated to himself the glory, the power, and the strength of this All, he now lays them within himself, makes them his own: that is why he mutters, while looking in the different directions.
16. They throw up to him bags of salt; for salt means cattle, and cattle is food; and he who offers theVājapeya wins food, for vāja-peya is the same as anna-peya: thus whatever food he thereby has gained, therewith now that he has gone to the supreme goal, he puts himself in contact, and makes it his own,--therefore they throw bags of salt up to him.
17. They (the pieces of salt) are done up in aśvattha [Page 34] (ficus religiosa) leaves: because Indra on that (former) occasion called upon the Maruts staying on the Aśvattha tree[9], therefore they are done up in aśvattha leaves. Peasants (viś) throw them up to him, for the Maruts are the peasants, and the peasants are food (for the nobleman): hence peasants throw them up. There are seventeen (bags), for Prajāpati is seventeenfold: he thus wins Prajāpati.
18. Thereupon; while looking down upon this (earth), he mutters, Homage be to the mother Earth! homage be to the mother Earth!' For when Bṛhaspati had been consecrated, the Earth was afraid of him, thinking, 'Something great surely has he become now that he has been consecrated: I fear lest he may rend me asunder[10]!' And Bṛhaspati also was afraid of the Earth, thinking, 'I fear lest she may shake me off!' Hence by that (formula) he entered into a friendly relation with her; for a mother does not hurt her son, nor does a son hurt his mother.
http://www.wisdomlib.org/hinduism/book/the-%C5%9Batapatha-br%C4%81hma%E1%B9%87a-part-iii/d/doc63270.html#note-t-36191

Binjor attests Vedic River Sarasvati as a Himalayan navigable channel en route to Persian Gulf

The fire altar, mahavedi for vajapaya shows an octagonal brick as detailed in the Satapatha Brahmana for Vajapeya and other Soma yaga.

चषालः *caṣāla* on *Yupa*, an Indus Script hieroglyph like a crucible to carburize ores into steel, hard alloys

चषालः caṣāla on Yupa, made of wheat straw, an Indus Script hieroglyph, signifies pyrolysis/carburization in smelting ores into steel/hard alloys

Yupa is a kunda, a pillar of bricks. This kunda signifies a fire-alter or agnikunda in Vedic tradition. A signifier of the pillar is a चषालः caṣāla as its top piece. This चषालः caṣāla (Rigveda) is made of wheat straw for pyrolysis to convert firewood into coke to react with ore to create hard alloys, e.g. iron reacting with coke to create crucible steel or carburization of wrought iron in a crucible to produce steel. See: https://en.wikipedia.org/wiki/Crucible_steel

The sacredness associated with चषालः caṣāla is demonstrated by the architectural splendour of ancient varaha sculptures in the Hindu tradition. On the varaha monolith in Khajuraho, the चषालः caṣāla is signified by Devi Sarasvati. On many other sculptures of varaha, the चषालः caṣāla is associated with Mother Earth भूदेवी *bhudevi.* A gallery of varaha sculptural splendour is embedded together with explanatory notes on the dcipherment of metal work catalog in a Rakhigarhi seal with a rhinoceros decorated with a scarf (dhatu 'scarf' rebus: dhatu 'ore').

The Indus Script hieroglyphic hypertexts get expanded into metaphors during the historical periods narrating Varaha as the third Avatara of Vishnu. In archaeometallurgical parlance, the चषालः caṣāla is the core pyrolysis process to create crucible steel and/or hard alloys in smelting processes.

See the yupa as a signifier on Kuwait gold disc with Indus Script hieroglyphs:

Hieroglyph: kunda = a pillar of bricks (Ka.); pillar, post (Tu.Te.); block, log (Malt.); kantu = pillar, post (Ta.)(DEDR 1723).

Rebus: kun.d. = a pit (Santali) kun.d.amu = a pit for receiving and preserving consecrated fire; a hole in the ground (Te.) kun.d.am, kun.d.a sacrificial fire pit (Skt.) kun.d.a an altar on which sacrifices are made (G.)[i] gun.d.amu fire-pit; (Inscr.)

caṣāla चषाल This is a Rigveda word (RV 1.162.6) which signifies the top-piece, ring on the Yūpa.

(22) **162** (म. 1, अनु. 22)

ऋषिः दीर्घतमाः औचथ्यः	छन्दः त्रिष्टुप् 1-2, 4-5, 7-22, जगती 3, 6	देवता अश्वः

मा नो मित्रो वरुणो अर्यमायुरिन्द्र ऋभुक्षा मरुतः परि ख्यन् ।
यद्वाजिनो देवजातस्य सप्तेः प्रवक्ष्यामो विदथे वीर्याणि ॥ 1 ॥
यन्निर्णिजा रेक्णसा प्रावृतस्य रातिं गृभीतां मुखतो नयन्ति ।
सुप्राङ्जो मेम्यद्विश्वरूप इन्द्रापूष्णोः प्रियमप्येति पाथः ॥ 2 ॥
एष च्छागः पुरो अश्वेन वाजिना पूष्णो भागो नीयते विश्वदेव्यः ।
अभिप्रियं यत्पुरोळाशमर्वता त्वष्टेदेनं सौश्रवसाय जिन्वति ॥ 3 ॥
यद्धविष्यमृतुशो देवयानं त्रिर्मानुषाः पर्यश्वं नयन्ति ।
अत्रा पूष्णः प्रथमो भाग एति यज्ञं देवेभ्यः प्रतिवेदयन्नजः ॥ 4 ॥
होताध्वर्युरावया अग्निमिन्धो ग्रावग्राभ उत शंस्ता सुविप्रः ।
तेन यज्ञेन स्वरंकृतेन स्विष्टेन वक्षणा आ पृणध्वम् ॥ 5 ॥
यूपव्रस्का उत ये यूपवाहाश्चषालं ये अश्वयूपाय तक्षति ।
ये चार्वते पचनं संभरन्त्युतो तेषामभिगूर्तिर्न इन्वतु ॥ 6 ॥

1.162.01 Let neither Mitra nor Varun.a, Aryaman, A_yu, Indra, R.bhuks.in,nor the Maruts, censure us; when we proclaim in the sacrifice the virtus of the swift horse sprung from the gods. [a_yu = va_yu (a_yuh satataganta_ va_yuh, vaka_ralopo va_); r.bhuks.in = Indra; but,here Praja_pati, he in whom the r.bhus,or the devas, abide (ks.iyanti); sprung from the gods: devaja-tasya = born as the type of various divinities, who are identified with different parts (e.g. us.a_ va_ as'vasya medhyasya s'irah: Br.hada_ran.yaka Upanis.ad 1.1.1); legend: the horse's origin from the sun, either direct, or through the agency of the Vasus: sura_d as'vam vasavo niratas.t.a].
1.162.02 When they, (the priests), bring the prepared offering to the presence (of the horse), who has been bathed and decorated with rich (trappings), the various-coloured goat going before him, bleating, becomes an acceptable offering to Indra and Pu_s.an. [The prepared offering: ra_tim-gr.bhi_ta_m = lit. the seized wealth; the offering to be made for the horse; pu_s.an = Agni; the goat is to be tied to the front of the horse at the sacrificial post, such a goat, black-necked, kr.s.nagri_va (a_gneyah kr.s.n.agri_vah: Taittiri_ya Sam.hita_ 5.5.22), being always regarded as an a_gneya pas'u, or victim sacred to Agni, and to be offered to him (Ka_tya_yana Su_tra 98). A black goat is also dedicated to pu_s.an, along with soma (Yajus. xxix.58; but, he is also to be attached to the na_bhi or middle of the horse (Yajus. xxiv.1)].
1.162.03 This goat, the portion of Pu+s.an fit for all the gods, is brought first with the fleet courser, to that Tvas.t.a_ may prepare him along with the horse, as an acceptable preliminary offering for the (sacrificial) food. [The portion of Pu_s.an: he is to be offered in sacrifice to

Pu_s.an or Agni; Tvas.t.a_ = sarvasyotpa_daka, the producer of all forms; tvas.t.a_ ru_pa_n.i vikaroti (Taittiri_ya Sam.hita_ 1.5.92); or, identified wiith Agni;preliminary offering purod.a_s'am = offering of cakes and butter; purasta_d-da_tavyam, that which is to be first offered].

1.162.04 When the priests at the season (of the ceremony), lead forth the horse, the offering devoted to the gods, thrice round (the sacrificial fire); then the goat, the portion of Pu_s.an, goes first, announcing the sacrificer to the gods. [The goat is to be first immolated]. 1.162.05 The invoker of the gods, the minister of the rite, the offerer of the oblation, the kindler of the fire, the bruiser of the Soma, the director of the ceremony, the saage (superintendent of the whole); do you replenish the rivers by this well-ordered, well-conducted, sacrifice. [The invoker of the gods: designations applied to eight of the sixteen priests employed at a solemn rite: the two first are: hota_ and adhvaryu; avaya_j = pratiprastha_ta_, who brings and places the offering; agnimindha = agni_dh, the kindler of the fire; gra_vagra_bha = the praiser of the stones that bruise the Soma,or he who applies the stones to that purpose; s'am.sta_ = pras'a_sta_; suvipra = Brahma_ (brahmaiko ja_te ja_te vidya_m vadatibrahma_ sarvavidyah sarva veditumarhati: Nirukta 1.8); replenish the rivers: vaks.an.a_ apr.n.adhvam, nadi_h pu_rayata, fill the rivers; the consequence of sacrifice being rain and fertility; or, it may mean, offer rivers of butter, milk, curds, and the like].

1.162.06 Whether they be those who cut the (sacrificial) post, or those who bear the post, or those who fasten the rings on the top of the post, to which the horse (is bound); or those who prepare the vessels in which the food of the horse is dressed; let the exertions of them all fulfil our expectation. [The post: twenty-one posts, of different kinds of wood, each twenty-one cubits long, are to be set up, to which the different animals are to be fastened, amounting to three hundred and forty-nine, besides two hundred and sixty wild animals, making a total of six hundred and nine (Ka_tya_yana); the text seems to refer to a single post: cas.a_lam ye as'vayu_pa_ya taks.ati: cas.a_la = a wooden ring, or bracelet, on the top of the sacrificial post; or, it was perhaps a metal ring at the foot of the post].

Satapatha Brāhmana describes this as made of wheaten dough (gaudhūma).

गौधूम [p= 369,3] *mf*(ई *g.* बिल्वा*दि)*n.* made of wheat MaitrS. i Hcat. i , 7 (*f*(आ).) made of wheat straw S3Br. v , 2 , 1 , 6 Ka1tyS3r. xiv , 1 , 22 and 5 , 7.
http://www.sanskritdictionary.com/agnir/961/6#sthash.aDu8onbZ.dpuf

"Pyrolysis has been used since ancient times for turning wood into charcoal on an industrial scale...Pyrolysis is used on a massive scale to turn coal into coke for metallurgy, especially steelmaking."
https://en.wikipedia.org/wiki/Pyrolysis In archaeometallurgical terms, the use of wheat straw to prepare the चषाल: caṣāla fixed atop a Yupa may relate to such pyrolysis process to convert charcoal used in the fire-altar (furnace) into charcoal/coke to react with the dhAtu in the earth subjected to smelting/melting process (e.g. iron reacting with coke in a crucible to be transmuted as steel).

చషాలము [caṣālamu] *chashālamu*. [Skt.] n. A chalice, or cup used in sacrifice. A ring attached to the sacrificial post in a horse sacrifice. రాజ మాయము నందు యూపస్తంభమునకు అడుగున తగిలించే కడియము.خلي *tsalaey*, s.m. (1st) A **ring** for the finger. 2. A pillar of mud or stones as a mark for land. 3. A butt or mark for arrows. 4. A mound or platform for watching a field. 5. A temporary building or shed. Pl. ي *ī*. See منا (Pashto)

चषाल [p= 391,2]*mn.* (g. अर्धर्चा*दि) a wooden ring on the top of a sacrificial post RV. i , 162 , 6 TS. vi Ka1t2h.xxvi , 4 (चशाल) S3Br. &c चषालः caṣālḥचषालः 1 A wooden ring on the top of a sacrificial post; **चषालं** ये अश्वयूपाय तक्षति Rv.1.162.6; चषालयूपत- च्छन्नो हिरण्यरशनं विभुः Bhāg.4.19.19.-2 An iron ring at the base of the post.-3 A hive.

In lokokti, the yupa is associated with potaraju. The word pota signifies casting or smelting of metal.

పోతురాజు or **పోతరాజు** *pōtu-rāḍsu*. n. The name of a rustic god, like Pan, worshipped throughout the Telugu, Canarese and Mahratta countries. He represents the male principle associated with the village goddesses Gangamma, Peddamma, &c. A proverb says పాడుఊరికి మంచపుకోడుపోతురాజు in a ruined village the leg of a cot is a god. cf., 'a Triton of the minnows' (Shakespeare.) పోత [pōta] *pōta*. [Tel. from పోయు.] n. Pouring, పోయుట. Casting, as of melted metal. Bathing, washing. Eruption of the small pox. ఆకుపోత putting plants into the ground. పెట్టుపోతలు శాశ్వతములుకావు meat and drink (literally, feeding and bathing) are not matters of eternal consequence. **పోత** *pōta*. adj. Molten, cast in metal. పోతచెంబు a metal bottle or jug, which has been cast not hammered.

పోతము [pōtamu] *pōtamu*. [Skt.] n. A vessel, boat, ship. ఓడ. The young of any animal. పిల్ల. శిశువు. An elephant ten years old, పదేండ్ల యేనుగు. A cloth,వస్త్రము. శుకపోతము a young parrot. వాతపోతము a young breeze, i.e., a light wind. **పోతపాత్రిక** *pōta-pātrika*. n. A vessel, a ship, ఓడ. "సంసార సాగరమతుల ధైర్యపోత పాత్రికనిస్తరింపుముకు మార." M. XII. vi. 222. **పోతవణిక్కు** or **పోతవణిజుడు** *pōta-vaṇikku*. n. A sea-faring merchant. ఓడను కేవుకు పుచ్చుకొన్నవాడు, ఓడ బేరగాడు. **పోతవహుడు** or **పోతనాహుడు** *pōta-vahuḍu*. n. A rower, a boatman, a steersman. ఓడనడుపువాడు, తండేలు.

"Lord Vishnu appeared in the form of a Boar in order to defeat Hiranyaksha, a demon who had taken the Earth (Prithvi) and carried it to the bottom of what is described as the cosmic ocean in the story. The battle between Varaha and Hiranyaksha is believed to have lasted for a thousand years, which the former finally won. Varaha carried the Earth out of the ocean between his tusks and restored it to its place in the universe. Vishnu married Prithvi (Bhudevi) in this avatar.The Varaha Purana is a Purana in which the form of narration is a recitation by Varaha." https://en.wikipedia.org/wiki/Varaha_Temple,_Khajuraho

वराह [p= 923,2]*m.* (derivation doubtful) a boar , hog , pig , wild boar RV. &c (ifc. it denotes , " superiority , pre-eminence " ; » g.व्याघ्रा*दि)N. of विष्णु in his third or boar-incarnation (cf. वराहा*वतार) TA1r. MBh. &c

वराह an array of troops in the form of a boar Mn. vii , 187 வராகம்² varākam, *n.* < *varāka*. Battle; போர். (யாழ். அக.)

கட்டிவராகன் kaṭṭi-**varākaṉ**, *n.* < கெட்டி +. A gold coin, the *varākaṉ*. கட்டிலோ மெத் தையோ கட்டிவராகனோ. (குற்றா. குற.).கருக்குவராகன் karukku-**varākaṉ**, *n.* < id. +. New pagoda coin on which the figures are well defined; புதுநாணயம்.

(W.)தங்கவராகன் taṅka-**varākaṉ**, *n.* < தங்கம் +. Pagoda, a gold coin = 3½ rupees; 3½ ரூபாய் பெறுமான வராகன் என்னும் நாணயம்.வராகன்[1] **varākaṉ**, *n.* < *Varāha.* 1. Viṣṇu, in His boar-incarnation; வராகரூபியான திருமால். (பிங்.) 2. Pagoda, a gold coin = 3½ rupees, as bearing the image of a boar; மூன்றரை ரூபாய் மதிப்**புள்ளதும்** பன்றிமுத்திரை கொண்டதுமான ஒரு வகைப் பொன்நாணயம். (அரு. நி.)

The Varaha shrine, built on a lofty plinth, is essentially similar in design to the Lalguan Mahadeva Temple, but is simpler and more modest. It is an oblong pavilion with a pyramidal roof of receding tiers, resting on fourteen plain pillars and enshrines a colossal monolithic (2.6 m long and 1.7 high) image of Yajna Varaha (incarnation of Vishnu) which is exquisitely finished to a glossy luster and is carved all over with multiple figures of gods and goddesses. The flat ceiling of the shrine is carved with a lotus flower of exquisite design in relief. The shrine built entirely of sandstone is assignable to circa 900-925.
http://asibhopal.nic.in/monument/chhatarpur_khajuraho_varahatemple.html#

Metaphors of ancient data mining for knowledge systems

Sarasvati with veena in her hands is shown on the चषाल 'snout (of boar).'

Devi Sarasvati: in Hindu civilization. Sarasvati on the lip (snout) of a Varaha monolithic sculpture.

Why is Sarasvati shown on the upper lip (snout) of Varaha? Varaha is the 3rd avatar of Vishnu, rescuing the earth and the Vedas from the pralayam. Sarasvati on the lip of Varaha is a metaphor for Vaak and Vedas (Knowledge).

Varaha is Veda purusha, the avatar who ensured the continued prevalence of the Knowledge embodied in the Vedas. It is a stellar example of ancient data mining for knowledge systems. चषाल as annam explains the hardening of soft metal (iron) into hard metal (steel?) by pyrolysis/carburization. The metaphor explains the ancient archaeometallurgical process of the Bronze Age.

The last image is the high water-mark of the knowledge system realized. The sculptural detail shows a kalas'a a signifier of nidhi. With the Soma Yaga hurling the चषाल caṣāla (snout of boar) rebus: 'thunderbolt, Vajra', rebus: annam (wheat chaff) on the top rung of Yupa, अमृत -इष्टका, octagonal brick, nidhi is realized; it is a metaphor for immortality with hardened iron (metal) with utilitarian and exchange value to create wealth.

In a creation myth, Vishnu took the form of a boar to rescue Bhuvedi, the Earth goddess from the depths of the primordial waters. In this sculpture, Bhudevi stands to the right of the boar's head, while a serpent-goddess (nagini) appears in front. Rows of sages, deities and other figures appear on the body of the cosmic boar. The prominent conch shell, discus and mace below are all symbols of Vishnu.

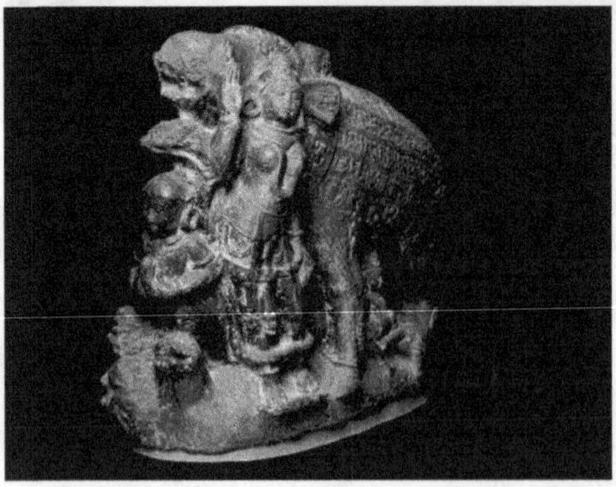

http://jameelcentre.ashmolean.org/object/EA1969.43

Stone carving. **Associated place**

Bihar (possible place of creation) north Madhya Pradesh (possible place of creation) **Date** 2nd half of the 9th century - 1st half of the 10th century CE **Material and technique** dark-brownish-grey stone **Dimensions** 64.8 x 87.5 x 28 cm max. (height x width x depth)

Data mining of metaphors and hieroglyphs to unravel ancient knowledge systems

Varaha is a metaphor signifying a Vedic yajna and pralaya (dissolution).

In the Vedic tradition, a boar anthropomorphic form signifies Rigvedamurti.

The choice of this metaphor is governed by the word चषाल *mn.* which signifies *n.* the snout of a hog MaitrS. i , 6 , 3, as the snout which lifts up the earth, dhAtu, to transmute into hardened alloy metal.

Thus the 'snout of the boar' renders चषाल atop a Yupa of yajna kunda which signifies (g. अर्धर्चा*दि) a wooden ring on the top of a sacrificial post RV. i , 162 , 6 TS. vi Kath. xxvi , 4 (चशाल) SBr. &c. This metaphor is layered by another meaning assigned as annam in Satapatha Brahmana composed of Go-dhuma गो--धूम *m.* (√गुध् Un2.) " earth-smoke " wheat (generally pl.) VS. TBr. i SBr.v (sg.) , xii , xiv SankhSr. Mn. &c. The use of wheat chaff is explained in metallurgical processes (pyrolysis and carburization) related to the infusion of carbon into soft iron to create hardened steel or metal for swords or weapons or hard metal implements. The metaphor of a 'serpent' nAga associated with these processes is related to the oxidation of lead from composite minerals in a process of cementation. Another metaphor relates to the shape of चषाल fixed like a ring atop an octagonal अष्टाश्रि 'with eight angles' yupa: the shape is like an octagonal hour-glass or Damaru drum shaped sheaf of wheat chaff which is also referred to as Vajra, 'thunderbolt' of Indra or Rudra. Thus layers of rebus renderings of hieroglyph-multiplexes constitute the rendering of a knowledge system related to the metallurgical processes in a smelter-furnace which is the yajna kunda for transmuting mere earth and stones (signified by Bhudevi) into metal products with exchange and utilitarian value, the process of creation of wealth arising out of an intense immersion in fire comparable to pralayam (dissolution caused by the hurling of the thunderbolt weapon or sudars'ana cakra or pavi) as a metaphor for purification of metals and transmutation of base resources into value or wealth, nidhi.

Thus, Varaha is a metaphor of Vedic Yajna; the processes involved are explained as the intermediation of divinities depicted on Varaha's body resulting in the production of carburized, hard alloys of metal. Hence, the depiction of a metal sword in front of a Varaha and depiction of warriors carrying swords, the ayudha purusha.

Apart from the metallurgical layer of explaining th metaphors and hieroglyphs, a number of ancient texts unravel the cosmic and spiritual significance of the processes of yajna or, in particular, Soma Yaga. These statements are integral parts of ancient cultural foundations which constituted the knowledge systems which unravel the wonders of divine interventions in transmutation processes which also extend to transformations for nihs'reyas, from Being to Becoming.

In this framework of knowledge systems, the iconographic renderings become self-explanatory renderings of transmutation: veda iyal (Tamil) or rasa-vAda, 'alchemy' with the hurling of the Vajra, 'thunderbolt' of Indra.

Armourer's work, mintwork, metalwork to produce metal implements, tools, weapons, coinage, pots and pans

Warriors. Hoysala. 11th cent. Karnataka.

Relief showing Varaha in front of a standing dagger.16th cent. Vijayanagar style temple.

Unaimancheri Rama temple, Kanchipuram.

Royal emblem of Chalukyas; Varaha, Shankha, Chakra and a mirror Durga Gudi complex. 5th cent. CE. Karnataka. Where Pulakeshin had performed As'vamedha Yaga.

Coin with Varaha (Vishnu Avatar) on a Gurjara-Pratihara coin 850-900 CE,British Museum.

Varaha. Sandstone. 10th century. Madhya Pradesh. **चषाल** as ring, Sudars'ana cakra.

Photographic prints at the Kern Institute Leiden

Excerpts from observations by GERDA THEUNS-DE BOER:

Nrvarah from Garhwa. ASI, 1909-1910 Silver gelatine developing out paper

Varaha: The Indian boar

Varaha from Badoh. ASI 1908-1909

Varaha The first photograph shows the Varaha from Badoh (Pratihara period, ninth century) kept in the Archaeological Museum, Gwalior. Varaha can be seen to lift the earth, which is personified as the goddess Bhu (meaning earth), with his right tusk. In front of Varaha are three small damaged figures: Garuda (Visnu's mount), a *naga* (a snake or water spirit) and a fly-whisk bearer. Between Varaha's legs we see the coils of Ananta Sesa (the endless serpent), the primeval serpent. Varaha's body is covered with 765 figures displayed in horizontal bands and three circles (vertebral column). These figures have puzzled researchers for a long time, both in concept and in serial and individual identification. Varaha is related to the concept of *yajna*. In order to visualize '*yajna*', specific components of *yajna* were personified and depicted chiefly on Varaha's head and limbs.

The second photograph depicts the lesser known Varaha from Muradpur, a small village on the borders of Madhya Pradesh. This Varaha, with an estimated height of 2.50 m, is worshipped even today.

Nrvaraha from Garhwa. ASI, 1909-1910. Silver gelatine developing out paper.

References:

Nagar, Shanti Lal, *Varaha in Indian Art, Culture and Literature*, New Delhi (1993).

Rangarajan, Haripriya, 'Varaha Images in Madhya Pradesh, Symbolism and Iconography', in: *Journal of the Asiatic Society of Bombay*, Mumbai (1997), pp. 100-119, Vol. 72.

http://www.iias.nl/iiasn/26/regions/26SA1.htm

Adivarahar Perumal temple. Kumbakonam. Utsava Beram.

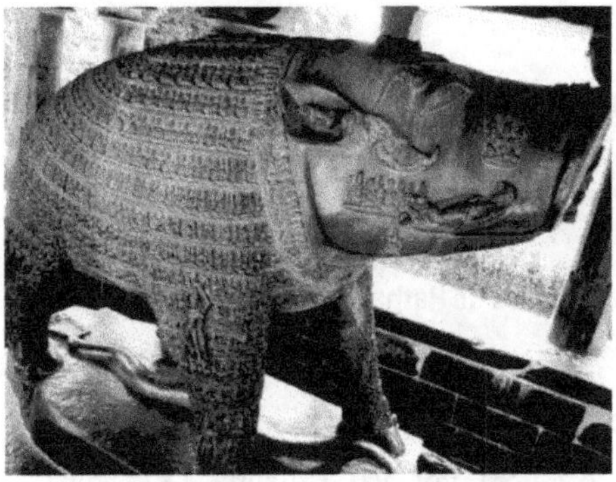

Built on lofty plinth, the Varaha shrine rests on fourteen plain pillars which houses a Yajna Varaha (incarnation of Vishnu) idol. All over the idol multiple figures of divinitie are carved. It faces the Lakshamana temple. It's said that this temple was built by Yashovarman. The serpent Sheshnag is at the pedestal. Chandela. Khajuraho.

Bhudevi. Varaha.

Close view of sculptures (Varaha, Sculpures of Varaha, Kurma and Kalki-avatara) in the pillared hall, Pathari, Bhopal State

Photograph of sculptures at Pathari, taken by Joseph David Beglar in 1871-72 and described in his 'Report of a tour in Bundelkhand and Malwa, 1871-72; and in the Central Provinces, 1873-74' (A.S.I. vol. VII, Calcutta, 1878), pp. 76-77, 'Close to the embankment and north-east of the great temple stands a group of ruins of several temples and pillared halls; the principal one appears to have consisted of a court-yard surrounded on three sides by pillared halls with an entrance on the west flanked by two small temples...The statues inside are numerous; there are, in fact, all the ten avatars of Vishnu except the fish; the tortoise incarnation is remarkable..."

Kurma (Vishnu as tortoise) is at the right (negative damaged in this portion of print), Varaha (Vishnu as boar) on the left, Kalki (future incarnation of Vishnu, on horseback) is at the centre of the photograph.

http://www.bl.uk/onlinegallery/onlineex/apac/photocoll/c/019pho000001003u01330000.html

Varaha. Udayagiri caves. Madhya Pradesh. Gupta period.

Varaha tramples the fallen daitya, Hiranyaksha (golden-eyed RV. Tar.) with Bhudevi on his shoulder, Hoysaleswara Temple.

Varaha Mahakuta, Deccan 7th C

Bhuvaraha. Srimushnam temple. 40 kms. from Chidambaram.

Varaha stands on a tortoise pedestal and has four hands. Two hands holds conch and wheel. Goddess earth sits on the left elbow of the lord Varaha. The right leg is bent and rests upon the jeweled hood of the serpent Adisesha. Vidyadhara on the holds garlands. Odisha State Museum. GM-OSM-75286

Varaha. Durga Temple, Aihole Vishnu's boar avatar lifts Bhu Devi on the crook of his arm, while suppressing the nagas (snakes) with his foot.

Badami #5 - Cave Temple 2 (c. late 6th century)

Varaha Temple (Tiruvadantai)

Nuapatna - Laxmi Nrusingha Temple - Parsvadevata Varaha

Chola period. Bronze. Varaha. Ca. 1300 CE

Varaha holding Bhudevi, 7th century CE,Mahabalipuram.

Varaha stands on Nagas, rises from the waters with the earth (Bhudevi) on his elbow, National Museum, New Delhi.

Bhubaneswar - Odisha State Museum - Vajrapani Avalokiteshvara

Vajrapāni (Sanskrit: "Vajra in [his] hand") is one of the earliest-appearing bodhisattvas in Mahayana Bauddham.

In Japan, Vajrapāni is known as "the head vajra-wielding god" (執金剛神 Shukongōshin?).

According to the scripture [Lotus Sutra], this deity (Narayana) is a manifestation of Avalokitesvara (Guanyin)
The Lotus Sutra passage reads: “To those who can be conveyed to deliverance by the body of the spirit who grasps the vajra (Vajrapāni) he preaches Dharma by displaying the body of the spirit who grasps the vajra.”

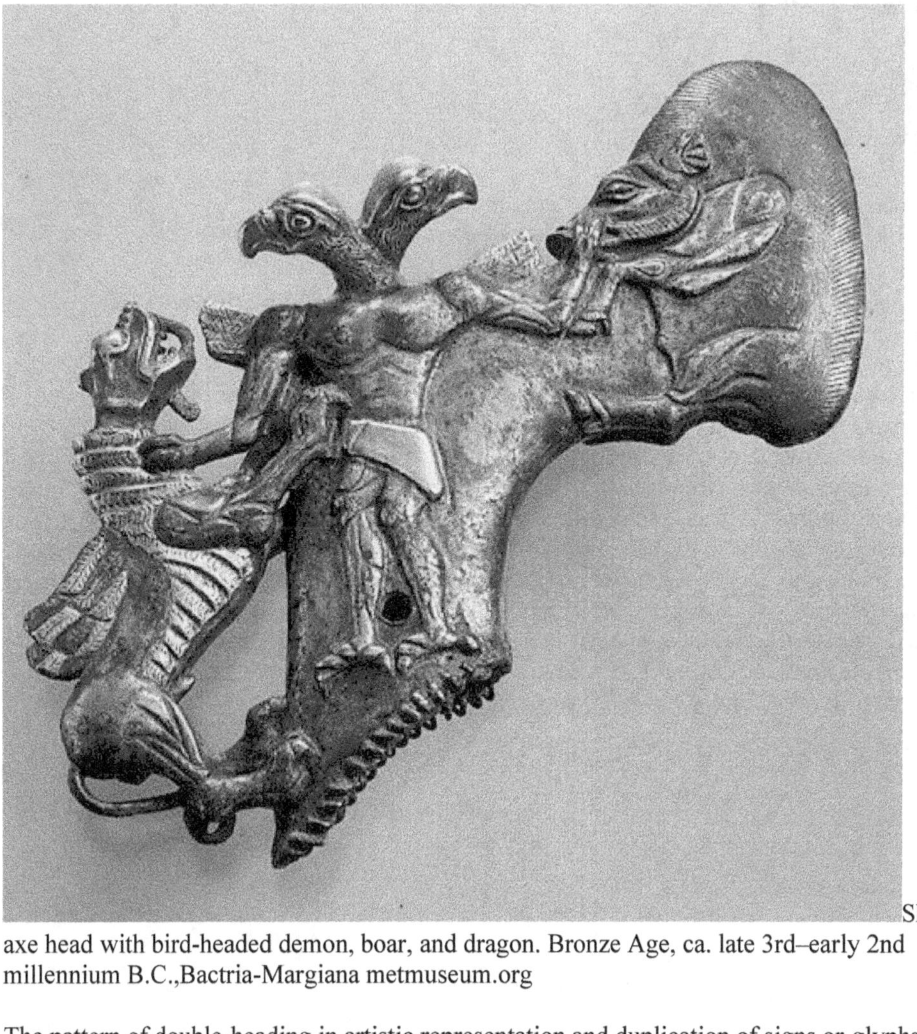

Shaft-hole axe head with bird-headed demon, boar, and dragon. Bronze Age, ca. late 3rd–early 2nd millennium B.C.,Bactria-Margiana metmuseum.org

The pattern of double-heading in artistic representation and duplication of signs or glyphs (e.g. two bulls facing each other) in an inscription have been explained in decoded Indus script as connoting dula 'pair'; rebus: dul 'casting (metal)'. If the eagle is read rebus using a lexems of Indian linguistic area to connote pajhar 'eagle' (rebus: pasra 'smithy'), the double-headed eagle can be read as: dul pajhar = metal casting smithy. The body of a person ligatured to the double-headed eagle can denote the smith whose metalworking trade is related to casting of metals. S'yena 'kite' rebus: ***sena***, *heṇa* ' thunderbolt ' (Sinhala) dula 'two' rebus: dul 'cast metal'. Kola 'tiger' rebus: kol 'working in iron' kambhaTa 'wing' rebus: kammaTa 'mint' varAha 'boar' rebus: 'gold coin'

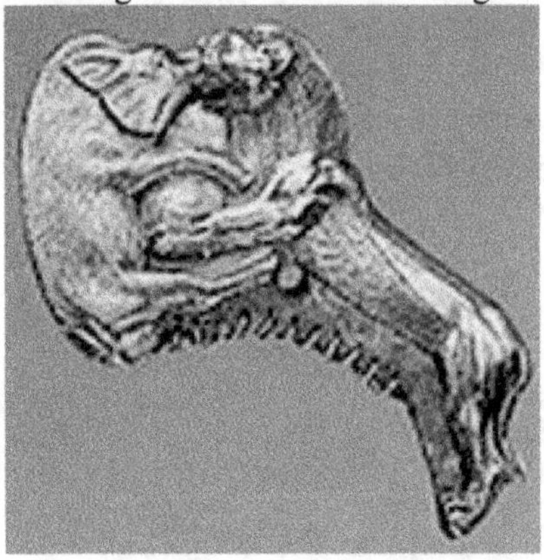

Gold sheet and silver, Late 3rd/early 2nd millennium B.C.E.

L. 12.68 cm. Ceremonial Axe Baktria,Northern Afghanistan http://www.lessingimages.com/search.asp?a=L&lc=202020207EE6&ln=Collection+George+Ortiz%2C+Geneva%2C+Switzerland&p=1 "The whole cast by the lost wax process. The boar covered with a sheet of gold annealed and hammered on, some 3/10-6/10 mm in thickness, almost all the joins covered up with silver. At the base of the mane between the shoulders an oval motif with irregular indents. The lion and the boar hammered, elaborately chased and polished. A shaft opening - 22 holes around its edge laced with gold wire some 7/10-8/10 mm in diameter - centred under the lion's shoulder; between these a hole (diam: some 6.5 mm) front and back for insertion of a dowel to hold the shaft in place, both now missing.
Condition: a flattening blow to the boar's backside where the tail curled out and another to the hair between the front of his ears, his spine worn with traces of slight hatching still visible, a slight flattening and wear to his left tusk and lower left hind leg. A flattening and wear to the left side of the lion's face, ear, cheek, eye, nose and jaw and a flattening blow to the whole right forepaw and paw. Nicks to the lion's tail. The surface with traces of silver chloride under the lion's stomach and around the shaft opening." https://www.flickr.com/photos/antiquitiesproject/4616778973

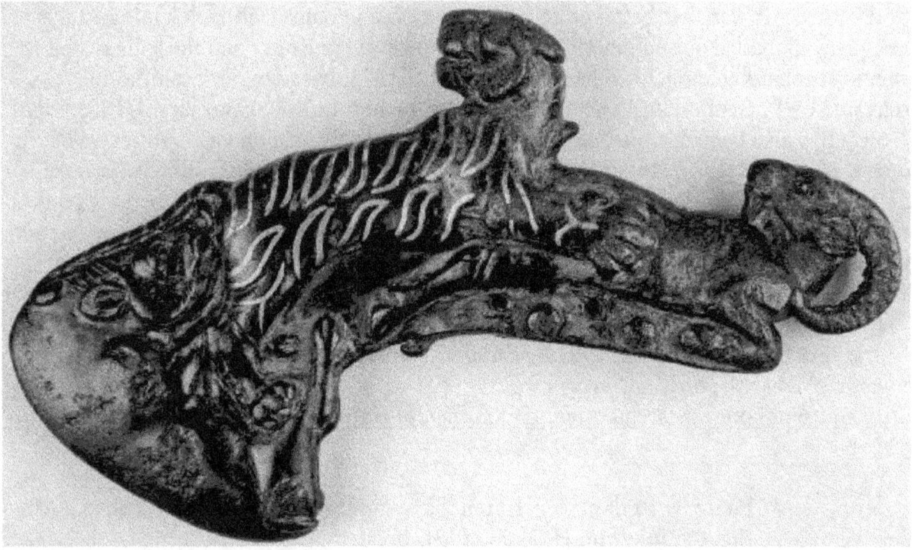

Cast axe-head; tin bronze inlaid with silver; shows a boar attacking a tiger which is attacking an ibex.ca. 2500 -2000 BCE Bactria-Margiana Archaeological Complex. Length: 17.8 cm (7 in). Weight: 675.5 g (23.82 oz). British Museum.ME 123268 (1913,0314.11913,0314.1) R. Maxwell-Hyslop, 'British Museum "axe" no. 123628: a Bactrian bronze', *Bulletin of the Asia Institute*, NS I (1987), pp. 17-26 *miṇḍā'l* ' **markhor** '(Tor)(CDIAL 10310) rebus: meD 'iron' Curator's comments: See RL file 6616 (29/6/1995); also Research Lab file 4992 of 12/09/1983 where XRF analysis of surface indicates composition as tin bronze with approx 10% tin and traces of arsenic, nickel, silver and lead. Dalton's inclusion in the 'Catalog of the Oxus Treasure' among a small group of comparative items has unfortunately led to recurrent confusion over the date and

provenance of this piece. It was first believed to be Achaemenid in date (Dalton, 'Catalog of the Oxus Treasure', p. 48), labelled as such in 1975 in the former Iranian Room and thus suggested to be an Achaemenid scabbard chape (P R S Moorey CORRES 1975, based on an example said to have been excavated by P. Bernard at Ai Khanoum or seen by him in Kabul Bazaar, cf. P. Bernard CORRES 1976). It has also been assigned a 4th-5th century AD Sasanian date (P. Amiet, 1967, in 'Revue du Louvre' 17, pp. 281-82). However, its considerably earlier - late 3rd mill. BC Bronze Age - date has now been clearly demonstrated following the discovery of large numbers of objects of related form in south-east Iran and Bactria, and it has since been recognised and/or cited as such, for instance by H. Pittmann (hence archaeometallurgical analysis in 1983; R. Maxwell-Hyslop, 1988a, "British Museum axe no. 123628: a Bactrian bronze", 'Bulletin of the Asia Institute' 1 (NS), pp. 17-26; F. Hiebert & C.C. Lamberg-Karlovsky 1992a, "Central Asia and the Indo-Iranian Borderlands",' Iran' 30, p. 5; B. Brentjes, 1991a, "Ein tierkampfszene in bronze", 'Archäologische Mitteilungen aus Iran' 24 (NS), p. 1, taf. 1).
http://www.britishmuseum.org/research/collection_online/collection_object_details.aspx?objectId=367862&partId=1

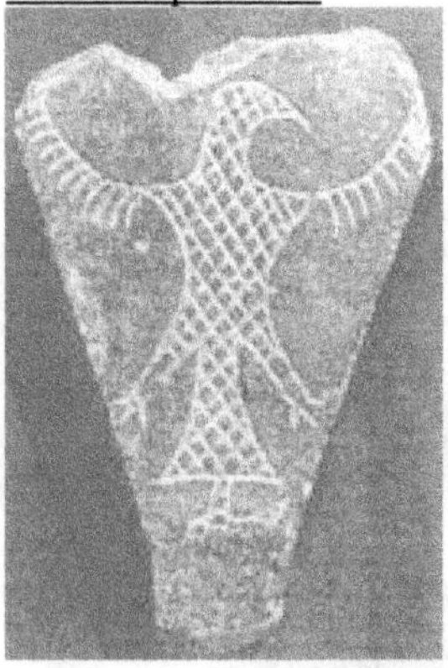

Eagle incised on a ceremonial axe made of chlorite. Tepe Yahya. (After Fig. 9.6 in Philip H. Kohl, 2001, opcit.)

चषालः caṣāla, 'snout of boar' as hieroglyph/metaphor of wheat chaff as annam as a ring, a cakra, a vajra on Yupa for Soma Yaga (e.g. Vajapeya), a metaphor of knowledge system, Sarasvati, vāk

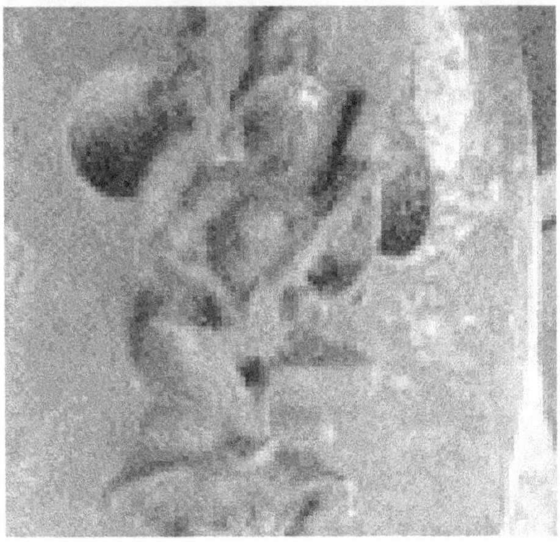

Zoom: Sarasvati depicted on the upper lip (snout) of Varaha.

Varaha temple. Khajuraho.

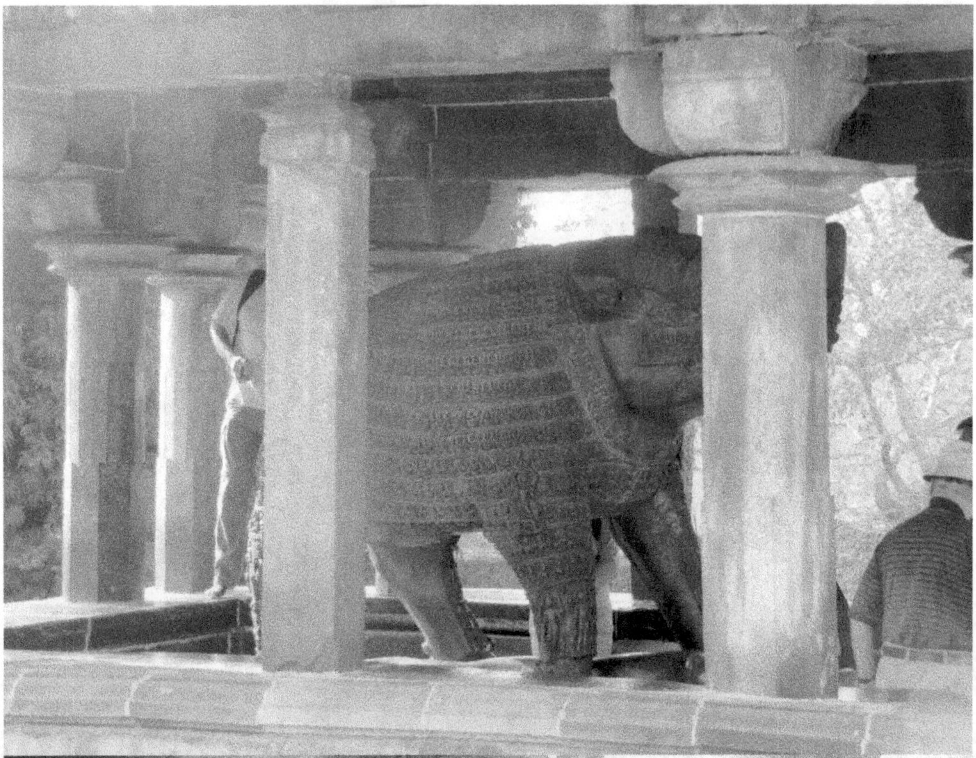

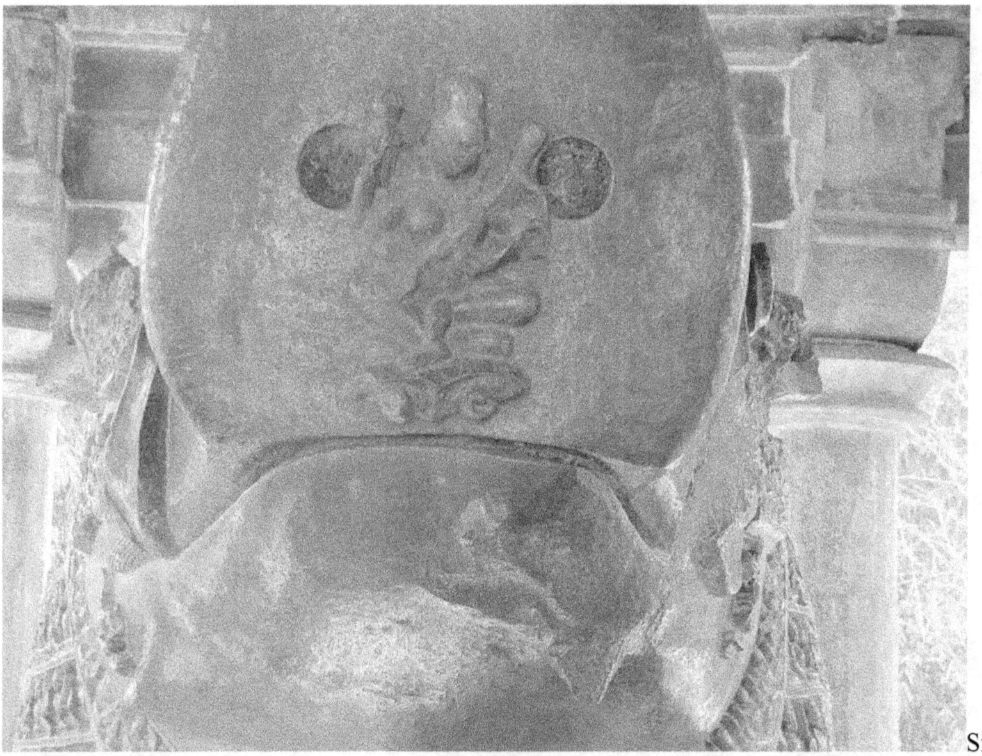

Site Name: Khajuraho
Monument: Varaha Mandir
<u>Subject of Photo: Varaha</u>
Locator Info. of Photo: SE of Laksmana temple courtyard
Photo Orientation: overview from SW looking NE
Iconography: Varaha
Dynasty/Period: Candella
Date: ca. latter half of the tenth century CE, 950 CE - 1000 CE
Material: stone
Architecture: structural

Zoom into Sarasvati image on the upper lip (snout) of Varaha

Along with various divinities, shown on the body of Viṣṇu's Varāhāvatara, third among incarnations, Sarasvatī figures appropriately on the mouth of Varāha Boar's monolithic image at Khajurāho (10th cent.)

Contemplating on pan-Indian tendencies of making images of Sarasvatī in the Hindu, Buddhist and Jaina pantheons, Catherine Ludvik, with her extensive researches on the theme[*], suggests two possibilities of Sarasvatī's feminine form : 1. the Mahābhārata narrative details, 2. Or, the other way around 'the female figure of Sarasvatī in the epic (Mahābhārata) might conceivably have been inspired from already existing, but no longer extant or known to be extant, representations of her' [Ludvik 107]. Thus the origin of Sarasvatī's iconographic conceptualization goes back to the third century bce. From then on gradually her human-like representations developed in the three different religions of the Hindu, Buddhist and Jain.
Vedābnāṁ mātaraṁ paśya matsthāṁ.

'Behold goddess Sarasvatī, the mother of Vedas enshrined in me' says Nārāyaṇa to Nārada [Vyasa's Mahābhārata, 12 : 326 : 5.]

Sarasvatīha vāgbhūtā śarīram te pravekṣyati Sarasvatī enters the body as speech - [supra 12 : 306 : 6.]

jihvāyām vāk Sarasvatī Sarasvatī dwells in the tongue [- ibid 12 : 231 : 8.].

devī jihvā sarasvatī 'goddess Sarasvatī is (your) tongue' says Bhīṣma, in veneration of Viṣṇu - [supra 6 : 61 : 56.].

parama jinendra-vāṇiye Sarasvatī the supreme Lord Jina's preaching is Sarasvatī - [Pampa, Ādipurāṇa, 1-16.].

The Mahābhārata has referred to Sarasvatī as vāc [12 : 306 : 6] and vaṇī [3 : 132 : 2]. Besides, her beautiful form and lovely celestial body is lauded [3 : 184 : 18].
rūpaṁ ca te divyam atyanta kāntam

http://www.herenow4u.net/index.php?id=68838

Srimad Bhagavatam Canto 3 Chapter 18

Canto 3: The Status Quo Chapter 18: The Battle Between Lord Boar and the Demon Hiranyaksha
Bhaktivedanta VedaBase: Srimad Bhagavatam

SB 3.18.1: Maitreya continued: The proud and falsely glorious Daitya paid little heed to the words of Varuna. O dear Vidura, he learned from Narada the whereabouts of the Supreme Personality of Godhead and hurriedly betook himself to the depths of the ocean.

SB 3.18.2: He saw there the all-powerful Personality of Godhead in His boar incarnation, bearing the earth upward on the ends of His tusks and robbing him of his splendor with His reddish eyes. The demon laughed: Oh, an amphibious beast!

SB 3.18.3: The demon addressed the Lord: O best of the demigods, dressed in the form of a boar, just hear me. This earth is entrusted to us, the inhabitants of the lower regions, and You cannot take it from my presence and not be hurt by me.

SB 3.18.4: You rascal, You have been nourished by our enemies to kill us, and You have killed some demons by remaining invisible. O fool, Your power is only mystic, so today I shall enliven my kinsmen by killing You.

SB 3.18.5: The demon continued: When You fall dead with Your skull smashed by the mace hurled by my arms, the demigods and sages who offer You oblations and sacrifice in devotional service will also automatically cease to exist, like trees without roots.

SB 3.18.6: Although the Lord was pained by the shaftlike abusive words of the demon, He bore the pain. But seeing that the earth on the ends of His tusks was frightened, He rose out of the water just as an elephant emerges with its female companion when assailed by an alligator.

SB 3.18.7: The demon, who had golden hair on his head and fearful tusks, gave chase to the Lord while He was rising from the water, even as an alligator would chase an elephant. Roaring like thunder, he said: Are You not ashamed of running away before a challenging adversary? There is nothing reproachable for shameless creatures!

SB 3.18.8: The Lord placed the earth within His sight on the surface of the water and transferred to her His own energy in the form of the ability to float on the water. While the enemy stood looking on, Brahma, the creator of the universe, extolled the Lord, and the other demigods rained flowers on Him.

SB 3.18.9: The demon, who had a wealth of ornaments, bangles and beautiful golden armor on his body, chased the Lord from behind with a great mace. The Lord tolerated his piercing ill words, but in order to reply to him, He expressed His terrible anger.

SB 3.18.10: The Personality of Godhead said: Indeed, We are creatures of the jungle, and We are searching after hunting dogs like you. One who is freed from the entanglement of death has no fear from the loose talk in which you are indulging, for you are bound up by the laws of death.

SB 3.18.11: Certainly We have stolen the charge of the inhabitants of Rasatala and have lost all shame. Although bitten by your powerful mace, I shall stay here in the water for some time because, having created enmity with a powerful enemy, I now have no place to go.

SB 3.18.12: You are supposed to be the commander of many foot soldiers, and now you may take prompt steps to overthrow Us. Give up all your foolish talk and wipe out the cares of your kith and kin by slaying Us. One may be proud, yet he does not deserve a seat in an assembly if he fails to fulfill his promised word.

SB 3.18.13: Sri Maitreya said: The demon, being thus challenged by the Personality of Godhead, became angry and agitated, and he trembled in anger like a challenged cobra.

SB 3.18.14: Hissing indignantly, all his senses shaken by wrath, the demon quickly sprang upon the Lord and dealt Him a blow with his powerful mace.

SB 3.18.15: The Lord, however, by moving slightly aside, dodged the violent mace-blow aimed at His breast by the enemy, just as an accomplished yogi would elude death.

SB 3.18.16: The Personality of Godhead now exhibited His anger and rushed to meet the demon, who bit his lip in rage, took up his mace again and began to repeatedly brandish it about.

SB 3.18.17: Then with His mace the Lord struck the enemy on the right of his brow, but since the demon was expert in fighting, O gentle Vidura, he protected himself by a maneuver of his own mace.

SB 3.18.18: In this way, the demon Haryaksha and the Lord, the Personality of Godhead, struck each other with their huge maces, each enraged and seeking his own victory.

SB 3.18.19: There was keen rivalry between the two combatants; both had sustained injuries on their bodies from the blows of each other's pointed maces, and each grew more and more enraged at the smell of blood on his person. In their eagerness to win, they performed maneuvers of various kinds, and their contest looked like an encounter between two forceful bulls for the sake of a cow.

SB 3.18.20: O descendant of Kuru, Brahma, the most independent demigod of the universe, accompanied by his followers, came to see the terrible fight for the sake of the world between the demon and the Personality of Godhead, who appeared in the form of a boar.

SB 3.18.21: After arriving at the place of combat, Brahma, the leader of thousands of sages and transcendentalists, saw the demon, who had attained such unprecedented power that no one could fight with him. Brahma then addressed Narayana, who was assuming the form of a boar for the first time.

SB 3.18.22-23: Lord Brahma said: My dear Lord, this demon has proved to be a constant pinprick to the demigods, the brahmanas, the cows and innocent persons who are spotless and always dependent upon worshiping Your lotus feet. He has become a source of fear by unnecessarily harassing them. Since he has attained a boon from me, he has become a demon, always searching for a proper combatant, wandering all over the universe for this infamous purpose.

SB 3.18.24: Lord Brahma continued: My dear Lord, there is no need to play with this serpentine demon, who is always very skilled in conjuring tricks and is arrogant, self-sufficient and most wicked.

SB 3.18.25: Brahma continued: My dear Lord, You are infallible. Please kill this sinful demon before the demoniac hour arrives and he presents another formidable approach favorable to him. You can kill him by Your internal potency without doubt.

SB 3.18.26: My Lord, the darkest evening, which covers the world, is fast approaching. Since You are the Soul of all souls, kindly kill him and win victory for the demigods.

SB 3.18.27: The auspicious period known as abhijit, which is most opportune for victory, commenced at midday and has all but passed; therefore, in the interest of Your friends, please dispose of this formidable foe quickly.

SB 3.18.28: This demon, luckily for us, has come of his own accord to You, his death ordained by You; therefore, exhibiting Your ways, kill him in the duel and establish the worlds in peace.

Varaha, rock carving from the early 5th century, in Udayagiri, Orissa, India. (Encyclopaedia Britannica).

On the Rakhigarhi seal, a fine distinction is made between two orthographic options for signifying an arrow with fine pronunciation variants, to distinguish between an arrowhead and an arrow: kaNDa, kANDa. The word kANDa is used by Panini in an expression ayaskANDa to denote a quantity of iron, excellent iron (Pāṇ.gaṇ) i.e., metal (iron/copper alloy). This expression ayas+ kāṇḍa अयस्--काण्ड is signified by hieroglyphs: aya 'fish' PLUS kāṇḍa, 'arrow' as shown on Kalibangan Seal 032. An allograph for this hieroglyph 'arrowhead' is gaNDa 'four' (short strokes) as seen on Mohenjo-daro seal M1118.

Rebus: ayaskāṇḍa 'a quantity of iron, excellent iron' (Pāṇ.gaṇ) aya = iron (G.); ayah, ayas = metal (Skt.)

Thus, the arrowhead is signified by the hieroglyph which distinguishes the arrowhead as a triangle attached to a reedpost or handle of tool/weapon.

As distinct from this orthographic representation of 'arrowhead' with a triangle PLUS attached linear stroke, an arrow is signified by an angle ^ (Caret; Circumflex accent; Up arrow) with a linear stroke ligatured, as in the Rakhigarhi seal. To reinforce the distinction between 'arrow' and 'arrowhead' in Indus Script orthography, a notch is added atop the tip of the circumflex accent. Both the hieroglyph-components are attested in Indian sprachbund with a variant pronunciation: khANDA. खांडा [kāṇḍā] m A jag, notch, or indentation (as upon the edge of a tool or weapon) (Marathi)

It is thus clear that the morpheme kANDa denotes an arrowhead, while the ^ circumflex accent hieroglyph is intended to signify rebus: kāṇḍā 'edge of tool or weapon' or a sharp edged implement, like a sword. In Indian sprachbund, the word which denotes a sword is *khaṁḍa* -- m. 'sword'(Prakritam).

In the hieroglyph-multiplex of Rakhigarhi seal inscription, the left and right parentheses are used as circumscript to provide phonetic determination of the gloss: *khaṁḍa* -- m. 'sword' (Prakritam), while the ligaturing element of 'notch' is intended to signify खांडा [kāṇḍā] 'A jag, notch, or indentation (as upon the edge of a tool or weapon)' Rebus: kaNDa 'implements' (Santali). Thus, the hieroglyph-multiplex is read rebus as kaNDa 'implements' PLUS *khaṁḍa* 'sword'. The supercargo is thus catalogd on the seal as: 1. arrowheads; 2. metal implements and ingots; 3. swords.

The hieroglyph 'rhinoceros is: kANDA rebus: kaNDa 'implements/weapons'.
The entire inscription or metalwork catalog message on Rakhigarhi seal can be deciphered: kaNDa 'implements/weapons' (Rhinoceros) PLUS खांडा [kāṇḍā] 'weapons' PLUS *mūhā* 'cast ingots'(Left and Right parentheses as split rhombus or ellipse).

Thus, the supercargo consignment documented by this metalwork catalog on Rakhigarhi seal is: metal (alloy) swords, metal (alloy) implements, metal cast ingots.

Rakhigarhi seal

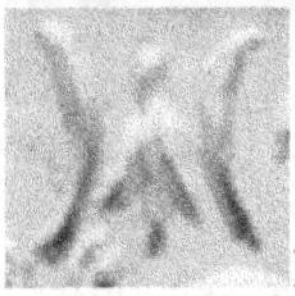
Hieroglyph-multiplex on Rakhigarhi seal.

M1118

Kalibangan032

This monograph deciphers m1429 Prism tablet with Indus inscriptions on 3 sides. Three Sided Moulded Tablet with a boat and crocodile+fish Indus inscription Fired clay L.4.6 cm W. 1.2 cm Indus valley, Mohenjo-daro,MD 602, Harappan,ca 2600 -1900 BCE Islamabad Museum, Islamabad NMP 1384, Pakistan.

One side of a Mohenjo-daro tablet.

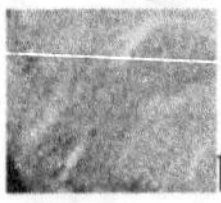
baTa 'quail' Rebus: bhaTa 'furnace' (i.e., supercargo out of furnace)

What was the cargo carried on the boat? I suggest that the cargo was Meluhha metalwork.

The shape of the pair of ingots on the boat (shown on the tablet) is comparable to following figures: 1. the ingot on which stands the Ingot-god (Enkomi); 2. Copper ingot from Zakros, Crete, displayed at the Heraklion Archaeological Museum But the script used on the tablet is NOT Cypro-Minoan or Cretan or Minoan but Meluhha:

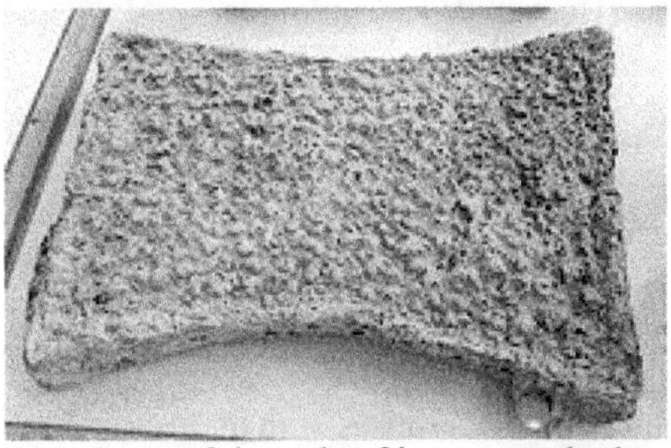

The shape of the pair of ingots on the boat (shown on the tablet) is comparable to following figures: 1. the ingot on which stands the Ingot-god (Enkomi); 2. Copper ingot from Zakros, Crete, displayed at the Heraklion Archaeological Museum But the script used on the tablet is NOT Cypro-Minoan or Cretan or Minoan but Meluhha: One side of a Mohenjo-daro prism tablet (Full decipherment of the three sided inscription is embedded). What was the cargo carried on the boat? I suggest that the cargo was Meluhha metalwork -- castings and hard copper alloy ingots. Together with the pair of aquatic birds, the metalwork is with hard alloys (of copper).

bagalo = an Arabian merchant vessel (Gujarati) *bagala* = an Arab boat of a particular description (Ka.); *bagalā* (M.); *bagarige, bagarage* = a kind of vessel (Kannada) Rebus: *bangala* = kumpaṭi = angāra śakaṭī = a chafing dish a portable stove a goldsmith's portable furnace (Telugu) cf. *bangaru* *bangaramu* = gold (Telugu)

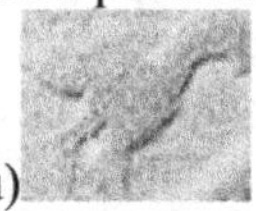

karaṇḍa 'duck' (Sanskrit) karaṛa 'a very large aquatic bird' (Sindhi) Rebus: करडा [karaḍā] Hard from alloy--iron, silver &c. (Marathi)

Side A: kāru a wild crocodile or alligator (Telugu) ghariyal id. (Hindi)
kāru 'crocodile' (Telugu) கராம் karām, n. prob. grāha. 1. A species of alligator; முதலைவகை. முதலையு மிடங்கருங் கராமும் (குறிஞ்சிப். 257). 2. Male alligator; ஆண் முதலை. (திவா.) కారుమొసలి a wild crocodile or alligator. (Telugu) Rebus: kāru 'artisan' (Marathi) kāruvu 'artisan' (Telugu) khār 'blacksmith' (Kashmiri)
[fish = aya (G.); crocodile = kāru (Telugu)] Rebus: ayakāra 'ironsmith' (Pali)

khār 1 खार् । लोहकारः m. (sg. abl. khāra 1 खार; the pl. dat. of this word is khāran 1 खारन्, which is to be distinguished from khāran 2, q.v., s.v.), a blacksmith, an iron worker (cf. bandūka-khār, p. 111b, l. 46; K.Pr. 46; H. xi, 17); a farrier (El.)

Text 3246 (l., to r.)

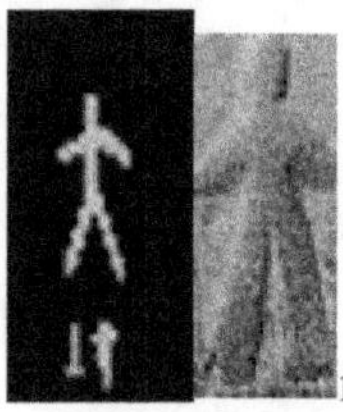mēd 'body' (Kur.)(DEDR 5099); meḍ 'iron' (Ho.) *karNika* 'rim of jar' Rebus: *karNI* 'supercaro'

*dula* 'pair' Rebus: *dul* 'cast metal' Thus the the pair of ellipses with an inscripted 'notch' hieroglyph component: *dul mūhā* 'cast ingot.

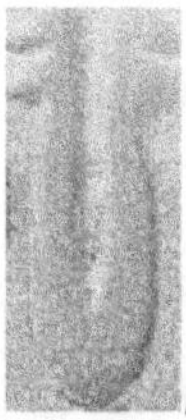*karNika* 'rim of jar' Rebus: *karNI* 'supercargo'
kárṇa— m. 'ear, handle of a vessel' RV., 'end, tip (?)' RV. ii 34, 3. [Cf. *kāra—6] Pa. kaṇṇa— m. 'ear, angle, tip'; Pk. kaṇṇa—, °aḍaya- m. 'ear', Gy. as. pal. eur. kan m., Ash. (Trumpp) karna NTS ii 261, Niṅg. kõmacr;, Woṭ. kanƏ, Tir. kana; Paš. kan, kaṇ(ḍ)— 'orifice of ear' IIFL iii 3, 93; Shum. kõmacr;ṛ 'ear', Woṭ. kan m., Kal. (LSI) kuṛõmacr;, rumb. kuŕũ, urt. kŕā̃ (< *kaṇ), Bshk. kan, Tor. k *l ṇ, Kand. kōṇi, Mai. kaṇa, ky. kān, Phal. kāṇ, Sh. gil. kọn pl. kọní m. (→ Ḍ kon pl. k *l ṇa), koh. kuṇ, pales. kuāṇƏ, K. kan m., kash. pog. ḍoḍ. kann, S. kanu m., L. kann m., awāṇ. khet. kan, P. WPah. bhad. bhal. cam. kann m., Ku. gng. N. kān; A. kāṇ 'ear, rim of vessel, edge of river'; B. kāṇ 'ear', Or. kāna, Mth. Bhoj. Aw. lakh. H. kān m., OMarw. kāna m., G. M. kān m., Ko. kānu m., Si. kaṇa, kana. — As adverb and postposition (ápi kárṇē 'from behind' RV., karṇē 'aside' Kālid.): Pa. kaṇṇē 'at one's ear, in a whisper'; Wg. ken 'to' NTS ii 279; Tir. kõ; 'on' AO xii 181 with (?); Paš. kan 'to'; K. kȧni with abl. 'at, near, through', kani with abl. or dat. 'on', kun with dat. 'toward'; S. kani 'near', kanā̃ 'from'; L. kan 'toward', kannũ 'from', kanne 'with', khet. kan, P. ḍog. kanē 'with, near'; WPah. bhal. k *l ṇ, °ṇi, k e ṇ, °ṇi with obl. 'with, near', kiṇ, °ṇiā̃, k *l ṇiā̃, k e ṇ° with obl. 'from'; Ku. kan 'to, for'; N. kana 'for, to, with'; H. kane, °ni, kan with ke 'near'; OMarw. kanai 'near', kanā̃ sā 'from near', kā̃nī̃ 'towards'; G. kan e 'beside'. Addenda: kárṇa—: S.kcch. kann m. 'ear', WPah.kṭg. (kc.) kān, poet. kanṛu m. 'ear', kṭg. kanni f. 'pounding—hole in barn floor'; J. kā'n m. 'ear', Garh. kān; Md. kan— in kan—fat 'ear' (CDIAL 2830)

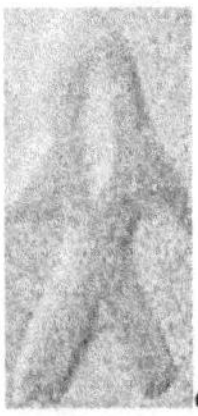*aya* 'fish' Rebus: *aya* 'iron' (Gujarati); *ayas* 'metal' (Rigveda)

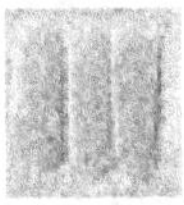*kolom* 'thre' Rebus: *kolami* 'smithy, forge'

*kolami mūhā* 'ingot (for)smithy,forget'

Thus, the message of the text on the Mohenjo-daro prism tablet of a boat + crocodile + fish is: supercargo of kolami mūhā 'smithy,forge ingots' dul mūhā 'cast metal ingots'. The metal is sinified as ayas.

mẽṛhẽt, meḍ 'iron' (Mu.Ho.)
mūhā mẽṛhẽt = iron smelted by the Kolhes and formed into an equilateral lump a little pointed at each of four ends (Santali)

Maysar c.2200 BCE Packed copper ingots. The shape of the ingots is an 'equilateral lump a little pointed at each of four ends' -- like an ellipse or rhombus. See:

See: http://nautarch.tamu.edu/pdf-files/JonesM-MA2007.pdf Michael Rice Jones' thesis of 2007 on the importance of Maysar for copper production.

An ingot may be signified by an ellipse or parenthesis of a rhombus. It may also be signified by an allograph: human face.

Hieroglyph: *mũhe* 'face' (Santali) mũhã̄ = the quantity of iron produced at one time in a native smelting furnace of the Kolhes; iron produced by the Kolhes and formed like a four-cornered piece a little pointed at each end; *kolhe tehen me~ṛhe~t mūhā akata* = the Kolhes have to-day produced pig iron(Santali) Rebus: *mūhā* 'ingot'; Compound formation: mleccha-mukha (Skt.) = milakkhu 'copper' (Pali)

Vāk and Mlecchita Vikalpa (Select inscriptions from Indus Script Corpora)

Note: Vāk refers to *sprachbund* (speech area) of ancient India on the banks of Rivers Sarasvati and Sindhu, two river basins of Himalayan glacial-fed rivers of ancient times. Mlecchita Vikalpa is a cipher, a writing system using hieroglyph-multiplexes to signify rebus Prakritam lexis of hieroglyphs and homonyms of glosses of metalwork.

A writing system is an intersection of speech and orthography. Speech is venerated in Rigveda as वाग्देवी, 'divinity of speech'. She declares, in a monologue that she is Rashtri, the lighted path for abhyudayam, for acquisition and movement of wealth by the first performers of yajna. The technological processes of yajna, Soma yaga, in particular, are signified by a writing system, Indus Script. This is called mlecchita vikalpa by Vatsyayana, to mean an alternative representation by mleccha (copper, metal) workers who documented their work. Each inscription is a metalwork catalog rendering the entire corpora *catalogus catalogorum* of metalwork.

वाग्देवी सूक्तम् ऋग्वेद 10.125

ऋषि वागाम्भृणी; devata: वागाम्भृणी (atmastuti); chanda: त्रिष्टुप्, 2 जगती

अहं रुद्रेभिर् वसुभिश् चराम्य् अहम् आदित्यैर् उत विश्वदेवैः ।
अहम् मित्रावरुणोभा बिभर्म्य् अहम् इन्द्राग्नी अहम् अश्विनोभा ॥
अहं सोमम् आहनसम् बिभर्म्य् अहं त्वष्टारम् उत पूषणम् भगम् ।
अहं दधामि द्रविणं हविष्मते सुप्राव्ये यजमानाय सुन्वते ॥ अहं राष्ट्री
संगमनी वसूनां चिकितुषी प्रथमा यज्ञियानाम् ।
ताम् मा देवा व्य् अदधुः पुरुत्रा भूरिस्थात्राम् भूर्य् आवेशयन्तीम् ॥
मया सो अन्नम् अत्ति यो विपश्यति यः प्राणिति य ईं शृणोत्य् उक्तम् ।
अमन्तवो मां त उप क्षियन्ति श्रुधि श्रुत श्रद्धिवं ते वदामि ॥ अहम्
एव स्वयम् इदं वदामि जुष्टं देवेभिर् उत मानुषेभिः ।
यं कामये तंतम् उग्रं कृणोमि तम् ब्रह्माणं तम् ऋषिं तं सुमेधाम् ॥
अहं रुद्राय धनुर् आ तनोमि ब्रह्मद्विषे शरवे हन्तवा उ ।
अहं जनाय समदं कृणोम्य् अहं द्यावापृथिवी आ विवेश ॥ अहं सुवे
पितरम् अस्य मूर्धन् मम योनिर् अप्स्व् अन्तः समुद्रे ।
ततो वि तिष्ठे भुवनानु विश्वोताम् द्यां वर्ष्मणोप स्पृशामि ॥
अहम् एव वात इव प्र वाम्य् आरभमाणा भुवनानि विश्वा ।
परो दिवा पर एना पृथिव्यैतावती महिना सम् बभूव ॥

RV_10,125.01a ahaṃ rudrebhir vasubhiś carāmy aham ādityair uta viśvadevaiḥ |
RV_10,125.01c aham mitrāvaruṇobhā bibharmy aham indrāgnī aham aśvinobhā||
RV_10,125.02a ahaṃ somam āhanasam bibharmy ahaṃ tvaṣṭāram uta pūṣaṇam bhagam |
RV_10,125.02c ahaṃ dadhāmi draviṇaṃ haviṣmate suprāvye yajamānāya sunvate ||
RV_10,125.03a ahaṃ rāṣṭrī saṃgamanī vasūnāṃ cikituṣī prathamā yajñiyānām |
RV_10,125.03c tām mā devā vy adadhuḥ purutrā bhūristhātrām bhūry āveśayantīm ||
RV_10,125.04a mayā so annam atti yo vipaśyati yaḥ prāṇiti ya īṃ śṛṇoty uktam |
RV_10,125.04c amantavo māṃ ta upa kṣiyanti śrudhi śruta śraddhivaṃ te vadāmi ||
RV_10,125.05a aham eva svayam idaṃ vadāmi juṣṭaṃ devebhir uta mānuṣebhiḥ|
RV_10,125.05c yaṃ kāmaye taṃ-tam ugraṃ kṛṇomi tam brahmāṇaṃ tam ṛṣiṃ taṃ sumedhām ||
RV_10,125.06a ahaṃ rudrāya dhanur ā tanomi brahmadviṣe śarave hantavā u |
RV_10,125.06c ahaṃ janāya samadaṃ kṛṇomy ahaṃ dyāvāpṛthivī ā viveśa ||
RV_10,125.07a ahaṃ suve pitaram asya mūrdhan mama yonir apsv antaḥ samudre |
RV_10,125.07c tato vi tiṣṭhe bhuvanānu viśvotāmūṃ dyāṃ varṣmaṇopa spṛśāmi||
RV_10,125.08a aham eva vāta iva pra vāmy ārabhamāṇā bhuvanāni viśvā |
RV_10,125.08c paro divā para enā pṛthivyaitāvatī mahinā sam babhūva ||

10.125.01 I proceed with the Rudras, with the Vasus, with the A_dityas, and with the Vis'vedeva_s; I support both Mitra and Varun.a, Agni and Indra, and the two As'vins.[Deity Prama_tma_: the word, or first of creatures].
10.125.02 I support the foe-destroying Soma, Tvas.t.a_, Pu_s.an and Bhaga; I bestow wealth upon the institutor of the rite offering the oblation, deserving of careful protection, pouring forth the libation.
10.125.03 I am the sovereign queen, the collectress of treasures, cognizant (of the Supreme Being), the chief of objects of worship; as such the gods have put me in many places, abiding in manifold conditions, entering into numerous (forms.
10.125.04 He who eats food (eats) through me; he who sees, who breathes, who hears what is spoken, does so through me; those who are ignorant of me perish; hear you who have hearing, I tell that which is deserving of belief.
10.125.05 I verily of myself declare this which is approved of by both gods and men; whomsoever I will, I render formidable, I make him a Brahma_, a r.s.i, or a sage. [A Brahman: Brahma_, the creator].
10.125.06 I bend the bow of Rudra, to slay the destructive enemy of the Bra_hman.as, I wage war with (hostile) men. I pervade heaven and earth.
10.125.07 I bring forth the paternal (heaven) upon the brow of this (Supreme Being), my birthplace is in the midst of the waters; from thence I spread through all beings, and touch this heaven with my body.
10.125.08 I breathe forth like the wind giving form to all created worlds; beyond the heaven, beyond this earth (am I), so vast am I in greatness.

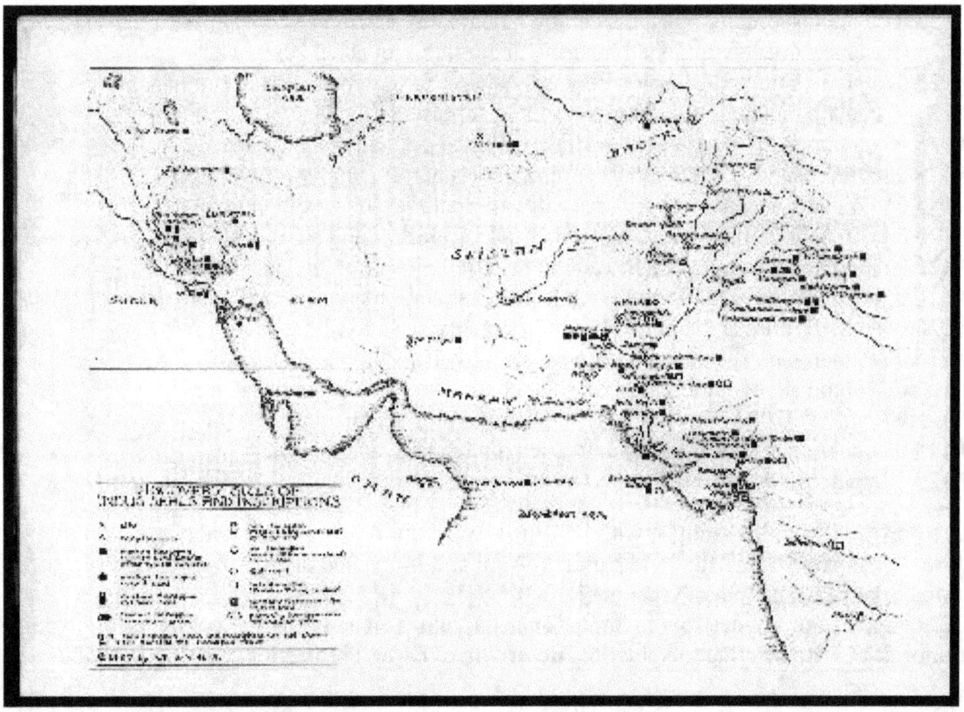

Discovery sites: Indus Script inscriptions

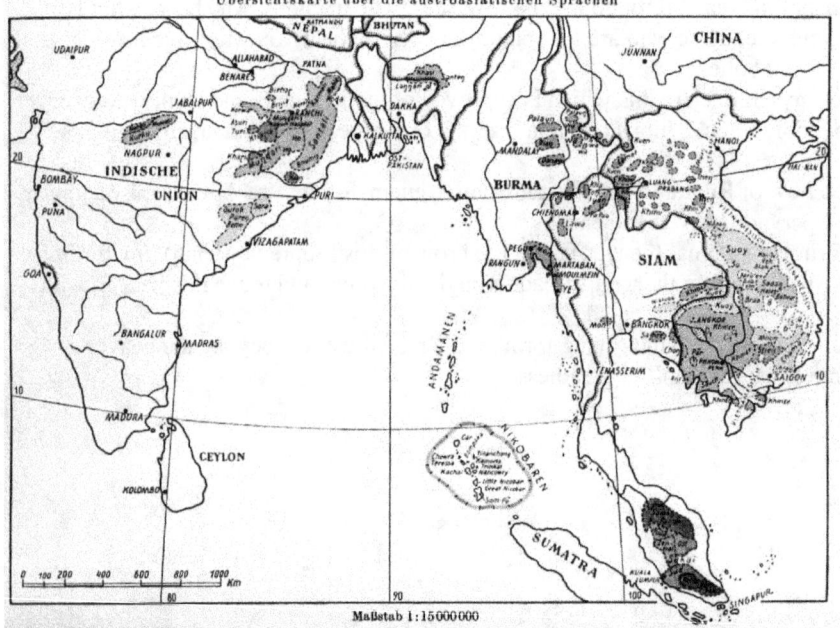

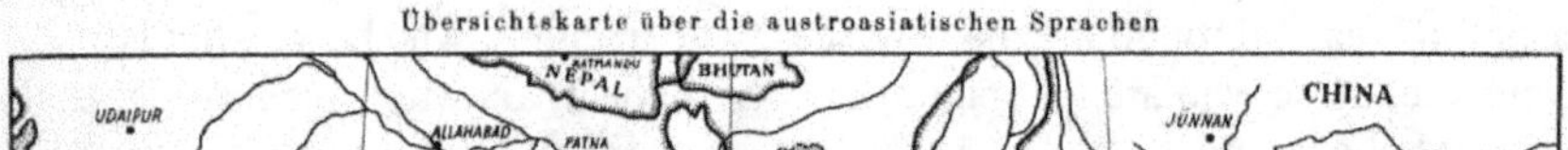

Pinnow's map of Austro-AsiaticLanguage speakers correlates with bronze age sites.[16] The areal map of Austric (Austro-Asiatic languages) showing regions marked by Pinnow correlates with the bronze age settlements in Bharatam or what came to be known during the British colonial regime as 'Greater India'. The bronze age sites extend from Mehrgarh-Harappa (Meluhha) on the west to Kayatha-Navdatoli (Nahali) close to River Narmada to Koldihwa- Khairdih-Chirand on Ganga river basin to Mahisadal – Pandu Rajar Dhibi in Jharia mines close to Mundari area and into the east extending into Burma, Indonesia, Malaysia, Laos, Cambodia, Vietnam, Nicobar islands. A settlement of Inamgaon is shown on the banks of River Godavari.

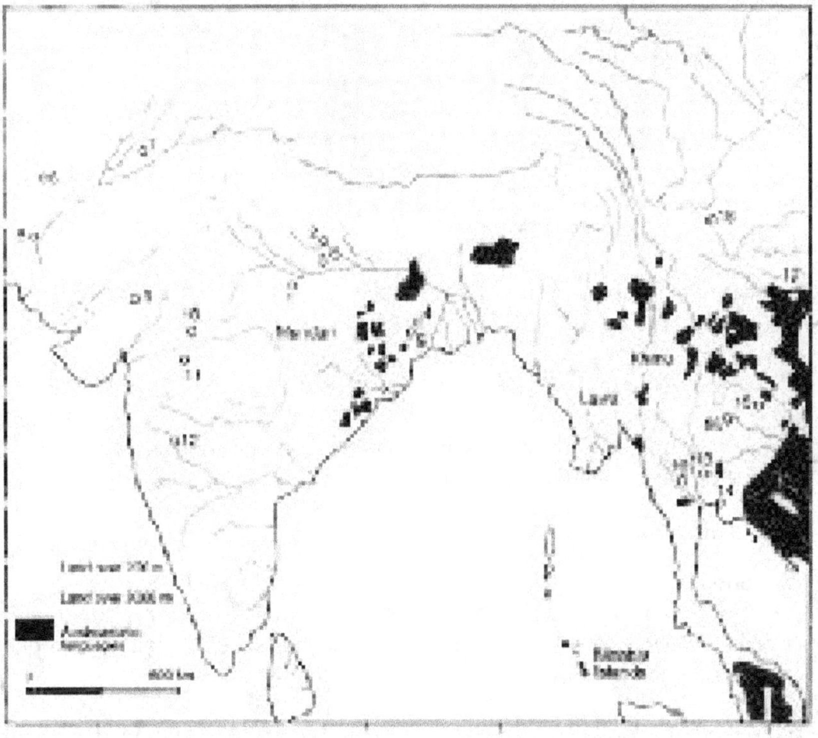

Bronze Age sites of eastern India and neighbouring areas: 1. Koldihwa; 2.Khairdih; 3. Chirand; 4. Mahisadal; 5. Pandu Rajar Dhibi; 6.Mehrgarh; 7. Harappa;8. Mohenjo-daro; 9.Ahar; 10. Kayatha; 11.Navdatoli; 12.Inamgaon; 13. Non PaWai; 14. Nong Nor;15. Ban Na Di andBan Chiang; 16. NonNok Tha; 17. Thanh Den; 18. Shizhaishan; 19. Ban Don Ta Phet [After Fig. 8.1 in: Charles Higham, 1996, The Bronze Age of Southeast Asia, Cambridge University Press].

Background

Seafaring meluhhan merchants used Indus Writing in trade transactions; artisans created metal artifacts, lapidary artificats of terracotta, ivory for trade. Glosses of the proto-Indic or Indus language are used to read rebus the Indus script inscriptions.

The glyphs of the Indus script or Indus Writing include both pictorial motifs and signs and both categories of glyphs are read rebus. As a first step in delineating the Indus language, an *Indian lexicon*[17] provides a resource, compiled semantically cluster over 1240 groups of glosses from ancient Indian languages as a proto-Indic substrate dictionary.

The evidence is remarkable that many single glyphs or glyptic elements of the Indus writing can be read rebus using the repertoire of artisans (lapidaries working with precious shell, ivory, stones and terracotta, mine-workers, stone-masons, metal-smiths working with a variety of minerals, furnaces and other tools) who created the inscribed objects and used many of them to authenticate their trade transactions. Many of the inscribed objects are seen to be calling cards of the professional artisans, listing their professional skills and repertoire. Many are veritable mining- and metal-work catalogs.

Continuing legacies of glyptic art noted by Huntington: "There is a continuity of composite creatures demonstrable in Indic culture since Kot Diji ca. 4000 BCE."[18]

The identification of glosses from the present-day languages of India on Sarasvati river basin is justified by the continuation of culture evidenced by many artifacts evidencing civilization continuum from the Vedic Sarasvati River basin, since language and culture are intertwined, resulting in a unique, logo-semantic writing system. .

Indus writing in Ancient Near East is a tribute to the Meluhhan artisans who have established an expansive contact area in Eurasia and left for posterity the bronze-age *harosheth hagoyim*, 'the smithy of nations.'

Concordance lists for epigraphs

Abbreviations and references to heiroglyphs and text transcripts

m-Mohenjodaro

h-Harappa

ABCDE at the end of a reference number indicate side numbers of an inscribed object. Multiple seal impressions on the same object are numbered 1 to 4.

At the end of the reference number:

'a' sealing; 'bangle' inscription on bangle or bangle fragment; other objects: shell, ivory stick, ivory plaque, ivory cube, faience ornament, steatite ornament; 'ct' copper tablet; 'Pict-' Pictorial motifs (0 to 145) described as illustrations of field-symbols in Appendix III of Mahadevan corpus (pp. 793 to 813); 'it' inscribed tablet; 'si' seal impression; 't' tablet.

Illegible inscribed objects are excluded in the following tabulations. Many potsherds Rahmandheri and Nausharo are excluded since the 'signs' are considered to be potters' marks; only those inscriptions which appear to have parallels of field symbols or 'signs' in the corpora are included.

Based on a number of resources and from the collections of inscribed objects held in many museums of the world, such as the Metropolitan Museum of Art, the Indus Writing Corpora include Sarasvati heiroglyphs, representing many facets of glyptic art of Sarasvati Civilization. The corporas also includes many texts of inscriptions, corresponding to the epigraphs inscribed on objects. The compilation is based mostly on published photographs in archaeological reports right from the days of Alexander Cunningham who discovered a seal at Harappa in 1875, of Langdon at Mohenjodaro (1931) and of Madhu Swarup Vats at Harappa (1940). The corpus includes objects collected in India, Pakistan, other countries and the finds of the excavations at Harappa by Kenoyer and Meadow during the seasons 1994-1995 and 1999-2000.

Framework for decoding epigraphs of Sarasvati Sindhu Civilization

This is also intended to serve as a pictorial and text index to Mahadevan Concordance and to the three volumes published so far of pictorial corpus of Parpola et al.

Many texts are indexed to the text numbers of Mahadevan concordance. The choice of this concordance is based on four factors: (a) the concordance is priced at a reasonable cost; (b) it is a true concordance for every sign of the corpus to facilitate an analysis of the frequency of occurrence of a sign and the context of other sign clusters/ sequences in relation to a sign and for researchers to cross-check on the basic references for the inscribed objects; (c) the exquisite nature of orthography is notable and 'readings' are authentic, even for very difficult to read inscriptions; and (d) signs and variants of signs have been delineated with cross-references to selected text readings.

Mahadevan concordance excludes inscribed objects which do not contain 'texts'; for example, this concordance excludes about 50 seals inscribed with the 'svastikā' pictorial motif and a pectoral which contains the pictorial motif of a one-horned bull with a device in front and an over-flowing pot. Parpola concordance has been used to present such objects which also contain valuable orthographic data which may assist in decoding the inscriptions. Many broken objects are also contained in Parpola concordance which are useful, in many cases, to count the number of objects with specific 'field symbols', a count which also provides some valuable clues to support the decoding of the messages conveyed by the 'field symbols' which dominate the object space.

Cross-references to excavation numbers, publications, photographs and the museum numbers based on which these texts have been compiled are provided in Appendix V: List of Inscribed Objects (pages 818 to 829) in Iravatham Mahadevan, 1977, *The Indus Script: Texts, Concordance and Tables*, Memoirs of the Archaeological Survey of India No. 77, New Delhi, Archaeological Survey of India. In most cases, these text numbers are matched with the inscribed objects after Asko Parpola concordance [1. Jagat Pati Joshi and Asko Parpola, eds., 1987, *Corpus of Indus Seals and Inscriptions: 1. Collections in India*, Memoirs of the Archaeological Survey of India No. 86, Helsinki, Suomalainen Tiedeakatemia; 2. Sayid Ghulam Mustafa Shah and Asko Parpola, eds., 1991, *Corpus of Indus Seals and Inscriptions: 2. Collections in Pakistan*, Memoirs of the Department of Archaeology and Museums, Govt. of Pakistan, Vol. 5, Helsinki, Suomalainen Tiedeakatemia]. *Memoir of ASI No. 96 Corpus of Indus Seals and Inscriptions, Vol. II* by Asko Parpola, B.M. Pande and Petterikoskikallio (containing copper tablets) (December 2001).

The debt owed by those interested in civilization studies to Iravatham Mahadevan, Asko Parpola, Archaeological Survey of India, Department of Archaeology and Museums, Govt. of Pakistan and Finnish Academy for making this presentation possible is gratefully acknowledged. I am grateful to Iravatham Mahadevan who made available to me his annotated personal copy of a document which helped in collating the texts with the pictures of inscribed objects. [Kimmo Koskenniemi and Asko Parpola, 1980, Cross references to Mahadevan 1977 in: *Documentation and Duplicates of the Texts in the Indus Script, Helsinki*, pp. 26-32].

Four epigraphs from Bhirrana from ASI website http://asi.nic.in and five epigraphs from Bagasra (Gola Dhoro) reported by VH Sonawane in *Puratattva*, Number 41, 2011 have also been included.

Pitfalls of normalising orthography of some glyphs

Parpola (1994) identifies 386 (+12?) signs (or graphemes) and their variant forms. Mahadevan (1977) identifies 419 graphemes; out of these 179 graphemes have variants totalling 641 forms.

Parpola observes: "...the grapheme count might be as low as 350...The total range of signs once present in the Indus script is certain to have been greater than is observable now, for new signs have kept turning up in new inscriptions. The rate of discovery has been fairly low, though, and the new signs have more often been ligatures of two or more signs already known as separate graphemes than entirely new signs." (Parpola, 1994, p. 79)

Many 'signs' are ligatures of two or more 'signs'.

In the process of normalizing the orthography of some glyphs to identify the core 'signs' of the script, some information is lost and at times, the process itself impedes the possibility of decoding the writing system. This can be demonstrated by (1) the 'identification' of a 'squirrel' glyph and (2) the failure to identify 'dotted circle' or 'stars' as glyphs.

It is, therefore, necessary to view the inscribed object as a composite message composed of glyphs: pictorial motifs and signs alike. Many scholars have noted the contacts between the Mesopotamian and Sarasvati Sindhu (Indus) Civilizations, in terms of cultural history, chronology, artefacts (beads, jewellery), pottery and seals found from archaeological sites in the two areas.

An outstanding contribution to the study of the script problem is the publication of the Corpus of Indus Seals and Inscriptions (CISI) Three volumes have been published so far:

> *Corpus of Indus Seals and Inscriptions, 1. Collections in India, Helsinki, 1987 (eds. Jagat Pati Joshi and Asko Parpola)*
>
> *Corpus of Indus Seals and Inscriptions, 2. Collections in Pakistan, Helsinki, 1991 (eds. Sayid Ghulam Mustafa Shah and Asko Parpola)*
>
> *Corpus of Indus Seals and Inscriptions, 3. 1 Supplement to Mohenjo-daro and Harappa, 2010 (eds. Asko Parpola, B.M. Pande and Petteri Koskikallio) in collaboration with Richard H. Meadow and Jonathan Mark Kenoyer. (Annales Academiae Scientiarum Fennicae, B. 239-241.) Helsinki: Suomalainen Tiedeakatemia.*

These volumes in which Asko Parpola is the co-author constitute the photographic corpus. The CISI contains all the seals including those without any inscriptions, for e.g. those with the geometrical motif called the 'svastika'. Parpola's initial corpus (1973) included a total number of 3204 texts. After compiling the pictorial corpus, Parpola notes that there are approximately 3700 legible inscriptions (including 1400 duplicate inscriptions, i.e. with repeated texts). Both the concordances of Parpola and Mahadevan complement each other because of the sort sequence adopted. Parpola's concordance was sorted according to the sign following the indexed sign. Mahadevan's concordance was sorted according to the sign preceding the indexed sign. The latter sort ordering helps in delineating signs which occur in final position. With the publication of CISI Vol. 3, Part 1, the total number of inscriptions from Mohenjo-daro totals 2134 and from Harappa totals 2589; thus, these two sites alone accounting for 4,723 bring the overall total number of inscriptions to over 6,000 from all sites (even after excluding comparable inscriptions on 'Persian Gulf type' circular seals from the total count).

Compendia of the efforts made since the discovery by Gen. Alexander Cunningham, in 1875, of the first known Indus seal (British Museum 1892-12-10, 1), to decipher the script appear in the following references:

A number of concordances and sign lists have been compiled, by many scholars, for the 'Indus' script:

> Dani, A.H., *Indian Palaeography*, 1963, Pls. I-II

Gadd and Smith, *Mohenjodaro and the Indus Civilization*, London,1931,, vol. III, Pls. CXIX-CXXIX

Hunter, G.R., *JRAS*, 1932, pp. 491-503

Hunter, G.R., *Scripts of Harappa and Mohenjodaro*, 1934, pp. 203-10

Langdon, Mohenjodaro and the Indus Civilization*, London, 1931, vol. II, pp. 434-55*

Koskenniemi, Kimmo and Asko Parpola, *Corpus of texts in the Indus script,* Helsinki, 1979; *A concordance to the texts in the Indus script*, Helsinki, 1982

Mahadevan, I., *The Indus Script: Texts, concordance and tables*, Delhi, 1977, pp. 32-35

Parpola et al., *Materials for the study of the Indus script, I: A concordance to the Indus Inscriptions*, 1973, pp. xxii-xxvi

Vats, *Excavations at Harappa*, Calcutta, 1940, vol. II, Pls. CV-CXVI

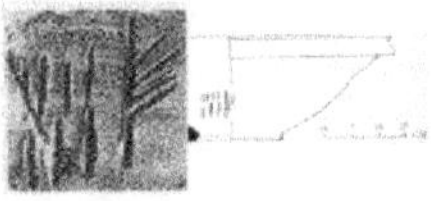

Alamgirpur Late

Harappan pottery, a three-legged chakala_(After YD Sharma)

Alamgirpur Agr-1 a(2) graffiti

9062

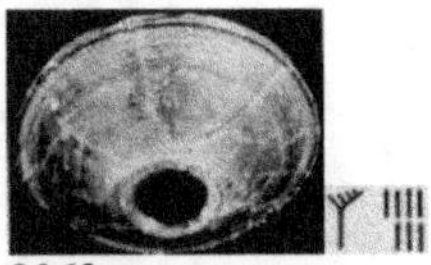

9063

Alamgirpur: Late Harappan pottery (After YD Sharma)

Alamgirpur2

Allahdino (Nel Bazaar)01

Allahdino (Nel Bazaar)02

Allahdino (Nel Bazaar)03

Allahdino (Nel Bazaar)04

Allahdino (Nel Bazaar)05

Allahdino (Nel Bazaar)06

Allahdino (Nel Bazaar)07

Allahdino (Nel Bazaar)08

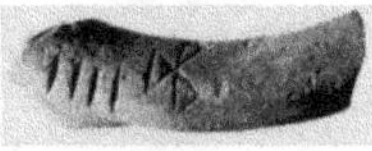

Allahdino (Nel Bazaar)09

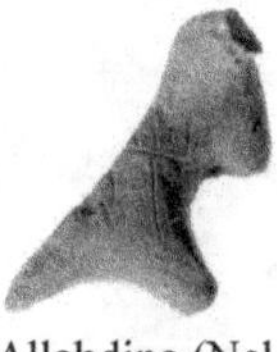

Allahdino (Nel Bazaar)11

9061

Amri

9084

Amri

9085

Amri06

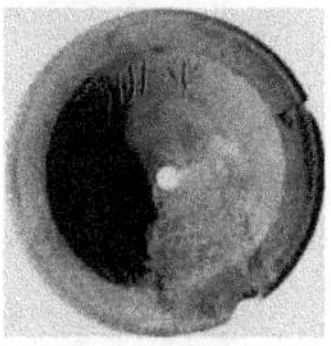

Amri07

Bagasra1 (Gola Dhoro)

Bagasra2 (Gola Dhoro)

Bagasra3 (Gola Dhoro)

Bagasra4 (Gola Dhoro)

Bagasra5 (Gola Dhoro)

Balakot01

Balakot 02

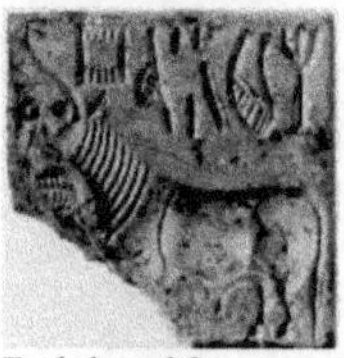

Balakot 03

Balakot 04

Balakot 05

Balakot 06 bangle

Balakot 06bangle

Balakot 06C

Banawali1

Banawali10 9204

Banawali11

Banawali12

Banawali13a

Banawali14

Banawali15 9203

Banawali16

Banawali 17

9201

Banawali 18a

Banawali19

Banawali2

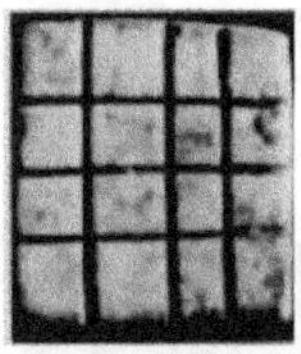
Banawali 20

Banawali 21a

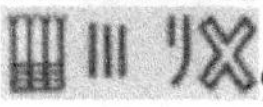9205

Banawali 23A

Banawali 23B

Banawali 24t

9211

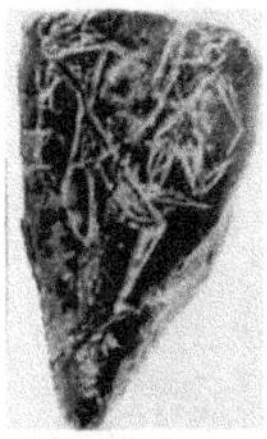
Banawali 26A

Banawali0026a

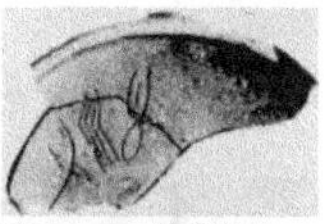
Banawali 28A

9221

Banawali 3

Banawali30

Banawali 4

Banawali 5

9203

Banawali 6

Banawali 7

Banawali 8

Banawali 9C

Bet Dwaraka 1

S'ankha seal. One-horned bull, short-horned bull looking down and an antelope looking backward.

Bhirrana1

Bhirrana2

Bhirrana3

Bhirrana4

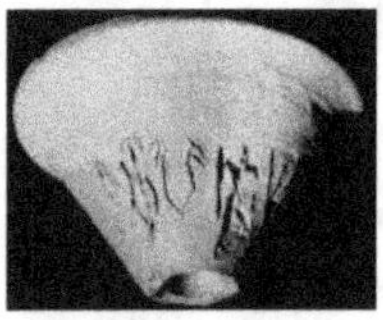
Chandigarh01
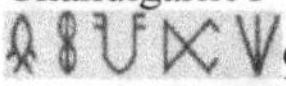9101

Chandigarh02
9102

Chandigarh
9103

Chandigarh
9104

Chanhudaro10

6129

Chanhudaro 11
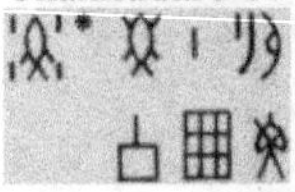 6220

Chanhudaro12a
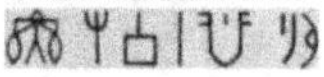

6231

Chanhudaro13
 6221

Chanhudaro14a
6108

Chanhudaro15a
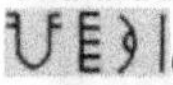6213

Chanhudaro16a
6222

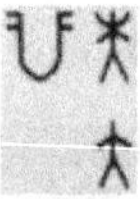
Chanhudaro17a
6122

Chanhudaro18a
6216

Chanhudaro1a

6125

Chanhudaro2
6128

Chanhudaro20
6210

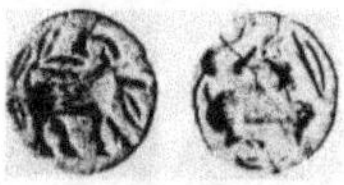
Chanhudaro Seal obverse and reverse. The oval sign of this Jhukar culture seal is comparable to other inscriptions. Fig. 1 and 1a of Plate L. After Mackay, 1943.

Chanhudaro21a
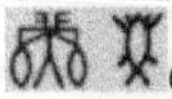6209

Chanhudaro22a 
6115

Chanhudaro23
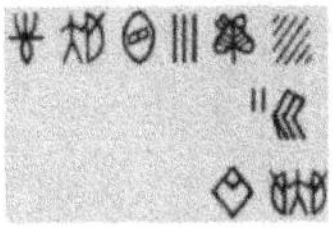

6402 Goat-antelope with a short tail.

The object in front of the goat-antelope is a double-axe.

Chanhudaro24a
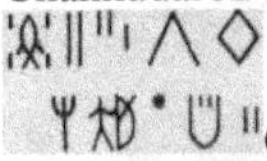 6116

Chanhudaro25

Chanhudaro26

 6405

Chanhudaro27

Chanhudaro28

Chanhudaro29
 6403

Chanhudaro3
 6230

Chanhudaro30
 6111

Chanhudaro32a
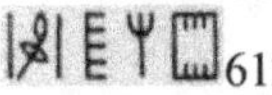 6123

Chanhudaro33a
 6104

Chanhudaro. Tablet. Obverse and reverse. Alligator and Fish. Fig. 33 and 33a. of Plate LII. After Mackay, 1943.

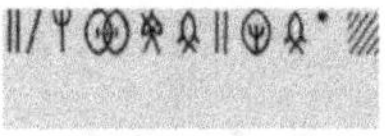

6233 Pict-67: Gharial, sometimes with a fish held in its jaw and/or surrounded by a school of fish.

 6303  6304

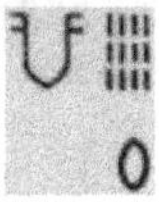

 6301

6305  6109

 6112

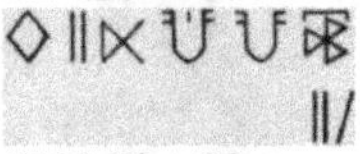

6113 Pict-98

 It is seen from an enlargement of the bottom portion of the seal impression that the 'prostrate person' may not be a person but a ligature of the neck of an antelope with rings on its necks or of a post with ring-stones. The head of the 'person' is not shown. So, I would surmise that this is an artist's representation of an act of copulation (by an animal) + a ligatured neck of another bovine or alternatively, a pillar with ring-stones ligatured to the bottom portion of a body. It is not uncommon in the artistic tradition to ligature bodies to the rump of, for example, a bull's posterior ligatured to a horned woman (Pict. 103 Mahadevan) or standing person with horns and bovine features (hoofed legs and/or tail) -- Pict. 86-88 Mahadevan.

Bison (gaur) trampling a prostrate person (?) underneath. Impression of a seal from Chanhujodaro (Mackay 1943: pl. 51: 13). The prostrate 'person' is seen to have a very long neck, possibly with neck-rings, reminiscent of the rings depicted on the neck of the one-horned bull normally depicted in front of a standard device. 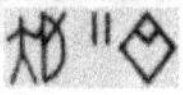
6114 Pict-108

 Person kneeling under a tree facing a tiger. [*Chanhudaro Excavations*, Pl. LI, 18]

 6118

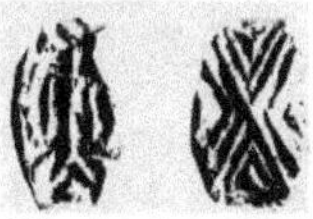

Chanhudaro Seal obverse and reverse. The 'water-carrier' and X signs of this so-called Jhukar culture seal are comparable to other inscriptions. Fig. 3 and 3a of Plate L. After Mackay, 1943.

 6120

Pict-40

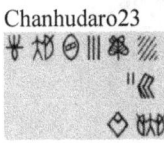

Ox-antelope with a long tail; a trough in front. 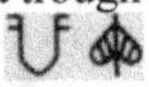 6121

Chanhudaro. Seal impression. Fig. 35 of Plate LII. After Mackay, 1943.

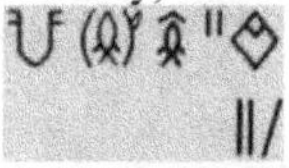 6124

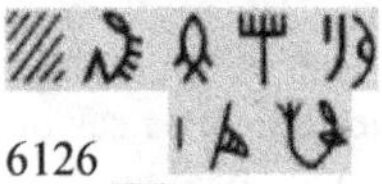

6126

6130  6131

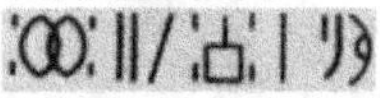

6133

6201

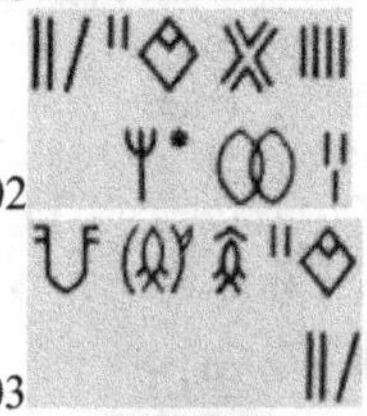

6202

6203

6204

6208 6211

6214

6215

6217

6218

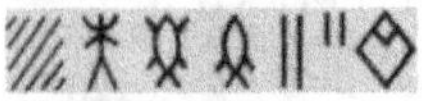

6219

6223

6224 6225

 6226

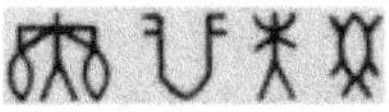

6228

6229 6232

Chanhudaro. Tablet. Fig. 34 of Plate LII. After Mackay, 1943.

 6234

Chanhudaro. Seal impression. Fig. 35 of Plate LII. After Mackay, 1943.

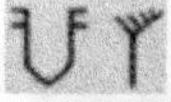 6235

Chanhudaro38A

Chanhujodaro

39A1

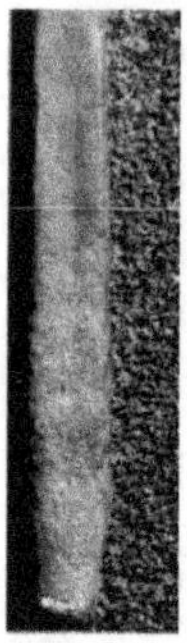

Chanhudaro

39A2

Chanhudaro4

 6206

Chanhudaro40A

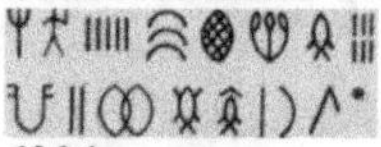

6306

Chanhudaro40B

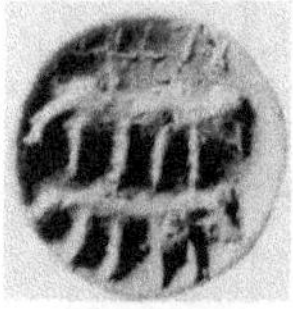

Chanhudaro41a

Chanhudaro42

Chanhudaro43

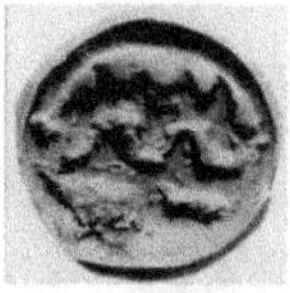

Chanhudaro46a

Chanhudaro46b

Chanhudaro47

Chanhudaro 48

Chanhudaro49A

Chanhudaro49B

Chanhudaro 5

6132

Chanhudaro50A

Chanhudaro50B

Chanhudaro 6

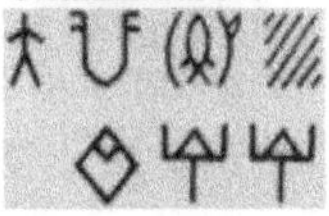

6205

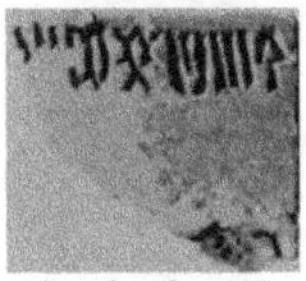
Chanhudaro 7

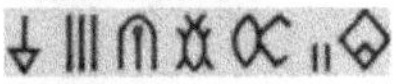
6207

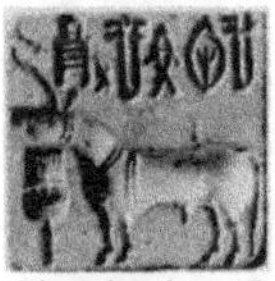
Chanhudaro 8

6227

Chanhudaro 9

6127

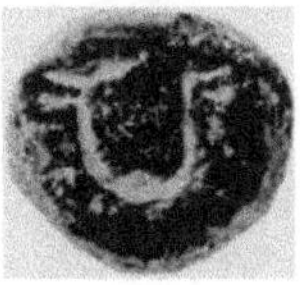

Daimabad1 
Sign342

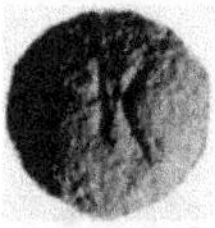
Daimabad
2a

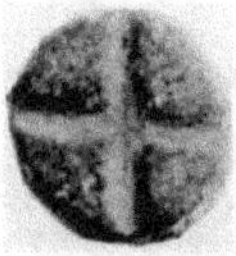
Daimabad
3A

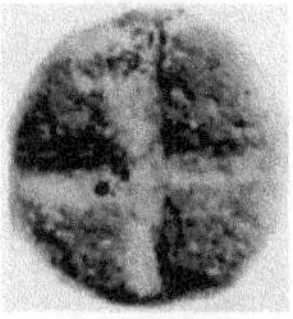
Daimabad 3B

Daimabad 4

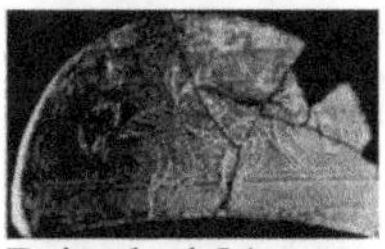
Daimabad 5A

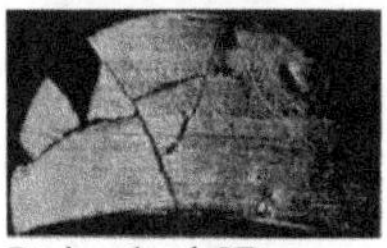
Daimabad 5B

Desalpur1a

9071Desalpur2

esalpur3

9073

Dholavira Sign-board mounted on a gateway.

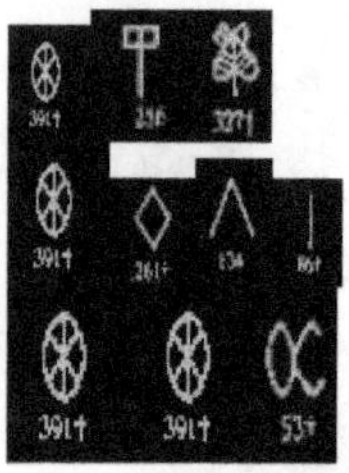

Dholavira (Kotda) on Kadir island, Kutch, Gujarat; 10 signs inscription found near the western chamber of the northern gate of the citadel high mound (Bisht, 1991: 81, Pl. IX).

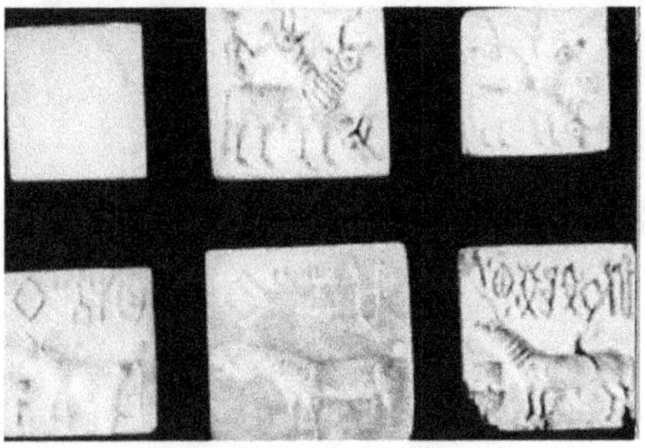

Dholavira: Seals (Courtesy ASI)

Dholavira1a

9121

Dholavira 2a

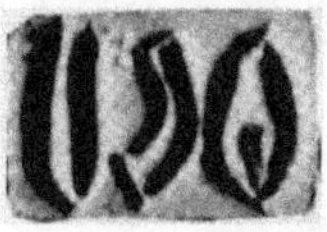

Gharo Bhiro (Nuhato) 01

Gumla10a

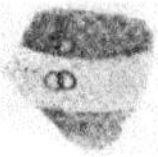

Gumla8a

h001a

4010

h002

4012

h003

4002

h004

4693

h005

4004

h006a

4006

h007

4008

h008

4001

h009

4009

h010a

4003

h011a

4038

h012

4005

h013

5055

h014

4106

h015

4053

h017

4052

h018

4071

h019

4694

h020

4019

h021

4022

h022

4023

h023

4047

h024

4013

h025

4081

h026

4016

h027

4017

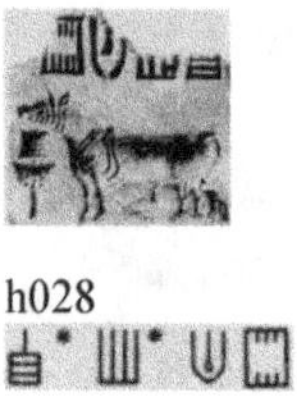

h028

4040

h029

4042

h030

4049

h031

4103

h032

4018

h033

5059

h035

5083

h036

4113

h037

4031

h038

4029

h039

h040

4072

h041

4178

h042

**4057

h043

4077

h044

4028

h045

4043

h046

4076

h047

4030

h048

4091

h049

4133

h050

4131

h051

4090

h052

4109

h053

 5089

h054

 4085

h055

4107

h056

4110

h057

 4086

h058

4105

h059

 5120

h060

5119

h061

4118

h062

4128

h063

 4142

h064 

h065 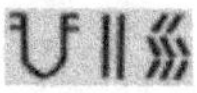

4094

h066 4130

h067 4115

h068

4141

h069 4146

h070 4122

h071 5054

h072 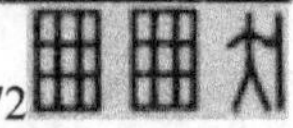
4120

h073

 4617 [An orthographic representation of a water-carrier].

h074 
4135

h075
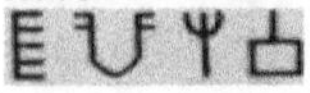

4161

h076

4241

h077

h078 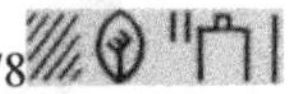

4244

h079

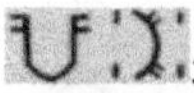 5060

h080
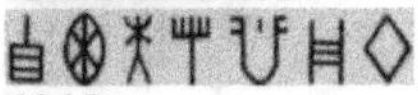
4245

h081

 5063

h082a
Text 4238

h083
 4236

h084

h085 

4232

h086

4233

h087

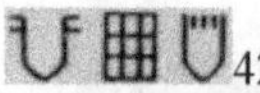 4240

h088

4253

h089

090
227

h091

4230

h092

4229

h093a

4231

h094 4246

h095

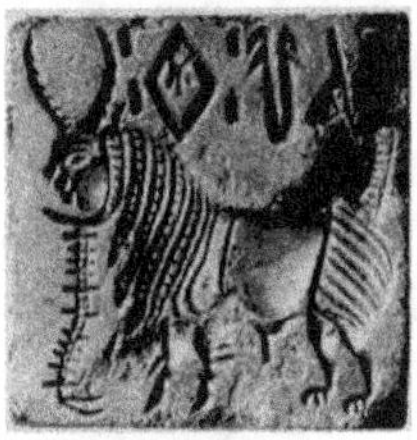

h096

4249

h097 Pict-95: Seven robed figures (with pigtails, twigs)

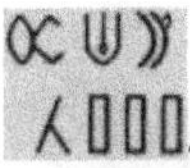

4251

h098

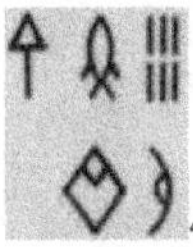

4256 Pict-122 Standard device which is normally in front of a one-horned bull.

h099

4223

h100

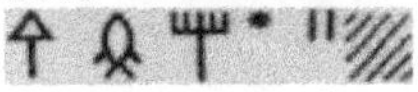

4258 One-horned bull.

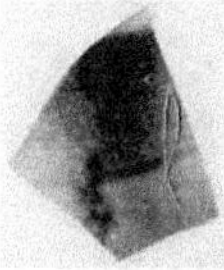

h1002

h1007

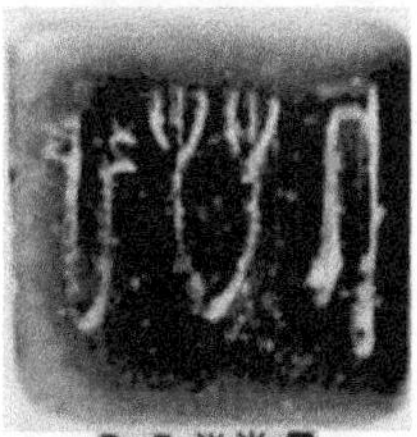

h101

5069

h1010bangle

h1011cone

5103

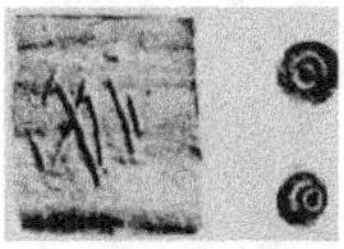

h1012cone

h1017ivorystick

4561

h1018copperobject Head of one-horned bull ligatured with a four-pointed star-fish (Gangetic octopus?)

h102A*

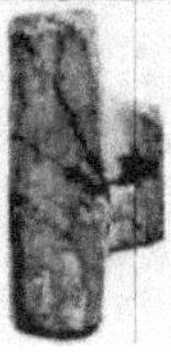

h102B

h102D

5056

h103

4254

h104

h105

h106

h107

h108

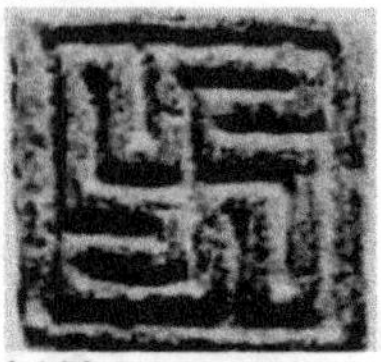

h109

h110

h111

h112

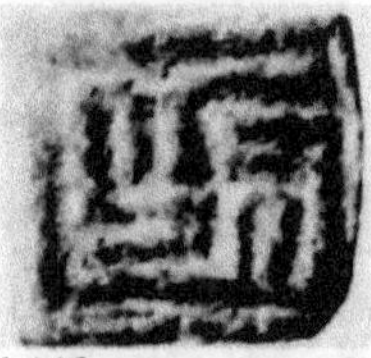

h113

h114

h115

h116

h117

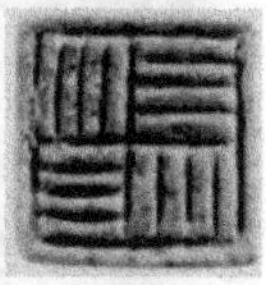

h118
h119

h120

h121

h122

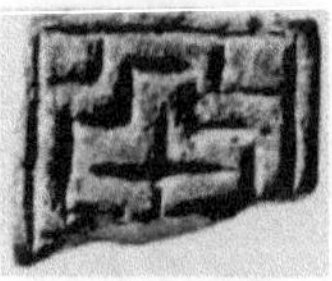

h123

h124

h125

h126

h127

h130

5096

h131 4271

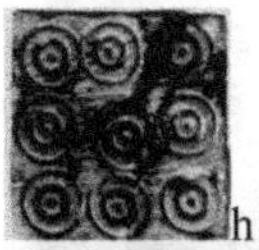
h128
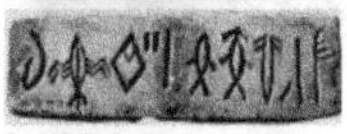
h129A
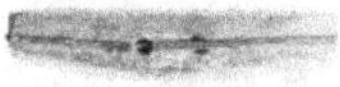
h129E

4269

h132
5052

h133
4261
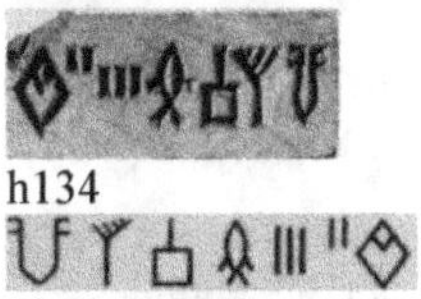
h134
4264

h135
4270

h136
4288

h137a
5058

h138a
5072

h139
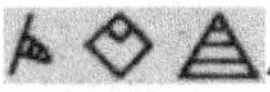
4267

h140
4268
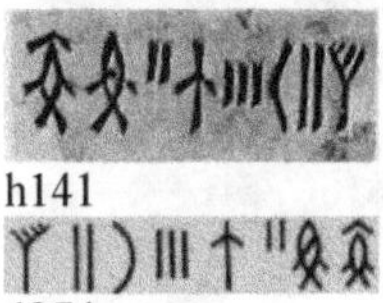
h141
4274
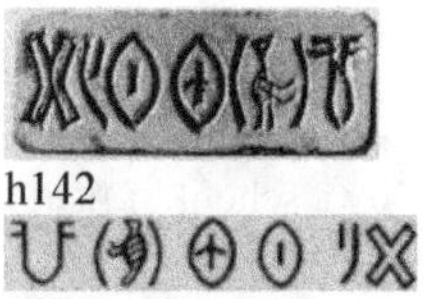
h142
4272

h143a
5101

h144

4280
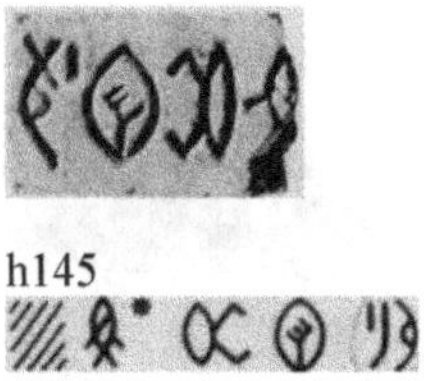
h145
5067

h146

4628
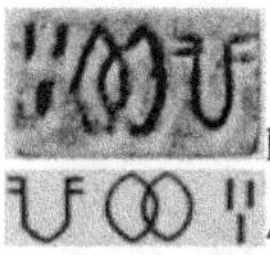
h147
4629
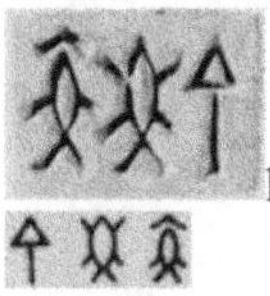
h148
4285

h149
4275

h150
4283
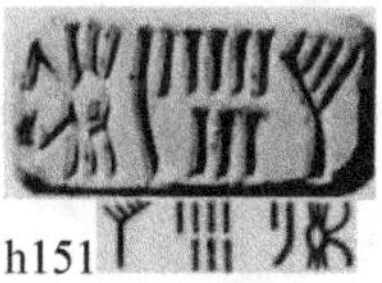
h151
5057

h152

5016

h153

4627

h154
4282

h155
4630
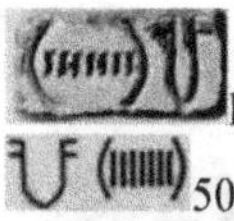
h156
5051

h157
4284

h158
4297
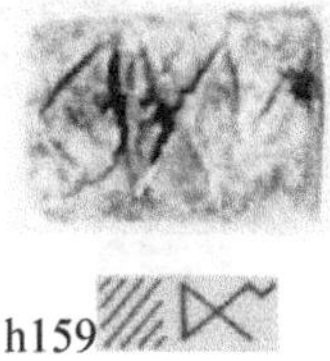
h159
4633

h160A
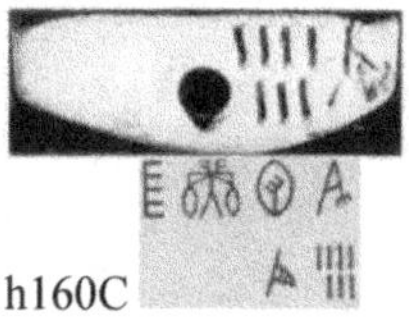
h160C
4276

h161

4262

h162

4294

h163

h164

5046

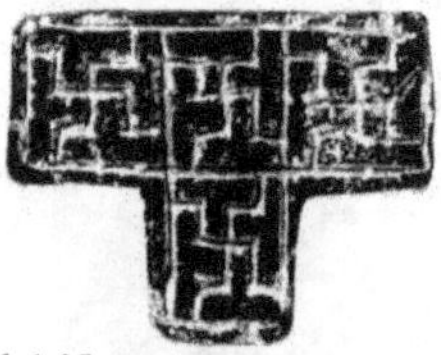

h165

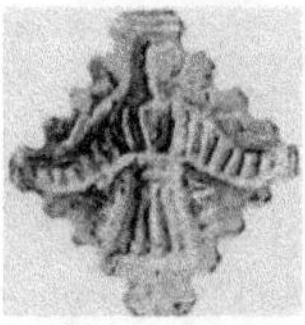

h166A

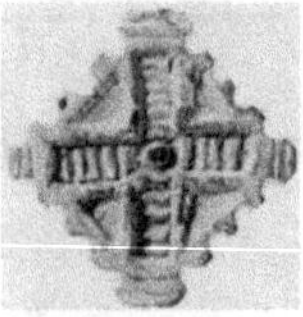

h166B

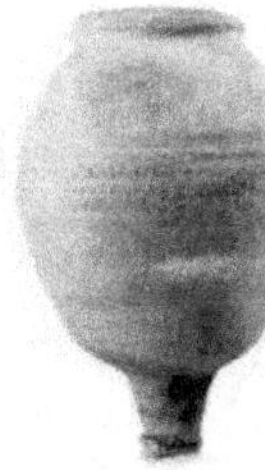

h167A

h167A2

5225

h168

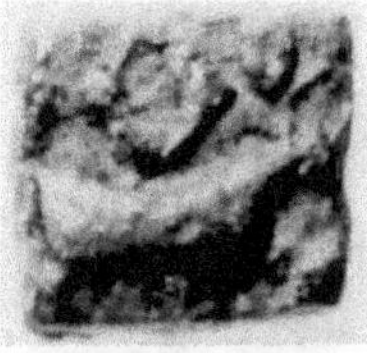

h169A

h169B

5298

h170A

h170B

4701

h171A

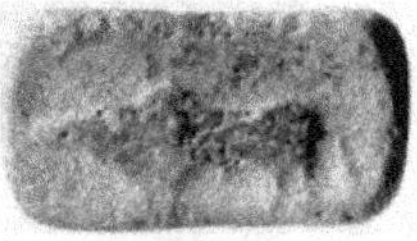

h171B tablet

4312

Buffalo.

h172A

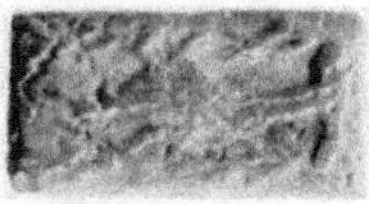

h172B

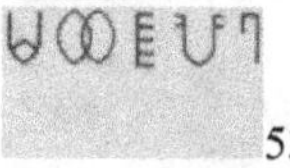

5305

Pict-66: Gharial, sometimes with a fish held in its jaw and/or surrounded by a school of fish.

h173A

h173B

4333

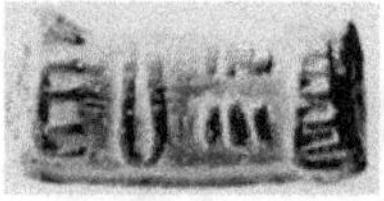

h174A

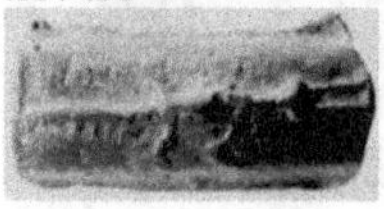

h174B

4338

h175A

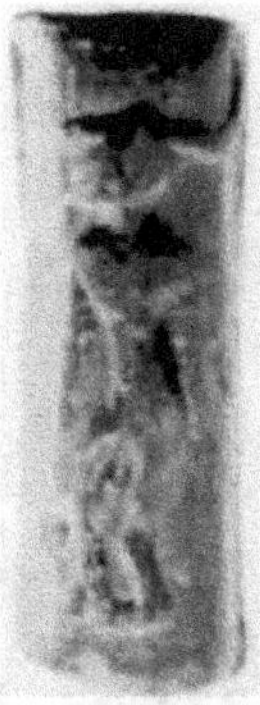

h175B Pict-87

4319 Standing person with horns and bovine features (hoofed legs and/or tail).

h176A

h176B

h176bb

4303

Tablet in bas-relief h176a Person standing at the centerbetween a two-tiered structure at R., and a short-horned bull (bison) standing near a trident-headed post at L. h176b

From R.—a tiger (?); a seated, pig-tailed person on a platform; flanked on either side by a person seated on a tree with a tiger, below, looking back. A hare (or goat?) is seen near the platform.

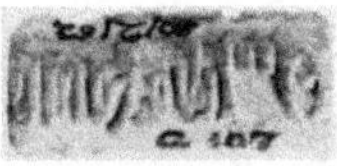

h177A

h177B

4316 Pict-115: From R.—a person standing under an ornamental arch; a kneeling adorant; a ram with long curving horns.

h178A

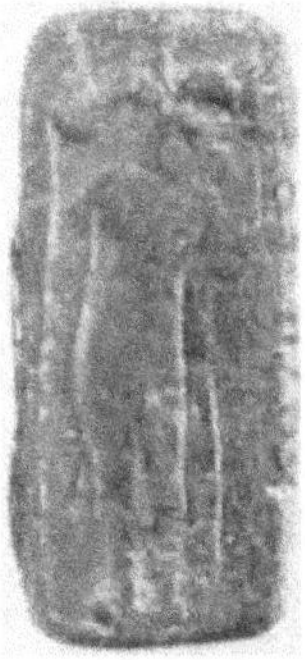

h178B

4318 Pict-84: Person wearing a diadem or tall head-dress (with twig?) standing within an arch or two pillars?

h179A

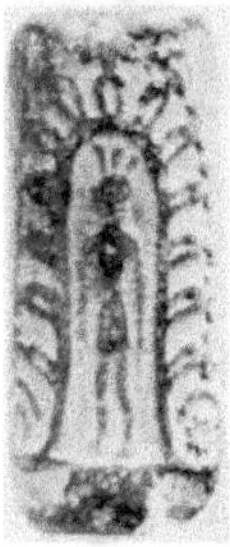

h179B

4307 Pict-83: Person wearing a diadem or tall head-dress standing within an ornamented arch; there are two stars on either side, at the bottom of the arch.

h180A

h180B

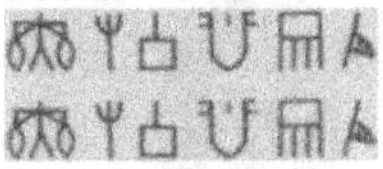

4304 Tablet in bas-relief h180a Pict-106: Nude female figure upside down with thighs drawn apart and crab (?) issuing from her womb; two tigers standing face to face rearing on their hindlegs at L. h180b Pict-92: Man armed with a sickle-shaped weapon on his right hand and a cakra (?) on his left hand, facing a seated woman with disheveled hair and upraised arms.

h181A

h181B

h182A

h182B

4306Tablet in bas-relief

h182a Pict-107: Drummer and a tiger.

h182b Five svastika signs alternating right- and left-handed.

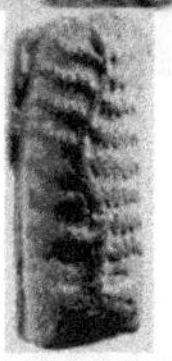

h183A

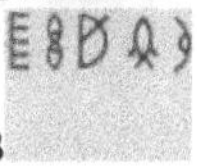

h183B

4327

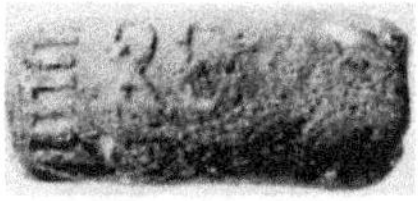

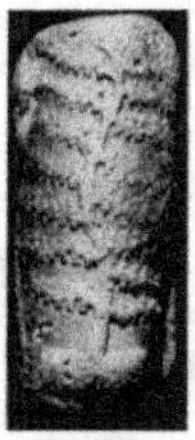

h184A

h184B

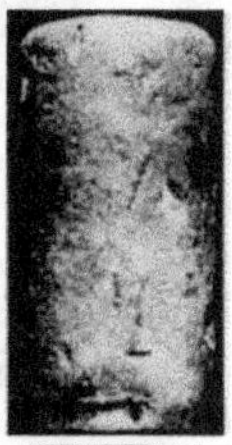

h185A

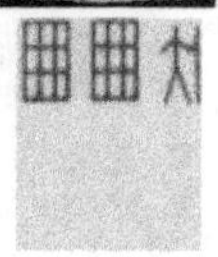

h185B

5279

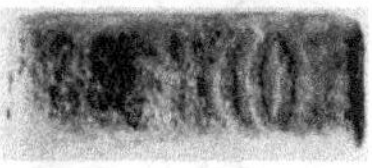

h186A

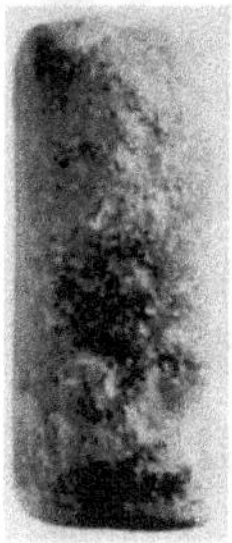

h186B

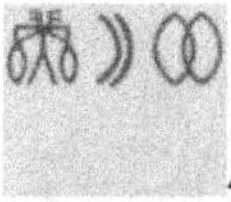

4329

h187A

h187B

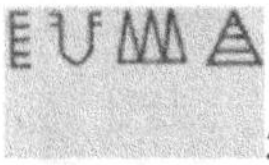

5282

Pict-75: Tree, generally within a railing or on a platform.

h188A

h188B
4325

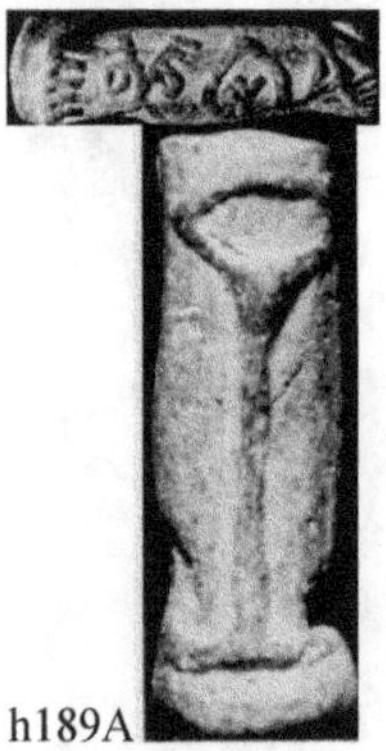

h189A
h189B

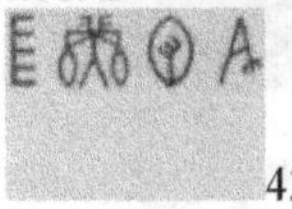

4341

Pict-126: Anchor?

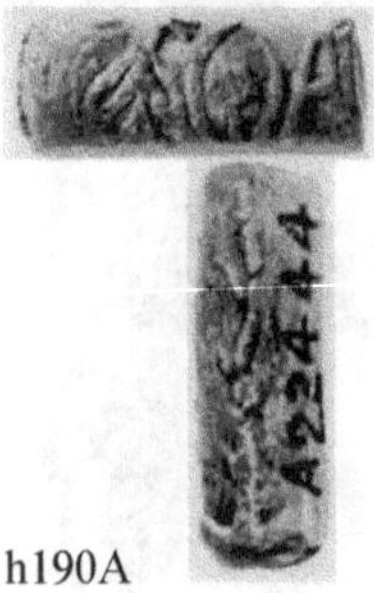

h190A

h190B
4323

h191A

h191B
4332

h192A
h192B

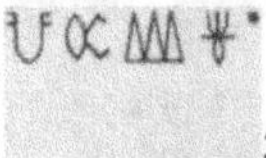

5340

h193A

h193B
5332

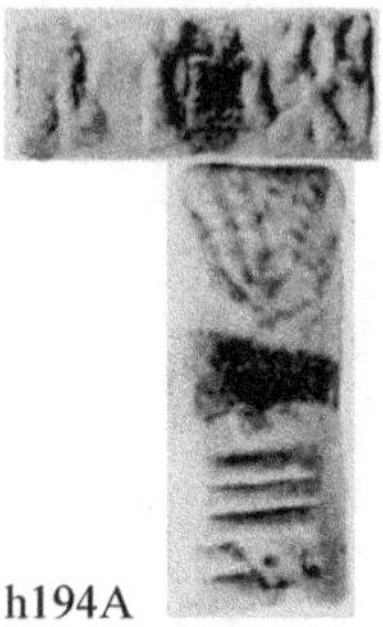

h194A
h194B

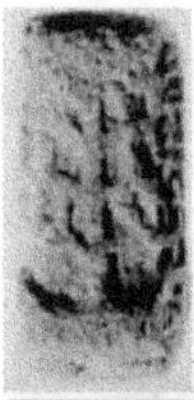

h195A

h195B

h196A

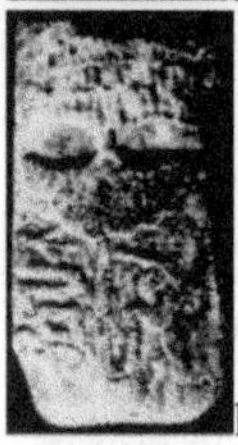

h196B

4309

Tablet in bas-relief

h196b
Pict-91: Person carrying the standard. h196a The standard.

h197A
h197B

5333

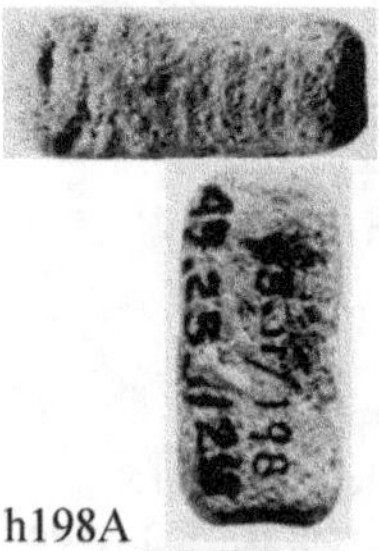

h198A

h198B

5331

h199A
h199B

5252

h200A

h200B
4321

h201A

h201B
5289
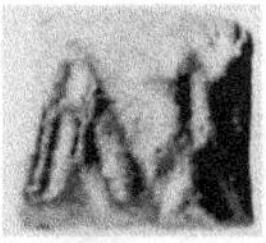
h202A
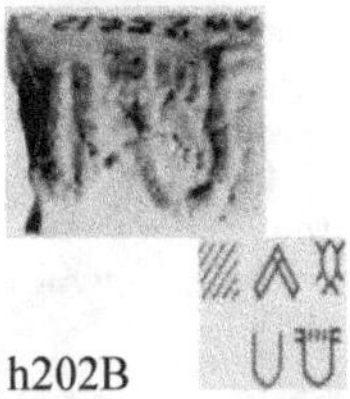
h202B
5334
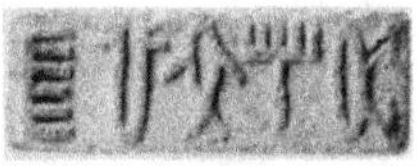
h203A

5226

5236

h204A
h204B

5211

h205A
h205B

5254

h206A
h206B
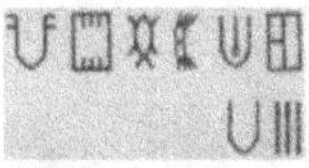
4345
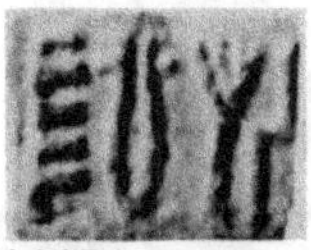
h207A
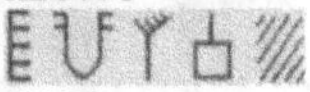
5297
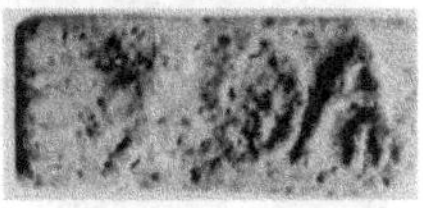
h208A

h208B
5296

h209A
h209B
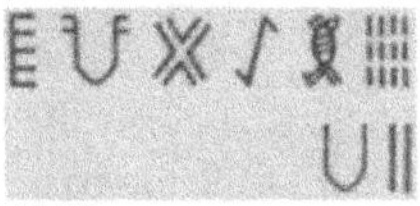
4348

h210A
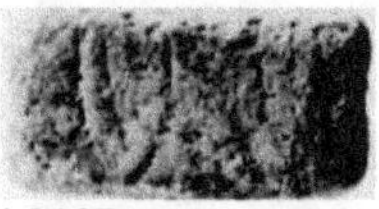
h210B
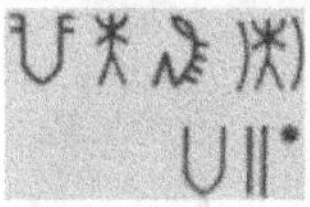
4355

h211A
h211B

5274

h212A

h212B
4357
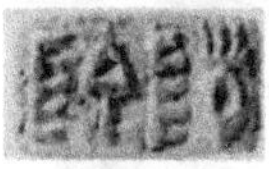
h213A
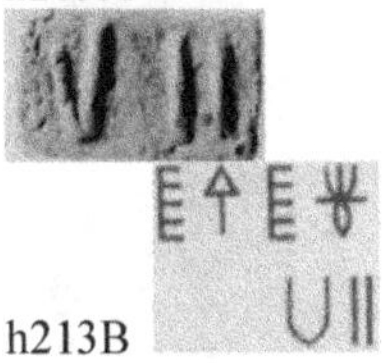
h213B
5270

h214A
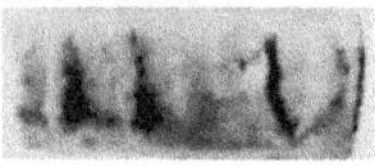

h214B
4684

h215A
h215B

5271

h216A
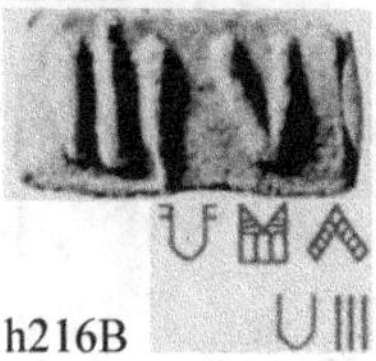
h216B
5335

h217A
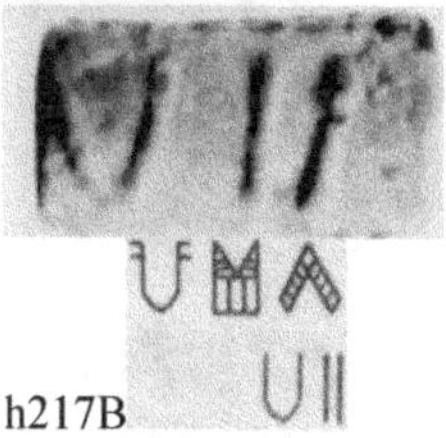
h217B
5336

h218A

h218B
5293

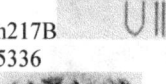

h219A

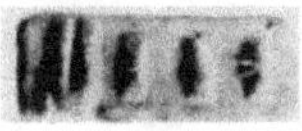

h219B
5269

h220A
5267

h221A

h221B
5265

h222A

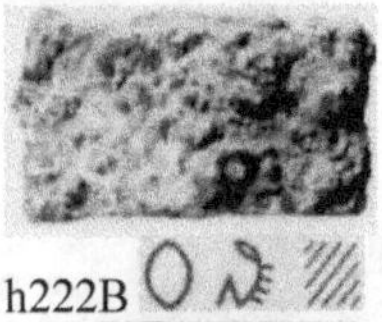

h222B

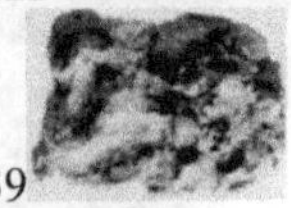

5339
h223A

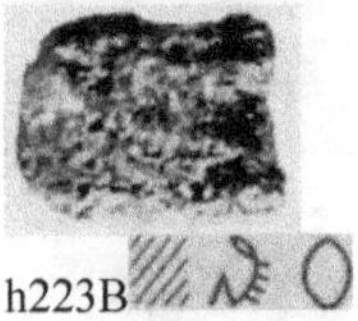

h223B
5221

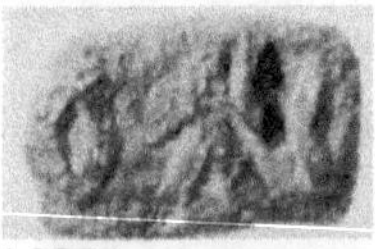

h225A

h226A

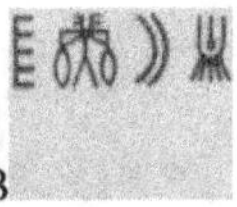

h226B
5243 Standard.

h227A

h227B
4322 Standard. Pict-123

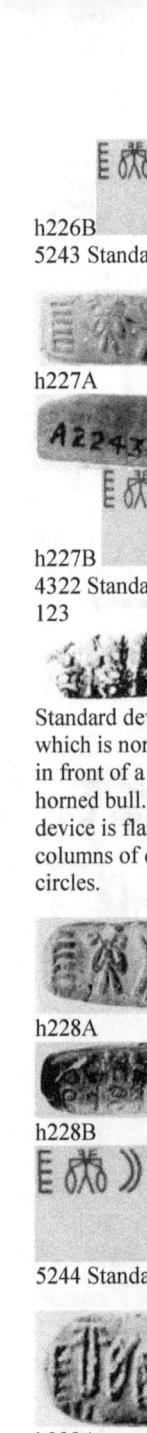

Standard device which is normally in front of a one-horned bull. The device is flanked by columns of dotted circles.

h228A

h228B

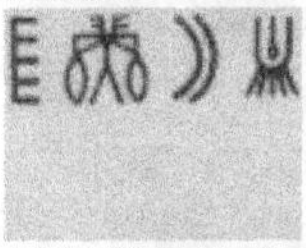

5244 Standard.

h229A

h229B

4674

h230A

h230B

h231A

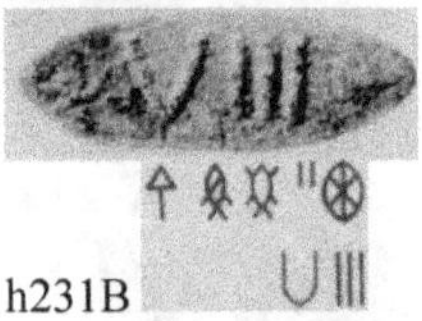

h231B
4673

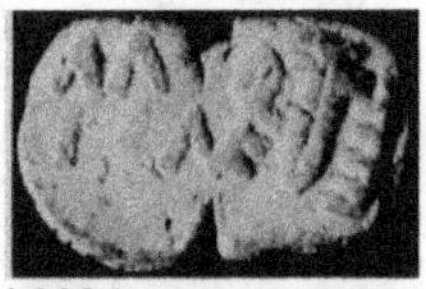

h232A

h232B tablet in bas

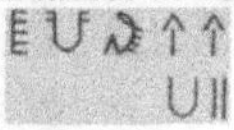

relief
4368 Inscribed object in the shape of a double-axe.

h233A

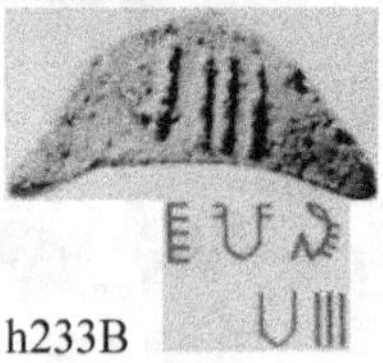

h233B
4387 Tablet in bas-relief. Sickle-shaped. Pict-131: Inscribed object in the shape of a crescent?

h234A

h234B

4717

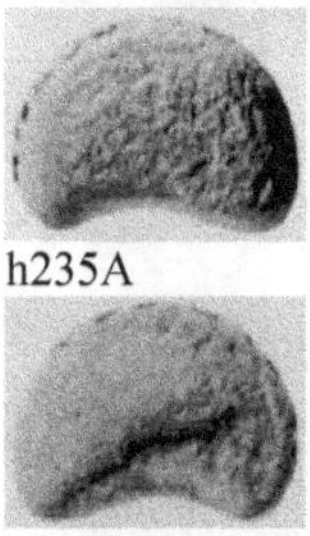

h235A
h235B

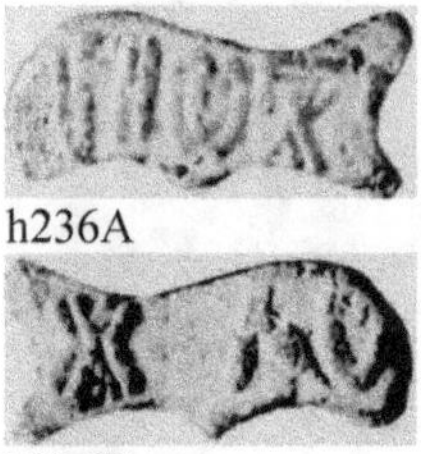

h236A
h236B

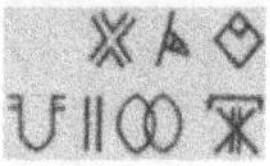

4658 Incised miniature tablet. Object shaped like fish or sickle? h825A h825B

h237A

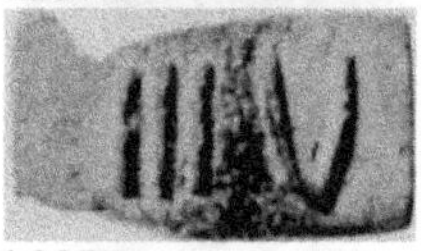

h237B

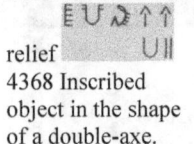

5337

h238A

h239A

h239B Tablet in bas

relief
4386

h240

4657

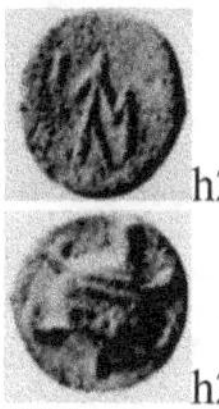

h241A
h241B

4663

Pict-69: Tortoise.

h242A

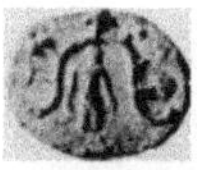

h242B

Pict-84

4317

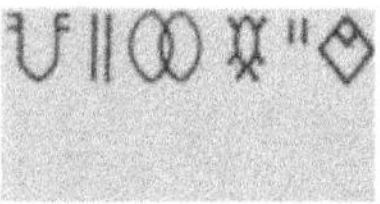

2863

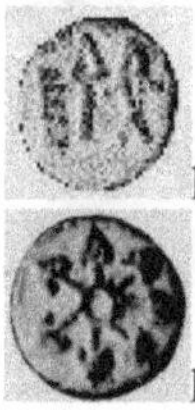

h243A
h243B
Tablet in bas-relief
Pict-78: Rosette of seven pipal (?) leaves.

4664

For See inscription: 4466

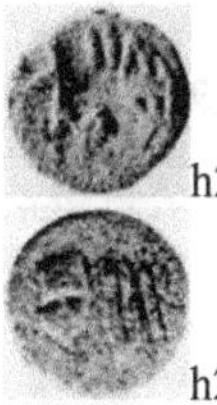

h244A
h244B

4665

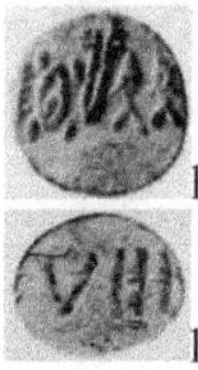

h245A
h245B

4702

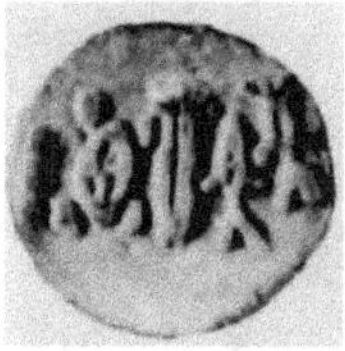

h246A

h246B

5283

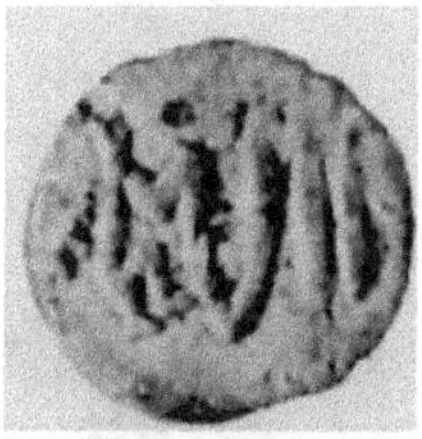

h247A

h247B Tablet in bas-relief

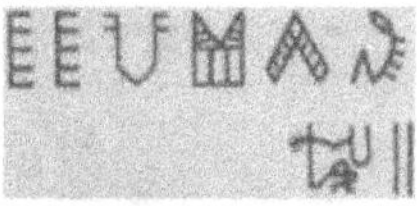

4372

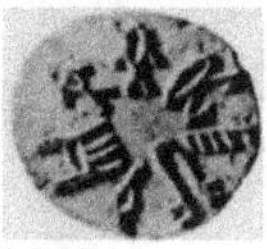

h248A

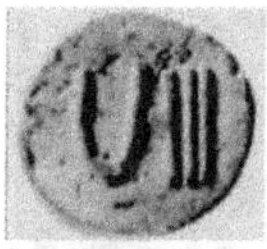

h248B Tablet in bas-relief

4371
See 3354.

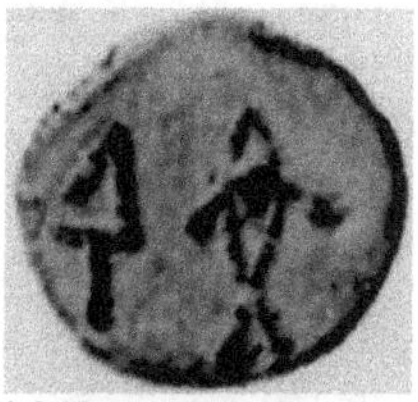

h249A

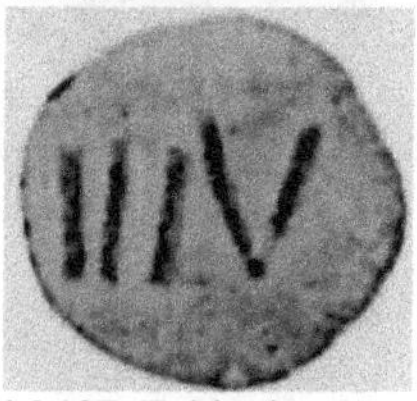

h249B Tablet in bas-relief

4374

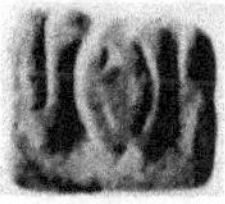

h250A

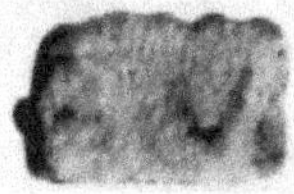

h250B

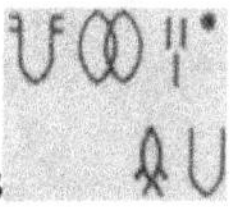

5250

h251A

h251B

h251C
4342 Tablet in bas-relief. Prism.
Bison (short-horned bull).

h252A

h252B

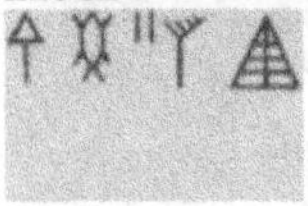

5215

h253A

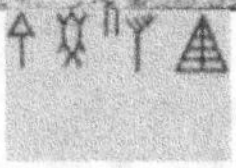

h253B
5219

h254A

h254B

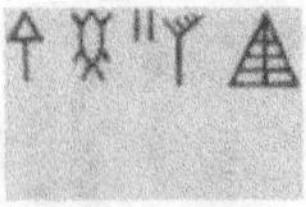

5214

h255A

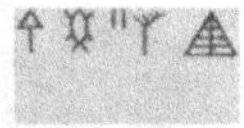

h255B
5208

h256A

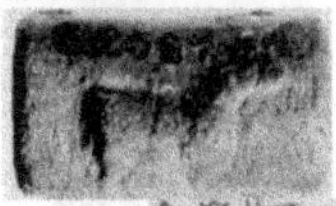

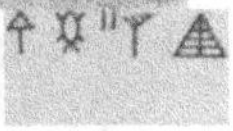

h256B
5213

h257A

h257B

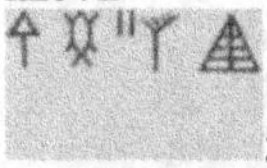

5216

h258A

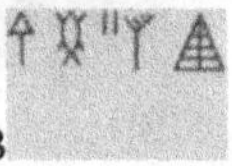

h258B
5217

h259A

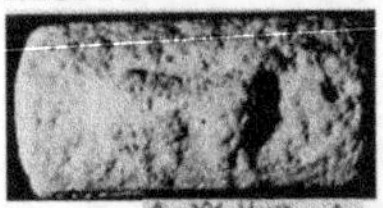

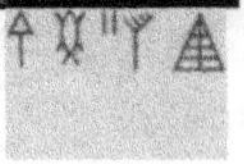

h259B
5218

h260A

h260B

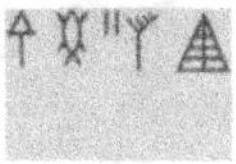

h261
5212

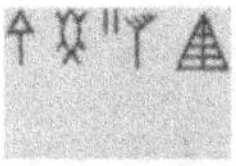

h262
5220

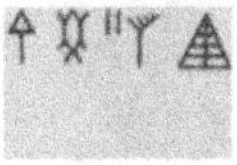

h263
5262

h264

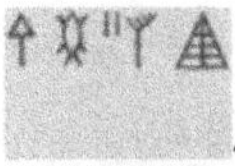

4315

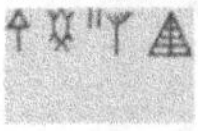

5207, 5208, 5209, 5210,
5212, 5213, 5214,5215, 5216, 5217,
5218,5219, 5220, 5262 Tablets in bas relief. The first sign looks like an arch around a pillar with ring-stones.
One-horned bull.
h252, h253, h255, h256, h257, h258, h259, h260,h261, h262, h263, h264, h265, h276, h277, h859, h860, h861, h862,h863, h864, h865, h866,h867, h868, 869, 870

h266
4011

h267
4007

h268

4020

h269

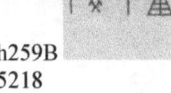

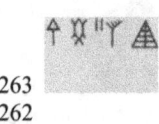

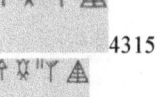

h270

4014

h271

4069

h272

4619

h273

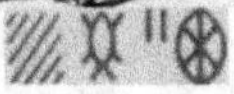

4176

h274

h275

h276A

h276B

h277A

h277B

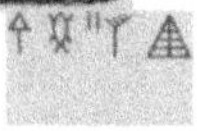

5207

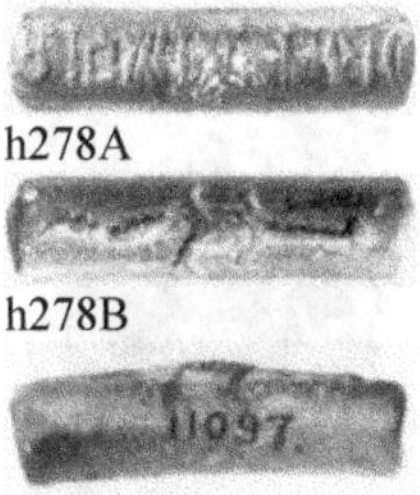

h278A

h278B

h278C

5205

h279A

h279B

5256

h280A

h280B

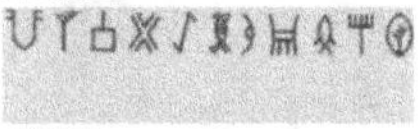

4335

h281A

h281B

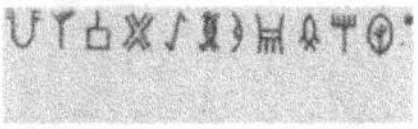

4336

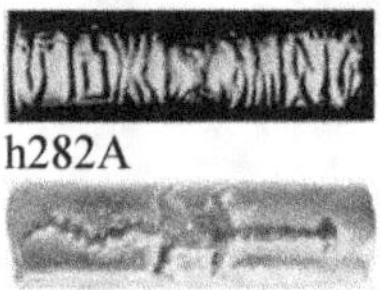

h282A

h282B

h283A

h283B

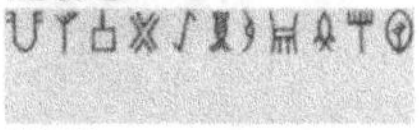

5253

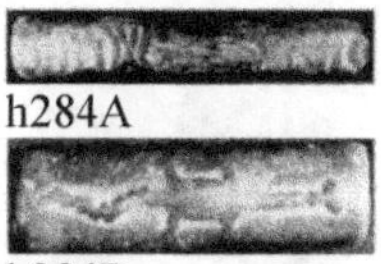

h284A

h284B

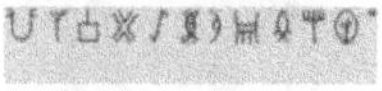

5229

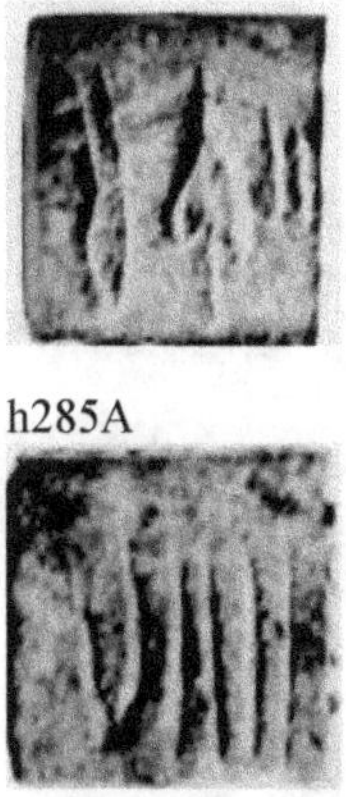

h285A

h285B

h286A

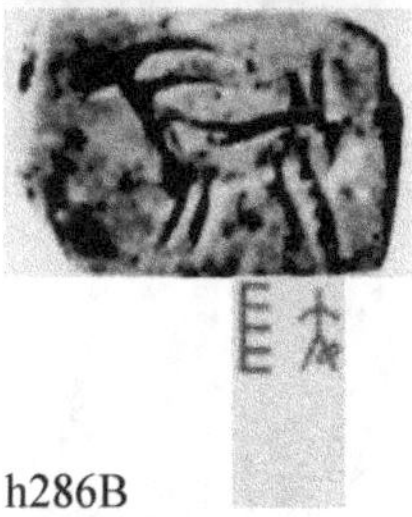

h286B

4429 Incised miniature tablet Goat-antelope with a short tail

h287A

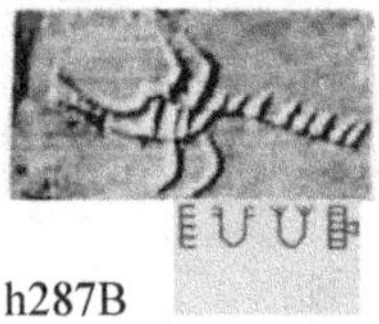

h287B

4430

h288A

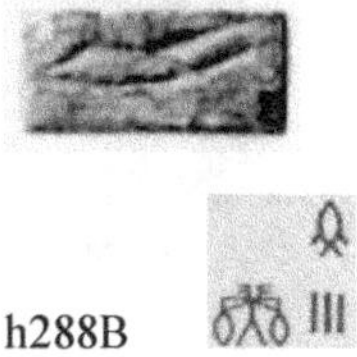

h288B

5463

h289A

h289B

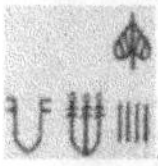

5467

h290A

h290B

5462

h291A

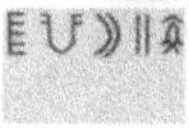

h291B

4440 Standard.

h292A

h292B
4443 Standard.

h293A

h293B
4441 Standard.

h294A

h294B
4442

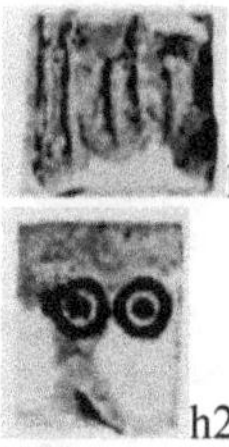

h295A

h295B

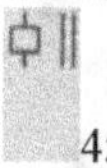

4505

h296A

h296B

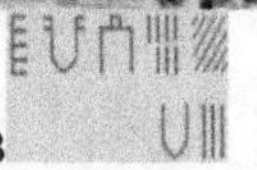

4457

h297A

h297B

5497

h298A

h298B

5473

h299A

h299B

4478

h300A

h300B

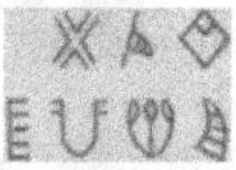

4454

h301A

h301B

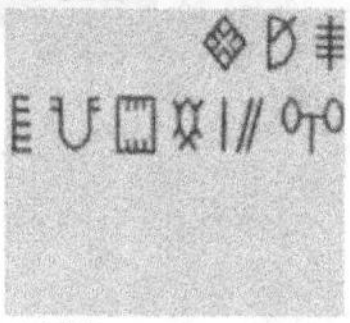

4450

h302A

h302B

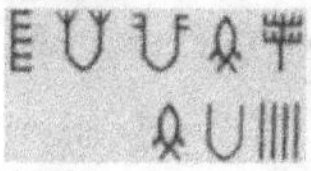

5460

h303A

h303B

4444

h304A

h304B

5401

h305A

h305B Text 5460

h306A

h306B

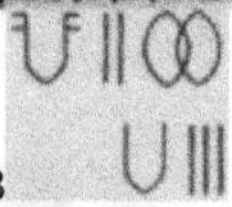

5474

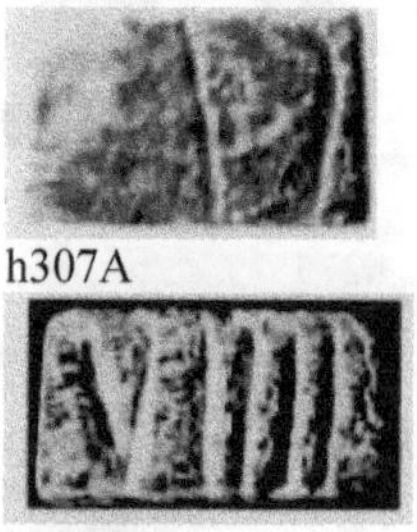

h307A

h307B

h308A

h308B

5427

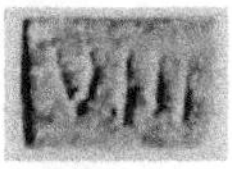

h309A
h309B

4403
4405, 4509, 4543, 5419, 5421, 5422, 5423, 5425, 5442, 5449

Incised miniature tablets h309, h311, h317, h932, h959, h935, h960

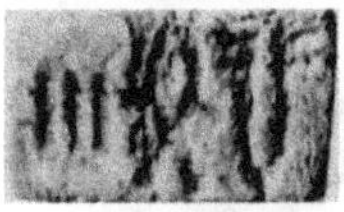

h310A

h310B 
5475

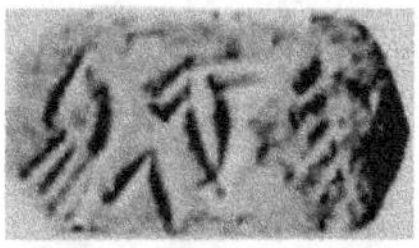

h311A

h311B
5421

h312B

h312Ac

5426

h313A

h313B

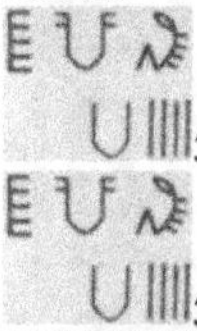

5432

5433

h314A

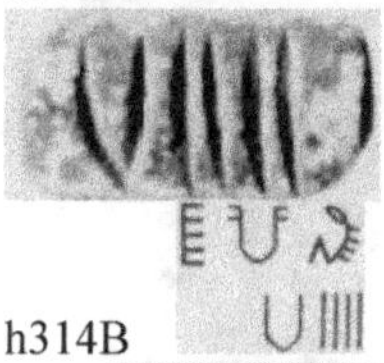

h314B

5447
h315A

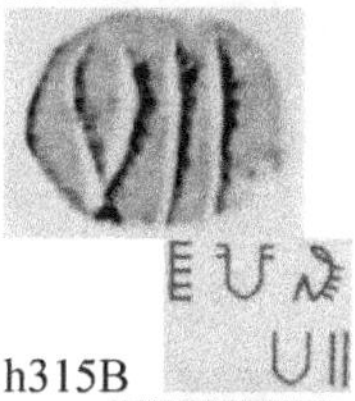

h315B

5464
h316A

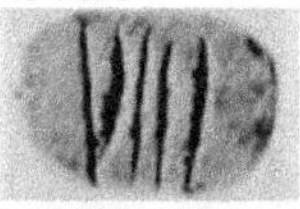

h316B

h317A

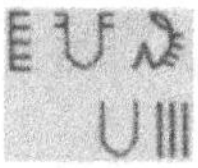

h317B
5442

h318A

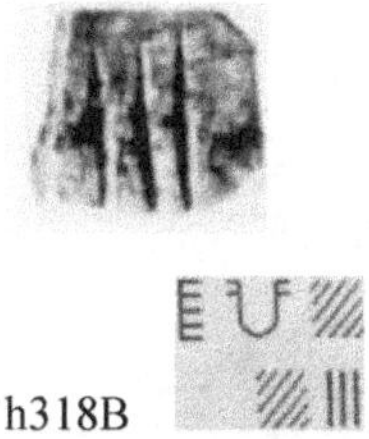

h318B
5451

h319A

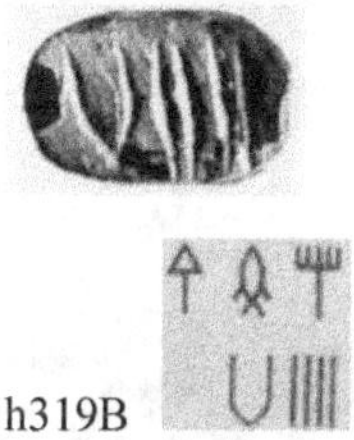

h319B
4544

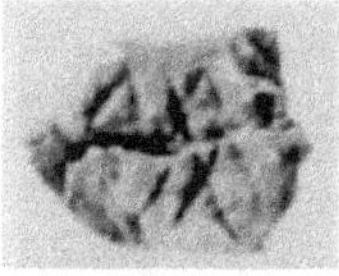

h320A

h320B
5450

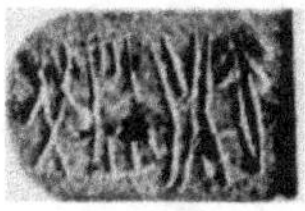

h321A

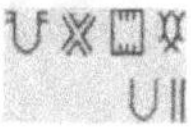

h321B
5402

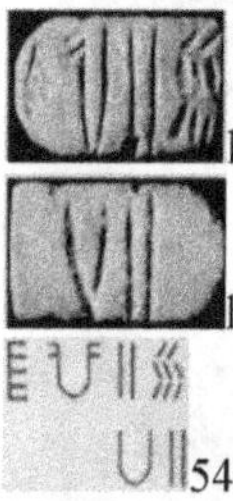

h322A

h322B

5498

h323A

h323B
4497

h324A

h324B
4484

h325A

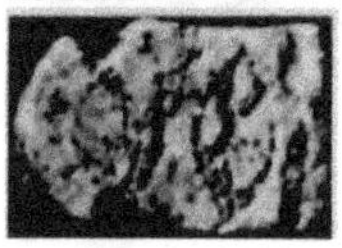

h325B

4416 Pict-130: Inscribed object in the shape of a writing tablet (?)

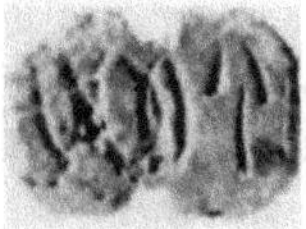
h326A

h326B 
4564 Double-axe?

h327A

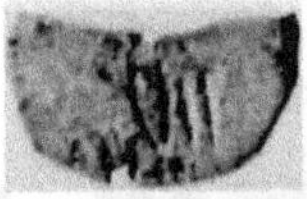
h327B 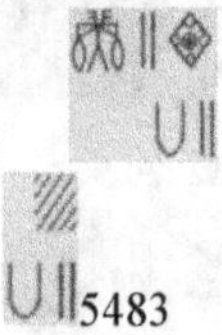
5472 5483
Shape of object: Blade of a weapon?

h328a

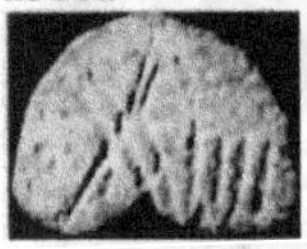

h328B 
4415 Shape of object: Bladeof weapon?

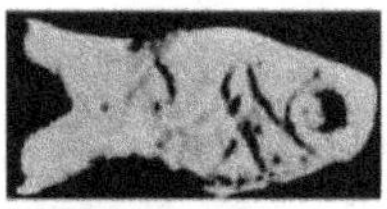
h329A

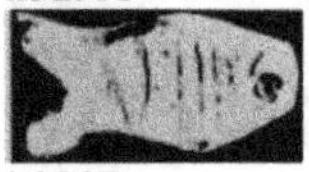
h329B

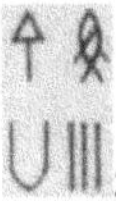 5496 Pict-68: Inscribed object in the shape of a fish.

h330A

h330B  4560

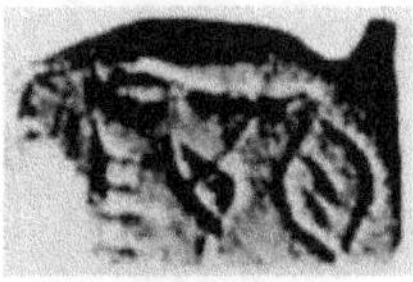
h331A Incised miniature tablet. 
4421, 4422, 4423

h332C 4885

h333A

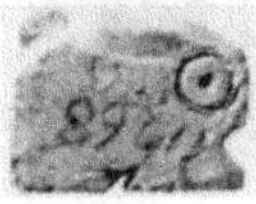
h333B

 4421

h334A

h334B

4423

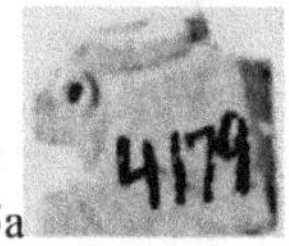
h335a

h335B 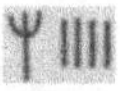
4425

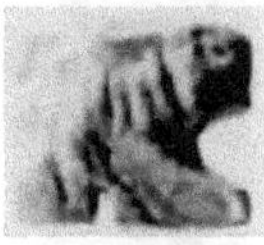
h336A

h336B

 4424

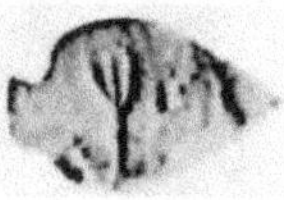
h337A

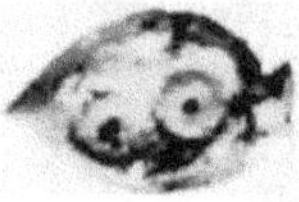

h337B 
4417 Pict-79: shape of a leaf. Dotted circle on obverse.

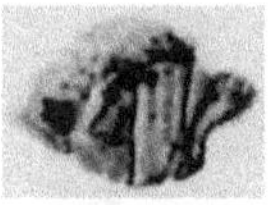
h338A

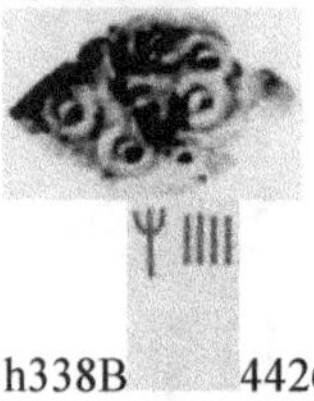
h338B 4426
Pict-39: Inscribed object in the shape of a tortoise (?) or leaf (?). Dotted circles on obverse.

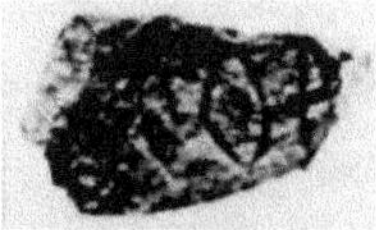
h339A

h339B

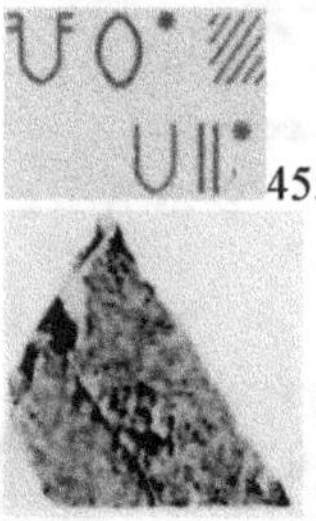
4559

h340A

h340B

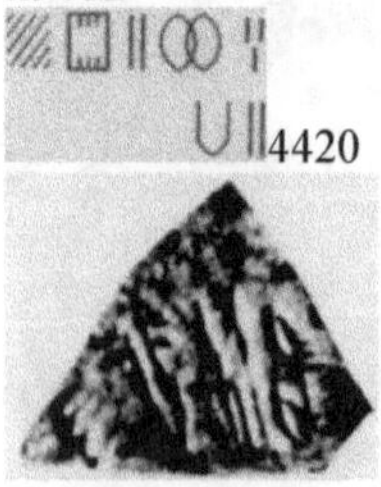
4420

h341A

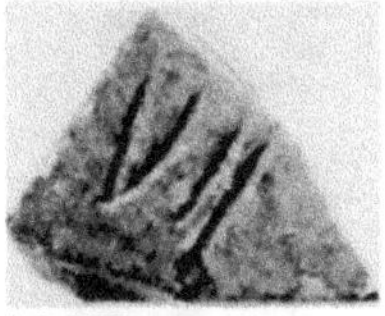

h341B

4419

h342A

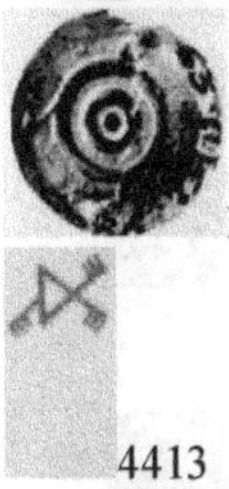

h342B

4413

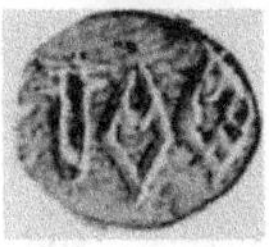

h343A

h343B
4549

h344A

h344B
4410

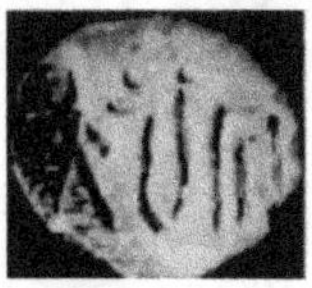

h345A

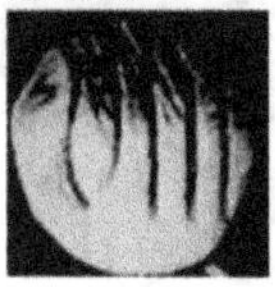

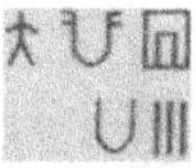

h345B
4550

h346A

h346B Incised miniature

tablet.
4412

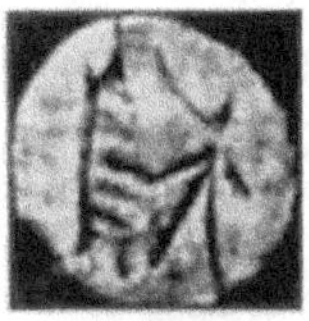

h347A  4414

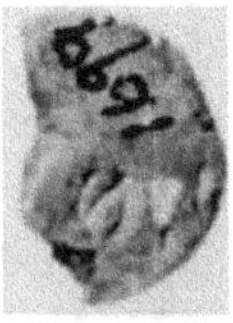

h348A

h348B
4552

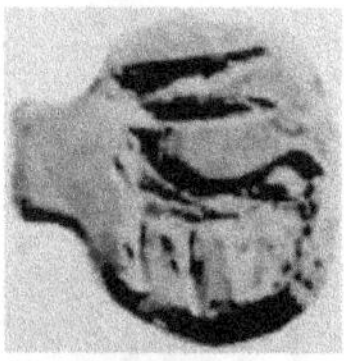

h349A

h349B

h350A

h350B

h350C

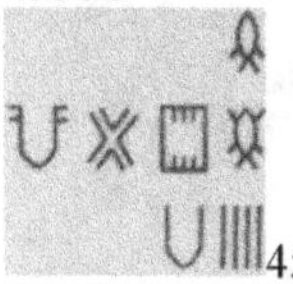

4576

h351A

h351B

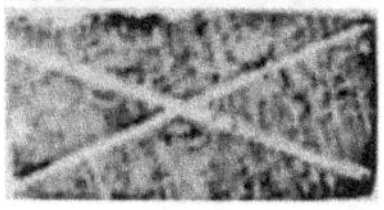

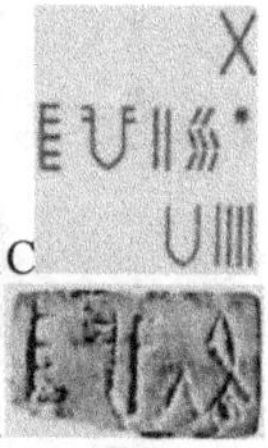

h351C

4581

h352A

h352B

h352C

4575 Pict-120: One or more dotted circles.

h353A

h353B

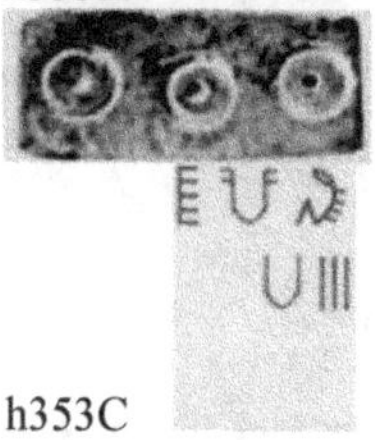

h353C
5416

h354A

h354B

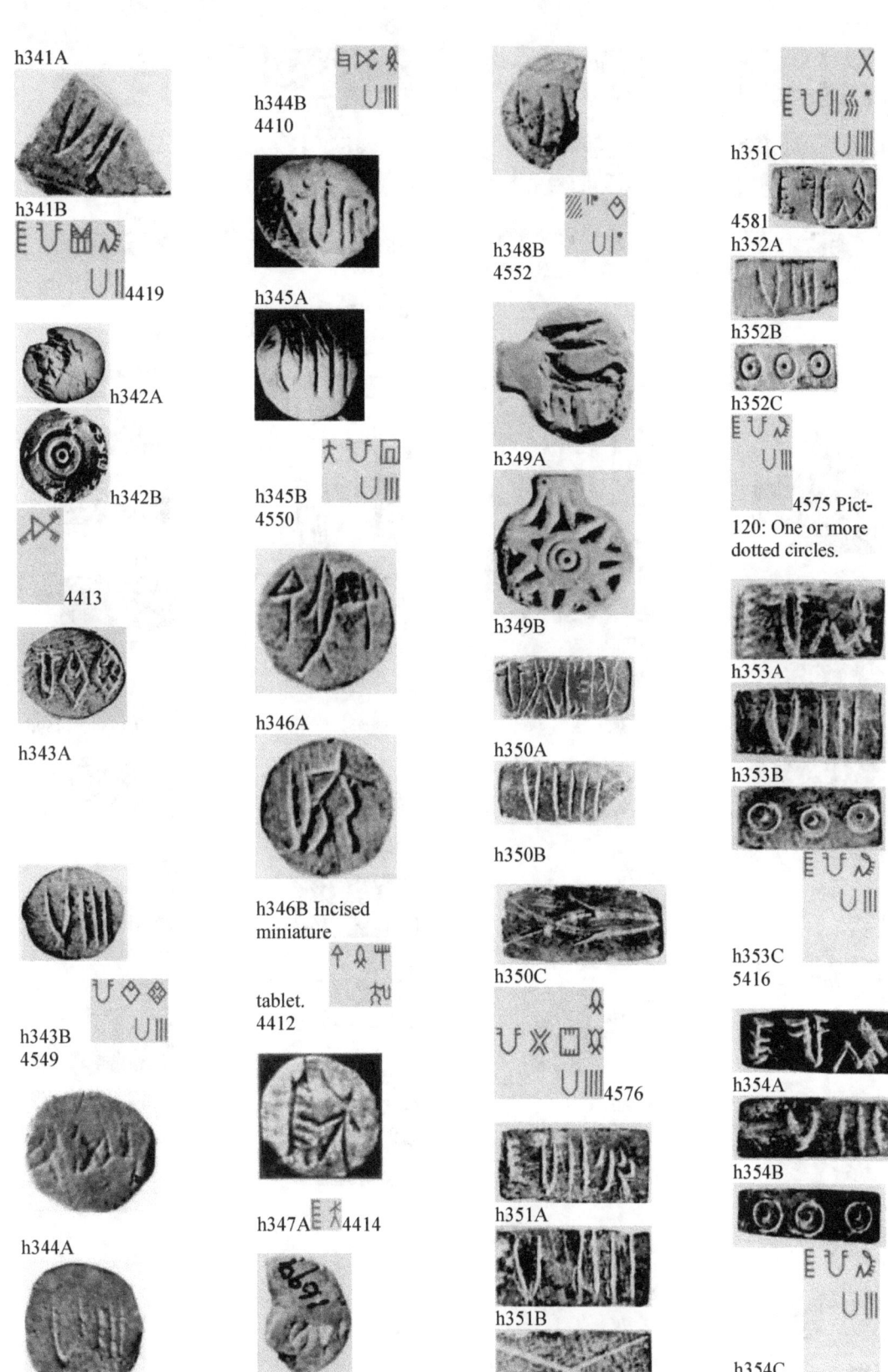

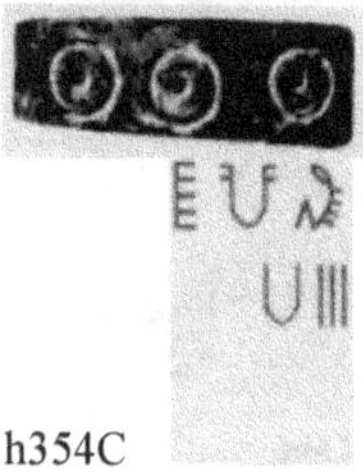

h354C
5499

h355A

h355B

h355C
5413

h356

h357

h358A

h358B
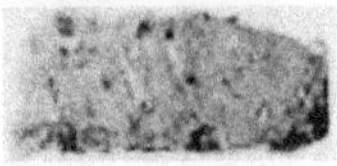
h358C

4579

h359a
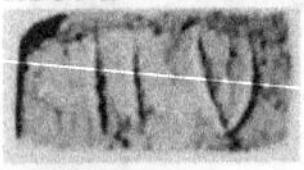
h359B
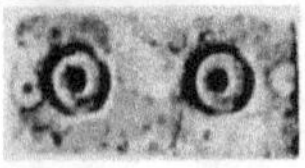
h359C

h360A

h360B

h360C
4584
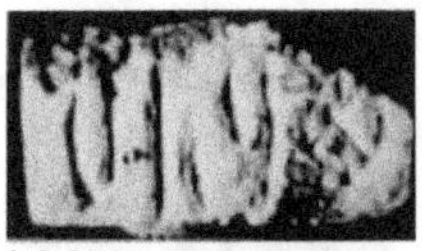
h361A

h361B

h361C
5476

h362A

h362B
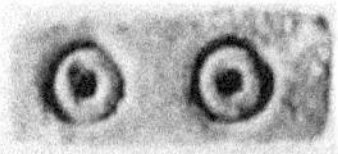

h362C
5466

h363A
h363B

h363C
h363E Pict-86

Pict-85 Standing person with horns and bovine features (hoofed legs and/or tail).

5471
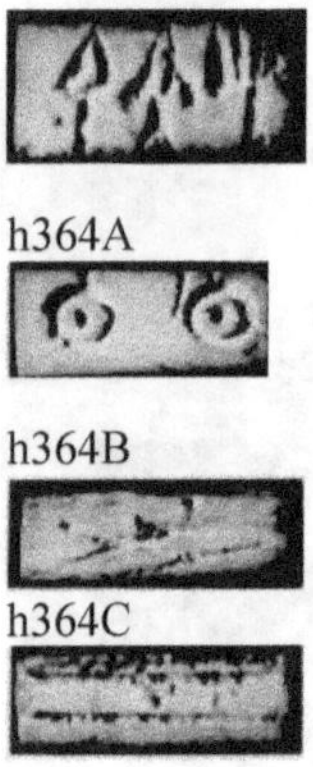
h364A
h364B
h364C
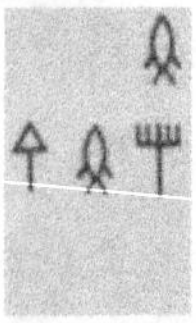
h364E
4635

h365A
h365B
h365C
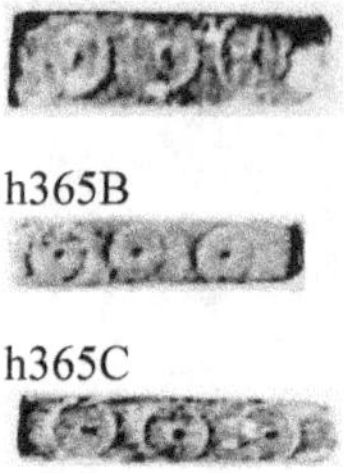
h365E
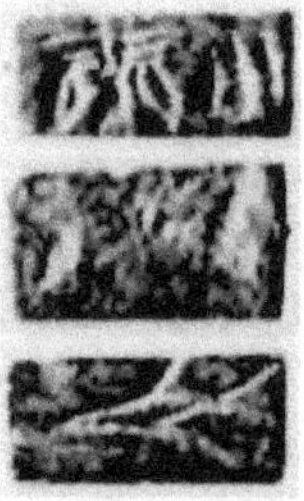
h366C
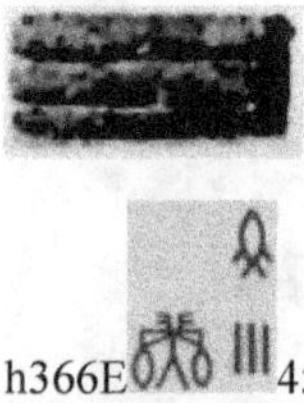
h366E 4590
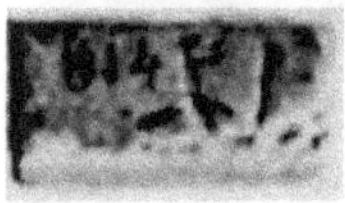
h367A
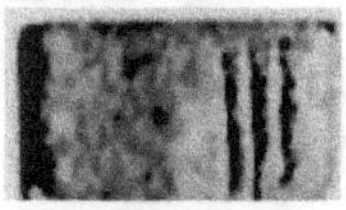
h367B

h367C
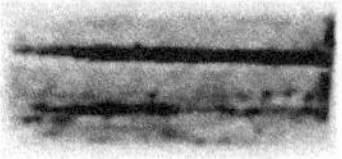

h367E 4401

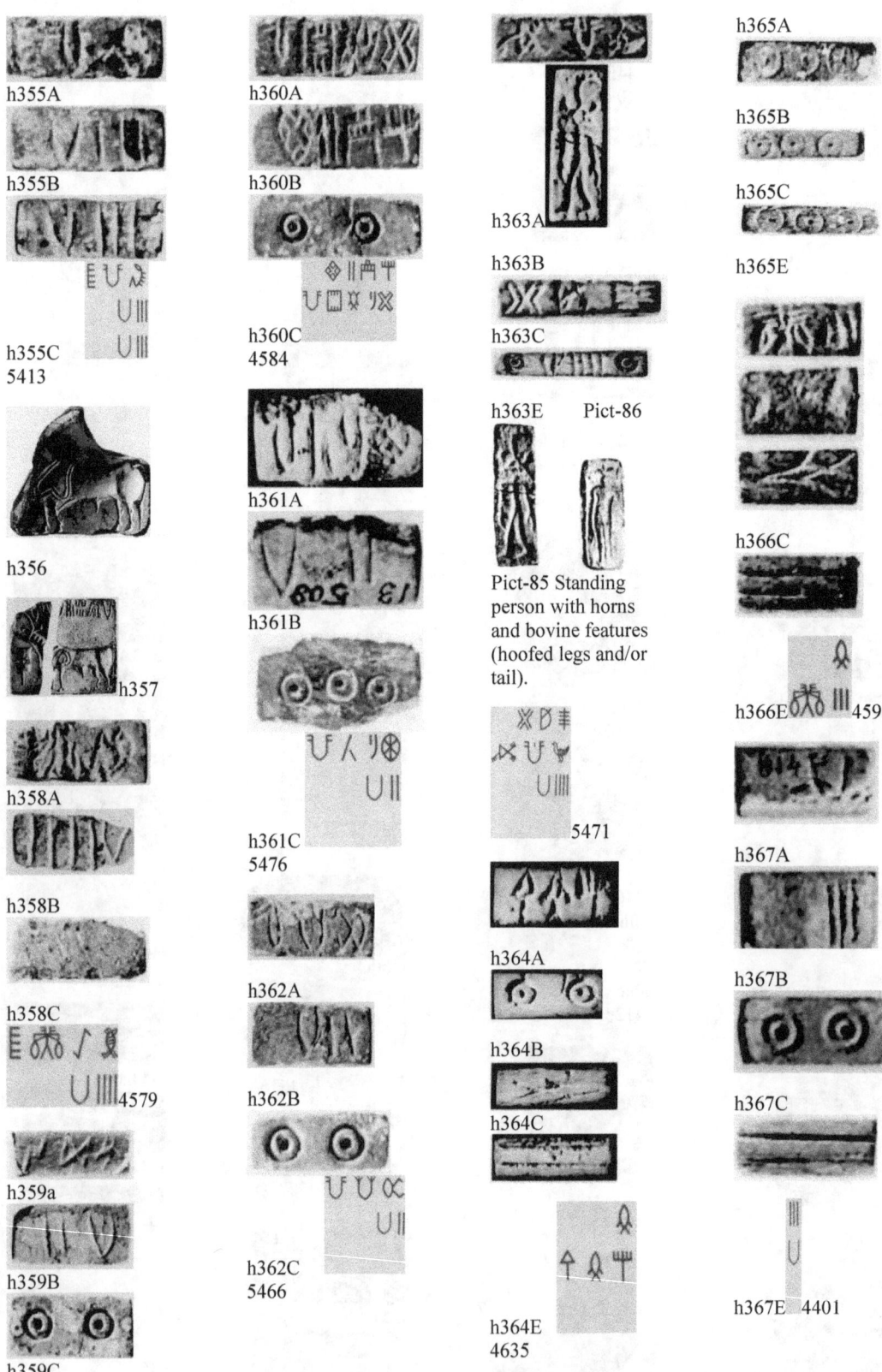

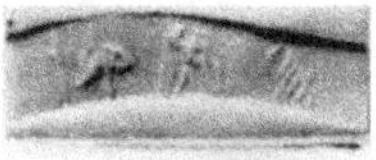
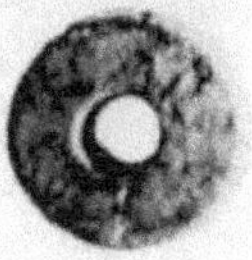
h368a

h368E 
4409

h369a

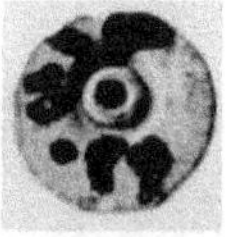
h369C

h369E
4718

h370A

h370A2

h371A

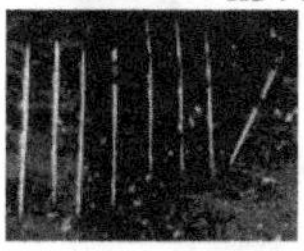
h371A2

h372A

h372A2

h374  4815

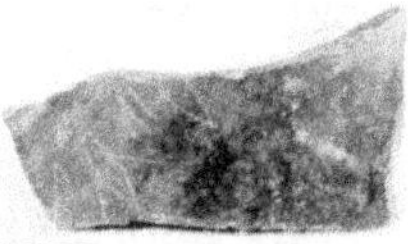
h375

4812

h377

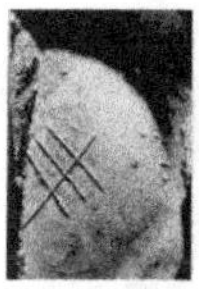
h378

h380 
4902 Bronze dagger

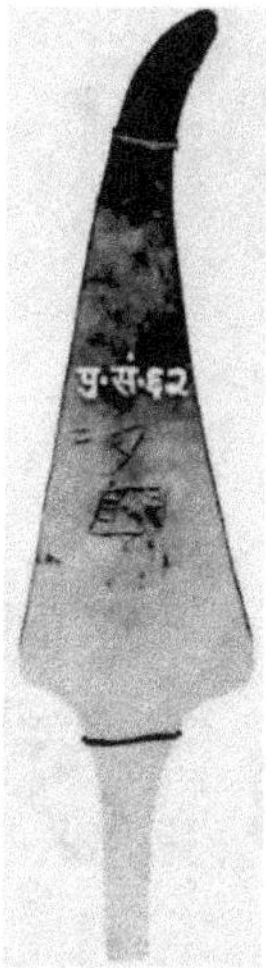

h381 
4901 Bronze dagger

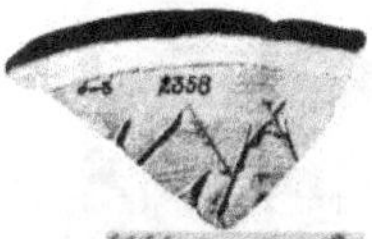
h382 
4818

h383 (Not shown).

4021

h384

h385

4045

h386

4025

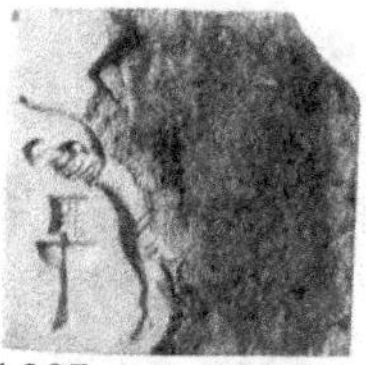
h387

h388

5062

h389

5090

h390

4024 [The second sign from right appears like a weaver's loom with three looped strings].

h391

5064

h392a  4207

h393

h394a 
5003

h395a

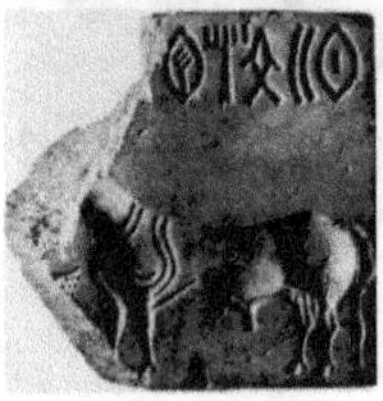
h396

4027

h397

h398

h399

h400

h401
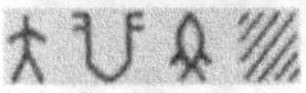
4168

h402

h403

h404

h405
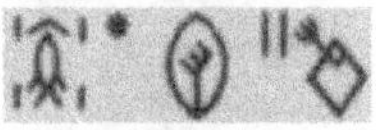
5091

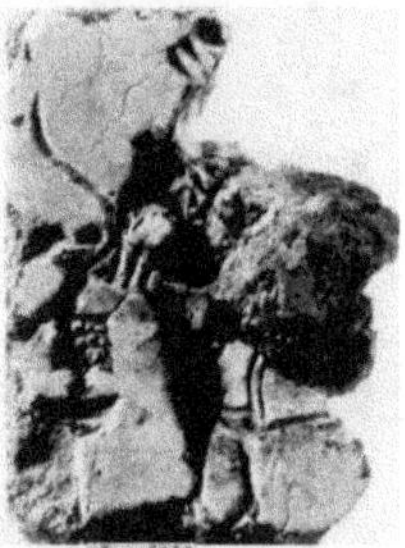
h406  5034

h407 
4126

h408

4079

h409

h410

4080

h411 
4078

h412
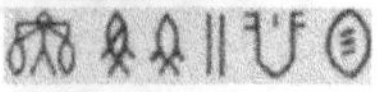
4036

h413
 4032

h414

h415
4204

h416
4059

h417
4051

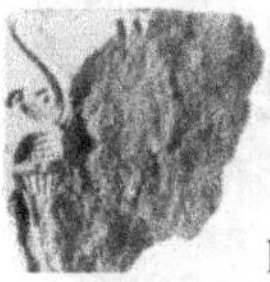

h418

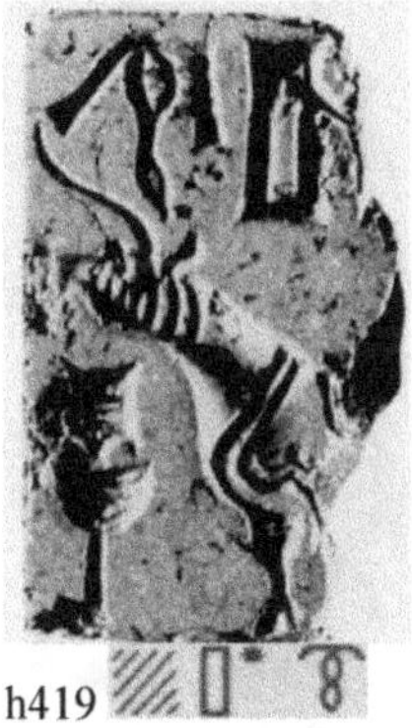

h419
5092

[ The first sign may be a squirrel as in Nindowaridamb 01 Seal].

h420

4614

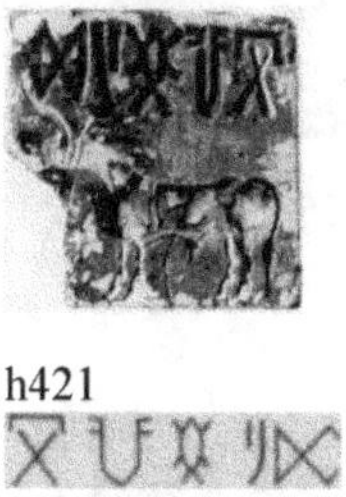

h421
4026

h422
4185

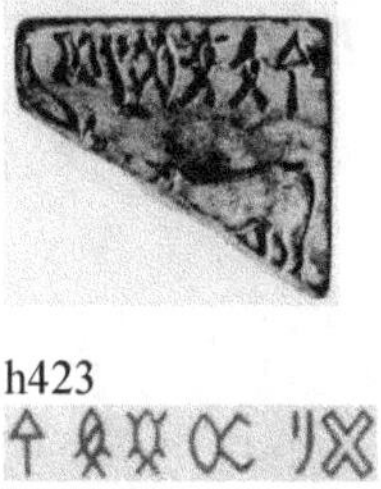

h423
4056

h424

h425

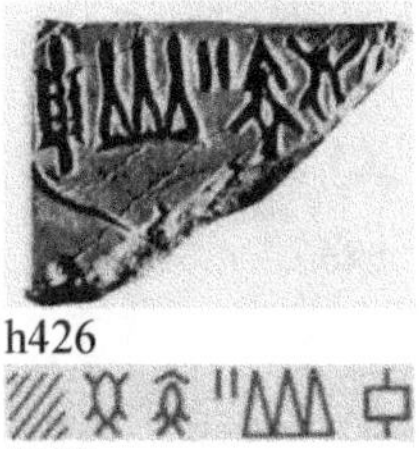

h426
4153

h427
4217

h428

h429

h430

h431
5068

h432
4616

h433

h434

h435

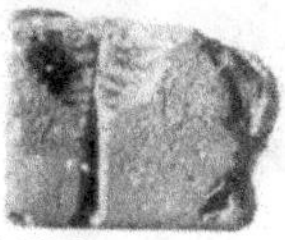

h436

h437

h438

h439

h440
4615

h441
4074

h442
4095

h443
4121

h444

h445 5110

h446
4034

h447
4089

h448
4054

h449
4082

h450
4084

h451
4137

h452a 4124

h453
4061

h454
4132

h455
4055

h456
4083

h457
5080

h458 4050

h459
4092

h460

h461
4037

h462
4620

h463

h464a
4100

h465 4181

h466
4111

h467
4624

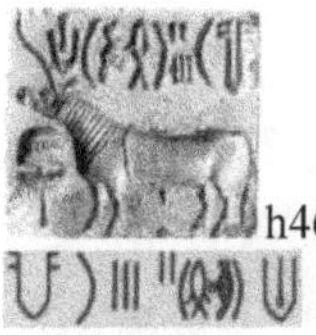
h468
4087

h469
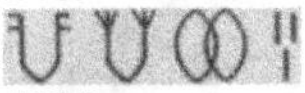
4138

h470
4186

h471
4145

h472

4152

h473
4096

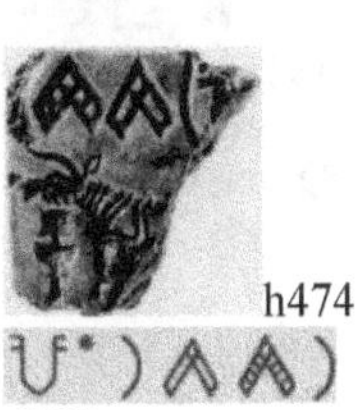
h474
4188

h475  4093

h476 
4102

h477

h478
4088

h479
4099

h480  4180

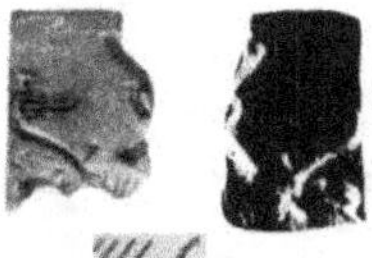
h482  4208

h483

h484
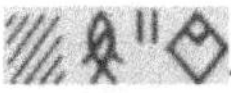 4154

h485

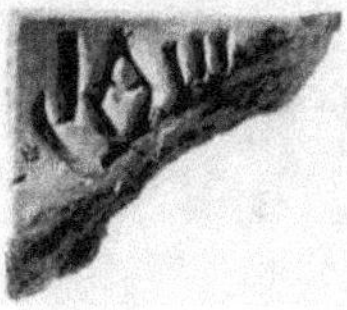
h486

h488 
4198

h489
4189

h490
h492

h493

h494

h495

h497

h498

h499
5093

h500

h501 
4112

h502
4143

h503
4129

h504
4183

h505 5094

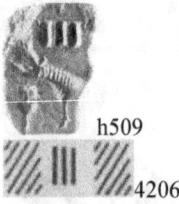

h506
4097

h507 4159

h508

h509
4206

h510
4139

h511
4165

h512a
4618

h513
4163

h514
4116

h515
4162

Text 4166
h516a

h517

h518 4160

h519
4147

h520 4127

h521 4155

h522

h523
5071

h524
4150

h525 4149

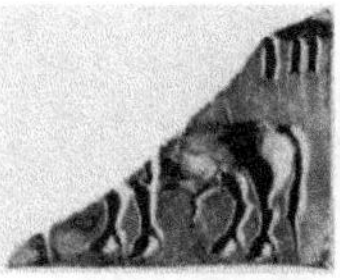

h526

h527

h528

h529

h530
4148 [May have to be arranged from right to left?]

h531

4172

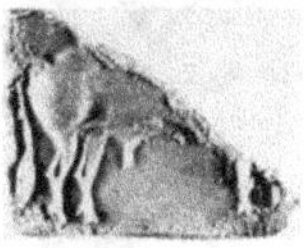
h532

h533

4625

h534

h535

h536
h537

4170

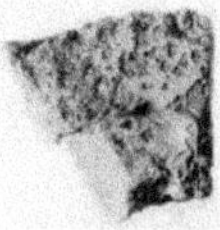
h538

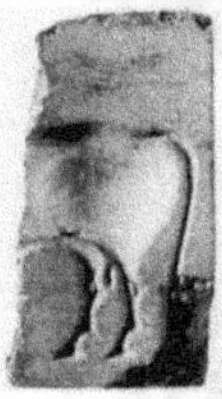
h539

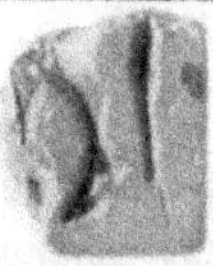
h541
h542

h543

4177

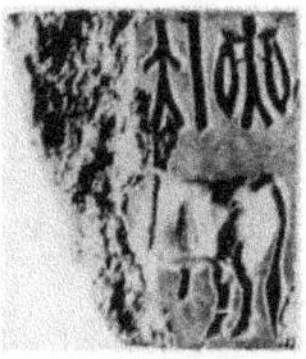
h544

4144

h545
4622

h546

4697

h547

h548

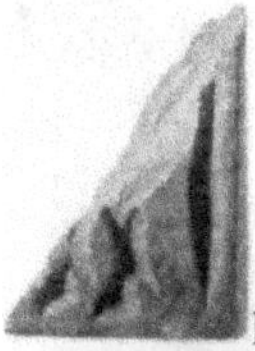
h549

h550
4211

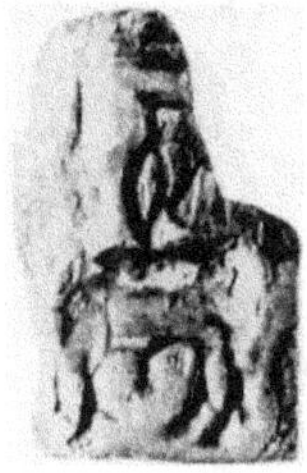
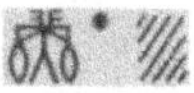
h551
4197

h552

h553

h554

h555

h556

h557

h558
4220

h559
4290

h561

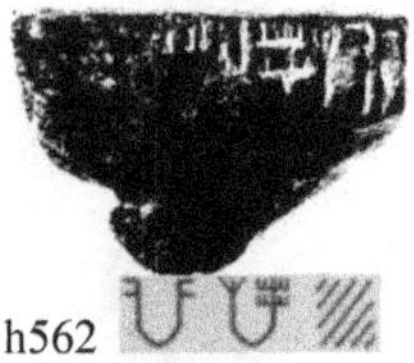

h562
5066

h563
5065

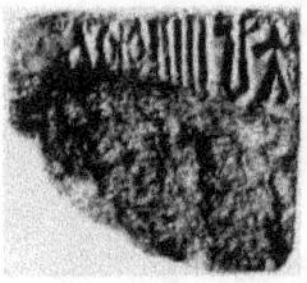

h565

4621

h566
4277

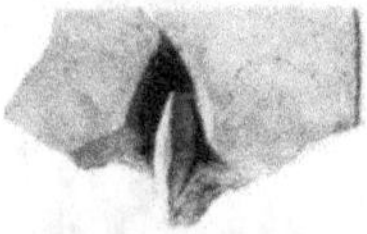

h567

h568

h569

4263

h570

4212

h571

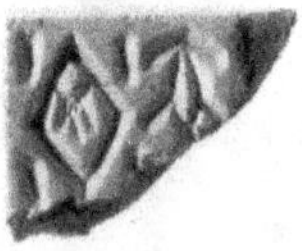

h572
4695

h574

4696

h575

h576

h577

4243

h578

h579

5109

h580

h581

h582

h583

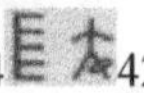

h584 4235
Bison.

h585

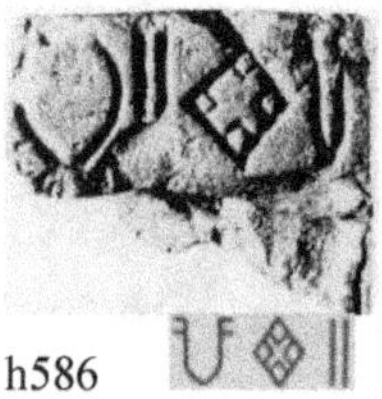

h586
4237

h587

h588

h589
4239

h590

h591
4228

h592
5081

h593

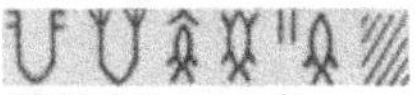

4250 [Composite animal].

h594 [Composite animal].

h595

4623

 h596a

4382 [One-horned bull].

h597A

h597D

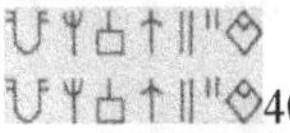 4075

h598A

h598D

5073 [The ligature in-fixed on the last sign of the second line may be Sign 54 ]

h599A

h599D

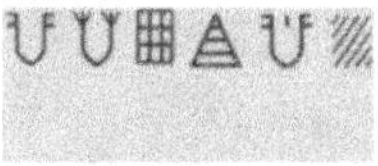

5076

h600 

4156 [The last sign may be a variant of Sign 51 ] .

h601

4044

h602a

 4169

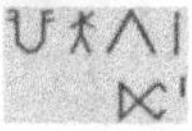

h603

4224

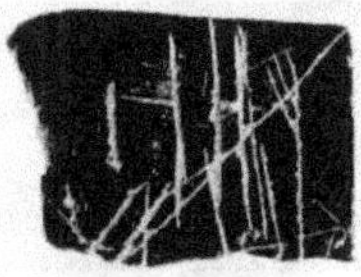

h604

h605

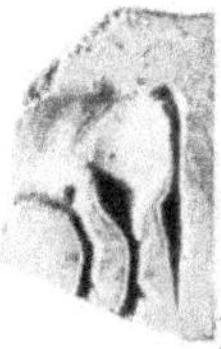

h606

 4167

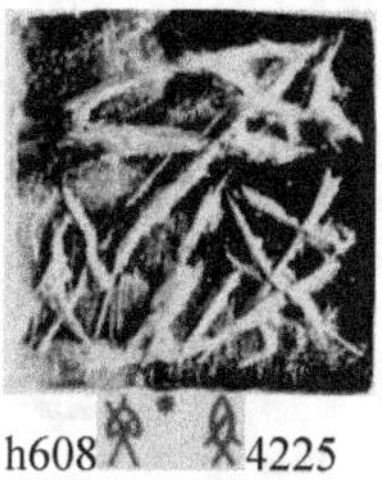

h608 4225

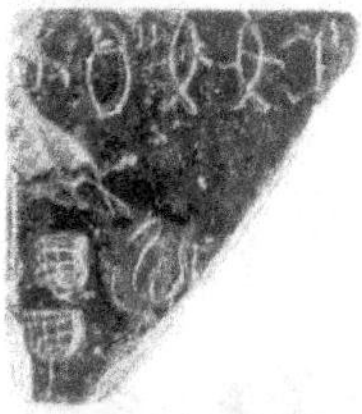

h609

4060

h610

4098

h611

4260 One-horned bull.

h612A

h612B

h612D

4123

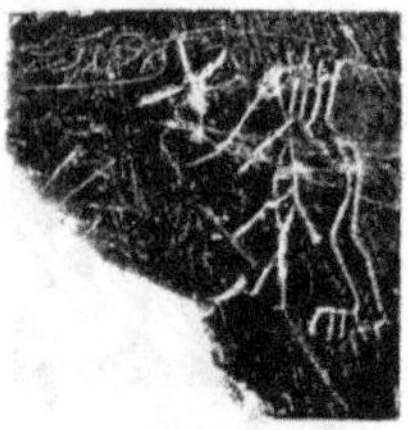

h613A

h613C

4259

Endless-knot motif?

h614

h616

h617

h618

h619

h620

h621

h622

h623

h624

h625

h626

h627

h628

h629

h630

h631

h632 h633

h634

h635

h636

h637

h638

h639

5061

h640

h641A

h641C

4698

h642

4266

h643

4273

h644

4299

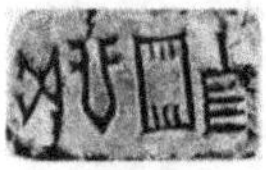

h645

4265

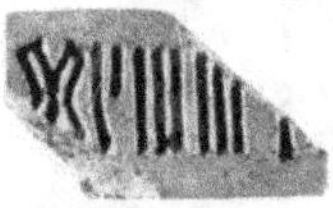

h646

5108

h647

4291

h648

h649

4281

h650A

h650C

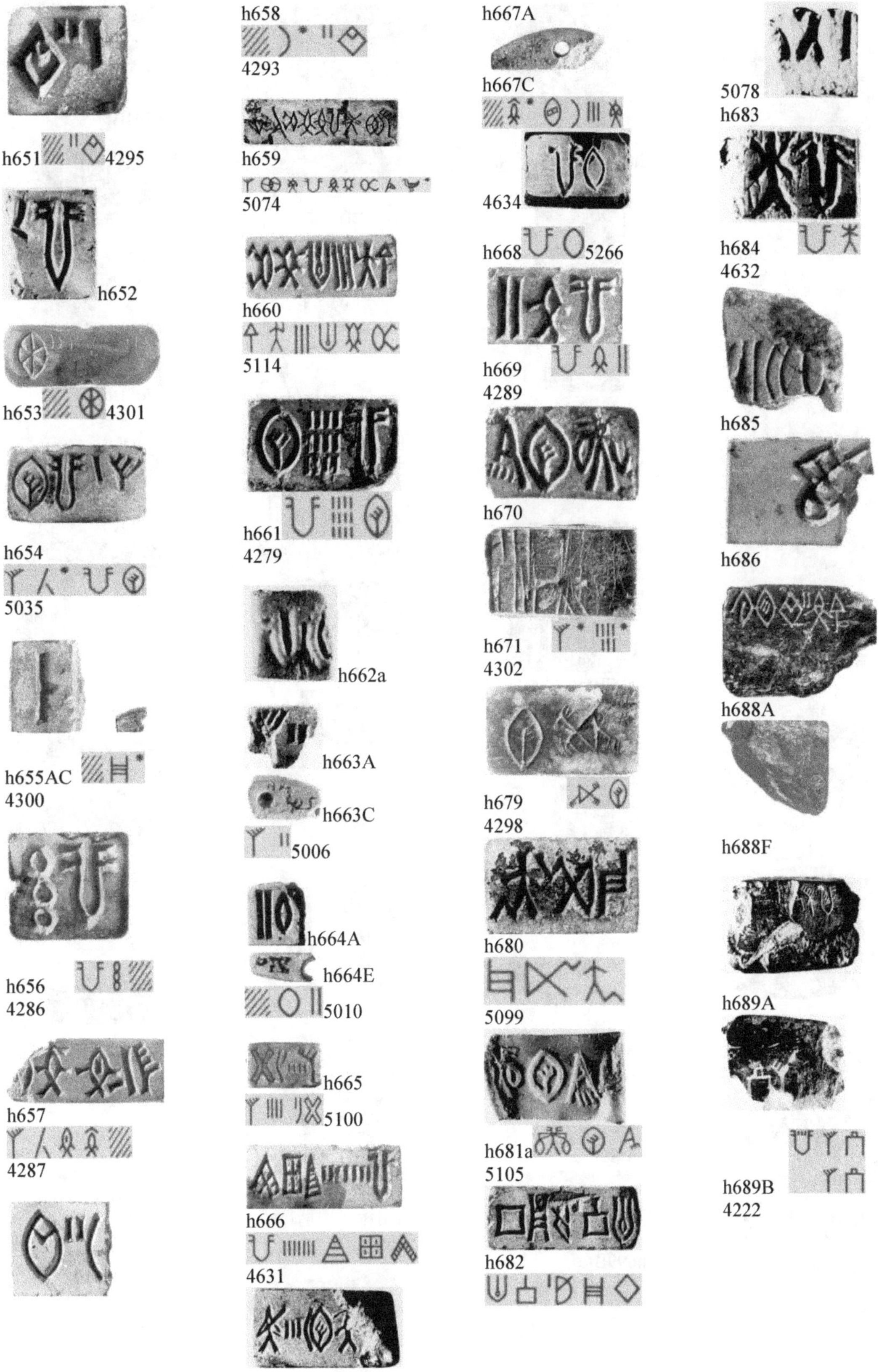
h651 4295
h652
h653 4301
h654
5035
h655AC
4300
h656
4286
h657
4287
h658
4293
h659
5074
h660
5114
h661
4279
h662a
h663A
h663C
5006
h664A
h664E
5010
h665
5100
h666
4631
h667A
h667C
4634
h668 5266
h669
4289
h670
h671
4302
h679
4298
h680
5099
h681a
5105
h682
5078
h683
h684
4632
h685
h686
h688A
h688F
h689A
h689B
4222

h690si  5304

h691A1si

h691A2si

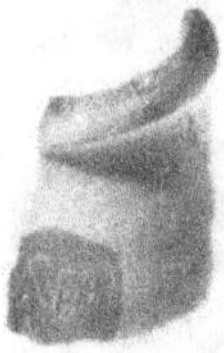

h692A1si

h692A2si

h693t

4707

h694t

h695t

h696At

h696Bt

4677

h697At

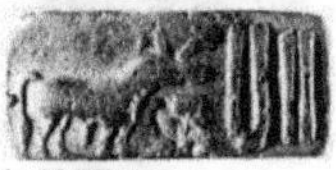

h697Bt

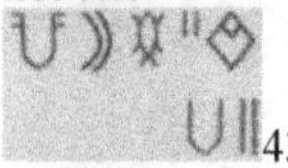

4314

h698At

h698Bt

4659

h699At

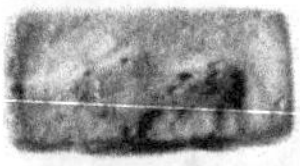

h699Bt

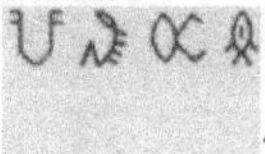

5288

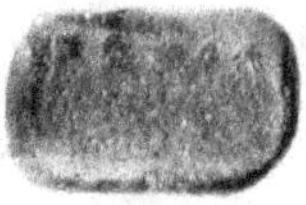

h700At

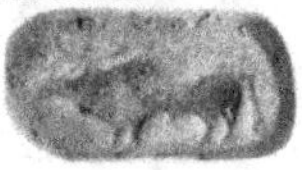

h700Bt

h701At

h701Bt

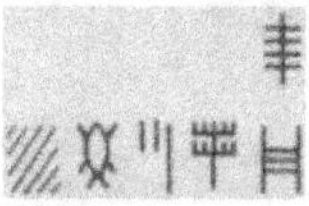

5329

h702At

h702Bt

4601

h703At

h703Bt

4595

h704At

h704Bt

h705At

h705Bt

4337

h706At

h706Bt

4340

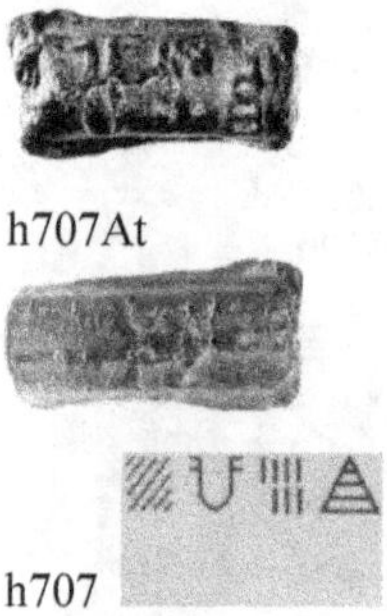

h707At

h707

4339

h708At

h708Bt

5280

h709 Text

5260

h710 Text
5249

h711 Text

4715

h713At

h713Bt

h714At

h714Bt

Standing person with horns and bovine features (hoofed legs and/or a tail) Icon of a person has bull's legs and a raised club.

h715At

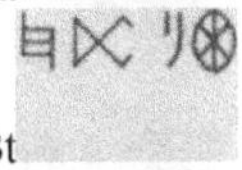

h715Bt

5299

h716At

h716Bt

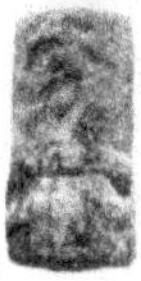

h717At

h717Bt

h718At

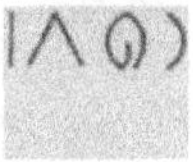

h718Bt
4328

h719At

h719Bt
4326

h720At
h720Bt

h722At
h722Bt

h723At

h723Bt

h724At

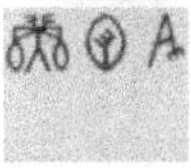

h724Bt
5255

h725At

h725Bt

h726At

h726Bt

h727At

h727Bt

h728At
h728Bt

h729At
h729Bt

4331

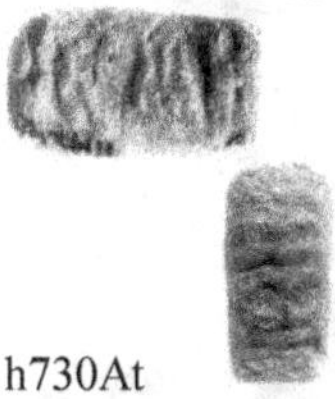

h730At
h730Bt

h731At

h731Bt

h732At
h732Bt

h733At

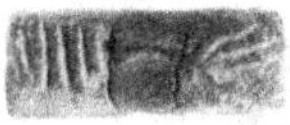

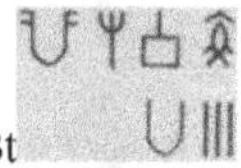

h733Bt
5222

h734At

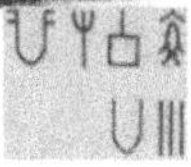

h734Bt
5286

h735At

h735Bt
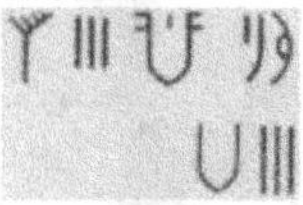
5310

h736At

h736Bt

h737At

h737Bt

h738At

h738Bt
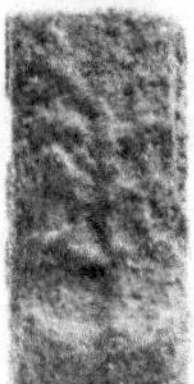
h739At

h739Bt

h740At
h740Bt
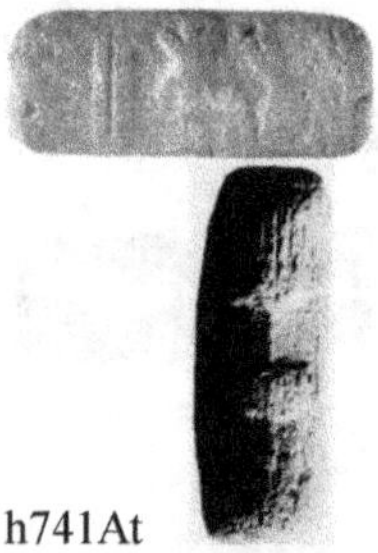
h741At
h741Bt
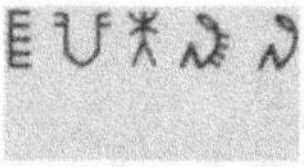
5263

h742At

h742Bt

4320
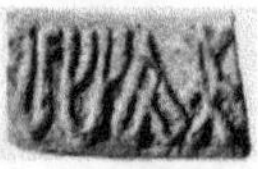
h743At

h743Bt

h744At
h744Bt

h745At

h745Bt
5257
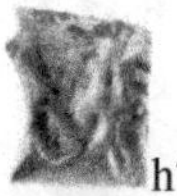
h746At

h746Bt

h747At
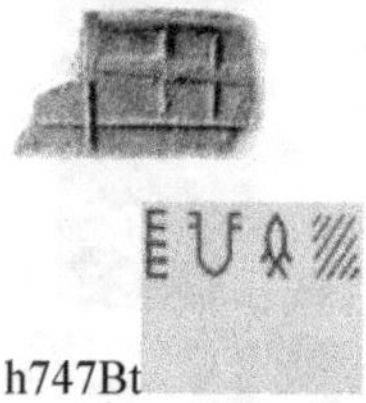
h747Bt
4656

h748At
4654

h749At

h750At

h751At

h752At
5275

h753At
5231

h754At
4716

h755At
5287

h756At
4669

h757At
4655

h758At
h759At

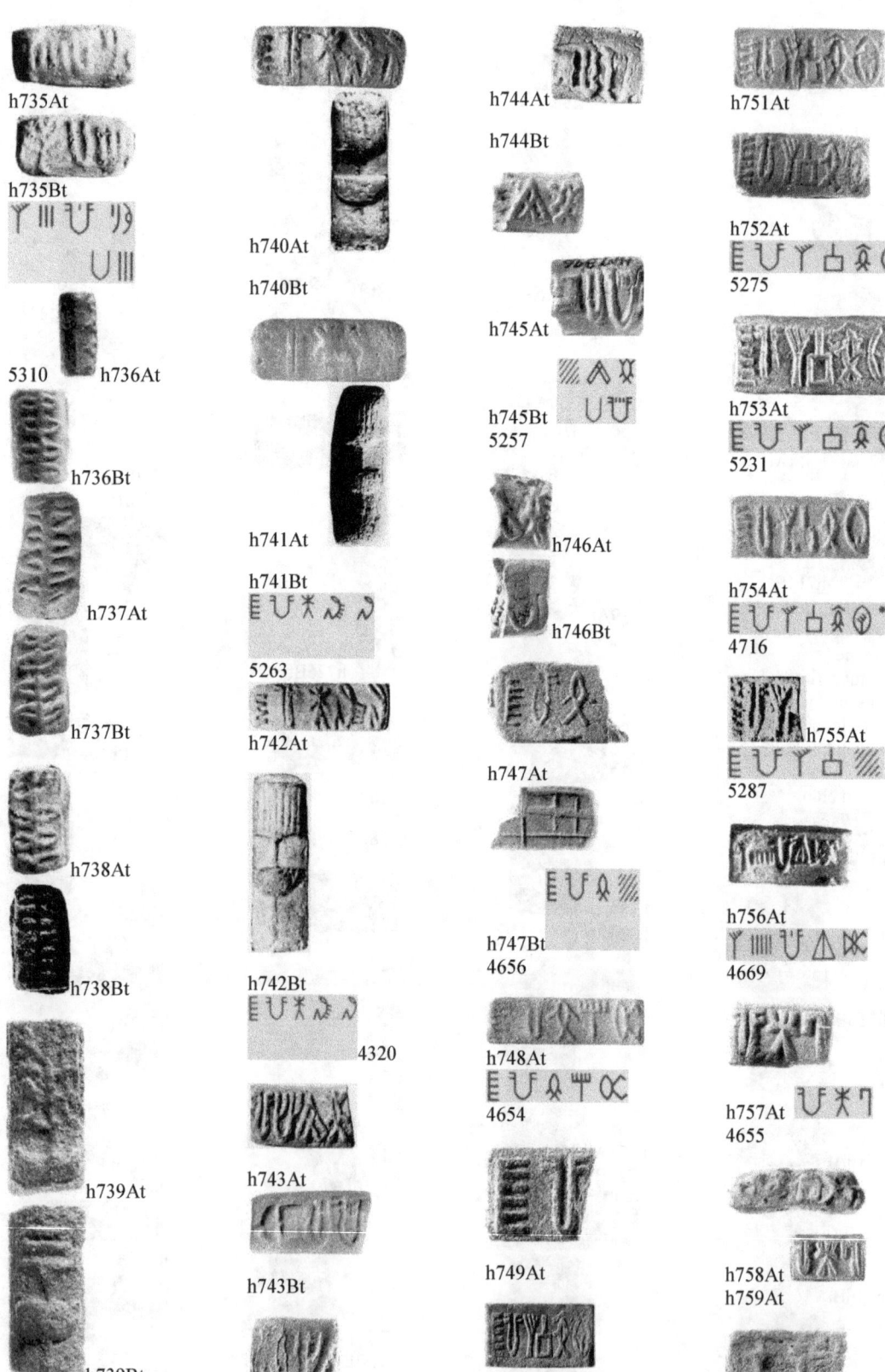

h760At

h760Bt

h761At

h761Bt

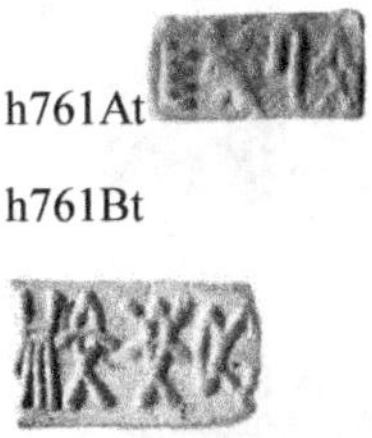

h762At

h762Bt Tablet in bas-relief.

4354

h763At

h763Bt

4661

h764At

h764Bt

h765At

h765Bt

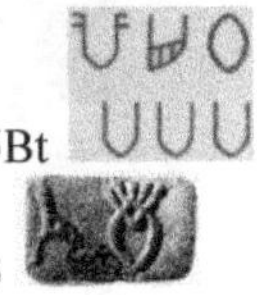

4653

h766At

h766Bt

4359

h767At

h767Bt

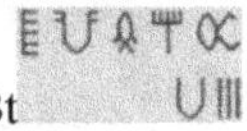

4352

h768At

h768Bt

4358

h769At

h769Bt

4667

h770At

h770Bt

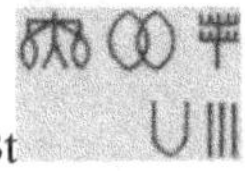

4353

h771At

h771Bt

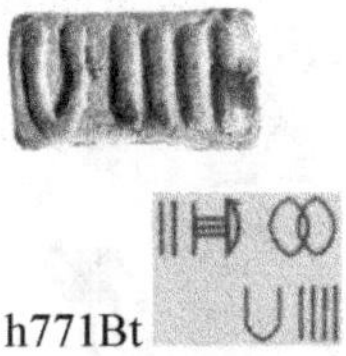

4678 [The second sign on line 1 is a squirrel

].

h772At

h772Bt

4660

h773At

h773Bt

4351

h774At

h774Bt

4672

h775At

h776At

h776Bt

4350

h777At

h777Bt

h778At

h778Bt

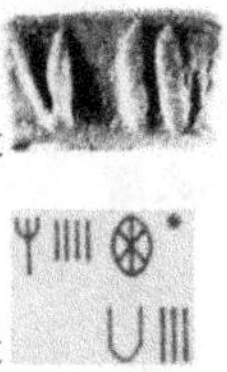

5322

h779At

h779Bt

h780At

h780Bt

4361

h781At

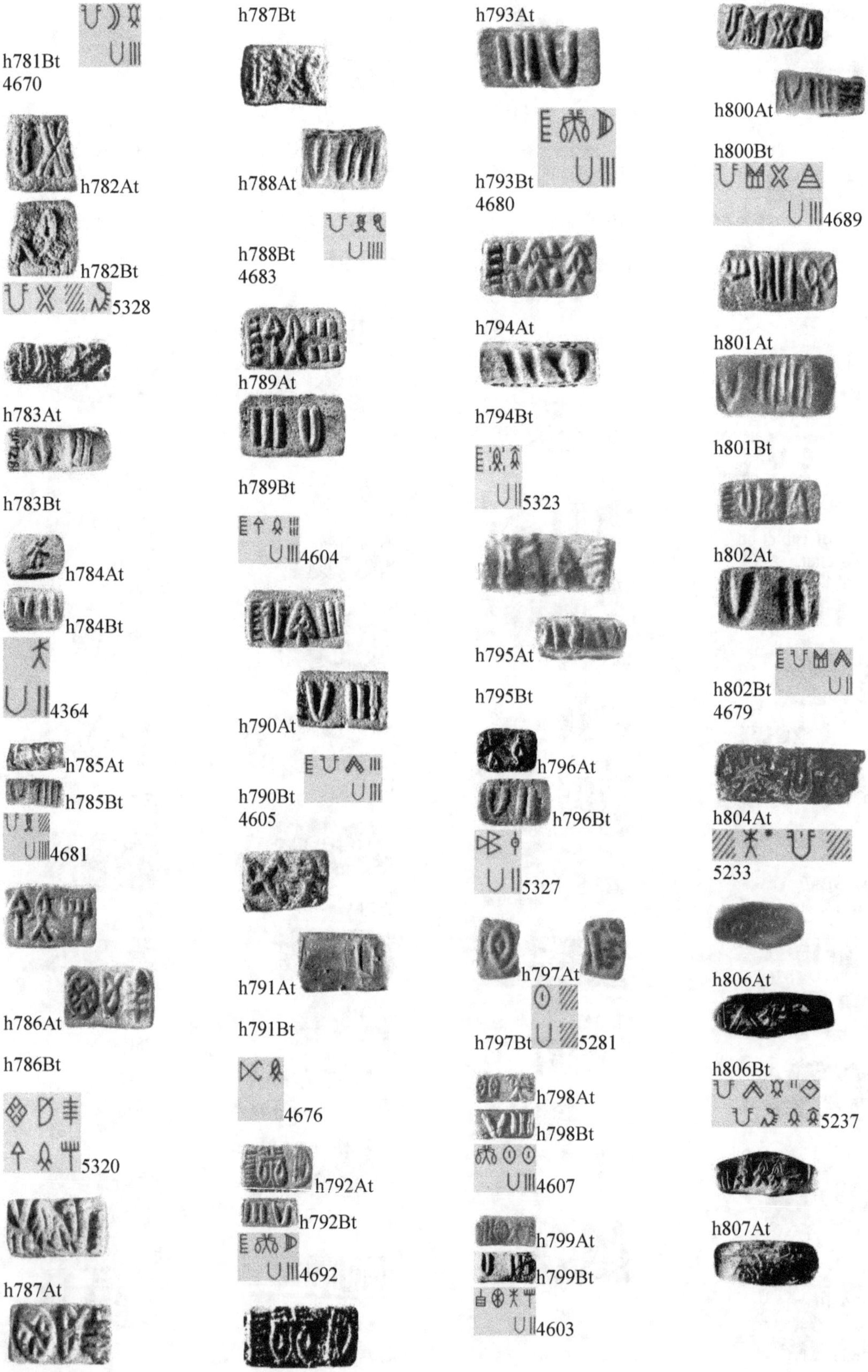

h781Bt
4670
h782At
h782Bt
5328
h783At
h783Bt
h784At
h784Bt
4364
h785At
h785Bt
4681
h786At
h786Bt
5320
h787At

h787Bt
h788At
h788Bt
4683
h789At
h789Bt
4604
h790At
h790Bt
4605
h791At
h791Bt
4676
h792At
h792Bt
4692

h793At
h793Bt
4680
h794At
h794Bt
5323
h795At
h795Bt
h796At
h796Bt
5327
h797At
h797Bt
5281
h798At
h798Bt
4607
h799At
h799Bt
4603

h800At
h800Bt
4689
h801At
h801Bt
h802At
h802Bt
4679
h804At
5233
h806At
h806Bt
5237
h807At

h807Bt

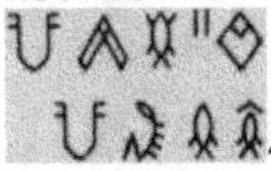 4343

One-horned bull.

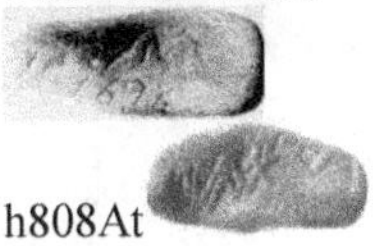

h808At

h808Bt

 5238

h810At

 4366

h811At

h811Bt

4349

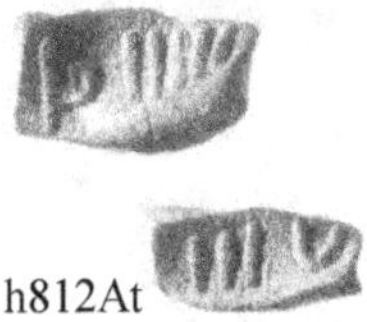

h812At

h812Bt

 4686

h813At

h813Bt

 4682

h814At

h814Bt 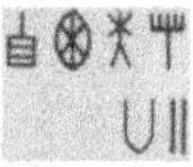

4606

h815At

h815Bt

h816At

h816Bt 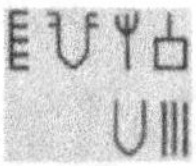

4602

h817At

h817Bt Inscribed object in the shape of a double-axe.One or more dotted circles.

h818At

h818Bt Inscribed object in the shape of a double-axe.

 4376

h819At

h819Bt Shape of object: Blade of a weapon?

 5302

h820At

h820Bt

h821At

h821Bt Shape of object: axe.

h822At

h822Bt Shape of object: axe.

 5319

h823At

h823Bt 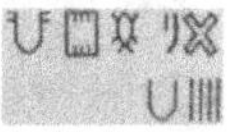

4346

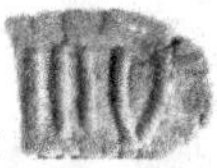

h824At

h824Bt 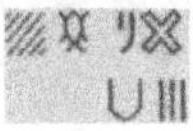

5278

h825At

h825Bt Shape of object: sickle?

 5324

h827At

h827Bt Shape of object: axe?

h829At

h829Bt

 5303

h830At

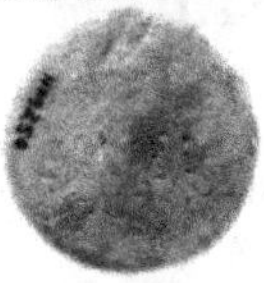

h830Bt Tablet in bas-relief. Bovid.

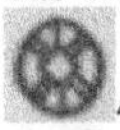4311

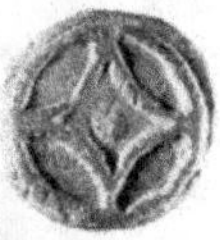

h832At

h832Bt Tablet in bas-relief
Pict-121: Lozenge within a circle with a dot in the center.

4377

h833At

h833Bt

4370

h834At

h834Bt

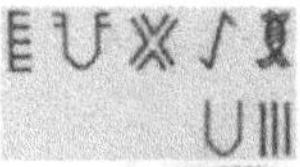

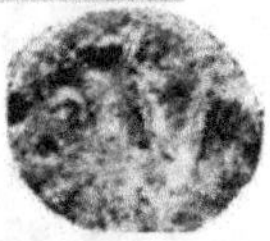

4666
h835Bt

h836At

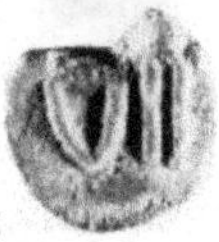

h837At
h837Bt

4381

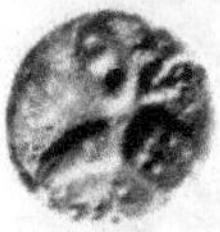

h838At

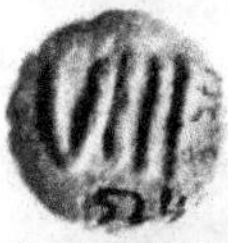

h838Bt

4375

h839At

h839Bt 4378

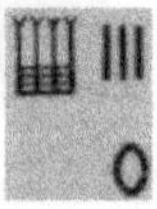

h840At
4380

h841At 
4379

h842At

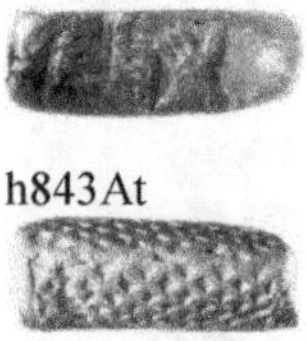

h843At

h843Ct

5326

h844At

h844Bt

h845At

h845Bt

h845Ct

h846At

h846Bt

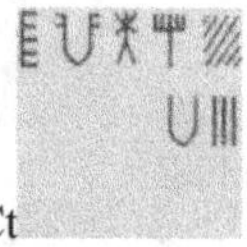

h846Ct
4641

h847At

h847Bt

h847Ct

h848At

h848Bt

h848Ct

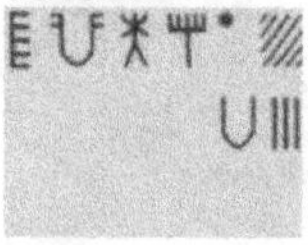

4597

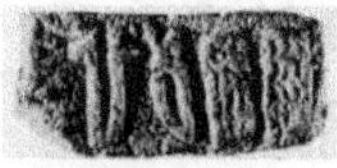

h849At

h849Bt

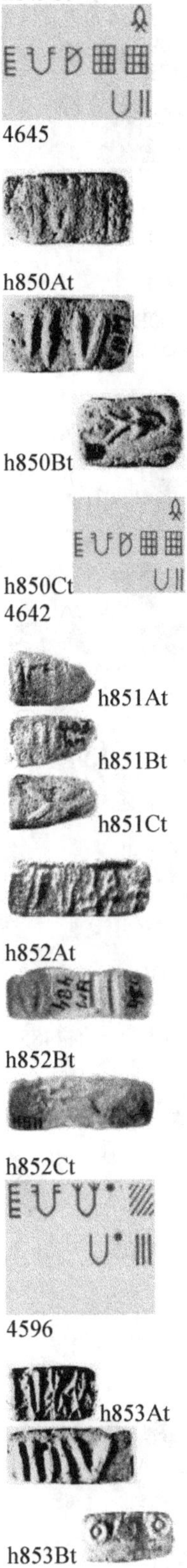

h849Ct
4645
h850At
h850Bt
h850Ct
4642
h851At
h851Bt
h851Ct
h852At
h852Bt
h852Ct
4596
h853At
h853Bt

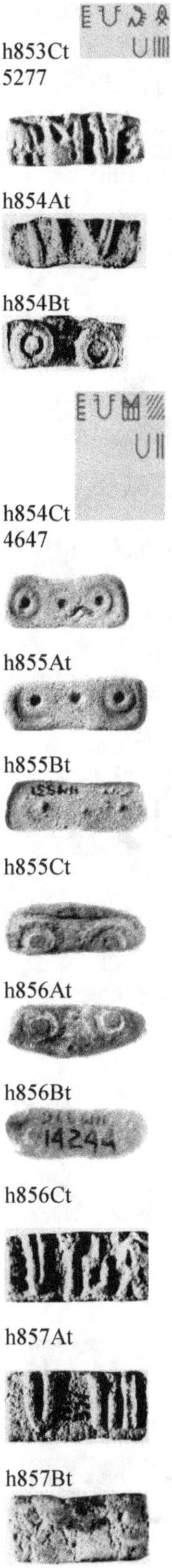

h853Ct
5277
h854At
h854Bt
h854Ct
4647
h855At
h855Bt
h855Ct
h856At
h856Bt
h856Ct
h857At
h857Bt

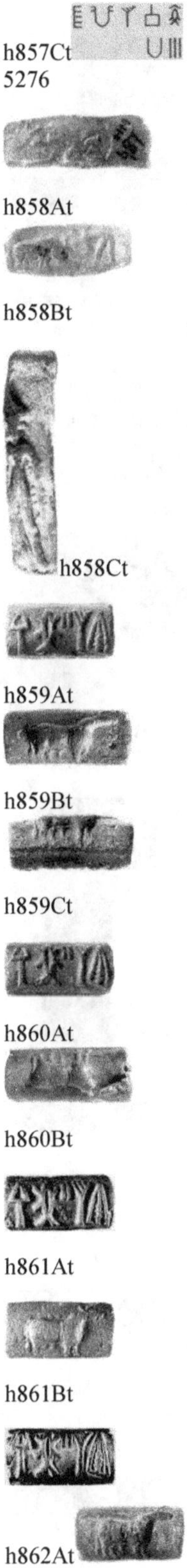

h857Ct
5276
h858At
h858Bt
h858Ct
h859At
h859Bt
h859Ct
h860At
h860Bt
h861At
h861Bt
h862At
h862Bt

h863ABt
h864ABt
h865ABt
h866ABt
h867ABt
h868ABt
h869ABt
h870ABt
h871Bt
5234
h872Bt
5230
h873At
h873Bt
5227
h874At

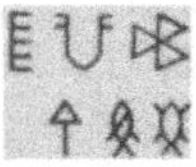
h874Bt
4362

h875At

h875Bt
4651

h876At

h876Bt
4675
h877At
h877Bt 4594

h878At
h878Bt
4687

h879Abit

h880ABit
4433

h881Abit
4434

h882Abit

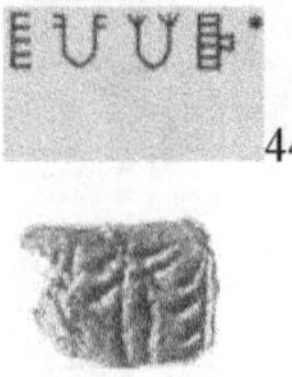
4436

h883Ait

h883Bit

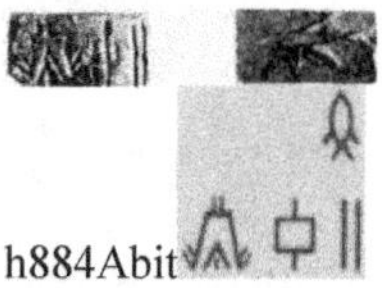
h884Abit
4437

h885Ait

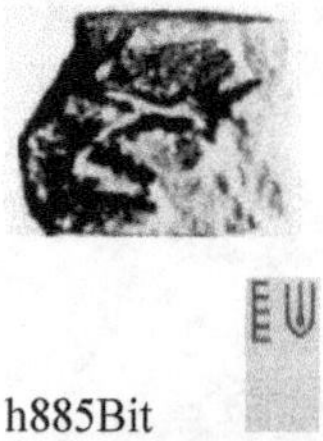
h885Bit
4530 Fish.

h887Ait
h887Bit

h888Abit
4466

h889Abit
5477

h890ABit

4446

h891ABit
h892ABit
4451

h893Ait
h893Bit
4522

h894ABit
4487

h895Ait
h895Bit

h896ABit
4480

h897ABit
h898ABit
4506

h899Ait

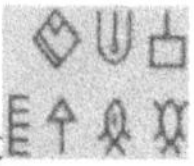
h899Bit
4471

h900Ait

h900Bit
4455

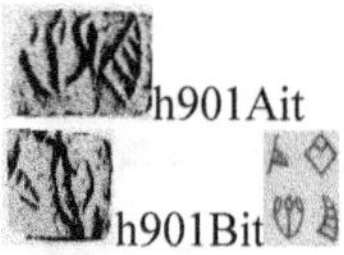
h901Ait
h901Bit
4460

h902Ait
h902Bit
4535

h903Ait

h903Bit
4485

h904Ait
h904Bit

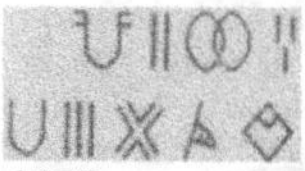
4477

h905ABit
4449

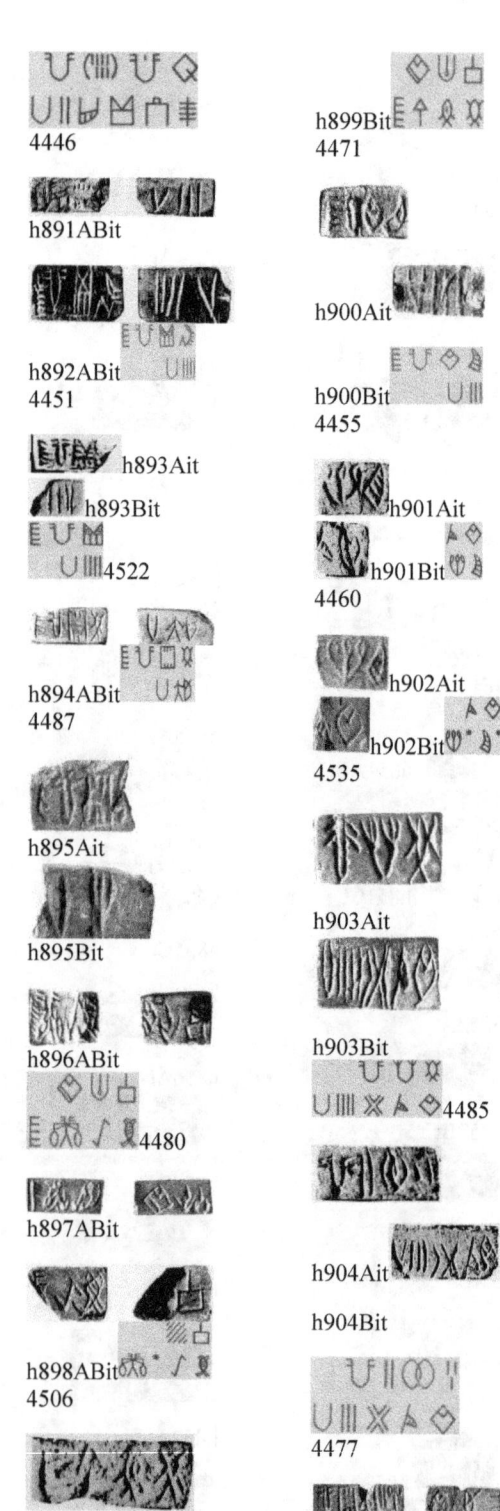

h906Ait

h906Bit

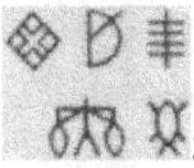

5494

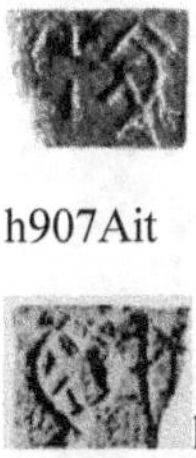

h907Ait

h907Bit

4537 The second sign on h907Ait may be a ligatured fish?

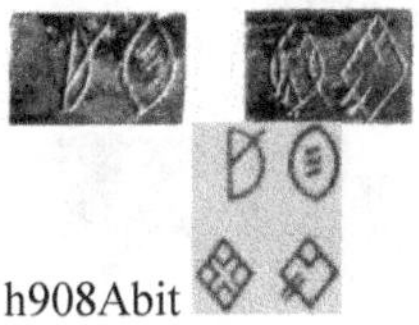

h908Abit
4488

h909ABit
5325

h910ABit

4470

h911Ait

h911Bit

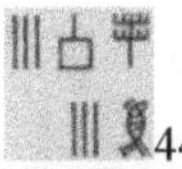

4486

h912Abit

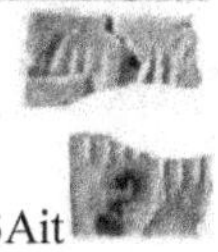

5461

h913Ait
h913Bit

h914Ait

h914Bit
4483

h916Ait

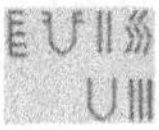

h916Bit
4456

h917Ait

h917Bit
4472

h918Ait

h918Bit
4481

h919Ait

h919Bit

h920Ait

h920Bit

4527

h921ABit
4514

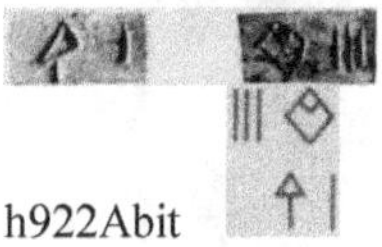

h922Abit
4518

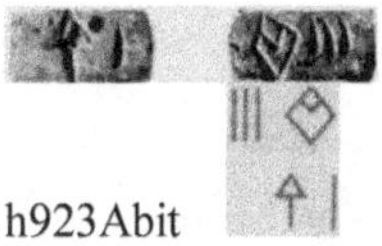

h923Abit
4474

h924ABit

h925Abit
4512

h926Abit
4519

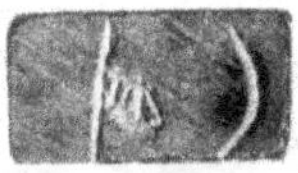

h927Ait

h927Bit 4502

h928Ait

h928Bit

h929Ait

h929Bit

h930Ait

h930Bit

4520

h931Ait

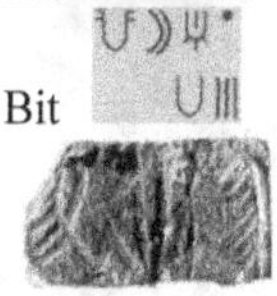

h931Bit

4511
h932Ait

h932Bit

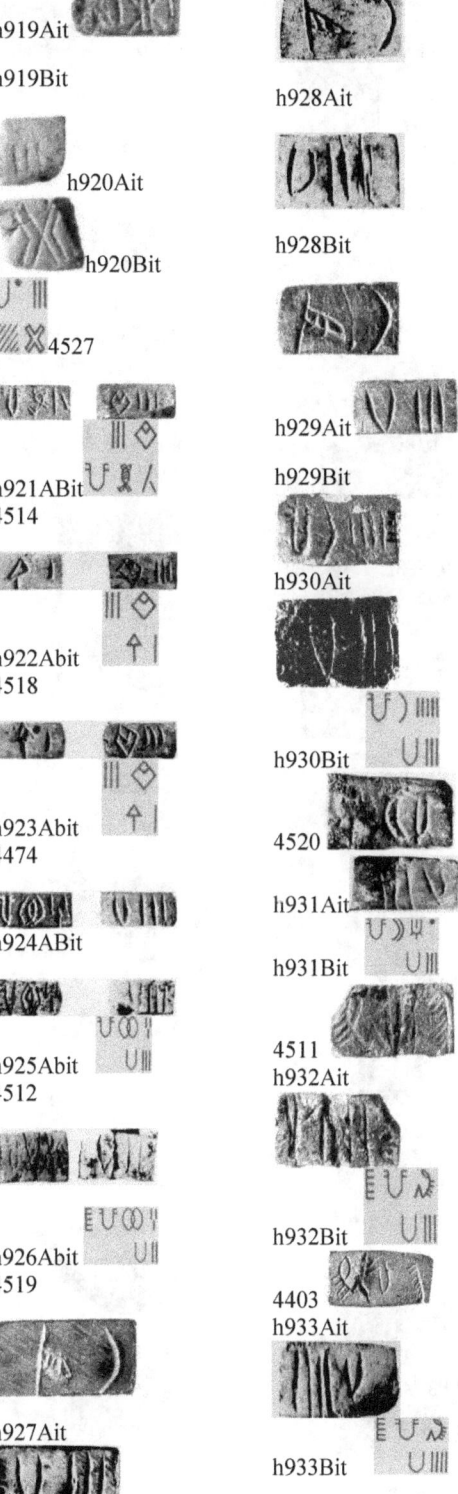

4403
h933Ait

h933Bit

4516

h934Ait
h934Bit
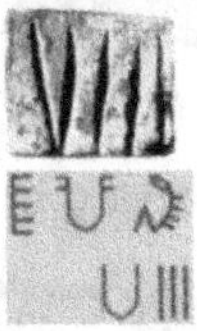
h935Ait
h935Bit
4509

h936Ait
h936Bit
5405

h937Ait

h937Bit
5458

h938Ait
h938Bit

h939Ait
h939Bit

h940Ait

h940Bit
4453

h941Ait

h941Bit
4464

h942Ait
h942Bit

4490

h943Ait
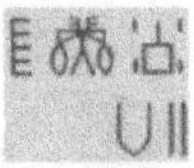
h943Bit
4461

h944Ait

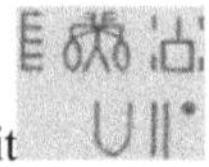
h944Bit
4475

h945Ait

h945Bit
4503

h946Ait

h946Bit
4501
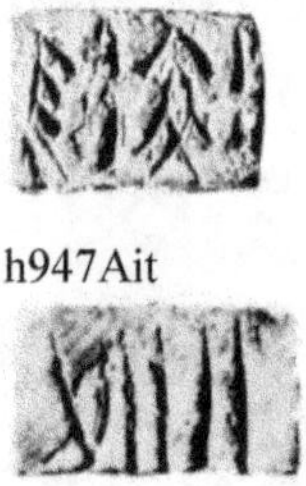
h947Ait

h947Bit
4493

h948Abit
4489

h949Abit
4479

h950ABit
4463

h951Ait
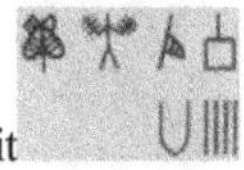
h951Bit
4498

h952Ait

h952Bit
4469

h953Ait
h953Bit

h954Ait

4467
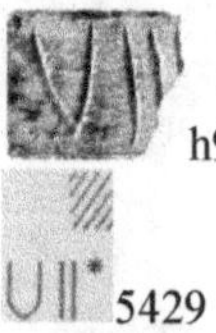
h955Bit
5429

h959Ait

h959Bit
4405

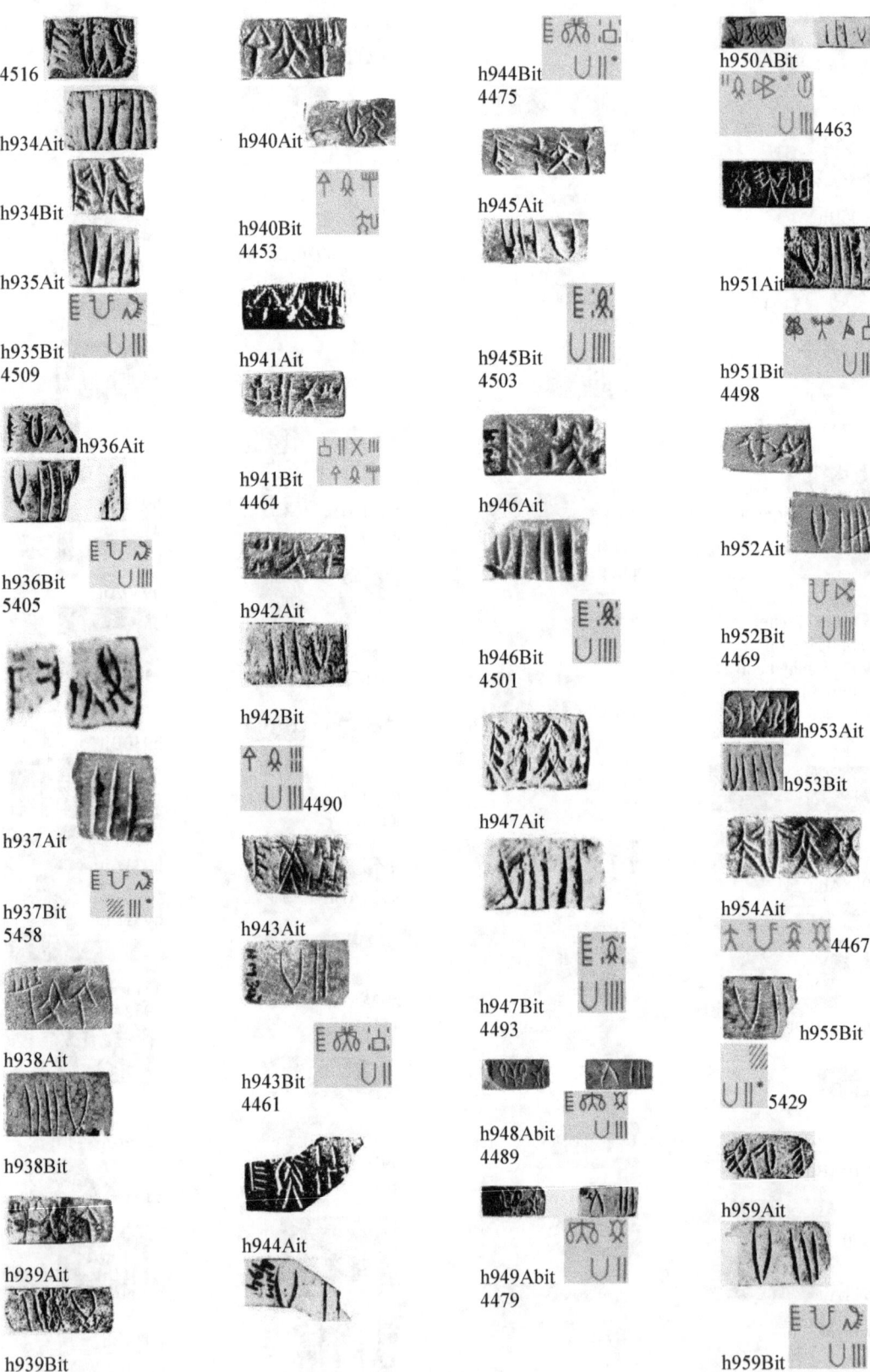

h960Ait

h960Bit

4543
h961Ait

h961Bit

5449
h962Ait

h962Bit

4548

h963Ait

h963Bit
5420

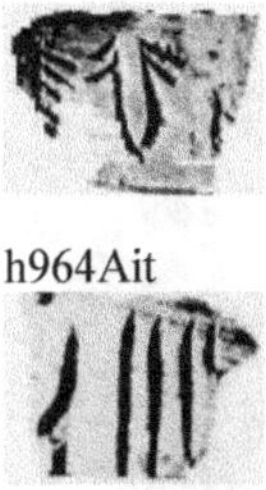

h964Ait

h964Bit
5456

h965Ait

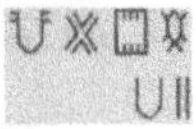

h965Bit
4562

h966Ait

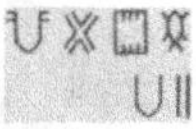

h966Bit
5479

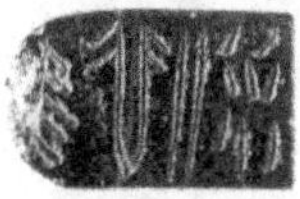

h967Ait

4563

h968Ait
h968Bit

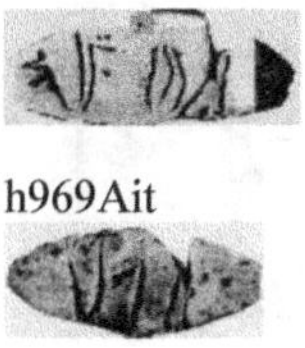

h969Ait

h969Bit
4555

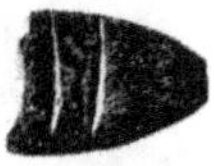

h970Ait

h970Bit
4553

h971Ait
h971Bit

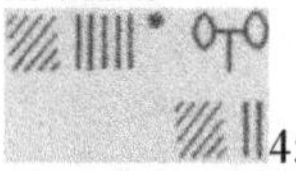

4557
Shape of object: double-axe?

h972Ait
h972Bit

4418 Pict-128: Inscribed object in the shape of a leaf? Dotted circles on obverse.

h973Ait

h973Bit
4411

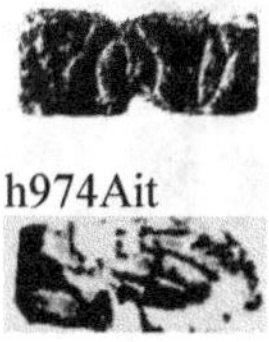

h974Ait

h974Bit

h974Cit
4592

h975Ait
h975Bit

h975Cit
4402

h976Ait
h976Bit

h976Cit
4588

h977Ait
h977Bit

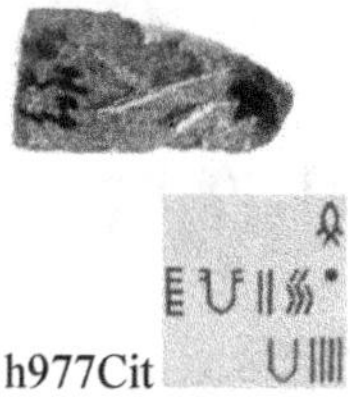

h977Cit
4591

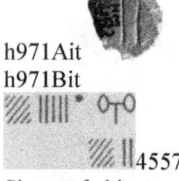

h978Ait

h978Bit

h978Cit
5412

h979Ait

h979Bit

h979Cit

h980Ait

h980Bit

h980Cit

h981Ait

h981Bit

h981Cit
5415

h982Ait

h982Bit

h982Cit
m4574

h983Ait

h983Bit

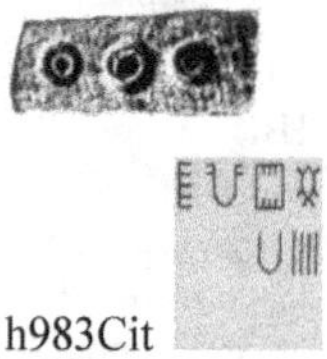

h983Cit
4582

h984Ait

h984Bit

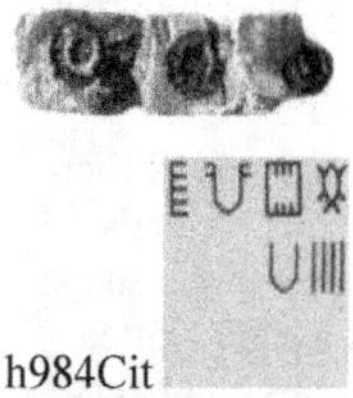

h984Cit
4587

h985Ait

h985Bit
4577

h987Ait

h987Bit

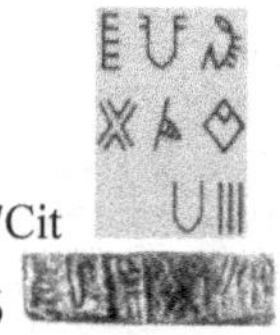

h987Cit

4586

h988Ait

h988Bit

h988B2it

h988Cit

h988Eit

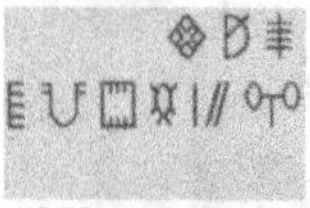

4573

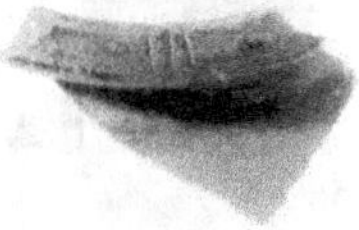

h990

h992

h994

h1020

h1021

h1022

h1023

h1024

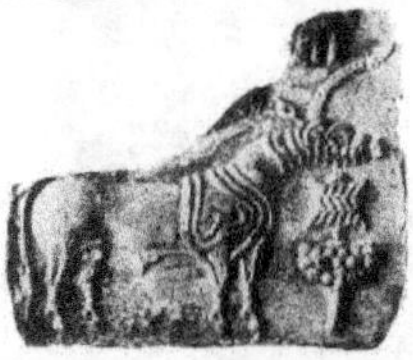

h1025a

h1027a

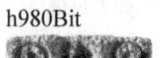

h1028

h1029a

h1030a

h1031

h1032a

h1033a

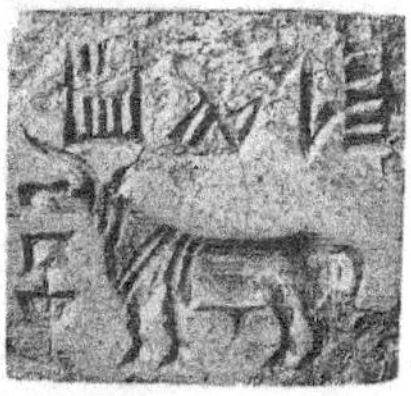

h1035

h1036

h1037

h1038

h1042a

h1043a

h1044a

h1045a

h1046

h1047a

h1048

h1049a

h1050

h1051

h1052

h1053a

h1056a

h1058a

h1059

h1064

h1065

h1066a

h1067a

h1068

h1071
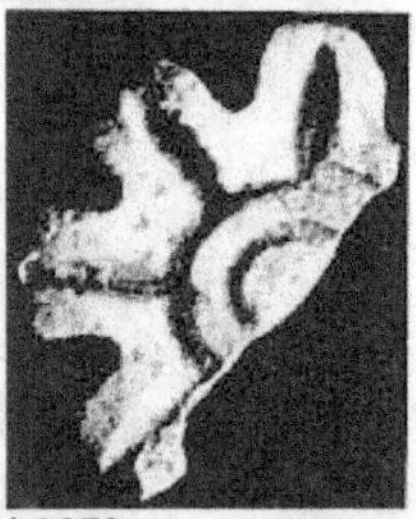
h1072
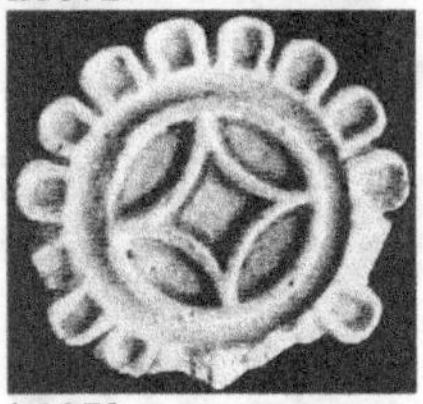
h1073

h1075
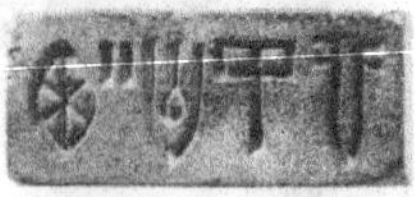
h1076

h1077

h1079a

h1080a
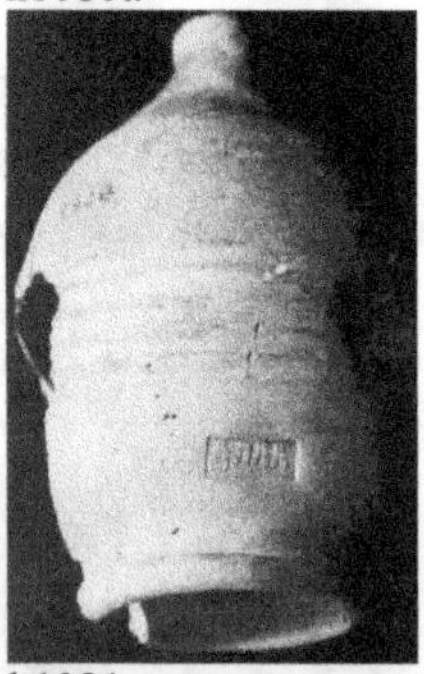
h1081
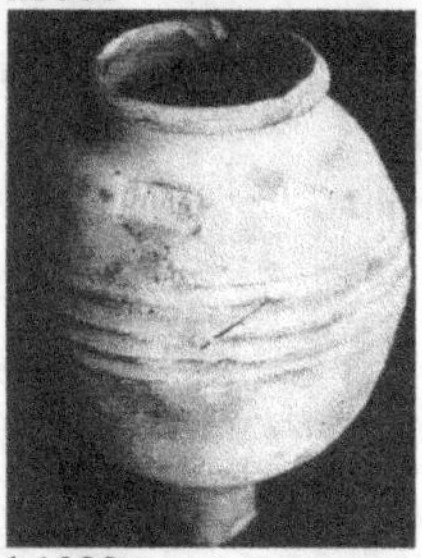
h1082

h1083
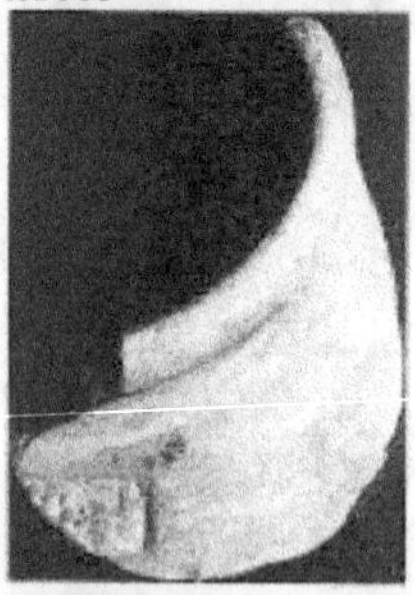
h1084
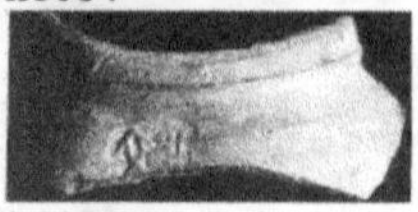
h1085

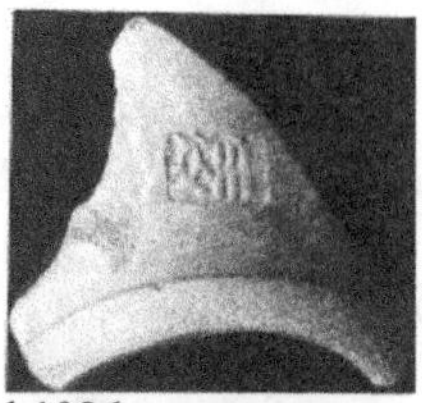
h1086
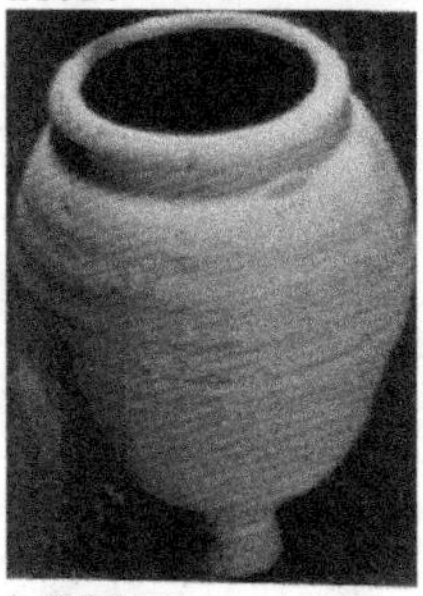
h1087

h1091
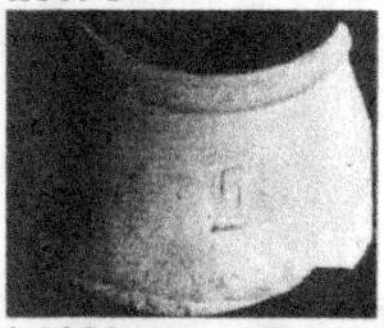
h1092
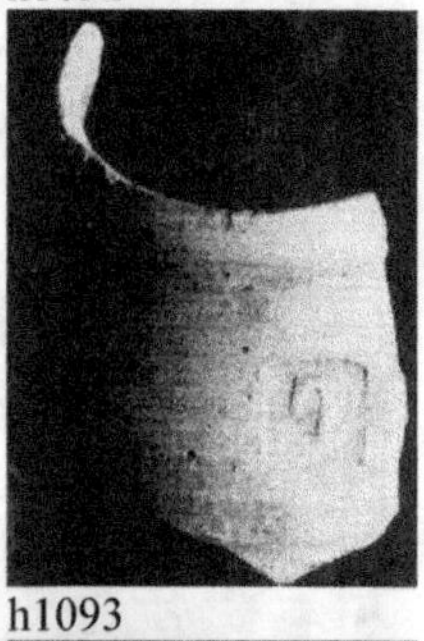
h1093
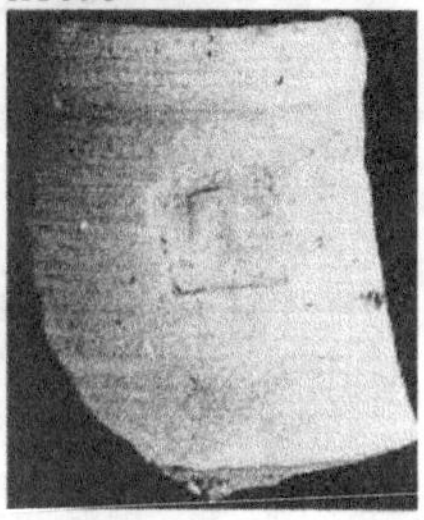

h1094
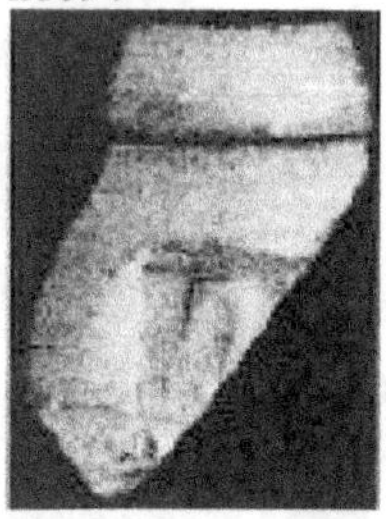
h1097
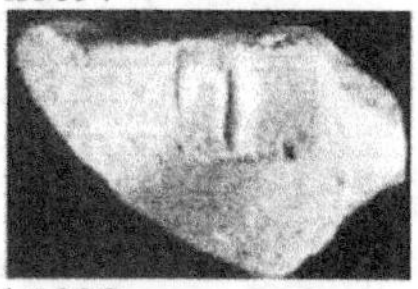
h1098

h1100A

h1100B

h1101A

h1101B

h1102A

h1102B

h1103A

h1103B

h1104A

h1104B

h1105A

h1105B

h1107A

h1107B

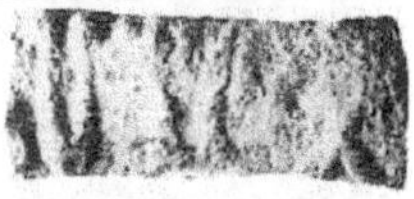
h1108A

h1108B

h1109A

h1109B

h1113A

h1113B

h1114B

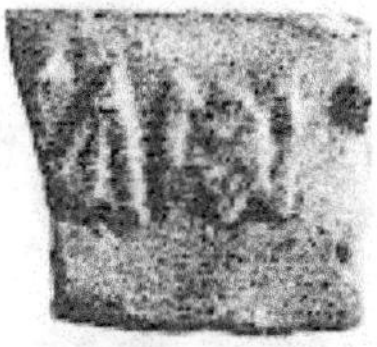
h1115A

h1116A

h1116B

h1117A

h1121A

h1121B

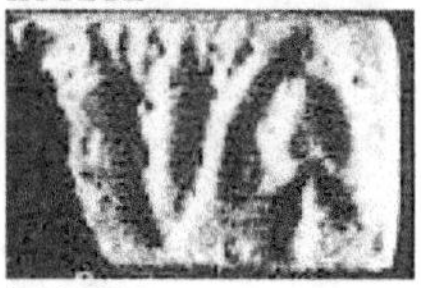
h1122A

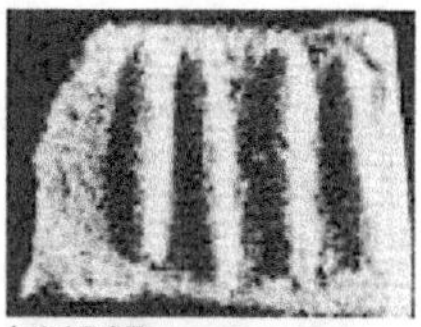
h1122B

h1123A

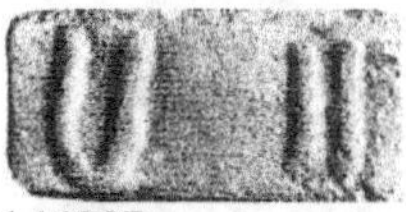
h1123B

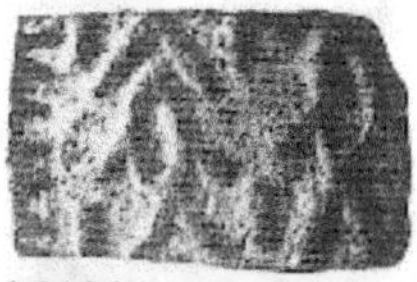
h1124A

h1124B

h1126A

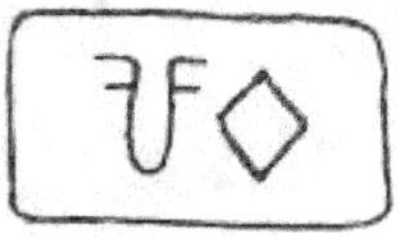
h1126B

h1130A

h1130B

h1131A

h1131B

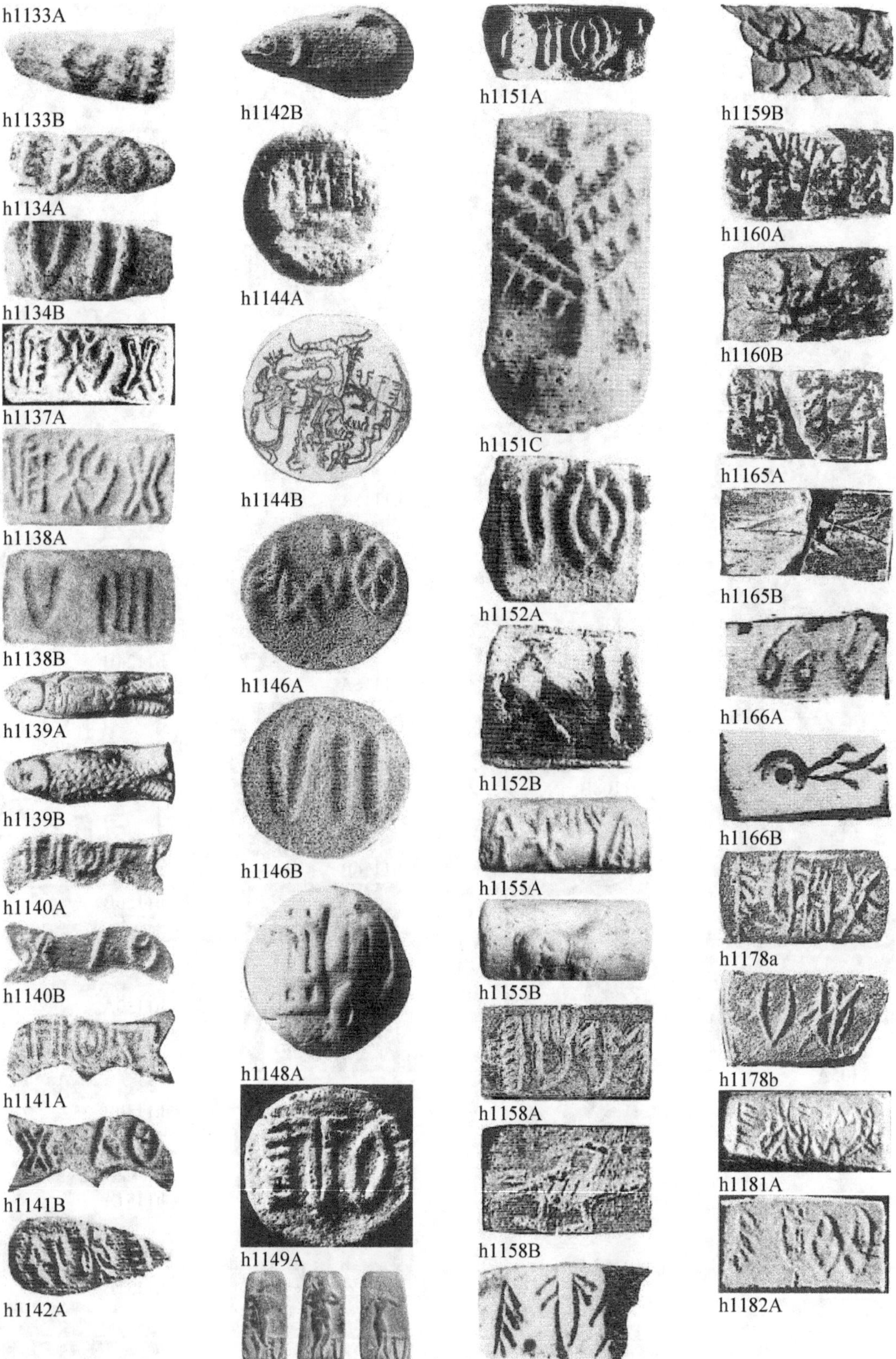

h1133A
h1133B
h1134A
h1134B
h1137A
h1138A
h1138B
h1139A
h1139B
h1140A
h1140B
h1141A
h1141B
h1142A
h1142B
h1144A
h1144B
h1146A
h1146B
h1148A
h1149A
h1150ABC
h1151A
h1151C
h1152A
h1152B
h1155A
h1155B
h1158A
h1158B
h1159A
h1159B
h1160A
h1160B
h1165A
h1165B
h1166A
h1166B
h1178a
h1178b
h1181A
h1182A

h1182B

h1184A
h1184B
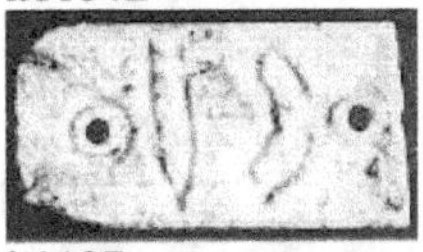
h1187a

h1187b

h1188A

h1188B

h1189A

h1189B

h1190A

h1190B

h1191A

h1191B
h1192A

h1192B

h1198A

h1198B

h1200-1258

h1261A
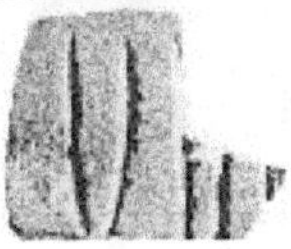
h1261B

h1272A

h1272B

h1273A

h1273B

h1274A

h1274B

h1275A
h1275B

h1284A

h1284B

h1287A

h1287B

h1289A
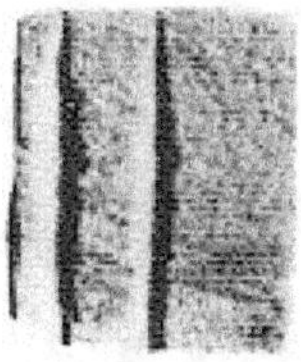
h1289B

h1293A

h1293B

h1294A

h1294B

h1302A

h1302B

h1303A

h1303B

h1304A
h1304B

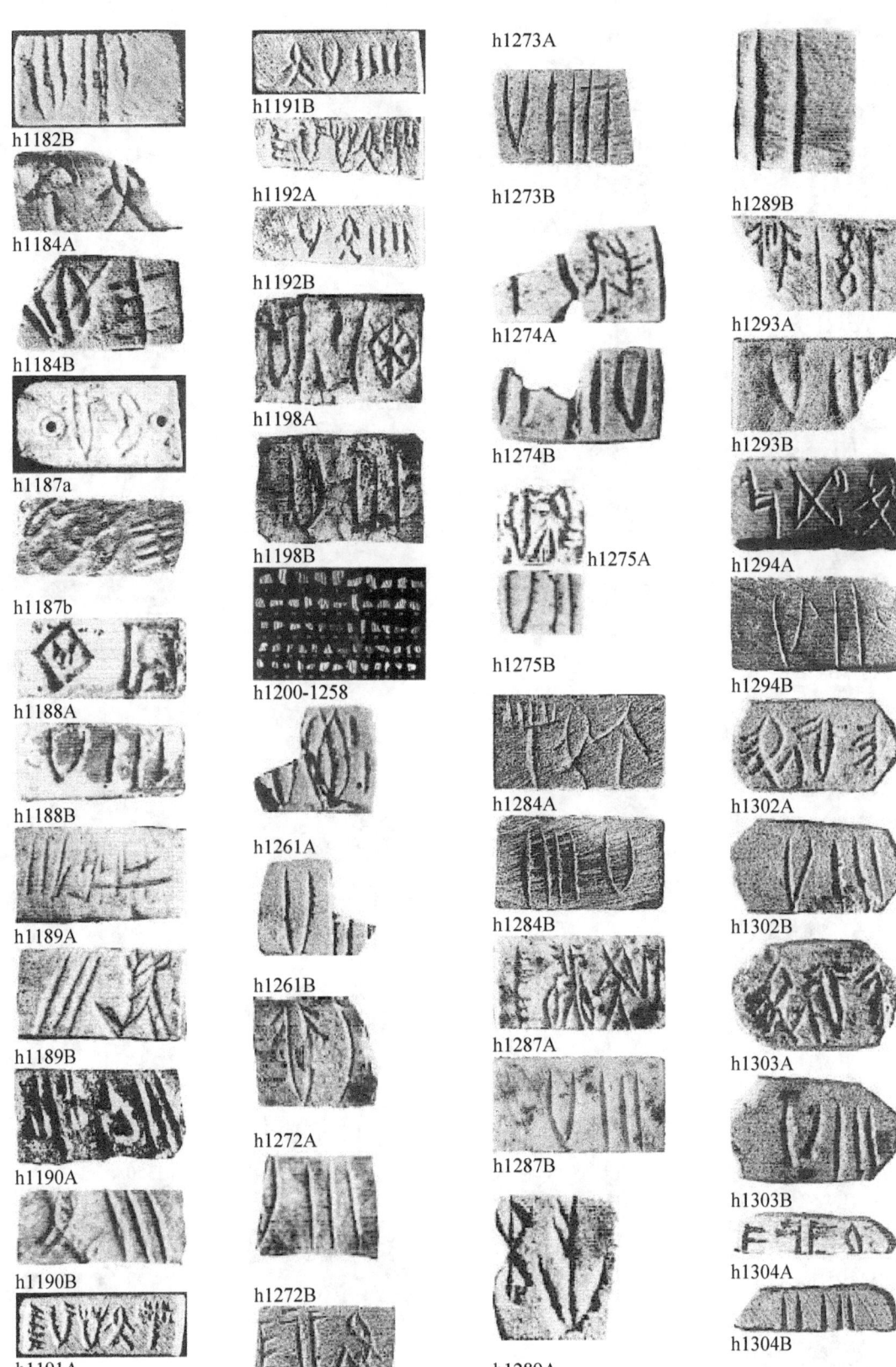

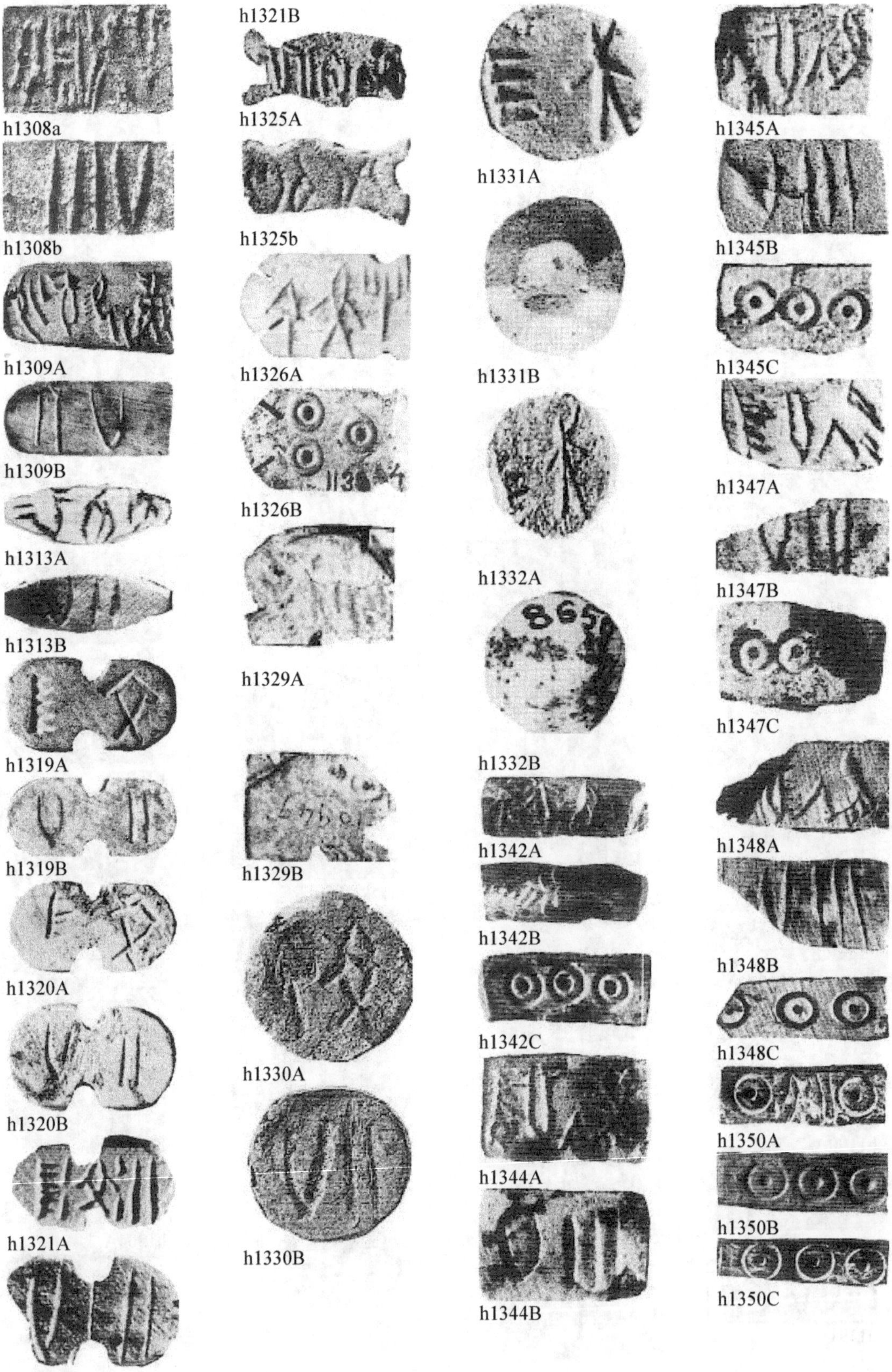

h1308a
h1308b
h1309A
h1309B
h1313A
h1313B
h1319A
h1319B
h1320A
h1320B
h1321A
h1321B
h1325A
h1325b
h1326A
h1326B
h1329A
h1329B
h1330A
h1330B
h1331A
h1331B
h1332A
h1332B
h1342A
h1342B
h1342C
h1344A
h1344B
h1345A
h1345B
h1345C
h1347A
h1347B
h1347C
h1348A
h1348B
h1348C
h1350A
h1350B
h1350C

h1353a

h1353b

h1353c

h1354A

h1354B

h1354C

h1354D

h1355a

h1355B

h1355c

h1355d

h1344C

h1357A

h1357b

h1366a

h1388A

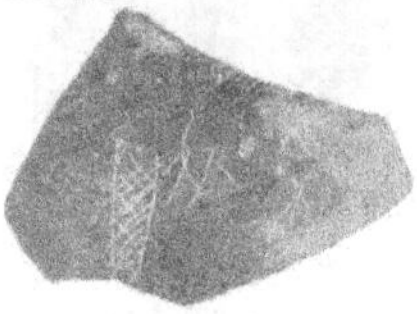
h1392A

h1393A

h1394A

h1397A

h1403A

h1404A

h1406A

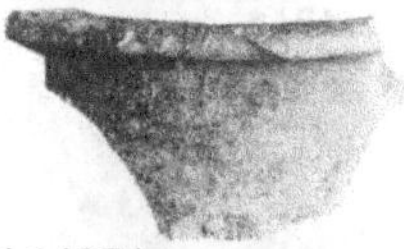
h1407A

h1408A

h1410A

h1411A

h1412A

h1421A

h1422A

h1424A

h1431A

h1433A

h1434A

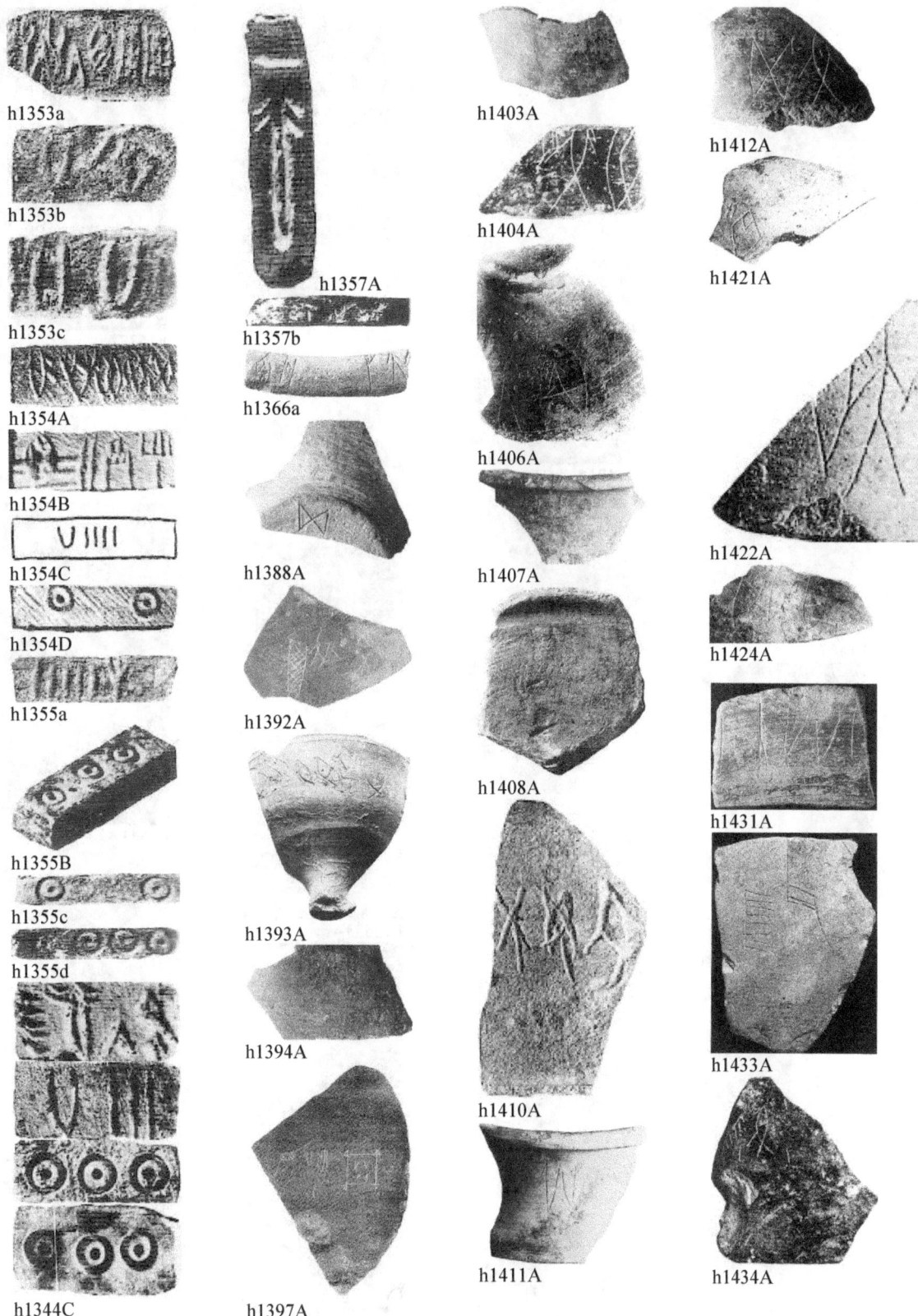

h1441A

h1444A

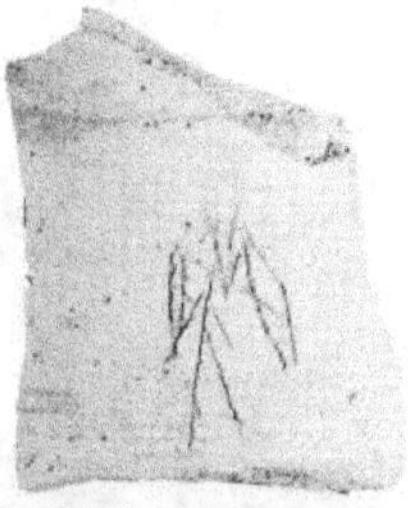

h1461A

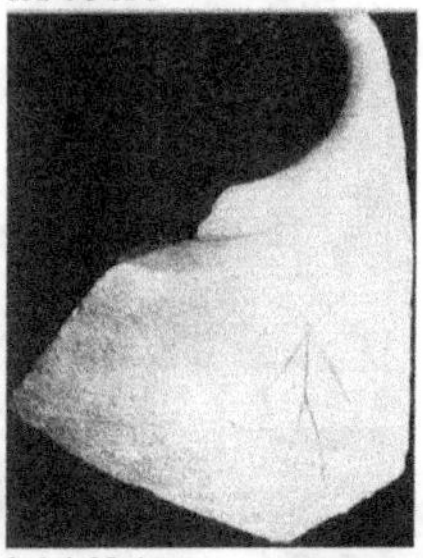

h1462A

h1464A

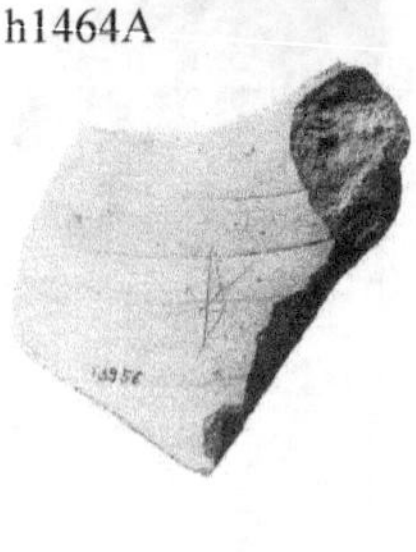

h1467A

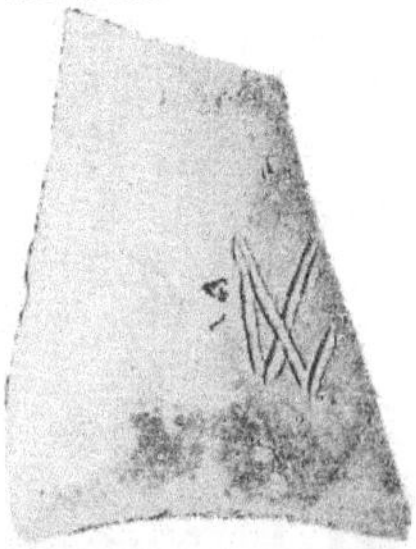

h1468A

h1471A

h1481A

h1487A

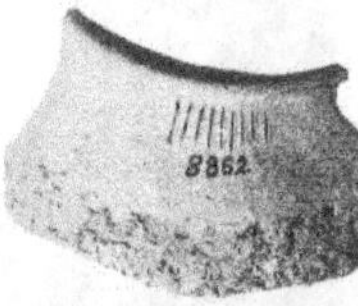

h1491A

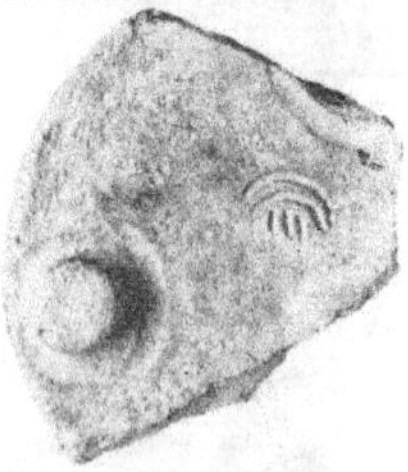

h1501A

h1506A

h1507A

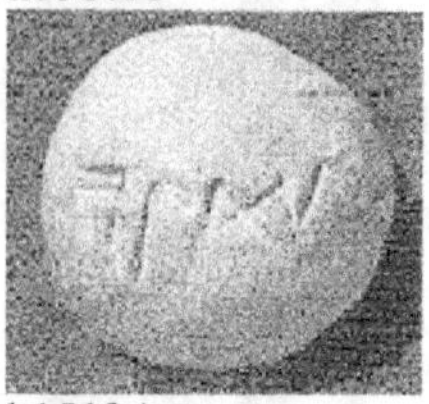

h1513A

h1516A

h1517A

h1518copperaxe

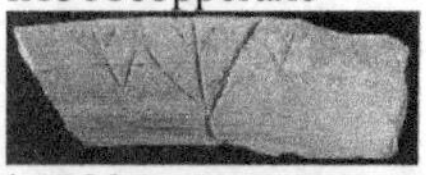

h1522A

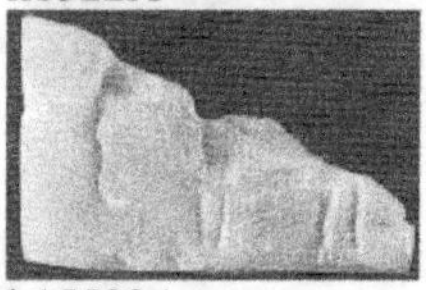

h15533A

h1534A

h1535A

h1536A

h1537A

h1537B

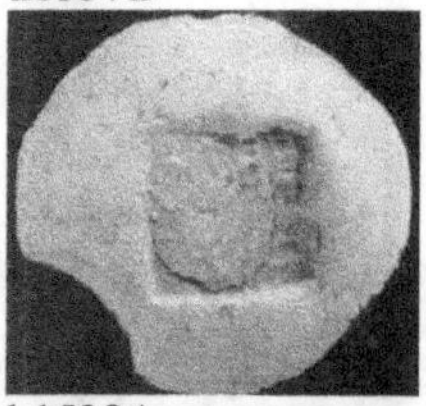

h1538A

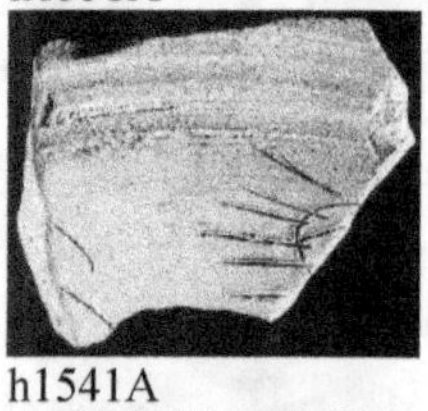

h1541A

h1544A

h1545A

h1547A

h1559A

h1586A

h1587A

h1657A

h1662A

h1663A

h1664A

h1666A

h1667A

h1669A

h1670A

h1671A

h1672A

h1673A

h1676A

h1677A

h1678A

h1679A

h1680A

h1681A

h1682A

h1684A

h1685A

h1687A

h1688A

h1690A

h1691A

h1692A

h1694A

h1695

h1696

h1697

h1698

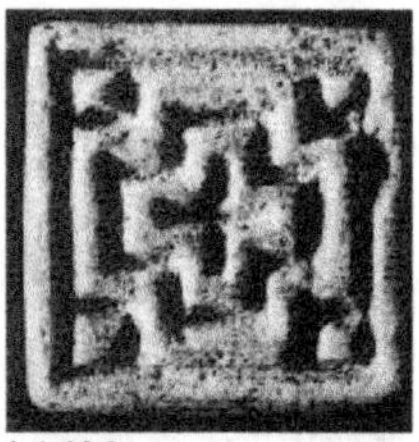

h1699

h1700

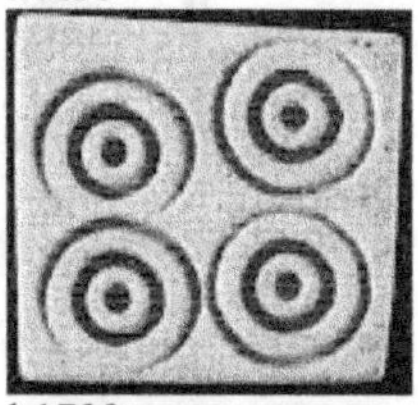

h1701

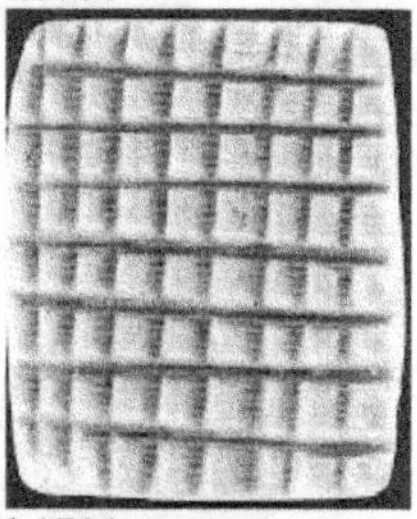

h1702

h1703

h1704

h1705

h1706

h1707

h1708

h1709

h1710

h1711

h1712

h1713

h1714

h1715

h1716

h1719A

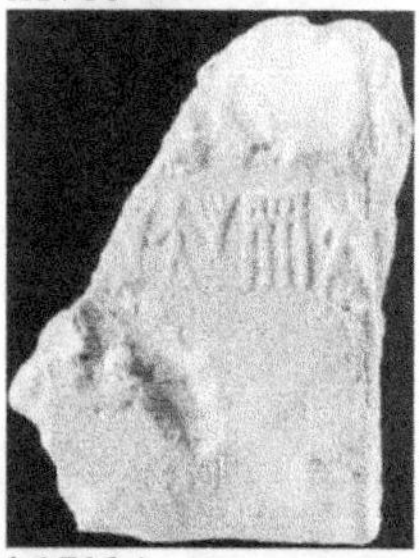

h1719B

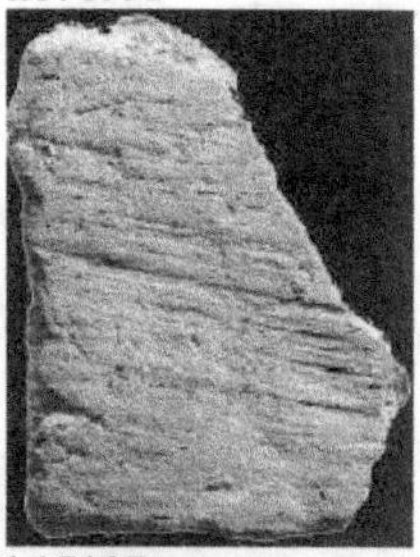

h1720A

h1720B

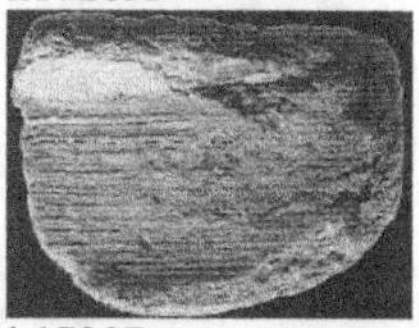

h1721A

h1721B

h1722A

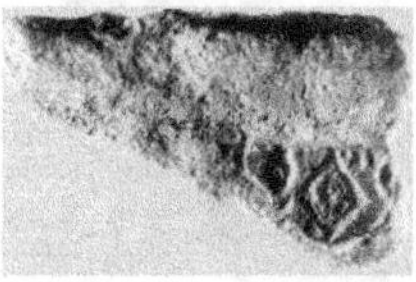
h1723

h1724

h1725A

h1726

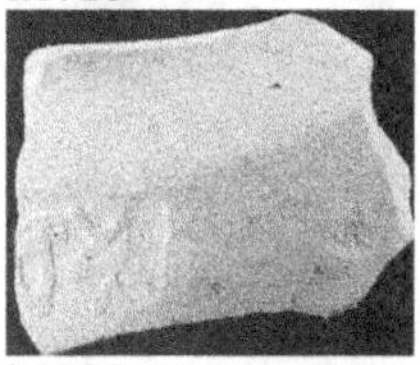
h1727

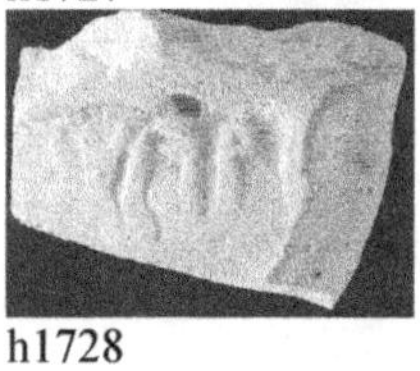
h1728

h1729

h1731

h1732

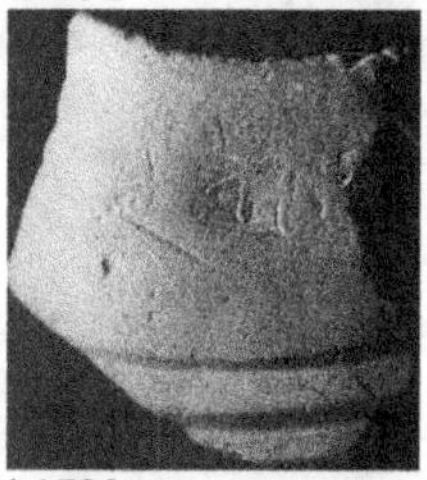
h1733

h1734

h1735

h1736

h1737

h1739

h1740

h1742

h1743

h1744

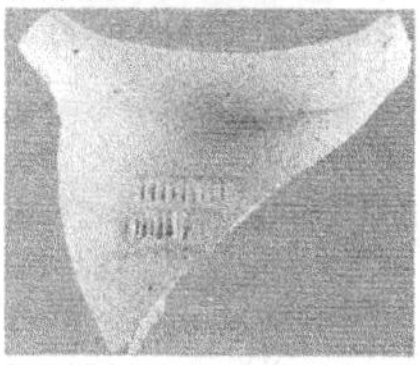
h1751

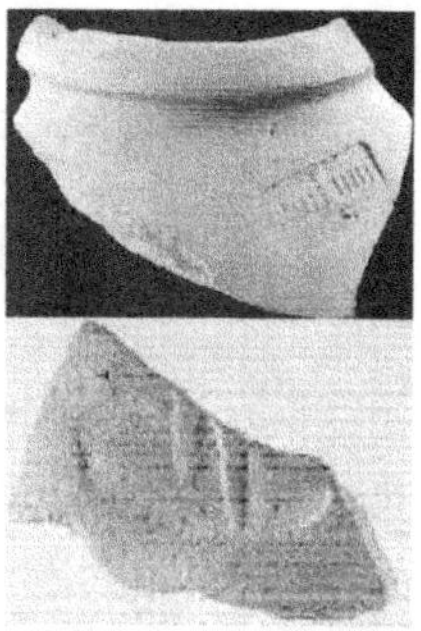
h1753

h1756

h1757

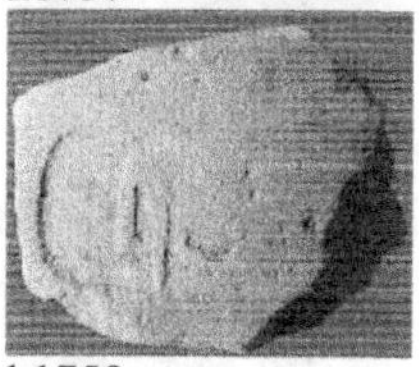
h1758

h1759

h1760

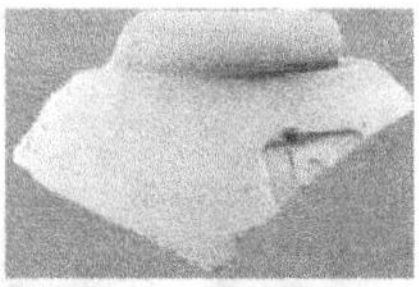
h1761

h1762

h1767A

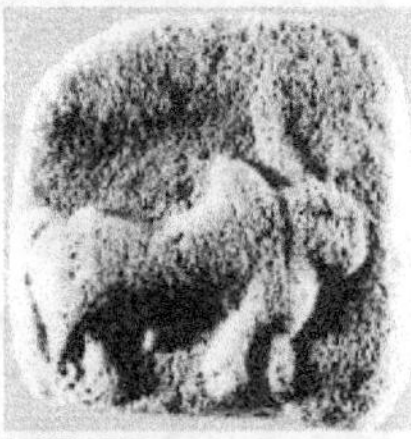
h1767B

h1768A

h1768B

h1770A

h1770B

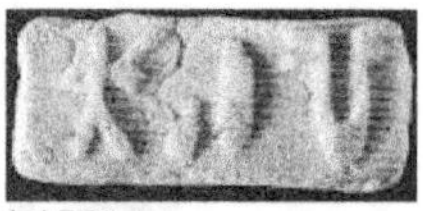
h1771A

h1771B

h1772A

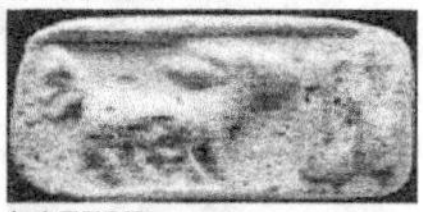
h1772B

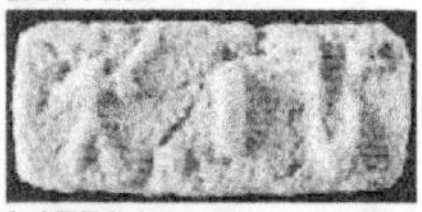
h1773A

h1773B

h1774A

h1774B

h1775A

h1775B

h1776A

h1776B

h1777A

h1777B

h1778A

h1778B

h1779A

h1779B

h1780A

h1780B

h1781A

h1781B

h1782A

h1783A

h1783B

h1785A

h1785B

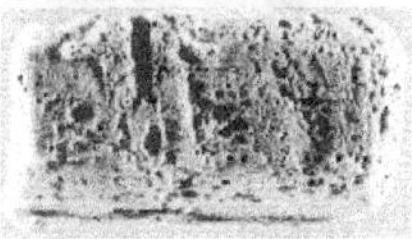

h1786A

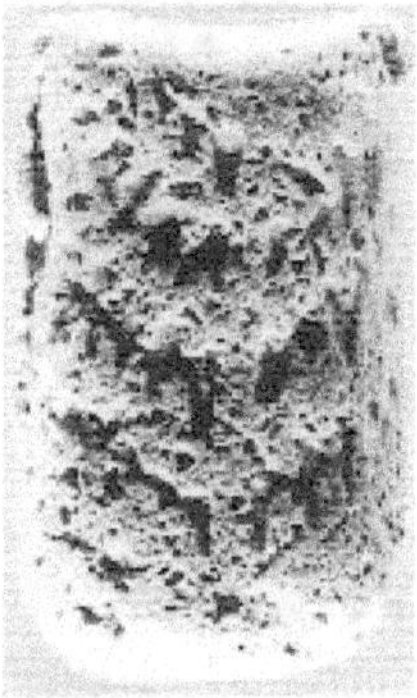

h1786B

h1787A

h1787B

h1788A

h1788B

h1791A

h1791B

h1792A

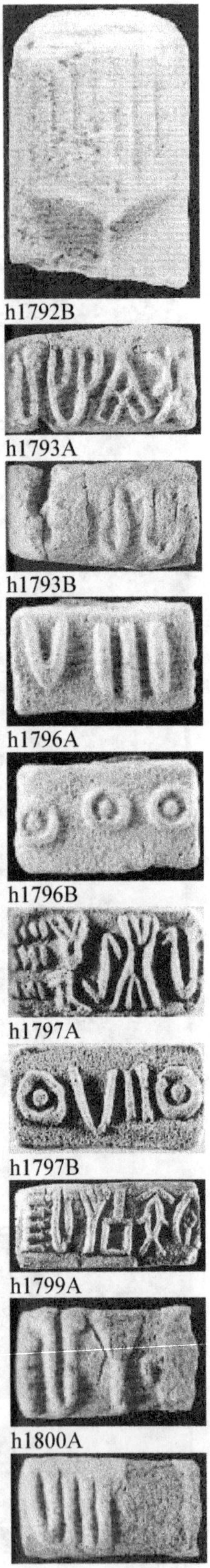

h1792B
h1793A
h1793B
h1796A
h1796B
h1797A
h1797B
h1799A
h1800A

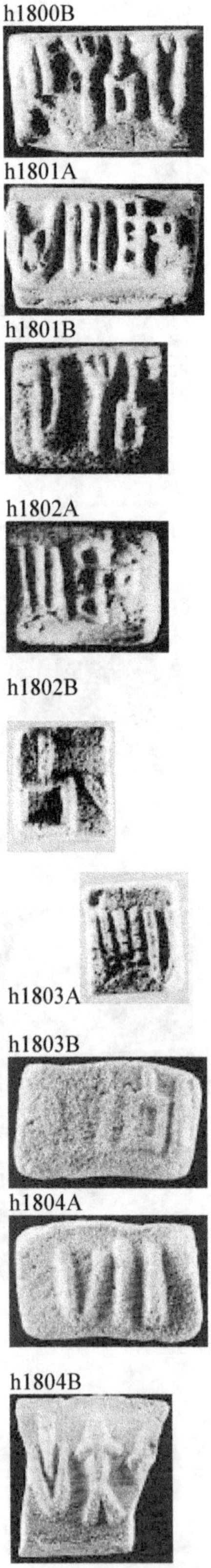

h1800B
h1801A
h1801B
h1802A
h1802B
h1803A
h1803B
h1804A
h1804B

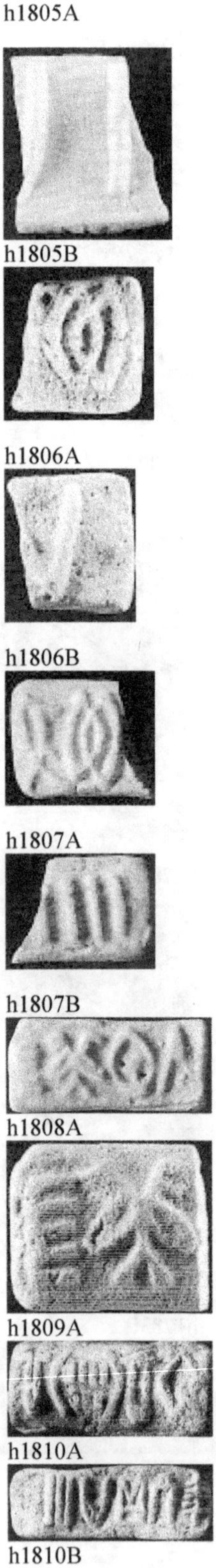

h1805A
h1805B
h1806A
h1806B
h1807A
h1807B
h1808A
h1809A
h1810A
h1810B

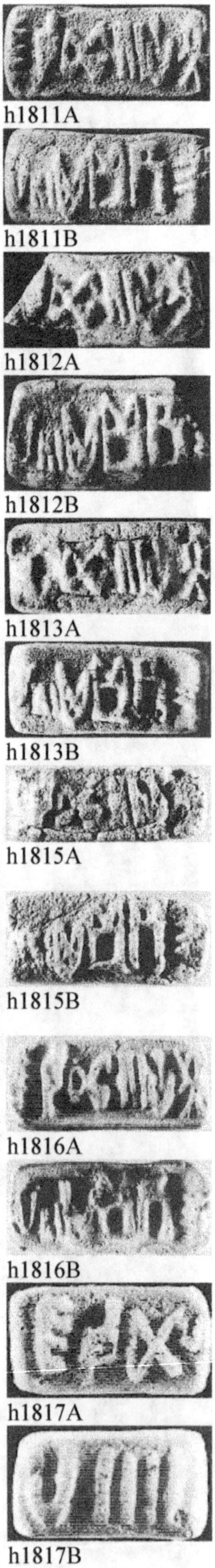

h1811A
h1811B
h1812A
h1812B
h1813A
h1813B
h1815A
h1815B
h1816A
h1816B
h1817A
h1817B

h1818A

h1818B

h1819A

h1819B

h1820A

h1820B

h1821A

h1821B

h1822A

h1822B

h1823A

h1823B

h1824A

h1824B

h1825A

h1825B

h1826A

h1826B

h1827A

h1827B

h1829A

h1829B

h1830A

h1830B

h1831A

h1831B

h1832A

h1832B

h1833A

h1833B

h1834A

h1834B

h1835A
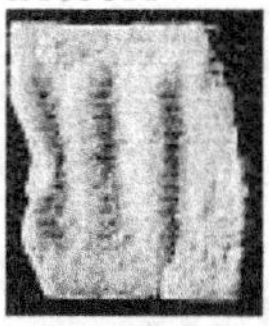
h1835B

h1836A
h1836B
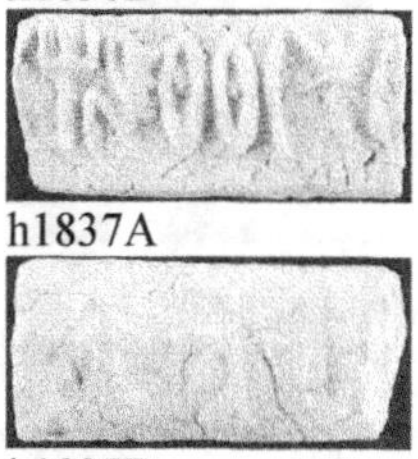
h1837A
h1837B

h1839A
h1839B

h1840A
h1840B

h1841A

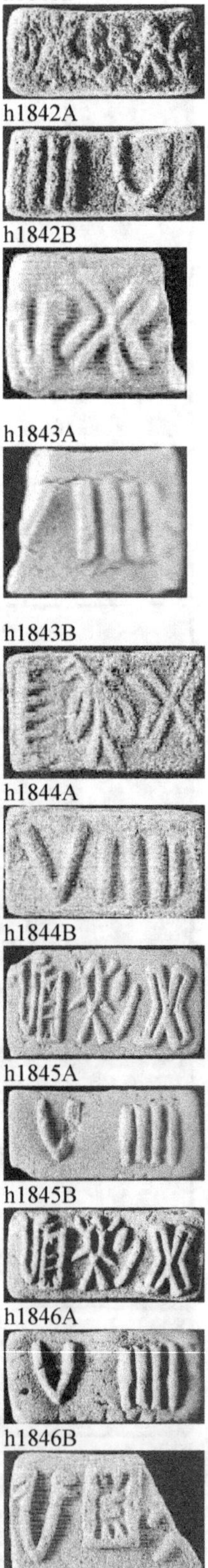

h1841B
h1842A
h1842B
h1843A
h1843B
h1844A
h1844B
h1845A
h1845B
h1846A
h1846B

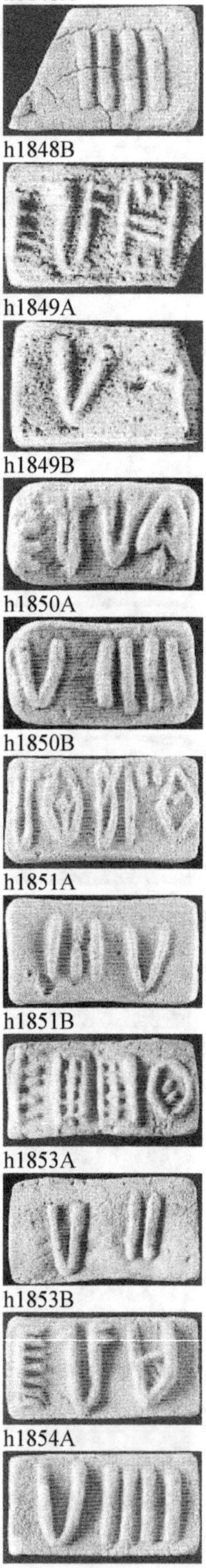

h1848A
h1848B
h1849A
h1849B
h1850A
h1850B
h1851A
h1851B
h1853A
h1853B
h1854A

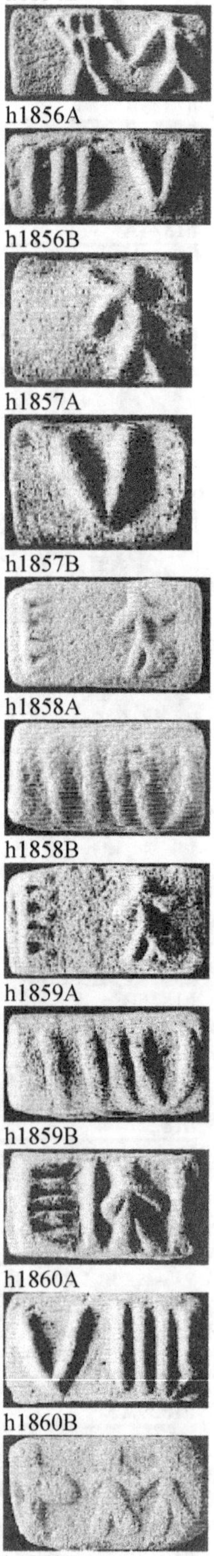

h1854B
h1856A
h1856B
h1857A
h1857B
h1858A
h1858B
h1859A
h1859B
h1860A
h1860B
h1861A

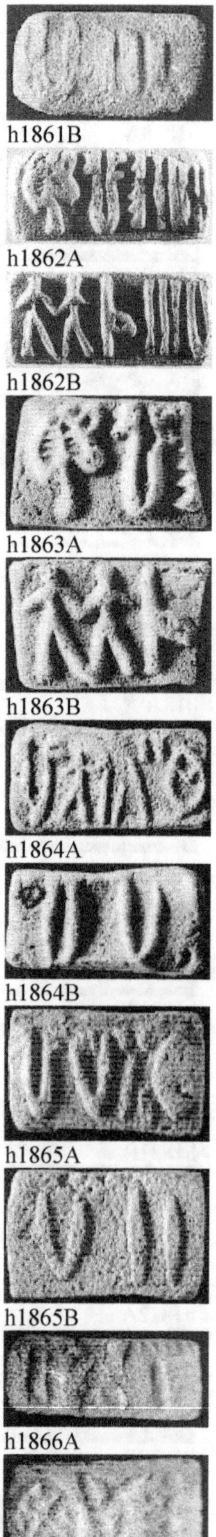

h1861B
h1862A
h1862B
h1863A
h1863B
h1864A
h1864B
h1865A
h1865B
h1866A
h1866B

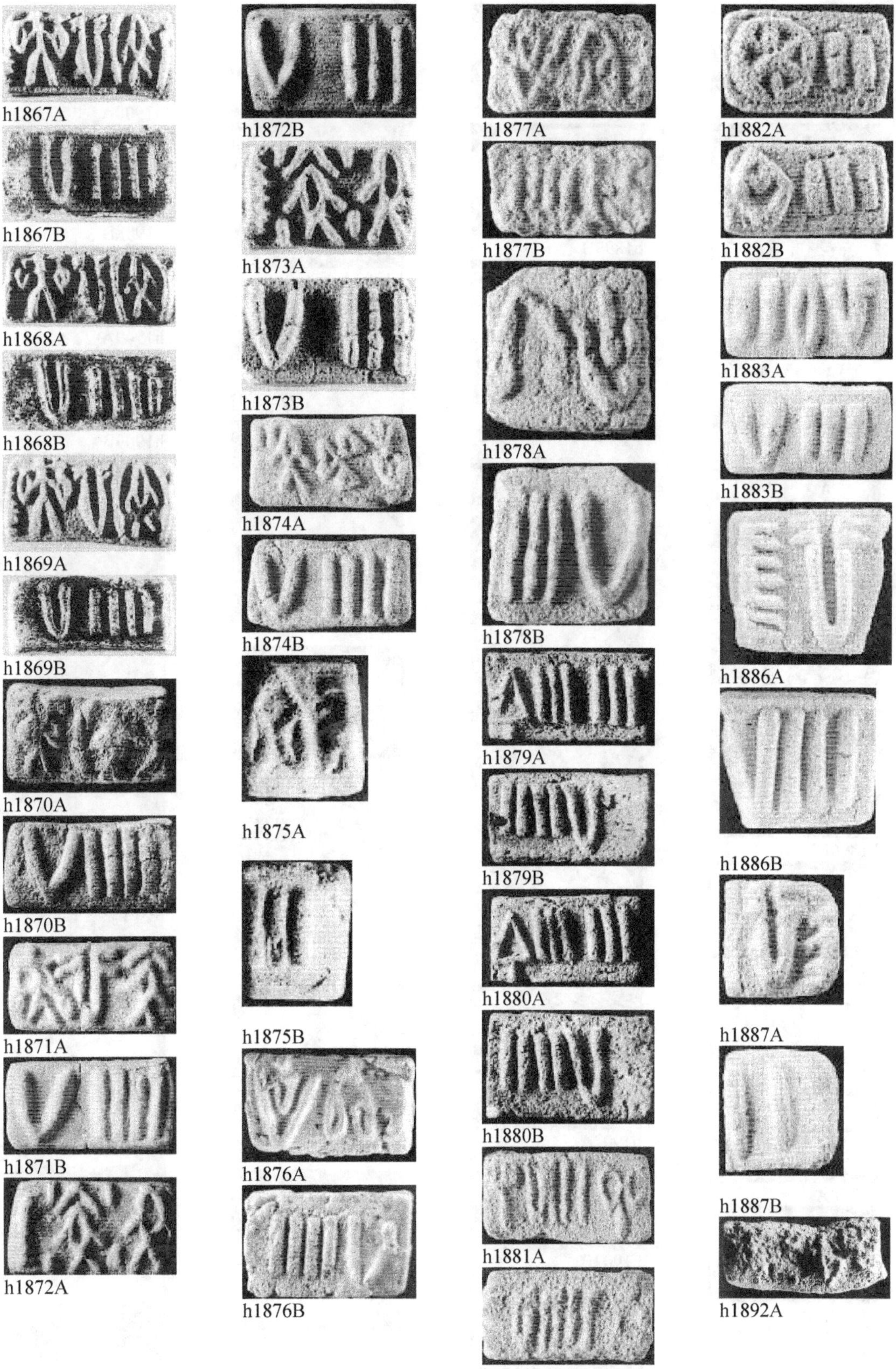

h1867A
h1867B
h1868A
h1868B
h1869A
h1869B
h1870A
h1870B
h1871A
h1871B
h1872A
h1872B
h1873A
h1873B
h1874A
h1874B
h1875A
h1875B
h1876A
h1876B
h1877A
h1877B
h1878A
h1878B
h1879A
h1879B
h1880A
h1880B
h1881A
h1881B
h1882A
h1882B
h1883A
h1883B
h1886A
h1886B
h1887A
h1887B
h1892A

h1892B

h1893A

h1893B

h1895A
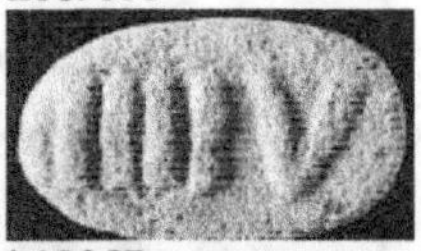
h1895B

h1896A

h1896B

h1897A

h1897B

h1898A

h1898B

h1899A

h1899B

h1900A

h1900B

h1901A
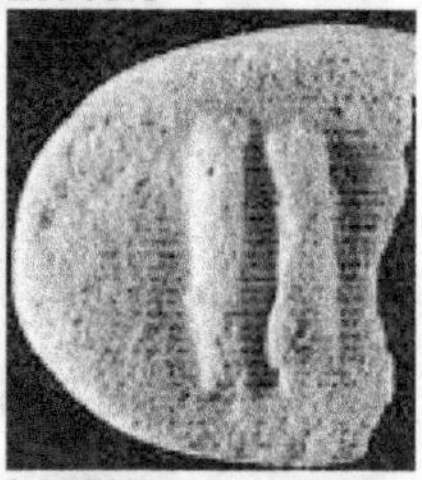
h1901B

h1902A

h1902B

h1903A
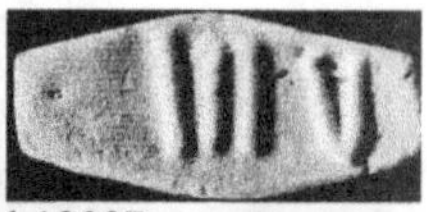
h1903B

h1904A
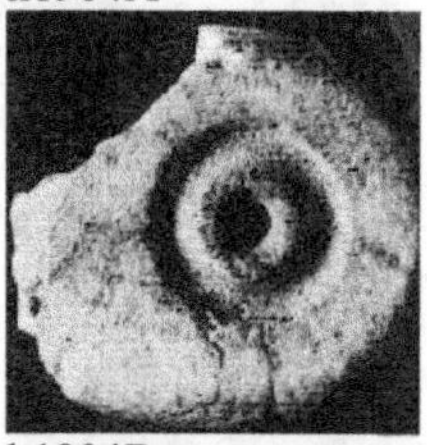
h1904B
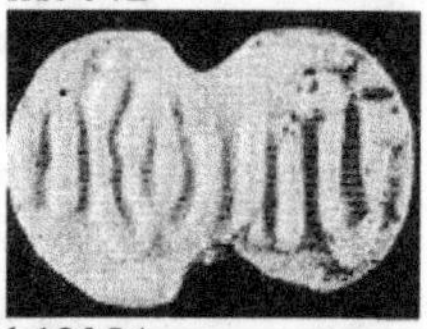
h1905A
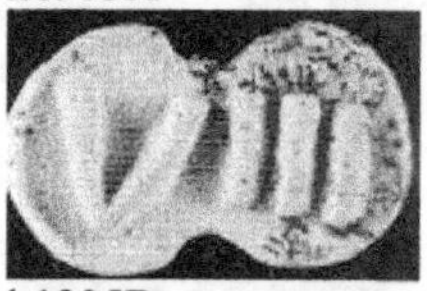
h1905B

h1906A

h1907A

h1907B
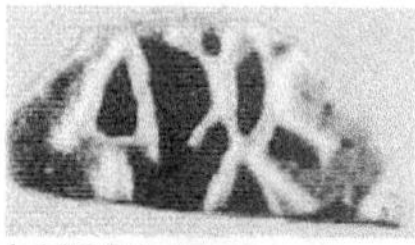
h1908A
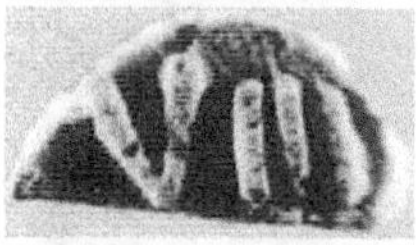
h1908B

h1909A

h1909B

h1910A

h1910B

h1911A

h1911B

h1912A
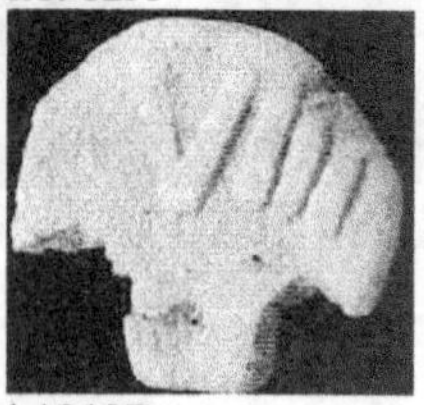
h1912B

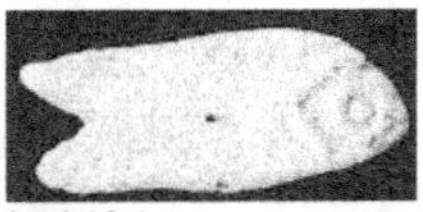
h1913A

h1913B

h1914A

h1914B

h1915A

h1915B

h1916A
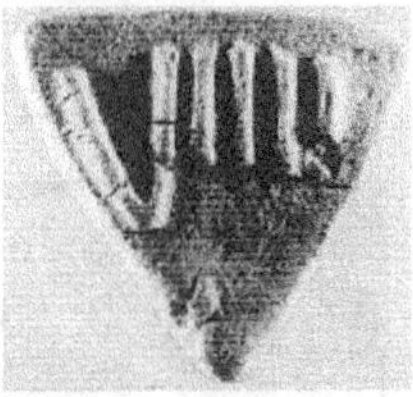
h1916B

h1917A

h1917B
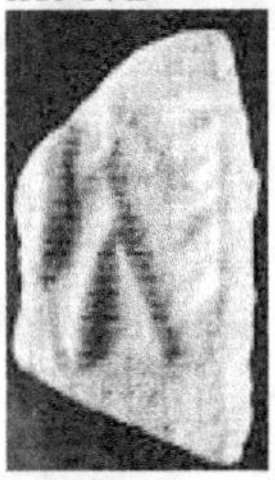
h1918A
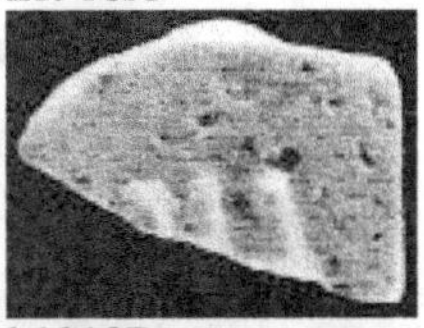
h1918B
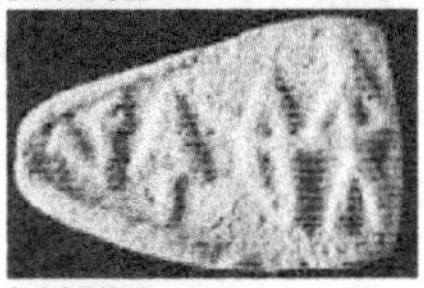
h1920A
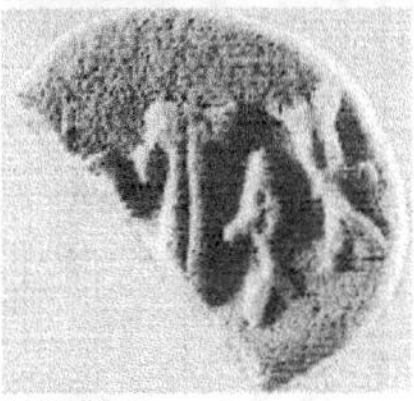
h1921A

h1921B

h1922A

h1922B

h1923A
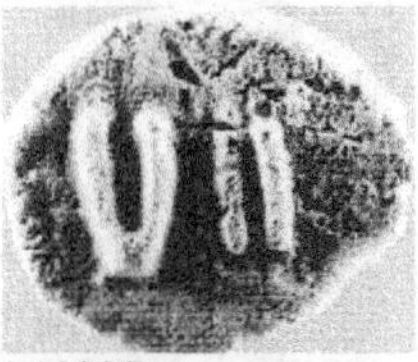
h1923B
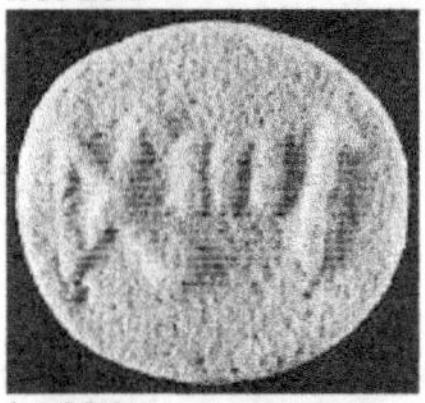
h1924A

h1924B

h1925A

h1925B

h1926A

h1927A

h1929A

h1929B

h1929C

h1930A

h1930B

h1930C

h1931A
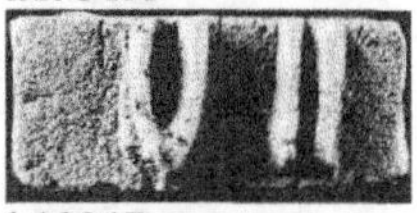
h1931B

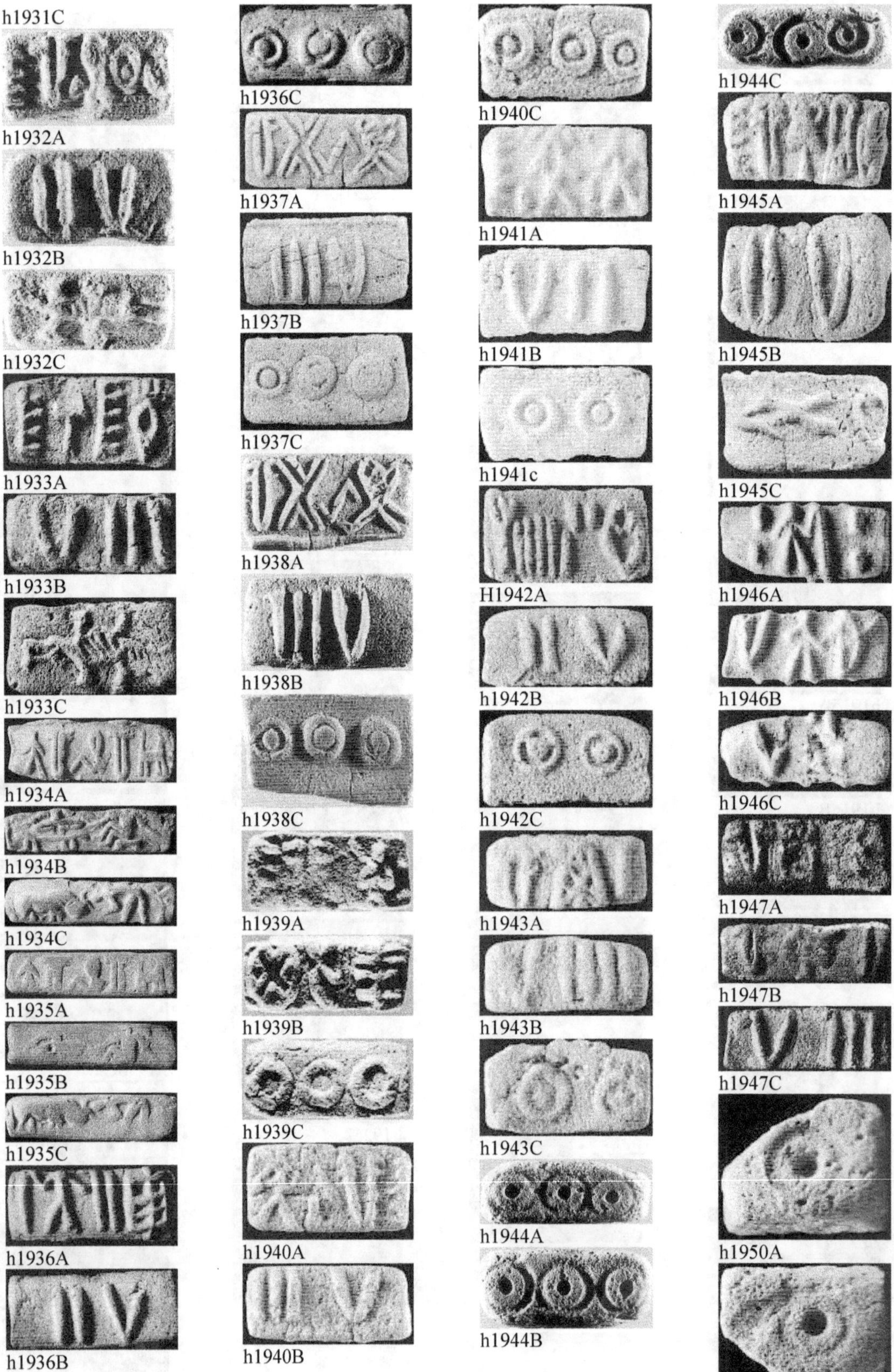

h1931C
h1932A
h1932B
h1932C
h1933A
h1933B
h1933C
h1934A
h1934B
h1934C
h1935A
h1935B
h1935C
h1936A
h1936B

h1936C
h1937A
h1937B
h1937C
h1938A
h1938B
h1938C
h1939A
h1939B
h1939C
h1940A
h1940B

h1940C
h1941A
h1941B
h1941c
H1942A
h1942B
h1942C
h1943A
h1943B
h1943C
h1944A
h1944B

h1944C
h1945A
h1945B
h1945C
h1946A
h1946B
h1946C
h1947A
h1947B
h1947C
h1950A

h1950B

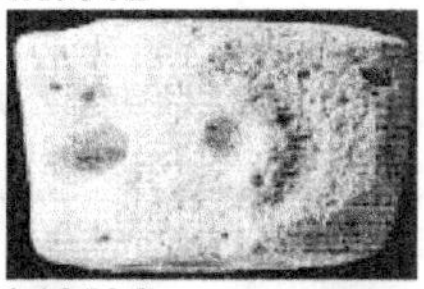

h1950C

h1950E

h1951A

h1951B

h1953A

h1953B

h1955A

(bird+fish)

h1955B

h1958A

h1958B

h1959

h1961A

h1961B

h1962A

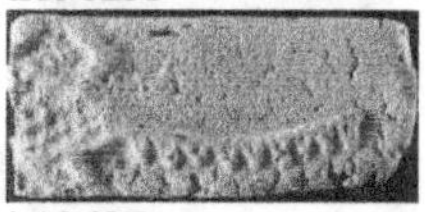

h1962B

h1963A

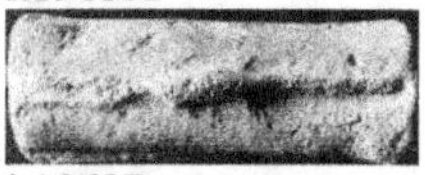

h1963B

h1964A

h1964B

h1966A

h1966B

h1967A

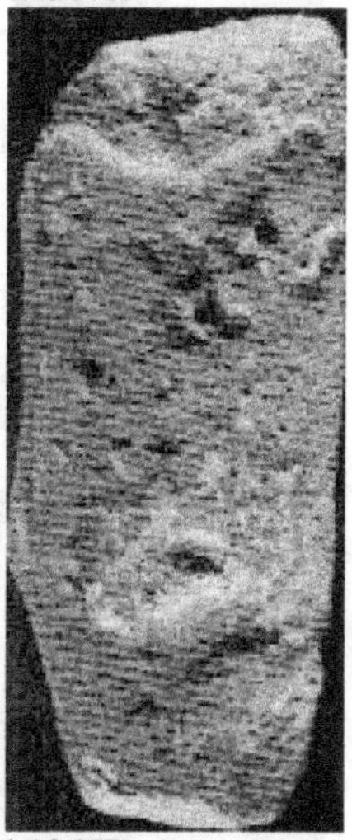

h1967B

h1968A

h1968B

h1969A

h1969B

h1970A

h1970B

h1971A

h1971B

h1972A

h1972B

h1973A

h1973B

h1974A

h1974B

h1975A

h1975B

h1976A

h1976B

h1977A

h1977B

h1978A

h1978B

h1979A

h1979B

h1980A

h1981B

h1981A

h1981B

h1985A

h1985B

h1987A

H1987B

h1988A, h1989A, h1990A

h1988B, h1989B, h1990B

h1991A

h1991B

h1992B

h1993A

h1993B

h1994A

h1994B

h1995A

h1995B

h1997A

h1997B

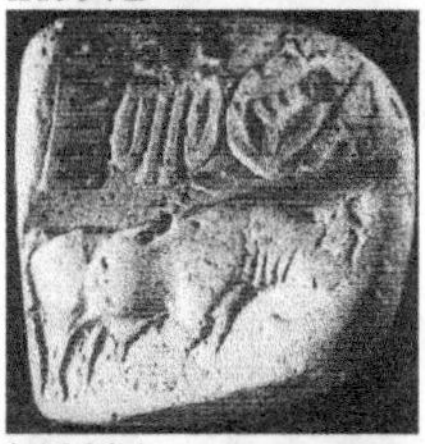
h1999A

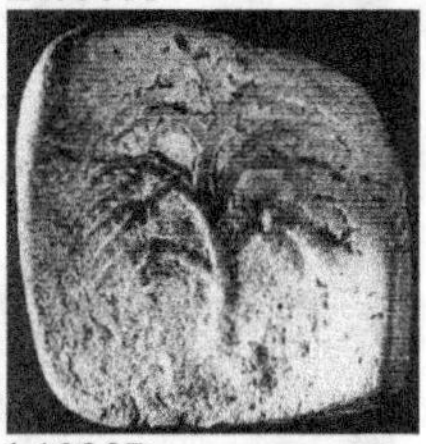
h1999B

h2002A

h2003Ah

h2003B

h2005A

h2005B

h2006A

h2006B

h2010A

h2010B

h2012A

h2012B

h2013A

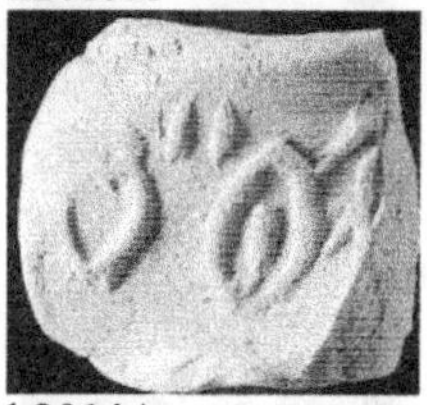
h2014A

h2014B

h2015A

h2015B

h2016A

h2018A

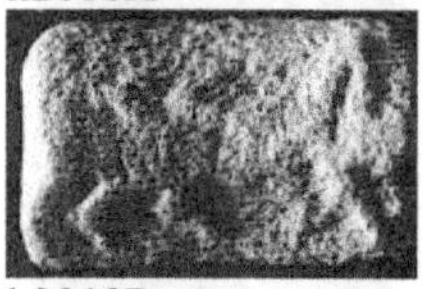
h2018B

h2019A

h2019B

h2019C

h2020A

h2020C

h2021A

h2021B

h2021C

h2022A

h2022B

h2022C

h2023A

h2023B

h2023C

h2024A

h2024B

h2024C

h2025C

h2026A

h2026B

h2026C

h2026D

h2027A

h2027B

h2027C

h2027D
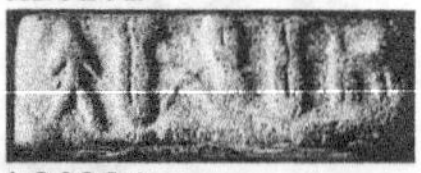
h2028A

h2028B

h2028C

h2028A

h2029A

h2029B

h2029C

h2029D

h2030A

h2030C

h2030D

h2031A

h2031B

h2031C

h2031D
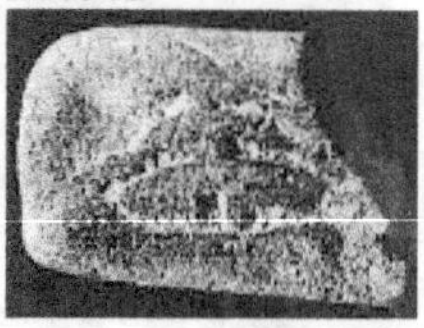

h2032B

h2032D

h2033A

h2033B

h2034A

h2034B

h2035A

h2035B

h2036A

h2036B

h2308A

h2038iB

h2039A

h2039B

h2040A

h2040B

h2041A

h2041B

h2043A

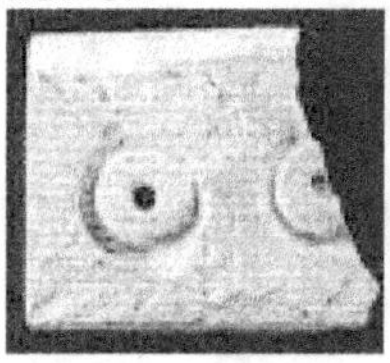

h2043B

h2044A

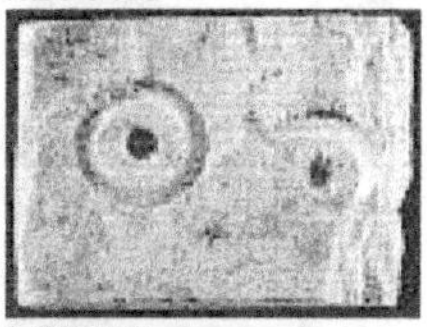

h2044B

h2045A

h2045B

h2046A

h2046B

h2047A

h2047B

h2048A

h2048B

h2049A

h2049B

h2050A

h2050B

h2051A

h2052A

h2053A

h2054B

h2055A

h2055B

h2056A

h2056B

h2057A

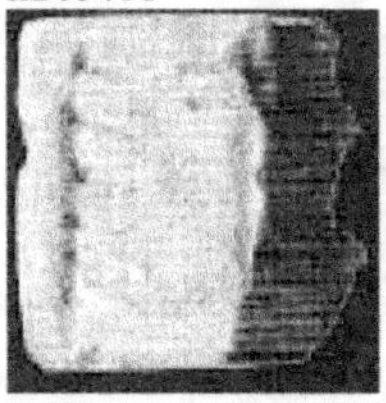

h2057B

h2058A

h2058B

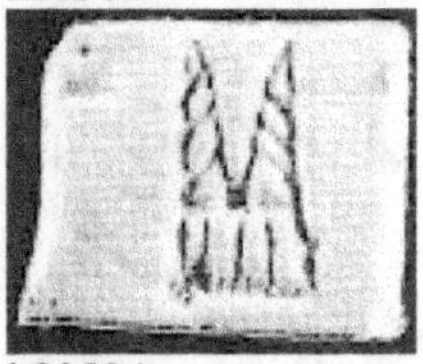

h2059A

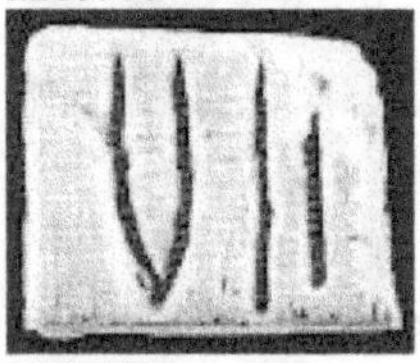

h2059B

h2062A

h2062B

h2063A

h2063B

h2064A

h2064B

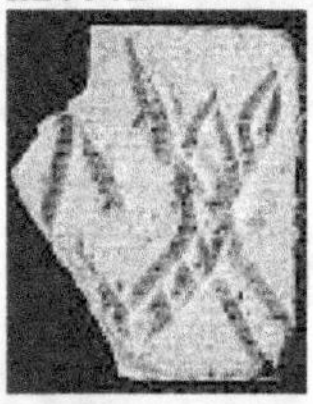

h2065A

h2065B

h2066A

h2066B

h2067A

h2067B

h2068A

h2068B

h2069A

h2069B

h2070A

h2070B

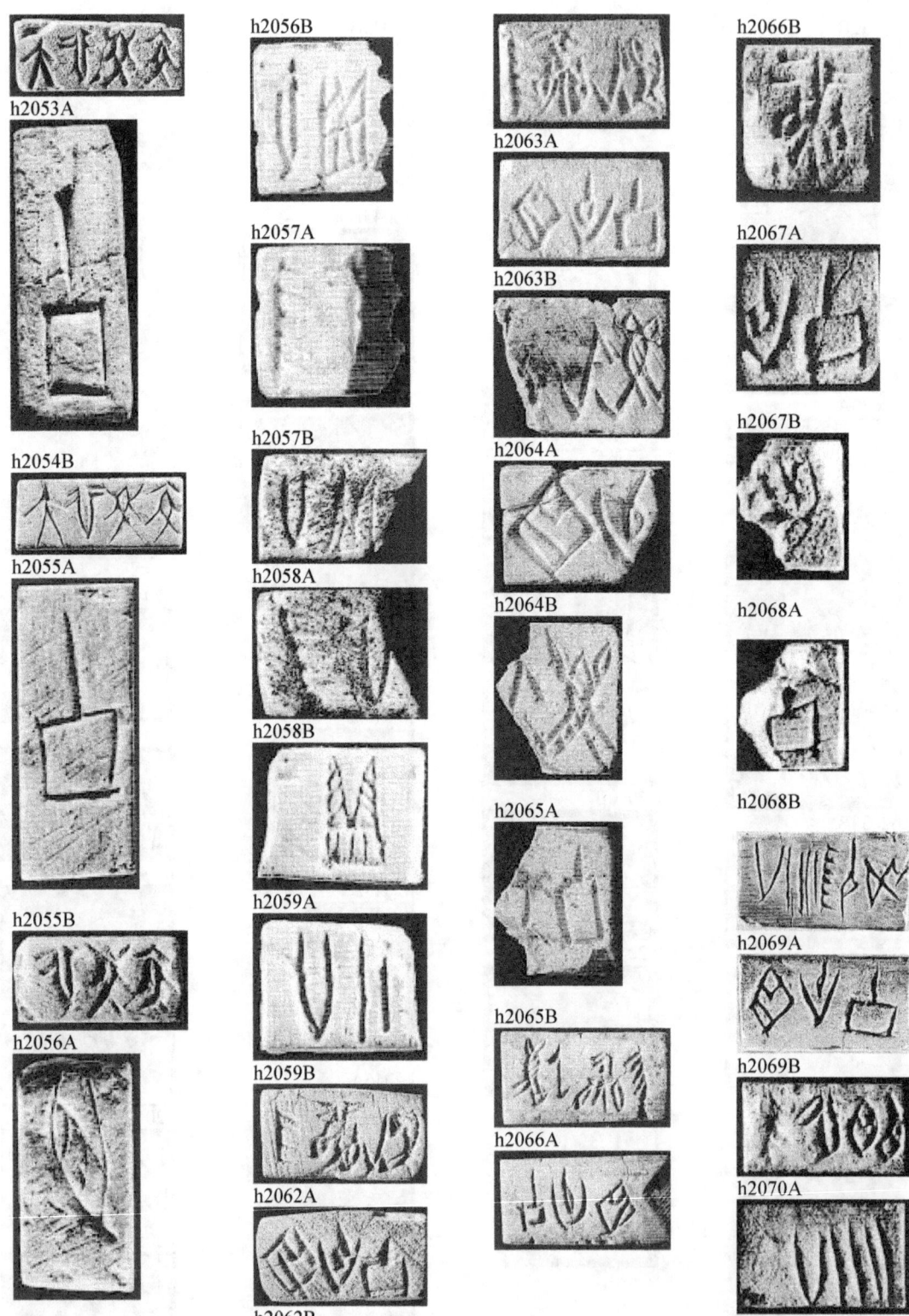

h2071A

h2071B

h2072A

h2072B
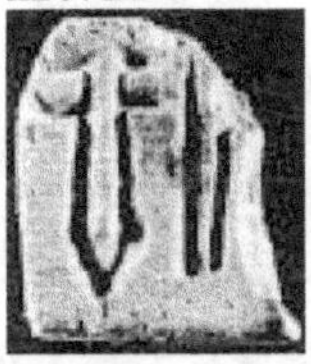
h2073A
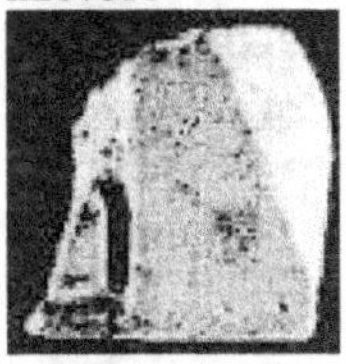
h2073B

h2074A

h2074B

h2076A
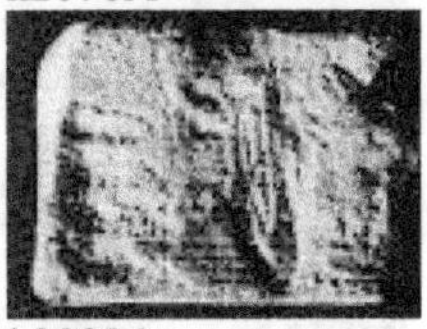
h2082A

h2082B

h2083A

h2083B

h2084A
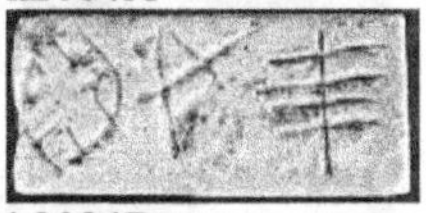
h2084B

h2085A

h2085B
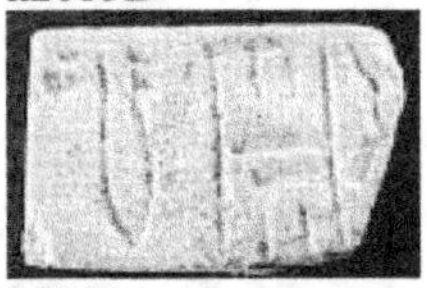
h2086A
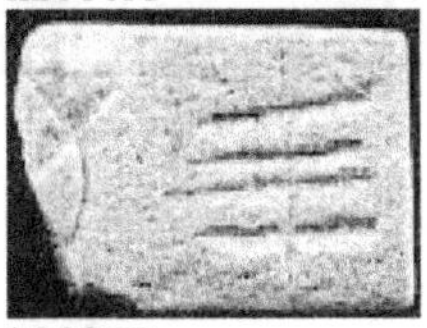
h2086B

h2089A

h2089B

h2090A

h2090B

h2091A

h2091B

h2092A

h2092B

h2093A

h2093B

h2094A

h2094B

h2095A

h2095B

h2096A
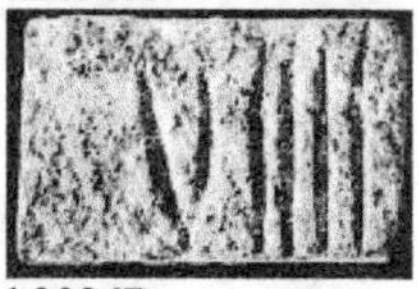
h2096B

h2097A

h2097B

h2098A

h2098B

h2099A

h2099B

h2102A

h2102B

h2104A

h2104B

h2105A
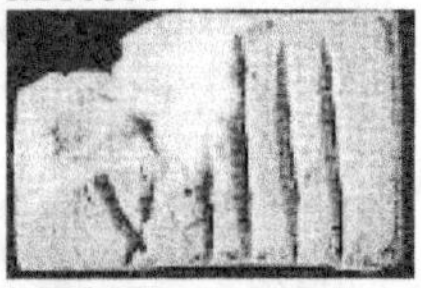
h2105B

h2106A
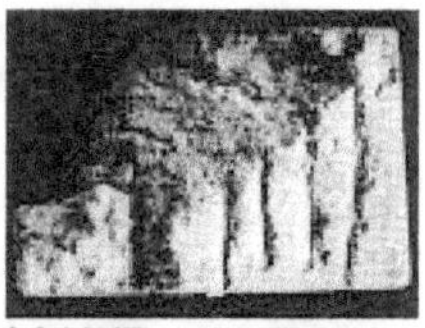
h2106B

h2107A

h2107B

h2108A

h2108B

h2109A1B2

h2109B1A2

h2110A

h2110B

h2111B

h2112A

h2112B

h2113A

h2113B

h2114A

h2114B

h2115A

h2115B

h2119A

h2119b
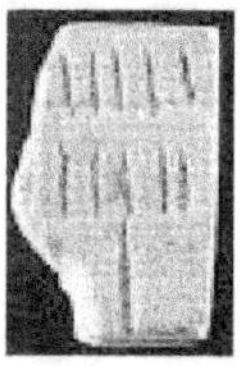
h2120A

h2120B

h2121A

h2121B

h2123A

h2123B
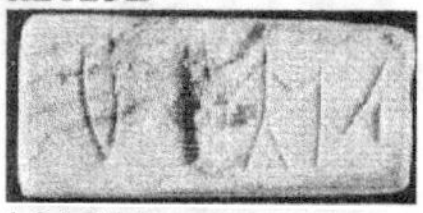
h2125A

h2125B

h2127A

h2127B

h2128A

h2128B

h2129A

h2129B

h2130A
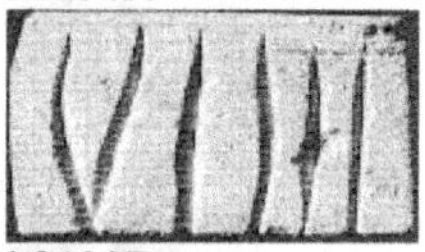
h2130B

h2131A

h2131B

h2132A

h2132B

h2133A

h2133B

h2134A

h2134B

h2135A

h2136A

h2137A

h2137B

h2138A

h2138B

h2139A

h2139B

h2140A

h2140B

h2141A

h2141B

h2142A
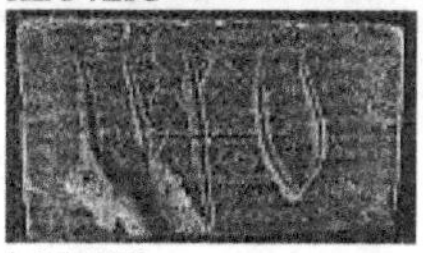
h2142B

h2143A

h2143B
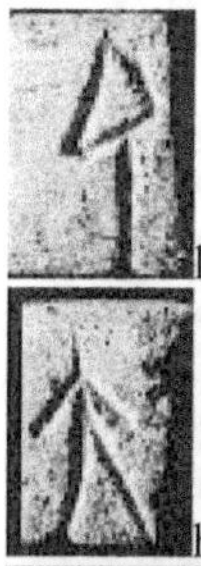
h2144A
h2144B

h2145A

h2145B

h2146A

h2146B

h2147A

h2147B

h2148A

h2148B

h2149A

h2149B

h2150A

h2150B

h2151A

h2151B

h2152A

h2152B

h2153A

h2153B

h2154A

h2154B

h2155A

h2155B

h2156A
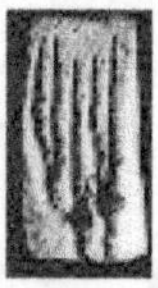
h2156B

h2158A

h2158B

h2159A

h2159B

h2160A

h2160B

h2173A
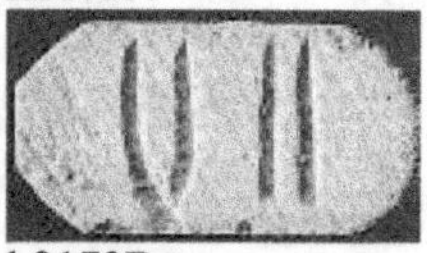
h2173B

h2174A
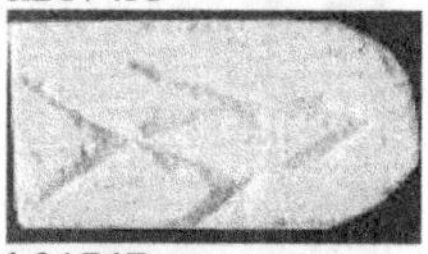
h2174B

h2175A

h2175B

h2176A
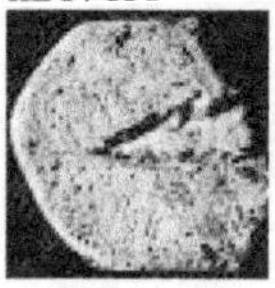
h2176B

h2177A
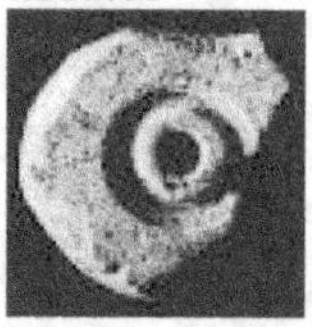
h2177B

h2178A
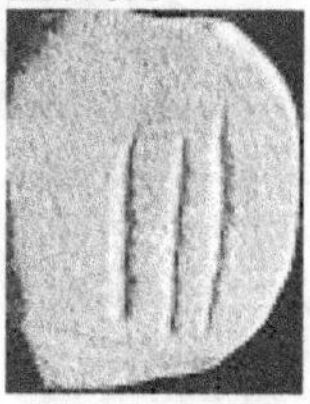
h2178B

h2180A
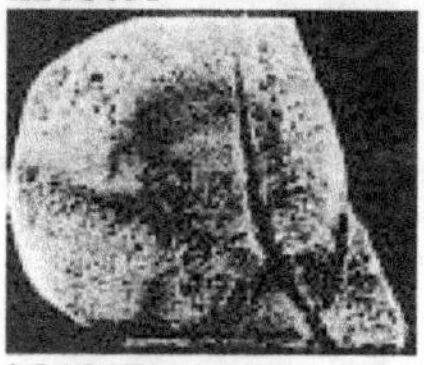
h2180B
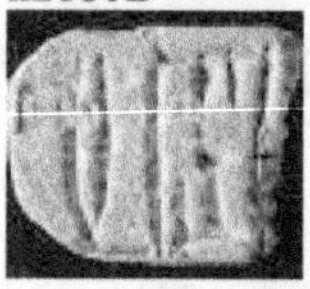

h2181A

h2181B

h2182A

h2182B

h2183A

h2183B

h2184A

h2184B

h2185A

h2185B

h2186A

h2186B

h2187A

h2187B

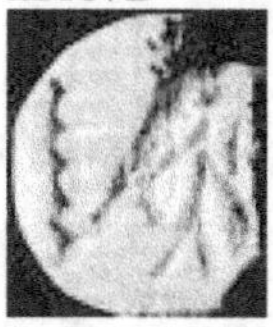

h2188A

h2188B

h2189A

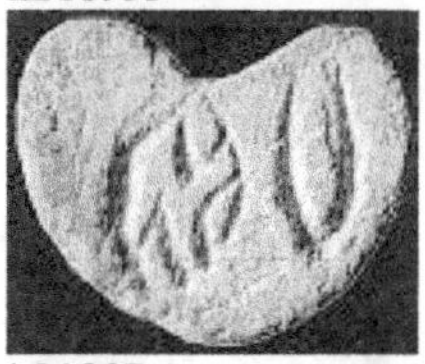

h2189B

h2190A

h2190B

h2192A

h2192B

h2193A

h2193B

h2194A

h2194B

h2195A

H2195B

h2197A

h2197B

h2198A

h2198B

h2200A

h2200B

h2200C

h2201A

h2201B

h2201C

h2204A

h2204B

h2204c

h2205A

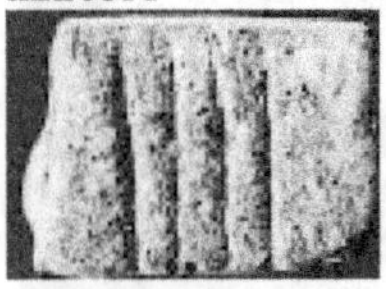

h2205B

h2205C

h2207A

h2207B

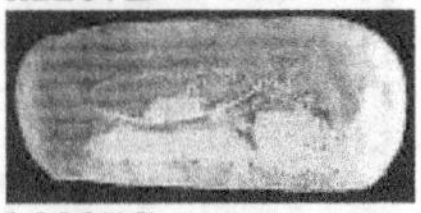

h2207C

h2208A

h2208B

h2208C

h2209A

h2209B

h2209C

h2210A

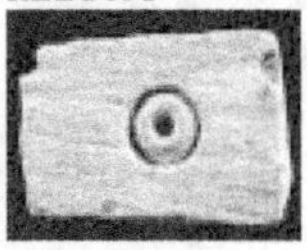

h2210B

h2210C

h2211A

h2211B

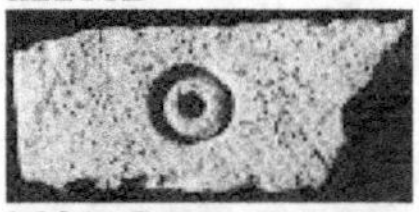

h2211C

h2212A

h2212B

h2212C

h2213A

h2213B

h2213C

h2214A

h2214N

h2214C

h2215B

h2215C

h2217A

h2217B

h2217C

h2218A

h2218B

h2218C

h2219A

h2219B

h2219C

h2220A

h2220B

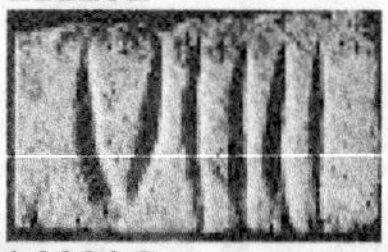

h2220C

h2221A

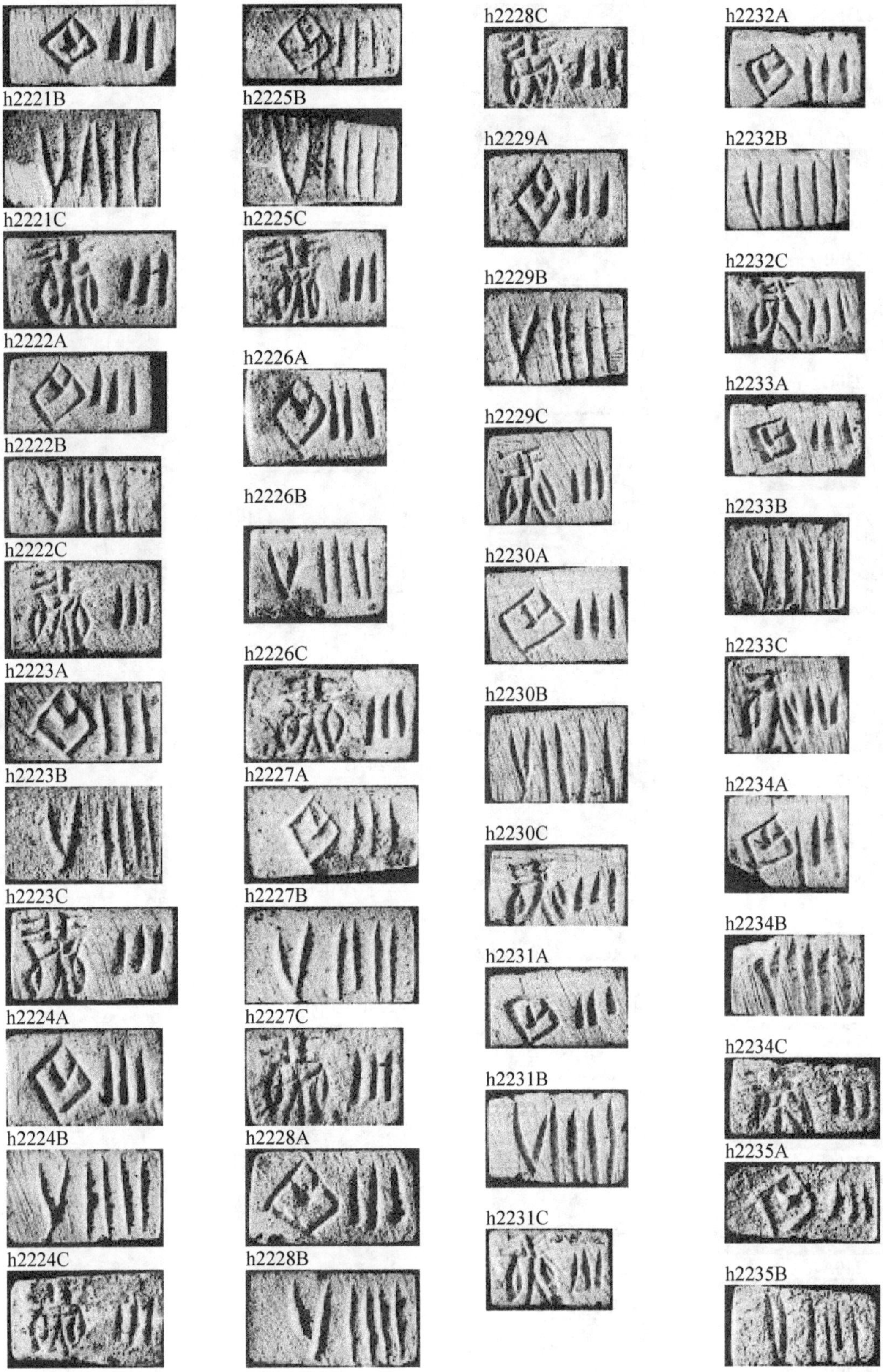

h2221B
h2221C
h2222A
h2222B
h2222C
h2223A
h2223B
h2223C
h2224A
h2224B
h2224C
h2225A

h2225B
h2225C
h2226A
h2226B
h2226C
h2227A
h2227B
h2227C
h2228A
h2228B

h2228C
h2229A
h2229B
h2229C
h2230A
h2230B
h2230C
h2231A
h2231B
h2231C

h2232A
h2232B
h2232C
h2233A
h2233B
h2233C
h2234A
h2234B
h2234C
h2235A
h2235B

h2235C

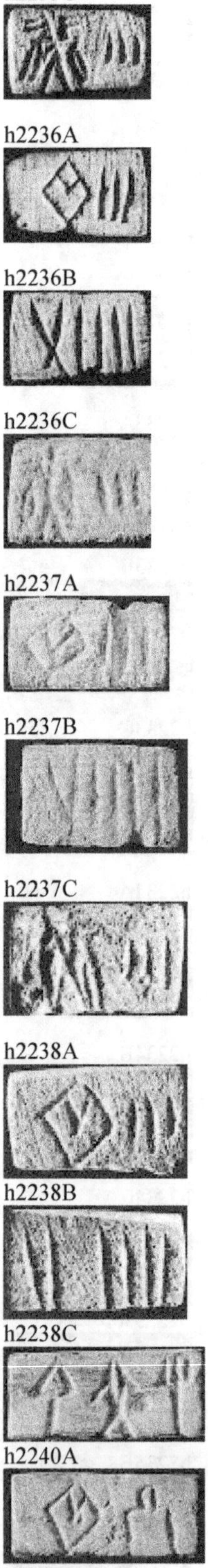

h2236A

h2236B

h2236C

h2237A

h2237B

h2237C

h2238A

h2238B

h2238C

h2240A

h2240B

h2240C

h2240E

h2241A

h2241B

h2241C

h2241E

h2243A

h2243B

h2244A

h2244B

h2244E

h2245A

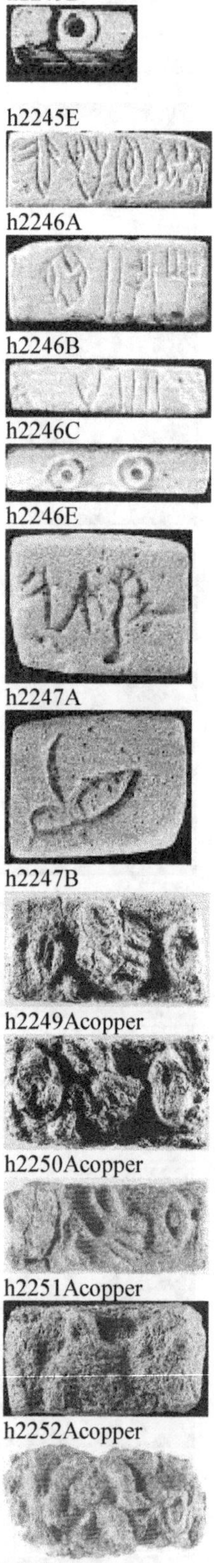

h2245B

h2245E

h2246A

h2246B

h2246C

h2246E

h2247A

h2247B

h2249Acopper

h2250Acopper

h2251Acopper

h2252Acopper

h2253Acopper

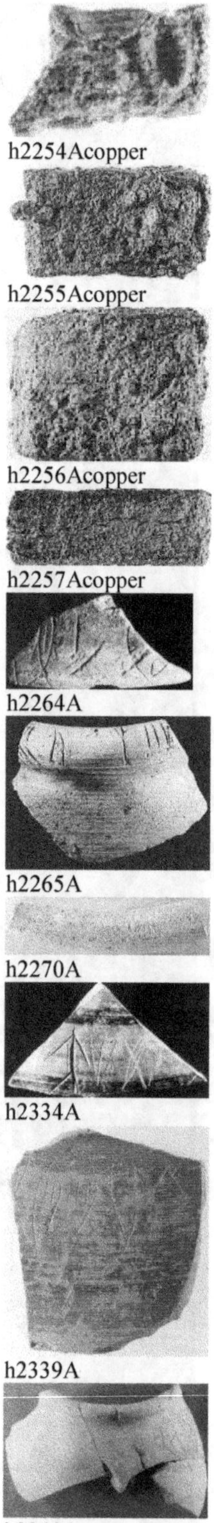

h2254Acopper

h2255Acopper

h2256Acopper

h2257Acopper

h2264A

h2265A

h2270A

h2334A

h2339A

h2340A

h2341A

h2345A

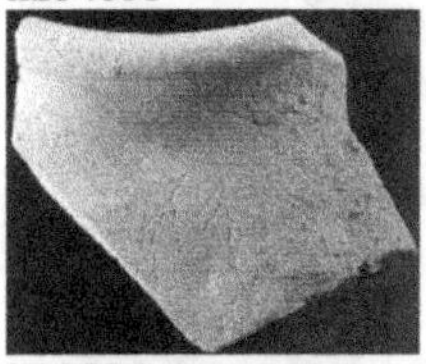
h2353A

h2354A

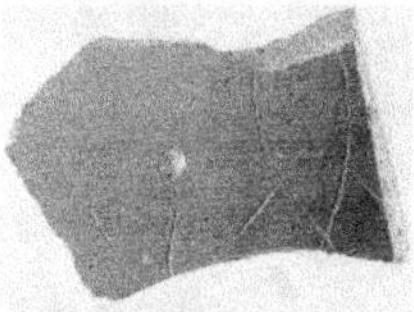
h2357A

h2358A

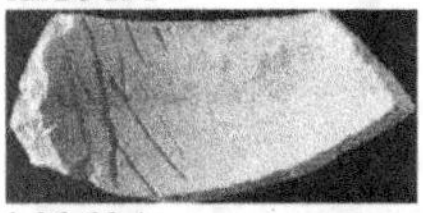
h2360A

h2367A

h2368A

h2373A

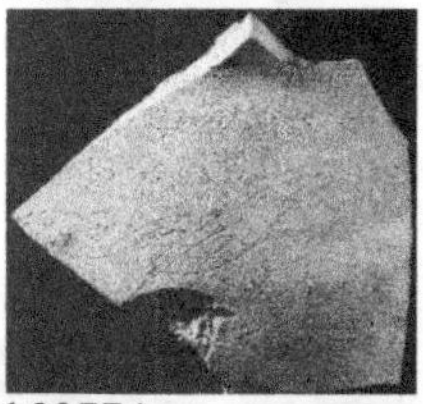
h2377A

h2380A

h2383A

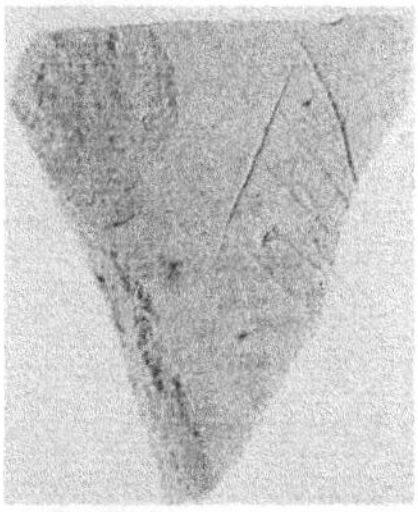
h2384A

h2390A

h2397A

j2398A

h2399A

h2400A

h2403A

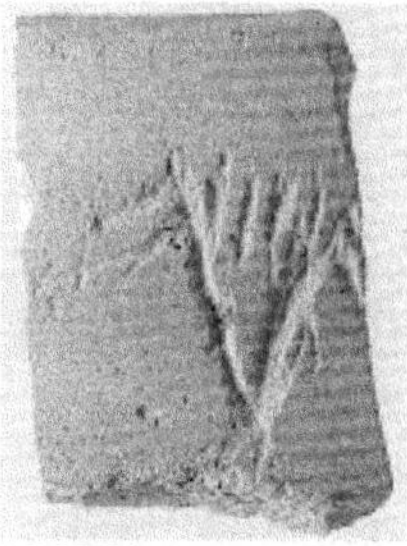
h2405A

h2548A

h2549A

h2586A

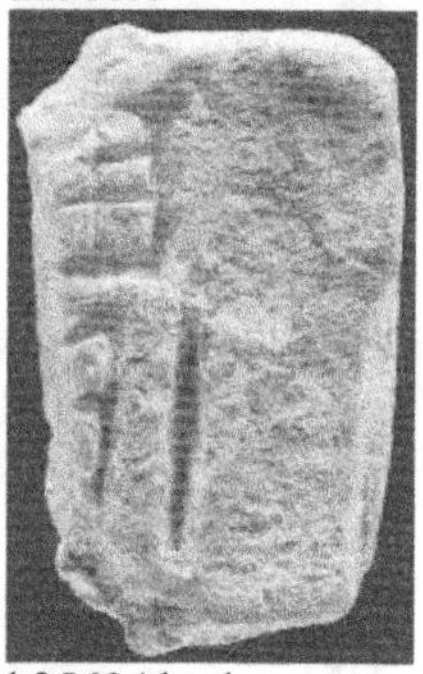
h2569Alead

h2570Abone

h2576Abangle

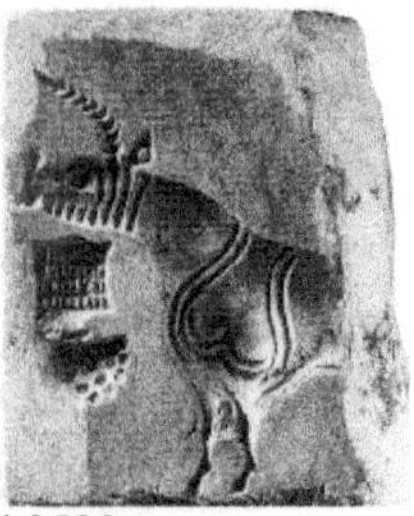

h2590

Harappa Texts (Either unmatched with inscribed objects or objects not illustrated)

4015

4033

4035

4046

4067

4073

4101

4108

4114

4117

4119

4134

4136

4140

4158

4164

4292

4296

4305

Pict-90: Standing person with horns and bovine features holding a staff or mace on his shoulder.

4324

4330

4334

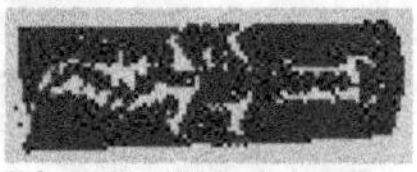

Pict-63: Gharial, sometimes with a fish held in its jaw and/or surrounded by a school of fish.

4343 Tablet in bas-relief One-horned bull

4344

4347

4356

4360

4363

4369

4373

4384

4404

4406

4407

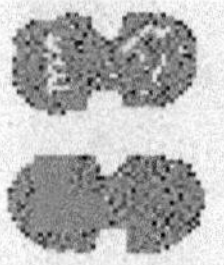

Pict-129: Inscribed object in the shape of a double-axe or double-shield?

4408

4422

4427

4428

4432

4435

4438

4439

4447

4448

4452

4458

4459

4462

4465

4468

4473

4476

Incised miniature tablet.

4491

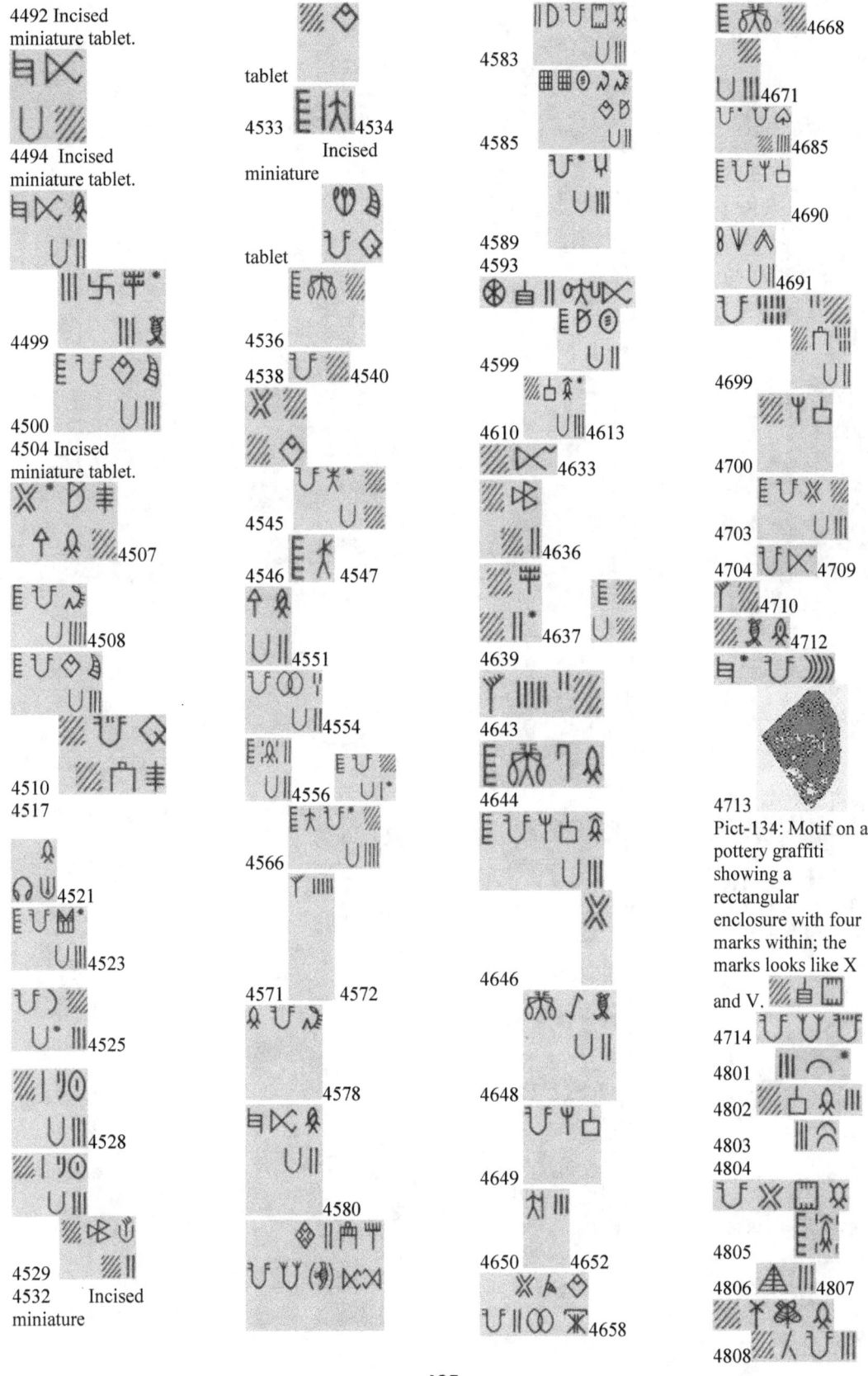

4492 Incised miniature tablet.

4494 Incised miniature tablet.

4499

4500

4504 Incised miniature tablet.

4507

4508

4510

4517

4521

4523

4525

4528

4529

4532 Incised miniature tablet

4533 4534 Incised miniature tablet

4536

4538 4540

4545

4546 4547

4551

4554

4556

4566

4571 4572

4578

4580

4583

4585

4589

4593

4599

4610 4613

4633

4636

4637

4639

4643

4644

4646

4648

4649

4650 4652

4658

4668

4671

4685

4690

4691

4699

4700

4703

4704 4709

4710

4712

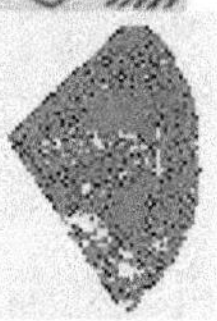

4713

Pict-134: Motif on a pottery graffiti showing a rectangular enclosure with four marks within; the marks looks like X and V.

4714

4801

4802

4803

4804

4805

4806 4807

4808

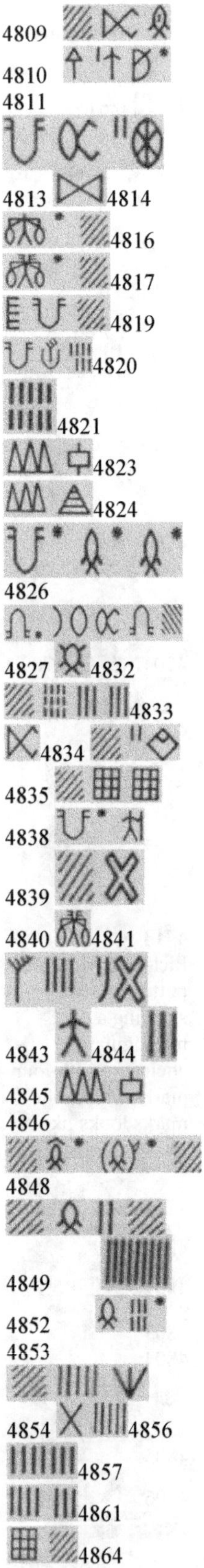
4809
4810
4811
4813
4814
4816
4817
4819
4820
4821
4823
4824
4826
4827
4832
4833
4834
4835
4838
4839
4840
4841
4843
4844
4845
4846
4848
4849
4852
4853
4854
4856
4857
4861
4864

4865
4868
4871
4873
4874
4875
4876
4877
4878
4879
4880
4881
4884
4905
5001
5017
5023
5031
5070
5077
5084
5085
5086
5087
5088
5102
5104
5107
5115
5123
5124
5201
5203

5204
5206
5209
5210
5223
5228
5232
5235
5239
5240
5241
5242
5245
5246
5251
5259
5261
5264

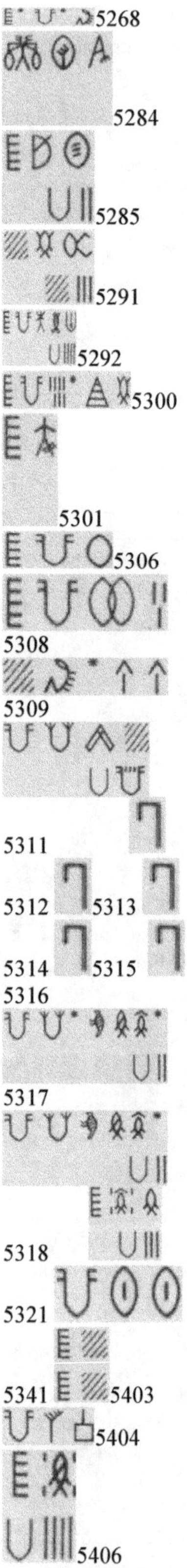
5268
5284
5285
5291
5292
5300
5301
5306
5308
5309
5311
5312
5313
5314
5315
5316
5317
5318
5321
5341
5403
5404
5406

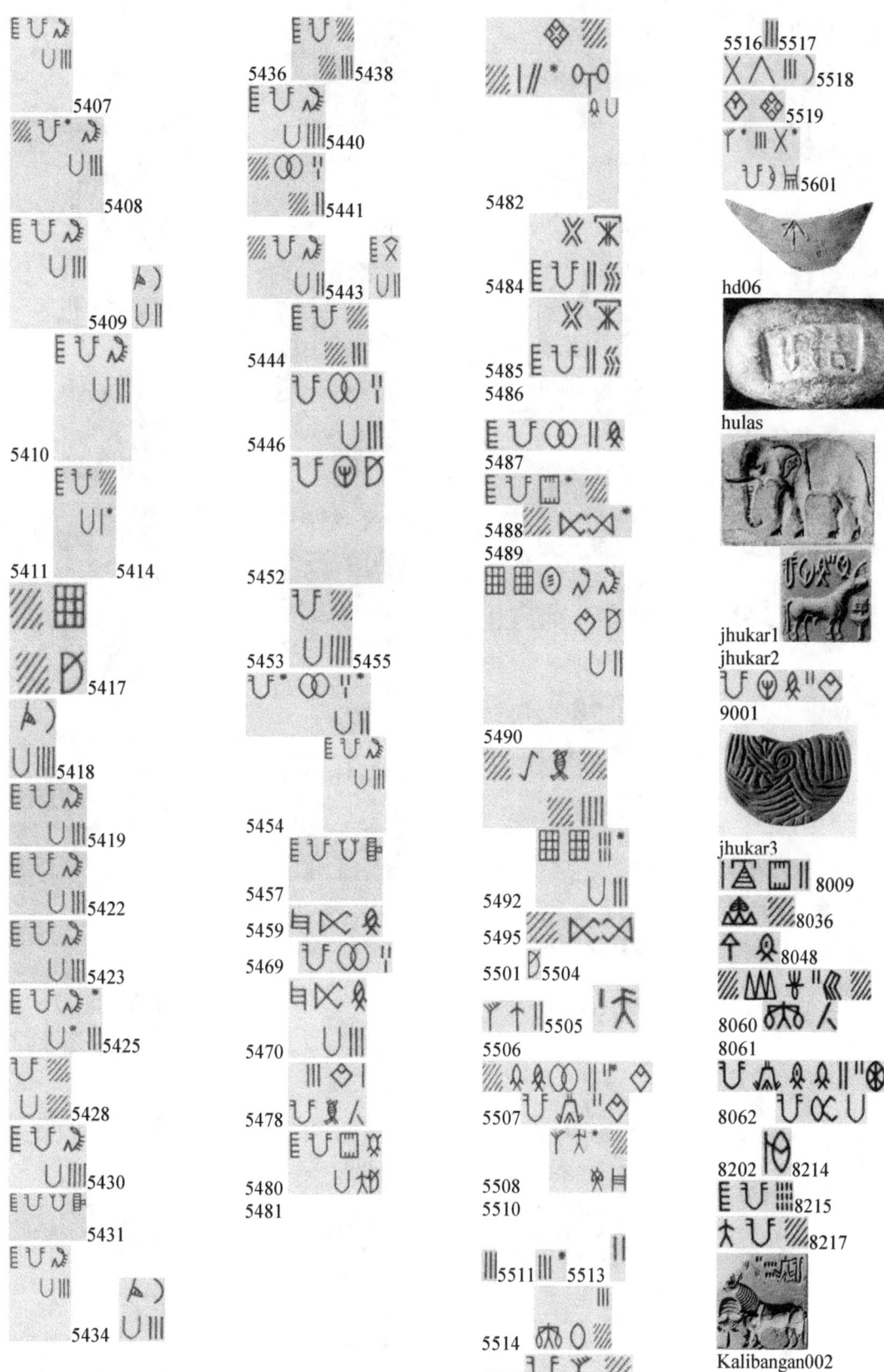

5407

5408

5409

5410

5411 5414

5417

5418

5419

5422

5423

5425

5428

5430

5431

5434

5436 5438

5440

5441

5443

5444

5446

5452

5453 5455

5454

5457

5459

5469

5470

5478

5480

5481

5482

5484

5485

5486

5487

5488

5489

5490

5492

5495

5501 5504

5505

5506

5507

5508

5510

5511 5513

5514

5515

5516 5517

5518

5519

5601

hd06

hulas

jhukar1

jhukar2

9001

jhukar3

8009

8036

8048

8060

8061

8062

8202 8214

8215

8217

Kalibangan002

8019

Kalibangan003

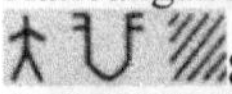

8030

Kalibangan004

8026

Kalibangan005

8017

Kalibangan006

8020

Kalibangan007

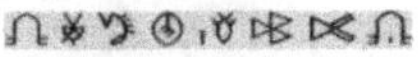

8043

Kalibangan008

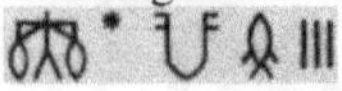

8041

Kalibangan009

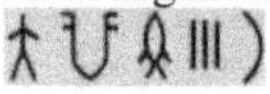

8021

Kalibangan010

8006

Kalibangan011

8034

Kalibangan012

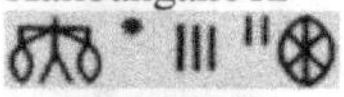

Kalibangan013

8051

Kalibangan014

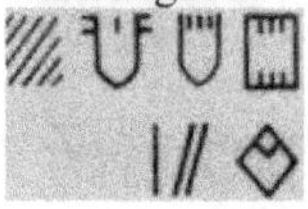

8012

Kalibangan015

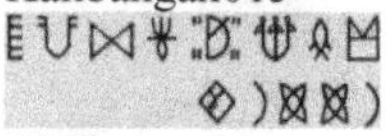

8056

Kalibangan016

8044

Kalibangan017

8027

Kalibangan018

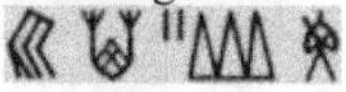

8040

Kalibangan019

8058

Kalibangan020

8047

Kalibangan021

Kalibangan022

8008

Kalibangan023

8029

Kalibangan024

Kalibangan025

8037

Kalibangan026

8071

Kalibangan027

8022

'Unicorn' with two horns! "Bull with

two long horns (otherwise resembling the 'unicorn')", generally facing the standard. That it is the typical 'one-horned bull' is surmised from two ligatures: the pannier on the shoulder and the ring on the neck.

Kalibangan028

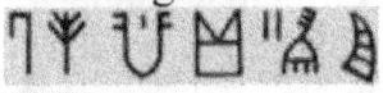

8038

Kalibangan029

8018

Kalibangan030

8002

Kalibangan031a

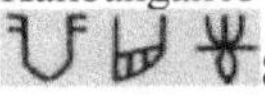8007

Kalibangan032a

Kalibangan033

8025

Kalibangan034

8052

Kalibangan035

Kalibangan036

Kalibangan037

8042

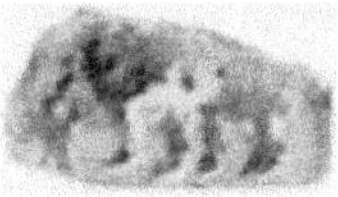

Kalibangan038

Kalibangan039

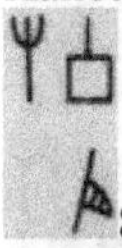8011

Kalibangan040

8072

Kalibangan041

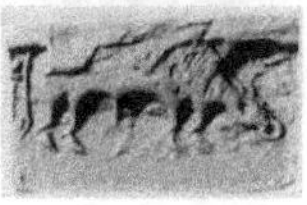

Kalibangan042a

Kalibangan043

8039 Pict-59:Composite motif: body of an ox and three heads: of a one-horned bull (looking forward), of antelope (looking backward), and of short-horned bull (bison) (looking downward).

Kalibangan044

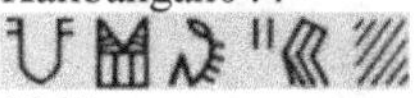

8045

Kalibangan045

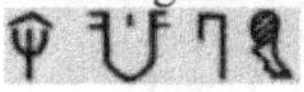

8054

Kalibangan046

8053

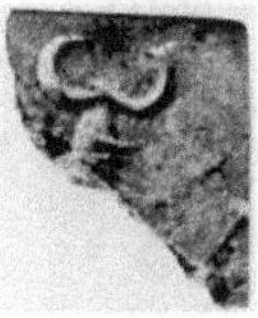

Kalibangan047

Kalibangan048

Kalibangan049

8013

Kalibangan050c

8031 Pict-53: Composition: body of a tiger, a human body with bangles on arm, a pig-tail, horns of an antelope crowned by a twig.

Kalibangan051 
8003

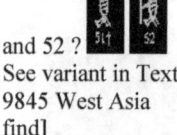

Kalibangan052
8015

Kalibangan053

Kalibangan054
8033

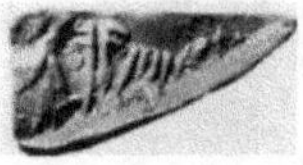

Kalibangan055a
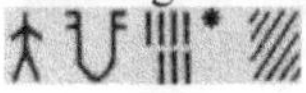

8035

Kalibangan056
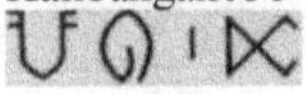

8004

Kalibangan057

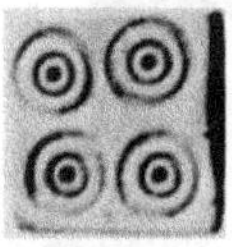

Kalibangan058

Kalibangan059
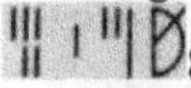8016

Kalibangan060
8059

Kalibangan061
8001

Kalibangan062
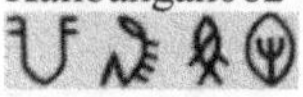

8023

Kalibangan063

8055

Kalibangan064

Kalibangan065a

Kalibangan065A6

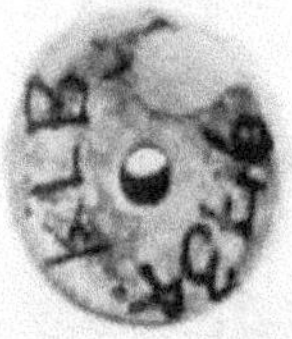

Kalibangan065E
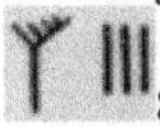8024 Pict-104: Composition: A tree; a person with a composite body of a human (female?) in the upper half and body of a tiger in the lower half, having horns, and a trident-like head-dress, facing a group of three persons consisting of a woman (?) in the middle flanked by two men on either side throwing a spear at each other (fencing?) over her head.

Kalibangan066

8102

Kalibangan067 
8121 Ox-antelope with a long tail; sometimes with a trough in front.

Kalibangan068A

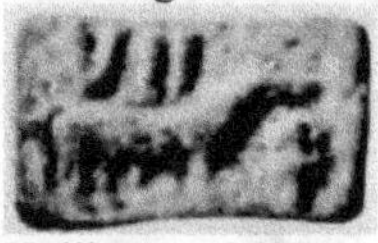

Kalibangan068B
8117 [Is it a bird or an India River Otter? Could be a scorpion, a model for Signs 51 and 52 ? 
See variant in Text 9845 West Asia find]

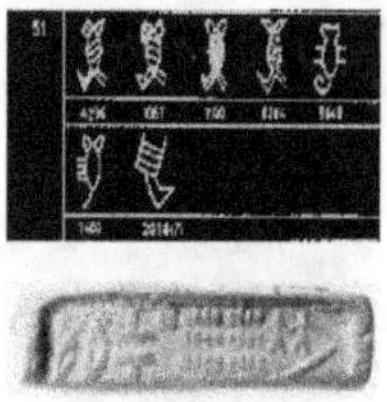

Kalibangan069A
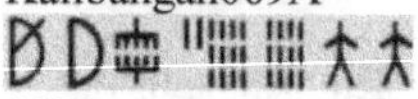
8109

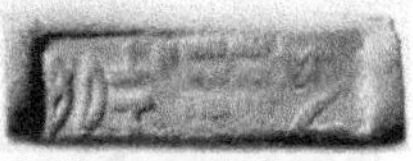

Kalibangan070A
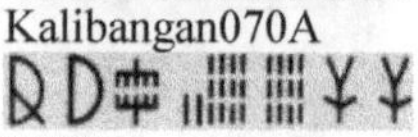
8108

Kalibangan071

8110

Kalibangan072

8111

Kalibangan073

8112

Kalibangan074

8115

Kalibangan075

8113

Kalibangan076A

Kalibangan076B

Kalibangan077A

Kalibangan077B
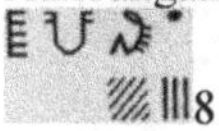
8118

Kalibangan078A
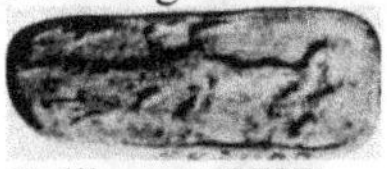
Kalibangan078B
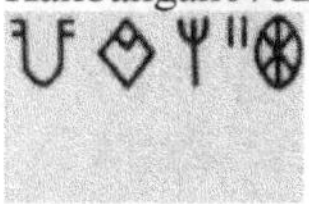

8104

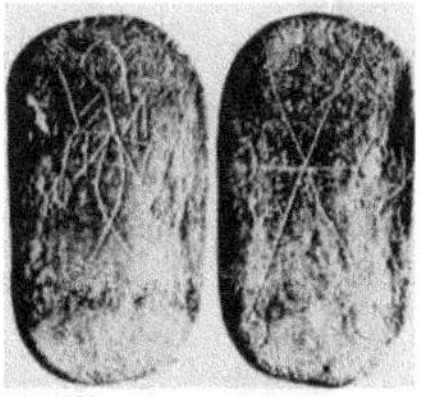
Kalibangan

079AB

Kalibangan080A
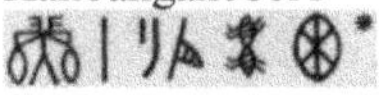
8120

Kalibangan081A

8105

Kalibangan082A
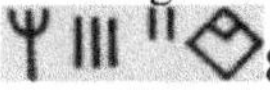
8122

Kalibangan

083A12

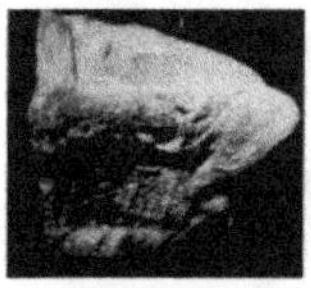

Kalibangan

084A12

Kalibangan

084A2 8103

Kalibangan

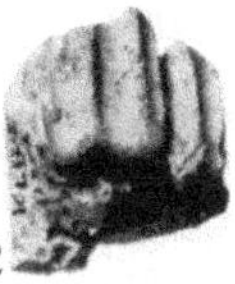
085A12

Kalibangan085B
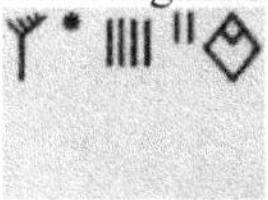

8106

Kalibangan086A14

8114

Kalibangan087A12

8116

Kalibangan

088A14

Kalibangan088B
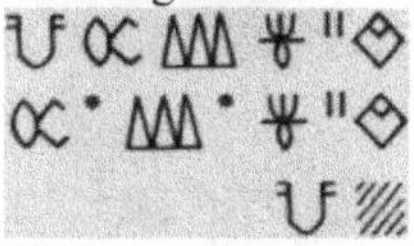
8119

Kalibangan089A14
c
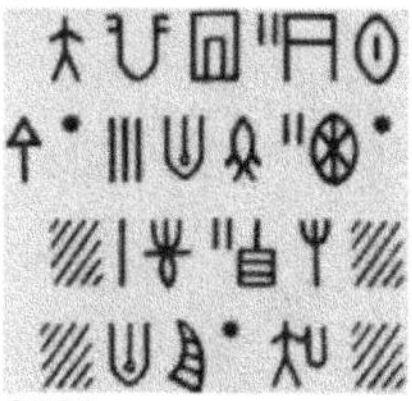
8101

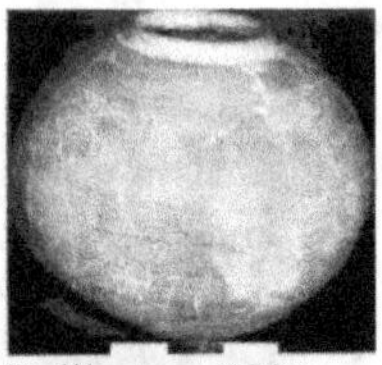
Kalibangan090A

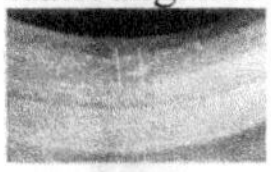
Kalibangan

090A1

Kalibangan

090A2 
8202

Kalibangan091A
 8212

Kalibangan092A
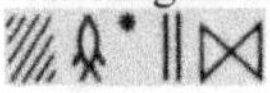

8210

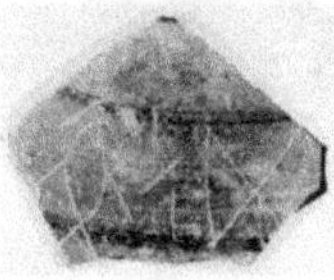
Kalibangan093A
 8219

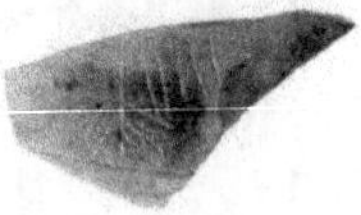
Kalibangan094A

Kalibangan095A

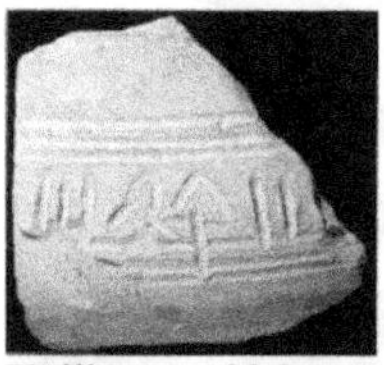
Kalibangan096c

8221

Kalibangan097A

 8213

Kalibangan098A

8201

Kalibangan099A
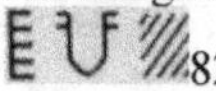 8208

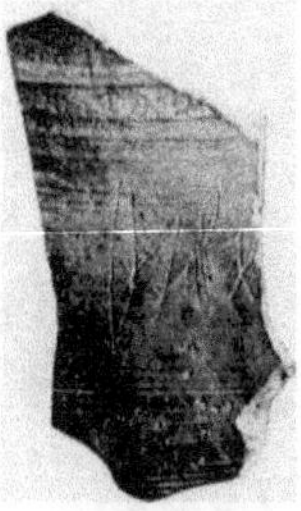
Kalibangan100A

Kalibangan101A
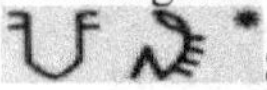 8205

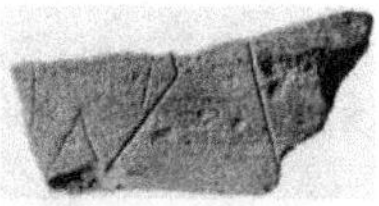
Kalibangan102A
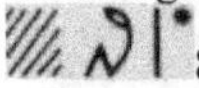 8207

Kalibangan103A 
8209

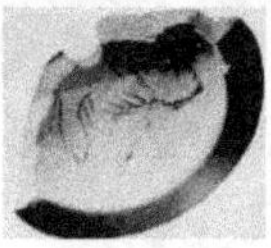
Kalibangan104A
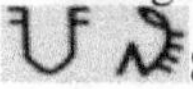 8218

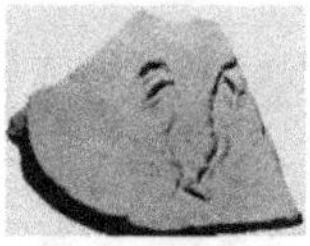
Kalibangan105A
 8216

Kalibangan106A
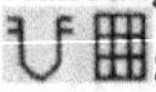 8204

Kalibangan107A

Kalibangan108A
 8206

Kalibangan109A

Kalibangan110A
 8211

Kalibangan111A

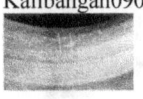

Kalibangan112A

Kalibangan118

Kalibangan119A

Kalibangan119B

Kalibangan120A

8220

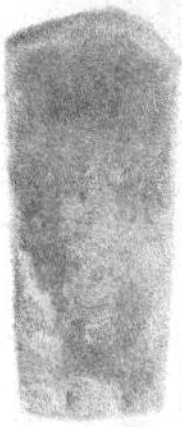

Kalibangan122B

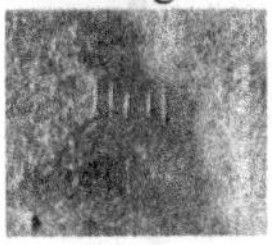

Kalibangan

122B2

Kalibangan

121A, B

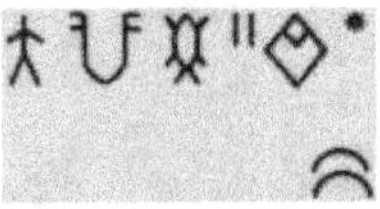

8302

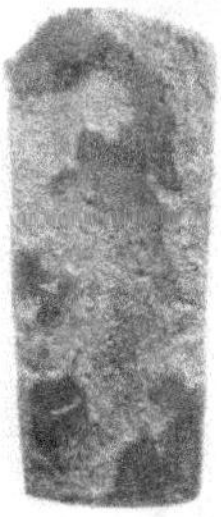

Kalibangan122A

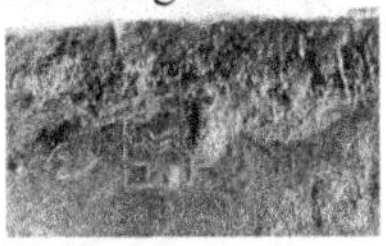

Kalibangan

122A2
8301

Kalako-deray 01

Kalako-deray 05

Kalako-deray 06

Kalako-deray 07

Kalako-deray 08

Kalakoderay10

Khirsara1a

Khirsara2a

9051 Kot-diji

Lewandheri01

Loebanr01

Lohumjodaro1a

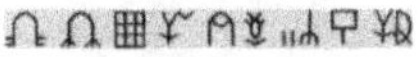

9011

Lothal001

7015

Lothal002

7031

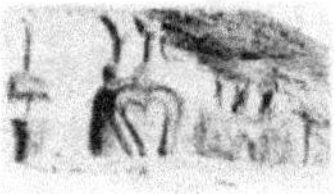

Lothal003

Lothal004a

7080

Lothal005

7044

Lothal006a

7038

Lothal007a

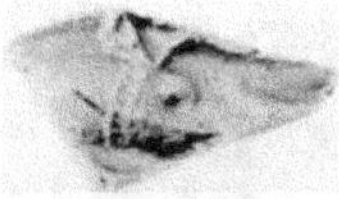

Lothal008a

Lothal009

7022

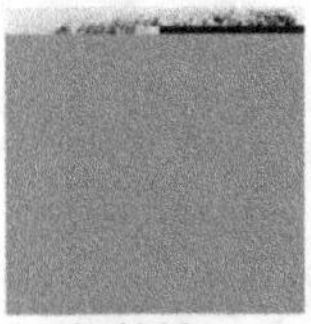

Lothal010

7009

Lothal011

7026

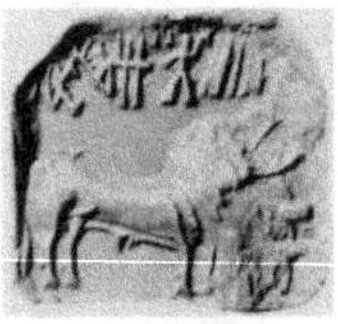

Lothal012a

7089

Lothal013

7050

Lothal014a

7094

Lothal015

7086

Lothal016

7002

Lothal017

7008

Lothal018

7096

Lothal019a

7092

Lothal020

7078

Lothal021

7047

Lothal022a

7035

Lothal023a

7043

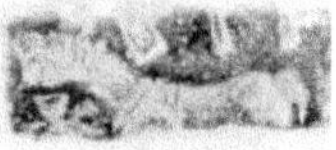

Lothal024

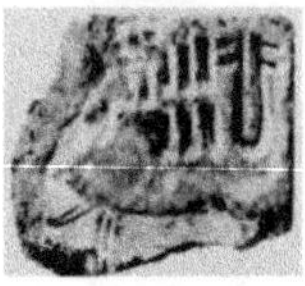

Lothal025

7104

Lothal026

7024

Lothal027

7036

Lothal028

7045

Lothal029

7005

Lothal030a

Lothal031

7076

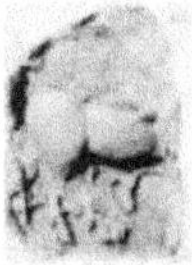

Lothal032a

Lothal033a

Lothal035

 7101

Lothal036a

7081

Lothal037

7034

Lothal038a

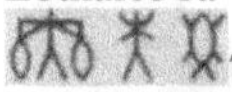 7053

Lothal039

7102

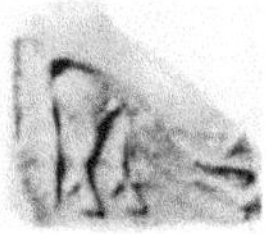

Lothal040a

Lothal041

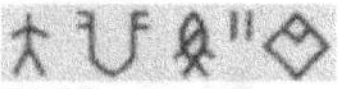

7066

Lothal042

Lothal043

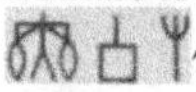 7049

Lothal044

Lothal045

7028

Lothal046

7107

Lothal047a

7074

Lothal048

 7025

Lothal049

Lothal050

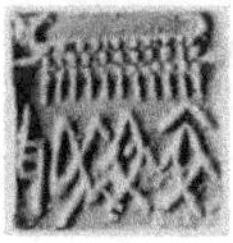

Lothal051a

 7057

Pict-127: Upper register: a large device with a number of small circles in three rows with another row of short vertical lines below; the device is horned. A seed-drill? [Is this an orthographic model for Sign 176?]

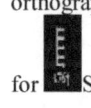

Lothal052

7011

Lothal054a

7099

Lothal055

7106

Lothal056

7100

Lothal057

7095

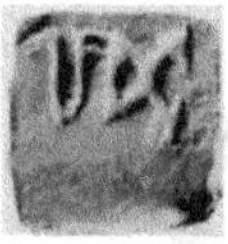

Lothal058a

7029

Lothal059

7097

Lothal060

7039

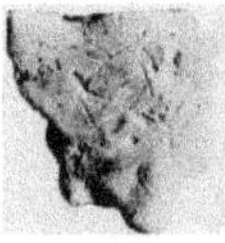

Lothal061

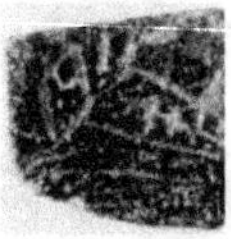

Lothal062

7054

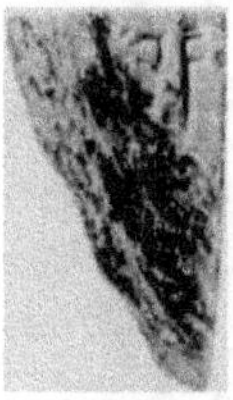

Lothal063

Lothal064

7030

Lothal065

7103

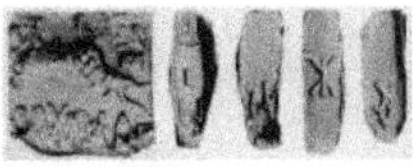

Lothal066acdef

7048

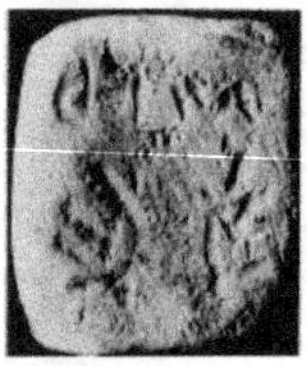

Lothal068

7070

Lothal069

Lothal070

Lothal071

Lothal072

Lothal075

Lothal076a

Lothal077

Lothal078

7077

Lothal079

7063

Lothal080a

Lothal081

7093

Lothal082

7105

Lothal083

7068

Lothal084

7112

Lothal085

Lothal086

7007

Lothal087

7021

Lothal088

7017

Lothal089

7090

Lothal090

7032

Lothal091

7111

Lothal092

7062

Lothal093

7064

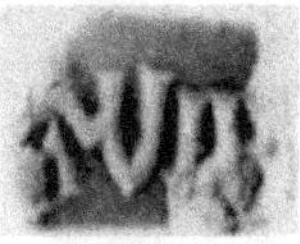
Lothal094a
7073

Lothal095
7042

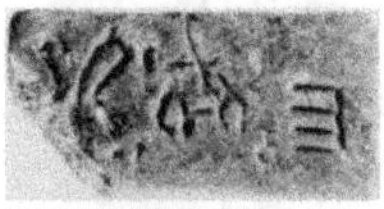
Lothal096
7023

Lothal097
7072

Lothal098
7082

Lothal099

Lothal100a

Lothal100B
7055

Lothal101
7001

Lothal102
7040

Lothal103
7018

Lothal104
7085

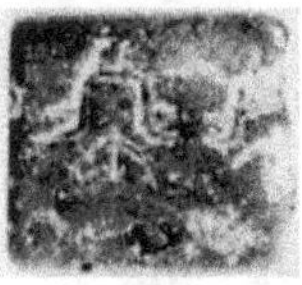
Lothal105
7016

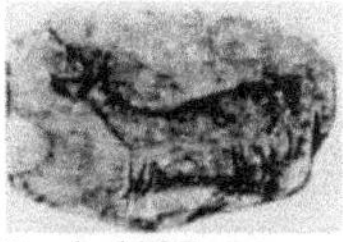
Lothal107

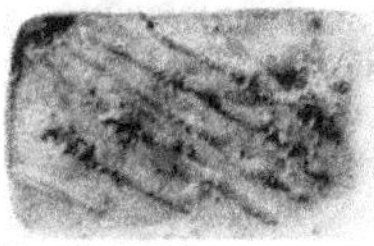
Lothal108

Lothal109a
7046

Lothal110
7006

Lothal111
7056

Lothal112
7020

Lothal113a
7004

Lothal114a
7013

Lothal115
7065

Lothal116
7027

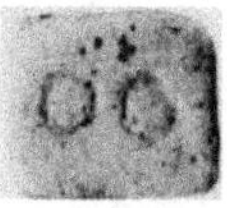
Lothal117
7075

Lothal118
7019

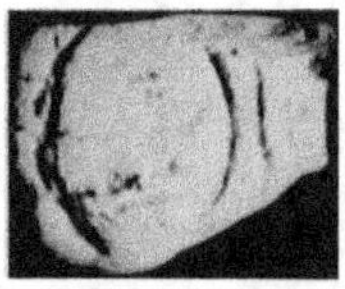
Lothal119

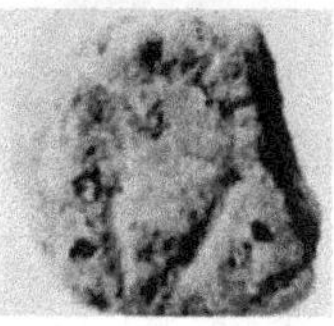
Lothal120

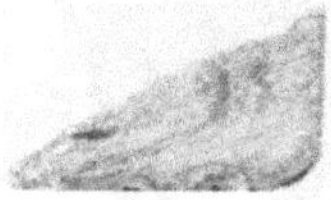
Lothal121

Lothal122
7069

Lothal123A

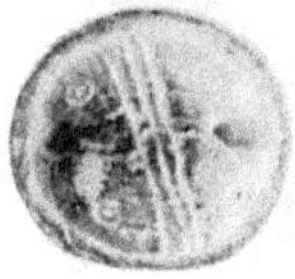

Lothal123B

Lothal124A

7224

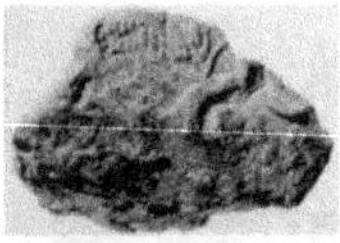

Lothal125A

7241

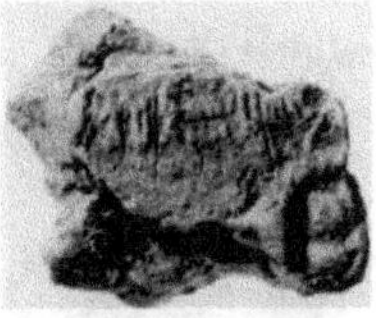

Lothal126A

7242

Lothal127A

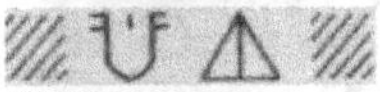

7221

Lothal128A

7239

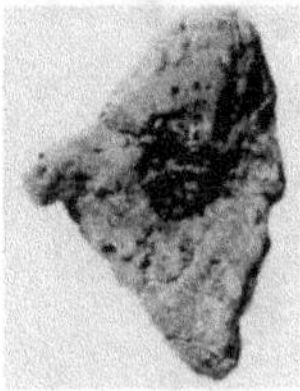

Lothal129A

Lothal130A

Lothal131A

7255

Lothal132A

7213

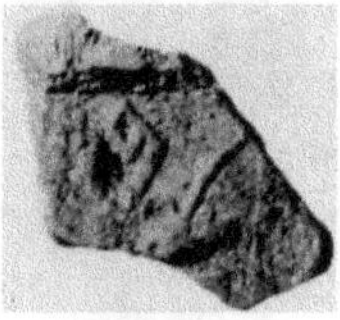

Lothal133A

7245

Lothal134A

7252

Lothal135A

7220

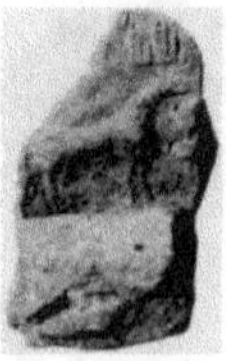

Lothal136A

7225

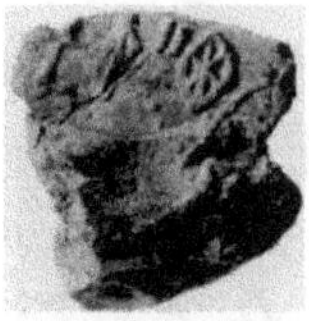

Lothal137A

7257

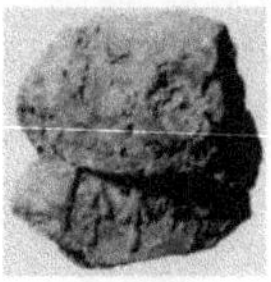

Lothal138A

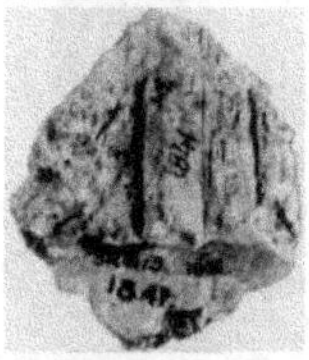

Lothal138B

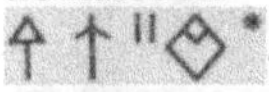

7214

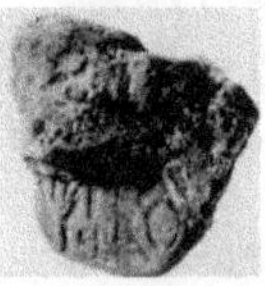

Lothal139A

7223

Lothal140A

7244

Lothal141A1

Lothal141A2

7280

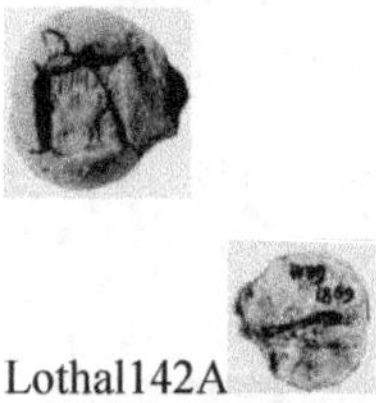

Lothal142A

Lothal142B

7204

Lothal143A

Lothal143B

7243

Lothal144A

7274

Lothal145A

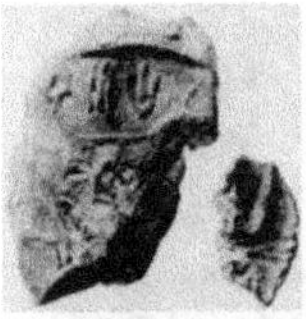

Lothal146AB
7279

Lothal147A
7260

Lothal148A
7270

Lothal149A
7272

Lothal150A
7268

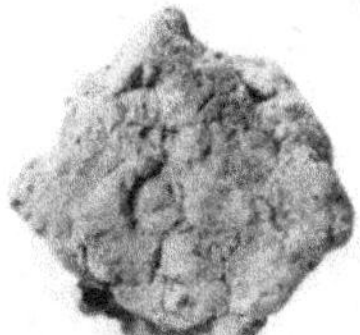

Lothal151A
7266

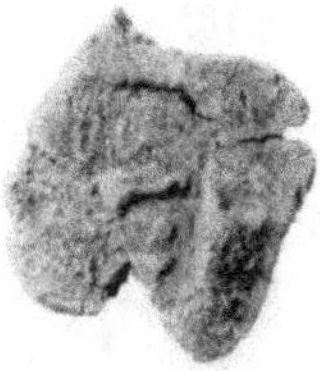

Lothal152A
7222

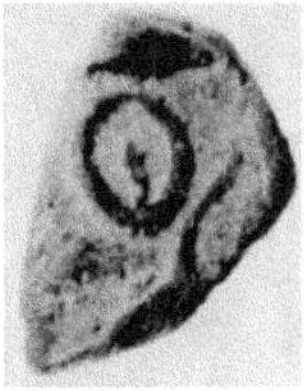

Lothal153A
7271

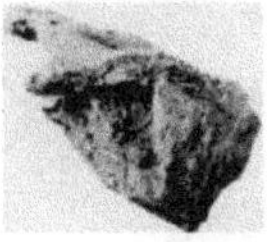

Lothal154A

Lothal155A

Lothal156A

Lothal157A

Lothal158A

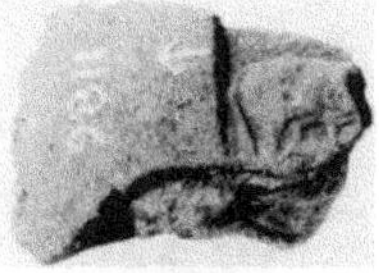

Lothal159A

Lothal160A

Lothal161A
7205

Lothal162A

Lothal162B

Lothal163A

Lothal163C
7228

Lothal164A
7230

Lothal165A
7203

Lothal166A
7206

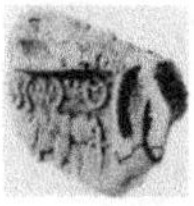

Lothal167A
7231

Lothal168A
7234

Lothal169A
7235

Lothal170A
7229

Lothal171A

Lothal172A

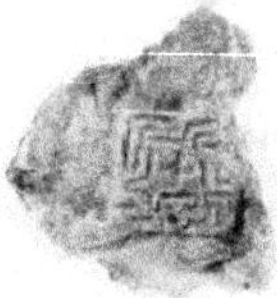

Lothal173A

Lothal174A

Lothal175A

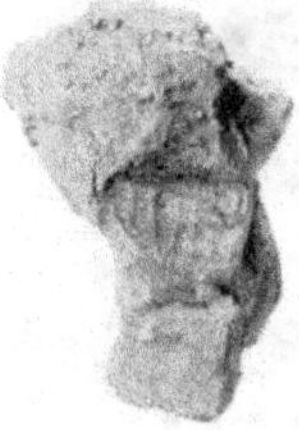

Lothal176A

7216

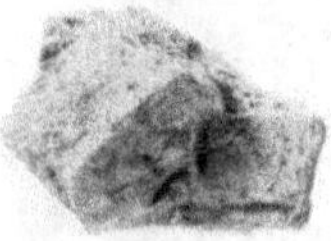

Lothal177A

7211

Lothal179A

Lothal180A

7240

Lothal181A

7273

Lothal182A

7238

Lothal183A

Lothal184A

Lothal185A

Lothal186A

7259

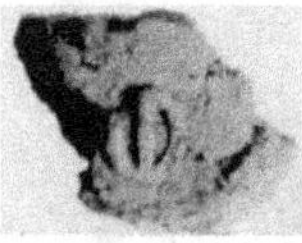

Lothal187A

7209

Lothal188A

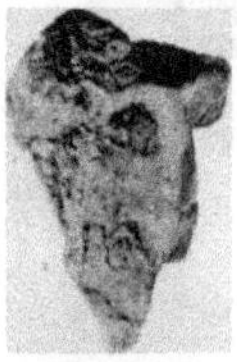

Lothal189A12

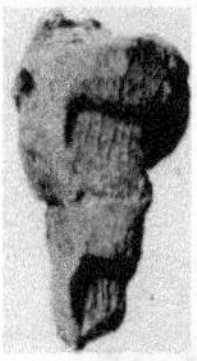

Lothal189A34

7217

Lothal190A13

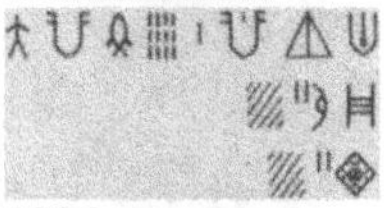

7236

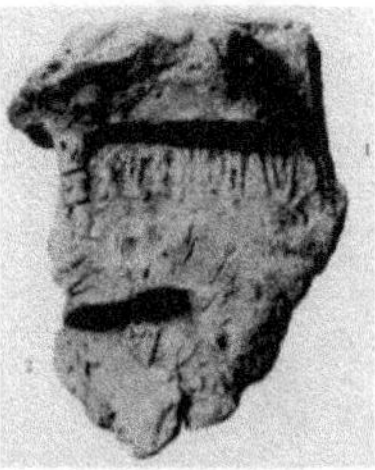

Lothal191A12

7249

Lothal192A12

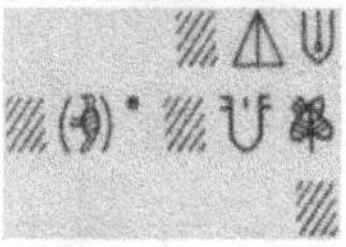

7227

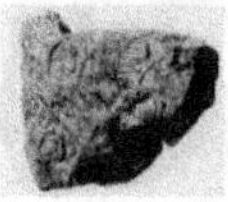

Lothal193A12

Lothal193A3

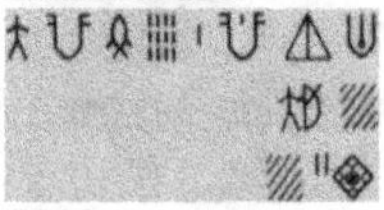

7253

Lothal194A1

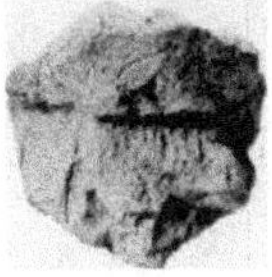

Lothal194A2

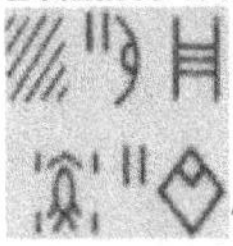
7251

Lothal195A12

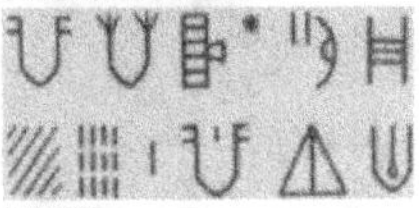
7258

Lothal196A12

7248

Lothal197A12

7237

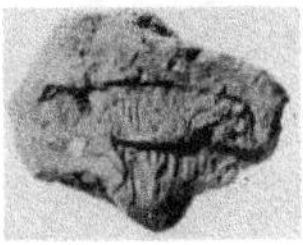

Lothal198A12

7215

Lothal199A12

7247

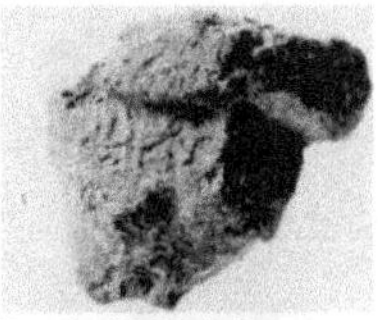

Lothal200A1

Lothal200A2

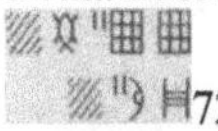
7219

Lothal201A12

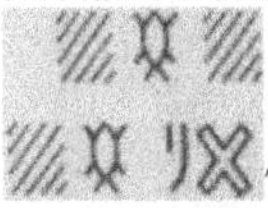
7263

Lothal202A12

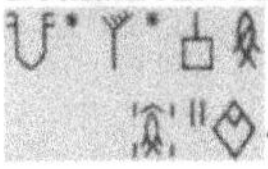
7267

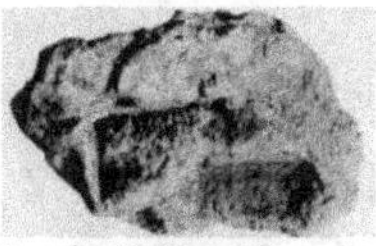

Lothal203A12

7246

Lothal204A

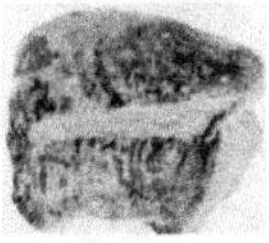

Lothal204F

7275

Lothal205A12

7218

Lothal206A12

7265

Lothal207A12

7281

Lothal208A12

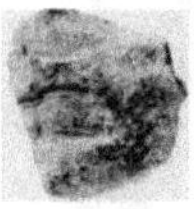

Lothal209A12

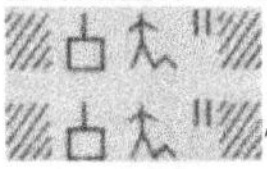
7262

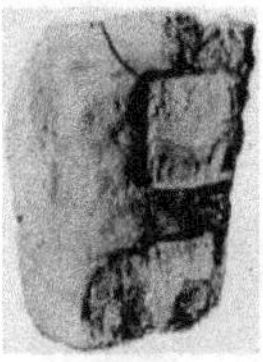

Lothal210A12

7201

Lothal211A13

7277

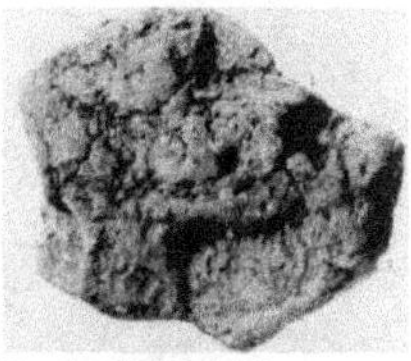

Lothal212A12

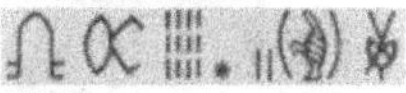
7261

Lothal213A2

7207
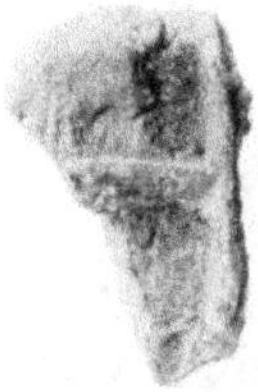
Lothal214A12

Lothal216D12

Lothal216E

7283
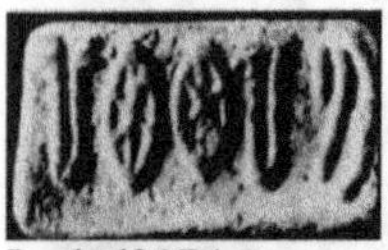
Lothal217A

Lothal217B

Lothal218A

7202
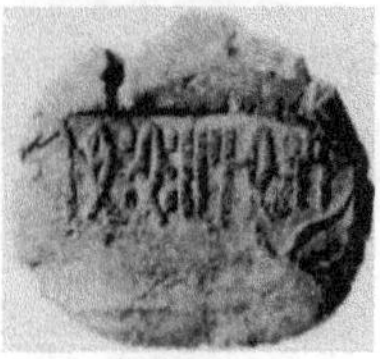
Lothal219A

7282

Lothal220A

7278

Lothal221A

Lothal222A
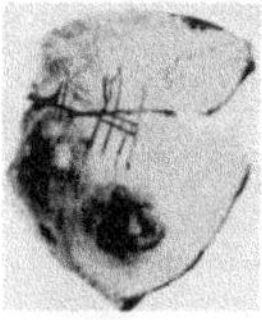
Lothal223A

Lothal224A

Lothal225A

Lothal227A

Lothal229A

Lothal230A
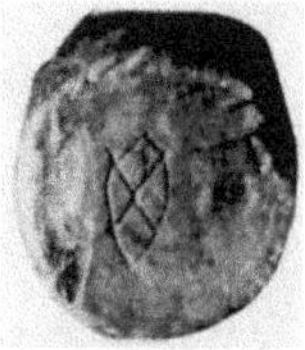
Lothal233A

Lothal246A
Lothal269A
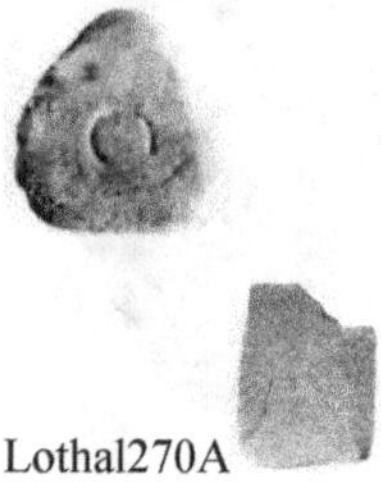
Lothal270A
Lothal272A
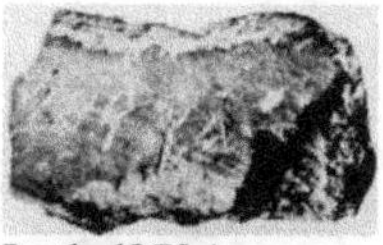
Lothal273A

7301

Lothal277A

Lothal280A

Lothal281A

7088

7098

7212
7232

7233
7269
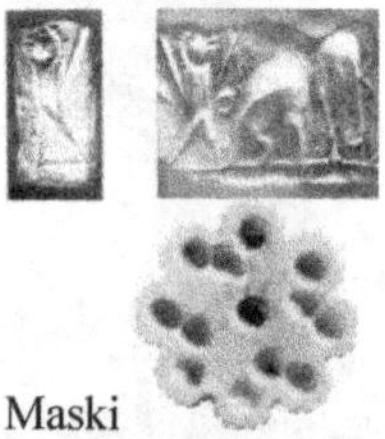
Maski
Mehi
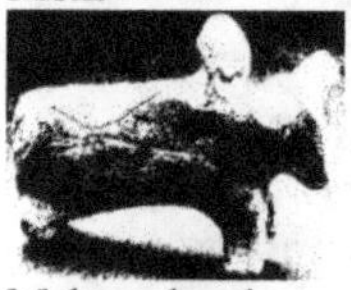
Mehrgarh zebu

Mehrgarh01

Mehrgarh04
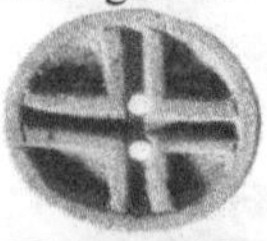
Mehrgarh05

Mehrgarh08

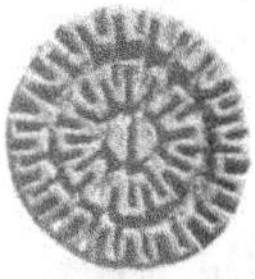
Mehrgarh10

Mehrgarh11
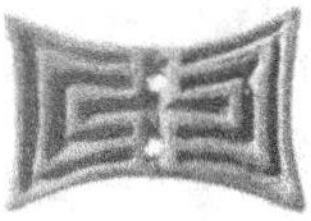
Mehrgarh12

Mehrgarh13

Mehrgarh14

Mehrgarh15

Mehrgarh16

Mehrgarh17

Mehrgarh18

m0001a

1067

m0002a

m0003a

2225

m0004a
3109

m0005
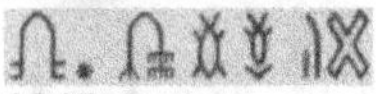
2247

m0006a

2422

m0007
1011

m0008a

1038

m0009a

2616

m0010
1006

m0011

m0012

3031

m0013

1069

m0014

1022

m0015

2177

m0016a

1037

m0017

1035

m0018Ac

1548

m0019a

1085

m0020a

1054

m0021a

2103

m0022a

1023

m0023a

2398

m0024

2694

m0025

1056

m0026a

2074

m0027a

2084

m0028a

2178

m0029a

2033

m0030a

2396

m0031

2576

m0032a

2180

m0033a

1042

m0034a

1058

m0035a

2333

m0036a

2455

m0037a

3103

m0039a

1544

m0040

1051 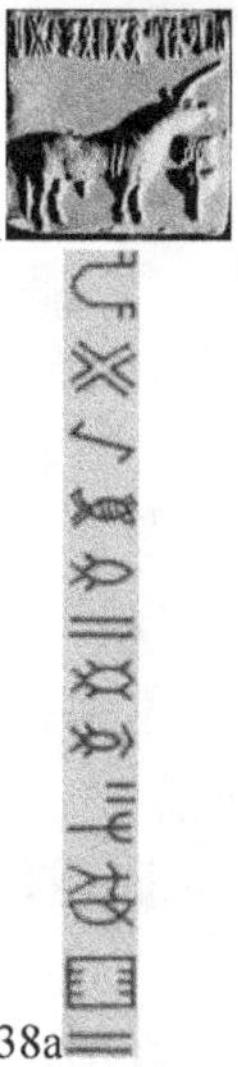

m0038a

1087

m0041

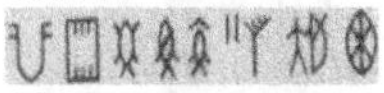

2271

m0042a

1096 

m0043

2584

m0044a

3110 

m0045a

1552

m0046a

3089

m0047a 

1098

m0048a

1186

m0049a

1047

m0050a

1557

m0051a

1555

m0052a

1540

m0053a

2128

m0054

2307

m0055a

2511

m0056

2406

m0057a

2340

m0058a

2680

m0059a

1029

m0060a

2124

m0061

m0062

3112

m0063

3068

m0064

2524

m0065

2440

m0066AC

1052

m0067

2264

m0068

3108

m0069

1095

m0070

1048

m0071a

3083 [The second sign from left is an orthographic representation of the thigh of a bovid, perhaps a bull].

m0072a

2085

m0073

1046

m0074

2353

m0075

1019

m0076

m0077

3111

m0078

3118

m0079a

2083

m0080

2635

m0081a

1180

m0082

2451

m0083a

2267

m0084a

1108

m0085a

2365

m0086

2208

m0087

2148

m0088

1075

m0089
3116

m0090
3039

m0091
2429

m0092
2407

m0093
2305

m0094
2594

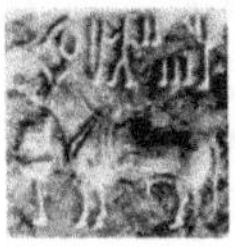

m0095
2657

m0096
2698

m0097
2549

m0098
2012

m0099
2475

m0100
1115

m0101
1537

m0102
1129

m0103
1076

m0104
2574

m0105
2337

m0106
2459

m0107
2593

m0108
1110

m0109
1151

m0110
2031

m0111
2029

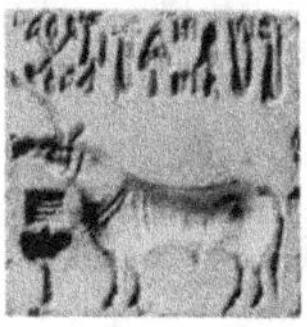
m0112
2099

m0113
2115

m0114

2166

m0115

3087

m0116

2481

m0117

1105

m0118

1104

m0119a

2018

m0120a

1099

m0121a

1188

m0122a

2015

m0123a

2702

m0124

1120

m0125

m0126

2311

m0127

1119

m0128a

2284

m0129

2193

m0130a

2285

m0131

2263

m0132

2082

m0133a

2052

m0134

2187

m0135

1168

m0136

2233

m0137

2261

m0138

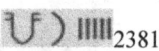

2381

m0139

2185

m0140

2563

m0141

2543

m0142

2630

m0143

2002

m0144

2048

m0145

1118

m0146

1100

m0147

3097

m0148

1245

m0149

1233

m0150

1236

m0151

2323

m0152

2102

m0153

2361

m0154

2373

m0155

1187

m0156

m0157

2022

m0158

2198

m0159

2355

m0160

2286

m0161

2088

m0162

2486

m0163

1543

m0164

2403

m0165

2687

m0166

1080

m0167.

1297

m0168a [The second sign may be an orthographic variant for a thigh of a bovid?]

2442

m0169

1113

m0170

2237

m0171

1149

m0172

1071

m0173

1161

m0174

1114

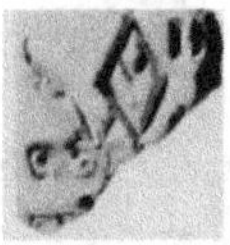

m0175

1291

m0176

1193

m0177

m0178

2354

m0179

m0180

2014

m0181

2490

m0182

2154

m0183

3113

m0184

2634

m0185

m0186

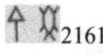

2161

m0187

2382

m0188

1287

m0189

1195

m0190

1205

m0191

1288

m0192

1206

m0193

2113

m0194

2254

m0195

2415

m0196

2474

m0197

2371

m0198

2363

m0199

2647

m0200

1148

m0201

2678

m0202

2625

m0203

1556

m0204

2623

m0205

1221

m0206

m0207

2458

m0208

2047

m0209

2375

m0210

2656

m0211

1214

m0212

2577

m0213

1150

m0214

2571

m0215

3081

m0216

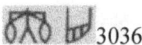

3036

m0217

2087

m0218

2175

m0219

2433

m0220a

3093

m0221a

3164

m0222

1194

m0223

1167 [The sign in front of the one-horned bull may be Sign 162

]

m0224

2215

m0225

2199

m0226

2152

m0227 2226

m0228

2502

m0229

3075

m0230.

1295

m0231

2444

m0232

2234 'Unicorn' with two horns! "Bull with two long horns (otherwise resembling the 'unicorn')", generally facing the standard. That it is the typical 'one-horned bull' is surmised from two ligatures: the pannier on the shoulder and the ring on the neck.

m0233

m0234.

1321

m0235

2689

m0236

2123

m0237

m0238AC

2534

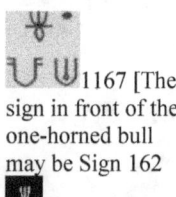

m0239

2238

m0240.

1324

m0241

1536

m0242

2216

m0243

2390

m0244

2399

m0245

2290

m0246.

1317

m0247

2298

m0248.

1310

m0249

2378

m0250.

1308

m0251

2370

m0252

2423

m0253

2701

m0254

2090

m0255

2409 [The second sign is diamond-shaped?]

m0256

1332

m0257

2314

m0258a.

1340

m0259

2132

m0260

2567

m0261

2535

m0262 Zebu

2249

m0263

1336

m0264

2607

m0265

2155

m0266.

1306

m0267 Water-buffalo

2257

m0268 Water-buffalo

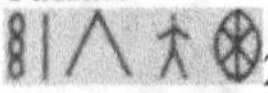
2445

m0269

2663

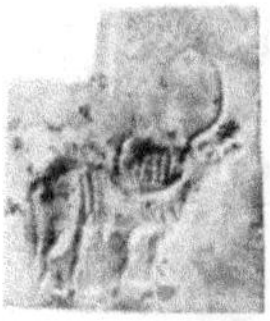

m0270

m0271 Goat-antelope with horns turned backwards and a short tail

m0272 Goat-antelope with horns bending backwards and neck turned backwards

2554

m0273 2673

m0274

1342

m0275

2131

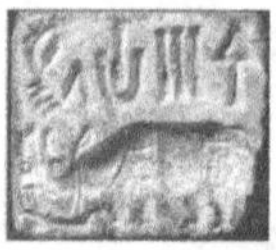

m0276AC

3122

m0277
2309

m0278
2648

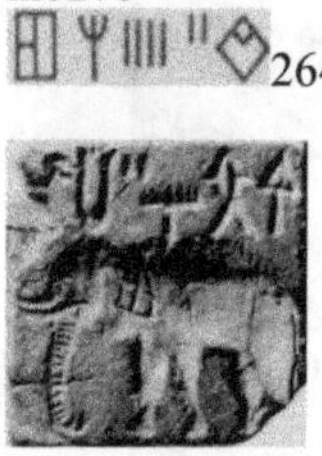

m0279

3060

m0280

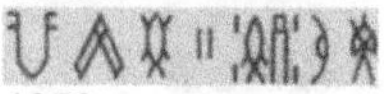
1373

m0281

3115

m0282
2304

m0283

2127

m0284

2195
m0285

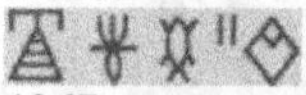
1367

m0286
2517

m0287

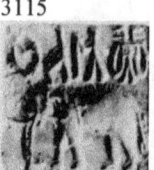

m0288

2518

m0289

3121

m0290

2527

m0291 Tiger

3069

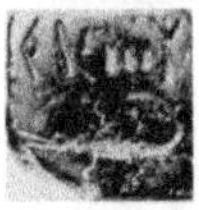

m0292 Gharial

1361

m0293 Gharial

1360

m0294 One-horned bull?; elephant

1376

m0295 Pict-61: Composite motif of three tigers joined together.

1386

m0296 Two heads of one-horned bulls with neck-rings, joined end to end (to a standard device with two rings coming out of the top part?), under a stylized pipal tree with nine leaves.

1387

m0297a Head of a one-horned bull attached to an undentified five-point symbol (octopus-like?)

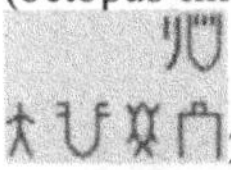
2641

m0298

m0299 Composite animal with the body of a ram, horns of a bull, trunk of an elephant, hindlegs of a tiger and an upraise serpent-like tail.

1381

m0300 Pict51: Composite animal: human face, zebu's horns, elephant tusks and trunk, ram's forepart, unicorn's trunk and feet, tiger's hindpart and serpent-like tail.

2521

m0301 Composite motif: human face, body or forepart of a ram, body and front legs of a unicorn, horns of a zebul, trunk of an elephant, hindlegs of a tiger and an upraised serpent-like tail.

2258

m0302 Composite animal with the body of a ram, horns of a bull, trunk of an elephant, hindlegs of a tiger and an upraise serpent-like tail.

1380

m0303 Composite animal.

2411

m0304B

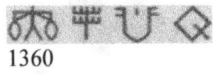

m0304AC Pict-81: Person (with three visible faces) wearing bangles and armlets seated on a platform (with an antelope looking backwards) and surrounded by five animals: rhinoceros, buffalo, antelope, tiger and elephant.

2420

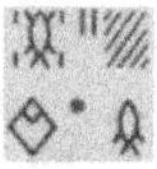

m0305AC

2235 Pict-80: Three-faced, horned person (with a three-leaved pipal branch on the crown with two stars on either side), wearing bangles and armlets.

m0306 Person grappling with two tigers standing on either side of him and rearing on their hindlegs.

2086

m0307 Person grappling with two tigers standing on either side of him and rearing on their hindlegs.

2122

m0308AC Pict-105: Person grappling with two tigers standing on either side of him and rearing on their hindlegs.

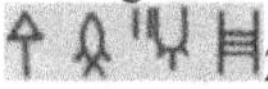

2075

[The third sign from left may be a stylized 'standard device'?]

m0309 Pict-109: Person with hair-bun seated on a tree branch; a tiger looks at the person with its head turned backwards.

2522

m0310AC

1355

m0311 Pict-52: Composite motif: body of a tiger, a human body with bangles on arms, antelope horns, tree-branch and long pigtail.

2347

m0312 Persons vaulting over a water-buffalo.

m0313

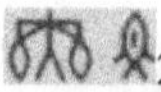

2637

m0314

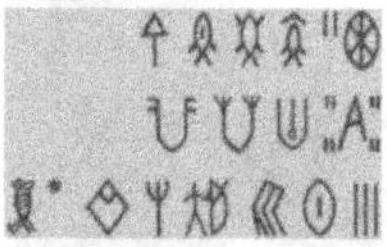

1400

m0315

1395

m0316

2408

m0317silver

2016

Mohenjodaro FEM, Pl. LXXXVIII, 316

2316

Mohenjodaro MIC, Pl. CVI,93

1093

Mohenjo-daro. Copper seal. National Museum, New Delhi. [Source: Page 18, Fig. 8A in: Deo Prakash Sharma, 2000, *Harappan seals, sealings and copper tablets*, Delhi, National Museum].

m0318

m0318B

2626

m0319

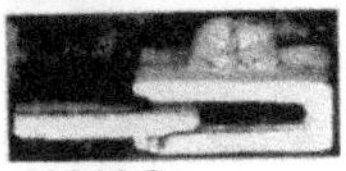

m0319C

2260

m0320

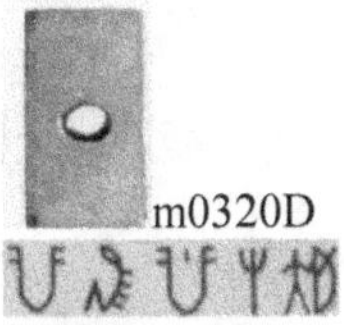

m0320D

2449

m0321

m0321D

2173

m0322

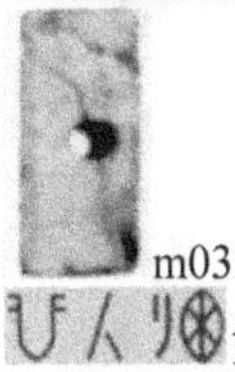

m0322D

1192

m0323

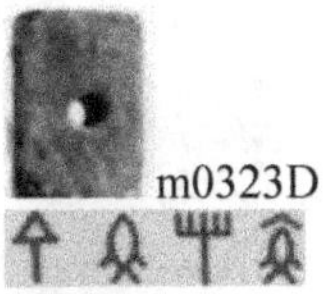

m0323D

1277

m0324A

m0324B

m0324D

1252

m0325A

m0325B

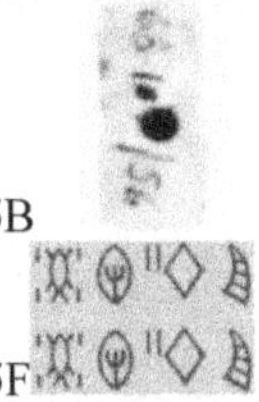

m0325F

3106

m0326A

m0326B

m0326C

m0326D

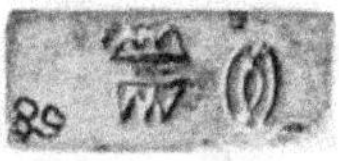

m326E

m0326F

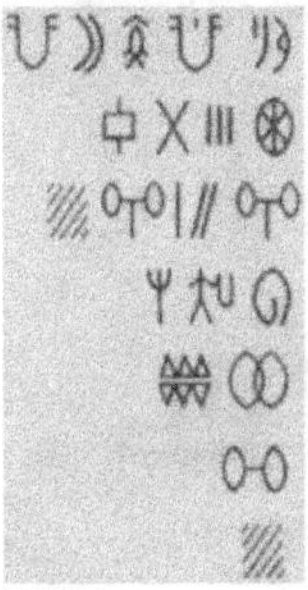

2405

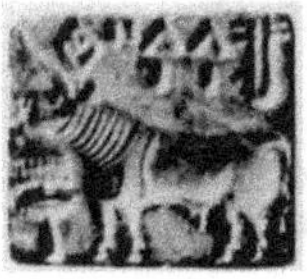

m0327

2631

m0328

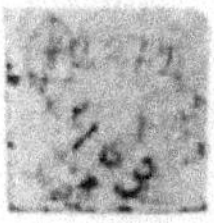

m0328B 

2108

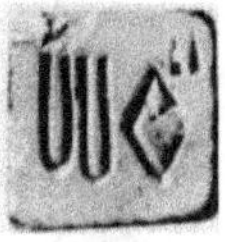

m0329

1477

m0330A

m0330B Perforated through the narrow edge of a two-sided seal

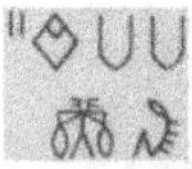

1475

m0331A

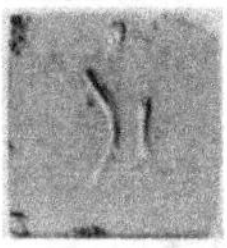

m0331B

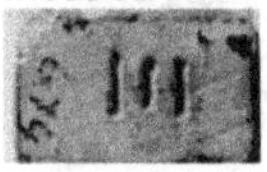

m0331D

m0331F Cube seal

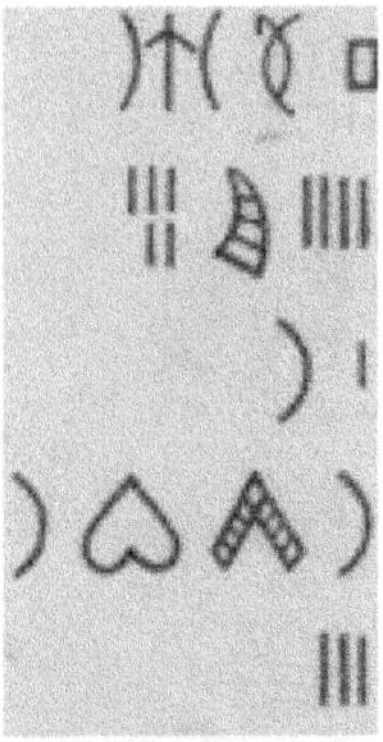
1471

m0332AC

m0333

m0334

m0335

m0336

m0337

m0338

m0339

m0340

m0341

m0342

m0343

m0344

m0345

m0346

m0347

m0348

m0349

m0350

m0351
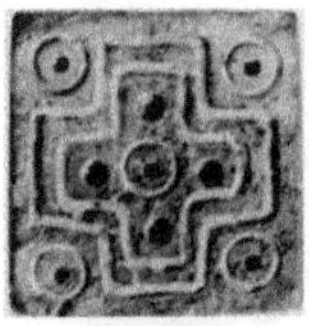
m0352A

m0352C
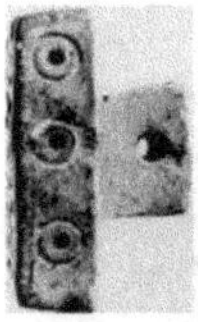
m0352D

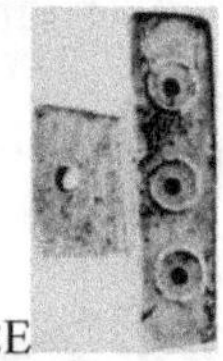
m0352E
m0352F
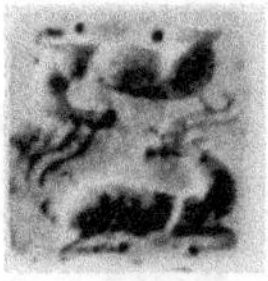
m0353

m0354

1403

m0356

1406

m0357

1401

m0358

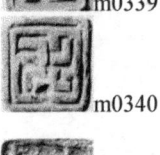

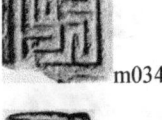

2297

m0360

3102

m0361

2101

m0362

1466

m0363

1469

m0364

1465

m0365

2273

m0366

2077

m0367

2044

m0368

2336

m0370

2138

m0371

2461

m0372

1438

m0373

2043

m0374

2097

m0375

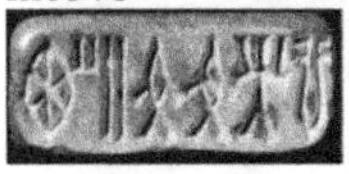
m375AC

m0376

1426

m0377

3120

m0378

1402

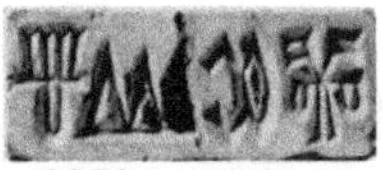
m0379

2159

m0380

2470

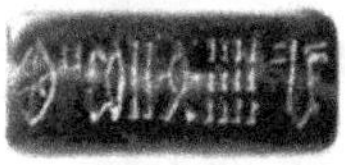
m0381

2162

m382AC

1437

m0383

2240

m0384

2302

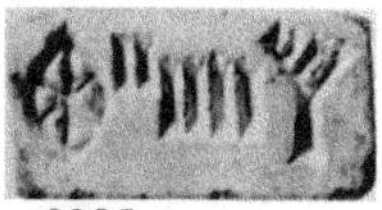
m0385

2387

m0386

1449

m0387

2041

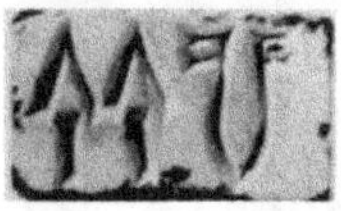
m0388

2200

m0389

2397

m0390

1444

m0392

2046

m393AC

2120

m0394

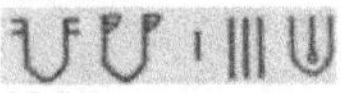

2213

m0395

2183

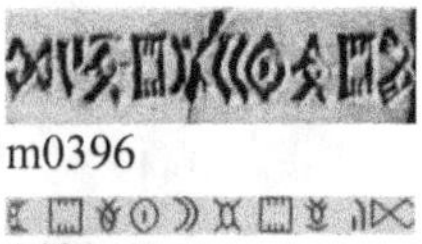

m0396

1421

m0397

1415

m0398

2308

m399AC

1414

m0400

3088

m0401

2346

m0402

2395

m0403

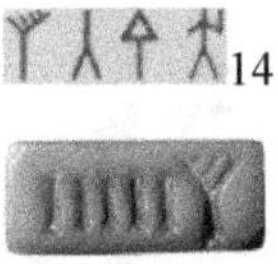

1410

m404AC 

1422

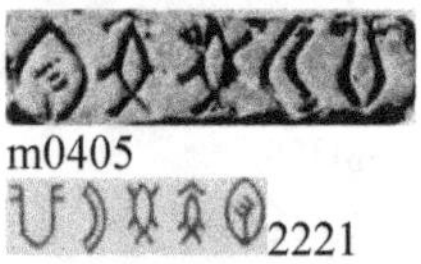

m0405

2221

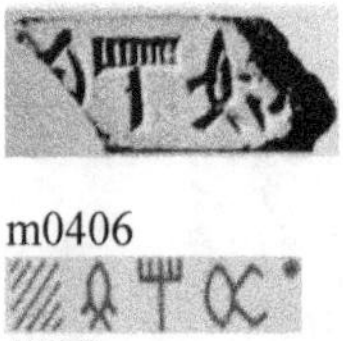

m0406

1399

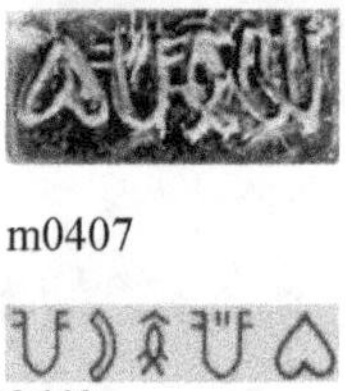

m0407

2643

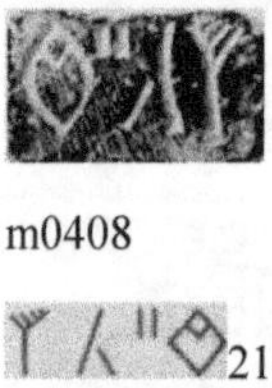

m0408

2100

m0409

2699

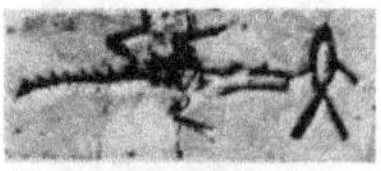

m0410 Pict-64: Gharial snatching, with its snout, the fin of a fish

2133

m0411

1431

m0412

1450

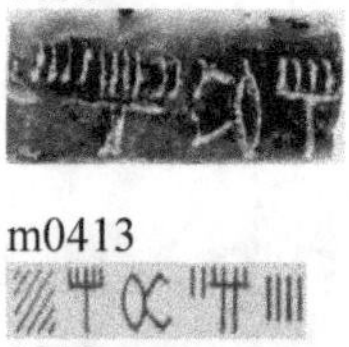

m0413

2319

m0414A

m0414B Seal with incision on obverse

2004

m0415a Bison

2500

m0416 Bison .

1309

m417AC Pict-62: Composition: six heads of animals: of unicorn, of short-horned bull (bison), of antelope, of tiger, and of two other uncertain animals) radiating outward from a hatched ring (or 'heart' design).

1383

m0418acyl

m0419acyl

m0419dcyl

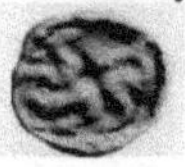

m0419fcyl

m0420A1si

m0420A2si

3236

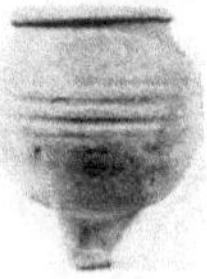

m0421A1si

m0421A2si

3237

m0422A1si

m0422A2si

m0423A1si

m0423A2si

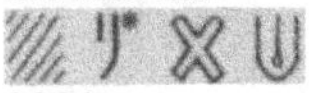

3221

m0424A1si

m0424A2si

m0425A1si

m0425A2si

m0426Asi

m0426Bsi
2809

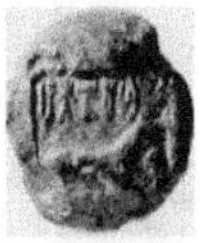

m0427t

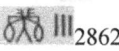

1630

m0428At

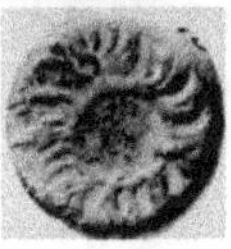

m0428Bt

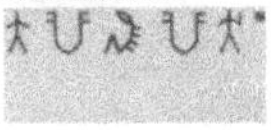1607

Pict- 132: Radiating solar symbol.

m0429 Text
2862

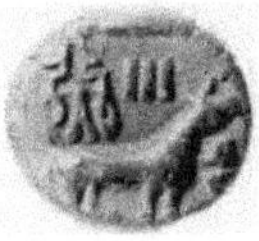

m0430At

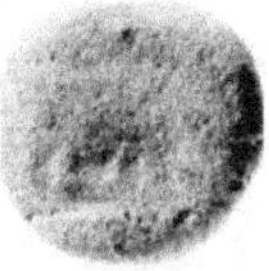

m0430Bt

2862

m0431At

m0431Bt

3239

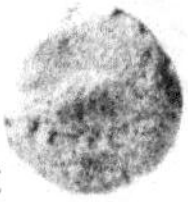

m0432At

m0432Bt

1624

m0433At

m0433Bt

3233

m0434At

m0434Bt

3248

m0435t

m0436At

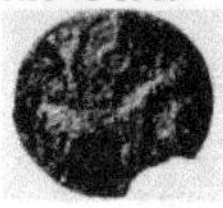

m0436Bt

2804

m0437t

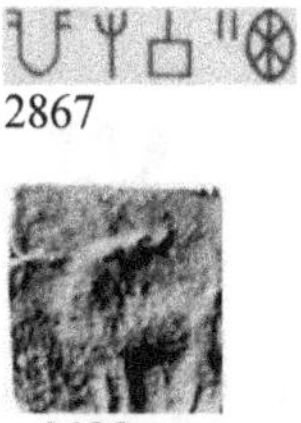

2867

m0438atcopper

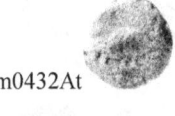

m0439t

m440AC

m0441At

m0441Bt

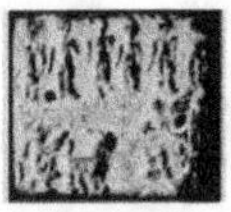

m0442At

m0442Bt

m443At

m443Bt

m444At

3223

m445Bt

m445AC

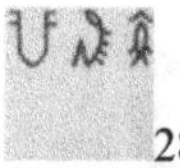

2821

m446At

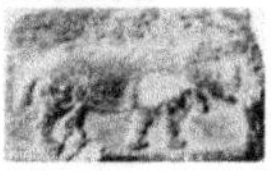

m446Bt

2854

m447At

m447Bt

m448t

m449Bt

m449AC

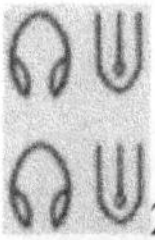

2836

m450At

m450Bt

2864

m0451At

m0451Bt

3235

m0452At

m0452Bt

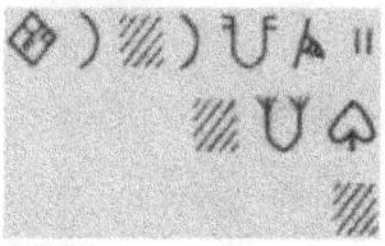

2855

m0453At

m453BC

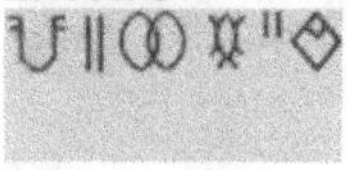

1629 Pict-82
Person seated on a pedestal flanked on either side by a kneeling adorant and a hooded serpent rearing up.

m0455At

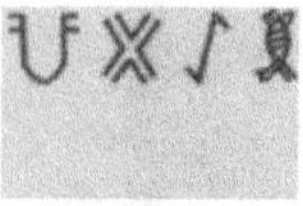

1619

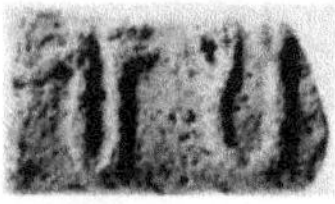

m0456At

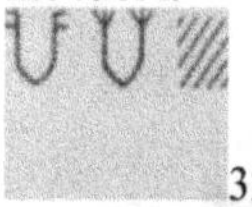

3219

m0457At

m0457Bt

m0457Et

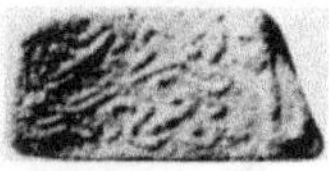

m0458At

m0458Bt

3227

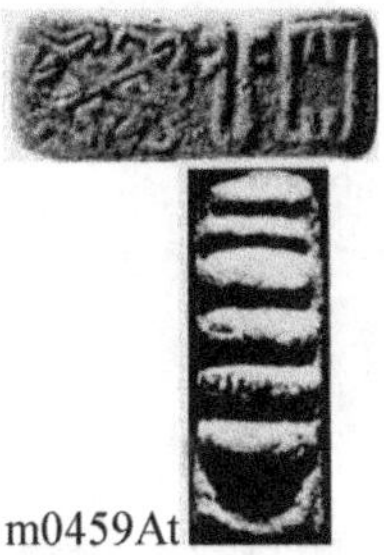
m0459At

m0459Bt

3225

m0460At

m0460Bt

3228

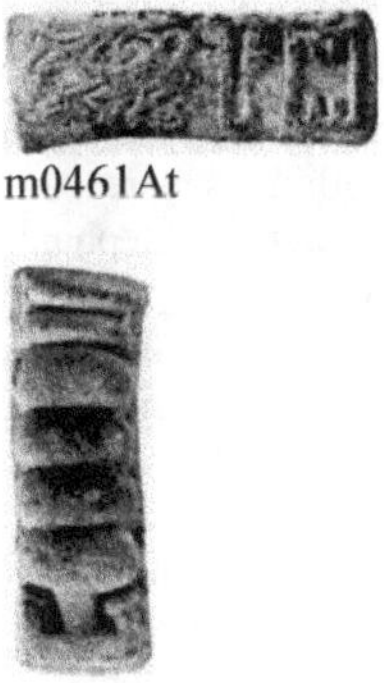
m0461At

m0461Bt

2806 Pict-73: Alternative 1. Serpent (?) entwined around a pillar with capital (?); motif carvd in high-relief. Alternative 2. Ring-stones around a pillar with coping stones in a building-structure as at Dholavira?

m0462At

m0462Bt

3215

m0463At

m0463Bt

2813

m0464At

m0464Bt

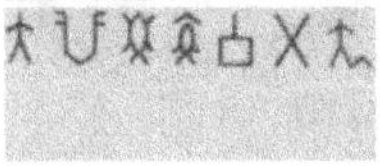
3216

m0465At

m0465Bt

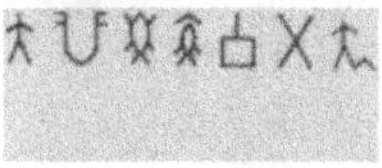
3220

m0466At

m0466Bt

m0467At

m0467Bt

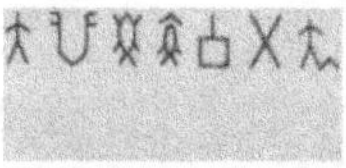
3209

m0468At

m0468Bt

3249

m0469At

m0469Bt

2830

m0470At

2810

m0471At

m0471Bt

3232

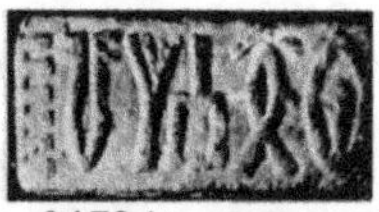
m0472At

1615

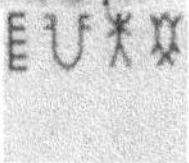
m0473At
2848

m0474At
3243

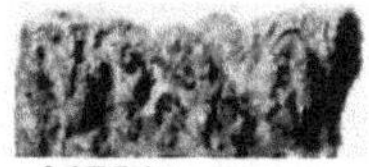
m0475Atcopper

3247

m0476At

m0476Ct

m0477At

m0477Bt

m0477Ct
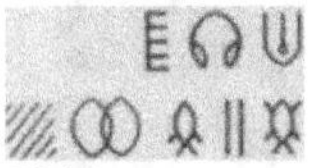
2844

Two rhinoceroses, one at either end of the text (Pict-29).

m0478At

m0478Bt

m0479At

m0479Bt

3224

m0480At
m0480Bt Tablet in bas-relief. Side a: Tree Side b: Pict-111: From R.: A woman with outstretched arms flanked by two men holding uprooted trees in their hands; a person seated on a tree with a tiger below with its head turned backwards; a tall jar with a lid.

Is the pictorial of a tall jar the Sign 342 with a lid?

Sign 45 seems to be a kneeling adorant offering a pot (Sign 328)

2815
Pict-77: Tree, generally within a railing or on a platform.

3230

m0481At

m0481Bt

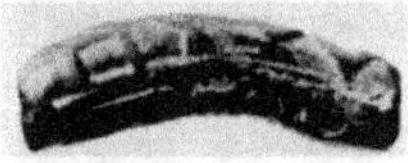
m0481Ct
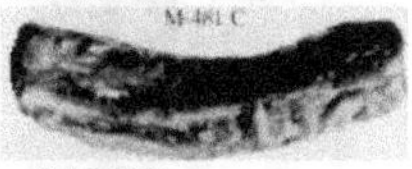

m0481Et

2846 Pict-41: Serpent, partly reclining on a low platform under a tree

m0482At
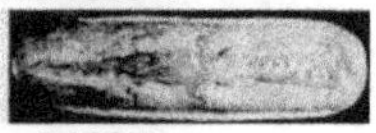
m0482Bt

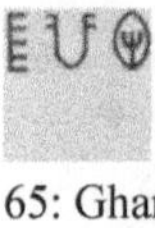
1620 Pict-65: Gharial, sometimes with a fish held in its jaw and/or surrounded by a school of fish.

m0483At

m0483Bt

m0483Ct
m0483Et
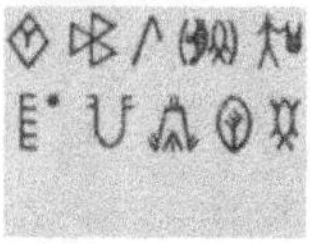
2866

Pict-145: Geometrical pattern.

m0484At

m0484Bt

2861

m0486at

m0486bt

m0486ct
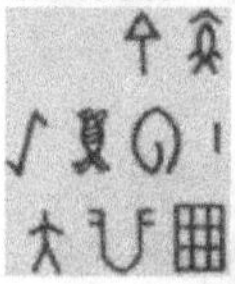
1625

m0487At

m0487Bt

m0487Ct
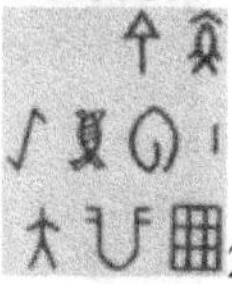
2852

m0488At

m0488Bt

m0488Ct
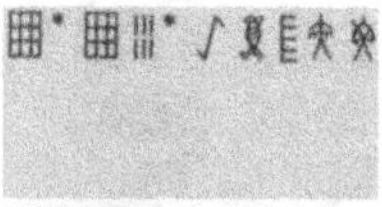
2802 Prism: Tablet in bas-relief. Side b: Text +One-horned bull + standard. Side a: From R.: a composite animal; a person seated on a tree with a tiger below looking up at the person; a svastika within a square border; an elephant (Composite animal has the body of a ram, horns of a zebu, trunk of an elephant, hindlegs of a tiger and an upraised serpent-like tail). Side c: From R.: a horned person standing between two branches of a pipal tree; a ram; a horned person kneeling in adoration; a low pedestal with some offerings.

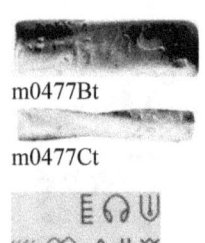

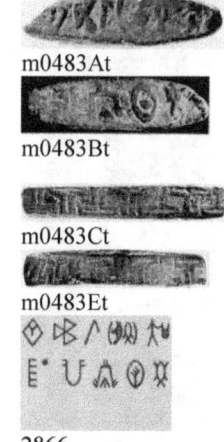

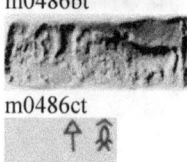

m0489At

m0489Bt

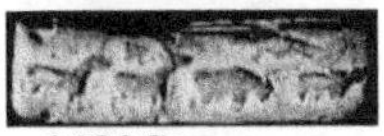

m0489Ct

m0490At

m0490BCt

1605

m0491At

m0491BCt

1608 Pict-94: Four persons in a procession, each carrying a standard, one of which has the figure of a one-horned bull on top.

m0492At

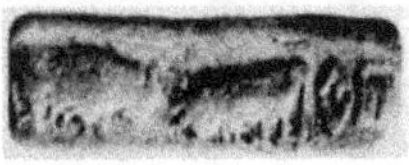

m0492Bt Pict-14: Two bisons standing face to face.

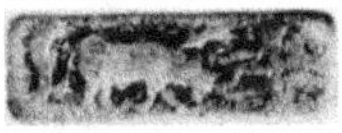

m0492Ct

2835 Pict-99: Person throwing a spear at a bison and placing one foot on the head of the bison; a hooded serpent at left.

m0493At

m0493Bt Pict-93: Three dancing figures in a row.

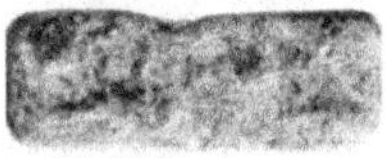

m0493Ct

2843

m0494At

m0494BGt Prism Tablet in bas-relief.

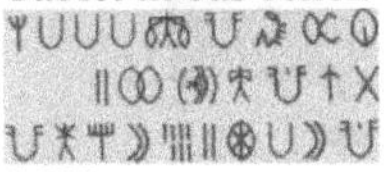

1623

m0495At

m0495Bt

m0495gt

2847b

m0496At

m0496Bt

m0496Dt

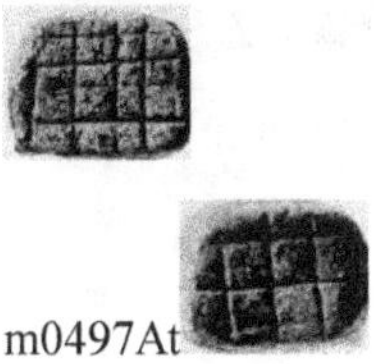

m0497At

m0497Bt

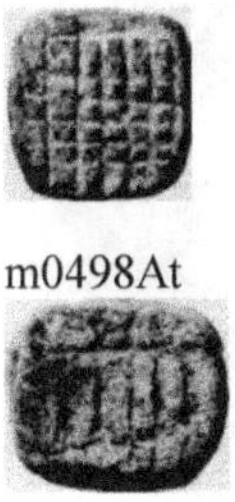

m0498At

m0498Bt

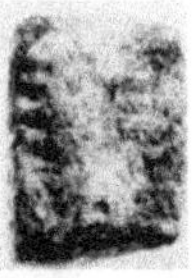

m0498Dt

m0499At

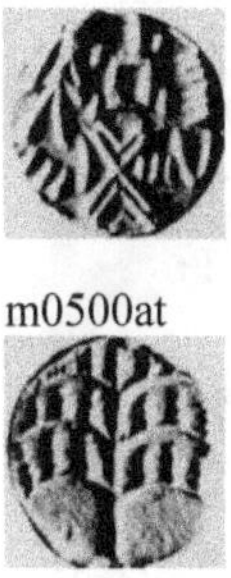

m0500at

m0500bt

2604

Pict-76: Tree, generally within a railing or on a platform.

m0501At

m0501Bt

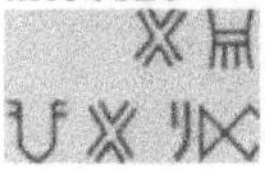

1412

m0502At

m0502Bt

3345

m0503 Text

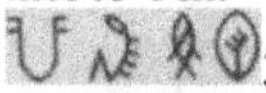

3346

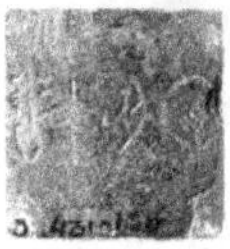

m0504At

m0504Bt

3323

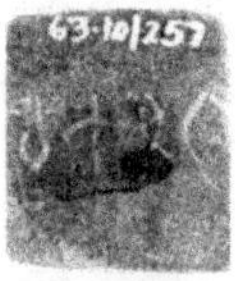

m0505At

m0505Bt

1702

m0507At

m0507Bt

3350

m0508At

m0508Bt

3352

m0509At

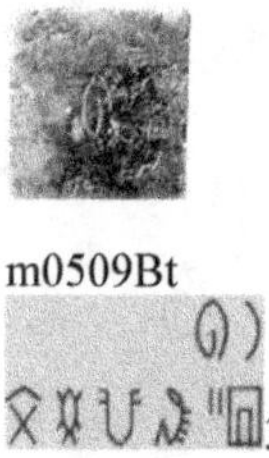

m0509Bt

3320

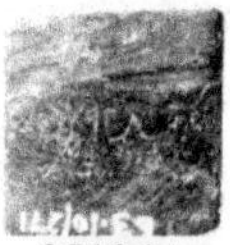

m0510At

m0510Bt

3319

m0511At

m0511Bt

2905

m0512At

m0512Bt

2906

m0513At

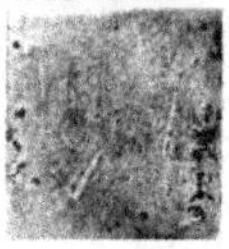

m0513Bt

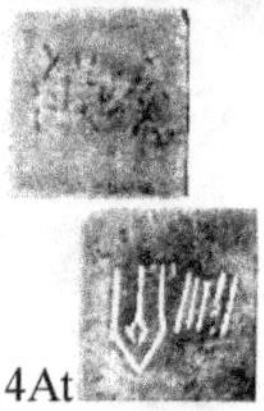

3364

m0514At

m0514Bt

3302

m0515 Text

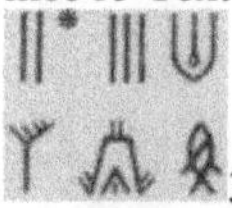

3335

m0516At

m0516Bt

3398

m0517At

m0517Bt

3334

m0519At

m0519Bt

1710

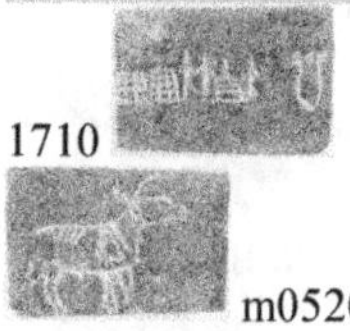

m0520

At, Bt

2916 m0521

3407

m0522At

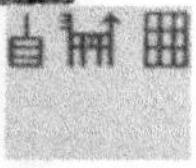

m0522Bt

3378

m0523At

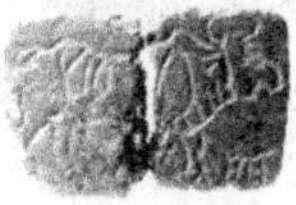

m0523Bt

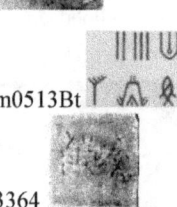

1714

m0524At

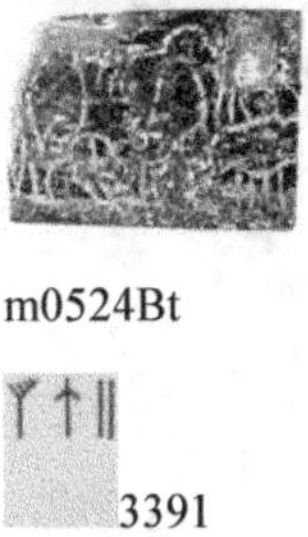

m0524Bt

3391

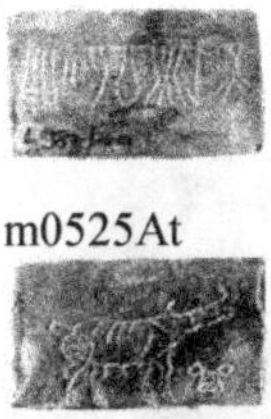

m0525At

m0525Bt

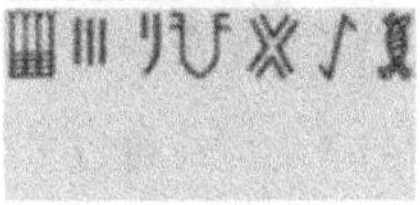

1713 Buffalo

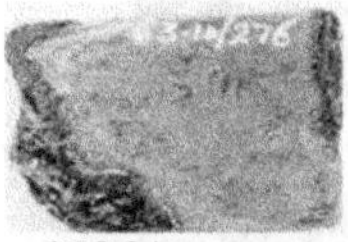

m0526At

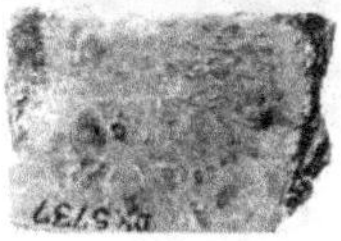

m0526Bt

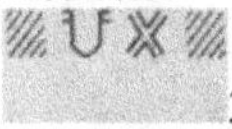

3329

Buffalo

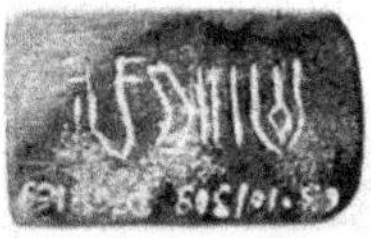

m0527At

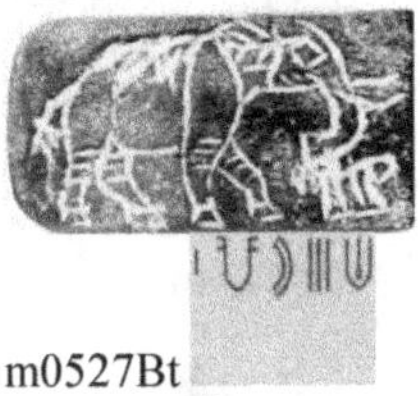

m0527Bt

3336

m0528At

m0528Bt

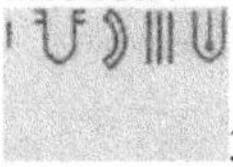

3368

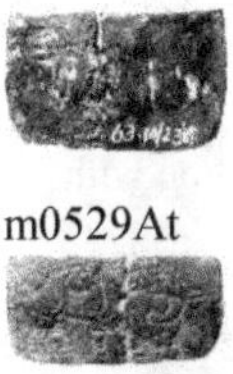

m0529At

m0529Bt

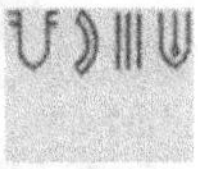

3392

m0530At

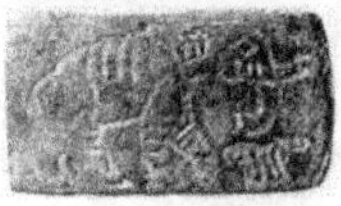

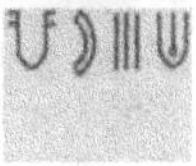

m0530Bt

3356

m0531At

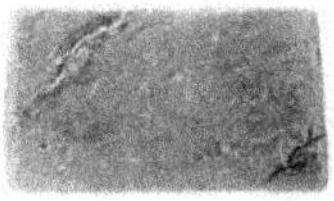

m0531Bt

m0532At

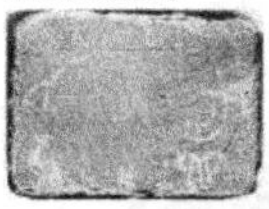

m0532Bt

3349

m0534At

m0534Bt

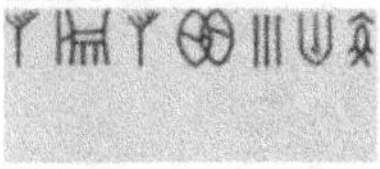

3304

m0535At

m0535Bt

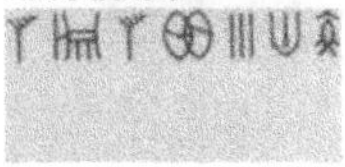

3355

m0536At

m0536Bt

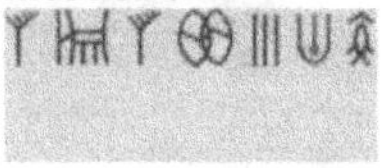

3312

m0537At

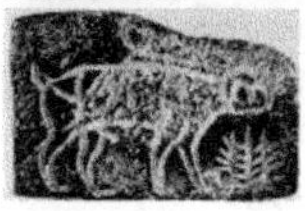

m0537Bt

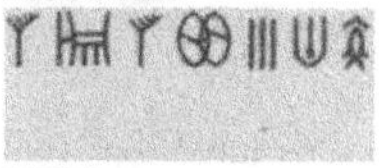

1705

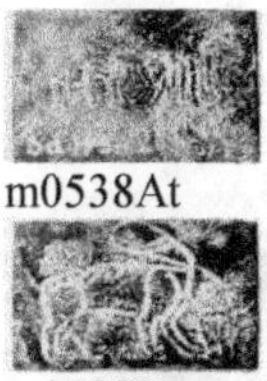

m0538At

m0538Bt

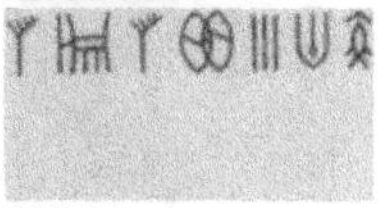

3384

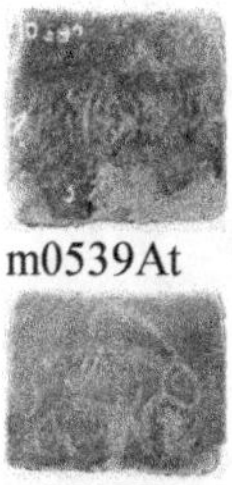

m0539At

m0539Bt

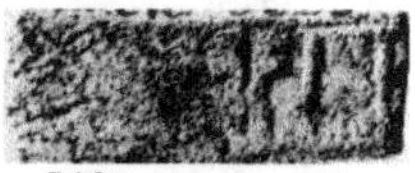

m540t

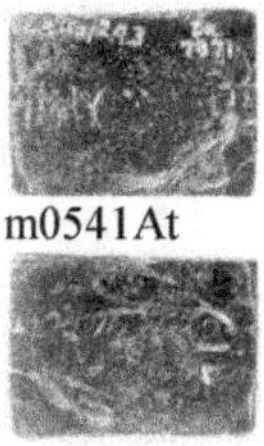

m0541At

m0541Bt

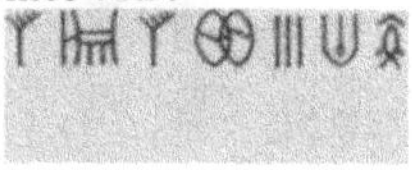

3331

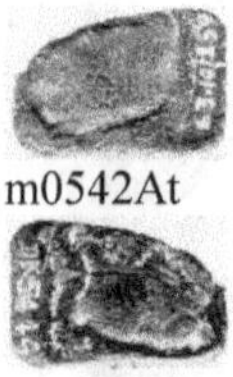
m0542At
m0542Bt

3326 Hare?

m0543At
m0543Bt

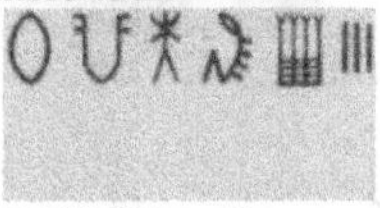
3363 [Note the 'heart' orthograph on the body of the antelope. This is comparable to Sign 323 ]

m0544At
m0544Bt

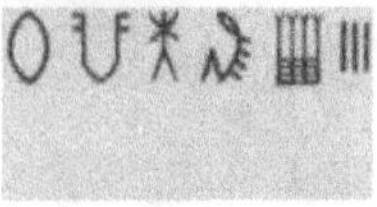
3357

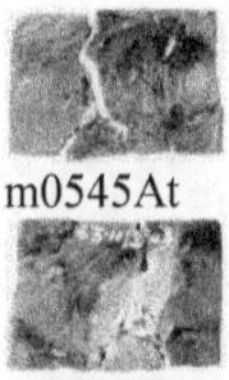
m0545At
m0545Bt

3301

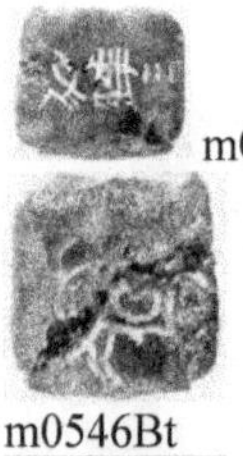
m0546At
m0546Bt

3383

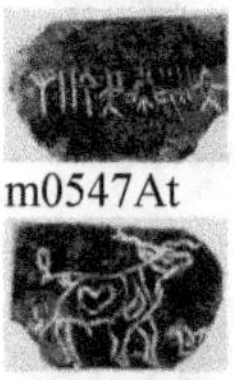
m0547At
m0547Bt

3303

m0548At
m0548Bt

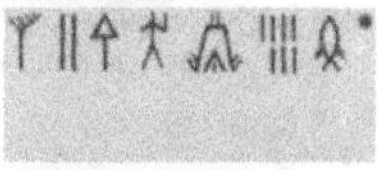
3305

m0549At
m0549Bt

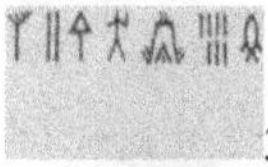
3373

m0550At

m0550Bt
3351

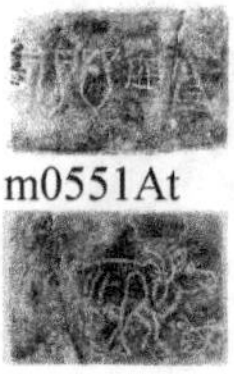
m0551At
m0551Bt

1708
Ox-antelope with long tail.

m0552At
m0552Bt

3306

m0553At
m0553Bt

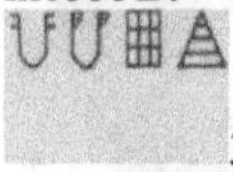
3353

m0554At

m0554Bt
1712

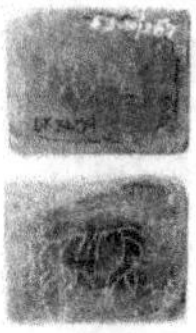
m0555At
m0555Bt

3314

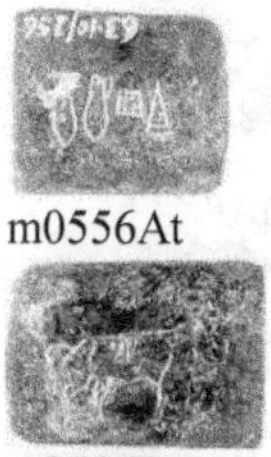
m0556At
m0556Bt

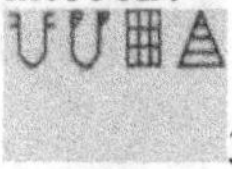
3404

m0557At
m0557Bt

3341

m0558At
m0558Bt

3342

m0559At

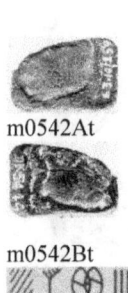

m0559Bt

2909

m0560At

m0560Bt

3386

m0561At

m0561Bt

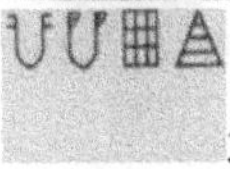

3339

m0562At

m0562Bt

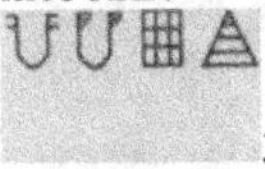

3361

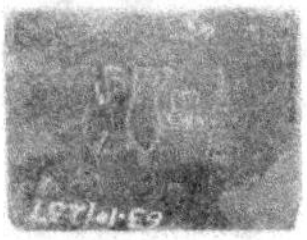

m0563At

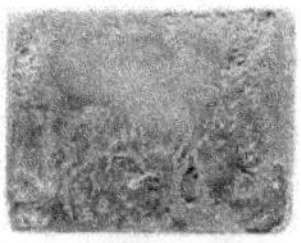

m0563Bt

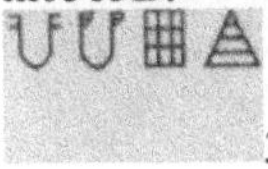

3379

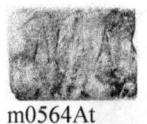

m0564At

m0564Bt

3371

m0565At

m0565Bt

3403

m0566At

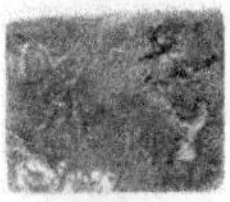

m0566Bt

3359

m0567At

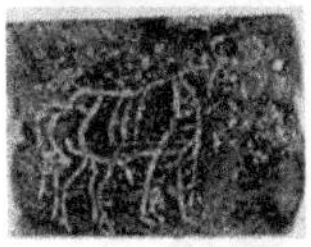

m0567Bt

3322

Bison.

m0568At

m0568Bt

3332 Tiger.

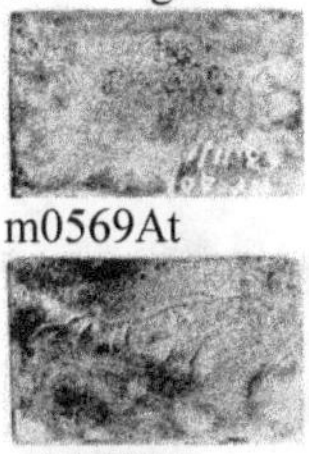

m0569At

m0569Bt

3372

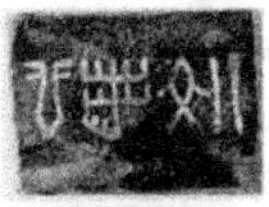

m0571At

m0571Bt

2913 Horned elephant. Almost similar to the composition: Body of a ram (with inlaid 'heart' sign), horns of a bull, trunk of an elephant, hindlegs of a tiger and an upraised serpent-like tail

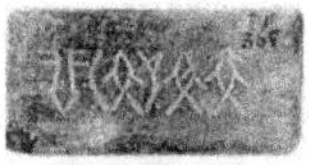

m0572At

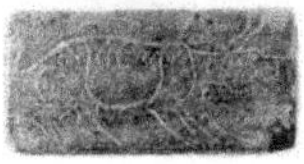

m0572Bt

3317

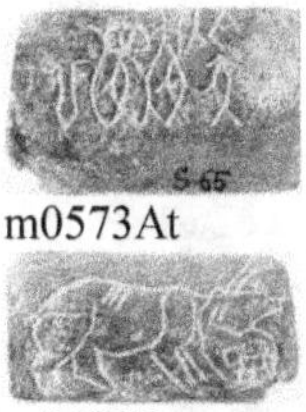

m0573At

m0573Bt

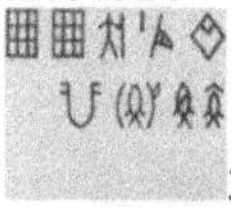

3415

m0574At

m0574Bt

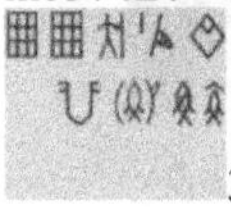

3318

m0575At

m0575Bt

3316

m0576At

m0576Bt

3344

m0577At

m0577Bt

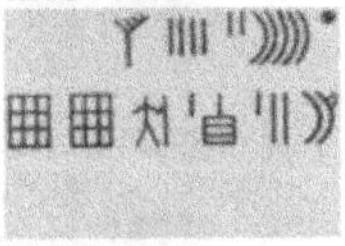

3347

m0578At

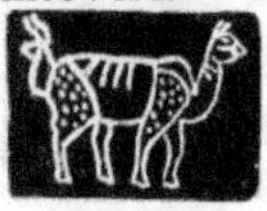

m0578Bt

2908

m0580At

m0580Bt

3321

m0581At

m0581Bt

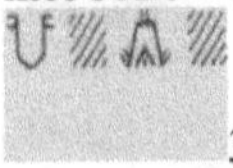

3340

2914

Pict-89: Standing person with horns and bovine features, holding a bow in one hand and an arrow or an uncertain object in the other.

m0582At

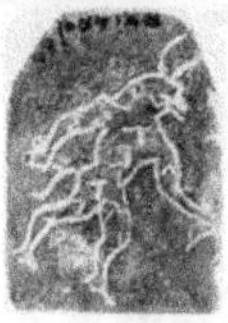

m0582Bt

3358

m0583At

m0583Bt

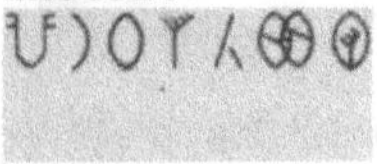

3387

m0584At

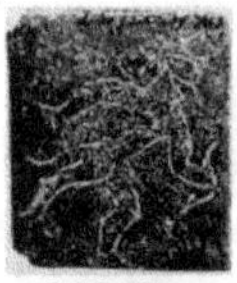

m0584Bt

m0585At

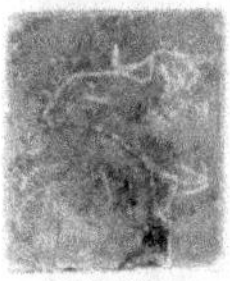

m0585Bt

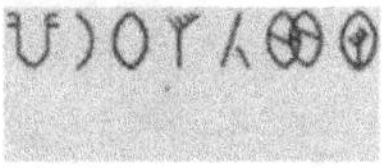

3369

m0586At

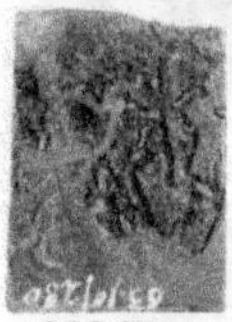

m0586Bt

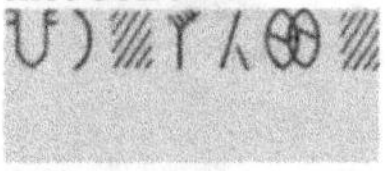

3406

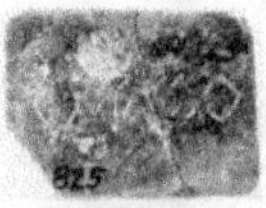

m0587At

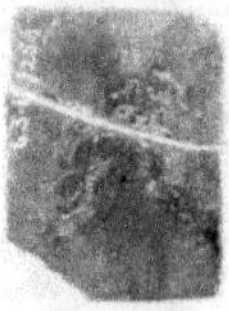

m0587Bt

3365 Horned Archer?

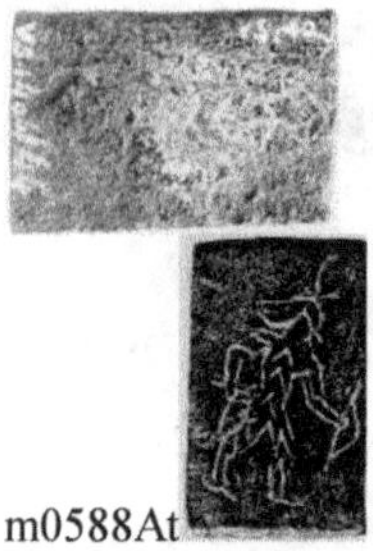

m0588At

m0588Bt Horned archer.

m0592At

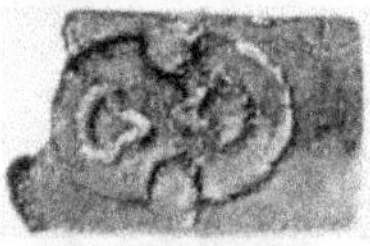

m0592Bt

3413 Pict-133: Double-axe (?) without shaft. [The sign is comparable to the sign which appears on the text of a Chanhudaro seal: Text 6402, Chanhudaro Seal 23].

m0593At

m0593Bt

3337

m0594At

m0594Bt

m0595A

m0595B

1010

m0596At

m0596Bt

3313

m0598 Text

3410

m0599At

m0599Bt

3360

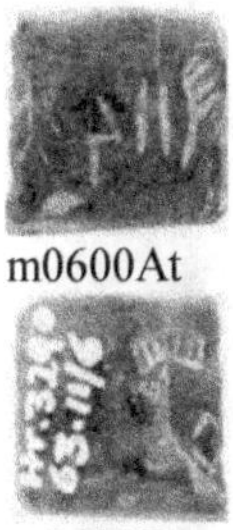
m0600At

m0600Bt

3375

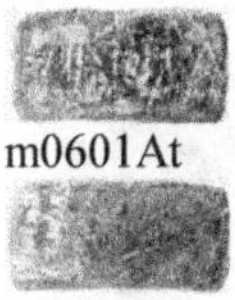
m0601At

m0601Bt

m0602At

m0602Bt

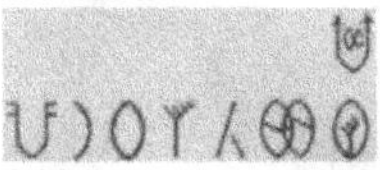
3414

m0604At

m0604Bt

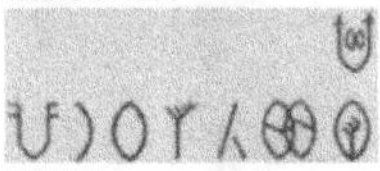
3315

m0605At

m0605Bt

2902

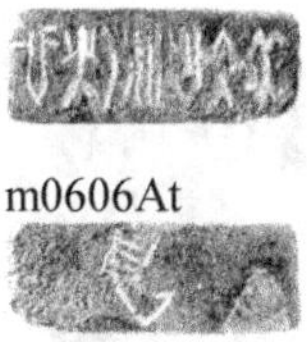
m0606At

m0606Bt

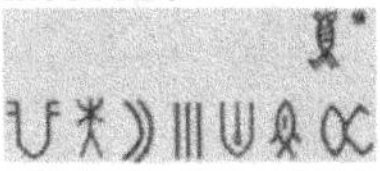
2918

m0608At

m0608Bt

m0614

1904

m0615

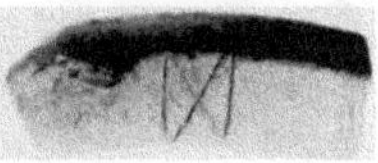
m0618

m0619

2939

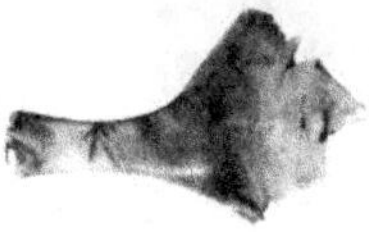
m0620

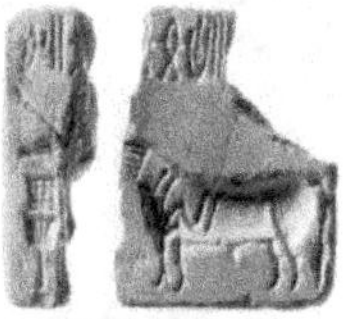
m0621

2367

m0622

m0623

m0624

1015

m0625

1027

m0626

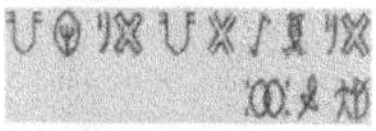
1012

m0627

1004

m0628

1033

m0629

m0630A

m0631

1008

m0632

1017

m0633

1016

m0634

2069

m0635a

m0636

2019

m0637

1034

m0638 One-horned bull

1404

m0639

m0640

m0641

m0642

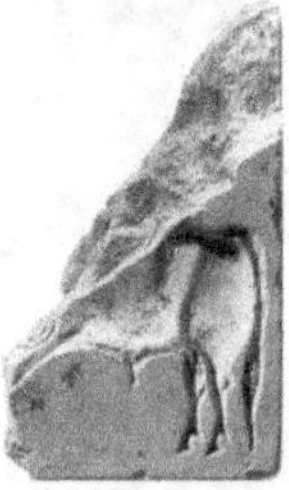
m0643

m0644

1553

m0645

m0646A1

m0646a12

m0646A2

2653

m0647

1024

m0648

3104

m0649

2530

m0650

1032

m0651

2578

m0652

m0653

1057

m0654

2561

m0655

2098

m0656

m0657

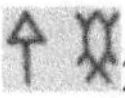
2026

m0658

1039

m0659

m0661

2207

m0662

1061

m0663
2597

m0664

2628

m0665
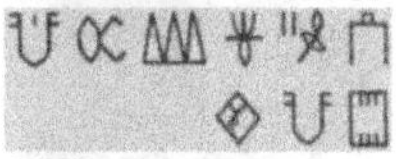
1139

m0666

2243

m0667

1111

m0668

2032

m0669

2686

m0670

1030

m0671

1021

m0672
1040

m0673

1025

m0674
1068

m0675
2197

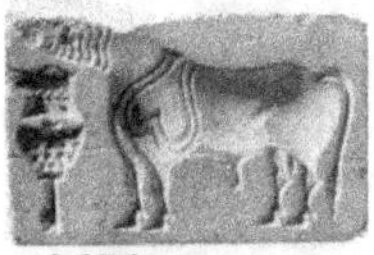
m0676

m0677

m0678
1066

m0679

m0680A1

m0681
2182

m0682

m0682A2

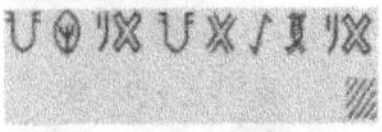

2690

m0683a

m0683A1

m0683A2

2174

m0684

m0685

1276

m0686
2324

m0687

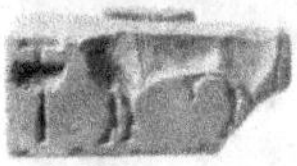

m0688

m0689

m0690

m0691

m0692

1031

m0693

m0694

m0695

m0696

m0697

m0698

m0699

1050

m0700

m0701

1059

m0702
2206

m0703

2438

m0704

2351

m0705

2272

m0706

1097

m0707

m0708
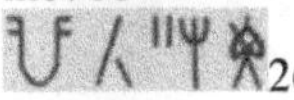2666

m0709

2071

m0710

3159

m0711

1166

m0712
1091

Note Sign391 ligatured on the animal's neck; this may be a logonym (i.e. two heiroglyphs – rings and spoked circle -- representing the same lexeme) for the rings on the neck?

m0713

2432

m0715

2681

m0716

2076 [Are there signs following these two signs?]

m0717
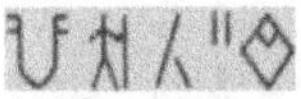
1078

m0714

2446
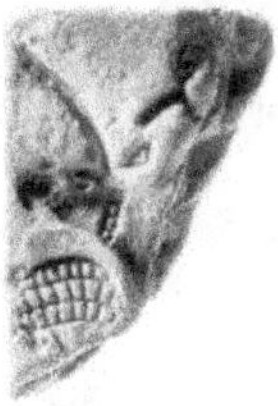
m0718

2209

m0719

2137

m0720

1082

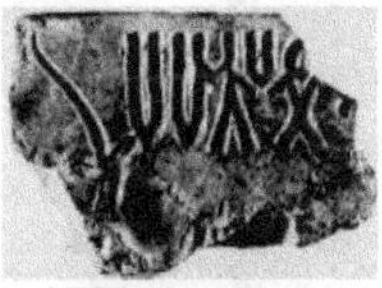
m0721
1165

m0722
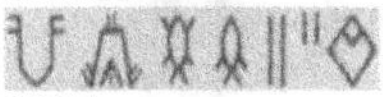
1014

m0723

2054

m0724

m0725

m0726

m0727a
m0727A1
m0727A2
2168

m0728
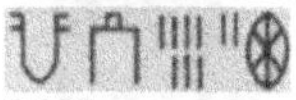
2691

m0729

1177

m0730

m0732
2674

m0733
2519

m0734
1539

m0735
1060

m0736
2562

m0737
1112

m0738
2644

m0739

m0740
1090

m0741
2421

m0742
2595

m0743

m0744

m0745
1175

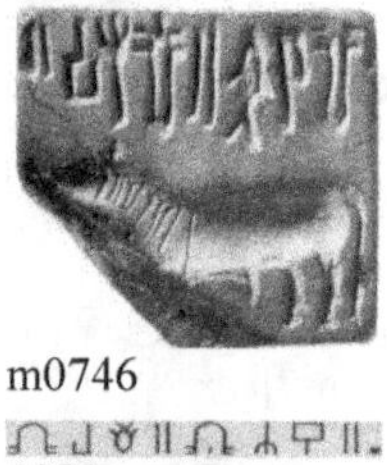
m0746
1081

m0747
2471

m0748
1135

m0749
2008

m0750
2065

m0751
1102

m0752a

m0753a

m0753A1

m0753A2
2589

m0754
1145

m0755

m0756a

1028

m0757

2507

m0758a

2184

m0759 One-horned bull.

2384

m0760

m0761 One-horned bull.

1417

m0762a

2645

m0763

m0764

m0765

m0766

m0767

m0768

1176

m0769

2034

m0770a

1138

m0771

2676

m0772
2453

m0773

m0774
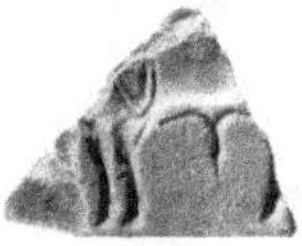
m0775

m0776
1146

m0777
2536

m0778
2425

m0779
2622

m0780
1178

m0781
2251

m0782
1122

m0783
1127

m0784
1128

m0785
1181

m0786
1107

m0787
2503

m0788

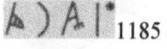

m0789
1185

m0790

m0791

m0792
2013

m0793

m0794
2067

m0795
1228

m0796
2105

m0797

m0798
1084

m0799 3015 or
3147

m0800

m0801
2104

m0802
1182

m0803
1131

m0804
2570

m0805
3041

m0806

m0807
2669

m0808
2146

m0809
2548

m0810
2364

m0811
2211

m0812
2629

m0813

m0814

2426

m0815

2555

m0816

2424

m0817

2435

m0818

1089

m0819

2081

m0820

m0821

1238

m0822

1249

m0823

1086

m0824

1164

m0825

1239

m0826

m0827

2513

m0828

2114

m0829

m0830

2274

m0831

2546

m0832

m0833

2281

m0834

2569b

m0835

2179

m0836

m0837

3085

m0838

2368

m0839

2476

m0840

2617

m0841

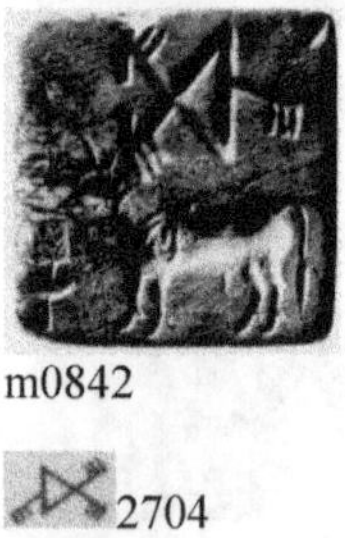
m0842
2704

m0843

m0844
1290

m0845
2202

m0846
1005

m0847
1156

m0848
2241

m0849
1121

m0850
2533

m0851
2660

99933333m0852a
2413

m0853
2255

m0854
2501

m0855
2473

m0856
1211

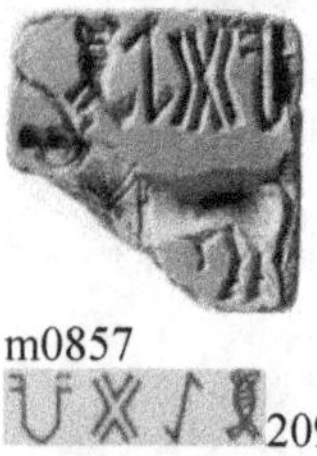
m0857
2091

m0858a
2189

m0859
2063

m0860

m0861
1123

m0862
2253

m0863
2621 Is the 'stubble' ligatured glyph a variant of Sign 162  ?]

m0864
1240

m0865

1109

m0866

2646

m0867

m0868

3160

m0869

m0870

1160

m0871

m0872

m0873

1170

m0874

3092

m0875

1189

m0876

m0877

m0878

1092

m0879

2121

m0880

m0881

1242

m0882
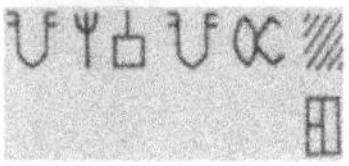
2312

m0883

m0884
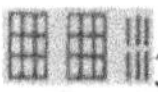
3158

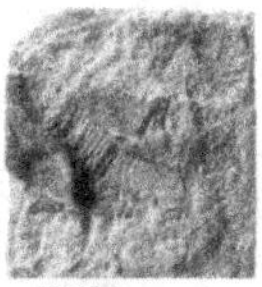
m0885

m0886
3072

m0887a
1169

m0888

1155

m0889
1126

m0890
2117

m0891
1073

m0892
1247

m0893

2659
One-horned bull.

m0894

2393

m0895

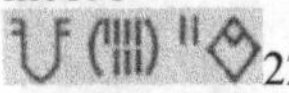
2262

m0896

2134

m0897

2545

m0898 2167

m0899

2242

m0900

2335

m0901

2276

m0902a

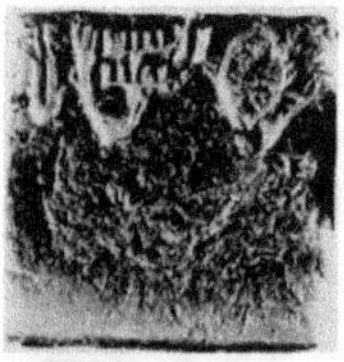
m0903a.

1294

m0904

m0905

m0906

m0907
2192

m0908

m0909

3028

m0910

m0911

m0914

2143

m0915

1218

m0916

1204

m0917
1224

m0918

m0919

2343

m0920

1219

m0921

m0922

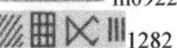

1282

m0923

m0924

2591

m0925

1292

m0926

2219

m0927

1171

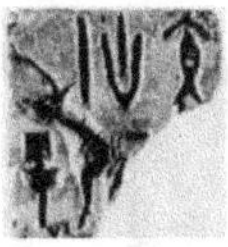

m0928

1202

m0929a

1144

m0930

3020

m0931

3091

m0932

3022

m0933

2160

m0934

1158

m0935

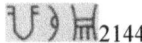

2144

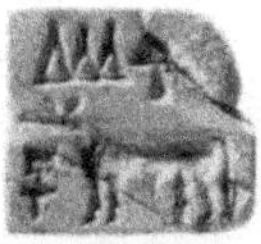

m0936

1197

m0937

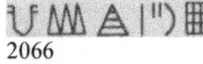

2066

m0938

2158

m0939a

2652

m0940a

2060

m0941

2256

m0942

1296

m0943

2282

m0944

2419

m0945

1208

m0946

2358

m0947

2404

m0948
2250

m0949A

m0949C
1271

Also, Sign 141

m0950a
1013

m0951
1263

m0952
2265

m0953
2582

m0954
1262

m0955
2547

m0956
1251

m0957
1026

m0958
2348

m0959
1147

m0960
1388

m0961
1163

m0962
3074

m0963
1232

m0964
2010

m0965
1222

m0966
2070

m0967
2460

m0968
2300

m0969
2239

m0970a
2116

m0971
1234

m0972a
2557

m0973a
2585

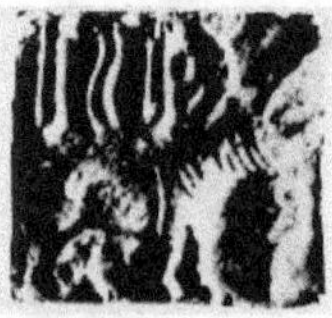
m0974a
2650

m0975
2295

m0976
1203

m0977
3152

m0978

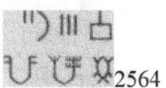

m0979
2564

m0980
2317

m0981

m0982a
2021

m0983

m0984
1143

m0985

m0986a
2341

m0987a
1007

m0988

m0989

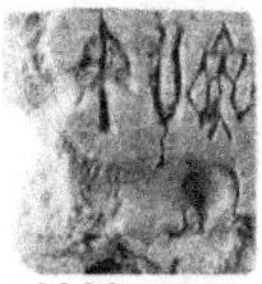
m0990
2472
One-horned bull.

m0991
2203

m0992
2464

m0993a
1267

m0994a
2165

m0995

m0996
2299 One-horned bull.

m0997a
3105

m0998
2176

m0999
2452

m1000a
1487 One-horned bull.

m1001a
1283

m1002

m1003
1275

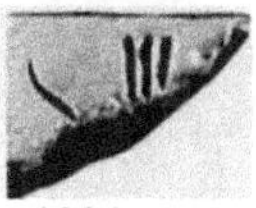
m1004

m1005

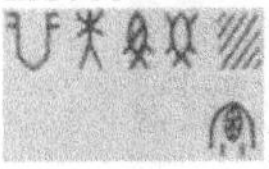

1001

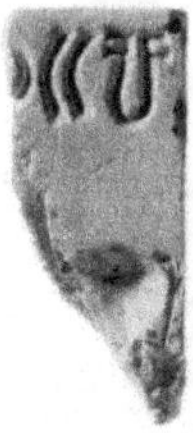

m1006

1499

Bovid.

m1007

m1008

m1009

2627

m1010

2672

Bovid.

m1011

m1012

m1013

m1014 One-horned bull?

1397

m1015

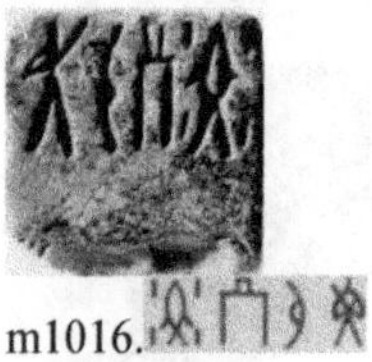

m1016.

1348

m1017.

1300

m1018a

2483

Bovid.

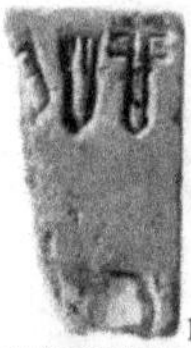

m1019.

1298

m1020

2496

m1021a.

1299

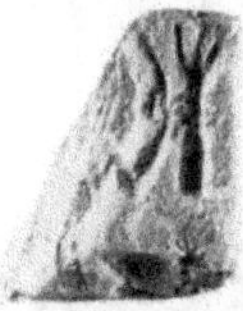

m1022

m1023

m1024

m1025a

m1026a.

1307

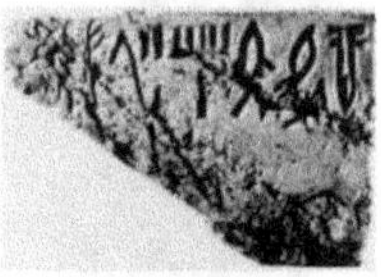

m1027

m1028

2671

Bovid.

m1029

1265

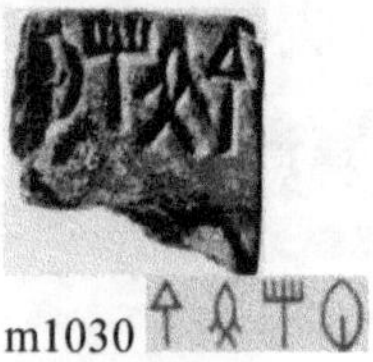

m1030

3145

m1031

2053

m1032
2217

m1033

m1034
2467

m1036

m1037

m1038

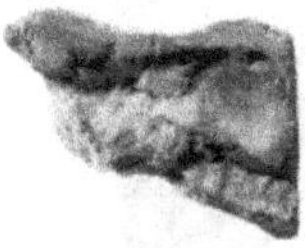
m1039

m1040

m1041

m1042

m1043

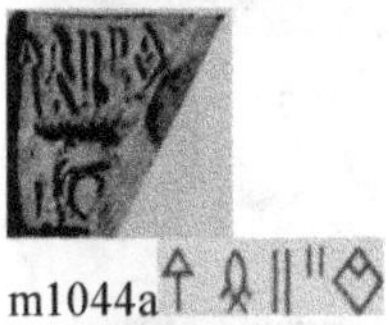
m1044a
1551 Bovid.

m1045
2447 Bovid.

m1046
3058

m1047
1281

m1048

m1049
3032

m1050
1196

m1051

m1052
3100

m1053
2163

m1054
2448

m1055
2529

m1057
2566

m1058a
1392

m1059

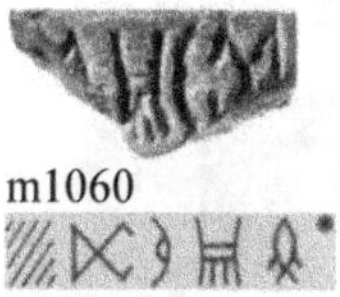
m1060
1497

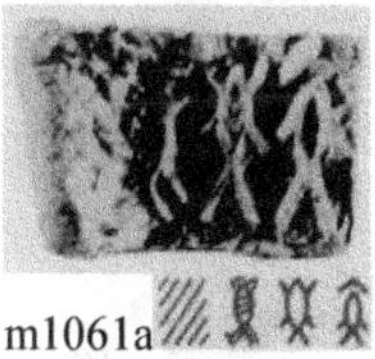
m1061a
1379

m1062
2089

m1063
2357

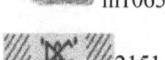

m1064 1492

m1065

2151

m1066

1547

m1067a

1496

m1068

m1069

1390

m1070

2040

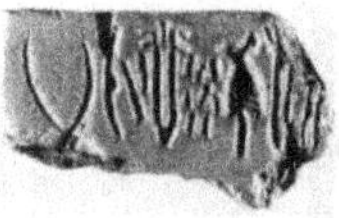

m1071

1488

m1072a

1443

m1073

1489

m1074

m1075a

1479

m1076

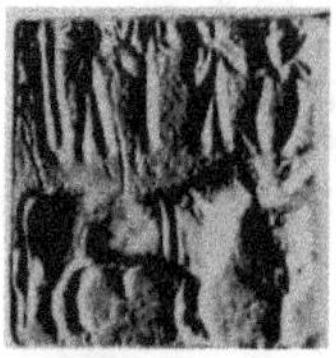

m1077a

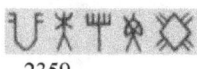

2359

m1078

m1079

2655

m1080

1542

m1081a

2129

m1082.

1349

m1083

m1084

1316 Bison.

m1085.

1322

m1086a

3070

m1087a.

1319

m1088

2268

m1089a.

1315

m1090

2675

m1091

m1092

1312

m1093

m1094

m1095

2495 Bison

m1096

2410

m1097

2313

m1098

1301

m1099

1313

m1100

2201

Bison

m1101

2431 Zebu.

m1102

m1103.

1337

m1104

1335

m1105

m1106

2331

Zebu

m1107a

2306

m1108

1339

m1109

1327 Zebu

m1110

1334

m1111.

1333

m1112

2366

Zebu.

m1113

2441

m1114.

1331

m1115

1328 Zebu

m1116.

1329

m1117a

2615

m1118

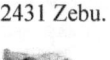

3157

m1119

2463

m1120

2362

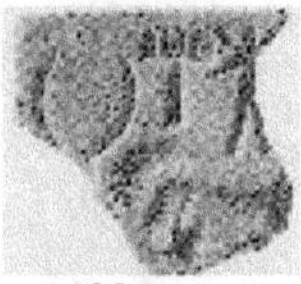
m1122

2610

m1126

2332

m1127

2696

m1128a

3163

m1129a .

1302 Markhor.

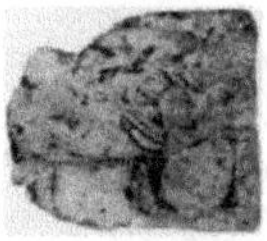
m1130

m1131

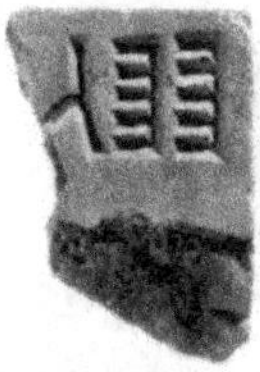
m1132

1545
Rhinoceros.

m1133

1343

m1134

2651

m1135

2140
Pict-50 Composite animal: features of an ox and a rhinoceros facing the standard device.

m1136

m1137

2531
Rhinoceros.

m1138.

1344

m1139.

1341

m1140a

2188 Rhinoceros.

m1141

2169

m1142

m1143

m1144

m1145

m146a

1374 Elephant

m1147

m1148

2590

m1149

1368 Elephant.

m1150

1534

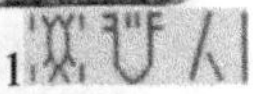
m1151
1535

m1152

1369

m1154

1362 Elephant.

m1155

2573

m1156

1370

m1157a

2110

m158

m1159
2171

m1160
2057

m1161

2504

m1162

2058

m1163
2640
Tiger.

m1164

2665 Tiger.

m1165a
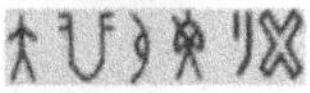
2064

m1166.
1351

m1167

2484
Tiger.

m1168

2360

Seal showing a horned tiger. Mohenjodaro. (After Scala/Art Resource).

Tiger with long (zebu's) horns?

1385

Pict-49 Uncertain animal with dotted circles on its body.

1626

Pict-47 Row of uncertain animals in file.

m1169a

2024

Pict-58: Composite motif: body of an ox and three heads: of a one-horned bull (looking forward), of antelope (looking backward), and of short-horned bull (bison) (looking downward).

m1170a
1382 Composite animal

m1171 Composite animal

m1172

m1173

1191

m1175a

2493

Composite animal: human face, zebu's horns, elephant tusks and trunk, ram's forepart, unicorn's trunk and feet, tiger's hindpart and serpent-like tail.

m1176

m1177

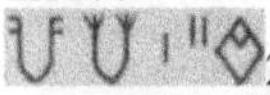2450

Composite animal: human face, zebu's horns, elephant tusks and trunk, ram's forepart, unicorn's trunk and feet, tiger's hindpart and serpent-like tail.

m1178

2559

m1179

2606 Human-faced markhor with long wavy horns, with neck-bands and a short tail.

m1180a .

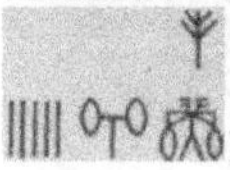1303

Human-faced markhor

m1181A

2222

Pict-80: Three-faced, horned person (with a three-leaved pipal branch on the crown), wearing bangles and armlets and seated on a hoofed platform

Padri . Head painted on storage jar from Padri, Gujarat (c. 2800 BCE). Details of body with multiple hands (?) Similar horned-heads painted on jars are found at Kot Diji, Burzhom and Kunal (c. 3rd millennium BCE). [Source: Page 21, Figs. 10A and B in: Deo Prakash Sharma, 2000, *Harappan seals, sealings and copper tablets*, Delhi, National Museum].

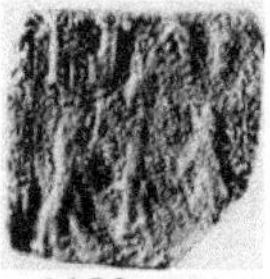

m1182a

m1183a

m1184

m1185

Pict-103 Horned (female with breasts hanging down?) person with a tail and bovine legs standing near a tree fisting a horned tiger rearing on its hindlegs.

1357

m1186A

2430

Composition: horned person with a pigtail standing between the branches of a pipal tree; a low pedestal with offerings (? or human head?); a horned person kneeling in adoration; a ram with short tail and curling horns; a row of seven robed figures, with twigs on their pigtails.

m1187

m1188

2228

m1189

1396

m1190

2558

m1191
1389

m1192

1495

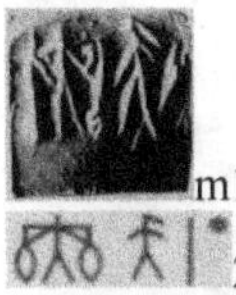
m1193a
2401

m1194a

3066

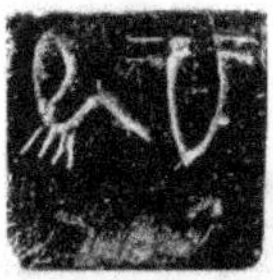
m1195

2181

m1196

m1197

m1198
1482

Silver
m1199A
2520

m1200A

m1200C

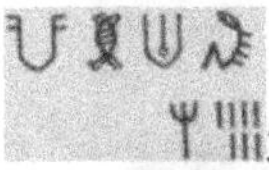
3078

m1201

m1202A
m1202C.

1325 Space on the side of the seal was used to inscribe a third line

m1203A

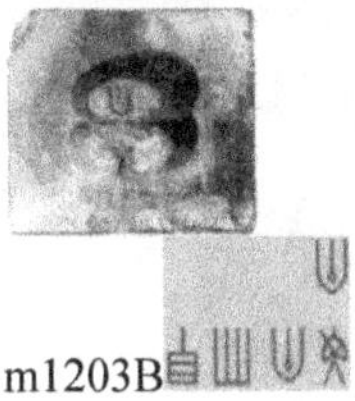
m1203B
1018

m1204

2095

m1205a

m1205c

m1205f

1293 + Two signs on the sides of the seal.

m1206AE

m1206e1

m1206F

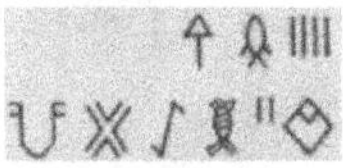
2229 Seal with a projecting knob containing the top three signs; m1206e is inscribed on the top edge of the lower indented frame which depicts the bison.

m1208

m1221

m1222

1268

m1223

2045

Pict-40: Frog.

2565

Pict-37 Goat-antelope with a short tail

m1224A
m1224B

1224

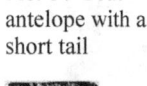

m1224e

Pict-88

1227
Standing person with horns and bovine features (hoofed legs and/or tail).

m1225A

m1225B.

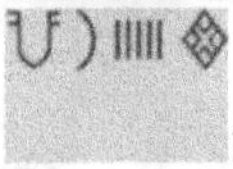
1311
Cube seal with perforation through the breadth of the seal Pict-118: svastika_ , generally within a square or rectangular border.

m1226A.

1326 Unfinished seal.

m1227

m1228a

1394

m1230a

1358

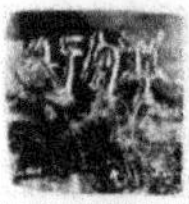
m1231

2321
Unfinished seal?

m1232a

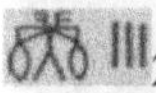
2497
Unfinished seal

m1233A
m1233B
m1233cd

2352

m1234a

m1234b

m1234d

m1234e

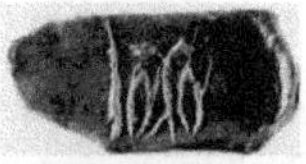
m1235a

m1235bc

2394
Unfinished seal

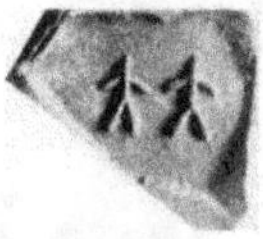
m1236

1483
Unfinished seal?

m1239
m1240
m1241
m1242

m1243
m1244
m1245
m1246

m1247
m1248
m1249

m125
0 m1251
m1252

m1253

m1254
m1255

m1256

m1257

m1258

m1259

m1260

m1261

m1262
2301

m1263
1391

m1264a
1405

m1265
2227

m1266
1470

m1267
1494

m1268
2288

m1269

m1270
1464

m1271
2603

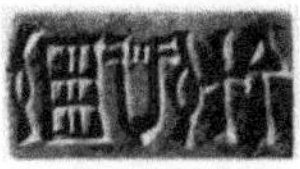
m1272

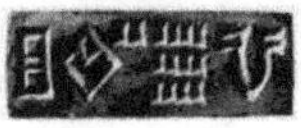
m1273
2679

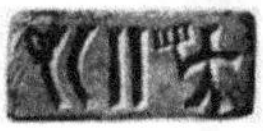
m1274
2106

m1275
3161

m1276
2428

m1277

m1278
2028

m1280a
1462

m1281
2266

m1282

m1283

m1284a
2477

m1285a
2204

m1286
1455

m1287
1454

m1288
3086

m1289
1452

m1290
1463

m1291a
2688

m1292
1461

m1293a
2388

m1294
2291

m1295
1458

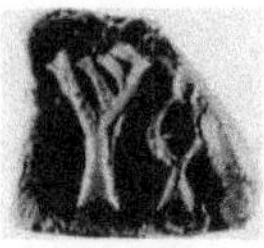
m1296a
3144

m1297
1445

m1298
3037

m1299a
1456

m1300
2350

m1301

m1302a
1432

m1303a
1398

m1304
1423

m1305
2289

m1306
1430

m1307

m1308
2697

m1309
2579

m1310
1418

m1311
2485

m1312
2318

m1313
2093

m1314a
1439

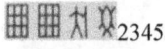

m1315
2345

m1316a

m1317
3095

m1318
1416

m1319

m1320
1447

m1321
1446

m1322a
3079

m1323
2006

m1324
2682

m1325
2118

m1326
3143

m1327
1408

m1328
2392

m1329A

m1329C

2439

m1330

1409

m1331a

2303

m1332

m1333

1434

m1334a

2170

m1335a

2072

m1336a

2515

m1337

2055

m1338a

2020

m1339

2025

m1340

2369

m1341

2092

m1342a

1393

m1343

1433

m1344

2315

m1346a

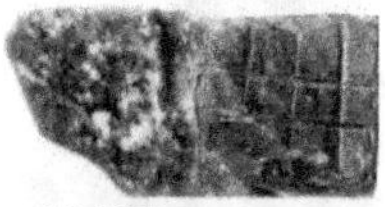

m1349B

m1349A

m1350

2599

m1351

2142

m1353

1459

m1354a

1498

m1355a

2568

m1356

m1357

2356

m1358

m1359

2575

m1360

1442

m1361a

1474

m1362A

m1362C

2230

m1363

2372

m1364A

m1364C

2542

m1365A

m1365B

2658 Cricket, spider or prawn?

m1366

2094

m1367a 
2661 Two bisons standing face-to-face

m1368

1460

m1369

1478

m1370a

2509 Cylinder seal; tree branch

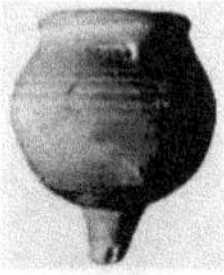

m1371A1

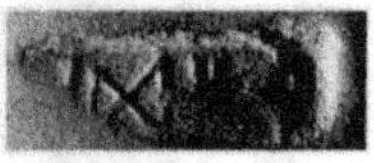

m1371A2

m1372A1

m1372A2

m1373A1

m1373A2

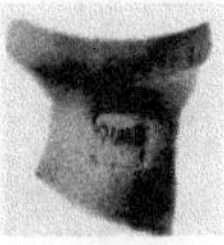

m1374A1

m1374A2

m1375A1

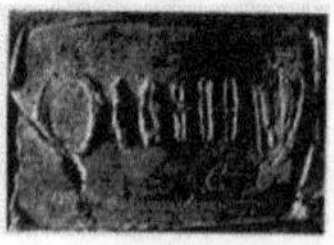

m1375A2

1560
Seal impression on pot

m1376A1

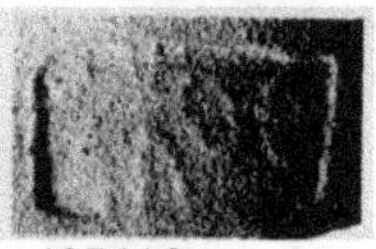

m1376A2

m1378A1

m1378A2

m1379A2

m1380A2

m1381A1

m1381A2

1559
Seal Impression on a pot

m1382A1

m1382A2 Seal impression on a potsherd

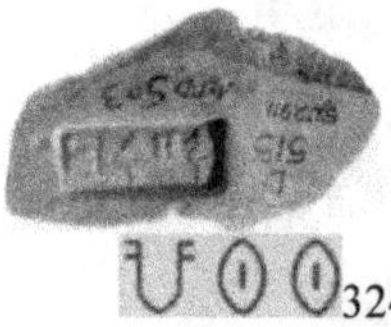3244

m1383

m1384si

m1385A14

m1385A2

m1385A3

m1386si

m1387t

m1388t

2856

m1389t

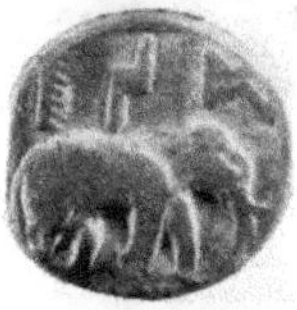

m1390At

m1390Bt

2868 Pict-74: Bird in flight.

m1391t

2826

m1392t

2837

m1393t

m1394t

m1395At

m1395Bt

m1396t

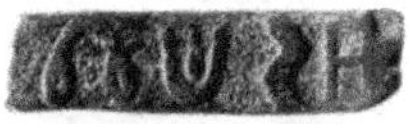

m1397At

m1397Bt

m1398t

2807

m1400At

m1400B

2851

m1401t

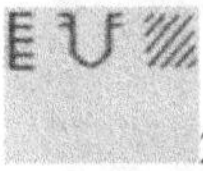

2822

m1402At

m1402Bt

m1403At

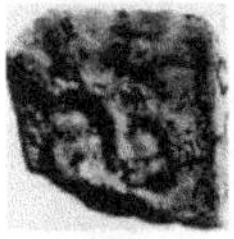

m1403Bt

m1405At Pict-97: Person standing at the center pointing with his right hand at a bison facing a trough, and with his left hand pointing to

the sign

Obverse: A tiger and a rhinoceros in file.

m1405Bt Pict-48 A tiger and a rhinoceros in file

2841

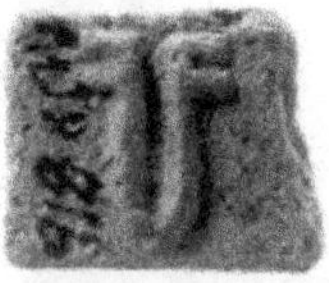

m1406At

m1406B  2827

Pict-102: Drummer and people vaulting over? An adorant?

m1407At

m1407Bt

m1408At

m1409At
m1409Bt Serpent (?) entwined around a pillar with capital (?) or ring-stones stacked on a pillar?; the motif is carved in high relief on the reverse side of the inscribed object.

m1410At
m1410Bt

m1411At
m1411Bt

m1412At

m1412Bt

m1413At

m1413Bt

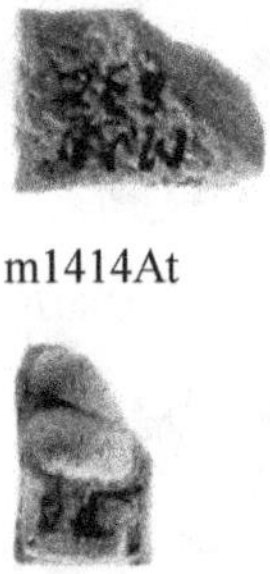
m1414At

m1414Bt

m1415At

m1415Bt

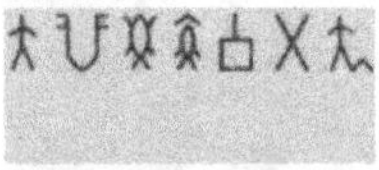
2825

m1416At

m1416Bt

2818

m1417t

3242

m1418At

m1418Bt

m1419At

m1419Bt

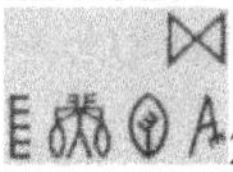
2812

m1420At
2865

m1421At

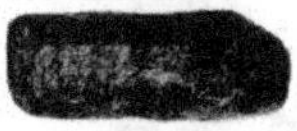
m1421Bt

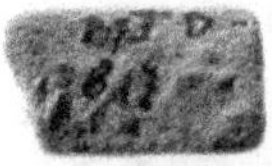

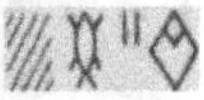
m1422At
2845

m1423At

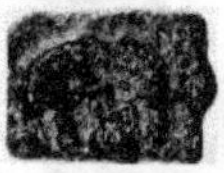
m1423Bt Elephant shown on both sides of the tablet.

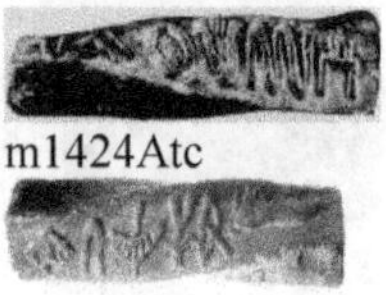
m1424Atc

m1424Btc

3234

m1425At

m1425Bt

m1427At

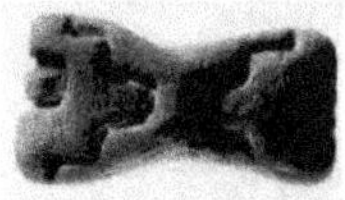
m1427Bt

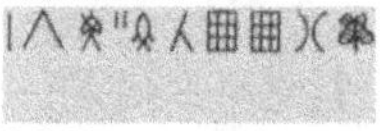
2860

m1428At

m1428Bt

m1428Ct

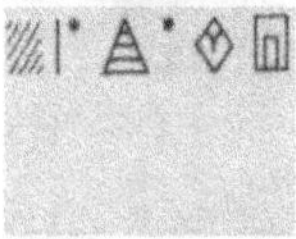
2842

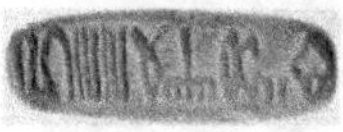
m1426

1621

m1429At

m1429Bt Pict-125: Boat.

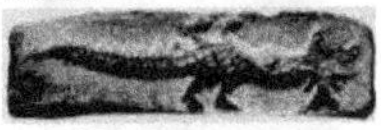

m1429Ct

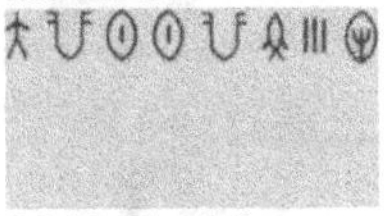

3246 Gharial holding a fish in its jaws.

Pict-100

Person throwing a spear at a buffalo and placing one foot on the head of the buffalo.

2279

m1430Bt

m1430C

m1430At Pict-101: Person throwing a spear at a buffalo and placing one foot on its head; three persons standing near a tree at the center.

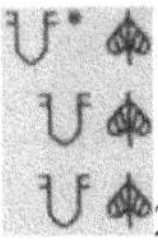

2819 Pict-60: Composite animal with the body of an ox and three heads [one each of one-horned bull (looking forward), antelope (looking backward) and bison (looking downwards)] at right; a goat standing on its hindlegs and browsing from a tree at the center.

m1431A

m1431B

m1431C

m1431E

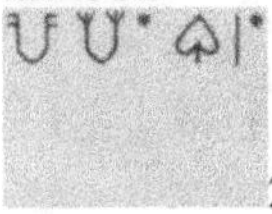

2805 Row of animals in file (a one-horned bull, an elephant and a rhinoceros from right); a gharial with a fish held in its jaw above the animals; a bird (?) at right. Pict-116: From R.—a person holding a vessel; a woman with a platter (?); a kneeling person with a staff in his hands facing the woman; a goat with its forelegs on a platform under a tree. [Or, two antelopes flanking a tree on a platform, with one antelope looking backwards?]

m1432At

m1432Bt

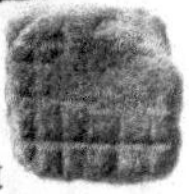

m1432Ct

m1433At

m1433Bt

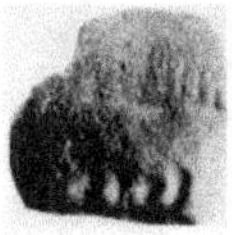

m1433Ct

m1436it

m1438it

m1439it

3132

m1440 it

2374

m1441it

m1442it

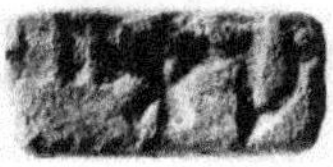

m1443it

3213

m1444Ait

m1444Bit

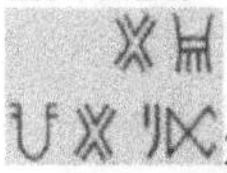

2339

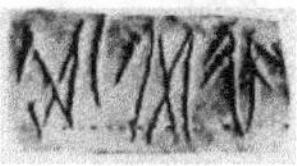

m1445Ait

m1445Bit

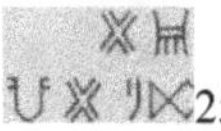

2505

m1447Ait

m1448Act

m1448Bct

m1449Act

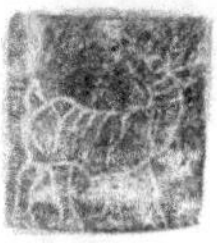

m1449Bct (obverse of inscription) Incised copper tablet (two sides) Markhor with head turned backwards

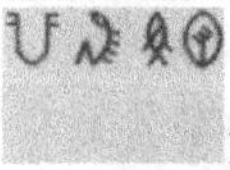

1801

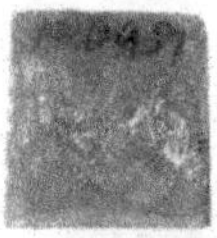

m1450Act

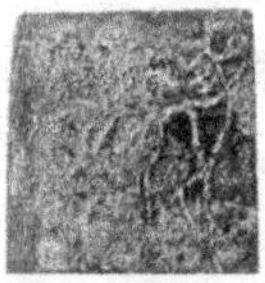

m1450Bct

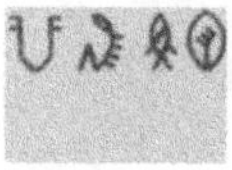

1701

m1451Act

m1451Bct

m1452Act

m1452Bct

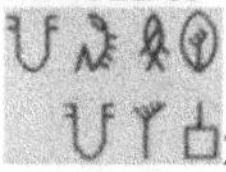

2912

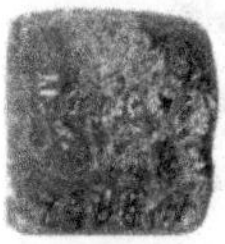

m1453Act

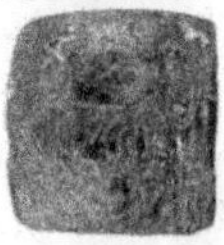

m1453Bct

m1456Act

1805

m1457Act

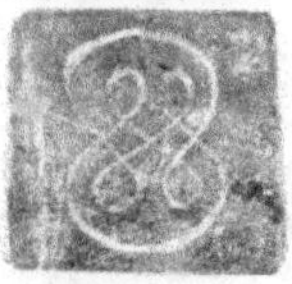

m1457Bct

2904 Pict-124: Endless knot motif.

m1458Act

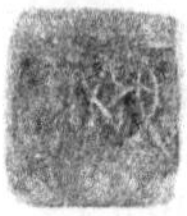

m1461Act

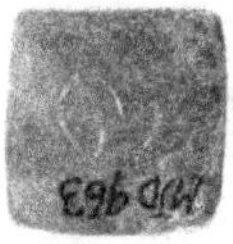

m1462Act

m1463ABct

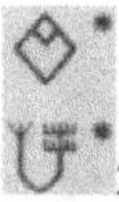

2919

m1465Act

2921

m1470Act

m1472Bct

m1474Act

m1474Bct

m1475Act

m1475Bct

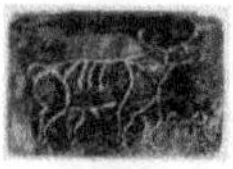

m1476Bct

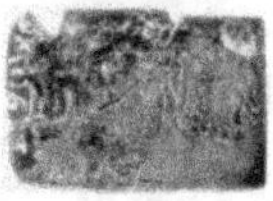

m1477Act

m1477Bct

m1482Act

m1482Bct

m1483Act

m1483Bct

m1484Act

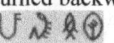

m1484Bct

m1485Bct

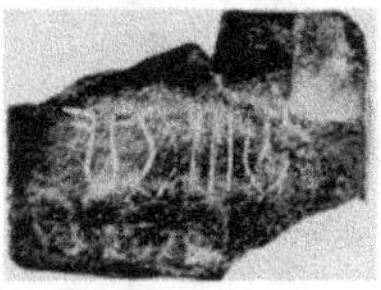

m1486Act

m1486Bct

1711

Incised copper tablets.Elephant

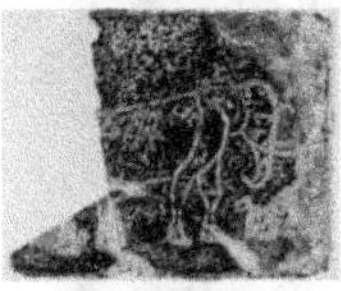

m1488Bct

m1491Act

m1491Bct

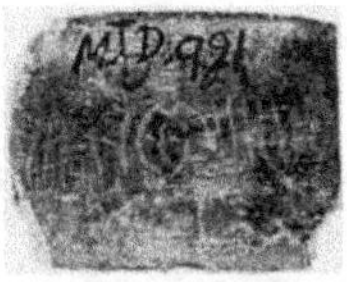

m1492Act

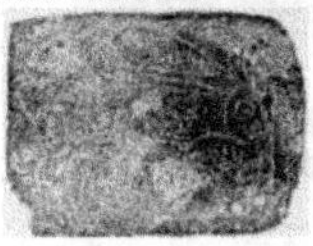

m1492Bct

m1493Bct

m1494

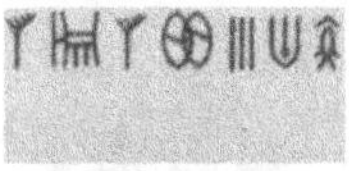

1706 Hare

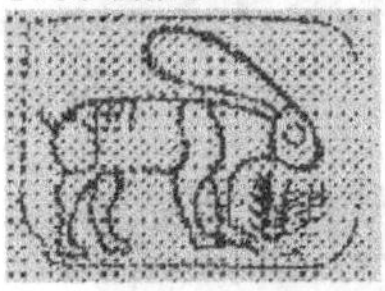

Pict-42

m1497Act

m1498Act

m1498Bct

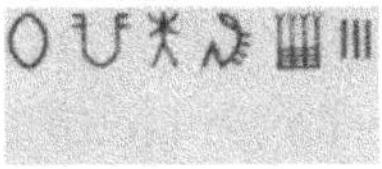

2917

1803

Pict-30

1804

Pict-39 Ox-antelope with a long tail; a trough in front.

m1501Bct

m1502Bct

m1503Act

m1503Bct

m1505Act

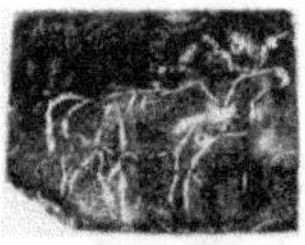

m1505Bct

m1506Act

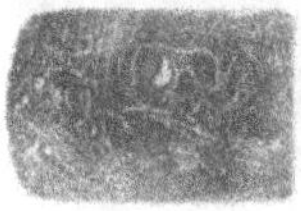

m1506Bct

m1508Act

m1508Bct

1708

m1511Act

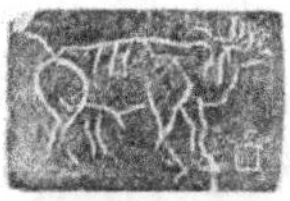

m1511Bct

m1512Act

m1512Bct

m1513

1712

m1514

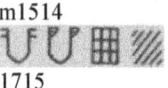

1715

m1515Act

m1515Bct

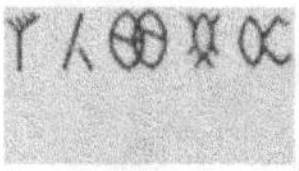
2910

m1516Act

m1516Bct

m1517Act

m1517Bct

m1518

1709

m1520Act

m1520Bct

2907

m1521Act

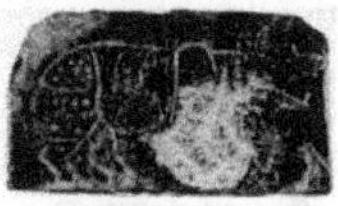
m1521Bct

m1522Act

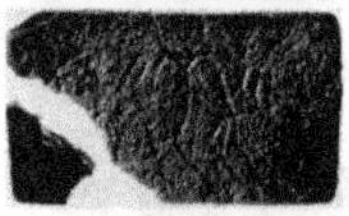
m1522Bct

m1523Act

m1523Bct

m1524

3396

m1528Act

m1529Act

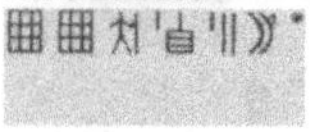
2920

m1529Bct

m1532Act

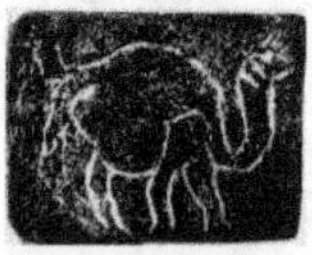
m1532Bct

m1534Act

m1534Bct

1703

Composition:

Two horned heads one at either end of the body. Note the dottings on the thighs which is a unique artistic feature of depicting a rhinoceros (the legs are like those of a rhinoceros?). The body apparently is a combination of two rhinoceroses with heads of two bulls attached on either end of the composite body.

m1535Act

m1535Bct

m1540Act

m1540

m1547Act

1547Bct

m1548A

m1548Bct

m1549Act

m1549Bct

m1563Act

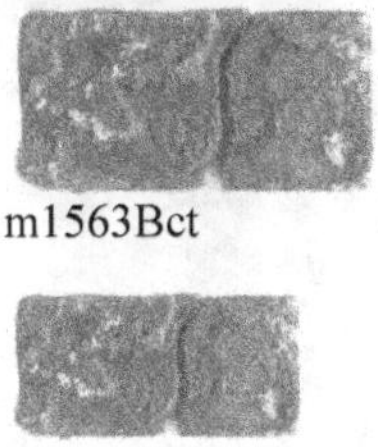

m1563Bct

m1566Bct

m1568Act

m1568Bct

m1569
3333

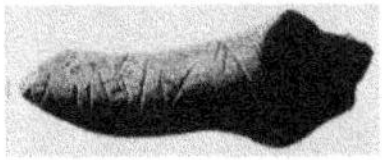

m1575

m1576

m1578
3251

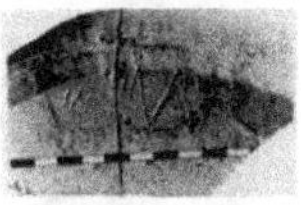

m1591

1592

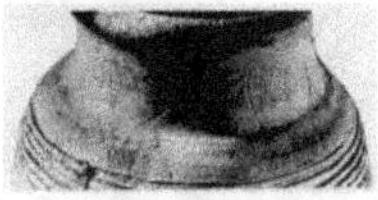

m1597

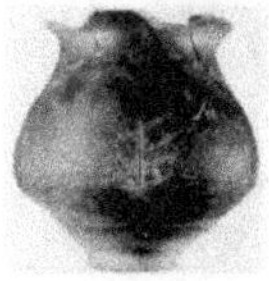

m1598

m1601

3252

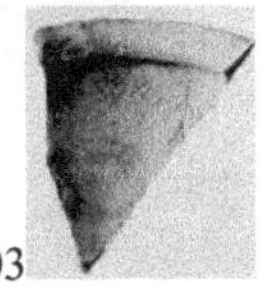

m1603

m1609

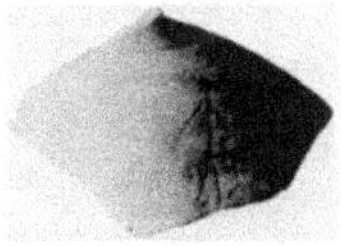

m1611

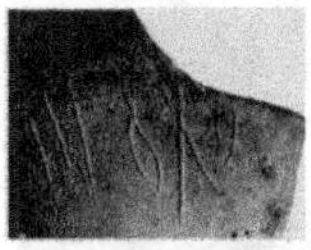

m1626
3245

m1629bangle

m1630bangle

m1631bangle

m1632bangle

m1633bangle

m1634bangle

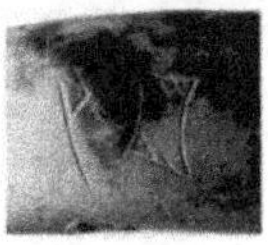

m1635bangle

m1636bangle

m1637bangle

m1638bangle

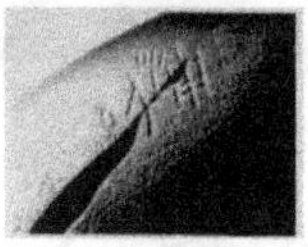

m1639bangle

m1640bangle

m1641bangle

m1643bangle

m1645bangle

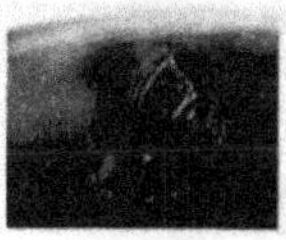

m1646bangle

m1647bangle

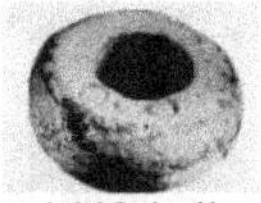

m1648shell

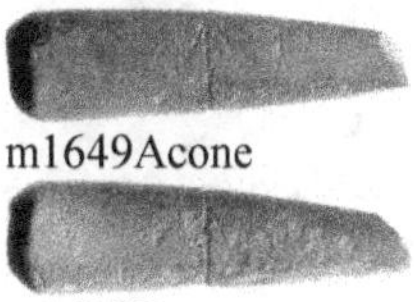

m1649Acone

m1649Bcone
3253

m1650ivory stick

3505

Pict-144:
Geometrical pattern.

Pict-141:
Geometrical pattern.

2942

Pict-142:
Geometrical

pattern.
2943 Ivory or bone rod

Pict-143:
Geometrical pattern.Ivory stick

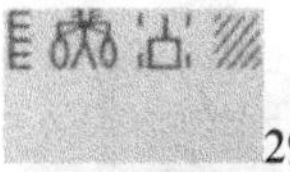
2948

Ivory rod, ivory plaque with dotted circles. Mohenjodaro. [Musee National De Arts Asiatiques Guimet, 1988-1989, *Les cites oubliees de l'Indus Archeologie du Pakistan.*]

m1652A ivory stick

m1653 ivory plaque

1905

m1654A ivory cube

m1654B ivory cube

m1654D ivory cube

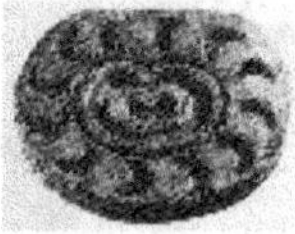
m1655faience ornament

m1656 steatite ornament

m1657A steatite

m1657B steatite

m1658AB etched bead

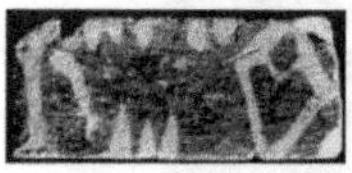

m1658
2952 Etched Bead

m1659 bangle

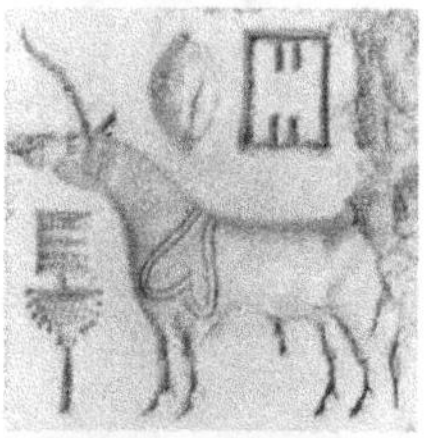
m1660

m1661a

m1662

m1663a

m1664a

m1665a

m1666a

m1667

m1668a

m1669a

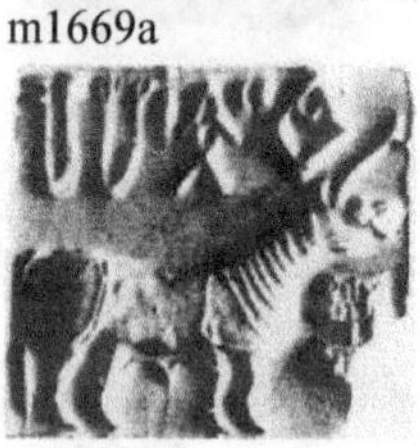
m1670a

m1671a

m1672

m1673a

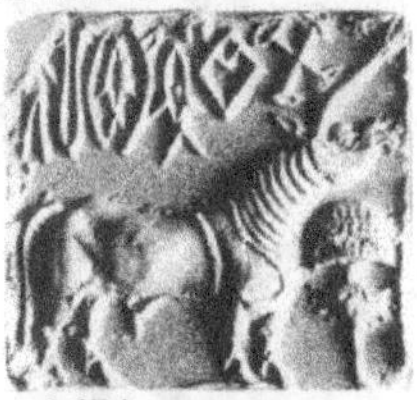
m1674a

m1675a

m1676a

m1677a

m1678a

m1679a

m1680a

m1681a

m1682a

m1683a

m1684a

m1685a

m1686a

m1687a

m1688a

m1689a

m1690a

m1691a

m1692a

m1693a

m1694a

m1695a

m1696a

m1697

m1698

m1699a

m1700a

m1701a

m1702a

m1703a

m17054

m1705a

m1706a

m1707a

m1708a

m1709a

m1710a

m1711a

m1712a

m1713a

m1714a

m1715a

m1716a

m1717a

m1718

m1719a

m1720

m1721

m1722a

m1723a

m1724a

m1725a

m1726a

m1727

m1728a

m1729a

m1730a

m1731a

m1732

m1733a

m1734

m1735

m1736a

m1737a

m1738

m1739a

m1740

m1741a

m1742

m1743

m17441

m1745a

m1746

m1747a

m1748

m1749a

m1750a

m1751a

m1752a

m1753a

m1754a

m1755a

m1756a

m1757a

m1758a

m1759a

m1760

m1761a

m1762a

m1763a

m1764a

m1765

m1766a

m1767

m1768a

m1769a

m1770a

m1771a

m1772a

m1773

m1774a

m1775a

m1776

m1777a

m1778

m1779a

m1780a

m1781a

m1782

m1783a

m1784a

m1785a

m1786a

m1787a

m1788a

m1789a

m1790a

m1791a

m1792a

m1793a

m1794

m1795a

m1796a

m1797

m1798a

m1799

m1800

m1801a

m1802

m1803a

m1804a

m1805a

m1806a

m1807a

m1808a

m1809a

m1810a

m1811a

m1812a

m1813a

m1814

m1815a

m1816a

m1817a

m1818

m1819

m1820

m1821a

m1822a

m1823

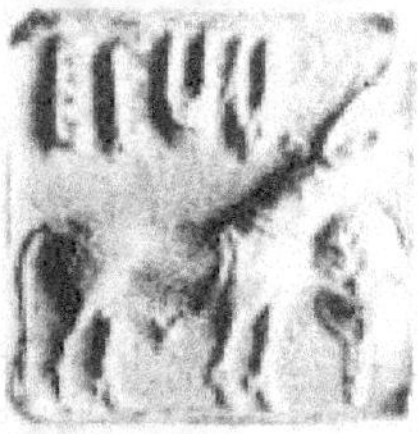
m1824a

m1825a

m1826

m1827

m1828a

m1829a

m1830

m1831a

m1832a

m1833a

m1834a

m1835a

m1836

m1837a

m1838a

m1839a

m1840

m1841a

m1842a

m1843a

m1844

m1845a

m1846a

m1847a

m1848

m1849

m1850a

m1851

m1852

m1853a

m1854a

m1855a

m1856a

m1857

m1858

m1860a

m1863a

m1864

m1865a

m1866

m1868a

m1869

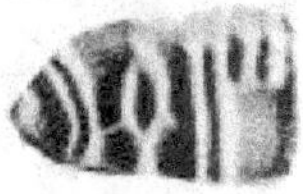

m1872a

m1876a

m1877

m1878a

m1879a

m1880a

m1881

m1882

m1883

m1884a

m1885a

m1886a

m1887

m1888a

m1889

m1890

m1891a

m1892a

m1893

m1894

m1895a

m1896a

m1897

m1898a

m1899a

m1900a

m1901

m1092a

m1903a

m1904a

m1905a

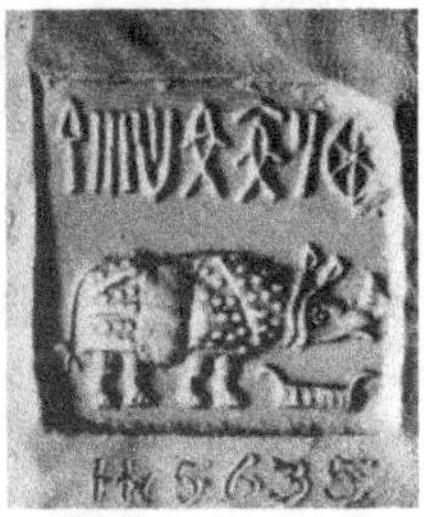
m1906

m1907a

m1909

m1910

m1911a

m1912

m1912

m1913

m1914

m1915a

m1916a

m1917

m1918a

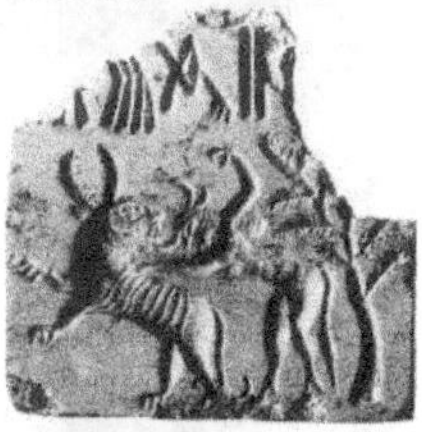
m1919

m1920a

m1921a

m1922a

m1923a

m1923c

m1923d

m1923e

m1927a

m1927b

m1928a

m1928b

m1930A

m1930B

m1931

m1932

m1933

m1934a

m1935

m1936

1937

m1938

m1939a

m1940

m1941a

m1942a

m1943a

m1944

m1945a

m1946

m1947a

m1948

m1950

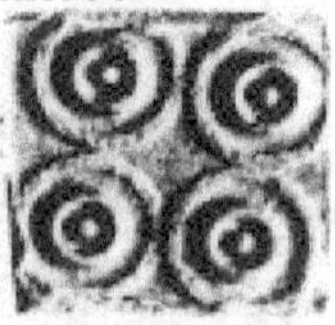

m1951a

m1953a

m1954a

m1955a

m1956a

m1957

m1958

m1959

m1960

m1961

m1962a

m1963a

m1964a

m1965a

m1966
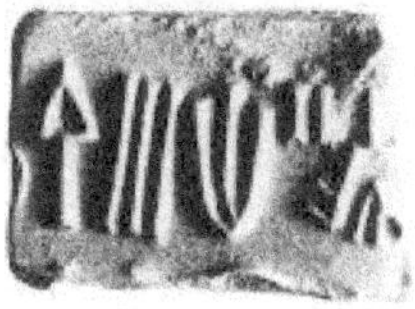
m1967a

m1968A+C
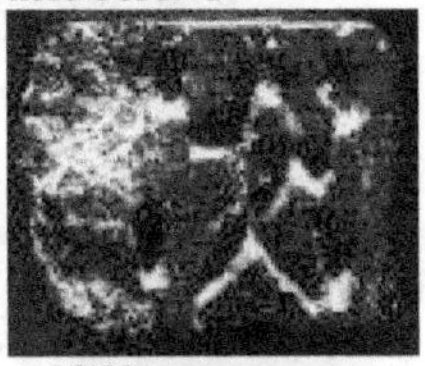
m1969
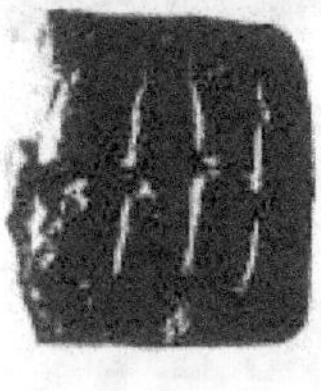
m1970

m1971a

m1972a

m1973a

m1974a

m1975a

m1976

m1977a

m1978a

m1979a

m1980

m1981a

m1982a

m1983a

m1984a

m1985a

m1986a

m1987a
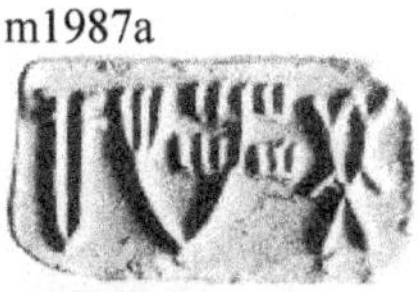
m1988a

m1989a

m1989b

m1990a

m1990b

m1991a

m1992a

m1993a

m1994A

m1995A

m1996A
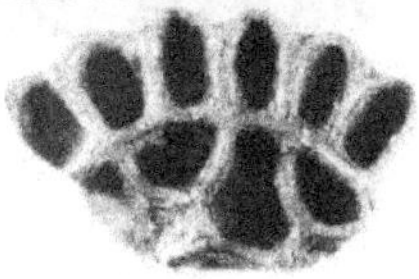
m1997A
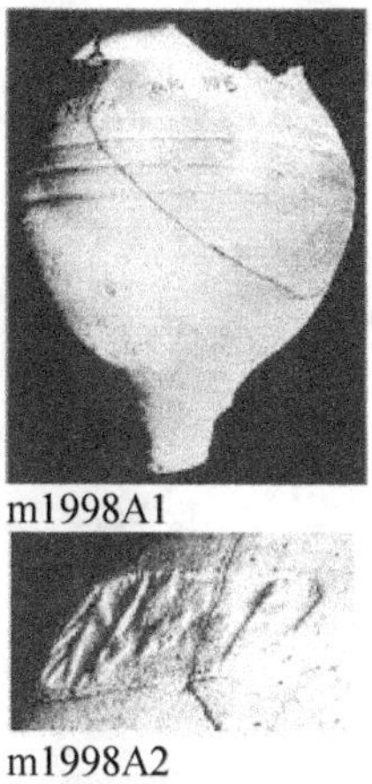
m1998A1
m1998A2
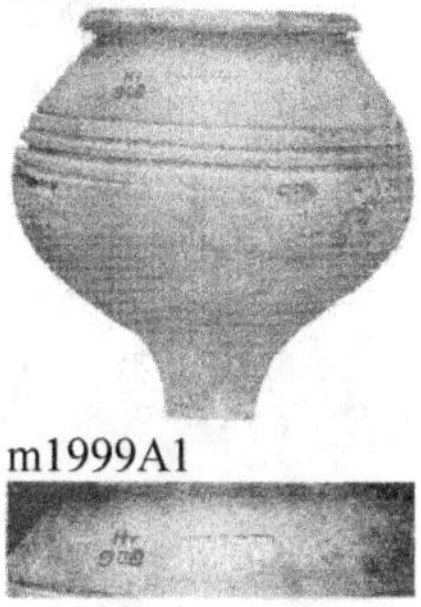
m1999A1
m1999A2
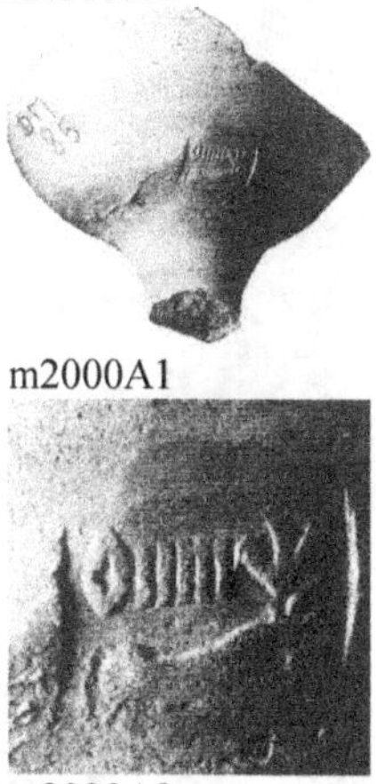
m2000A1
m2000A2
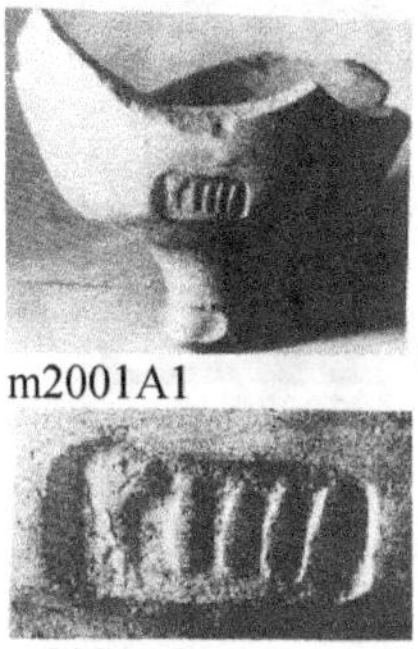
m2001A1
m2001A2

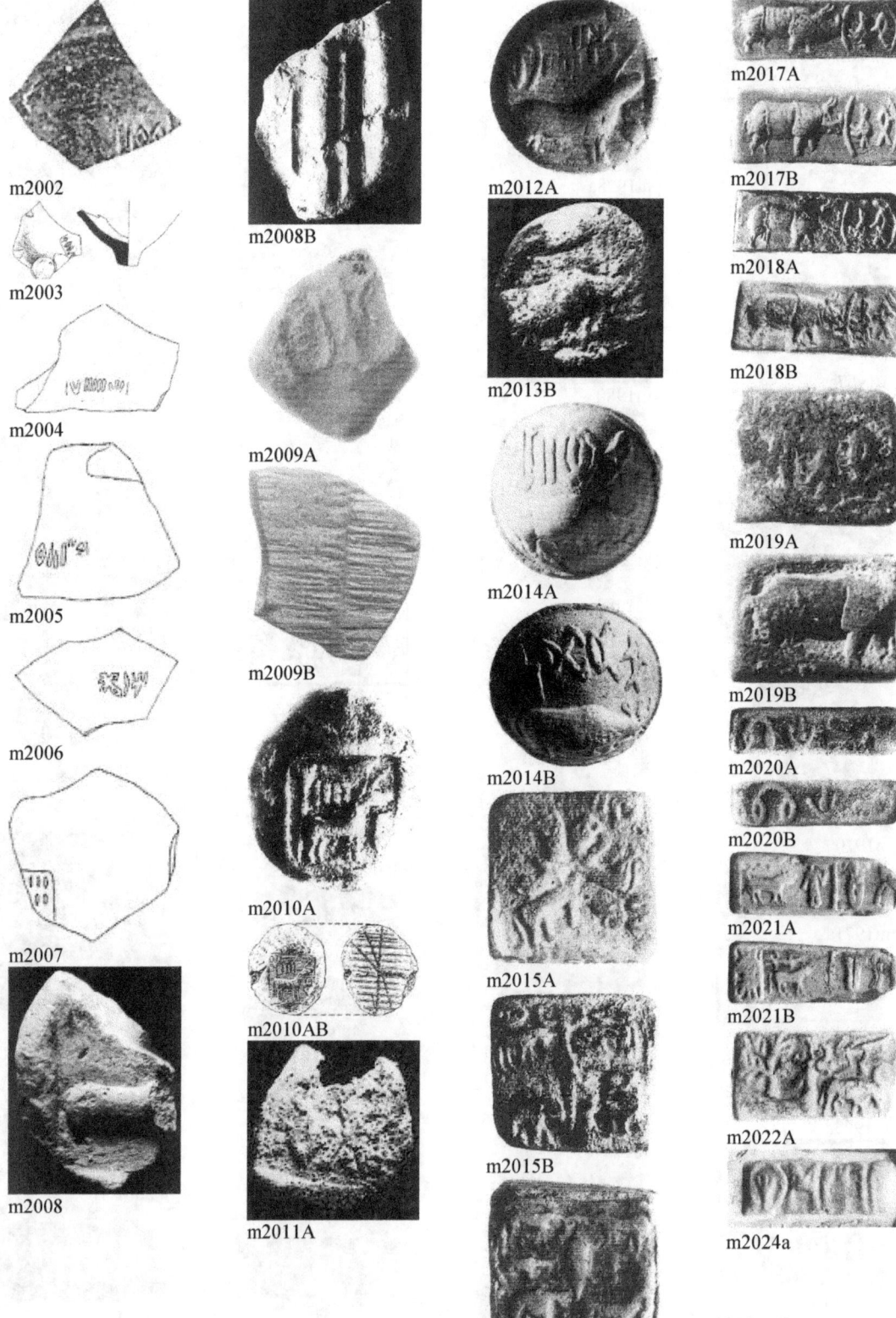

m2002

m2003

m2004

m2005

m2006

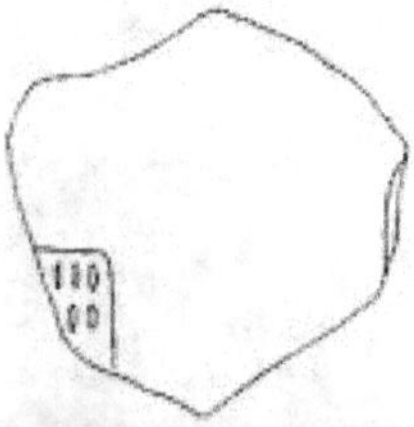
m2007

m2008

m2008B

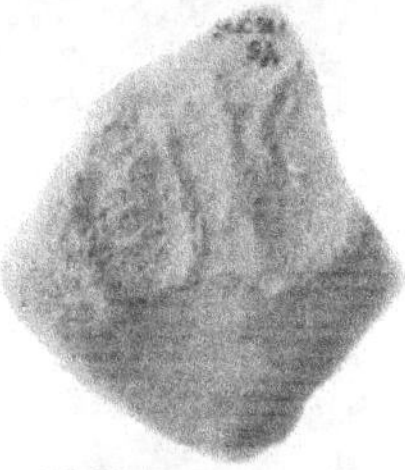
m2009A

m2009B

m2010A

m2010AB

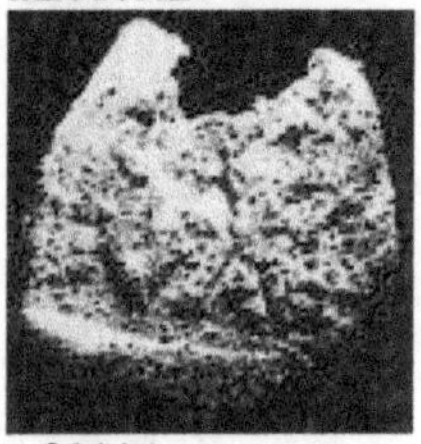
m2011A

m2012A

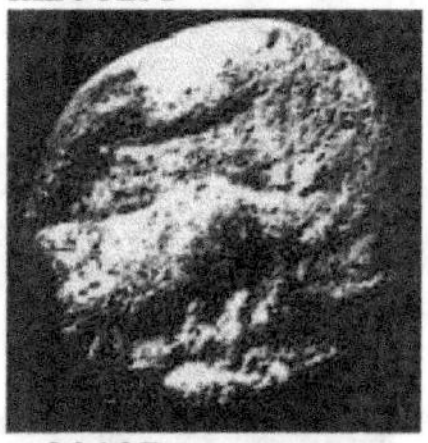
m2013B

m2014A

m2014B

m2015A

m2015B

m2016A

m2017A

m2017B

m2018A

m2018B

m2019A

m2019B

m2020A

m2020B

m2021A

m2021B

m2022A

m2024a

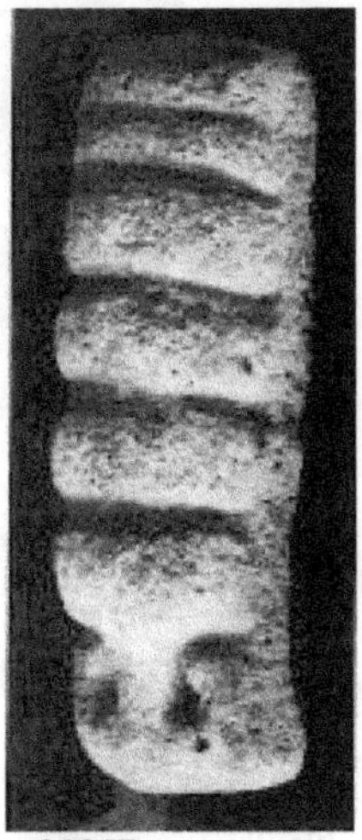
m2025B
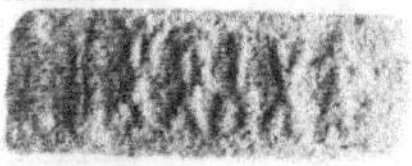
m2026A

m2026B

m2027A

m2027B

m2028A

m2028C

m2029A4

m2029B

m2029B1

m2030A

m2030B

m2032A

m2033A

m20333B

m2033C

m2034c

m2035A

m2035B
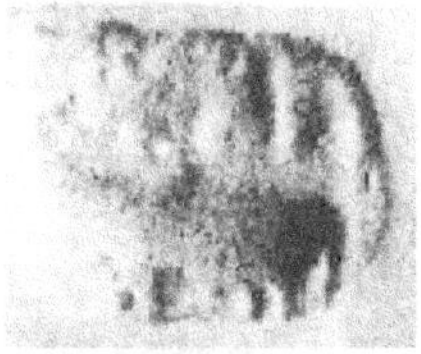
m2035d

m2036A

m2036F

m2037A

m2038F
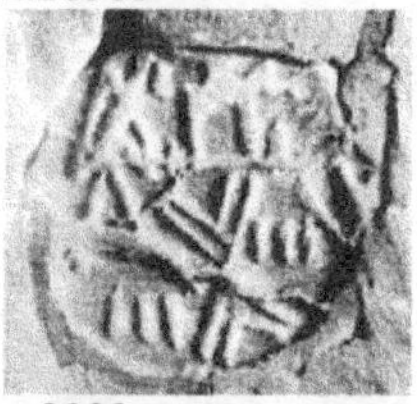
m2039a
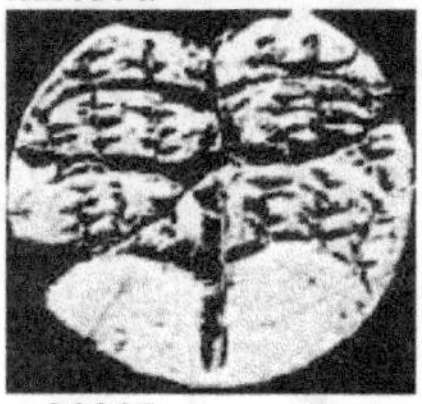
m2039B

m2040a

m2040b

m2041a

m2041b

m2042A

m2042B

m2044B

m2045A

m2045B

m2046A

m2046B

m2047A

m2047B

m2048A

m2048B

m2049A

m2049B

m2050A

m2050B

m2053A

m2053B

m2054A

m2054B

m2055A

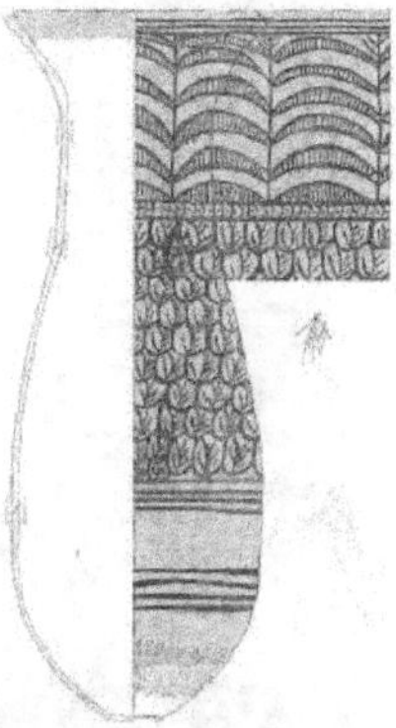
m2059A

m2060A

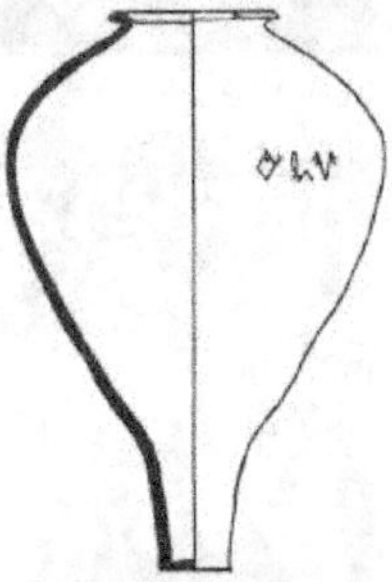
m2060A1+2

m2060b

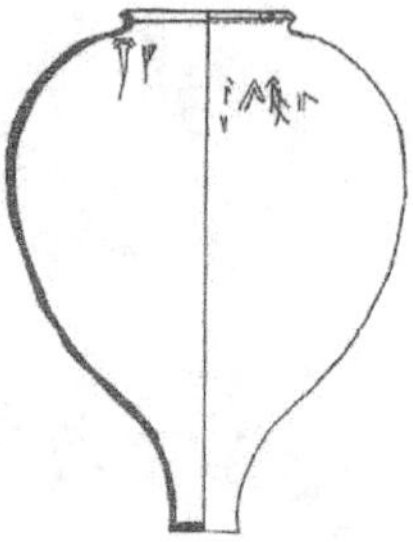
m2061A1+2

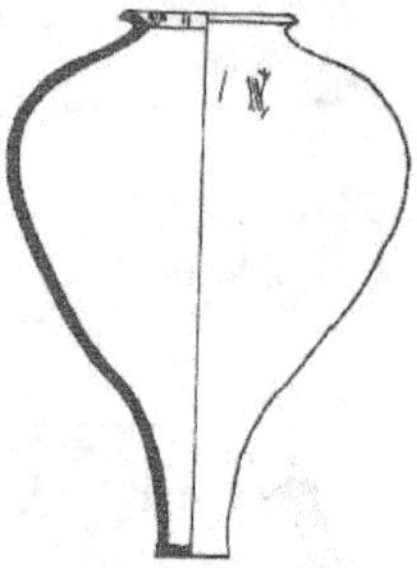
m2062A1+2

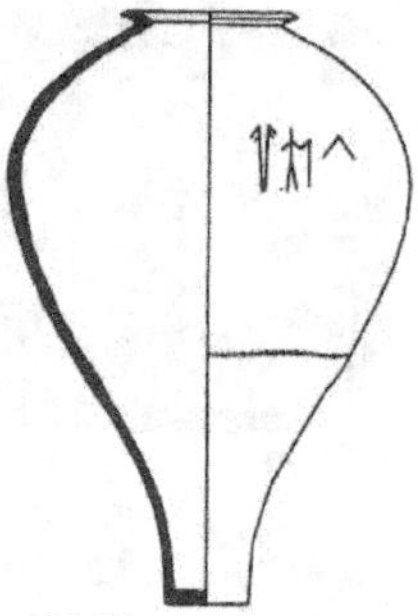
m2063

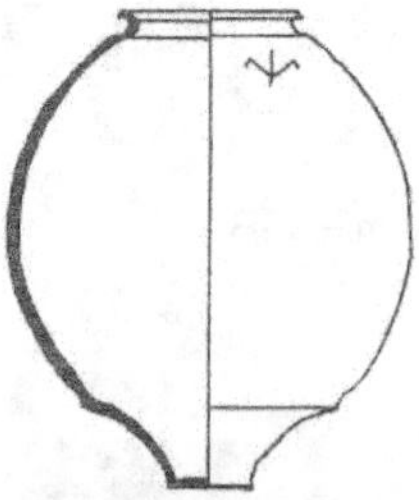
m2065

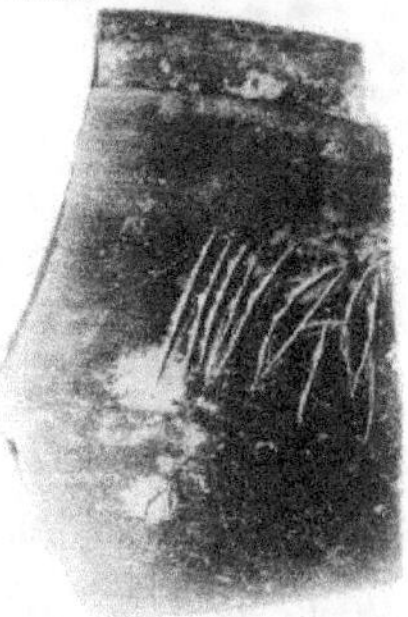
m2065

m2078

m2079

m2080

m2086

m2089A

m2089BC

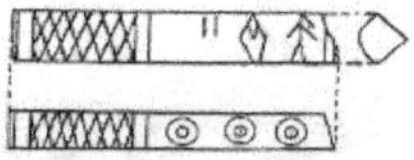
m2090

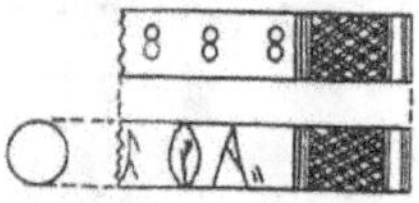
m2091

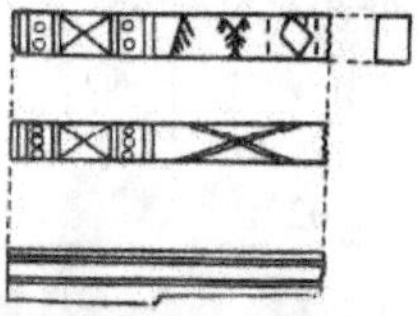
m2092

m2093

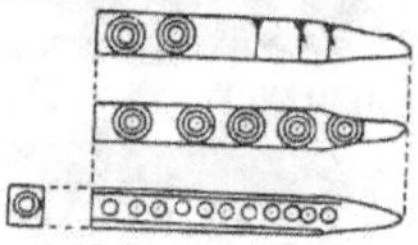
m2094

m2094A

m2095

m2096

m2097a

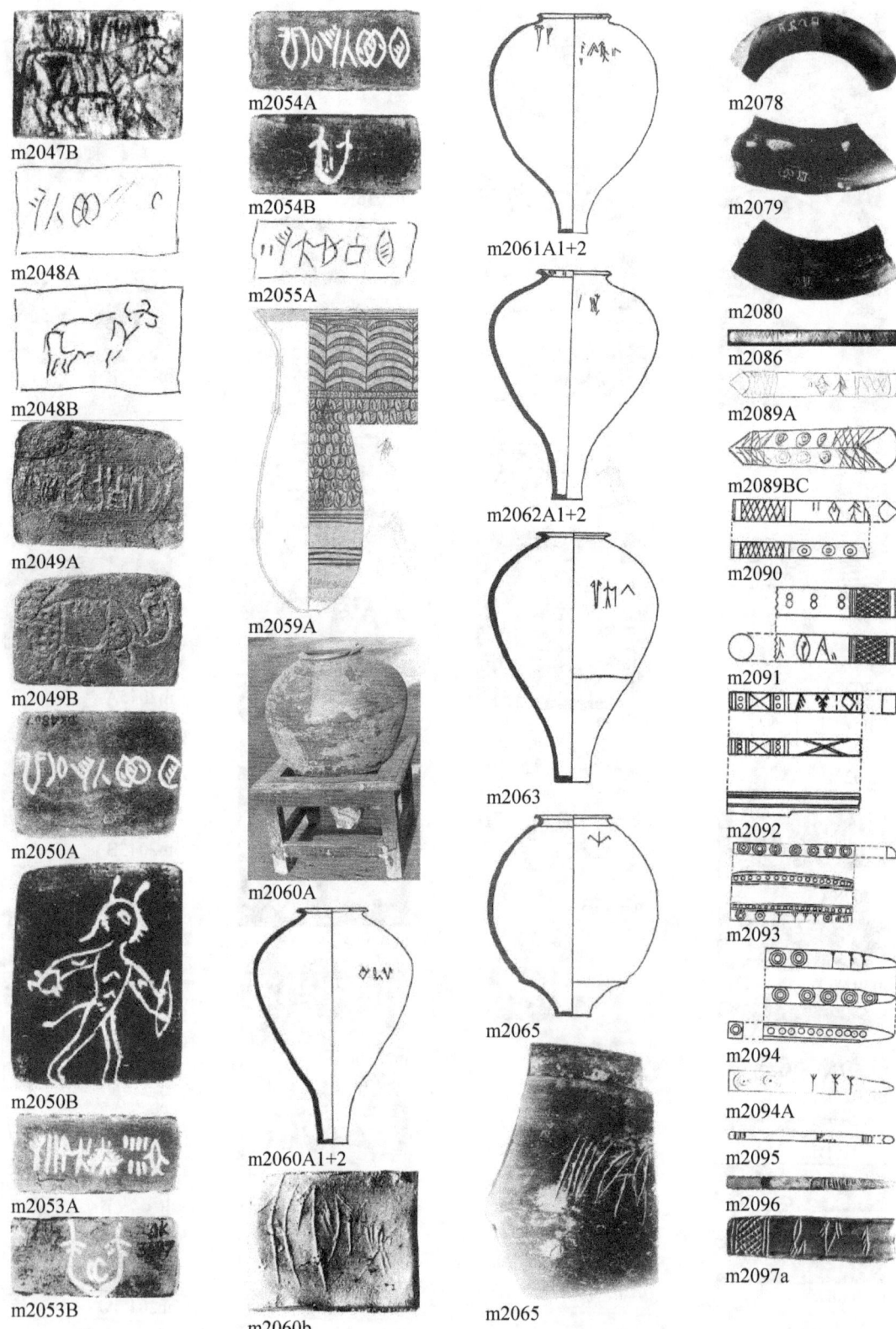

m2098a

m2099

m2102a

m2103a

m2104a

m2105

m2106D

m2107a

m2108a

m2109a

m2110

m2111

m2112a

m2113ABD

m2114

m2115

m2116
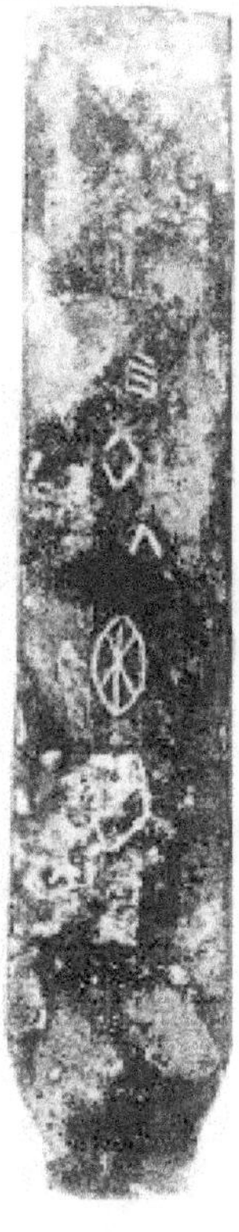

m2118a

m2118B

m2121A

m2121B
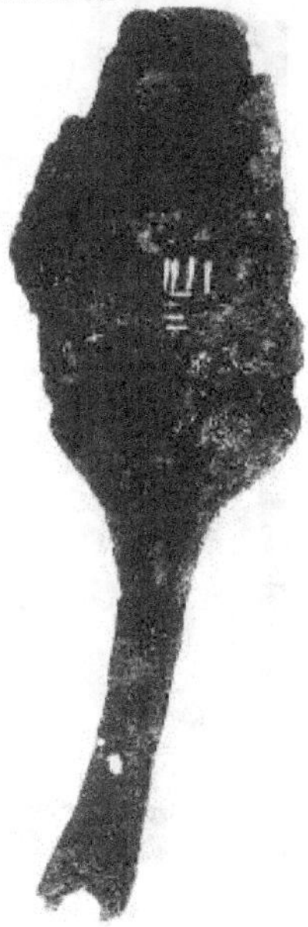
m2123

m2124

m2125

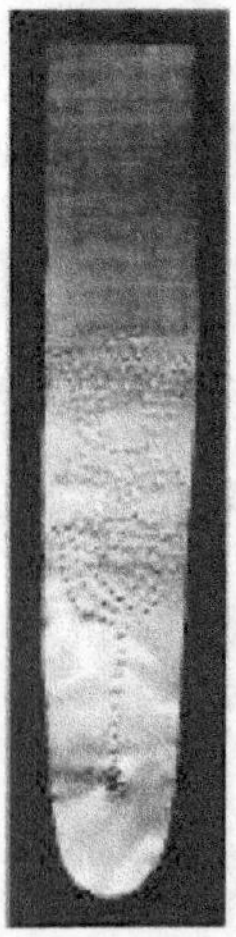

m2125A1

m2128A1

m2129A1

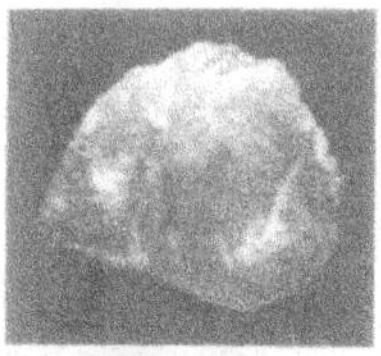

M-2131 A

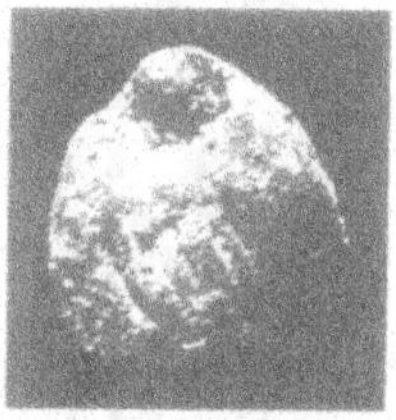

M-2131 B

Photograph from ASI: Sindh series Photo archive of ASI, Janpath, New Delhi. Si. 5:6639, 5:6640. Rattle? Bulla?

Mohenjodaro Texts either not illustrated or not linked with inscribed objects:

1002

1003

1020

1036

1041

1043 1044

1045

1049

1053

1055

1065

1070

1072

1074

1077

1079

1083

1088

1094

1101

1103

1106

1116

1117

1125

1130

1429

m1651Aivory stick

m1651D

m1651F

2947

1132

1133

1134

1136

1137

1141

1142

1154

1157

1159

1162

1172

1173

1174

1179

1183
1190
1198
1199
1200
1201
1207
1209
1212
1213
1215
1217
1220
1225
1226
1229
1231
1235
1237
1243
1244
1246
1248
1253
1254
1255
1257
1260
1261
1266
1269

1270
1272
1273
1274
1278
1279
1285
1286
1289
1305
1314
1318
1320
1323
1330
zebu bull
1338
1345
1346
1347
1350
1365
1366
1372
1407
1411
1419

1420
1424
1425
1427
1435
1436
1441
1448
1451
1453
1457
1467
1468
1480
1484
1486
1490
1491
1527
1529
1530
1531
1532
1533
1538
1541
1549

1550
1554
1558
1561
1563
1602
1604
1609
1610
1611
1613
1616
1622
1628
1704
1707
1802
1806
1813
1902
1903
2005
2007

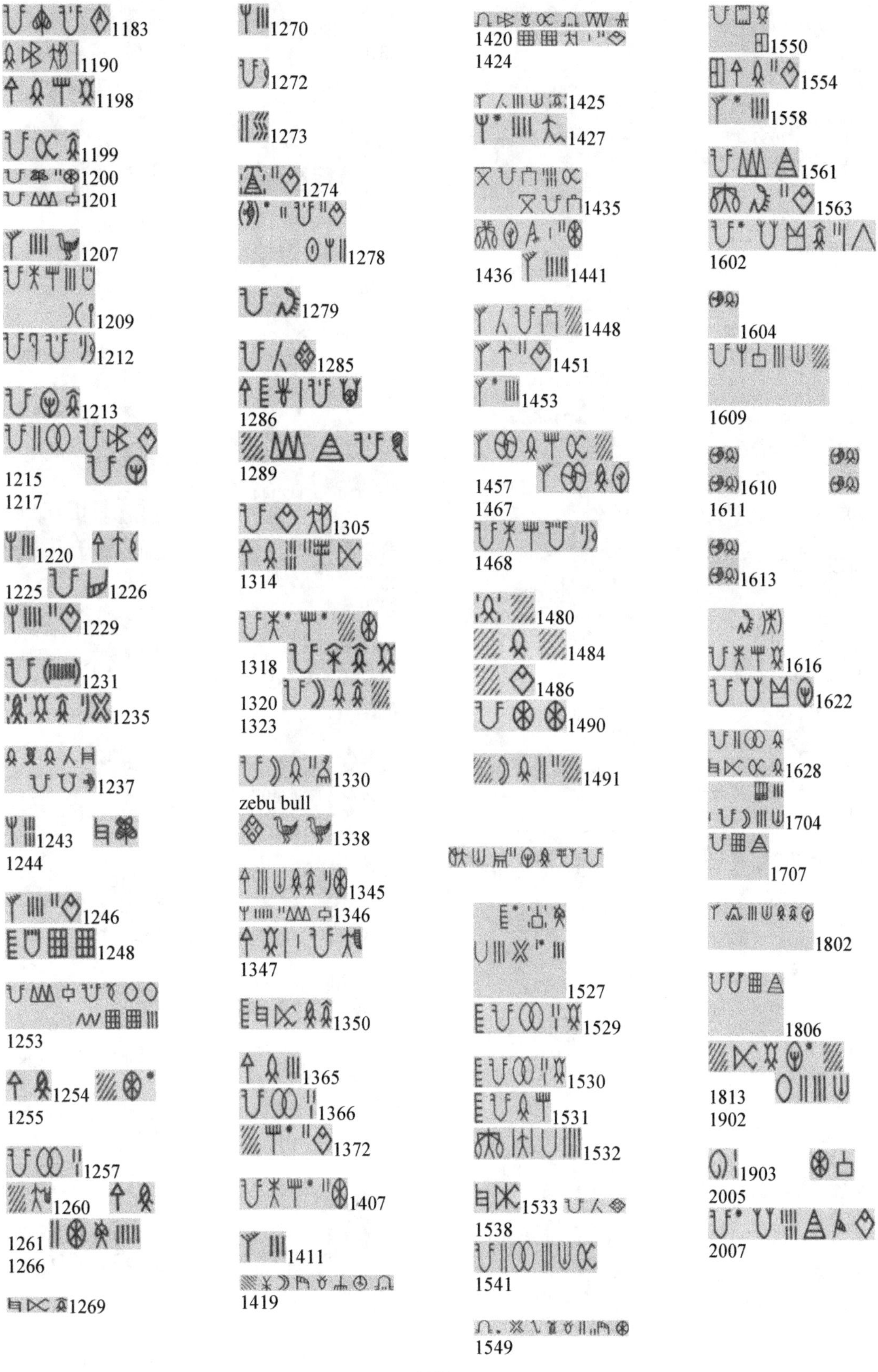

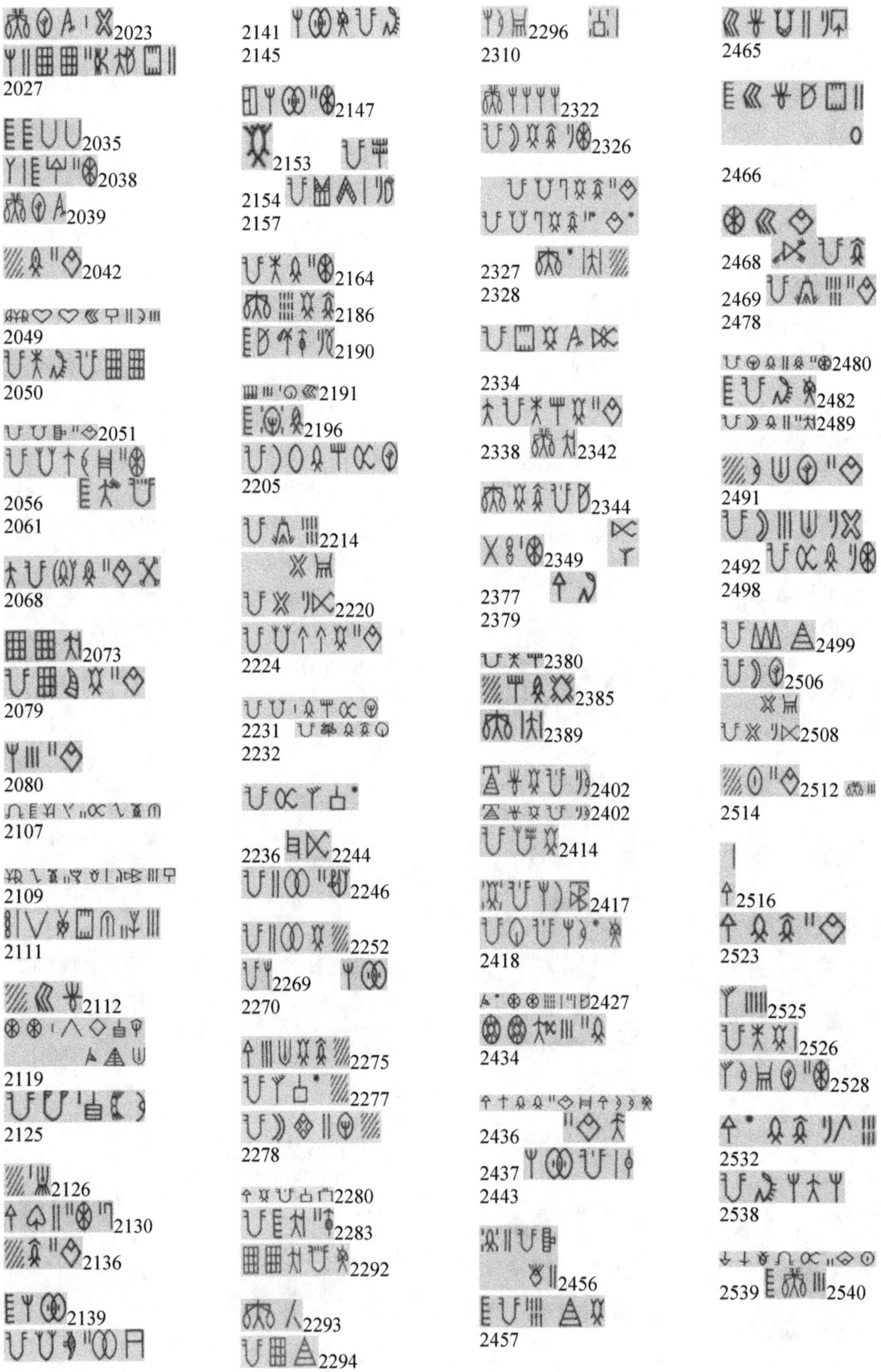
2023
2027
2035
2038
2039
2042
2049
2050
2051
2056
2061
2068
2073
2079
2080
2107
2109
2111
2112
2119
2125
2126
2130
2136
2139
2141
2145
2147
2153
2154
2157
2164
2186
2190
2191
2196
2205
2214
2220
2224
2231
2232
2236
2244
2246
2252
2269
2270
2275
2277
2278
2280
2283
2292
2293
2294
2296
2310
2322
2326
2327
2328
2334
2338
2342
2344
2349
2377
2379
2380
2385
2389
2402
2402
2414
2417
2418
2427
2434
2436
2437
2443
2456
2457
2465
2466
2468
2469
2478
2480
2482
2489
2491
2492
2498
2499
2506
2508
2512
2514
2516
2523
2525
2526
2528
2532
2538
2539
2540

2541
2551

2552

2556
2560

2572
2580

2581

2583

2587

2588

2592

2596

2598
2600

2601

2602
2605
2608

2609

2611
2612

2613
2614

2618
2620
2632

2633
2636 2638

2639

2662
2664

2667

2677
2683

2684

2685
2692
2693

2695
2700
2705

2706

2808
2814

2820

2824

2831
2839

2849

2857

2858

2901
Incised copper tablet

2903 Incised copper tablet

2911 Incised copper tablets. Markhor.

2915

2923
Inscribed bronze implement (MIC Plate CXXVI-2)

2924
Inscribed bronze implement (MIC Plate CXXVI-3)

2925
Inscribed bronze implement (MIC Plate CXXVI-5)

2926
Inscribed bronze implement (MIC Plate CXXVII-1)

2928
Inscribed bronze implement (MIC Plate CXXXIII-1)

2929 Incised on pottery

2930 Graffiti on pottery

2931 Graffiti on pottery

2934 Graffiti on pottery

2935 Graffiti on pottery

2936 Graffiti on pottery

2937 Seal impression on pot

2938Mohenjodaro, Pottery graffiti. Boat.

2940 Ivory or bone rod

2941 Ivory or bone rod Geometrical patterns followed by inscription.

2944
Ivory or bone rod

2945 Ivory or bone rod

2947

2949 Dotted circles

2950

2951

3001

3002

3010

3016

3019

3021

3023

3024

3035

3038

3042

3044

3051

3052

3056

3063

3064

3067

3069

3080

3090

3094

3096

3098 3099

3114

3123

3151

3153

3154

3155

3156

3162

3165

3202

3203

3206

3207

3217

3218

3222

3226

3238

3307

3309

3310

3318

3325

3326

3328

3343

3354

3362

3367

3374

3376

3385

3388

3390

3393

3395

3401

3405

3501

3502

3503

3504

3506

3507 3508

3509

3510

3511

3512 3513

Nindowari-damb01

 Squirrel sign

Nindowari-damb02

Nindowari-damb03

Nausharo01

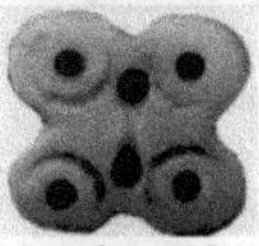

Nausharo02

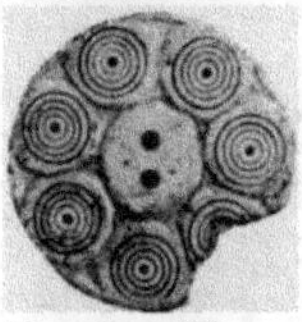

Nausharo03

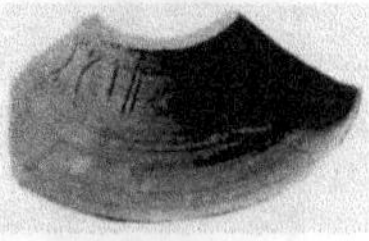

Nausharo04

Nausharo05

Nausharo06

Nausharo07

Nausharo08

Nausharo09

Nausharo10

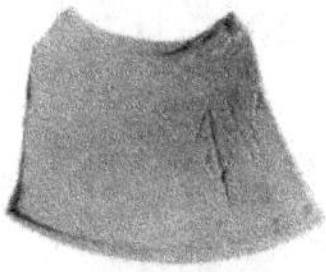

Naro-Waro-dharo01

Naro-Waro-dharo02

Naro-Waro-dharo03

Pabumath

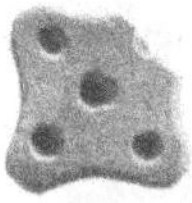

Prabhas Patan (Somnath) 1A

Prabhas Patan (Somnath)1B

Pirak1

Pirak12

Pirak13

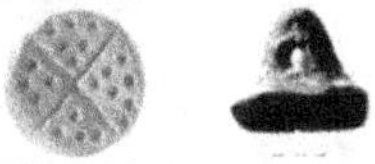

Pirak15

Pirak16

Pirak17

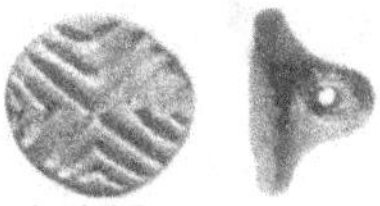

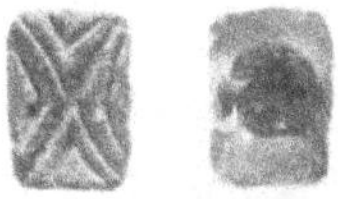

Pirak18

Pirak18A

Pirak19

Pirak2

Pirak20

Pirak24

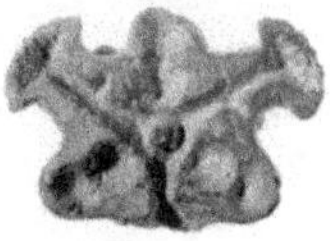

Pirak26Ac

Pirak27

Pirak28

Pirak35

Pirak38

Pirak3 post-harappan

Pirak40

Pirak4

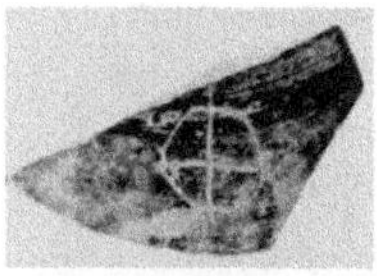

Rangpur

Rakhigarhi1

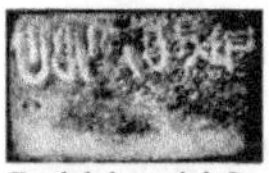

Rakhigarhi 2

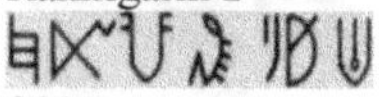

9111

Rakhigarhi 65

Rahman-dheri01A

Rahman-dheri01B

Rahman-dheri120

Rahman-dheri126

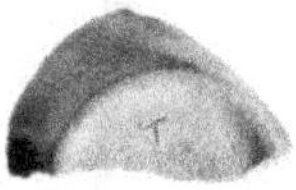

Rahman-dheri127

Rahman-dheri150

Rahman-dheri153

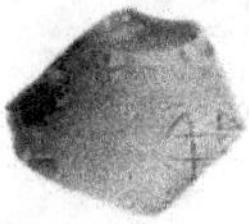

Rahman-dheri156

Rahman-dheri158

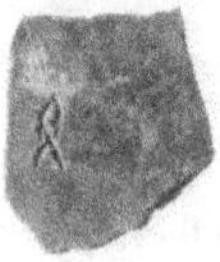

Rahman-dheri216

Rahman-dheri241

Rahman-dheri242

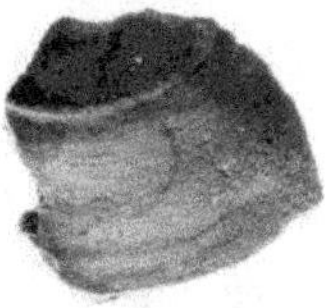

Rahman-dheri243

Rahman-dheri254

Rahman-dheri255

Rahman-dheri257

Rahman-dheri258

Rahman-dheri259

Rahman-dheri260

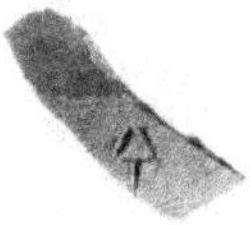

Rahman-dheri90

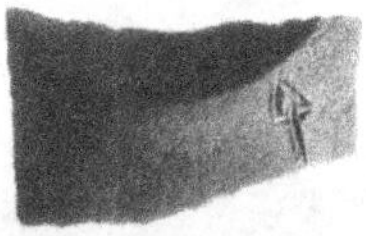

Rahman-dheri92

Rohira1

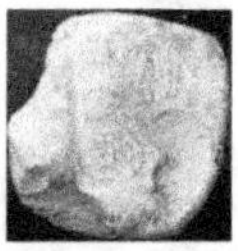

Rohira2

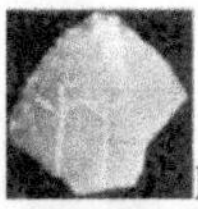

Rojdi

9041

9042

Rupar1A

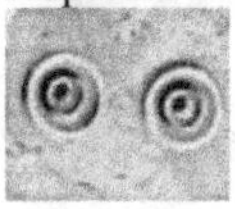

Rupar1B

9021

9022

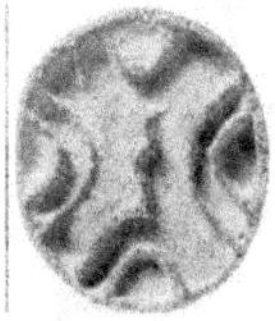

Shahi-tump

Sibri-damb01A

Sibri-damb01B

Sibri-damb02a

Sibri-damb02E

Sibri-damb03a

sibri cylinder seal zebu

Surkotada1

9091

Surkotada 2

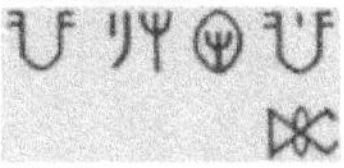

9092

Surkotada3c

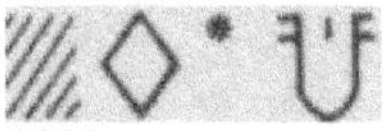

9093

Surkotada 4
9094

Surkotada 6

9095

Surkotada 7

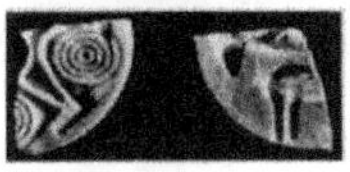

Tarkhanewala-dera1AB

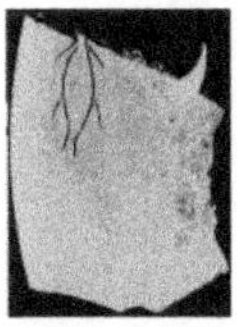

Tarkhanewala-dera 3

9031

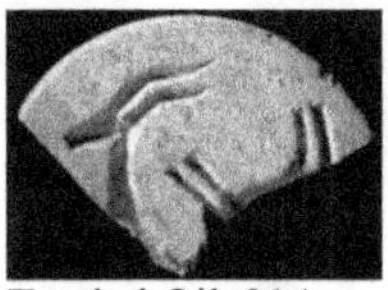

Tarakai Qila01A

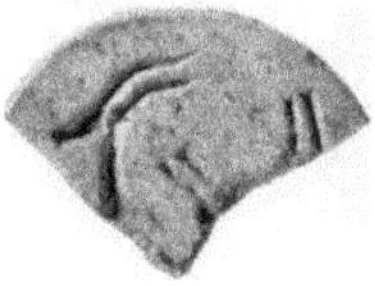

Tarakai Qila01B

Tarakai Qila02

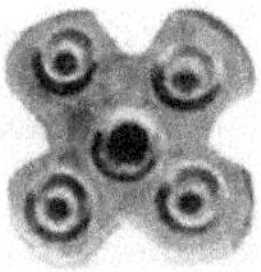

Tarakai Qila03

Tarakai Qila04

Tarakai Qila06

(provenance)
unkn01

Lakhonjodaro

unkn02

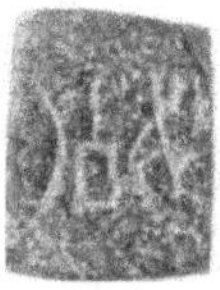

*****

unkn03

unkn04 unkn05A
unkn06

Seau l'nde. Musee des Arts Asiatique, Guimet, France

Mohenjo-daro. Copper tablet DK 11307 (SC 63.10/262).

Mohenjodaro; limestone; Mackay, 1938, p. 344, Pl. LXXXIX:376.

Mohenjodaro; Pale yellow enstatite; Mackay 1938, pp. 344-5; Pl. XCVI:488; Collon, 1987, Fig. 607.

Rakhigarhi: Cylinder Seal (ASI), Lizard or gharial?

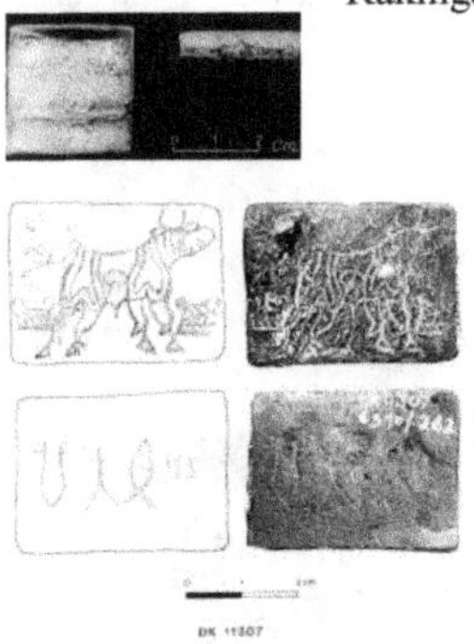

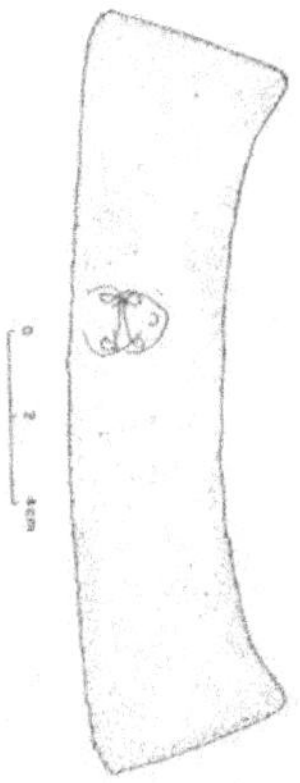

Rojdi. Ax-head or knife of copper, 17.4 cm. long (After Possehl and Raval 1989: 162, fig. 77

m0355

2654

m0359

2325

m0369

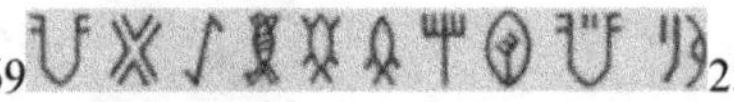
2537

m0391

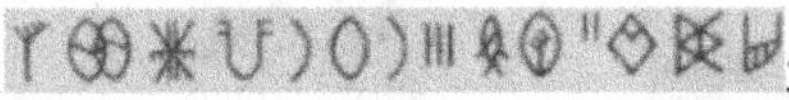
310

agate, 180
Akkadian, 64, 65, 174, 210, 241, 253, 259, 263, 272, 295, 298, 317, 318
alligator, 309, 392, 397
allograph, 174, 237, 395, 399
alloy, 6, 8, 9, 13, 29, 52, 55, 66, 87, 99, 100, 101, 109, 119, 129, 130, 139, 152, 153, 154, 155, 156, 162, 165, 166, 167, 168, 176, 196, 197, 198, 202, 212, 214, 215, 216, 221, 222, 227, 236, 237, 241, 259, 266, 267, 282, 285, 289, 290, 291, 295, 302, 303, 311, 322, 324, 330, 332, 335, 348, 394, 395, 397
alloying, 64, 83, 166, 293, 318
amśu, 237, 239, 240
ancu, 6, 240
antelope, 3, 25, 121, 168, 173, 174, 195, 241, 285, 287, 288, 289, 292, 293, 295, 309, 329, 410, 411, 412, 429, 499, 500, 524, 525, 526, 530, 538, 561, 563, 571, 573
antimony, 309
Anzu, 240, 282
archer, 27, 112, 150, 159, 199, 223, 224, 226, 322, 325, 540
arrow, 25, 26, 27, 159, 201, 210, 214, 237, 239, 330, 338, 394, 395, 540
arsenic, 83, 252, 274, 318, 381
artifact, 157, 297, 298, 313
artifacts, 403, 404
artisan, 8, 9, 28, 30, 66, 77, 98, 99, 101, 120, 128, 138, 172, 180, 195, 201, 206, 209, 214, 218, 219, 235, 243, 267, 288, 298, 312, 397
awl, 82
axe, 3, 31, 111, 131, 132, 170, 200, 209, 220, 303, 379, 381, 382, 411, 426, 432, 451, 457, 494, 540
ayas, 120, 149, 169, 181, 196, 197, 198, 200, 201, 203, 204, 206, 213, 214, 215, 216, 217, 226, 235, 237, 238, 239, 240, 268, 271, 272, 296, 307, 309, 330, 395, 399
ayo, 238, 296, 307, 309, 324
backbone, 27, 100, 122, 165, 196, 197, 198, 214, 215, 221, 291, 312
bangle, 44, 47, 404, 409, 576
beads, 10, 27, 37, 47, 154, 172, 210, 273, 293, 297, 345, 350, 406
bell-metal, 4
bird, 85, 117, 135, 136, 137, 141, 146, 178, 192, 236, 240, 241, 274, 282, 283, 284, 296, 301, 319, 320, 379, 397, 479, 500, 571
Bisht, 105, 414
bison, 139, 140, 422, 499, 530, 535, 561, 563, 569, 571
blacksmith, 13, 14, 28, 52, 55, 59, 63, 87, 96, 99, 119, 121, 123, 128, 138, 139, 140, 148, 172, 179, 199, 202, 205, 212, 213, 215, 216, 218, 222, 230, 232, 234, 239, 241, 243, 268, 272, 284, 285, 295, 298, 312, 318, 326, 336, 397
boar, 192, 358, 359, 379, 380, 381, 383, 392, 393, 394
boat, 99, 197, 220, 227, 338, 358, 396, 397, 399
body, 11, 15, 54, 63, 98, 103, 109, 117, 121, 125, 127, 159, 160, 161, 162, 163, 164, 165, 169, 171, 175, 179, 182, 192, 194, 196, 202, 204, 209, 210, 214, 217, 219, 253, 263, 267, 283, 288, 295, 300, 303, 325, 331, 345, 379, 391, 392, 393, 398, 401, 411, 499,500, 525, 526, 534, 538, 561, 562, 571, 574
bos gaurus, 139
bos indicus, 122, 140, 146
bovine, 62, 84, 85, 86, 119, 122, 289, 411, 422, 434, 447, 494, 540, 562, 564
brass, 4, 34, 100, 101, 102, 129, 131, 160, 164, 178, 197, 203, 204, 213, 220, 223, 230, 231, 232, 233, 241, 252, 259, 263, 267, 282, 283, 288, 296, 318, 324, 325, 332, 335
brazier, 4, 9, 51, 100, 117, 131, 200, 201, 203, 204, 205, 206, 210, 211, 213, 214, 215, 216, 217, 219, 226, 231, 286, 291, 295, 296
bronze, 3, 6, 25, 33, 60, 77, 83, 100, 101, 102, 112, 123, 129, 130, 145, 149, 157, 161, 164, 169, 170, 178, 182, 189, 202, 203, 204, 206, 207, 212, 213, 215, 217, 219, 222, 223, 230, 231, 234, 237, 240, 252, 253, 275, 288, 289, 292, 293, 297, 298, 307, 310, 318, 334, 338, 381, 402, 404, 595
buffalo, 28, 62, 63, 121, 139, 140, 141, 211, 283, 284, 296, 330, 524, 525, 526, 571

bull, 4, 28, 31, 84, 100, 119, 121, 140, 141, 168, 175, 176, 209, 210, 215, 219, 227, 230, 233, 234, 241, 242, 263, 283, 288, 290, 295, 296, 297, 298, 299, 300, 301, 302, 317, 325, 326, 334, 335, 336, 405, 410, 411, 419, 422, 426, 428, 443, 447, 451, 494, 499,516, 522, 525, 530, 534, 535, 539, 542, 547, 552, 555, 556, 561, 571, 593
bush, 26
carnelian, 180, 273
carpenter, 100, 237
cast, 83, 85, 87
casting, 8, 64, 82, 100, 101, 149, 161, 164, 195, 196, 199, 202, 203, 206, 215, 218, 223, 284, 293, 309, 312, 358, 379
cipher, 3, 4, 40, 65, 81, 82, 93, 146, 166, 210, 227, 241, 253, 302
citadel, 85, 414
comb, 9, 295, 301
community, 64, 77, 119, 148, 200, 209, 253, 292, 293
composite animal, 87, 119, 289, 534
conch, 43, 44, 45, 47, 48
copper, 3, 6, 8, 9, 13, 25, 28, 39, 64, 65, 66, 77, 78, 81, 83, 87, 88, 91, 93, 94, 95, 97, 98, 99, 100, 101, 102, 111, 112, 119, 121, 128, 129, 131, 132, 138, 140, 143, 146, 147, 149, 150, 151, 153, 154, 155, 156, 157, 160, 161, 162, 164, 165, 166, 167, 168, 170, 174, 175, 176, 181, 184, 185, 189, 195, 196, 197, 198, 199, 200, 201, 202, 203, 204, 205, 206, 207, 210, 212, 213, 214, 215, 216, 219, 220, 221, 222, 223, 224, 225, 226, 227, 228, 229, 230, 231, 232, 233, 234, 237, 241, 243, 252, 258, 259, 260, 262, 263, 266, 267, 272, 273, 275, 277, 278, 282, 283, 284, 285, 288, 289, 290, 291, 295, 298, 302, 303, 305, 306, 307, 308, 312, 313, 318, 319, 320, 321, 322, 324, 325, 326, 329, 330, 331, 332, 334, 335, 337, 345, 351, 394, 397, 399, 400, 404, 405, 526, 562, 572, 573, 595, 600
copulation, 172, 411
crab, 149, 150, 159, 198, 199, 200, 201, 202, 204, 216, 223, 224, 227, 228, 423
crocodile, 28, 138, 140, 268, 297, 298, 302, 396, 397, 399
crucible, 63, 91, 272, 322, 324, 329, 353, 354, 357
currycomb, 130
curve, 164, 203, 204, 206, 207, 212, 219, 223
curved, 55, 84, 101, 102, 120, 164, 196, 199, 212, 213, 215, 226, 236, 296, 307, 346
dagger, 131, 188, 322, 435
dance, 13, 51, 55, 59, 60, 61, 64, 81, 112, 114, 128, 163, 346
deer, 121, 173, 199, 213, 288
dhokra, 312
Dilmun, 183, 275, 281, 292, 293, 297
dotted circle, 13, 14, 15, 20, 210, 289, 293, 297, 351, 406, 426, 433, 451, 561, 576
drill, 12, 505
drum, 3, 22, 100, 129, 165, 324, 338
duck, 180, 236, 237, 397
eagle, 82, 135, 243, 250, 252, 256, 262, 263, 266, 267, 274, 277, 282, 283, 345, 351, 379
Egyptian, 84, 85
electrum, 83, 240
eraka, 99, 101, 138, 160, 202, 213, 230, 241, 252, 262, 282, 289, 303, 324, 325, 330, 332, 333, 334, 335
Failaka, 183, 242, 293
ficus glomerata, 202, 226, 227, 229, 230, 231, 234
ficus religiosa, 118, 163, 230, 234, 341, 352
fin, 237, 530
fish, 9, 82, 96, 104, 117, 141, 149, 169, 171, 181, 194, 196, 197, 198, 200, 201, 203, 204, 206, 213, 214, 215, 216, 217, 218, 219, 226, 227, 229, 232, 235, 236, 237, 238, 239, 272, 288, 294, 295, 296, 302, 307, 308, 309, 311, 317, 318, 319, 320, 324, 327, 330, 395, 396, 397, 399, 411, 419, 422, 426, 432, 455, 479, 494, 530, 534, 571
flag, 92, 164, 182, 215, 217, 218, 256, 272, 273, 301, 318, 322, 324, 331
forge, 3, 13, 14, 64, 81, 87, 99, 105, 121, 123, 129, 130, 139, 149, 164, 165, 169, 179, 196, 197, 198, 200, 201, 202, 203, 204, 206, 207, 210, 211, 212, 213, 214, 215, 216, 218, 219, 222, 241, 243, 259, 275, 282, 285, 288, 291, 295, 296, 318, 322, 325, 329, 334, 335, 399
fox, 232
furnace, 9, 13, 14, 27, 29, 59, 60
Gadd, 407

gimlet, 210, 334, 335
gloss, 61, 81, 111, 119, 120, 121, 138, 141, 146, 165, 222, 226, 235, 237, 240, 241, 253, 254, 263, 268, 271, 297, 298, 318, 321, 330, 395
glosses, 403, 404
glyph, 82, 87, 403
glyptic, 403
goat, 3, 29, 77, 102, 134, 162, 205, 210, 213, 222, 231, 273, 275, 284, 285, 295, 307, 311, 342, 356, 411, 423, 571
gold, 4, 10, 21, 83, 101, 105, 112, 115, 121, 146, 149, 156, 157, 169, 192, 193, 194, 199, 232, 233, 240, 284, 293, 294, 297, 301, 313, 322, 325, 342, 345, 354, 358, 380, 397
guild, 6, 119, 181, 209, 211, 213, 214, 215, 217, 233, 286, 292, 333, 334, 335
Haifa, 4, 6, 80, 123, 173, 174, 184, 288, 294, 317, 338
hare, 213, 423
harrow, 162, 206, 216, 295
hieroglyphic, 85, 86
hieroglyphs, 85
hill, 176, 205, 211, 215, 231, 259, 274, 286, 301
hood, 87, 119, 122, 139, 140, 148, 210, 318, 322, 323
horn, 9, 12, 87, 96, 101, 118, 172, 182, 196, 209, 216, 217, 218, 219, 226, 227, 235, 288, 290, 296, 325, 326
horns, 84
ibex, 111, 288, 294, 381
implements, 66, 77, 81, 91, 122, 132, 159, 168, 169, 172, 176, 181, 196, 197, 201, 202, 205, 206, 209, 210, 211, 214, 215, 217, 218, 219, 230, 233, 234, 259, 268, 282, 286, 329, 330, 395
ingot, 8, 9, 13, 54, 99, 103, 109, 119, 120, 121, 129, 140, 149, 163, 164, 165, 167, 174, 176, 177, 180, 182, 196, 198, 201, 202, 203, 204, 206, 210, 212, 213, 216, 218, 237, 259, 260, 288, 296, 314, 324, 331, 345, 397, 398, 399
iron, 6, 7, 9, 10, 13, 19, 25, 26, 28, 29, 33, 34, 39, 54, 55, 60, 61, 63, 64, 66, 85, 87, 88, 95, 96, 97, 98, 99, 100, 101, 102, 103, 111, 112, 114, 119, 120, 121, 122, 126, 127, 128, 129, 130, 131, 138, 139, 140, 148, 149, 152, 157, 159, 161, 162, 163, 164, 167, 169, 179, 181, 196, 197, 198, 199, 200, 201, 202, 203, 204, 205, 206, 209, 211, 212, 213, 214, 215, 216, 217, 218, 219, 222, 226, 227, 229, 230, 231, 232, 233, 234, 235, 236, 237, 238, 239, 240, 241, 242, 243, 253, 254, 258, 259, 260, 262, 266, 267, 268, 270, 271, 272, 282, 285, 286, 288, 291, 295, 296, 298, 304, 307, 309, 311, 314, 316, 318, 321, 322, 323, 325, 326, 330, 331, 345, 346, 350, 351, 353, 357, 358, 394, 395, 397, 398, 399
iron ore, 159, 161, 179, 241, 253, 267, 268, 270, 271, 350
jackal, 99, 124, 139, 282
jar, 9, 27, 53, 99, 102, 128, 160, 170, 177, 182, 200, 201, 203, 204, 206, 211, 213, 214, 215, 216, 217, 219, 240, 241, 242, 243, 274, 286, 289, 291, 313, 318, 319, 320, 534, 562
Kalyanaraman, 2, 166, 173
kamaḍha, 99, 159, 198, 201, 204, 234, 325
Kenoyer, 40, 43, 47, 48, 123, 140, 147, 154, 155, 156, 169, 170, 174, 185, 187, 194, 404, 406
ladder, 292, 295, 339
lapidaries, 403
lapidary, 403
lapis lazuli, 156, 172, 180, 273, 300
lathe, 4, 31, 129, 130, 172, 209, 210, 215, 219, 227, 231, 233, 234, 317, 332, 334, 335, 351
leafless tree, 9, 138
ligature, 21, 60, 61, 104, 164, 165, 226, 228, 237, 307, 411, 443
lion, 82, 117, 176, 241, 250, 259, 262, 263, 267, 277, 282, 380
logo-semantic, 404
Mackay, 77, 167, 170, 175, 189, 410, 411, 412, 599
Magan, 303
makara, 307, 309
Marshall, 12, 169, 194
mason, 100, 234, 334
Meluhha, 3, 6, 13, 27, 31, 40, 63, 64, 65, 66, 77, 81, 95, 111, 120, 121, 126, 128, 129, 130, 131, 138, 157, 166, 173, 174, 181, 184, 210, 222, 227, 233, 241, 253, 254, 271, 292, 293, 296, 302, 306, 310, 318, 321, 329, 333, 334, 335, 336, 396, 397, 403

merchant, 29, 30, 77, 91, 119, 121, 125, 163, 165, 172, 174, 187, 216, 231, 295, 297, 298, 307, 311, 312, 358, 397
metal, 83, 85, 87, 403
metals, 100
metalsmith, 83, 176, 202, 234, 335
mineral, 4, 13, 52, 53, 55, 85, 97, 101, 109, 119, 122, 159, 169, 173, 174, 198, 199, 200, 204, 209, 210, 211, 226, 227, 240, 241, 242, 243, 252, 254, 260, 262, 263, 267, 271, 284, 285, 289, 296, 329, 334, 335, 348, 351
mine-worker, 403
mleccha, 6, 31, 60, 64, 65, 66, 77, 81, 112, 119, 120, 128, 222, 231, 233, 295, 399, 400
monkey, 241
mould, 100
mountain, 164, 176, 177, 205, 211, 215, 218, 231, 240, 241, 242, 243, 286, 288, 296, 301, 307, 329
Muhly, 83
Munda, 26, 28, 54, 55, 60, 95, 102, 103, 111, 112, 119, 121, 130, 163, 164, 197, 235, 236, 238, 258, 282, 307, 320, 321, 325, 330, 332, 335, 345, 346, 351
Narmer, 82, 83, 84, 85
native metal, 99, 120, 138, 140, 160, 162, 216, 226, 237, 238, 268, 293
neck, 10, 27, 119, 121, 192, 209, 210, 219, 234, 279, 325, 326, 329, 411, 499, 522, 524, 525, 545, 562
numeral, 131, 194, 222, 253, 325
ore, 7, 8, 13, 27, 28, 95, 96, 97, 98, 101, 119, 138, 149, 159, 163, 173, 179, 197, 198, 199, 200, 203, 204, 211, 216, 221, 226, 227, 230, 232, 234, 237, 238, 239, 240, 241, 242, 243, 252, 260, 267, 268, 271, 274, 282, 284, 296, 297, 307, 325, 334, 351, 353, 354
oval, 182, 206, 218, 380, 410
overthrow, 393
pectoral, 405
penance, 99, 102, 119, 120, 140
Persian Gulf, 4, 91, 183, 273, 292, 294, 353, 406
pewter, 8, 9, 29, 64, 66, 100, 101, 121, 138, 140, 167, 168, 196, 197, 198, 203, 204, 210, 211, 212, 213, 214, 215, 221, 222, 223, 290, 291, 295, 312
phonetic, 84, 85
pictorial motif, 403
platform, 29, 52, 105, 145, 178, 181, 185, 187, 197, 231, 357, 423, 424, 525, 534, 535, 562, 571
Possehl, 146, 151, 600
Prakrit, 99, 291
present, 3, 12, 91, 135, 136, 147, 149, 176, 253, 295, 404, 405
Przyluski, 127
punch-marked, 4, 123, 128, 177, 181
ram, 29, 83, 87, 101, 102, 111, 120, 121, 138, 165, 174, 213, 214, 288, 295, 297, 298, 307, 309, 311, 312, 423, 525, 534, 539, 562
rebus, 84, 288, 403
rhinoceros, 145, 181, 211, 217, 218, 268, 286, 354, 395, 525, 560, 569, 571, 574
Rigveda, 5, 66, 81, 105, 113, 114, 120, 121, 169, 222, 239, 241, 263, 268, 272, 298, 330, 346, 353, 356, 399, 400
rim of jar, 9, 27, 99, 102, 122, 160, 167, 177, 182, 196, 197, 198, 200, 201, 203, 204, 205, 206, 211, 213, 214, 215, 216, 217, 219, 241, 286, 288, 291, 313, 326, 398
rimless pot, 60, 98, 162, 163, 165, 176, 178, 204, 206, 207, 212, 213, 215, 216, 218, 228
road, 4, 40, 53, 169, 331
safflower, 332, 336
Sarasvati, 2, 3, 5, 6, 7, 13, 30, 37, 38, 39, 40, 64, 66, 77, 78, 81, 89, 91, 93, 102, 105, 112, 114, 142, 146, 147, 165, 166, 173, 176, 181, 184, 233, 241, 253, 298, 302, 353, 354, 359, 383, 391, 400, 404, 406
Sarasvati river basin, 404
scarf, 85, 101, 119, 122, 165, 327, 329, 334, 335, 354
scribe, 9, 27, 30, 31, 35, 36, 102, 128, 160, 167, 181, 196, 200, 201, 203, 204, 205, 206, 211, 214, 215, 216, 217, 219, 241, 286, 288, 313, 326
serpent, 119, 139, 140, 272, 275, 317, 318, 322, 323, 324, 525, 532, 534, 535, 539, 562
shawl, 4, 11, 12, 15, 95
silver, 5, 21, 83, 112, 129, 130, 162, 166, 175, 180, 192, 199, 233, 236, 240, 252, 262, 266, 274, 278, 280, 291, 293, 322, 380, 381, 397

smelter, 13, 14, 40, 52, 54, 55, 87, 88, 96, 98, 99, 103, 104, 105, 113, 123, 130, 133, 138, 139, 140, 160, 177, 180, 204, 211, 212, 213, 215, 216, 218, 226, 259, 268, 275, 282, 293, 295, 297, 298, 314, 318, 325, 345, 346
smiths, 403
smithy, 3, 13, 55, 60, 64, 81, 87, 88, 99, 101, 104, 105, 121, 123, 128, 129, 130, 148, 164, 165, 169, 196, 197, 198, 200, 201, 202, 203, 204, 206, 207, 210, 211, 212, 213, 214, 215, 216, 218, 219, 222, 232, 233, 235, 241, 243, 254, 275, 285, 288, 291, 292, 295,296, 318, 322, 329, 333, 334, 379, 399, 404
spinner, 148
spokes, 160, 220, 332, 335
sprachbund, 6, 13, 66, 121, 123, 131, 149, 174, 210, 241, 253, 263, 282, 395, 400
spy, 99, 101, 138
stalk, 26, 199, 223, 231, 242
steel, 288
step, 403
stool, 29, 102, 119, 159, 258, 259
stump, 9, 179
substrate, 403
Sumer, 83, 121, 253, 261, 263, 317, 321
Sumerian, 42, 64, 82, 83, 86, 121, 231, 240, 251, 253, 321
summit, 164, 177, 301
Susa, 148, 235, 236, 262, 274, 292, 318, 319, 320
svastika, 95, 96, 222, 223, 289, 291, 406, 423, 534, 564
tablet, 7, 8, 9, 59, 86, 94, 95, 96, 97, 98, 99, 101, 102, 132, 139, 150, 151, 167, 169, 170, 180, 181, 185, 189, 201, 222, 223, 225, 274, 287, 334, 396, 397, 399, 404, 422, 426, 429, 432, 433, 494, 495, 570, 572, 595, 599
tail, 87, 96, 101, 104, 119, 122, 139, 285, 287, 288, 296, 380, 411, 412, 422, 429, 434, 447, 499, 500, 524, 525, 534, 538, 539, 562, 563, 564, 573
temple, 3, 7, 11, 13, 20, 21, 35, 51, 55, 56, 64, 81, 83, 86, 93, 101, 104, 105, 121, 123, 125, 128, 140, 141, 250, 266, 269, 280, 281, 300, 301, 302, 303, 318, 319, 320, 327, 332, 334, 343, 385, 390
Tepe Yahya, 130, 274, 382
terracotta, 87, 88, 94, 114, 122, 147, 157, 170, 180, 326, 345, 346, 403
tiger, 28, 64, 83, 86, 87, 88, 99, 119, 138, 157, 171, 215, 216, 222, 259, 282, 381, 411, 423, 499, 500, 525, 526, 530, 534, 539, 561, 562, 569
tin, 4, 6, 8, 9, 29, 30, 64, 66, 83, 98, 100, 101, 102, 112, 121, 123, 129, 138, 140, 156, 164, 165, 166, 167, 168, 172, 173, 174, 184, 196, 197, 198, 203, 204, 206, 207, 209, 210, 212, 213, 214, 215, 219, 221, 223, 241, 252, 267, 273, 285, 288, 290, 291, 292, 293, 294, 295, 296, 298, 309, 311, 312, 317, 318, 322, 381
Tocharian, 6, 240
trader, 231
tree, 7, 9, 13, 26, 40, 52, 54, 94, 98, 99, 103, 104, 105, 133, 138, 177, 180, 226, 228, 230, 231, 234, 238, 242, 259, 260, 293, 295, 301, 314, 332, 341, 342, 345, 352, 411, 423, 500, 525, 526, 534, 562, 568, 571
turner, 9, 98, 102, 129, 130, 138, 149, 162, 168, 204, 215, 227, 230, 231, 234, 236, 243, 267, 288, 290, 298, 299, 332, 334, 335
twig, 99, 101, 140, 179, 325, 423, 499
unsmelted metal, 9, 162, 182, 200, 206, 213, 217, 218, 268, 271
Uruk, 82, 84, 231
Vats, 53, 143, 186, 187, 189, 404, 407
Vedic, 85, 404
warehouse, 101, 220, 235, 329
Warka, 4, 318, 319, 320, 327
wing, 83, 237, 241, 252, 262, 282, 303
zebu, 119, 122, 138, 139, 140, 142, 146, 170, 189, 241, 242, 243, 259, 294, 295, 351, 512, 525, 534, 561, 562, 593, 598
zinc, 29, 66, 95, 96, 98, 100, 101, 138, 165, 196, 197, 198, 212, 214, 215, 221, 222, 223, 252, 267, 291, 312, 318, 330

---

[1] http://xoomer.virgilio.it/francescoraf/hesyra/palettes/narmerp.htm
[2] http://en.wikipedia.org/wiki/Narmer_Palette#cite_note-13

[3] http://www.nemo.nu/ibisportal/0egyptintro/2aegypt/index.htm
[4] Mallowan 1947; Crawford, op.cit., p. 134.
[5] Wilkinson, Toby A.H. *Early Dynastic Egypt*. p.6, Routledge, London. 1999.
[6] http://xoomer.virgilio.it/francescoraf/hesyra/palettes/narmerp.htm
[7] Brier, Bob. *Daily Life of the Ancient Egyptians*, A. Hoyt Hobbs 1999, p.202.
[8] http://en.wikipedia.org/wiki/Narmer_Palette#cite_note-13
[9] Wengrow, David, *The Archaeology of Ancient Egypt* Cambridge University Press.
[10] Janson, Horst Woldemar; Anthony F. Janson *History of Art: A Survey of the Major Visual Arts from the Dawn of History to the Present Day* Prentice Hall 1986.
[11] Breasted, , James Henry. *Ancient Records of Egypt*, Chicago 1906, part Two, §§ 143, 659, 853; part Three §§ 117, 144, 147, 285 etc.
[12] http://en.wikipedia.org/wiki/Narmer_Palette

[13] Donald P. Hansen, Erica Ehrenberg, 2002, *Leaving no stones unturned: essays on the ancient Near East and Egypt in honor of Donald P. Hansen*, Eisenbrauns, p.220.
[14] Originally published as fig. 368c in WIlliam Hayes Ward, *The Seal cylinders of Western Asia*, Washington 1910. Reprinted as fig. 3 under the heading *The Caduceus an the God Ningishzida* in A. L. Frothingham, *Babylonian Origin of Hermes the Snake-God, and of the Caduceus I*, American Journal of Archaeology, Vol. 20, No. 2 (Apr. - Jun., 1916), pp. 175-211 (p. 181). 1910 drawing of a vase of green steatite found at Telloh (Lagash), now ath the Louvre (De Sarzec, *Découvertes en Chaldée*, Paris 1883, pl. 44, fig. 2, pp. 234-236).
[15] V. Gordon Childe, 1929, *The most ancient East: the oriental prelude to European history*, London, Kegan Paul, Trench, Trubner and Co. Ltd., Fig. 72b.

[16] http://www.ling.hawaii.edu/faculty/stampe/aa.html
See http://kalyan97.googlepages.com/mlecchal.pdf
[17] http://www.scribd.com/doc/2232617/lexicon linked at http://sites.google.com/site/kalyan97/indus-writing
[18] [http://huntingtonarchive.osu.edu/Makara%20Site/makara

www.ingramcontent.com/pod-product-compliance
Lightning Source LLC
Chambersburg PA
CBHW081001180426
43192CB00041B/2710